Song

A Guide to Art Song Style and Literature

REVISED EDITION

Carol Kimball

HAL•LEONARD®
CORPORATION

7777 W. BLUEMOUND RD. P.O. BOX 13819 MILWAUKEE, WI 53213

ISBN-13: 978-1-4234-1280-9
ISBN-10: 1-4234-1280-X

Originally published in 1996 by Pst...Inc.

Published in 2006 by:
Hal Leonard Corporation
7777 W. Bluemound Road
P.O. Box 13819
Milwaukee, WI 53213

Library of Congress Cataloging-in-Publication Data

Kimball, Carol
  A guide to art song style and literature / Carol Kimball. — Rev. ed.
    p. cm.
  Includes bibliographical references (p.   ) and index.
  ISBN-13: 978-1-4234-1280-9
  ISBN-10: 1-4234-1280-X
  1. Songs—Analysis, appreciation. 2. Songs—History and criticism. I. Title.
  MT120.K56 2005
  782.42168—dc22
                              2006030389

Printed in the U.S.A.

Revised Edition

Visit Hal Leonard Online at **www.halleonard.com**

Song:
A Guide to Art Song Style
and Literature

TABLE OF CONTENTS

PART II   LITERATURE

An asterisk (*) indicates a song cycle.

FRENCH COMPOSERS

AMERICAN COMPOSERS

BRITISH COMPOSERS

Acknowledgements

This book is the product of many people—colleagues, composers, teachers, and students—who generously contributed helpful advice, sent scores, shared materials in their areas of expertise, and generally helped shape my ideas about content and scope.

I am grateful to the following colleagues for their contributions to the first edition of *Song* and/or this revision: Alfonse Anderson, Gary Arvin, Wanda Brister, Judith Cloud, Michael Cochran, Katharine DeBoer, Mary Day, Mary Dibbern, Tod Fitzpatrick, Thomas Grubb, Warren Hoffer, Amy Hunsaker, Serdar Ilban, Mary MacKenzie, Valerie Ore, Chloe Owen, Paul Kreider, Karen Peeler, Mary Pendleton, Harriett McCleary, Robin Rice, Debra Siebert, Christine Seitz, Stephanie Thorpe, and Roza Tulyaganova. I wish to thank the following composers who responded to my inquiries and offered materials for my use: Geoffrey Bush, Richard Faith, Daron Hagen, Lori Laitman, Libby Larsen, Stephen Paulus, and Jacques Leguerney.

Special thanks are due Debra Greschner, who served as a sympathetic sounding board for ideas and content during the formative stages of *Song*, and to Kathleen Marx and Jeanette Fontaine, who chased down elusive details in the library. Cheryl Taranto and Lamont Downs, the music librarians at UNLV, were always ready to help find scores and references that I needed. I am indebted to Juline Barol-Gilmore for her thoughtful suggestions about this edition, and for her keen pair of eyes reading many of its pages. I extend sincere thanks to Richard Walters and Christopher Ruck at Hal Leonard, whose encouragement and patience during this project made it seem less daunting. Ralph Kimball, who has been there for all my projects, was a special source of strength during this one.

Finally, I dedicate this book to all of my students, past and present. I hope the material offered here will help you in your studies, in your performances, and in your teaching. May it spark new exploration and research into that most amazing treasure house of music...song literature.

Carol Kimball
University of Nevada, Las Vegas
October, 2006

Bright is the ring of words
When the right man rings them.
Fair the fall of songs
When the singer sings them.

–Robert Louis Stevenson

Preface

Song, which first appeared in print in 1996, is the product of my passion for listening, performance, research, and teaching. Since that time, composers have continued to write songs, and new publications of vocal music have become available to singers and teachers. The ever-expanding list of CDs and DVDs offers opportunities to hear and become acquainted with unfamiliar literature, and the explosion of information available on the Internet—accurate and inaccurate—about music and composers, helps fuel song lovers and singers' appetites to explore and learn about new literature.

This new and expanded edition of *Song* contains the following additions: eighteen new composer sections; eighty-five single songs with annotations; and fifteen additional song cycles/collections. The sections on Italian, Russian, Scandinavian, and American literature have been enlarged. Appendices have been modified to make them as "user-friendly" as possible. Bibliographies in the composers' sections and the appendices have been updated to reflect new and pertinent publications. Russian and Czechoslovakian song titles are given in their original languages.

FORMAT

The focus of *Song: A Guide to Art Song Style and Literature* is to provide materials for the study of song literature, highlighting the fusion of poetry and music inherent in the form. The book is designed to be useful either as a textbook for initial study or quick referral, or as a reference source. As a text of study for vocal literature classes, it provides material, directions, and ideas that may be flexibly incorporated into a number of classroom situations.

Song is divided into two main sections. The first is a concise guide to learning about composers' song styles, and the musical details that reveal each composer's "soundprint." The second part of the book presents song literature grouped by national areas (German, French, American, British, Italian, Russian, Scandinavian, Spanish, South American, and eastern European). For each composer, there is a concise biography and descriptive annotations for representative songs. At the end of each composer unit there is a list of songs for further study as well as a bibliography of books and articles specific to that composer's work.

Style sheets for selected composers address specific compositional approaches in their songs. Information in these charts is grouped by melody, harmony, rhythm, accompaniment, and poets/texts. Additional material on styles can be found in composers' biographies. Readers are encouraged to add to the style sheets provided and to develop style sheets on their own.

SONG LITERATURE AND ANNOTATIONS

In attempting to define a basic body of song literature, the following were omitted: opera arias, vocal chamber works, and concert pieces with orchestra. In a few cases voice-piano versions of orchestrated vocal works are discussed; those regularly programmed on the recital platform have been included. For example, arias from the operas of Handel and Gluck appear with great frequency in recital performance, and are included here as works representative of their compositional style. There are a few annotations of pieces for voice with instruments; these have also been included as stylistic illustrations.

Subjectivity is undeniably a factor in compiling any list. Some readers will question the inclusion of certain songs and composers and the omission of others. The author has chosen songs and cycles for annotation with the following criteria in mind:

- songs generally accepted as comprising a broad overview of song literature—a "generic" list of well-known songs and cycles

- songs that are representative examples of each composer's compositional style

- songs that are generally available in published form

- songs that may be accessed on recordings—compact discs, cassettes and long-playing records

Annotations do not provide a complete stylistic or theoretical analysis of each piece, but emphasize information that might provide direction for further exploration or create interest in an unknown work or composer. The annotated format should also prove helpful to the teacher in assigning listening outside the classroom. The list of works and bibliography at the end of each unit provides material for further study and/or class assignments.

This book is a guide, not a chronological history of the evolution of song as a genre. For in-depth historical study there are excellent references in specific areas of the literature that offer thorough discussions and analyses; the reader should access those for detailed study.

Style

> Song must not be thought of as either music or poetry but rather as an amalgam that shares significantly in both arts and is equally dependent upon both. It is possible to discuss the poetry, in form and content, and it is possible to discuss the music, in form and content. But in a truly successful song they *function* concurrently.
>
> —Donald Ivey[1]

Music is often praised for its poetic expression, and poetry for its musical sound. Music without words has its own sense, its own causes, meanings, and aesthetics, which we can study and explore. Poetry also has its own sensibilities—and they are different from those of music, although some of the terms are similar. But in an art song, a composer blends music and poetry in such a way that it is impossible to think of them apart. We do not hear poetry set to music—we hear a *song*.

When combined, poetry and music create a new kind of sensibility, with unique qualities to notice and study. Our task is to learn to study this distinctive art form, to find the underlying sense of it as neither just music nor just poetry, but as an overall expression of both.

When we hear a song, we experience it as a complete entity—we get an overall impression. Our understanding of the song's art is stimulated by the images in the song, which composers create with words, melodies, harmonies, and rhythms. All the images of the poem merge with the images in the music, creating the distinctive overall images of the song—a unique blend of word and sound, poetry and music. As we listen, we respond to those images, we form mental pictures and experience emotions, or even tastes, smells, and physical sensations.

In order to understand these images at a deeper level, we need to probe into the parts of the song that create them. How do we study a song to discover the underlying causes of the imagery in it? We learn to look at the song's style.

What Is Style?

Style is easier to describe than to define. It is a combination of all the song's parts—its melodies, harmonies, rhythms, and text. If we look at a song's vocal line, we may see that the composer has written long melodic phrases and that they contain large interval leaps. We thus identify one chief component of style of this song—its *melody*—and begin to distinguish the details that define its character. We develop an even stronger sense of style as we notice that the melodic line contains patterns that vividly illustrate specific words in the poem—such as leaping an augmented fourth under the word "angst."

Flipping through the music, we might note the various elements of the song and observe their characteristics: we might see the *melody* and notice that it sets the text syllabically; the *rhythm*, and notice that it is complex; the *accompaniment*, and see that it uses chordal patterns, but also shares melodic material with the vocal line; the *text*, and see that the most poignant words are highlighted by some detail of melody, harmony, or rhythm.

1

Since every song has the same kinds of components (melody, harmony, rhythm, accompaniment, text), when we study a song's style, we need to examine the distinctive way the composer handles these elements. We can describe the song's components in finer and finer detail and compile and categorize them in a list—a *style sheet*. As we read through our style sheet, we can begin to get an idea of not only the overall design of a song, but also the composer's particular method of working with the song's various parts. We will begin to understand, how, cumulatively, all facets of the song create the imagery of the song, which ultimately inspires the performer and stimulates the listener.

At first glance, just identifying a song's style in a list may not seem very useful. We may wonder why noticing, for example, that a song has *stepwise melodies* is relevant. But just as knowing whether a book is fiction or nonfiction categorizes its overall contents for the reader, knowing whether the melody basically moves stepwise or in large intervals begins to categorize the overall melodic content for the singer. Once all the details of the melody, harmony, rhythm, accompaniment, and text are identified, we can begin to understand how each part of the songs works in combination with the others. We can start to see the underlying blueprint of the song, to see how the composer constructed the song, and to see the source of the imagery in the song.

The song's style—this detailed list of how the composer treats the melody, harmony, rhythm, and text—gives us a structure on which we can build a detailed interpretation for performance. Since all the details of a song's style create the imagery in the song, we can begin to discriminate which qualities to articulate, which images to emphasize, which elements of the song to give our focus and special handling.

We can also learn to recognize composers by their style, so that, even without knowing the song, we can make an intelligent guess about who wrote it. In the same way that Van Gogh painted with similar brush strokes, colors, perspectives, and subjects, Schumann composed with similar melodies, harmonies, rhythms, accompaniments, and texts. And just as Van Gogh's details all add up to a characteristic, recognizable style, so too does Schumann's work. We can say the composer's style leaves a distinctive *soundprint*, like a fingerprint. This soundprint is created by the individual way a composer treats each of the parts of a song, so that when we hear an unfamiliar song, we can identify it as Schumann, Brahms, Ives, Poulenc, or Britten.

Style can also orient you to a country, historical eras, aesthetic trends, and national characteristics. Spanish song contains musical features strongly rooted in the folk songs and rhythms of Iberia. Obviously, the sound of a language is also an immediate way to recognize songs of a particular country. Although they are both French composers, Poulenc's *mélodies* do not sound like Gounod's because during the eighty-one years that separate their births, French song developed and evolved—but Gounod's songs and Poulenc's songs do share certain style characteristics of their own French contemporaries.

Learning to look at the song's style also gives us a way to understand large numbers of songs. With style in mind, it is easy to seach beyond the songs we already know and explore more songs from the riches of song literature. Unfamiliar works can immediately seem more familiar, which can help increase our repertoire more easily.

Components of Style

The broad parameters of style are *melody, harmony, rhythm, accompaniment*, and *poets/texts*. These broad components can be broken into smaller subsections to help define the way a composer creates the song's imagery in each component. For example, the melody can be broken down into its contours and shapes, its phrase lengths, or its motives. As you analyze each component and its subsections separately, a pattern will ultimately emerge, helping to define and characterize the "song style" of that composer.

However, since a song blends all these components into one complete whole, melody, harmony, rhythm, accompaniment, and text all overlap, which can make them difficult to separate. So, in studying these components, it is important to look at each one by itself and then in combination with the others.

MELODY

Melody is the first broad component of style. When we listen to a song, we generally hear the vocal line and text most easily, so melody is usually a dominant focus for the listener. Melody is not confined only to the vocal line; melodies can also be found in the piano accompaniment or in the harmonic structure, in the form of small melodic motives, pitch "cells," or melodic fragments. A composer may use these elements to emphasize a dramatic moment, accentuate an emotion, or sustain tension.

Melodic shape and vocal articulation are also important in enhancing poetic content. The opening vocal phrase of Strauss's "Morgen!" is like a murmuring recitative, a narrow range of five notes that gently emerges from the piano prelude, rising like the newly dawning day to complete the emotional mood even as the song begins. Melodic lines can be highly dramatic, as in Duparc's "Le Manoir de Rosemonde," portraying the despair of one in a desperate search for an unattainable goal; or they can be romantic, soaring phrases, as in Liszt's "Oh! quand je dors."

Melody and rhythm are closely linked in creating imagery. When we look at a vocal phrase, we see a range of pitches, but also the rhythms assigned to those pitches. For instance, a composer may stress an important word or words in a poetic line by using notes of longer duration or employing striking interval changes within the melodic phrase.

Melodic Contour/Phrase Shape

How has the composer constructed the contours and shapes of the melody? A melody may be very fluid, with many changes of direction, evoking a lover's ardent message as in Brahms' "Botschaft"; or a melody may be relatively static, creating a quietly expressive mood as in Quilter's "Now sleeps the crimson petal." The melody's contours and shapes determine its character and, in a song, are usually connected to the text.

Different melodic shapes may reflect different images in the poetry or express contrasting emotional moods. Is the melody built stepwise in scale passages, or is the melody line disjunct, with large interval leaps? Do the phrases contain sequences (patterns repeated at different pitch levels), or is the vocal range very narrow with little movement? Has the composer used extended intervals at points of high emotion?

Poulenc begins "Nous avons fait la nuit" (*Tel jour, telle nuit*) with a stepwise melody that rises calmly to set the initial mood—"we have made the night." Musorgsky uses angular, jerky melody shapes to bring to life the exasperated Nurse in the second song of his cycle *The Nursery*; Dowland portrays a lover's desire in "Come again, sweet love doth now invite" with five sequential repetitions of a rising interval, creating a phrase of breathless expectation that finally releases on a long extended note. Granados evokes a *maja's* deep grief as she cries for her dead lover with a vocal line of large intervals that rise and fall like an anguished wail. Argento's spiky vocal phrases in "Winter" (*Six Elizabethan Songs*) leave no doubt in the listener's mind that the weather is freezing cold.

Phrase Length

It is important to notice the length of melodic phrases. Are they long or short? A composer may use a broad-lined melody for an exalted or deeply expressive text and shorter phrases for a poem that portrays breathless excitement. Contrast Schubert's stately melodic line in "An die Musik" with the breathless, bouncy vocal phrases in Schumann's "Aufträge." Also notice that the texts of "Aufträge" and Brahms's "Botschaft" both deal with lovers' messages, but the length of the melodic phrases in each makes the emotional mood of the two songs quite different.

Range and Tessitura

Range and tessitura are not usually tied to the poetry. *Range* is an overall measurement and refers to the highest and lowest notes of the song; *tessitura* is used to specify the pitch levels that predominate throughout the entire song.

Songs of certain composers often have tessituras that favor one voice type or seem suited to one particular vocal timbre. Some composers wrote with specific voices or voice types in mind: most of Richard Strauss's songs were written for his wife, soprano Pauline de Anha. Duparc's *mélodies* were composed for what he called a "violin-voice"; and the range of Brahms's *Lieder* makes them a treasure-trove for rich-textured medium and low voices.

Chromaticism

"Chromatic" comes from the Greek word meaning *"color."* A composer often colors or embellishes a melody with notes foreign to the key, or uses chromatic alterations within a particular phrase, usually to illustrate the meaning of the poem. Look at the first vocal phrase of Schumann's "Mondnacht" for an example of a chromatic melodic passage that perfectly illustrates the serenity of the poetic text. However, chromaticism may not always relate to the text. Notice Berg's *Vier Lieder*, Op. 2, where his highly chromatic melodic writing is tied more to his twelve-tone style than to specific poetic content.

Motives

Often a composer will use a motive (a small melodic pattern) that repeats throughout the song. Motives can symbolize characters, emotions, or dramatic situations, or they can stand on their own simply as musical units. Look for recurring motives in a song and try to define their function in the musical texture.

Motives in song literature tend to be short. Hugo Wolf uses many tiny motives in his *Lieder*; the *Italienisches Liederbuch* contains many examples of his skillful use of these patterns. A small motive may be used for the foundation of an entire song (one example is "Das verlassene Mägdlein") or it may appear throughout the song in varied forms—perhaps it may have a different rhythm, or it may begin on a higher or lower pitch, or it may be embedded in the piano accompaniment. Dominick Argento uses melodic fragments in each song of his cycle *From the Diary of Virginia Woolf*, then reprises them in the final song of the cycle.

Vocal Articulation

Vocal articulation, like melodic shape, is closely connected to text setting. Melodies can be written in several styles having certain vocal characteristics, although the term "vocal articulation" refers more to the musical features of the vocal line than to the way it is sung. Below are some examples of different vocal articulation:

RECITATIVE. *Recitative* (also called *parlando*, or "declamatory recitative") refers to a style in which the composer has closely approximated speech rhythms in the vocal line. In song literature, recitative is not the same as the *secco* (dry) recitative found in opera; usually the composer combines a straightforward recitative line with some lyricism in the accompaniment so that the voice is supported by some melodic material. Examples of "reciting" vocal lines underscored with simple chords can be found in the opening measures of Schumann's last song of *Frauenliebe und –leben* ("Nun hast du mir den ersten Schmerz getan") or the final phrase of Schubert's "Erlkönig" ("In seinen Armen das Kind war tot").

LYRIC RECITATIVE. Numerous songs contain recitative-like passages or melodies; many of these have substantial melodic contours or expressive melodic patterns are also likely to contain more organized rhythms. An early example of this technique is found in "Der Leiermann," the final song of Schubert's *Winterreise*. Schubert gives the vocal line a little melodic design, but retains its recitative-like quality by setting it over open fifths in the piano. Since the overall line is declamatory in nature, yet is still within a more lyric format, the term "lyric recitative" may be used to categorize this type of melody.

Claude Debussy brought this technique to new heights in his mature *mélodies*. Prime examples of his lyric declamation can be found in *Chansons de Bilitis*: see for example the opening measures of "La Flûte de Pan" ("Pour le jour des Hyacinthies, il m'a donné une syrinx faite de roseaux bien taillés") or "Le Tombeau des naïades" ("Je suis la trace du satyre. Ses petits pas fourchus alternent comme des trous dans un manteau blanc. Il me dit: 'Les satyres sont morts' ").

MELISMAS. *Melismas* are expressive melodic figures used to set one syllable of text. Georges Bizet ends his *mélodie* "Adieux de l'hôtesse arabe" with long melismas for the voice, fashioned of sensual dance-like rhythms.

LYRIC MELODY. Lyric melodies are beautifully "tuneful" within the phrase structure. There are myriad examples of lyric melodies, including Ralph Vaughan Williams's "Silent Noon"; Schubert's "An die Leier" (this *lied* also contains alternating sections of declamatory recitative); Strauss's "Cäcilie"; Bellini's "Vaga luna che inargenti"; Rorem's "The Lordly Hudson"; Rakhmaninov's "Ne poy, krasavitsa pri mne"; Obradors's "Del cabello más sutil"; and Poulenc's "C."

Text Painting

Composers sometimes use the melody to "paint" or illustrate the text by using certain intervals, rhythms, or melodic patterns that capture the sense and sound of the words. Franz Schubert paints a chilling picture with the last two notes of "Der Tod und das Mädchen": as Death sings the word "schlafen" (sleep), Schubert drops the melody down into the deepest part of the voice, sinking the maiden into eternal sleep. Henry Purcell's songs contain vivid examples of text painting: see the skittering eighth-note figure on the word "fly" ("I Attempt from Love's Sickness to Fly"), and look at the melodic movement on the words "tear," "roaring," and "rainbow from the sky" in "I'll Sail Upon the Dog Star"—text painting *par excellence*.

Selected Examples for Listening and Study
Richard Strauss: Morgen!
Henri Duparc: Le Manoir de Rosemonde
Samuel Barber: The Monk and His Cat (*Hermit Songs*)
Claude Debussy: La Chevelure (*Chansons de Bilitis*)
Franz Schubert: Erlkönig
Franz Schubert: Ganymed
Franz Liszt: Oh! quand je dors
Alban Berg: Die Nachtigall (*Sieben frühe Lieder*)
Maurice Ravel: Le Grillon (*Histoires naturelles*)
Henry Purcell: I'll Sail Upon the Dog Star
John Dowland: Come again, sweet love doth now invite
Dominick Argento: Winter (*Six Elizabethan Songs*)
Francis Poulenc: C'est ainsi que tu es (*Métamorphoses*)
Hugo Wolf: Mein Liebster singt (*Italienisches Liederbuch*)
John Duke: Loveliest of Trees

HARMONY

Harmony in a song is usually tied to the expressive qualities of the poetry, and is a key component in creating imagery. How a composer organizes harmonic materials is important in creating a mood, reinforcing the drama, or illustrating the poetic elements. Thick harmonic textures can create a luxurious, sensuous atmosphere; sparse textures can illustrate a lighter, buoyant mood. A composer can illustrate text through harmonic color or by harmonic movement; harmonic sequences can heighten the drama of the text and dissonances can highlight words or groups of words. Although we can analyze chord structures and harmonic progressions theoretically, when we listen to a song, the most striking effect of the harmony will be connected to the words.

Harmony combined with melody and rhythm can produce momentum in a song, create tension, sustain intensity, or provide release. Melodic climaxes, as well as rhythmic stresses, are usually related to important harmonic changes within a piece. Gabriel Fauré was a master of harmonic movement, using shifting harmonies without reaching a stable key center, to sustain mood and interest (for examples of Fauré's fluctuating harmonic style, see "Soir," "Arpège," or *L'Horizon chimérique*). Hugo Wolf also used harmony to underscore the conversation between the lover and his heart in "Heut Nacht erhob ich mich um Mitternacht" (*Italienisches Liederbuch*). The harmonic center fluctuates with the words of each participant; chords punctuate pauses in the conversation and emphasize the emotion of each speaker. Francis Poulenc's cycle *La Fraîcheur et le feu* contains excellent examples of varied harmonic textures that depict a wide variety of moods.

Harmonic Texture

How does the composer organize harmonic materials in the song? The sum total of all the harmonic elements in the song is called *texture*. Texture is a large umbrella covering many sub-elements. Is the texture tonal or atonal? Are the harmonies chordal, or a combination of chords and broken figures? Is the harmony created by intersecting lines? Are the harmonies primarily diatonic, chromatic, modal, twelve-tone, or combinations of these? Do they sustain tension, control forward movement, or supply release? What key centers has the composer chosen? Do modulations outline the song's form, or signal a change in mood?

Tonality

All of the melodic and harmonic elements of a musical work are related to a common tonal center or a tonality. A number of patterns are commonly used for tonal organization:

DIATONIC. *Diatonic* harmony used in the strict sense does not deviate from the notes in the major or minor scales.

CHROMATIC.[*] A composer may make chromatic alterations to a chord to modulate from key to key, or to give dramatic emphasis to the text. He may write chromatic passages in the vocal line or in the piano accompaniment to emphasize an intensely tonal color to a phrase or section or to highlight a specific word.

[*]A chromatic scale is built in half-steps within the octave.

MODAL HARMONY (MODALITY). Ottman[*] defines the term "mode" as "the arrangement of whole steps and half steps (or sometimes other intervals) to form a scale. In contrast to the present common use of major and minor modes, pre-17th century music was largely based on a system of six different modes. Modes can be transposed to begin on any pitch or letter name." In medieval music, modes were classified by plainsong melodies used in the early church. They were given Greek names and may be represented by the white notes on the modern keyboard.

Modal melodies may contain altered tones or have some steps of the scale missing. A composer will sometimes use modal patterns (usually pitches of a flat-sixth or flat-third within the major mode) for contrast or to add a distinctive tonal color to a phrase or section. Fauré composed his *mélodie* "Lydia" in the Lydian mode. Modal harmonies may be found in some of the songs of Debussy, Ravel, Sibelius, and Vaughan Williams, among others.

7

Twentieth-century composers used modes in their music with great frequency. Modality is also very common in folk music of the Western world.

*Robert W. Ottman, *Music for Sight-Singing*. 3rd edition (Englewood Cliffs, Prentice-Hall, 1986), 229.

TWELVE-TONE (SERIAL). This term refers to a composition style originated by Arnold Schoenberg around 1921. The twelve tones of the chromatic scale are placed into a tone row, in a particular order. The row order is always used in complete form, although it may be inverted, used backwards (retrograde), or used in a combination (retrograde inversion). Alban Berg used twelve-tone techniques in his songs, but organized his tone rows in melodic cells so the listener feels a sense of tonality within the atonal organization.

Tonal vs. Atonal

Tonal refers to music that has a key center. Tonal centers can shift (modulate) during a song, or they can remain the same. Tonal centers have related, secondary tonalities that a composer can use for contrast or tension; these are usually the major tonic/key of dominant, or minor tonic/key of relative major. These combinations are common in earlier song; toward the end of the nineteenth century, composers began to use less closely related keys to create tension or structural divisions.

Atonal refers to the absence of key feeling or centered tonality. Some twentieth-century songs have fragments of atonality within a tonal-based harmonic structure; some songs lack any tonal center. For an example of an atonal song, see "Warm die Lüfte," the last song in Alban Berg's *Vier Lieder*, Op. 2.

Dissonance vs. Consonance

Dissonance refers to a state of tension between various tones in a chord, which generally produces an unsettled, often disagreeable sound. A composer may use dissonant intervals in harmonic structures to produce or sustain dramatic tension. Dissonant intervals or chords have a restless quality that is highly important for a song's sense of movement and energy. Hugo Wolf's skillful use of dissonance in "Herr, was trägt der Boden hier" effectively underscores the anguish of the conversation between Christ and the sinner. Schubert uses dissonant chords in the first section of "An die Leier" to accompany the bard who wanted his lyre to accompany only dramatic songs of heroes. A composer does not always use dissonance to illustrate agony or sorrow; Falla's "Nana" (*Siete canciones populares españolas*) is full of soft dissonances created by two lines in the piano, moving in opposite motion and intersecting the vocal line in random fashion.

Consonance is the opposite of dissonance; consonant intervals sound stable and complete; consonant chords contain harmonious, compatible sounds. Bellini's *bel canto* melodies and Granados's tuneful *Tonadillas* are among the numerous examples of consonance in song literature.

Recurring Harmonies

In any song you may find harmonies that are used more often than others. Mozart, Haydn, and Beethoven were fond of using the diminished 7th chord to illustrate the text, or just as often, for musical reasons. The songs of Debussy, Poulenc, and other twentieth-century composers are full of extended tertian harmonies (7th, 9th, 11th, 13th chords).

Major, minor, diminished, and augmented chords can all be used for text illustration or to highlight dramatic mood. It is important to notice the structure of chords in a song, and the kinds of harmonic progressions used.

Key Scheme/Modulations/Cadences

Key scheme refers to the way a composer organizes the tonal centers within a piece. A composer may use one tonality or key center for a song, or several. Key centers are the primary way a composer can delineate the sections in a song or effectively point up an emotional change in the poetry. Check the composer's key scheme for a song. What keys are used and what is their relationship to one another? Do they form a pattern? When a key change occurs, check the poetry to see why the composer might have made this choice.

Cadences are chord progressions that indicate closure, either temporary or complete. Cadences occur at the ends of periods (two musical phrases), the ends of musical sections, or at the end of a complete song. There is no limit to the possible variations of cadences available to a composer. A composer might write an interrupted or inconclusive cadence that "leaves you hanging." Look at the cadences in the songs of Charles Ives for examples of unorthodox cadences, or examine the songs in Robert Schumann's *Dichterliebe* and notice the skill with which Schumann handles cadences.

Contrasts of Major/Minor

Look for places in the song where the composer has alternated between major and minor keys. This may be at the end of a large formal section, or can happen at a specific point within a section. How does this change relate to the poetic text at that particular moment?

Schubert was fond of creating sections in his *Lieder* by using major-minor alternations and modulations to key centers a third apart, although these modulations did not always signal a change of mood. An example is "Der Musensohn," which seesaws from major to minor, but only as a means of dividing sections; the song never loses its happy buoyancy. Major-minor contrasts are found on a smaller scale in "Lachen und Weinen" (Laughter and Tears), where a major key highlights laughter, and a minor key highlights tears.

Text Illustration Through Harmonic Means

A composer can suggest mood, atmosphere, or dramatic content by using specific harmonies or harmonic progressions. A beautiful example of how harmony can illustrate poetic atmosphere is found in Richard Strauss's "Die Nacht." The song begins with a single repeated note in the piano. As the singer enters, the accompaniment gradually becomes two notes, then three, heralding the soft approach of the night. Without losing momentum or changing rhythmic pattern, these harmonies shift imperceptibly throughout the song. Another example of harmonic text painting is the third song of *Chansons de Bilitis,* in which Claude Debussy illustrates the text "Le long du bois couvert de givre, je marchais" through a repeated harmonic pattern over a pedal point, evoking Bilitis's plodding steps along an icy path.

Selected Examples for Listening and Study

Robert Schumann: Mondnacht
Hector Berlioz: Le Spectre de la rose (*Les Nuits d'été*)
Francis Poulenc: Dans l'herbe (*Fiançailles pour rire*)

Charles Ives: Tom Sails Away
Hugo Wolf: Herr, was trägt der Boden hier (*Spanisches Liederbuch*)
Hugo Wolf: Anakreons Grab
Peter Warlock: Sleep
John Musto: Recuerdo
Edvard Grieg: En svane
Samuel Barber: Solitary Hotel (*Despite and Still*)
Xavier Montsalvatge: Cuba dentro de un piano (*Cinco canciones negras*)
Modest Musorgsky: Kolybel'naya (*Songs and Dances of Death*)
Johannes Brahms: Wenn ich mit Menschen... (*Vier ernste Gesänge*)
Alban Berg: Schlafen, schlafen (*Vier Lieder*, Op. 2)
Claude Debussy: En Sourdine (*Fêtes Galantes I*)
Francis Poulenc: *La Fraîcheur et le feu*

RHYTHM

Rhythm has been called the "backbone of music," since it is the underlying pulse of a musical work. But the rhythmic duration of tones within a musical work also functions to organize tension and relaxation in the piece.

In looking at the rhythm in a song, you will find that it is closely tied to melody, since rhythm organizes the word stress or versification of the words within the melodic line. The design of rhythm patterns and tones within a melodic phrase can determine its dramatic character. Rhythm can describe a character (see Wolf's quicksilver rhythmic patterns in "Der Rattenfänger" that vividly paint the slippery Pied Piper), illustrate specific sound qualities in the poem (the ragtime rhythms in waltz meter that Richard Hundley uses in "Moonlight's Watermelon" complement the poems cheerful wordplay), or create an emotional atmosphere (Schubert's throbbing rhythmic design in "Rastlose Liebe" describes love's despair and joy).

Like a chameleon, rhythm also combines with harmony; rhythmic patterns found in the harmonic texture are important in creating a mood or highlighting a particular image in the poem. A simple unchanging rhythm of repeated chords can create a serene, dreamlike atmosphere (as in Fauré's "Après un rêve") or plunge us immediately into a dramatic scene (Strauss's "Schlechtes Wetter" begins with rain and snow slapping rhythmically against a windowpane). The regal tread of the peacock in Ravel's "Le Paon" (*Histoires naturelles*) is set in a stately rhythmic pattern, which paints the pompous peacock in unmistakable detail. In "Le Grillon," the second song of *Histoires naturelles*, several tiny rhythmic figures blend in various combinations to picture the little cricket and his movements. Schubert uses an urgent, driving rhythmic pattern in the opening phrase of "Erlkönig" to set the stage for the tense drama about to unfold. Duparc builds "Le Manoir de Rosemonde" on a syncopated rhythmic pattern in the piano—stark repeated octaves that illustrate another despairing journey on horseback.

Tempo

Tempi in songs are usually more complicated than "slow" or "fast." Clues to the composer's perception of the text can also be found sprinkled through the score in metric indications or in tempo markings. Often a composer will designate an interpretive mood, as well as a metronomic marking at the beginning of the piece. Here are some examples of those "indicators":

Aaron Copland: I felt a funeral in my brain (*Twelve Poems of Emily Dickinson*)

Rather fast (♩=80)
Heavy, with foreboding, blurred, uneven ♪)

Charles Ives: The Greatest Man
Moderato (In a half boasting and half wistful way; not too fast or too evenly)

Claude Debussy: La Flûte de Pan (*Chansons de Bilitis)*
Lent et sans rigueur de rythme (Slow and with no rigor in rhythm)

Leonard *Bernstein*: The Pennycandystore Beyond The El (*Songfest*)
Leggiero (like a quick, dark dream) (♪.=100)

Francis Poulenc: Aussi bien que les cigales (*Calligrammes)*
Aussi vite que possible; dans un tourbillon de joie (♩=120)
(As fast as possible in a whirlwind of joy)

Hugo Wolf: Mignon
Langsam und sehr ausdrucksvoll (Slowly and with great expression);
Ruhiger (more calmly)
Belebt (animated); *Leidenschaftlich hingebend* (surrending to passionate emotion)

Metric Organization*

How does the composer organize various meters within the song? He may choose to displace regular rhythmic accents by juxtaposing different meters, as in Virgil Thomson's "Sigh no more, ladies," or John Musto's "Recuerdo." Meters that change frequently are usually tied to poetic stress, but can be used by the composer to create tension or surprise for the listener.

Is the song written in simple meter, compound meter, or irregular meter? All meters have accented beats (for example, in $\frac{2}{4}$ the downbeat is always accented, but in $\frac{4}{4}$ there is a secondary stress on the third beat), and these have implications for text setting. A composer generally ties meter to word stress in the poetry, but always has the choice to bend those stresses for dramatic or musical emphasis.

SIMPLE METERS.
Simple duple meter: $\frac{2}{2}$, $\frac{2}{4}$, $\frac{2}{8}$, $\frac{2}{16}$ (one duple group in each measure)

Simple triple meter: $\frac{3}{2}$, $\frac{3}{4}$, $\frac{3}{8}$, $\frac{3}{16}$ (one triple group in each measure)

Simple quadruple meter: $\frac{4}{2}$, $\frac{4}{4}$, $\frac{4}{8}$, $\frac{4}{16}$ (one quadruple group in each measure)

COMPOUND METERS.
Duple compound meter: $\frac{6}{4}$, $\frac{6}{8}$, $\frac{6}{16}$ (two triple groups in each measure)

Triple compound meter: $\frac{9}{4}$, $\frac{9}{8}$, $\frac{9}{16}$ (three triple groups in each measure)

Quadruple compound meter: $\frac{12}{4}$, $\frac{12}{8}$, $\frac{12}{16}$ (four triple groups in each measure)

IRREGULAR METERS. *Irregular meters* have an odd number as the upper figure in the meter signature (5, 7, 9). Five and seven are encountered most frequently in songs. All these numbers divide into groups of two and three, but the odd number of beats in the measure allows the composer flexibility in handling rhythm, harmony, and melody. Chausson's "Le Colibri" is a *mélodie* in $\frac{5}{4}$ meter; the irregular number of beats forces the song forward and illustrates the movements of the hummingbird. Chausson has written the song so that rhythmic stresses within the vocal line seem to call for a sixth beat, which is missing, creating a feeling of anticipation for the listener.

In some instances, a composer may insert a measure of irregular meter into a phrase (usually at the end) to accommodate poetic meter, or to balance whatever rhythmic organization he has given the phrase.

NONMETRIC, IMPROVISATORY METERS. Some twentieth-century works have improvisatory, non-traditional notation that requires improvisatory techniques from the performer. In this type of notation, the great staff is not used in the traditional manner, nor is the vocal part barred in regular meter. A staff of several measures with precise pitches or a staff with implied pitches may be used. George Crumb's chamber works, such as *Night of the Four Moons* and *Ancient Voices of Children*, use non-traditional notation; Berio's *Sequenza for Voice* is a famous improvisatory solo work; and some of Bernard Rands's vocal pieces use non-traditional elements. In works of this type, real time, rather than metered time, becomes the guideline for performance, and musical units, large and small, are organized as "gestures" or "events."

* In describing these terms, the author used William F. Lee's Music Theory Dictionary: The Language of the Mechanics of Music (New York: Charles Hansen, 1966). This is a succinct but precise reference for the student.

Rhythmic Patterns

Does the composer use simple or complex rhythmic patterns in the song? Check the vocal line and the accompaniment to see the degree of complexity or simplicity of the rhythms. Are the patterns rigid or flexible? A composer may choose an unvarying rhythmic pattern for the accompaniment of a piece, or use combinations of flexible rhythmic patterns to perpetuate or illustrate movement.

Rhythm is closely bound to the word stresses in the poetry; the songs of Claude Debussy, Hugo Wolf, Modest Musorgsky, and Ned Rorem are outstanding examples of a close blend of speech rhythms and musical rhythm. A composer may also choose to make a word longer using a longer note value or a rhythmic pattern, or he may displace normal word stresses to create a special effect.

Rhythms that Unify

Composers have built complete songs on a rhythmic motive. Hugo Wolf often constructed an entire song around a rhythmic cell. His famous *lied* "Das verlassene Mägdlein" is built on a rhythmic figure in the accompaniment that never varies throughout the song; Wolf uses variations of this figure in the vocal line as well. The result is a highly unified song in which rhythm perpetuates the tension in the poetry. Another song built on a single rhythmic pattern is Fauré's "Les Berceaux"; here the rhythm in the accompaniment creates motion that evokes two pictures simultaneously—rocking cradles and ships riding on the tide.

Ostinato

An *ostinato* is a motive, phrase, or short theme repeated many times at the same pitch level. A composer generally uses an ostinato pattern to sustain a mood, create tension, or unify structure in a song. Ostinati may be long or short; patterns may consist of several notes, a complete phrase, or an octave pattern that continuously repeats.

Ostinati are normally found in the piano accompaniment. One of the most common ostinato patterns is a ground bass, or a constantly repeated bass phrase. Henry Purcell frequently used this musical device; the great lament "When I am Laid in Earth" from *Dido and Aeneas* and the song "Music for a while" are well-known examples of Purcell's use of the ground bass.

Rhythms that Reinforce the Text

Composers commonly use rhythms to paint the text. These patterns or features are often found in the accompaniment, but a composer may choose to highlight a single word in the vocal line with a specific rhythmic treatment as well. He may deviate from a normal metric pattern to intentionally create tension or ambiguity, and thus expressively illustrate the text. Some examples of these rhythmic patterns are:

SYNCOPATION AND SUSPENSION. *Syncopation* and *suspension* are highly important as a means of emotional expression, tension, and release. Syncopation accents or stresses a normally weak or unaccented beat within a metric line. Look at the stressed beats in the vocal line of Charles Ives's "The Circus Band" or in the accompaniment figures of the B section of Schubert's "Lied der Mignon." Suspensions are another form of syncopation; here, an expected tone (usually in the melodic line) is delayed, then held or suspended (see, for an example, Schumann's "Seit ich ihn gesehen" in *Frauenliebe und –leben*).

DOTTED RHYTHMS. *Dotted rhythms* of all types are often used to expressively illustrate the text. A representative example is Henry Purcell's "Sweeter than Roses," in which the word "victorious" is lengthened by a dotted rhythm to highlight and accent the meaning of the word.

HEMIOLA. *Hemiola* is another form of rhythmic interruption, which produces tension by temporarily altering the metric pattern. Hemiola upsets the normal rhythmic flow by constantly accenting a weak beat, which changes the meter momentarily (usually making $\frac{3}{4}$ become $\frac{2}{4}$ or vice versa). Hemiola is frequently found in the *Lieder* of Johannes Brahms (for an example, see "O wüsst ich doch den Weg zurück").

POLYRHYTHMS/CROSS-RHYTHMS WITH THE VOICE. *Polyrhythm* (or *cross-rhythm*) refers to the simultaneous use of contrasting rhythms in different lines of the musical texture. Cross-rhythms interrupt the flow of regular rhythmic accents, creating a sense of distortion or imbalance. Cross-rhythms can occur in the piano accompaniment or can be used between the piano and the voice. Two examples of cross-rhythms between voice and piano are Dvořák's "Als die alte Mutter" (Songs My Mother Taught Me) from his *Zigeunermelodien* and Ginastera's "Gato," a highly rhythmic song from *Cinco canciones populares argentinas*.

Selected Examples for Listening and Study:
Johannes Brahms: Brauner Bursche (*Zigeunerlieder*)
Antonin Dvořák: Als die alte Mutter (*Zigeunermelodien*)
Gabriel Fauré: Les Roses d'Ispahan
Paul Bowles: Once a Lady Was Here
Hugo Wolf: Das verlässene Mägdlein
Ernest Chausson: Le Colibri
Claude Debussy: Le Tombeau des naïades (*Chansons de Bilitis*)
Virgil Thomson: Sigh no more, ladies
Richard Struass: Die Nacht
Dominick Argento: War (June, 1940) (*From the Diary of Virginia Woolf*)
Alberto Ginastera: Gato (*Cinco canciones populares argentinas*)
Jacques Leguerney: A son page
Charles Ives: The Circus Band
Aaron Copland: Going to Heaven! (*Twelve Poems of Emily Dickinson*)
Richard Hundley: Moonlight's Watermelon
Maurice Ravel: Le Paon, Le Grillon, La Pintade (*Histoires naturelles*)

ACCOMPANIMENT

In examining a song's accompaniment, first notice the type of figurations used. Block chords, broken chords, arpeggiated materials—each of these figures is capable of transmitting a mood, highlighting a phrase of text, or enhancing the vocal material. Block chords may evoke a somber or regal mood, or underlie the menacing voice of Death as in Schubert's "Der Tod und das Mädchen"; broken chords may express innocence or picture the uncaring steps of the little shepherdess in Mozart's "Das Veilchen"; arpeggiated figures can paint buoyant emotion as found in Debussy's "Green" or the shimmer of soft light on Dutch canals as found in Duparc's "L'Invitation au voyage." A composer may also enrich accompaniment patterns by articulating them in a specific way—legato versus staccato.

Figures in the piano can set the emotional or dramatic mood of the song, or become a participant in the poetic texture—Gretchen's spinning wheel, the hoof beats of a galloping horse, the flirtatious movements of a temptress, the quiet serenity of a graveyard, rain slapping against a windowpane, a Spanish guitar, the grasping fingers of phantoms, the whispering leaves of a tree.

The texture of the accompaniment is important as well. The texture may be thought of as the fabric of the song, woven to support and define the poetry. It can be dense and thick or light and clear, conceived in linear form or chordal form. All of these variations create different sounds and colors, and, when coupled with the words, can transmit different images to the listener.

Predominant Accompaniment Figures

Piano figures may indicate a composer's response to the poem. Does he use block chords, arpeggiated figures, or broken chords to illustrate and support the words? Does the song begin with one figuration and change to another? Does this change occur at a significant dramatic point in the text, or does it merely signal a different musical section?

Prominent Sections Without the Voice

Composers sometimes include prominent sections in the song without the voice. These sections are called *preludes*, *interludes*, and *postludes*, and are often found in songs written by composers who were also excellent pianists. For example, Robert Schumann regularly used preludes, interludes, and postludes in his *Lieder*—an important factor in identifying a Schumann song.

PRELUDE. A *prelude* is a musical introduction to a song that is longer than a few measures. When is a prelude a prelude and not an introduction? The term prelude is usually used when the introductory material to a song has substantial length and is almost a mini-musical form of its own. One example of a song with an extended prelude for the piano is Haydn's "She Never Told Her Love."

INTERLUDE. An *interlude* is a connecting passage used between sections of a song. Long interludes are found less frequently in song form, but a composer can sectionalize a piece easily by inserting a piano interlude, or use an interlude to "comment" on what has gone before or to introduce what is coming next.

POSTLUDE. A *postlude* is a section of music for the piano that closes the song. Postludes are found more frequently than preludes and interludes. A postlude can serve as a moment of reminiscence by bringing back melodic, rhythmic, or harmonic material heard before. Francis Poulenc ended his cycle *Tel jour, telle nuit* with an expansive postlude that ends the work with beautiful serenity. Richard Hundley's "Astronomers" features an ethereal postlude that evokes a starry night viewed from the quiet of a graveyard. A famous example of a postlude is found in Schumann's *Frauenliebe und –leben,* in which the first song is recalled in its entirety at the end of the cycle.

Shared Material with the Voice

The accompaniment often shares musical material with the voice; this collaboration is usually tied to the meaning of the poem. The shared material may be a motive or melodic fragment that is bandied back and forth between voice and piano, or is used afterwards as a gesture of recall. The accompaniment and voice can share rhythmic figures as well; these are often heard as "echoes." The composer may also double the vocal line in the accompaniment to intensify an emotion or illustrate the text.

Use of Motives

Locate any cells, motives, or longer themes that the composer has used in the piano accompaniment. Notice their length and their shape, and try and tie this to text illustration if it seems to fit. Are there patterns found in the vocal line as well?

Text Illustration in Piano Patterns—Word, Mood, Atmosphere

Melody, harmony, and rhythm can all be used to illustrate the text. Since the accompaniment integrates all these components, the piano plays a supportive and active part in text illustration. Try to identify the places in a song where the piano accompaniment plays the dominant role in illustrating the poetry, and pinpoint whether the text painting involves a word, creates a mood, or sustains an atmosphere.

15

Accompaniment Texture

Texture generally refers to the density or sparseness of the piano accompaniment. A glance at the musical score will confirm whether the accompaniment is thick or thin. Texture is the accompaniment fabric, woven with harmony, lines of melody, or other distinctive figures. It may contain a few threads or many, numerous strands of color or a monochromatic hue. Texture can also indicate combinations of musical elements such as the melody and the harmony and how they relate to one another.

LINEAR TEXTURE. This texture is sparse, fashioned of only a single line in each hand of the piano accompaniment. This texture usually evokes clarity, elegance, and control. Often a composer will begin a song with linear texture, and then expand into a fuller sound. See the opening of Gabriel Fauré's "Clair de lune," in which the piano opens with two fluid lines that intertwine and then expand into a fuller texture.

CONTRAPUNTAL TEXTURE. Contrapuntal texture is "in the style of counterpoint." A contrapuntal accompaniment will contain independent melodies used simultaneously.

Distinctive Dramatic Effects

In some songs, the composer writes striking effects for the piano that point up text or action in the text. Charles Ives's song "Charlie Rutlage" contains a number of these moments, especially the full-fisted chord clusters the pianist plays as Charlie's horse falls on him during the roundup. Look in the accompaniment of a song to see if there are instances of the accompaniment becoming an active participant in the dramatic action.

Selected Examples for Listening and Study

Franz Schubert: Gretchen am Spinnrade
Franz Schubert: Die Forelle
Henri Duparc: L'Invitation au voyage
Johannes Brahms: Von ewiger Liebe
W. A. Mozart: Das Veilchen
Francis Poulenc: C
Maurice Ravel: D'Anne jouant de l'espinette
Enrique Granados: El tra la la y el punteado (*Tonadillas*)
Jacques Leguerney: Epipalinodie
Reynaldo Hahn: A Chloris
Richard Strauss: Schlectes Wetter
Ned Rorem: Rain in Spring
Robert Schumann: Der Nussbaum
Ralph Vaughan Williams: Silent Noon
Benjamin Britten: A Charm (*A Charm of Lullabies*)

POETS • TEXTS

Composers approach their texts in many different ways. Many composers have a penchant for creating a melody that closely corresponds to the natural inflection and stress of the words. Other composers approach their texts without regard for the natural inflection and stress of the words—either by choice or lack of sensitivity. One only has to study musical settings of the same poem by different composers to appreciate how the poetry sparked different emotional or interpretive responses (for example: "Feldeinsamkeit" as set by Johannes Brahms and Charles Ives; "C'est l'extase," by Claude Debussy and Gabriel Fauré).

Choice of Texts

How do composers choose their texts? What draws them to a particular poem, poet, or poetic theme? Most composers of song have a strong love of literature and a wide knowledge of the best choices to be made in choosing words to set to music. Often a composer will set poetry by colleagues and contemporaries; for example, the three great poets of Francis Poulenc (Guillaume Apollinaire, Louise de Vilmorin, Paul Eluard) were people he knew well; Paul Goodman, a close friend of Ned Rorem, provided poetry for many Rorem songs; Johann Wolfgang von Goethe was a contemporary of Franz Schubert; and so on.

In many cases, a composer is strongly attracted to poetry from a specific period in history—with few exceptions, Jacques Leguerney used Renaissance poetry for all his *mélodies*; other composers are similarly drawn to texts from other historical periods.

Some composers prefer the works of specific poets; for instance the work of William Shakespeare, Emily Dickinson, and Paul Verlaine is found in numerous songs.

Still other composers prefer highly dramatic poems. Carl Loewe is chiefly remembered for his stirring ballads, which present gripping stories of high intensity and emotion.

Prose Settings

Not all songs have poems for texts; some composers also use prose texts. *From the Diary of Virginia Woolf, The Andrée Expedition*, and *Casa Guidi* are three cycles by American composer Dominick Argento based on prose texts taken from varied sources—the diaries of author Virginia Woolf, the journals of a Swedish explorer trying to reach the North Pole by balloon, and the letters of poet Elizabeth Barrett Browning written during her stay in Italy. Maurice Ravel's *Histoires naturelles* uses prose texts by Jules Renard. Because they lack regular poetic meter, prose texts in musical settings will be quite different in metric organization, and in other musical elements as well.

Treatment of Prosody

Prosody literally refers to the study of poetic meters and versification. Some composers are said to have a "heightened sense of prosody"—that is, they are instinctively able to set poetic meter in the melodic line without sacrificing the natural stresses of the words or language. When a composer sets a poem musically, he creates an entirely new frame of reference for the words. If the composer is s ensitive to prosody, he can achieve a true synthesis of music and poetry. He can find the images, emotions, and sensations in the poetry and translate them musically. He can use the resonances, colors, and shapes of the words to create a work of art that fuses two artistic mediums into one, so that it is impossible to think of one without the other.

Pierre Bernac comments on this fusion of words and music in *The Interpretation of French Song*, his classic reference to French *mélodie*:

> In vocal music, the sonority and the rhythm of the words are an integral part of the music itself. The word is itself a musical sound. The sonority and stress and rhythm of words inspire music no less, and at times even more, than the emotion they express...the music *of* the poem is as important as the music set *to* the poem. The music of the words and the music itself are one and the same; they should not be disassociated.[2]

Composer Virgil Thomson took this one step farther, declaring the words in a song to be the dominant factor in the blend of sound and text:

> If songs really need words (as indeed they mostly do, since the human voice without them is just another wind instrument) then there has to be in the marriage of words and music a basic compatibility in which the text's exact shape and purpose dominate the union, or seem to.[3]

Response to the Poem

This category is subjective, but can be approached through study of the musical setting of the same poem by more than one composer. Just as no two people respond to a piece of music, a painting, a book, or any other audio/visual stimuli in the same way, no two composers respond to a poem in the same manner. Each responds musically to the imagery, rhythmic patterns, accents, and variations of tempo within the poem in different ways.

TEXT SETTING. The text in a poem has natural stresses and accents, but there is more than one way to place those within a melodic line. Because the melodic line, with its own stresses and accents, will deepen some of the text's natural stresses and accents, the composer chooses parts of the poem to emphasize.

How has the composer set the text to the melodic line? He may have chosen a syllabic setting, using just one syllable per note, or a melismatic setting, which takes one syllable and sets it to more than one note in a rather florid style. He might have combined these styles in various places in the song. Perhaps he embellished or ornamented the melodic line with grace notes, appoggiaturas, or turns. Usually his choices will be closely tied to his response to the poem.

Different composers have set the poems listed below. Read each poem aloud. Next read the poem in the rhythm of the melody by each composer. Also, to get each composer's sense of inflection as you read the poem, let your inflection rise when the melody rises, and fall when the melody falls. Finally, listen to the poetry set as a song. (Foreign texts should be read in the original language and then in translation.).

Poems (Poets)	Composers*
C'est l'extase (Paul Verlaine)	Claude Debussy, Gabriel Fauré
Clair de lune (Paul Verlaine)	Claude Debussy (two settings) Gabriel Fauré
Das verlassene Mägdlein (Eduard Möricke)	Hugo Wolf, Robert Schumann Hans Pfitzner
Erlkönig (Johann Wolfgang von Goethe)	Franz Schubert, Carl Loewe
Kennst du das Land (Goethe)	Hugo Wolf, Franz Schubert Ludwig van Beethoven Robert Schumann Franz Liszt Fanny Mendelssohn Hensel
I'm Nobody (Emily Dickinson)	Vincent Persichetti, Arthur Farwell Ernst Bacon, Lori Laitman
Is My Team Ploughing? (A.E. Housman)	George Butterworth, Charles Orr
in just-spring (e. e. cummings)	Dominick Argento, John Duke

* Some of the poems listed above have been set by other composers as well. The list above reflects a representative selection for the purpose of studying text setting.

SECONDARY FACTORS OF STYLE

In addition to the primary elements of melody, harmony, rhythm, accompaniment, and poetry, other secondary factors should also be used in examining song style.

Unifying Elements in a Song or Song Cycle

Composers sometimes unify a composition with elements from the music or the poetry inside a single song, or across several songs in a song cycle. They may use musical motives, rhythmic cells or patterns, or harmonic progressions, which may be found in the vocal line, the accompaniment, or both. Linked themes and motives are usually used as symbols of remembrance, and cause the listener to connect what is being heard with something heard previously. Sometimes composers will overlap these motives or cells, or use more than one at a time. They may use the poetic or dramatic story, as Schubert does in *Winterreise* and *Die schöne Müllerin* in which the poems tell a story. Some stories are not as long as these two cycles, as with Fauré's *Poème d'un jour*—three songs that chronicle a brief relationship that lasts just one day. Or the composer may link the songs—as Schumann does in *Frauenliebe und –leben*—by having the piano play the first song of the cycle in its entirety as a postlude to the cycle.

Some composers link a work with elements from both the poetry and music. Poulenc's *La Fraîcheur et le feu* is seven songs, based on the poetic divisions of one long poem by poet Paul Eluard. Poulenc also unifies the cycle by reprising the opening piano introduction at the end of the cycle.

Some song sets are related by a particular group of poets (example: Dominick Argento's *Six Elizabethan Songs* uses poetry specifically from the Elizabethan era, but by several different poets; William Bolcom's *I Will Breathe a Mountain* is a group of eleven songs using poems by American women poets). A poetic theme is another unifying element that can serve to link a group of songs. Dominick Argento's *songs about spring* on poems of e.e. cummings is a group of poems all dealing with springtime; another example is Francis Poulenc's *Le Travail du peintre*, a series of poems about cubist painters. Poulenc illustrates the poetic images about their paintings into musical images that strengthen the theme even further.

Not all sets of songs are cyclic, that is, they cannot all be called "song cycles." Many are simply grouped together under a single title, or are unified by virtue of the poetry, which might have been written by the same poet (examples: Aaron Copland's *Twelve Poems of Emily Dickinson* or Benjamin Britten's *Seven Sonnets of Michelangelo*).

Try to identify a recurring pattern in a song or song cycle. Has the composer used it for poetic emphasis? Musical emphasis? Or to unify the musical structure?

Form

Since structure of the poem usually determines form of the song, many forms may be found in song literature. Here are a few of the most common:

STROPHIC FORM. *Strophic form* refers to songs with several poetic verses, in which the composer repeats the same music for each verse, with little or no change.

MODIFIED STROPHIC. To create interest, the composer often makes changes to the music that accompanies each verse; this form is referred to as *modified strophic*. These changes may be subtle or small or they may be substantial. A composer might change a key, the rhythm of the melodic line, or the piano figures to create variety.

THROUGH-COMPOSED (*DURCHKOMPONIERT*). A song is *through-composed* when there is virtually no repetition of sections or phrases. Both the poem and the music unfold, moving forward through the song without really restating the musical material. A famous example of a through-composed song is Schubert's "Erlkönig."

BINARY, TERNARY. Binary form divides a song into two parts, usually AB, but more complex variations are possible, as AA'BB'. Ternary form divides a song into three musical sections, usually ABA or ABA'. You will find many songs in ternary form in literature from all countries. Ternary structure provides a nicely balanced formal design that allows a composer to vary the middle section and still bring back the opening section in an exact repeat, or with slight variations.

Other Forms

The list above contains the forms commonly encountered in song literature, but it is by no means complete. There are as many forms possible as there are formal poetic designs.

THEME AND VARIATIONS. *Theme and variations* is not a formal design usually found in song; however, Franz Schubert used theme and variations form as a basis for "Im Frühling."

RONDO FORM. *Rondo form* refers to a design that features a recurring section that alternates with a number of different sections, as ABACA or ABACADA.

PALINDROME FORM. *Palindrome form* (ABCBA, ABBA, ABCDCBA) is a formal design, which reads the same backward as it does forward. Alban Berg was fond of using this form in his music, but it is not confined exclusively to contemporary song. There are instances of palindrome structure in Franz Schubert's *Lieder*. This form is sometimes referred to as *Bogenform*, or "bow" form, indicating the arch shape of the sections. As in all forms, there are many variations possible.

Influences on the Composer

Just as any human being is the sum total of his experience and knowledge, a composer's music reflects—in varying degrees—the influences of his teachers, his own study, his life experiences and personality. His songs may also mirror his national background; for example, Chopin's musical style reflects his native Poland, and Villa-Lobos's music is steeped in the rhythms and sounds of Brazil. Therefore, a composer's biography will provide clues for where to find patterns in his song style. Specific influences on a composer's work are important to note when working with that composer's songs.

COMPONENTS OF STYLE OVERLAP

No matter how thoroughly you study the structure and component parts of a song,yet [you] must discover that strangely enough the whole is greater than the sum of its parts.

—James Husst Hall[4]

As you study the component parts of song, you will find it difficult to separate them from the expressive intent of the poem. In the best songs, melody, rhythm, and harmony function singly and together to strengthen the emotional/dramatic content of a poem. It is simpler to study them on the page than to isolate them in the performance of a song, for it is in performance that they blend into a unified whole to become the artistic experience.

Notes

1. Donald Ivey, *Song: Anatomy, Imagery, and Styles* (New York: The Free Press, 1970), 96.
2. Pierre Bernac, *The Interpretation of French Song* (New York: W. W. Norton & Co., Inc., 1978), 3-4.
3. Virgil Thomson, *Music With Words: A Composer's View* (New Haven: Yale University Press, 1989), 1.
4. James Husst Hall, *The Art Song* (Norman, OK: University of Oklahoma Press, 1953), 9.

Developing Style Sheets

CREATING STYLE SHEETS FOR SINGLE SONGS

- After you have looked carefully at all the components in a song and broken down their characteristic qualities into subsections, you can pull all these details together and create a style sheet for the song. It is important to note that *each style sheet will be different for every song*, since every song a composer writes will be slightly different.
- Using the broad components of style as categories, list the information you have gathered about the song in the proper category on the style sheet. Use the subsections that apply for that particular song, for example:

Melody	*Phrase shape / Length*	•	fluid melodic line, sustained phrases
		•	uses large intervals for dramatic emphasis
Harmony	*Texture*	•	fairly dense texture; striking harmonies that illustrate the text
	Key scheme	•	modulations used for expressive quality
Rhythm	*Rhythmic patterns*	•	extremely flexible, varied patterns
	Tempo	•	tempo fluctuates, precise metric directions
Accomp.	*Preludes, interludes, postludes*	•	extended postlude sustained mood of the text
	Texture	•	writing for the piano is rich and virtuosic
	Shared material with the voice	•	some countermelodies with the voice in left hand of piano
Poets / Texts	*Prosody*	•	excellent sense of prosody
	Choice of texts	•	poetry rich in imagery Elizabethan poet John Fletcher (give dates and any other information you wish to add)

As you study more songs, begin style sheets for them, and add new information as you study the music and listen to the songs. Consider these style sheets "works in progress."

CREATING STYLE SHEETS FOR INDIVIDUAL COMPOSERS

- Choose a composer whose songs interest you.
- Make a list of songs by that particular composer (five to ten songs is a good number).
- Using the guidelines above, create a style sheet for each song. Keep your data specific and succinct. As you collect more songs and develop style sheets for them, you will begin to identify patterns in the way that composer handles the broad components of style.
- Enter these patterns into a style sheet that addresses that particular composer's overall song style. Note: You may find information that doesn't seem

to fit neatly under one particular heading, but is a characteristic typically found in that composer's music. This information can be placed in a "General" heading in the style sheet.

STYLE SHEET EXAMPLES FOR SELECTED COMPOSERS

Listed below are style sheets for representative composers from six national areas. Look at the range of qualities and the number of different details within each component category: *melody, harmony, rhythm, accompaniment*, and *poets/texts*.

As you read the style sheets, you will notice that the information in each begins to form a blueprint of the composer's overall song style. As you explore the songs of these composers, add to these style sheets, and practice creating your own style sheets for other composers.

GERMAN

Franz Schubert (1797-1828)

General		• first to explore possibilities of the *Lied* as a genre
		• songs characterized by a heightened sense of drama
Melody	*General*	• supreme melodist; *Lieder* full of beautiful melodies
	Melodic Contour/Phrase Shape	• melodies natural, balanced, lyric
	Vocal Articulation	• variety of vocal styles: arioso, declamatory, recitative, lyric, etc.
	Text Painting	• melodic rhythms and direction illustrative
Harmony	*Harmonic Texture*	• harmonic sequences, particularly chromatic
	Tonality	• tonality linked to mood, emotion
	Dissonance vs. Consonance	• dissonant chords and some unlikely key relations
	Recurring Harmonies	• German and Neapolitan sixth-chords
	Key Scheme/Modulations/Cadences	• movements to distant tonal center are often unprepared • enharmonic modulations • fond of modulations to keys with third relationships • deceptive resolutions, often for modulation purposes
	Contrasts of Major/Minor	• fondness for major/minor vacillation
	Text Illustration through Harmonic Means	• modulations signal characterization in some songs
Rhythm	*Metric Organization*	• extraordinary control of rhythm
	Rhythmic Patterns	• flexible rhythms of great variety
	Rhythms that Unify	• accompaniment patterns
	Ostinato	• rhythm patterns used as ostinati, but at varying pitch levels
	Rhythms that Reinforce the Text	• rhythmic patterns in accompaniment highly illustrative

Accomp.	*General*	• treatment of accompaniment unique for his time • programmatic accompaniments that illustrate and unify
	Predominant Figures	• movement of the bass line under repeated chords characteristic
	Preludes, Interludes, Postludes	• preludes, postludes and interludes used in songs • principal musical material stated in piano introduction
	Shared Material with the Voice	• some interweaving of vocal and piano lines
	Text Illustrations in Patterns	• accompaniments used to color text • tone painting: water figures, storm scenes, evocations of nature • piano sets the scene, comments on action, anticipates or echoes the vocal phrase • incredible variety of piano figures that suggest mood, connect dramatic textual ideas
	Texture	• exploited and explored range possibilities of the piano • accompaniment unifies the stanzas, but is subordinate to voice in general
Poets/Texts	*Choice of Texts*	• settings of approximately ninety poets texts with Romantic themes: night, dreams, death, wanderlust, mystery, unfulfilled longing • best-known *Lieder*: texts of Goethe, Schiller, Müller (Schubert's two monumental cycles use Müller's poems: *Die schöne Müllerin, Winterreise*)
	Response to Poetic Content	• instinctive response to poetry
Form		• strophic, strophic variation, ternary, through-composed, binary, each with their modifications
Influences		• ballads of Johann Zumsteeg • classical form and function • Beethoven

Robert Schumann (1810-1856)

Melody	*Melodic Contour / Phrase Shape*	• lyric vocal phrases • repetition of phrases, some sequences (usually varied) • pianistic figures in vocal lines (turns, *appoggiaturas*)
	Phrase Length	• melodies of considerable length, fragmented between voice and piano
	Chromaticism	• chromaticism in melodic lines
	Vocal Articulation	• melodic techniques continued from Schubert • avoids use of recitative, using a lyric declamation instead
	Text Illustration	• chromatic passing tones, *appoggiaturas* add expression
Harmony	*Harmonic Texture*	• contrapuntal textures in some songs, and in postludes
	Tonality	• key centers frequently blurred by chromatics, sequences
	Key Scheme / Modulations / Cadences	• modulations for expressive purposes • modulation by enharmonic change • cadences illustrate text • interrupted vocal cadences, with overlapping material in piano

Contrasts of Major / Minor	•	key changes a major third apart (like Schubert)
Text Illustration through Harmonic Means	•	momentary changes of tonality for word-painting
	•	syncopation, chromaticism often dramatizes the text
Rhythm *Rhythmic Patterns*	•	triplets used for expressive purposes
Rhythms that Reinforce the Text	•	dotted rhythms on weak beats
Polyrhythms / Cross-Rhythms with the Voice	•	rhythmic patterns are used to perpetuate movement, textual mood
Accomp. *General*	•	piano on a completely equal footing with the voice for first time
	•	rich accompaniments
Predominant Figures	•	rich variety of figures
Preludes, Interludes, Postludes	•	preludes, postludes, interludes integral parts of most songs
Use of Motives	•	motives allow for continuous movement (examples: "Aufträge," "Das ist ein Flöten und Geigen")
Text Illustrations in Patterns	•	descriptive figures significant in text illustration
Texture	•	close interconnection of voice and piano, one often completes the other's line (For an excellent example of Schumann's tight-knit integration of voice and piano, see *Dichterliebe*.)
Poets/Texts *Choice of Texts*	•	wide literary interests drew him to translations of poetry of other countries (Spain, Scotland, England, Denmark) as well as German texts
	•	fond of picturesque description
	•	majority of texts lyrical
	•	many texts of Heine (41) and Eichendorff (16); also Goethe, Schiller, Möricke, Rückert (22), Chamisso, Mosen, Kerner
Response to Poetic Content	•	strong literary orientation coupled with newly available poetry significant in song style
	•	often grouped songs by poet, subject, or mood
Form	•	modified strophic, rondo-like structures which use repetition in varied ways

Johannes Brahms (1833-1897)

Melody *General*	•	melody of paramount importance
Melodic Contour / Phrase Shape	•	fluent, expressive, rhythmic vocal phrases
	•	melodies often inspired by folk songs, but with freer phrase shapes
Phrase Length	•	broad, long-lined phrases
Motives	•	voice and piano often linked by similar motives
Vocal Articulation	•	lyric expression
Text Illustration	•	details in text not illustrated
Harmony *Harmonic Texture*	•	rich harmonies appeal directly to senses, emotions
	•	harmonic extension through repetitions
	•	Baroque devices: counterpoint, pedal point, augmentation
Dissonance vs. Consonance	•	dissonances for tension

	Recurring Harmonies •	polarity of melodic line and bass line, each with linear freedom
Rhythm	*Metric Organization* •	rhythm always a controlling element
	Rhythmic Patterns •	rhythms do not shift to accommodate poetic rhythms
	Rhythms that Reinforce the Text • •	syncopations in accompaniment rhythms hemiola characteristic throughout his songs; also augmentation, diminution, alternating meters
	Polyrhythms / Cross-Rhythms •	cross-rhythms between voice and piano promote musical movement
Accomp.	*Predominant Figures* • • •	the arpeggio a basic accompaniment pattern frequent bare octaves in bass syncopations in chordal patterns frequently used
	Shared Material with the Voice •	some interplay between voice and bass line
	Use of Motives •	motives not generally found in accompaniment
	Texture •	complex harmonic contrapuntal textures
Poets/Texts	*Choice of Texts* • •	not scrupulous in choosing poems; some songs use second and third-rate poetry texts of loneliness, longing, lost love, despair (All the standard Romantic poetic themes are found in Brahms's *Lieder*.)
	Treatment of Prosody • •	prosody less important (Musical elements were more important to Brahms than accuracy of text setting; some of his texts have incorrect accents in deference to musical considerations.) text often repeated for effect
Form	• •	symmetry of form always present fond of strophic folksong but invested it with numerous variations
Influences	•	Schubert

Hugo Wolf (1860-1903)

General		• • • •	poetry is the ultimate element from which all musical design springs Ivey: "the interdependence of voice and piano usually reaches such a high degree that one without the other is greatly impoverished."* *Lieder* contain psychological intensity songs usually unified by one motive

*Donald Ivey, *Song: Anatomy, Imagery, and Styles*, 210.

Melody	*Melodic Contour / Phrase Shape* •	voice part of overall texture; generated by the poetry
	Chromaticism •	dissonant melodic figures of all types
	Vocal Articulation •	styles vary widely—simple tonal melodies, highly chromatic phrases, speech-like declamation, Wagnerian lyric recitative
Harmony	*Harmonic Texture* •	bold use of harmony, dictated by poetry
	Tonality •	often highly chromatic
	Dissonance vs. Consonance •	dissonances for emotional intensity and poetic effect, many unresolved

	Key Scheme / Modulations / Cadences	• verbal associations linked with keys, key-signatures*
		• free modulations, usually unprepared
		• fluctuating tonal centers

*See Eric Sams, *The Songs of Hugo Wolf* for a discussion of motives and keys.

Rhythm	*Rhythmic Patterns*	• extremely diverse rhythms
	Rhythms that Unify	• extensive use of rhythmic motives
	Rhythms that Reinforce the Text	• syncopations and rests create variety and highlight poetry
	Polyrhythms / Cross-Rhythms	• rhythmic cross-relations with the voice
Accomp.	*Use of Motives**	• rhythmic and melodic motives expand and develop motives create atmosphere, mood, and unity
		• motives generate entire songs
	Text Illustrations in Patterns	• accompaniment often dominant element, commenting on poem
	Texture	• source of musical atmosphere
		• usually independent of the voice

*The reader is directed to Eric Sams: *The Songs of Hugo Wolf* (pp.18-42) for a discussion of Wolf's motives, which Sams codifies as to emotional and expressive symbolism.

Poets/Texts	*Choice of Texts*	• worked with one poet at a time, in "songbooks" or collections; his concentration on the work of one poet allowed him to penetrate the poet's style
		• set Möricke, Eichendorff, Goethe, translations of Spanish and Italian texts
		• on principle, would not set any poem set by his predecessors unless he felt they had not done justice to it
	Response to Poetic Content	• deeply sensitive to literature—"Poetry supplies me with the electricity I need to compose."
		• titled his collections with the poet's name in deference to the poetry
Influences		• Wagner

FRENCH

Henri Duparc (1848-1933)

General		• Duparc composed skillfully for the voice
Melody	*Melodic Contour / Phrase Shape*	• extremely flexible, expressive melodic phrase
		• at climactic points: a chord outline, descending
	Range and Tessitura	• chose high voice for most of his songs
		• phrases of considerable range
Harmony	*Harmonic Texture*	• rich harmonic style a hallmark of Duparc's *mélodies*
		• bass pedal frequently found in harmonic structure
	Dissonance vs. Consonance	• embellishments and passing notes used as dissonances
	Key Scheme / Modulations / Cadences	• unexpected harmonic progressions
		• melodic line often pivots around the dominant of the key

Rhythm	Rhythmic Patterns	• fluid, flexible rhythm patterns
	Rhythms that Reinforce the Text	• melodic lines often carry syncopation across the bar line
Accomp.	Preludes, Interludes, Postludes	• short preludes and recurring piano sections
	Use of Motives	• short phrases (rhythmic, melodic, harmonic) used as *leitmotivs* (These develop into themes and become a unifying factor in many songs.)
	Texture	• accompaniments often dense-textured, orchestral in conception • a number of songs orchestrated, principally by Duparc
Poets/Texts	Choice of Texts	• all Parnassian poets (Duparc was interested in living poets, but cared little for their school of thought.) • Charles Baudelaire the greatest poet of Duparc
Form		• determined by poetic structure

Gabriel Fauré (1845-1924)

Melody	Melodic Contour / Phrase Shape	• classical lyricism in his melodic phrases • early *mélodies* have an immediate melodic appeal • vocal phrases grow out of the harmonies; Fauré referred to it as *mélodico-harmonique*
	Vocal Articulation	• later songs (after *La Bonne chanson*) have a leaner vocal line, based more closely on speech
	Text Painting	• vocal line does not attempt to interpret text melodically • vocal line is combined with subtly changing harmonies in the piano
Harmony	Harmonic Texture	• harmonies create vocal phrases (see Melody) • coloristic, pliable harmonies • considerable contrapuntal interest, seldom obvious
	Tonality	• modality, influence of plainchant seen at times • last songs characterized by tonal ambiguity, avoidance of stable key feeling
	Recurring Harmonies	• chains of 7ths and 9ths used frequently
	Key Scheme / Modulations / Cadences	• expressive modulations through subtle changes in piano figures • unexpected modulations to distant keys and unconventional returns
Rhythm	Metric Organization	• rhythmic patterns fall into regular groupings
	Rhythmic Patterns	• rhythmic framework structured to allow supple phrasing
Accomp.	Predominant Figures	• detailed patterns, demands excellent pedaling • wide variation: broad arpeggiated patterns, dramatic textures, subtle undulating figures
	Preludes, Interludes, Postludes	• introductions and postludes (when used) are rather short; few independent interludes
	Use of Motives	• repetition of a single figure or variant unifies songs, particularly in last period

29

Text Illustrations in Patterns	•	accompaniment often a mood poem that serves to create proper atmosphere
Texture	•	transparent textures
	•	accompaniment often develops freely with its own thematic material
	•	no countermelodies in usual sense of term

Poets/Texts	*Choice of Texts*	•	development of literary taste in style periods: Romantics to Parnassians to Symbolist poets
		•	avoided texts containing distinct colorful verbal descriptions or tense dramatic situations
		•	searched for poetry rich in atmosphere and musical possibilities
	Response to Poetic Content	•	musical elements (thematic motives, rhythms in vocal line, harmonies) emerged from repeated readings of a text

Claude Debussy (1862-1918)

Melody	*Melodic Contour / Phrase Shape*	•	early songs are tuneful and simple in texture
		•	subtle and delicately shaded melodic lines
		•	generally avoids strongly emotional melodic intervals
	Vocal Articulation	•	*mélodies* masterpieces of musical declamation
		•	declamatory (parlando) style, closely resembling French speech inflections in mature songs
Harmony	*Harmonic Texture*	•	harmony important and unique element of Debussy's songs
		•	exotic harmonies: interlocking whole tone scales, pentatonic scales, chromatic and diatonic patterns
	Tonality	•	movement away from key feeling in his middle style
	Key Scheme / Modulations / Cadences	•	fluid harmonic structures result from shifting tonal relationships
		•	freedom of dynamics, phrase, rhythm result in free tonal motion
	Text Illustration through Harmonic Means	•	harmonic color paramount, motivated entirely by the text
		•	shifting harmonies complement poetic symbolism
Rhythm	*Metric Organization*	•	feeling of bar line is erased
	Rhythmic Patterns	•	flowing, non-pulsated rhythmic patterns
	Polyrhythms / Cross-Rhythms with the Voice	•	elements of polyrhythms present in some songs
Accomp.	*General*	•	songs require an excellent pianist
	Text Illustrations in Patterns	•	involved texture of tonal elements, provides a complementary foundation for the voice, but also contributes its own text images
	Texture	•	early songs: simple textures, patterns
		•	mature style: accompaniments generally independent of the vocal line
		•	melodic interest seldom in accompaniment, recedes when voice enters

Poets/Texts	*Choice of Texts*	•	early songs: Parnassian poets
		•	enthusiastic interest in poetry led him to become an integral part of the Symbolist movement
		•	chose texts from twenty-three poets, and wrote his own texts for the *Proses lyriques*
		•	almost half of his songs use verses of the great French poets: Verlaine, Baudelaire, Charles d'Orléans, Mallarmé, François Villon, Tristan L'hermite
		•	set Verlaine more than any other poet

| | *Treatment of Prosody* | • | poetic rhythm set perfectly in musical rhythms |

| | *Response to Poetic Content* | • | great sensitivity to texts (Debussy's extreme interest in literature and poetry as well as his critical writings on music contributed to this.) |

| **Influences** | | • | early songs: Massenet, Gounod, and the voice of Mme. Marie-Blanche Vasnier, a gifted amateur singer with whom he was in love |

Francis Poulenc (1899-1963)

Melody	*General*	•	melody the prime ingredient in a Poulenc song
	Melodic Contour / Phrase Shape	•	favorite intervals: minor sixth leaps, sevenths; extended intervals used at points of high emotion
	Phrase Length	•	generally short melodic phrases, developed as antecedent-consequent
		•	longer phrases infrequent
	Motives	•	frequent melodic motives
	Vocal Articulation	•	simple direct melodies, many with recitative-like declamation
		•	rhapsodic lyric themes, declamatory vocal phrases

Rhythm	*General*	•	extreme contrasts in texture, tempo, timbre, dynamics
		•	fond of terraced dynamics
		•	all dynamic markings should be strictly observed
	Tempo	•	tempos remain constant until change is indicated (Poulenc abhorred *rubato*)
		•	precise metronome markings
	Rhythmic Patterns	•	simple patterns including dance and music-hall rhythms
		•	few rhythmic difficulties in vocal lines
	Text Illustration	•	rhythms conform to dictates of the text, used illustratively
	Polyrhythms / Cross-Rhythms with the Voice	•	mixed meters sometimes appear

Harmony	*Harmonic Texture*	•	eclectic harmonic style that maintains traditional diatonicism
		•	textures generally homophonic, counterpoint rare
	Recurring Harmonies	•	stacked sonorities of tertian structure a hallmark of his style
	Harmonic Text Illustration	•	harmony always structured to highlight aesthetic intent of the poetry
	Tonal vs. Atonal	•	shifting tonalities, and frequent, fluid modulations (A sense of tonality is always present, despite harmonic fluctuations.)

Dissonance vs. Consonance	•	many non-harmonic tones in chords
Chordal Preferences	•	repetitive sequenced patterns
Key Scheme / Modulations / Cadences	•	juxtaposed keys frequent; gradual modulations rare (Poulenc shifted tonal centers in response to textual demands, rarely using modulations.)

Accomp.

General	• •	piano shares equal role with voice in any Poulenc song accompaniments reflect his excellence as a pianist
Predominant Figures	• •	designs mixed, varying in sonority, density, and rhythm usual figures: repeated chords, arpeggios, scale figures, always employed with subtle, individual treatment
Text Illustrations in Patterns	•	accompaniment always enhances content of text and melody
Texture	•	substantial use of pedal ("In a halo of pedals" is a frequent direction in Poulenc's songs.)

Poets/Texts

Choice of Texts	• • • •	impeccable literary taste set contemporary poets almost exclusively major poets: Guillaume Apollinaire, Paul Eluard, Louise de Vilmorin other poets: Max Jacob, Jean Cocteau, Jean Racine, Pierre Ronsard, Maurice Carême, Federico Garcia-Lorca
Treatment of Prosody	•	fastidious attention to prosody; fidelity to the poetry paramount
Response to Poetic Content	•	profound feeling for the inherent drama in texts

Form

- poetry always determines structure
- binary and ternary forms; some songs in one section
- preferred sectional composition to pure through-composed style

AMERICAN

Charles Ives (1874-1954)

Melody *Melodic Contour / Phrase Shape* • melodies change key feeling rapidly

Chromaticism	•	highly chromatic vocal lines
Vocal Articulation	• •	naturalistic declamation in text setting repeated, adjacent notes, non-metrical notation, spoken passages (Ives wrote vocal lines as "informal speech" lines, meant to reflect the spoken sentence.)
Text Painting	• •	borrowed material (quotation) a central element of compositional style (Ives used quotation as musical reminiscence, a sort of stream-of-consciousness device that brings up old tunes with their associative nostalgia and emotion.) fragmented quotations of familiar tunes (hymns, minstrel songs, college songs, etc.)

Harmony	*Harmonic Texture*	• dense harmonic structures mix simplicity with complexity • polychord and polytonal harmonic textures
	Tonality	• Ives: "...why tonality as such should be thrown out for good, I can't see. Why it should be always present, I can't see."
	Dissonance vs. Consonance	• free dissonant counterpoint • tone clusters used in a percussive manner
	Key Scheme / Modulations / Cadences	• extended the harmonic system far beyond traditional harmony • frequent modulations, rarely resolved dissonances
Rhythm	*Metric Organization*	• complex meters and rhythms; irregular meters, unusual accents, including off-beats and syncopation; no regular metrical organization; bar lines and key signatures frequently omitted
	Rhythmic Patterns	• additive rhythms (Ives used rhythmic ideas one after another, each provoking another, until the end of the song is reached.)
Accomp.	*Predominant Figures*	• complex accompaniments more frequent than accompaniments with simple chord patterns
	Use of Motives	• recurring rhythmic figures or brief ostinati in accompaniment rather than vocal line
	Distinctive Dramatic Effects	• surprising piano effects in many songs
Poets/Texts	*Choice of Texts*	• incredibly eclectic choices of texts and poetry—Keats, Stevenson, Lindsay, Browning, poems by his wife (Harmony Twichell Ives), German, French, Italian poems, and his own texts
	Treatment of Prosody	• complex rhythms often obscure the text

Samuel Barber (1910-1981)

Melody	*Melodic Contour / Phrase Shape*	• fluid, flexible melodies of expressive lyricism • early songs: romantic vocal lines • later songs: adds angular phrases
	Phrase Length	• long-lined vocal phrases, carefully suited to word rhythm and stress.
Harmony	*Harmonic Texture*	• contrapuntal textures form a vivid part of his *oeuvre* • dramatic and expansive
	Tonality	• tonal center often masked
		• lyricism always present within tonality
Text Illustration through Harmonic Means		• intervals as unifying devices; sometimes used as seeds for the entire work, chief thematic material, and important structural points
	Dissonance vs. Consonance	• more dissonant chromatic harmonies after 1939
	Contrasts of Major / Minor	• constant shift between major and minor harmony in early works

33

Rhythm	Metric Organization	• meter changes tied to prosody
	Rhythmic Patterns	• active rhythms of many types
Accomp.	Predominant Figures	• varied, wide-ranging figurations
	Text Illustrations in Patterns	• accompaniment describes, comments, or explains the text
	Texture	• variety of accompaniments: some dense-textured and difficult; others lean-lined and simpler
Poets/Texts	Choice of Texts	• lyrical, romantic poetry a preference • diverse texts (dramatic, humorous, atmospheric) always set with lyricism • wide range of texts from eighth century poets to James Joyce, including James Stephens, A.E. Housman, W.B. Yeats, Gerard Manley Hopkins
	Treatment of Prosody	• natural word rhythms always preserved
	Response to Poetic Content	• extreme sensitivity to literature translated into highly expressive settings music always adapted to fit text
Form		• text dictates song form • strong feeling for classical form • large works rooted in principles of sonata construction, but varied to suit style

Ned Rorem (b. 1923)

General		• composes in an essentially lyric style; several songs are in a more popular vein • neo-classic idioms prevalent part of his songs • incorporates twentieth century idioms into a highly individual style, avoiding extremes of the *avant-garde* • his songs evolve with his maturity—later songs are more complex harmonically, rhythmically, pianistically
Melody Melodic Contour / Phrase Shape		• lyrical, smooth, flowing, romantically conceived melodies • understands and writes well for the voice • nature of text determines contour of melody
	Vocal Articulation	• melodic lines follow natural speech inflection
Harmony	Harmonic Texture	• some contrapuntal techniques • chords used in a melodic manner, giving them a melodic character
	Tonality	• rich tonal range
Polyrhythms / Cross-Rhythms with the Voice		• polytonality, extended tritone chords in some works
Rhythm	Metric Organization	• shifting time signatures ("musical meter can literally illustrate the poet's meter")*
	Rhythmic Patterns	• uncomplicated rhythms; relatively few songs depend on rhythmic complexities for primary effect
Polyrhythms / Cross-Rhythms with the Voice		• polyrhythms in some songs

*Quoted in Philip L. Miller, "The Songs of Ned Rorem," *Tempo* 127 (December 1988), 29.

Accomp.		
	General	• accompaniments always enhance and emphasize vocal line, but are not virtuosic
	Predominant Figures	• imitative passages for piano and voice occur in a strict canonic manner • ostinato figures, both rhythmic and melodic
	Texture	• relatively sparse linear construction; some songs dense and thick-textured

Poets/Texts		
	Choice of Texts	• poets from all literary periods set prior to 1950s • since 1950, texts generally confined to twentieth century American poets: Paul Goodman, Theodore Roethke, Kenneth Koch, Howard Moss, Witter Bynner, Walt Whitman
	Response to Poetic Content	• great concern for treatment of text, although poetry as art seems not to interest him as much as its connection to music ("I don't need to understand a poem [whatever that means] so much as to react kinetically to it; sometimes the very act of setting it reveals a meaning...perhaps different from the poet's own.")* • Rorem: "My aim towards poetry is, I suppose, to intensify rather than reinterpret."**

*"*The NATS Bulletin* Interviews Ned Rorem," *The NATS Bulletin* 39:2 (Nov/Dec 1982), 5.
**Ned Rorem, *Pure Contraption* (New York: Holt Rinehart & Winston, 1974), 142.

Influences		
		• French influence in his song style (Rorem's great admiration for Poulenc shows in the elegance, wit, and clarity of his songs.)

BRITISH

Henry Purcell (1659-1695)

Melody		
	General	• overall effect of supreme refinement whether the mood is simple or highly dramatic
	Melodic Contour / Phrase Shape	• rising and falling intervals used for emotional effect • Italian and French operatic traditions influenced melodic writing • words and phrases repeated for dramatic effect
	Vocal Articulation	• flexible declamatory style (Purcell often began a phrase using recitative-like declamation which he developed into a freer *arioso* style.)
	Text Painting	• expressive text painting, often on verbs

Harmony		
	Harmonic Texture	• extensive use of repeated ground basses, used strictly (In his later songs, Purcell writes ground basses in more varied forms.)
	Key Scheme / Modulations / Cadences	• well-controlled modulations in response to dramatic/poetic content • common key relationships: dominant, subdominant, relative major and minor
	Text Illustration	• chromaticism for dramatic/emotional effect within common tonal relationships

Rhythm	Metric Organization	• meter changes linked to changing moods in the poetry
	Rhythmic Patterns	• English speech patterns set with unerring accuracy in rhythms
	Ostinato	• frequent rhythmic ostinati
	Rhythms that Reinforce the Text	• various rhythmic figures (including rests) used for "affect" and dramatic illustration
Accomp.	Predominant Figures	• ground basses in many accompaniments
	Text Illustrations in Patterns	• accompaniments rely strongly on interplay between melody and bass
	Texture	• modern piano accompaniments often do not do justice to Purcell's songs—a more authentic sound is the harpsichord, lute or guitar
Poets/Texts	Choice of Texts	• most songs attached to theatrical productions ("semi-operas")
	Treatment of Prosody	• incontestably set the English language better than anyone else • sense of the word always projected musically

Benjamin Britten (1913-1976)

General		• clarity, precision, and economy of form always present themes of youth, lost innocence, pacifism, good and evil, and death (Britten had impulsive sympathy for the struggle of the human being against the establishment.) • melody, harmony, counterpoint used in unique and varied ways in vocal works
Melody	Melodic Contour / Phrase Shape	• essentially a lyricist with a spontaneous melodic gift • melodies written as purely musical structures, often largely an adjunct of meter and rhythm, containing melismas and other melodic elaboration • melodic sequences used frequently (see also Rhythm and Harmony) • abundance of melodic invention and fondness for vocal cadenzas
	Vocal Articulation	• declamatory quality in vocal lines—some melodies quasi-recitative
Harmony	Harmonic Texture	• harmonies used with extreme versatility • chord outlines used skillfully, without predictable "squareness" • simultaneous layers of tonic and dominant harmony (For an example, see "Echo," the first song of *The Poet's Echo*)
	Tonality	• generally tonal vocal lines
	Dissonance vs. Consonance	• more dissonance in later works
	Text Illustration through Harmonic Means	• harmony and counterpoint comment on text harmonic sequences (see also Melody and Rhythm)

Rhythm *Rhythms that Reinforce the Text*	<ul><li>dotted rhythms of many types and variations</li><li>rhythmic sequences used frequently (see also Melody and Harmony)</li><li>subtle contrapuntal techniques for illustration (These are never used overtly, but establish a mood or an emotion before they're really recognized.)</li></ul>
Accompaniment *Use of Motives*	<ul><li>Britten often uses short melodic motives contrapuntally</li></ul>
Accompaniment Texture	<ul><li>texture in later works *(The Poet's Echo, Songs and Proverbs of William Blake)* becomes more austere</li><li>after *A Charm of Lullabies,* compositions exhibit a growing reliance on melodic independence in accompaniments</li></ul>
Poets/Texts *Choice of texts*	<ul><li>eclectic poetic choices (Arthur Rimbaud, Thomas Hardy) a result of his highly developed literary sense</li><li>reflective poets for mature works (Examples: Michelangelo, John Donne)</li></ul>
Treatment of Prosody	<ul><li>speech-rhythms carefully set, but do not dictate form of melodic phrases</li><li>musical effect takes precedence over precise word-setting (Britten's musical setting adds another dimension to the words in an abstract sense, rather than by actual word-painting or other illustrative devices.)</li></ul>
Response to Poetic Content	<ul><li>texts approached on an intellectual basis (Britten's goal was to create in music the same idea the poet had created in words.)</li><li>immediate response to poetic mood</li><li>sensitivity to all kinds of texts (His long and close association with tenor Peter Pears sharpened his sensitivity to a wide range of literature.)</li></ul>

German Song

The "birthday" of the *Lied*[1] is said to be October 14, 1814—the day Schubert composed "Gretchen am Spinnrade." Schubert's *Lieder* produced a near-revolution in song composition, influencing composers of the *Lied* for the remainder of the century. Robert Schumann (1810-1856), Johannes Brahms (1833-1897), and Hugo Wolf (1860-1903) continued to develop and shape what is known as the "High Romantic *Lied*," each adding his distinctive style to the maturing form: Schubert's descriptive and coloristic accompaniments, coupled with his prodigious gift of melody, underlined the expressive possibilities of the *Lied*; Schumann's *Lieder* highlighted the accompaniment and elevated it to full partnership with the voice; Brahms's *Lieder* emphasized melody and bass lines within a classic tonal plan for form; and Hugo Wolf's songs exemplified his deep sensitivity to literature, revealed in subtle details, bringing about the closest possible fusion of word and tone. These important composers not only shaped the High Romantic *Lied* during the nineteenth century, but also charted the course for its further development.

The German *Lied* has been a traditional form for German composers since the minnesingers[2]; however, the seeds of the High Romantic *Lied* began to sprout in the eighteenth century in the form of the *volkstümliches Lieder*. These *Lieder* often appeared in German theatrical *Singspiels*. They were self-contained strophic songs with simple accompaniments and tuneful melodies that were easily remembered by audiences. The *volkstümliches Lieder* served as a model for early song composers.[3] Over 750 collections of *Lieder* with keyboard accompaniment were published in Germany during the second half of the eighteenth century.[4]

Both Johann Sebastian Bach (1685-1750) and George Frideric Handel (1685-1759) composed songs, but their greatest vocal music is found in their choral and dramatic works. C.P.E. Bach (1714-1788), the most important composer of the first Berlin School, composed some solo songs, much simpler in their style than his father's contrapuntal textures. C.P.E. Bach's younger brother, Johann Christian Bach (1735-1782), settled in London and his thirty-odd songs are set to English texts. German song continued to develop through the eighteenth century, acquiring more sophistication in the works of Christoph Willibald Gluck (1714-1787), Franz Joseph Haydn (1732-1809), Wolfgang Amadeus Mozart (1756-1791), and Ludwig van Beethoven (1770-1827). Gluck, Haydn, and Mozart were only marginally interested in the *Lied*, although their songs showed a higher level of sophistication in the interplay between the voice and piano. Beethoven was a transitional figure in the development of the *Lied*; his accompaniments exploited the capabilities of the "new" piano and greatly influenced Schubert.

In the late eighteenth century, a new type of song appeared in Germany—the ballad, modeled after the popular ballads of England and Scotland. Johann Rudolf Zumsteeg (1760-1802) wrote numerous dramatic ballads; these influenced Carl Loewe (1796-1869), who became well known for his ballads, and Franz Schubert, who seized upon the dramatic qualities inherent in the ballad form. To illustrate the emotions and the dramatic story line in the ballad, an expanded piano texture was needed. Ballads were thus an agent in widening the dramatic scope of the *Lied* and developing a closer relationship between voice and piano.

By the nineteenth century, the German *Lied* was ripe to mature because of several significant factors: the advent of the new German lyric poetry; the pianoforte with its wider range of expressive effects and musical sonorities; and changes in the social and political climate of Germany.

NEW POETRY. Johann Wolfgang von Goethe (1749-1832) was significant in launching the new lyricism in German poetry—freer, more expressive forms, and lyrical verse full of personal expression and awareness of self. Goethe, Heinrich Heine (1797-1856), Joseph von Eichendorff (1788-1857), Friedrich Rückert (1788-1856), and Eduard Möricke (1804-1875) were poets whose texts played an important part in the development of German song. The themes found in Romantic poetry—nature, night, longing, moonlight, fantasy, and magic—offered composers limitless possibilities for their songs.

MORE EXPRESSIVE PIANO. By the end of the eighteenth century, the piano had replaced the clavichord and harpsichord as a solo instrument and as an accompanying instrument for song. The technical and expressive possibilities of the pianoforte played a large part in the development of the *Lied*. Since by definition the *Lied* is a synthesis of poetry and music, the accompaniment contributes significantly to the overall artistic effect. Mozart's early song accompaniments are simple, doubling the vocal line, but his later songs use the piano to achieve mood and illustrate text. Beethoven wrote his accompaniments from an instrumental standpoint; they are full of the same originality and expressive power found in the rest of his music. In his *An die ferne Geliebte*, considered to be the first song cycle, there is an unprecedented interplay of accompaniment and vocal motives. Schubert firmly established a partnership between voice and piano. In his *Lieder*, the piano accompaniment takes on a larger role in developing mood and illustrating poetic content. Imaginative patterns of all types are found in Schubert's accompaniments – figures that play a large part in establishing mood and partnering the voice illustratively. Robert Schumann was a successful composer for the piano, and in his *Lieder*, the voice and piano sing duets. The piano assumes a prominence that places it on an equal footing with the voice; Schumann's songs contain preludes, interludes, and postludes that come close to being tiny piano pieces. Brahms maintains a balance between accompaniment and voice in his *Lieder*; his accompaniments often have sumptuous textures, but play a somewhat limited role in illustrating poetry. Hugo Wolf called his songs "poems for voice and piano"; his accompaniments are full of motives that illustrate text, and textures that show Wagnerian influence. He sought to compose accompaniments that created a background for the poem and expressed emotions that the voice could not.

SOCIAL AND POLITICAL CLIMATE. The popularity of the pianoforte affected music making in the homes of the middle class, where women in particular spent time pursuing cultural activities—singing, playing the piano, and learning to draw or paint. A tradition of domestic music making was established, and with it, a profitable market for accessible keyboard music and keyboard-accompanied song.

As the century progressed, Germany's middle and lower classes acquired social mobility and began to look for entertainment outside the home in theaters and concert halls.

Although the *Lied* was a small form complete in itself, composers sought to expand its scope in some way, while retaining its unique qualities. The *song cycle* developed naturally from the *Lied*. By grouping songs with a common poetic theme or story into a connected set of songs, composers extended the miniature *Lied* into a larger, more impressive work. Schubert's *Die schöne Müllerin* and *Winterreise*, and Schumann's *Dichterliebe*, are examples of the nineteenth-century song cycle. The length of this "new" vocal form, however, made it unsuitable for drawing-room concerts, and, in the mid-nineteenth century, it began to move into the concert halls. By the end of the century, composers were orchestrating songs originally written for the piano; this practice led to the independently conceived orchestral song cycle. Mahler's *Lieder eines fahrenden Gesellen* (Songs of a Wayfarer) is an example of an orchestrally conceived song cycle.

The *Lied* declined as a form in the twentieth century. Composers continued to create orchestral song compositions, and began to explore new techniques with tonal colors and sonorities. Richard Strauss and Gustav Mahler orchestrated many of their songs, and also wrote extended vocal compositions for voice and orchestra. Strauss and Alban Berg added new works to the operatic repertory as well.

Twentieth-century German composers continued to write songs, though the golden age of the High Romantic *Lied* had passed. The songs of Arnold Schoenberg, Alban Berg, Paul Hindemith, Joseph Marx, Hans Pfitzner, and Kurt Weill are examples of individual styles that blended contemporary techniques into existing formal patterns.

The great body of High Romantic *Lied* produced during the nineteenth century by Schubert, Schumann, Brahms, and Wolf had far-reaching influence on song composers throughout Europe and the United States. This literature continues to be studied, sung, and cherished by countless performers and audiences.

Notes

1. The German word for song is *Lied* (pl. *Lieder*). The word is also used to identify the German art song that evolved in the late eighteenth century and became a dominant vocal genre of nineteenth-century Romanticism.
2. Poet-composers of the twelfth and thirteenth centuries.
3. *Volkstümlichkeit*, a term that encompasses both the idea of "folk quality" and "national character," was the ideal of the composers of the second Berlin School (Johann Abraham Peter Schultz, Johann Friedrich Reichardt, and Carl Friedrich Zelter were the most prominent names). Their songs were strophic, with simple textures and harmonies and tuneful melodies.
4. Donald Jay Grout, *A History of Western Music*, 479.

FRANZ JOSEPH HAYDN (1732-1809)

> All of his works are characterized by lucidity, perfect finish, studied moderation, avoidance of meaningless phrases, firmness of design, and richness of development.
>
> —Carl F. Pohl and William H. Husk[1]

Haydn composed about forty songs, and although pleasantly tuneful and charming, they are not representative of his writing for the voice. His true vocal style may be most clearly seen in the arias in his oratorios, *The Seasons* and *The Creation*, and in his operas.

Haydn's earliest vocal work, *Lieder für das Klavier,* dates from 1781. This set may be performed with voice and keyboard or, with the exception of two songs, by keyboard alone, which illustrates Haydn's rather low opinion of the importance of text. He often set pedestrian verses given to him by friends or acquaintances; many of his songs are strophic and sometimes tedious.

The *English Canzonettas* of 1794 contain some of his most charming songs, although the relationship between the poetry and the music is only skin-deep and does not progress beyond a rather superficial union.

Although Haydn's song accompaniments are generally predictable, he wrote them with more independent musical interest from the voice part than did previous composers. For instance, he often presented the coming vocal phrases in the introductory material in the piano. Haydn was one of the first composers to write out his song scores in three staves instead of two, thus paving the way for the development of the piano accompaniment that was to flower in the nineteenth-century German *Lied.*

She Never Told Her Love   1795
(William Shakespeare. *Twelfth Night,* Act II)

Haydn assigns the piano the lion's share of this song—Shakespeare's text is nearly buried in the piano texture. Viola, disguised as a boy, tells the Duke of her love for him in an allegory ("My father had a daughter lov'd a man"). Haydn's setting is through-composed, without verse organization. Vocal phrases are short, organized in word groups corresponding to Shakespeare's declamation; these phrases tend to interrupt and punctuate the piano accompaniment rather than dominate it. Nonetheless, this song is one of Haydn's best-known and most-performed songs and should be cited as an early example of an attempt to involve the piano equally with the voice to establish a dramatic atmosphere.

A Pastoral Song   1794
(Anne Hunter)

Haydn's *English Canzonettas* are settings of twelve texts by Anne Hunter, wife of a prominent London doctor, whom he had met on his first visit to London in 1791. In 1794, he made a second visit to London and renewed the acquaintance. Anne Hunter was then widowed, and Haydn's mastery of elementary English made a warm friendship possible. Hunter's poems are uneven, as are Haydn's settings—understandable due to his superficial understanding of English—but the set contains some of Haydn's most-performed songs.

Often titled as the first line of text, "My mother bids me bind my hair," this song is one of Haydn's most familiar efforts in the genre. The original title of this verse was "Pastorale," and it is occasionally called "Shepherd's Song." Anne Hunter had originally set this verse to an *Andante* from a sonata by Pleyel, a common practice of that day.[2] Haydn's settings do little to soften the sentimentality of Hunter's verses; rather, they often intensify it. There are two verses, set identically. The song displays an ease of musical expression, lilting melody, and a close relationship between voice and piano. This piece was a favorite of celebrated coloratura Jenny Lind, who performed it as a dramatic scene.

The Spirit's Song   **1795**
(Anne Hunter)

The text of this *canzonetta* was no doubt inspired by the Gothic romances that were wildly popular in London at that time. While the text is overly dramatic, it is also romantically dark; the spirit of a dead lover counsels his lamenting loved one not to grieve, for "My spirit wanders free/And waits 'til Thine shall come."

Haydn's musical setting in this song is more complex and developed. There are four verses, set in through-composed form. Haydn uses elements of the sonata principle and shares material between the voice and piano. Interludes and transitions in the piano are beautifully constructed. Accompaniment from the first verse is used for the last verse. The epilogue contains a unifying factor, a pedal point on the tonic note, embellished with a turn borrowed from the interlude that precedes the B section.

Extended Study List
   O Tuneful Voice • Lob der Faulheit • Das Leben ist ein Traum • The Mermaid's Song • The Sailor's Song • Piercing Eyes

Selected Reading
   Karl Geiringer with Irene Geiringer, *Haydn: A Creative Life in Music* (Berkeley: University of California Press, 1982).
   H.C. Robbins Landon, *Haydn: Chronicle and Works* (Bloomington: Indiana University Press, 1978). A four-volume study of Haydn and his works. Volume 2 includes the years at the Esterházy Palace and the operas composed and performed there.
   Nick Rossi, "Joseph Haydn and Opera," *Opera Quarterly*, 1:1 , Spring 1983, 54-78.

Notes
   1. Carl F. Pohl and William. H. Husk, "Joseph Haydn," *Grove's Dictionary of Music and Musicians*, ed. Eric Blom. 5th edition , 164.
   2. James Husst Hall, *The Art Song*, 30.

WOLFGANG AMADEUS MOZART (1756-1791)

> Mozart wrote everything with such ease and speed as might first be taken for carelessness or haste; also he never went to the pianoforte while composing. His imagination held before him the whole work clear and lively once it was conceived. When he received the text for a vocal work he went about with it for some time, thought himself thoroughly into it, and gave it all the powers of his fantasy. Then he worked out his ideas fully on the pianoforte and then for the first time sat down to write. Consequently, the writing was for him an easy task during which he often joked or chattered.
>
> —Niemetschek[1]

Although songs do not figure prominently in Mozart's catalog of compositions, the best of them still exhibit his intuitive sense of blending music and drama. He set German, French, and Italian poetry with an unerring sense of musical style that elevated his best songs above rather pedestrian texts. With the exception of Goethe, he did not use the greatest poetry of the day; his oft-quoted statement that "poetry must be altogether the obedient daughter of the music" holds true in his songs as well as in his operas.

Mozart composed comparatively few songs and considered them fairly insignificant—in one instance giving one away to a friend who later claimed it as his own work.[2] His earliest songs in the *volkstümliches Lied* (folk song) tradition—charming strophic miniatures composed primarily for home entertainment—are little more than a melody with a bass line, with few inner voices. Mozart often obliged a host or hostess with a song composed on the spot. These songs are beautiful in the sense that Mozart was incapable of writing a poorly crafted work, no matter how small; however, the body of strophic songs do not stand out as Mozart's best.

After 1775, most songs are through-composed and begin to exhibit operatic characteristics. His most significant songs were written around the time of *Le nozze di Figaro* and *Don Giovanni*. His best-known song "Das Veilchen," a masterful setting of Goethe's poem, is a little operatic scene cast in song form. In his last years, the songs are a mixture of styles, some elaborate, some still simple. The final songs are simple text repetitions, entirely strophic, and restricted in vocal range.

Ridente la calma, K. 152 **Contentment Reposes. 1772-1775**
(Anonymous)

As Mozart's interest in operatic composition blossomed, his songs took on quite a different character and musical expression, moving away from a folk song format toward a more elegant Italianate style. This is one of the songs he wrote in Salzburg, in his teens. By this time, Mozart had composed seven Italian operas; this song falls between his operas *Lucio Silla* (1772) and *La finta giardiniera* (1775).

The song is in ABA form; its vocal phrases are longer, spun-out, and more emotionally expressive. Accompaniment figures are discreet and supportive.

Dans un bois solitaire, K. 308   **In a Dark and Lonely Wood. 1777**
(Antoine Ferrand)

Mozart set two French texts during his visit to Mannheim (1777-78) for Mlle. "Gustl " (Auguste) Wending, the daughter of his hosts —this *"chanson"* and the one titled "Oiseaux, si tous les ans." Both songs exhibit French elegance and style. Einstein refers to this song as "Watteau in music," [3] and it is not unlike the rococo spirit of the minuetto of the "Haffner" *Serenade in D major*, K. 250/248b, composed a year earlier.

Like "Als Luise die Briefe" (see below), this is a little dramatic scene, quasi-operatic in style. The music is full of operatic devices, used tastefully and scaled to miniature form. The opening section is repeated at the end of the song.

While wandering in the woods, a girl comes upon a sleeping cupid. She is drawn to him because he reminds her of her past faithless love. He awakens and shoots his arrow through her heart; she will love her faithless lover forever for having dared to wake him.

Das Veilchen, K. 476   **The Violet. 1785**
(Johann Wolfgang von Goethe)

"Das Veilchen" was not Goethe's most famous poem, but it is Mozart's best-known song, justly famous for its synthesis of music and poetry. It is through-composed, a miniature drama that has the economy and thematic unity of the true *Lied*. As the story unfolds, the musical treatment of both voice and piano highlights the dramatic scene: the tripping gait of the little shepherdess, the longing lyric lines of the violet, the careless trampling of the tiny flower. Mozart's highly developed theatrical sense is nowhere more visible than in the passage that illustrates the death of the violet: At "Es sank, und starb, und freut' sich noch," the voice line descends in recitative; the harmonic and rhythmic progressions in the piano shift to illustrate the little drama, and then smoothly segue into figures of increased movement. In a tiny postscript, Mozart repeats two short poetic phrases at the end of the song: "Das arme Veilchen! es war ein herzigs Veilchen."

Als Luise die Briefe, ihres ungetreuen Liebhabers verbrannte, K. 520
On Louise's burning her faithless lover's letters. 1787
(Gabriele von Baumberg)

"Als Luise..." is a tiny operatic *scena*, intensely dramatic and full of passion. Mozart's treatment of the text is highly theatrical; piano figures illustrate the crackling flames and Luise's emotional state which fluctuates from bitter anger to poignant despair. The form is through-composed but with a musical structure that progresses so naturally and dramatically that it seems perfectly rounded. This song and "Abendempfindung" were composed in 1787, the year of *Don Giovanni*.

Abendempfindung, K. 523   **Evening Thoughts. 1787**
(Joachim Heinrich Campe)

An Italianate vocal line crowns this beautiful song. The song's format is through-composed with varied accompaniment figures that point up the dramatic/poetic content. Vocal phrases are long-lined and reminiscent of Mozart's arias; they have a cumulative effect, increasing in intensity and passion to the final measures. Operatic devices found in the vocal line include ornamentation, vocal roulades, and some declamatory phrases. In this song, Mozart anticipated the Romantic style and the *Lieder* of Schubert that were yet to come.

Extended Study List
Der Zauberer • Die Zufriedenheit • Oiseaux si tous les ans • Gesellenreise • Lied und Trennung • An Chlöe • Komm, liebe zither • Sehnsucht nach dem Frühling

Selected Reading
Brigid Brophy, *Mozart the Dramatist: a New View of Mozart, his Operas and his Age* (London: Faber and Faber, 1964. 2nd edition 1988).
Edward Dent, *Mozart's Operas* (London: Oxford University Press, 2nd edition, 1960).
Alfred Einstein, *Mozart: His Character, His Work*, trans. Arthur Mendel and Nathan Broder (New York: Oxford University Press, 1962).
William Mann, *Mozart's Operas* (New York: Oxford University Press, 1977).
W.J. Turner, *Mozart: The Man and His Work*, rev. and ed. by Christopher Raeburn (New York: Barnes & Noble, 1966).

Notes
1. Quoted in W.J. Turner, *Mozart: The Man and His Work,* 282.
2. Alfred Einstein, *Mozart: His Character, His Work* , 377-378.
3. Ibid., 374.

LUDWIG VAN BEETHOVEN (1770-1827)

Strength is the morality of the man who stands out from the rest, and it is mine.

—Ludwig van Beethoven[1]

Beethoven is a transitional figure in his songs, as in other musical forms. Although his songs exhibit his interest in experimentation, as a group they fall into the eighteenth-century idiom rather than the nineteenth. He composed about sixty-six songs of a variety of types; fifty-nine to German texts, and seven to texts in Italian, including the concert aria, "Ah! perfido." His contribution to song literature includes short folk-like songs as well as a number of extended pieces, often in the form of a scene and aria. Beethoven's songs come closer in style to Haydn's than to Mozart's songs.

Several factors would influence the explosion of *Lied* composition: the new pianoforte, the quality of romantic poetry, and changes in the social and political climate. It was the piano that made Beethoven's experiments with song both interesting and ingenious. In his songs, one senses the *Lied* poised on the brink of development.

Although Beethoven wrote songs throughout his life, they were not paramount in his overall output; he once remarked to a friend that he didn't like composing them. In spite of his predilection for larger instrumental forms, his songs are important for introducing creative ideas that were to flower in the works of Schubert and Schumann. His expanded harmonies and his concept of the song cycle influenced the great *Lied* composers who followed.

Adelaide, Op. 46   1795-96
(Friedrich von Matthisson)

"Adelaide" is undeniably Italianate in style, reflecting the influence that Italian music was exerting on early song composers. Beethoven was no exception; both he and Schubert had studied composition with Antonio Salieri. Some of Beethoven's early songs are on texts of Metastasio, and he submitted them to Salieri to have the word setting checked.

The extended length and style of this song has made it difficult to categorize—is it a traditional *andante-allegro* form, a miniature dramatic concert aria, a little cantata, a "lyrical fantasia"? Certainly in length, musical freedom, and text structure, it resembles a solo cantata or concert aria. Beethoven bends Matthison's poetry to meet his musical needs, repeating Adelaide's name fourteen times (the original poem has four repetitions).

The work is in three sections. The first is accompanied by a smooth broken-chord figure in triplets; the second section develops dramatically, its final measures transitional to the concluding *allegro* section. This section is an assertive blend of lyric expression and dramatic suggestion in both voice and piano. Beethoven's varied accompaniment figures maintain variety throughout; the vocalism is broadly phrased and beautifully lyric.

Wonne der Wehmut,* Op. 83, No. 1   Bliss of Sadness. 1811
(Johann Wolfgang von Goethe)

Tears of eternal love...tears of unhappy love...at the heart of Goethe's poem is this sentiment: tears provide emotional release that express life's pain and make the desolate world easier to endure.

Goethe's poem is short—six lines of irregular meter. Beethoven extends its length by repeating the text. This *Lied* is an early example of the independence of the piano accompaniment; Beethoven gives it a descriptive voice of its own, which functions to highlight the poetry. Vocal phrases seem similarly independent, but only in the little recitative-like utterance "Trocknet nicht"; all other phrases are doubled by the piano.

Beethoven was not above text illustration; a descending figure in the accompaniment calls to mind flowing tears, and is used like a tiny motive. "Trocknet nicht" (Dry not) is given a repetitive rhythm that binds the vocal phrases together; here the writing is declamatory and quite free. The voice has a lovely extended climactic phrase "Tränen unglücklicher Liebe!" four measures from the end of the song.

*This poem was also set by Robert Franz, Johann Reichardt, Franz Schubert, and Carl Friedrich Zelter.

An die ferne Geliebte, Op. 98
(Aloys Jeitteles)

To the Distant Beloved. 1816

Auf dem Hügel sitz' ich spähend (I sit on the hill, looking) • Wo die Berge so blau
(Where the mountains so blue) • Leichte Segler in den Höhen (Clouds lightly
sailing on high) • Diese Wolken in den Höhen (These clouds high overhead)•
Es kehret der Maien, es blühet die Au' (Maytime is coming, the meadow
blooms)• Nimm sie hin dann, diese Lieder (Accept them then, these songs)

Although Beethoven wrote other songs of quality, Op. 98 is a most important
work, since it may be considered the first song cycle. Although flawed dramatically, *An die ferne Geliebte* is connected through musical materials, pointing the way
for future song cycles. The first edition carries this phrase, printed below the title:
Ein Liederkreis * *von Al. Jeitteles.*

Aloys Jeitteles (1794-1858) was a young medical student and musical amateur
whose works had been published in current periodicals. The poems of *An die ferne
Geliebte* recount the thoughts of a forlorn lover on his departed beloved. Jeitteles's
poetry contains a predominance of Romantic themes prevalent in poetry of the day:
love, pain, nature (forest/brook/birds), longing.

The merit of *An die ferne Geliebte* must be attributed to Beethoven's musical
setting, not the poetry. As with all of his compositions, Beethoven's extraordinary
individuality is clearly evident. The work is a series of themes and variations,
notable for the extensive involvement of the piano in the form and mood of the
piece. Each of the six sections or "songs" is linked to the next by transitional material in the piano, which prepares or introduces key changes and figures to be used
in the next song. Beethoven further unifies the *Lieder* by using music from the
beginning of the work to close the cycle, varying it to highlight the emotion of the
text, anticipating Schumann's *Frauenliebe und -leben,* which uses the same technique. The first and last songs end with the same poetic line "und ein liebend Herz
erreichet, was ein liebend Herz geweiht!" The cycle is a little over fourteen minutes
in length and must be performed as a unit.

*A garland, or circle of songs.

Der Kuss
(Christian Weisse)

The Kiss. Sketched 1798-99
Published 1822

"Ariette" was Beethoven's title for this charming little song, a flirtatious scene
in which a boy and girl coyly exchange a kiss. The action: boy asks girl if she will
give him a kiss, girl replies she will scream if he kisses her. She does scream—but
a long time later. Beethoven repeats the key word "lange" almost ten times to drive
the point home.

The setting is fresh and tunefully pastoral until Chloe's scream, which ushers
in more reinforced, dramatic accompaniment and an extended explanation.

"Der Kuss" was the last known song by Beethoven.

Extended Study List

Mailied • *Sechs geistliche Lieder,* Op. 48 (von Christian Gellert): Bitten / Die Liebe des Nächsten / Vom
Tode / Die Ehre Gottes aus der Natur / Gottes Macht und Vorschung / Busslied • Neue Liebe, neues
Leben • Ich liebe dich • Che fa il mio bene? (L'amante impaziente I, Op. 82, No. 3/also Op. 82, No. 4)

• An die Hoffnung • La Marmotte • In questa tomba oscura • Dimmi, ben mio • T'intendo, sì mio cor • Kennst du das Land • Aus Goethes Faust (Floh-Lied) • Sehnsucht • Mit einem Gemalten Band

Selected Reading

Anneliese Landau, *The Lied: The Unfolding of Its Style* (Lanham: University Press of America, 1980).

Jack M. Stein, *Poem and Music in the German Lied from Gluck to Hugo Wolf* (Cambridge: Harvard University Press, 1971).

Notes

1. Quoted in Harold Schonberg, *The Lives of the Great Composers*, 104.

JOHANN CARL GOTTFRIED LOEWE (1796-1869)

> The ballad requires a mystical touch, by which the mind is brought into that frame of undefined sympathy and awe which men unavoidably feel when face to face with the miraculous or with the mighty forces of nature.
>
> —Johann Wolfgang von Goethe[1]

Carl Loewe was born a few months before Schubert and outlived him by forty years. Loewe composed approximately 400 songs, varied in quality and in character. Loewe was organist at St. Jacobus church in Stettin and lived there for forty-six years, traveling frequently to the capitals of Europe. Although he set a number of beautiful *Lieder*, he is chiefly remembered as a composer of ballads, his most significant works. Loewe felt ballads were more important than *Lieder* because "they proffer action instead of narration, and approach the higher realm of dramatic art."[2]

A ballad may be defined as a narrative song-poem with a rhythm adapted for singing. An earlier definition was tied to dance—"a song to dance to." The word *ballad* traces to *balade*, from the old French, which had itself borrowed the word from the Provençal *balad*, from the verb *balar*—to dance.[3]

Ballads are the epitome of *Drama im kleinen* (miniature drama). They are dramatic dialogues, born from the traidition of oral poetry. These ballads inspired a number of late eighteenth-century composers (Zumsteeg, Zelter, Reichardt) to set them to music. Loewe, however, was the first to create musical settings that equaled the quality of the text. In addition to Loewe's settings, most of the major German *Lieder* composers set ballads; some examples: Schumann's "Die beiden Grenadiere," Schubert's "Erlkönig," and the dialogue ballad "Der Tod und das Mädchen," Brahms's "Edward," Wolf's "Der Rattenfänger" and "Der Feuerreiter."

Loewe's highly developed sense of drama drew him to texts of dramatic quality, especially those with supernatural subjects. He also set many translations of English, Irish, and Scottish ballads, which were much admired by composers of the day. Wagner was among them, and he often played and sang them for his guests. Loewe's use of musical motives in his ballads no doubt attracted Wagner's attention.

Loewe's flair for melodic invention was not startling, but he made effective use of piano accompaniments in creating musical characterization. His narrative ballads are his best vocal works, extraordinarily original and communicative vehicles for the text. In addition to his ballads and *Lieder*, Loewe composed symphonies, concertos, numerous piano pieces, five operas, over a dozen oratorios, and chamber works. Most all of the instrumental works remain in manuscript, never published.

Edward,* Op. 1, No. 1   1818
(Scottish Ballad, translated by Johann Gottfried Herder)

"Edward" is one of Loewe's earliest efforts and was published with two other pieces (one being "Erlkönig") as Op. 1. The text is a German form of the tragic Scottish ballad of the same name. Obviously, the Scottish dialect does not transfer to German, but Herder's skillful translation retains the general verse design and metric scheme of the original poem, including the exclamation "O" at the end of each stanza.

Each stanza of the gruesome ballad is a question-and-answer exchange between Edward and his mother. Tension builds as the cross-exmination progresses, each verse providing more information leading to the discovery of the horrible deed that Edward has committed—the murder of his father. The poem has a tinge of the supernatural about it; Edward committed murder, presumably on the counsel of his mother, but his motives for doing so are veiled and only suggested.

Loewe delineates the characters by setting the mother's questions in $\frac{6}{8}$ and her son's replies in $\frac{2}{4}$, and by giving each a separate melodic theme. Vocal phrases are set syllabically, creating a mood of breathlessness. Edward's vocal phrases are somewhat varied to illustrate his agitation. With each repetition, the characters' themes are slightly varied.

Loewe repeats this basic design, varying the accompaniment figures, melody and rhythm in keeping with the text until the final verse, which uses arpeggios in contrary motion. Although the form of the ballad is through-composed, Loewe's variances in accompaniment, rhythm, melody and harmony combine to retain the impression of stanza form.

*This text was also set by Franz Schubert and as a duet by Johannes Brahms and Piotr Il'yich Tchaikovsky.

Erlkönig, Op. 1, No. 3   Erlking. 1818
(Johann Wolfgang von Goethe)

Goethe's original poem was used in a *Singspiel** titled "Die Fischerin" (1782). As the curtain rises, the heroine Dortchen is mending nets and singing "Erlkönig." The music to which the poem was sung was composed by Corona Schröter, the actress who played Dortchen in the first performance at Weimar.

Loewe's ballad was composed in 1818, three years after Schubert's setting of the poem (and three years before its publication). It is one of the best examples of Loewe's skill in blending music and drama. Curiously, both composers chose G minor as the key for their settings of the poem.[4]

Loewe sets the stage immediately by a *tremolando* chord pattern over the tonic pedal which depicts the shimmering branches of the willow trees. The singer's line is doubled in octaves in the bass line of the accompaniment. Loewe changes the accompaniment for each stanza, introducing the new material in a brief interlude between verses. The narrator sings the outer stanzas; the father, the second stanza; the Erlking has the third, fifth, and seventh; and the child sings the fourth and sixth. There are periodic changes of key and mode (major-minor) as well.

Loewe unifies the work with the tremolo pattern, which continues through nearly all of the song. He constructs the vocal phrases in stepwise and chordal patterns. The concluding four words are in recitative with the piano providing the last eerie chords, over an octave tremolo. Loewe's ending is less melodic than Schubert's and more chilling in its stark intervals.

Goethe is said to have preferred Schubert's setting to Loewe's; however, this musical interpretation has much to commend it.** In it, Loewe has preserved the folk quality of the poetry[5] within a highly dramatic atmosphere.

*A play with spoken dialogue, interspersed with songs.
**Loewe's setting should be compared with that of Franz Schubert, composed three years earlier.

Herr Oluf, Op. 1, No. 2   1821
(Johann Gottfried Herder)

This ballad is subtitled "Whoever Danced with the Elves Would Feel Such Joy That He Would Not Stop Dancing Until He Fell Dead." Herder's dramatic story of the encounter of Herr Oluf with the Erlking's daughter on the eve of his wedding is reminiscent of the supernatural confrontation found in Schumann's "Waldesgespräch."

Loewe's skill as a musical storyteller is clearly apparent in his innovative writing for voice and piano. Narrator, fairy princess and Oluf are differentiated by vocal phrase shapes, accompaniment, and texture. Descending octaves in the bass are part of a "riding music" pattern that introduces Oluf's journey to invite friends to his wedding; "dancing music" in the upper octaves heralds the Erlking's daughter before she appears vocally. Her voice is accompanied by agitated fluttering figures, a magical dance designed to charm and kill.

After refusing her invitation to dance, the fairy princess strikes Oluf a mortal blow. He slowly returns home, accompanied by a short, rolling chromatic figure in the piano. When he reaches his house, he speaks with his mother is in the minor key; she responds in the major.

The last section is a somber *andantino* wedding-march; wide unsettled intervals in the vocal line and the piano belie the fact that something is wrong. The discovery of the dead Oluf by his bride is chillingly intoned by the narrator in close intervals that descend to a final low E on the word "dead."

Extended Study List

Odins Meeresritt • Archibald Douglas • Der Nöck • Elvershöh • Der Mummelsee • *Frauenliebe* (Seven settings from Chamisso's *Frauenliebe und –leben*) • Der Mohrenfürst auf der Messe • Wanderers Nachtlied • Tom der Reimer • Die wandelnde Glocke • Hinkende Jamben

Selected Reading

James Elson, "Carl Loewe and the Ninteenth Century German Ballad," *The NATS Bulletin,* (October 1971).
Hans Joachim Moser, *The German Solo Song and the Ballad.* Ed. K.G. Fellerer (Köln: Arno Volk Verlag, 1958).
Sydney Northcote, *The Ballad in Music* (New York: Oxford University Press, 1942).
Jürgen Thym, "Crosscurrents in Song: Five Distinctive Voices," in *German Lieder in the Nineteenth Century*, ed. Rufus Hallmark (New York: Schirmer Books, 1996), 153-185.

Notes

1. Goethe, writing of an "ideal ballad," quoted in James Husst Hall, *The Art Song*, 56.
2. Paul Hamburger. Liner notes. *Great German Songs,* Vol. 2. Hans Hotter, bass-baritone, Gerald Moore, pianist. Seraphim LP 60065.
3. Elaine Brody and Robert Fowkes, *The German Lied and Its Poetry*, 182.
4. The two versions were published in the same year, although Schubert's composition preceded Loewe's by three years. Loewe had no knowledge of Schubert's version.
5. In Jack M. Stein, *Poem and Music in the German Lied from Gluck to Hugo Wolf*, 63-64.

FRANZ SCHUBERT (1797-1828)

I have come into the world for no purpose but to compose.

—Franz Schubert[1]

Schubert's contribution to both romanticism and song are immeasurable. He took the forms, the harmonic and melodic devices, the rhythmic possibilities, and the poetic expressiveness of his predecessors and contemporaries and molded them into a heightened sort of brief lyrical exclamation that anticipated most of the song composition of the entire century.

—Donald Ivey[2]

The songs of Franz Schubert form the great cornerstone of nineteenth-century German *Lieder*. Brahms wrote: "There is not a song of Schubert's from which one cannot learn something."[3] He composed over 600 songs, setting texts by approximately ninety poets. The High Romantic *Lied* and its composers—Schumann, Loewe, Mendelssohn, Brahms, Liszt, Mahler, Wolf—all looked back to Schubert for influence and inspiration. By mid-century, over half of his songs had been published in France. According to Noske, their popularity helped to advance the heightened dramatic-musical content of the emerging *mélodie*.[4]

Artistic conditions in Germany were at their optimum for the Schubertian *Lied* to take root and flower. The sudden proliferation of German verse by poets like Schiller, Heine, Goethe, Müller, Rückert provided Schubert, a voracious reader, with a range of poetic choices; the development of the pianoforte offered a more expressive instrument for blending voice, accompaniment, and text.

Schubert's songs develop and anticipate every formal structure: strophic, strophic variation, through-composed, declamatory. He lavished equal care on the tiniest lyric song or an extended dramatic scene. He produced the first great German song cycles of remarkable character and quality (*Die schöne Müllerin* and *Winterreise*), which influenced song composers who succeeded him.

His vast catalog of songs explored the myriad possibilities of style and structure. His treatment of the accompaniment was unique for his time and looks ahead to the vocal works of Schumann. He had an intuitive melodic gift and the ability to gauge the essence of a poem and transform it melodically, from the simplest text to the most intensely dramatic. As a result, his *Lieder* display an extraordinary range of musical characterizations, moods, and styles. Schubert's melodies are fresh, inventive, and spontaneous—they seem inevitably "right."

In a Schubert song, the piano is an active supporter of the voice. It unifies stanzas and sets the scene. Schubert's arsenal of piano figures used as tone painting is legion: water figures of all types, patterns evoking nature (whispering winds, rustling leaves), and inanimate objects and their sounds (a whirring spinning wheel, a creaky weather-vane, a bubbling brook, and so on). Conceivably Schubert's piano accompaniments were influenced by figures and style found in Beethoven's piano works, which he greatly admired. In addition to creating atmosphere, the piano often comments on the action and sometimes anticipates or echoes the vocal phrase. It remained for Schumann to elevate the piano to equal stature with the voice, but Schubert's *Lieder* contain clear directions for development.

His pathetically short life was occupied with composition. The boy Schubert, a schoolmaster's son, became a member of the Imperial Choir of Vienna, where he received early training. His earliest surviving song was written in 1811; it was shown to Antonio Salieri and in the course of time, Schubert became his pupil. He composed his first masterpiece, "Gretchen am Spinnrade," at age sixteen.

For the next fifteen years he created continuously, writing 250 songs during the years of 1815 and 1816. His sense of inspiration was like a hair trigger; by age nineteen he had written nearly one-half of his entire output. In addition to his *Lieder*, he composed numerous chamber works, piano music, symphonies, operas, and choral music. After a disastrous stint as a schoolmaster, Schubert settled in Vienna where he attempted to make a living as a composer. He was aided by many friends who sought to disseminate his compositions by literary evenings in private homes ("Schubertiads"). This small circle of devoted friends prided themselves on universal artistic tastes ranging from music to poetry to painting. In Johann Michael Vogel, a distinguished singer of the day, Schubert found an interpreter for his songs as well as a critical artist.[5] They formed a close friendship; Vogel helped Schubert financially whenever he could and performed Schubert's songs frequently in the homes where regular musical evening concerts were held. At the time of his death, Schubert's songs and other music were gaining ever-widening recognition outside his own circle.

Of Schubert's *Lieder*, distinguished pianist-accompanist Gerald Moore wrote: "Their simplicity and purity defeat us and hold us...eternally...through our inability to explain why or how they are so sublime."[6]

Gretchen am Spinnrade	**Gretchen at the Spinning Wheel. 1814**
D. 118 from *Faust*, Part I.	
(Johann Wolfgang von Goethe)	

Schubert's first great masterpiece in song, this work is a landmark in the history of the form. Young Schubert's first setting of Goethe produced what must be considered the first modern *Lied*. He was to set Goethe's texts seventy-three times. He had been reading *Faust* and was obviously seized by the story. A few weeks later, he set the Church Scene (Szene aus *Faust*) to music for two soloists and chorus.

Gretchen sits in what we may imagine as a closed and cramped room, alone with her spinning wheel and her remembrance of Faust. The incessant whir of the turning wheel and her almost unvaried vocal phrases create a sense of confinement, and it is high drama when the voice breaks free from its repetitive phrase shapes. The song is tightly bound together by the rhythmic pattern of the spinning wheel and the treadle, which maintains dramatic and emotional tension.

Schubert's attention to dramatic detail is extraordinary. Gretchen's inner feelings are painted in masterful touches: her breathless gasp "Ich finde. ich finde sie nimmer"; the sudden shifts of vocal register from "Die ganze Welt ist mir vergällt" to "Mein armer Kopf ist mir verrückt"; her remembrance of Faust's kiss, so ecstatic a picture that the wheel stops turning; the searing intensity of her vocal phrases building to another climax at "an seinen Küssen vergehen sollt"; and finally, her despairing repetition of "Meine Ruh ist hin" before the final measures.

Schubert's genius for dramatic characterization is clearly seen in "Gretchen" and "Erlkönig," both early songs. Notice the vivid imagery after "Und ach...sein Kuss!" The treadle comes to a stop as the moment of rapture is relived. There are two unsuccessful tries to restart her wheel—the pattern begins, then falters—and it takes an extra bit of energy to get it moving again. But the sensuous memory is too much; at "Mein Busen drängst sich nach ihm hin" her agitation builds again, her foot is heavier on the treadle (intervals in the left hand rather than a single note), and her mind can only focus on recapturing the passion of that moment. Schubert expands this final climax by repeating "an seinen Küssen vergehen sollt," then lets the passionate moment cool down with a final repetition of the first two poetic lines ("Meine Ruh' ist hin/Mein Herz ist schwer") as Gretchen sinks into melancholy again, and the song ends.

Erlkönig, D. 328 (published as Op. 1)   Erlking. 1815?
(Johann Wolfgang von Goethe)

This is surely the best known of all Schubert's *Lieder*; its publication and performance helped spread his reputation during his lifetime and after his death. Although it is more often than not performed by men, it is not solely their domain. Goethe was much taken by a performance by Wilhelmine Schröder-Devrient, a female singer of formidable dramatic talent.

This great ballad poem is based on the Danish tale of the Ellerkrone (Elf Woman) but was changed to the Elf-King by an unknowing translator. In Schubert's hands, the fantastic tale takes on the quality of being frighteningly real. Like "Gretchen am Spinnrade," this song is also unified by the piano accompaniment, although perhaps less subtly. Schubert's opening bars in the piano not only represent the journey on horseback but establish an ominous tone that immediately draws us into the drama.

A narrator, who sings the first and the last stanza, introduces the three characters in the story. There is the father, galloping home with his small son in his arms. The child is panic-stricken as the Erlking, figure of Death, menaces him with tempting pictures and is finally successful in literally frightening him to death.

Each character is different vocally: the father sings in mid-range, his lines are comforting and positive; the child's tessitura is pitched higher, and rises with each fearful encounter with the Erlking, "Mein Vater, mein Vater!"; the voice of the Erlking is the most frightening, disembodied and temptingly beautiful as he describes delights that await the child if he will accompany him. Despite his enticing images, the Erlking's voice (which only the boy hears) repels and terrifies the child.

Dramatic tension is sustained throughout by the relentless accompaniment figures. In addition to the opening pattern, Schubert accompanies the Erlking with a gay little *Totentanz*, a maniacal *Ländler* which dances eerily under his sinister vocal phrases. As he moves in the for the kill, his last stanza is preceded by the opening motive and then retains the repeated chords in the right hand, underlined by octaves in the left. As the narrator finishes the story, an *accelerando* launches the last frenzied moments of the gallop home. Stark recitative ends the song: "in seinen Armen das Kind war tot."

It is rather daunting to imagine the frenzy of the eighteen-year-old Schubert as he excitedly put this song on paper after reading Goethe's ballad aloud to Spaun and Mayrhofer.* He had no piano; after the song was completed, the three friends had to go to the Konvikt to play and sing it. The teenage genius had created a gripping musical narrative that is one of the great German songs of all time. The power of the Erlking remains irresistible.

*Goethe's poem fascinated a number of composers. For comparison, see settings by Loewe, Reichardt, and Zelter. Liszt made two transcriptions of Schubert's song, one for piano, one for orchestra.

Ganymed,* D. 544   **Ganymede. 1817**
(Johann Wolfgang von Goethe)

In Greek legend, Zeus, in the guise of an eagle, takes the beautiful Trojan youth Ganymede from Mount Ida to become the cup bearer to the gods. Goethe's poem, steeped in symbolism, uses this legend to illustrate man's emotional bond with nature, one of the primary themes of nineteenth-century German Romantic music. "Spring enfolds me in his loving arms. I lie in his bosom while the morning breeze fans me and the nightingale calls from the glade. God descends, and he will take me up with him through the clouds."

The song begins with an invocation to spring and ends with Ganymede's assumption through the clouds to the bosom of the "Alliebender Vater" (All-loving Father). Ganymede's innocence is also tinged with eroticism; the music is full of passion.

"Ganymed" is a prime example of one of Schubert's through-composed songs in which the music changes in response to the poem. Key changes are subtly accomplished and delineate dramatic events in the poetry; the scheme is rambling: A-flat major, E major, F major.

A sprightly walking rhythm heard in the introduction expands into two additional patterns, all mirroring Ganymede's buoyant spirits as he surveys the beauty of the spring morning with all the ardent emotions of a lover for his sweetheart. Rhythmic stresses on the second beat maintain a feeling of springy step and upward movement. The second section begins with a key change ("Du kühlst den brennenden Durst..."). This section contains some imaginative accompaniment figures that illustrate the morning breeze and the nightingale's call.

"Ich komm" initiates a running figure of alternating chords as Ganymede begins his journey upward. Intensity builds at "Hinauf!" with another key change. His agitation and ecstasy mount towards his final assumption into the heavens, culminating with two expansive phrases of longer note values that crown the dramatic moment with a majestic calm. Schubert sets the words "all-loving Father" with religious fervor; its considerable breadth and elastic shape make it one of the most daunting "vocal phrase endurance tests" in all of song literature.

*Also see the setting by Hugo Wolf.

An die Leier, D. 737   **To My Lyre. 1822-23**
(Franz von Bruchmann)

Franz Bruchmann was a school fellow of Schubert's, the son of a well-to-do family at whose house the "Schubertiads" were often held. Bruchmann's verse is an imitation of a poem of the Greek poet Anacreon (fl. sixth-century BC). "I would sing of Atreus's sons and Cadmus and Alcides's victorious march...but my strings bring forth only sounds of love. Farewell, then heroes. Instead of threatening with heroic songs, my strings bring forth only sounds of love."

This wonderful song is unjustly neglected. Its two sections are an example of Schubert's effective combination of dramatic recitative with long-lined cantilena. A majestic fanfare of chords and broken chords issues from the minstrel's lyre, heralding his song. His bardic, somewhat pompous declamation is followed with patterns from the opening sequence. His lyre, however, has a mind of its own, and bit by bit the broken chords change harmonies and dissolve into gentle arpeggios that accompany an intensely expressive melody. Schubert uses supporting melodic fragments in the bass line at several points. When the verse is finished, the piano takes up the last phrase passionately, in octaves, but breaks off suddenly. There is a bar of silence.

Now the bard is more insistent. He has changed the strings of the lyre; his stormy song is extended and more intense; his accompaniment is laced with chromaticism. Again, his lyre responds only to songs of love. The B section returns, also extended. The coda bids farewell to the heroes, their leave-taking accompanied by a very low-range bass melody, descending into the depths of the piano. The last phrase "nur Liebe im Erklingen" is again echoed by the piano, but this time the song of love is completed.

Rastlose Liebe,* D. 138   **Restless Love. 1815**
(Johann Wolfgang von Goethe)

Schubert responded to Goethe's fast-flying text with a setting of breathless quality. No brakes are applied to the non-stop sixteenth-note figures in the piano, urged along by staccato notes in the bass line. At the word "ertragen," Schubert modulates to another key using his favorite formula, a key relationship of a third. In this section, the sixteenth-note patterns give way to triplets and the melodic line repeats sequentially .

Schubert expands the poem and the musical structure at "Alles vergebens! Krone des Lebens, Glück ohne Ruh, Liebe bist du." Repeating "Alles vergebens!", he returns to the opening tonality and, using the last two lines of verse in repetition, creates an ending section almost as long as everything that has preceded it (forty-four measures as compared to forty-eight). The turbulent rhythm leads to a climactic last phrase with an exuberant extended note on "Liebe." Piano figures tumble headlong over one another in their rush to the end of the song.

*Goethe's text was also set by Robert Franz, Othmar Schoeck, and Carl Friedrich Zelter.

Ständchen, D. 957   **Serenade. 1827-28**
(Ludwig Rellstab)

This song is part of *Schwanengesang*, a collection of fourteen songs published posthumously on texts by Rellstab, Heine, and Seidl. It is perhaps Schubert's most celebrated song, an ardent outpouring of desire and youthful enthusiasm. The melody, like that of "Ellens Gesang III" (Ave Maria), is one of Schubert's "art song hits."

The song's five stanzas are structured in the common German folk poetry pattern a/b/a/b. For musical reasons, Schubert repeats lines 6, 8, 14, 16 and 20. A lightly plucked guitar-like accompaniment escorts the serenade to the beloved's window. The pleading quality of the text seems perfectly caught in the shape of the vocal melody. Phrases are flexible, always drifting upward, and are given extra impetus on their flight by a three-note turn that launches the movement towards the window. The piano pattern echoes between the phrases in two-bar fragments while, as Capell observes, "The serenader seems to hold his breath to listen for a sign from the balcony and hears only the echo of his own cadence taken up...by the nocturnal breeze and the rustling foliage."[7]

An die Musik, D. 547   To Music. 1817
(Franz Schober)

This strophic setting of two stanzas is a hymn to the holy art of Music. The poet offers his thanks to Music for brightening his hours of sadness, transporting him to a better world, and promising a better world to come. Schubert has transformed a rather simple set of words into an eloquent and intense tribute. It is impossible to pinpoint what makes this song perfectly express the inexpressible. Its simplicity is profound; its phrases are both exalted and bittersweet.

A bass line melody below a chordal accompaniment creates a feeling of breadth and nobility. It begins in the first two bars of the piano, but is not allowed to finish, as the opening vocal phrase begins, echoing the piano's melody and extending it to a longer expressive line. A steady pulse of repeated triads creates a devotional tone, and allows for flexible, free and sweeping vocal phrases throughout.

For many, this superb song is inextricably bound up with their deepest feelings for the essence of Music and for its inexpressible gifts. Graham Johnson writes: "The music has the force of the still, small voice which can hush the world."[8]

Die Forelle, D. 550   The Trout. 1817?
(Christian Friedrich Daniel Schubart)

An angler in the stream tries vainly to catch a trout, which darts and flicks through the clear water. The singer watches the duel and is disgusted when the fisherman resorts to muddying the stream in order to hook the little fish.

The accompaniment is one of Schubert's most familiar and famous water figures. Sinuous movements of the little trout are captured in Schubert's graceful, curving piano pattern, which simultaneously creates the motion of the water and the leaping movements of the trout. Graham Johnson describes it as "utter delight—the joy in being free and full of energy."[9] Schubert sets the story in a modified strophic form. The first two stanzas are identical, fashioned with a tuneful lyric vocal melody with a folk-like simplicity.*

Impatient with waiting, the angler takes action in the third stanza. Vocal phrases become less flexible and more static, although the fish's playful pattern still persists. Schubert's vocal line mirrors the tension in the scene as the angler readies for the kill, with a series of repeated notes in the vocal line ("Er macht das Bächlein tükkisch trübe") followed by a string of repeated chords to drive the point home ("Und eh ich es gedacht"). A quick flick of the angler's wrist (mirrored in the biting consonants "So zuckte seine Rute"), the fish struggles on the line, and all is over. The last vocal phrases repeat the last two phrases of the opening stanza.

Despite the demise of the trout, the scene and the song remain lighthearted and charming, one of Schubert's best.

---

*Schubert used this tune as the basis for the variation movement in the *Piano Quintet in A-flat*, known as the "Trout" Quintet. The original poem contained a moralizing last stanza, which Schubert omitted— a warning to young ladies to avoid "fishy young men."

Der Musensohn, D. 764   The Son of the Muses. 1822
(Johann Wolfgang von Goethe)

It is difficult to imagine a more vibrant musical setting than "Der Musensohn." The son of the Muses is ostensibly the poet. Radiantly boyish, he gaily trips over fields and through woods. As he journeys, all Nature keeps time to his beat. He sings and pipes of spring, in season and out of season, inspiring the young people to dance and flirt to his tunes. But, he asks the gracious Muses, when will he at last find rest on *his* darling's bosom?

His breathless vocal phrases dance rhythmically through the song, not pausing until the final chord. Only the poetic content offers a chance for color and nuance. There are five stanzas, in simple cyclical form: ABABA. As the stanzas change, so do the tonalities, an alternation of major and minor, shifting without pause from G major into B major without preparation for modulation. The new key bursts upon us via the pivot note of B-natural, common to both tonic chords. Like the voice, the gaily dancing accompaniment dares not pause for breath. The same rhythmic pattern is common to the two sections, but the fragmented melody in the A section sets it apart from the slightly more static B section. The key changes seem to infuse new energy into the poet's song. His vocal phrases are rhythmic, and, although the two sections are related melodically, they are different. Dynamics alternate in A and B sections from *mf* to *pp*. There is the slightest *ritardando* on the word "Busen" (bosom) before he jubilantly closes his whirlwind melody.

This celebrated song comes by its reputation honestly. It is enchanting.

Auf dem Wasser zu singen, D. 774   To Be Sung On the Water. 1823
(Count Friedrich Leopold Graf zu Stolberg)

"Our boat glides over the lake in the evening sun. The waves dance, the trees beckon from the shore. Alas, with dewy wings, Time vanishes on the rocking waves."

This graceful barcarole with vocal obbligato is another of Schubert's famous water songs. Capell calls it "the idealization of Viennese river-pleasures."[10] Count Friedrich zu Stolberg, translator of Homer and Plato and a friend of Goethe, provided Schubert with seven poems for songs; this is the best known of the settings.

Schubert's rippling accompaniment has its own melodic pattern and is really worthy of being categorized as a solo piano piece. Like Fauré's "Clair de lune," the vocal part exists apart from the piano, yet both share similar patterns—drooping melodic apoggiaturas and the rhythmic water pattern.[*] The synthesis of vocal line and accompaniment captivates the listener and unifies the song.

The key is A-flat minor with modulations to and from C-flat major. There are three stanzas, set strophically. The repetitions never pall, for the glittering movement and hypnotic melody beg another hearing.

Despite the ongoing movement in piano and voice, the water remains placid, the waves gently lap on the sides of the boat, and the reeds murmur. The last stanza relates the entire serene picture to the passing of time and the ultimate journey "on shimmering wings" upward. The year 1823 is the year Schubert composed *Die schöne Müllerin*, and also marks a crisis in his health. He had only five years left to live.

*Schubert's mastery of accompaniment figures depicting water is legion. A few other Schubert "water-fig-ures" worth investigating: "Am Meer," "Auf dem See," "Die Forelle," "Meeres Stille," "Fischerweise," "Der Schiffer," "Der Jüngling an der Quelle," and the numerous examples found in *Die schöne Müllerin*.

Nacht und Träume, D. 827   Night and Dreams. 1822?
(Matthäus von Collin)

"Holy night, you sink down. Dreams, like moonlight, float down through space, through the silent hearts of men." This is one of Schubert's most famous songs, a beautiful hymn to the night and the peace and rest it brings. A quiet nocturnal mood is immediately created by a flowing accompaniment of alternating chords. Despite the undulating pattern, there is a feeling of suspension, a motionless sort of wonder.

In long phrases, the vocal line floats above the piano lines, which remain in the bass clef throughout the song. Melodic phrases are two measures long, but in Schubert's slow sustained tempo they create an unearthly serenity. Indeed, the night's calm peace in this poem also bears some connection with eternal rest.

Melodic material is shared in piano and voice. The second vocal phrase is from the piano introduction, and this melody is repeated for the third vocal phrase. Schubert splits the poem into two parts, beginning the second section with a dif-ferent melody, created from the vocal shapes from the first. Also at this point there is an unprepared modulation from B to G. The last two melodic phrases slip back into the original tonality; these are the last two phrase melodies from the first stanza, reprised to bring the song to a quiet close.

For interpretive as well as technical reasons, this is one of the most difficult of Schubert's *Lieder* to perform.

Die junge Nonne, D. 828   The Young Nun. 1824-25
(Jacob Nicolaus Craigher de Jachelutta)

A storm rages outside a convent. Inside, a young nun agonizes as she remem-bers her indecision to give her life to Christ. She likens the storm to the turmoil she felt, but now she is at peace, fervent and steadfast in her religious devotion.

Schubert underlines the agitation of the young novice with another of his mas-terful melodic/rhythmic patterns: a tremolo figure in the right hand with the melodic motive in the bass, punctuated by the ringing of the church bell. The entire song grows from this fragment.

Everything is seen and heard through the mind of the nun. The tolling of the bell is like a tiny leitmotiv, a still small voice of calm amidst the turbulent accom-paniment pattern. Her melodic line mirrors the emotional tumult she experienced before finding reassurance and strength in her faith; the phrases sweep from high to low, echoing or anticipating the pitch of the chiming bell. Melodic material alter-nates between voice and piano. The vocal line ranges over an octave and a fifth.

The song is like a dramatic *scena*, a mix of Romantic drama with traditional song style. The first two stanzas are strophic repetition, with the remainder of the song through-composed. Stanza 1 describes the external scene: storm, wind, thunder, clattering rafters, and lightning, all frightening in their intensity. In Stanza 2, the young novice compares the storm outside to the one that once raged within her, relating each element of the tempest to her inner agitation. In Stanza 3, she discards the comparison and affirms her faith and the inward calm it has brought her. "Nun tobe, du wilder, gewaltger Sturm/im Herzen ist Friede, im Herzen ist Ruh" (Now rage, wild, mighty storm/In my heart is freedom and peace) elicits an immediate key change to the major tonality. In Stanza 4, she calls upon the Savior to come and take the bride. At the line "Erlöse die Seele von irdischer Haft" (Free the soul from earthly bonds), the tolling bells that were silent in Stanza 3 begin to ring again. In the last four lines of the poem, the nun's religious fervor reaches ecstatic heights. "Alleluia!" signals the end of this immortal song.

Despite the turbulent accompaniment figures and the emotional text, dynamic levels reach *fortissimo* only three times in the entire song. Although the storm is turbulent, it is viewed from inside the convent walls and so a mixture of violence and calm coexist side by side as the young nun's innermost thoughts are revealed.

Another interpretation of this *Lied* is offered by Marjorie Wing Hirsch: the poem is based on the legend of St. Agnes, a favorite Romantic theme. St. Agnes was martyred at age thirteen for refusing to marry. Although her chastity was violated, she remained a virgin. Keats and Tennyson based two poems on her legend; in Tennyson's text, as in Craigher's, the girl is a nun.[11] Using this point of departure, the young nun eagerly awaits the coming of her Savior, and the vision of her impending holy marriage with Christ sends her into a state of ecstasy. Suddenly the tolling of the tower bells announces His arrival. As the bells continue ringing, calling her up to heaven, the enraptured nun sings out a joyful "Alleluia," as the raging turmoil of her life at last surrenders to the eternal comfort of death.[12]

"Die junge Nonne" is a massive song. Schubert's illustration of the grandeur of nature's elements unleashed in a storm is truly Romantic in conception. Capell describes this *Lied* as coming "strangely near being a hymn to the storm."[13] In essence, the song contains some of the strongest characteristics of Romantic song: dramatic power, psychological depth, and poetic communication with nature. We know that "Die junge Nonne" was one of the Schubert songs that Beethoven read and reread in his last illness.

Im Frühling, D. 882   In Spring. 1826
(Ernst Schulze)

Schulze's poem is a remembrance of a springtime the poet enjoyed with his sweetheart. "This spring is beautiful as ever...the flowers, the fields, the sun...but the happiness of love has passed, and only love remains...with sorrow. Oh, if I were only a bird in the meadow...I would sing a sweet song about her all summer long."

Schubert imaginatively sets this rather lightweight text in variation form—one of the few times he uses the technique. Both voice and piano have separate melodic material; the piano accompaniment is in variation form, and the voice has variants of the piano's opening phrases from stanza to stanza. These melodic strands are cross-threaded in a charming, fresh texture, that perfectly captures the poetic atmosphere.

The piano accompaniment is given the variation; the theme is introduced in a buoyant introduction. Vocal phrases are equally melodic, with graceful, flexible shapes. Two poetic stanzas pass, compressed into an extended musical section, before Schubert reprises the introductory material, presented now in variation (measure 17), its melody decorated in broken chord figures. Two more stanzas with varied melodic material are sung; Schubert retains the variation figure as accompaniment.

As the poet recalls the dissolution of the relationship, Schubert introduces an episode in G minor (measure 33) for the next stanza, and abandons the gaily dancing broken chord figure for more somber chords in a syncopated pattern. This is accompanied by a broken chord figure reminiscent of the variation material. A brief modulation takes us back to G major (measure 41); the variation figure blossoms again as the voice takes up material from the first section, also varied.

Blondel zu Marien, D. 626   Blondel to Mary. 1818
(Author unknown, erroneously attributed to Grillparzer)

Schubert composed this song during his summer stay in Zseliz, Hungary, where he was music tutor to the young daughters of the Count and Countess Esterházy. The song is enigmatic in that its text is from an anonymous author and its style quite a bit removed from Schubert's usual musical approach.

Blondel de Nesles was a twelfth-century *trouvère** famed for his rescue of the imprisoned King Richard the Lion-Hearted. His minstrel song is addressed to Mary, probably a sweetheart to whom he attributes Madonna-like qualities. In the age of the troubadours and *trouvères*, the tradition of courtly love held women as objects of adoration. Blondel's song is highly romantic—probably a *lai*, a form of medieval French poetry, whose texts are usually addressed to the Virgin or to a lady.

Schubert's expansive ornamented vocal lines are redolent of Italian opera. "In gloom of night, when anguish envelops my tender heart..." —the first phrase clearly defines this as a melancholy night piece. A five-measure piano introduction sets the scene for the first somber vocal phrases in E-flat minor. Rising phrase shapes appear at "Da leuchtet fern" (A distant light) and move toward the penultimate phrase "Ein holder Stern" (A fair star), which is then repeated. The second verse is a variation of the material in the first stanza, but this time presented in the major key.

"Blondel zu Marien" is exceptional for its vocal *fioriture*, which some have taken to be embellishments added by Vogl, whose normal practice was to ornament Schubert's vocal phrases when he performed them. Capell suggests that Schubert associated the ornaments with "artificial expression from his lavish use of them in his graceful little Italian pastiche, *La Pastorella* (1817), on a text by Goldoni."[14] A more likely explanation is offered by Graham Johnson: the vocal melismas might have been Schubert's attempt to suggest the style of a twelfth-century minstrel song—"a Schubertian equivalent of troping and hocking."[15] The coloratura figures seem to be part of a Gothic tapestry, an effort at evoking the rich atmosphere of a medieval court.

Trouvères were twelfth and thirteenth-century poet-musicians active in northern France. They imitated the movement begun by the Provençal troubadours. Blondel de Nesles (b.c. 1155) was instrumental in developing the *trouvère* movement.

An dem Mond, D. 259   To the Moon. 1819?
(Johann Wolfgang von Goethe)

Schubert set this Goethe text twice, the first time in strophic form, crowned with one of his captivating melodies. Several years later, he turned again to the poem, giving it a more searching, complex treatment. This time the moon engenders several different musical moods, all tinged with melancholy, but never crossing the line into despair.

In this romantic setting, Schubert plumbs the poet's reflections of joy, sadness, and loneliness. A serene, limpid melody is used for verses 1 and 2, then is repeated for verses 3 and 4. Verse 5 matches verses 1 and 3 and was not set in Schubert's first version of this song. Verses 6 and 7 describe the movement of the river (an allegory for life). Here the opening melodic material is supplanted with new lines. Verse 8 is like verse 1, with a poignant departure for text illustration at the word "Busen" (bosom/heart). In the last verse, the voice is assigned a declamatory descant, letting the melody sing in the piano. The singer's line finally descends into the lower depths for the last phrase, "wandelt in der Nacht" (wanders in the night), then, like a moonlit benediction, repeats again, an octave higher.

Suleika I (Was bedeutet die Bewegung?), D. 720   Zuleika I. 1821
(Marianne von Wellemer /
attributed to and adapted by Goethe, from the *West-östlicher Divan*)

"Suleika" I and II are both poems by Marianne von Wellemer, the third wife of a banker friend of Goethe. When Goethe first met her, she was thirty and he was in his sixties. For fourteen months, Goethe and Marianne were in contact, carrying on an extensive correspondence using the pseudonyms "Hatem" and "Suleika." So expert were her replies as "Suleika" that Goethe incorporated them into the oriental collection titled *West-östlicher Divan*, published in 1819. It is a tribute to Marianne's artistry that Goethe included five of her poems in the set, acknowledging her contributions only after his death.

Both Suleika songs are addresses to two winds of love, East and West. Form in each seems to be divided into halves, held together by inner tension. "Suleika I" reads like an operatic *scena*, although its musical style is grounded squarely in song style. It is vibrant with life, desire, and passion, entwined in a musical representation of nature. In an atmosphere of veiled sensuality, Suleika speaks to the East wind, which bears messages from her lover.

We immediately hear the East wind in the piano, as a moving chromatic line begins in the bass clef and wafts into the treble, finally reaching a resting place on a chord that resolves like a sigh. The meter is $\frac{3}{4}$; Schubert's unifying link is a rhythmic pattern in the accompaniment (dotted quarter/three eighths) repeated, with few exceptions, throughout the song. Open fifths and octaves suggest the insistent beating of a tambour, an exotic touch that keeps the oriental image before us.

For Suleika's last stanza, Schubert abandons the dotted rhythmic pattern and replaces it with a line of repeated eighth notes, all on F-sharp. Suleika's ill-disguised passion is mirrored in this insistent pedal point, which is joined to a repeated rhythm in the right hand, submerging into the overall texture for the last vocal phrases.

Verses 1 and 3 are identical vocally; the last two poetic lines are blended into an undulating phrase that suggests Suleika's desire. In Verse 2, the right hand accompaniment is varied; now we hear the buzzing insects, driven by the wind into the vines—a subtle sound picture that also enforces Suleika's mood. Schubert also employs this turning figure for verse 4, in which the vocal line adopts more flexible, sinuous shapes as Suleika anticipates the arrival of her lover. Verses 5 is more dramatic—here is the passionate climax of the verse that preceded it; verse 6 is the aftermath of that passion. Graham Johnson describes it as "...Schubert's 'extase langoureuse' and 'fatigue amoureuse' long before Verlaine and Debussy attempted to capture the post-coital mood...in the musical language of French impressionism."[16] The stanza is repeated twice, and Suleika repeats her languid phrase "Ach, die wahre Herzenslaunde" (O the true message of the heart) a third time to end the song.

Of this great *Lied*, Robert Franz wrote: "I...would find fault with even the greatest genius who wanted to emulate Schubert's setting of Suleika's song, for he has extracted every ounce of musical marrow from the poem."[17] Brahms thought "Suleika I" was the "loveliest song ever written."[18] This text was also set by Felix Mendelssohn.

Die schöne Müllerin,   **The Miller's Beautiful Daughter. 1823**
Op. 25, Nos. 1-20, D. 795
(Wilhelm Müller)

Das Wandern (Wandering) • Wohin? (Whither?) •
Halt! (Halt!) • Danksagung an den Bach (Song of Thanksgiving to
the Brook) • Am Feierabend (When Work is Over) • Der Neugierige
(The Inquisitive One) • Ungeduld (Impatience) • Morgengruss
(Morning Greeting) • Des Müllers Blumen (The Miller's Flowers) •
Tränenregen (Rain of Tears) • Mein! (Mine!) • Pause (Pause) • Mit
dem grünen Lautenbande (With the Green Lute-Ribbon) • Der Jäger
(The Hunter) • Eifersucht und Stolz (Jealousy and Pride) • Die liebe
Farbe (The Beloved Color) • Die böse Farbe (The Evil Color) • Trockne
Blumen (Withered Flowers) • Der Müller und der Bach (The Miller and
the Brook) • Des Baches Wiegenlied (The Brook's Lullaby)

The following sources should be used to study this cycle in depth:

Susan Youens. *Schubert: Die schöne Müllerin* (Cambridge: Cambridge University Press, 1992). Cambridge Music Handbooks.
Gerald Moore. *The Schubert Song Cycles, with Thoughts on Performance* (London: Hamish Hamilton, 1975).
Charles Rosen, *The Romantic Generation* (Cambridge: Harvard University Press, 1995). Chapter 3: "Mountains and Song Cycles."

Charles Rosen observes that "the song cycle is the most original musical form created in the first half of the nineteenth century. It most clearly embodies the Romantic conception of experience as a gradual unfolding and illumination of reality in place of the Classical insistence on an initial clarity."[19]   Schubert's *Die schöne Müllerin*, composed in 1823, must be considered the first great song cycle of the nineteenth century. It was composed eight years after Beethoven's *An die ferne Geliebte* , but unlike Beethoven, who had linked songs together to form a continuous work, Schubert structured his cycle so that each song is complete in itself, but also an essential part of the whole.

Wilhelm Müller, who conceived much of his verse as poetry for music, provided Schubert with the poetry for both his song cycles. Müller's diary contains this entry:

> I can neither play nor sing, yet when I write verses, I sing and play after all. If I could produce the melodies, my songs would be more pleasing than they are now. But courage! perhaps there is a kindred spirit somewherewho will hear the tunes behind the words and give them back to me.[20]

Müller's poems tell a tragic love story, simple and rustic. A young journeyman miller wanders along a stream, following its path. He eventually comes to the next watermill and apprentices himself to the master miller. He falls in love with the miller's beautiful daughter, and convinces himself that she returns his feelings, but comes to realize that she loves a huntsman instead. Overwhelmed by sorrow and despair, he drowns himself in the brook. The brook sings a lullaby over the dead miller.

Principal characters in the cycle are the young miller, the beautiful daughter of the master miller, and the huntsman. The most important character is not human; it is the all-pervading brook, graphically represented by a variety of musical figures throughout the cycle. For the young miller, the millstream is a living entity, a friend and confidant that he addresses as the story unfolds. Only the brook speaks to the miller during the cycle and it is the brook's voice that is heard in the final song, singing him a last lullaby. The relationship between miller and millstream reinforces his strong identification with nature and his sense of isolation from other human beings.

With the exception of the brook's last song, the cycle's "story" is narrated solely by one person, the miller. We do not meet the master miller's daughter during the cycle; she is only described to us. Her distance from the action reinforces her identity as an unattainable object, a figure to be worshipped from afar.

Musical and poetic elements unify the songs in the cycle. Most important is a series of musical "water" figures in the accompaniment that define and illustrate the brook. Color is a secondary but significant symbol in the cycle; the colors green, white, and blue are mentioned prominently in the poems. Green is the "hated color" for the miller; it is the color of the hunter's clothing, and the forest in which he lives. It is also the color of the ribbon on the miller's lute, a symbol for springtime and new love, and finally, green is the color he will dress in as he contemplates death. White stands for the miller—the flour he mills and the purity of his love. Blue is the color of the maiden's eyes and the color of the brook and the flowers growing by its side.

A kaleidoscope of emotions turns slowly throughout the cycle—from buoyant cheerfulness to bleak despair. The songs contain an extraordinary range of moods within a seemingly simple dramatic frame.

Almost half the songs in *Die schöne Müllerin* are in strophic form, giving the story great clarity and maintaining a simplicity of style throughout. The story's folk-like quality is preserved by syllabic text setting. Regular musical phrase shapes predominate, as do strong, energetic rhythms. Several of the songs have opening phrases with similar shapes (examples: Songs 3, 7 and 8; Songs 2 and 9).

Cyclic elements in *Die schöne Müllerin* exist as unifying links rather than a highly structured series of tonalities or motives. Tonality in the cycle seems tied to poetic narrative, in which songs can be grouped together by dramatic or emotional mood. Youens observes that "tonalities are also used to separate songs, to heighten changes of place, tone, time, and temper by means of tonal disjunction."[21] Youens groups Songs 1-12 under the heading "romantic illusions," and classifies Songs 13-20 as "disillusionment and death."[22]

Song 12 ("Pause") serves as the natural dividing point in the cycle, separating the opening songs of happier, hopeful mood from Song 13 onwards, in which the appearance of the hunter signals disillusionment and a progression toward the tragic conclusion.

Introduction. We meet the miller and are infected by his enthusiastic cheerfulness.
Song 1: Das Wandern   (B-flat major)

The next three songs group themselves into closely related major keys, and describe the miller's journey, his arrival at the mill, and his thanks to the brook for leading him to the beautiful maid of the mill.

Song 2: Wohin?	(G major)
Song 3: Halt!	(C major)
Song 4: Danksagung an den Bach	(G major)

These songs follow the wooing of the maiden by the young miller: his attempts to get her to notice him, his impatience and uncertainty, his growing devotion to his beloved, and the progress of the relationship. The last song in this group is the only poem in the cycle written in the past tense. In it, the miller remembers the magical moments sitting with his beloved by the side of the brook. The poem ends with her callous comment that it is about to rain and she is going home.

Song 5: Am Feierabend	(A minor)
Song 6: Der Neugierige	(B major)
Song 7: Ungeduld	(A major)
Song 8: Morgengruss	(C major)
Song 9: Des Müllers Blumen	(A major)
Song 10: Tränenregen	(A major/A minor)

At midpoint in the cycle, the miller rejoices at having triumphed in his suit. He has won his beloved. "Mein!" bursts with his energy of his ardor and joy.

Song 11: Mein!   (D major)

Song 12 is unified throughout by an ostinato motive in the piano, presented in the first two measures. Its title is apt; it acts as a dividing point in the cycle, a resting place before the final progression toward the story's tragic conclusion.

Song 12: Pause   (B-flat major)

Songs 13-15 follow in closely related keys. The ribbon-band on the miller's lute fades and he gives it to his lover to wear in her hair. The hunter appears and we witness the jealousy of the miller.

Song 13: Mit dem grünen Lautenbande	(B-flat major)
Song 14: Der Jäger	(C minor)
Song 15: Eifersucht und Stolz	(G minor/G major)

As the miller gives way to despair and disillusion, his emotions lead him nearer to suicide. All the songs in this group alternate between minor and major tonalities. Rosen points out the shocking harmonic shift from Song 18 to 19 (E major to G minor), signaling the moment of utmost despair and the miller's decision to commit suicide.[23] In the final song, the brook pronounces the ultimate benediction. In the waters' never-ending flow, the miller reaches eternal peace.

Song 16: Die liebe Farbe	(B minor/B major)
Song 17: Die böse Farbe	(B major/B minor)
Song 18: Trock'ne Blumen	(E minor/E major/E minor)
Song 19: Der Müller und der Bach	(G minor/G major/G minor)
Song 20: Des Baches Wiegenlied	(E major)

Schubert was twenty-six when he composed *Die schöne Müllerin*. He had already composed some 300 songs, including such masterpieces as "Gretchen am Spinnrade" and "Erlkönig." In a sense, 1823 marked the beginning of the end for Schubert. Health problems began to manifest themselves, and the venereal disease that was to kill him five years later was diagnosed. His last cycle, *Winterreise*, was to mark the end of his life. Both cycles share the poetic theme of human isolation, and the narratives of both works moves inexorably toward death.

Winterreise, Op. 80, Nos. 1-24   Winter's Journey. 1827
D. 911
(Wilhelm Müller)

Gute Nacht (Good Night) • Die Wetterfahne (The Weather-Vane) •
Gefrorne Tränen (Frozen Tears) • Erstarrung (Numbness) •
Der Lindenbaum (The Linden Tree) • Wasserflut (On the Stream) •
Auf dem Flusse (Flood Waters) • Rückblick (Backward Glance) • Irrlicht
(Jack-o'-Lantern) • Rast (Rest) • Frühlingstraum (Dream of Spring) •
Einsamkeit (Loneliness) • Die Post (The Post) • Der greise Kopf
(Grey Head) • Die Krähe (The Crow) • Letzte Hoffnung (Last Hope) •
Im Dorfe (In the Village) • Der stürmische Morgen (Stormy Morning) •
Täuschung (Delusion) • Der Wegweiser (The Sign-Post) • Das
Wirtshaus (The Inn) • Mut (Courage) • Die Nebensonnen (Mock Suns) •
Der Leiermann (The Organ-Grinder)

The following sources should be used to study this cycle in depth:

Susan Youens. *Retracing a Winter's Journey: Schubert's Winterreise* (Ithaca: Cornell University Press, 1991).

Gerald Moore. *The Schubert Song Cycles with Thoughts on Performance* (London: Hamish Hamilton, 1975).

Schubert set the first twelve poems of *Winterreise* in February of 1827. He had discovered the collection in a publisher's annual magazine called *Urania*; the second set of twelve poems was found and set in October of the same year. He wrote the cycle for a high voice and perhaps had his own countertenor voice in mind while he composed the songs.

Joseph Spaun described Schubert's first performance of the cycle:

> One day he said to me, "Come over to Schober's today, and I will sing you a cycle of horrifying songs. I am anxious to know what you will say about them. They have cost me more effort than any of my other songs." So he sang the entire *Winterreise* through to us in a voice full of emotion. We were utterly dumbfounded by the mournful, gloomy tone of these songs, and Schober said that only one, "Der Lindenbaum" had appealed to him. To this Schubert replied, "I like these songs more than all the rest, and you will come to like them as well."[24]

Winterreise is a monodrama. As its songs unfold, the tragic wanderer speaks to no one; he is alone and his narrative is introspective, addressed to himself. We are voyeurs who accompany him on his journey, eavesdropping on his melancholy soliloquies. We do not know his name or his destination. Youens comments that this is one of the principal sources of the cycle's power and serves to create and maintain tension throughout the work.[25]

Like the miller in *Die schöne Müllerin*, the wanderer of *Winterreise* is a loner. He is tortured by regrets and haunted by memories and dreams. His reminiscences and emotions are triggered by the landscapes he passes through, which mirror his bleak despair. His journey is truly terrifying because it has no goal.

As the cycle opens, the events that caused him to undertake his journey have already taken place. We are not told what they were, but his first words are clues: "I arrived a stranger/A stranger I depart." He mentions a girl who spoke of love and her mother, who talked of marriage, but the relationship is obviously dissolved and he leaves, writing "good night" on her gate so she will know he thought of her.

Rosen declares "*Winterreise* is unsurpassed in the art of musical representation."[26] The cumulative power of the cycle is stunning, moving inexorably toward the final song Images and situations described in the cycle seem like a series of paintings in a gallery. Even though the wanderer is a part of their landscape and action, his participation is curiously detached. Psychologically, he seems resigned to his state, too numb emotionally to show outward feeling; there are only four songs among the twenty-four in which he sheds tears ("Gefrorne Tränen," "Erstarrung," "Wasserflut," and "Letzte Hoffnung").

As we follow the bleak journey, we are seldom aware of how much time passes between songs or even the time encapsulated within one song. The wanderer describes what he sees, thinks and feels at each stage of his journey.[27]As the cycle progresses, he seems to grow older and increasingly tired. His travels exist in a void; with each new song, life seems to have less meaning. As the cycle winds toward its close, the traveler draws nearer to death. The last five songs contain ominous signs: the road sign that points the way down an unknown road from which there is no return; the cemetery that symbolizes an inn, its green wreaths inviting travelers into its coolness; the forbidding suns whose setting forecasts light departing from life; and finally, the mysterious organ-grinder, whose presence might symbolize death itself. Müller's poems do not provide an ending for the grim story; we are left to supply that for ourselves.

Until Schubert composed *Winterreise*, a theme of such intense grief had not been explored in song form. Feelings of doubt, gloom, despair, and pessimism are expressed throughout practically every song; the mood of unrelieved gloom binds the cycle together emotionally and dramatically. Poetic images of stillness pervade the twenty-four songs: wintry figures, frozen images, numbing cold, vast landscapes. Schubert hoards his lovely melodies in this cycle and appends them to happy reminiscences: "Der Lindenbaum" (No. 5) and "Frühlingstraum" (No. 11).

One recurring musical image in the cycle is that of walking patterns; the wanderer's footsteps appear in different figures, almost always in $\frac{2}{4}$ time and in minor keys. Songs 1, 3, 7, 10, and 12 all have an easygoing gait usually associated with a walk in the countryside. Vocal articulations are varied, but all display an affinity with speech patterns. Youens identifies four vocal contours found throughout the cycle: bold, wide-ranging triadic phrases with intervallic leaps; declamatory melodic writing; lyrical melodies of folk song character, and lyric style that uses grace-note ornamentation and dance rhythms.[28] Song forms in *Winterreise*, as contrasted with those of *Die schöne Müllerin,* are predominantly varied strophic structures that allow for variations of poetic detail and emotion.

Schubert's accompaniments are lean-textured, pared down to the lowest common denominator to create the barest support and maintain the dramatic atmosphere. Schubert also creates a monochromatic effect by writing much of the accompaniment in the mid-range of the piano. His manipulation of rhythms and accompaniment patterns is also calculated to support dramatic ends.

The old organ-grinder is not easily dismissed from memory. He is the only other living being the traveler meets during his wintry pilgrimage. He stands in the numbing cold, his hurdy-gurdy playing a single repetitive droning tune. Schubert uses this and two variants to create his portrait of the old man. Vocal phrases are barely accompanied; only the drone of the hurdy-gurdy is heard beneath them. The harmony teeters back and forth from tonic to dominant. Alternating phrases between voice and piano have the effect of a macabre conversation between the two men, although one does not speak. Is the organ grinder a symbol for death? Is he a kindred spirit for the traveler, another outcast to whom he can relate?

When he finished *Winterreise*, Schubert's own death was only a year away. In light of this fact, the last two phrases of the hurdy-gurdy seem particularly poignant: "Wunderlicher Alter, soll ich mit dir gehn?/Willst du meinen Liedern, deine Leier drehn?" (Wonderful old man, shall I go with you? Will you play my songs on your hurdy-gurdy?)

Winterreise is an unsettling experience for the listener; it requires total immersion into a bleak world of loss and despair. It is difficult because its subject explores themes that disturb us, and remind us of our mortality.

Extended Study List

Ständchen • Seligkeit• Erlafsee • Auf dem See • Auflösung • Die Allmacht • Der Jüngling an der Quelle • Nähe des Geliebten • An Sylvia • Schäfer's Klagelied • Der Doppelgänger • Die Taubenpost • Dem Unendlichen • Das Fischermädchen • Am Meer • Harfenspieler I, II, III • Heiss mich nicht reden • Nachtviolen • Der Schiffer • Im Abendrot • Aufenhalt • Wanderer's Nachtlied • Der Tod und das Mädchen • Frühlingsglaube • Meeres Stille • Der Zwerg • Heidenröslein • Der Hirt auf dem Felsen (soprano, clarinet, piano) • Ihr Bild • Der Atlas • Krieger's Ahnung

Selected Reading

A. Craig Bell, *The Songs of Schubert* (London: Alston Books, 1954).

Maurice Brown, *Schubert Songs.* BBC Music Guides (Seattle: University of Washington Press, 1967). Brief overview of Schubert's songs.

Richard Capell, *Schubert's Songs* (New York: MacMillan and Company., London: Gerard Duckworth and Company, Ltd., 1966). Classic reference to Schubert's songs, in historical- biographical context.

Dietrich Fischer-Dieskau, *Schubert's Songs: A Biographical Study* (New York: Alfred A. Knopf, 1977).

Otto Deutsch, *The Schubert Reader: A Life of Franz Schubert in Letters and Documents* (New York: W. W. Norton, 1947).

_____, *Schubert: Memoirs by his Friends* (New York: Macmillan, 1958). Interesting collection of authentic recollections of Schubert, with commentaries by Deutsch. Recreates the historical period.

Marjorie Wing Hirsch, *Schubert's Dramatic Lieder* (Cambridge: Cambridge University Press, 1993).

Graham Johnson. Liner notes to *The Hyperion Schubert Edition.* A series of compact discs containing all of Schubert's songs (including ensembles, partsongs, alternative settings and fragments). Hyperion Recordings Limited. London, England.

Gerald Moore, *The Schubert Song Cycles* (London: Hamish Hamilton, 1975). Thoughts on performance and interpretation for *Die schöne Müllerin* and *Winterreise.*

John Reed, *The Schubert Song Companion* (New York: Universe Books, 1985). With prose translations by Norma Deane and Celia Larner. Reference to Schubert's songs.

Charles Rosen, *The Romantic Generation* (Cambridge: Harvard University Press, 1995). Chapter 3: "Mountains and Song Cycles."

Susan Youens, *Retracing a Winter's Journey: Schubert's Winterreise* (Ithaca: Cornell University Press, 1991). Schubert's cycle with analysis of each song, overview of poetry, and biographical information about Müller.

_____, Schubert: *Die schöne Müllerin* (Cambridge: Cambridge University Press, 1992). Softcover edition. Genesis of the cycle from poetry to song cycle, romantic illusion of the poems, discussion of musical settings.

_____. "Franz Schubert: The Prince of Song," in *German Lieder in the Nineteenth Century,* ed. Rufus Hallmark (New York: Schirmer Books, 1996), 31-74.

Richard Wigmore, *Schubert: The Complete Song Texts* (London: Victor Gollancz, 1988). Complete texts and translations for all of Schubert's *Lieder.*

Notes

1. Quoted in Harold Schonberg, *The Lives of the Great Composers,* 105.
2. Donald Ivey, *Song: Anatomy, Imagery and Styles,* 196.
3. Quoted in S. S. Prawer, ed. *The Penguin Book of Lieder,* 33.
4. Frits Noske, *French Song from Berlioz to Duparc* . See "Schubert and the German *Lied,*" 25-39.
5. Dietrich Fischer-Dieskau, *Schubert's Songs: A Biographical Study,* 102.
6. Quoted in Lorraine Gorrell, *The Nineteenth Century German Lied,* 107.
7. Richard Capell, *Schubert's Songs,* 51.
8. Graham Johnson. Liner notes to *The Hyperion Schubert Edition.* No. 21. Edith Mathis/Graham Johnson. Hyperion Records. Compact disc CDJ33021, 1994.
9. Ibid.
10. Capell, 185.
11. Marjorie Wing Hirsch, *Schubert's Dramatic Lieder,* 117, 164.
12. Ibid., 117.
13. Capell, 208.
14. Capell, 146-47.
15. Graham Johnson, *The Hyperion Schubert Edition,* Vol. 21.
16. Graham Johnson. Liner notes to *The Hyperion Schubert Edition,* Vol. 19. Felicity Lott/Graham Johnson. Hyperion Records. Compact disc CDJ 33019, 1993.
17. Quoted in Dietrich Fischer-Dieskau, *Schubert's Songs,* 146.
18. Quoted in Graham Johnson, *The Hyperion Schubert Edition,* Vol. 19.
19. Charles Rosen, *The Romantic Generation,* 194.
20. Quoted in Susan Youens, *Schubert: Die schöne Müllerin,* 10.
21. Ibid., 73.
22. Ibid., 31, 55.
23. Rosen, *The Romantic Generation,* 192-93.
24. Quoted in Susan Youens, *Retracing a Winter's Journey,* 27.
25. Susan Youens, "Retracing a Winter Journey: Reflections on Schubert's *Winterreise,*" *Nineteenth Century Music,* 9:2 (Fall 1985), 129. This article forms the basis for both the title of Youen's book (see footnote 24) and its second chapter.
26. Rosen, 201.
27. Youens, 129.
28. Ibid., 80.

FANNY MENDELSSOHN HENSEL (1805-1847)

You must become more steady and collected, and prepare more earnestly
and eagerly for your real calling, the only calling of a young woman—
I mean the state of a housewife.

—Letter from Abraham Mendelssohn
to his twenty-three-year-old daughter Fanny
on her birthday, 1828.[1]

Her songs are distinguished by tenderness, warmth, and originality; some
which I heard were exquisite...

—Review in *The Harmonicum* of 1830[2]

Fanny Mendelssohn Hensel composed 300 *Lieder*, many of which are at last
seeing publication. Although she composed prolifically, she did not have a career as
a composer. We know of Fanny's compositions and of many details of the remarkable Mendelssohn family from her diaries. During her lifetime, the reputation of
her younger brother, Felix Mendelssohn would have assured her music of being
published and having good sales. But Felix discouraged her publishing her songs,
and since his professional opinion was very important to her, her compositions
have languished until recent decades. Her father Abraham Mendelssohn also
opposed the public dissemination of Fanny's music: "Music will perhaps become
Felix's profession; whilst for you it can and must only be an ornament, never the
root of your being and doing."[3]

Both the Mendelssohn children were gifted musically. Fanny received the
same extensive education in music and the arts as Felix; both studied music with
Karl Friedrich Zelter and liberal arts with K.W.L. Heyse. She began to compose
songs as child. Although Fanny was not allowed to publish her compositions or to
perform in public, she played at the concerts sponsored in the Mendelssohn household each Sunday. Abraham Mendelssohn often hired instrumentalists to accompany Felix and Fanny. Audience members read like a "who's-who" in artistic circles of
the day: Liszt, Hegel, Paganini, Heine. In his *Memoires*, Charles Gounod penned
this description of Fanny Hensel:

Mme. Hensel was a first-rate musician—a very clever pianist,
physically small and delicate, but her deep eyes and eager glance
betrayed an active mind and restless energy. She had rare powers
of composition, and many of the "Songs without Words," published
among the works and under the name of her brother, were hers.[4]

In 1829 Fanny married painter Wilhelm Hensel, who encouraged her (as did her mother) to publish her music . Only one song was published in 1837, but it was well-received in a performance in Leipzig attended by Felix. He made it clear to Fanny and to his mother that he still opposed Fanny's publishing music: "She is too much all that a woman ought to be for this...I am, as I said, quite ready to assist her so far as I can, but to encourage her in what I do not consider right, is what I cannot do."[5]

Ten years later, and only a year before her death, Fanny allowed publication of what she considered to be her best works: two books of songs for voice and piano, four books of piano music, and one book of partsongs. When Felix finally communicated with her about the pubication of these works, she wrote this entry in her diary: "At last Felix has written, and given me his professional blessing in the kindest manner. I know that he is not quite satisfied in his heart of hearts, but I am glad he has said a kind word to me about it..."[6]

Hensel's musical compositions were influenced by folk songs; her earliest songs are strophic, and use syllabic text setting and repetitive rhythms. Songs from her mature period are more diverse and musically developed. Most are through-composed; the piano assumes a more active role and vocal lines become more expressive. There is a high degree of interaction between piano and voice in these songs.

Hensel wrote lyrical, broad-lined melodies of extensive range. Vocal lines contain chromaticism and some recitative-like declamation; irregular phrase shapes are also characteristic of her melodic style. She often composed accompaniments using chordal figures or arpeggios of all types; many double the vocal line (these are probably a reflection of her studies with Zelter who felt that poetic content should dominate the song). She chose poetry by numerous contemporary poets, including Eichendorff, Uhland, Lenau, Hölty, Heine, Rückert, Müller, and Grillparzer, but set the largest number of poems by Goethe (a total of twenty-five).

Fanny Mendelssohn Hensel died in 1847, leaving about 500 compositions. The last lines of "Bergelust," the song she wrote the day before her death, are engraved on her tombstone: "Thoughts and songs pass until they reach the heavenly kingdom."

Nachtwanderer, Op. 7, No. 1   Night Wanderer
(Joseph von Eichendorff)

"Nachtwanderer" is an excellent example of Hensel's skillful handling of voice and piano texture, in a beautiful nocturne setting of Eichendorff. She could hardly have chosen a poem with more typical Romantic themes: nature and mystery..." O magical nightsong..." Hensel's sophisticated approach features sensitive melodic writing for both voice and piano, with free exchange of melodic materials.

The wanderer, strolling through the still night, is illustrated clearly by the constantly changing interaction between voice and piano. Vocal phrases vary in shape and length, and piano phrases show similar variety. Although the accompaniment maintains a chordal style, strands of melody in the piano appear in both bass and treble voices in an imitative fashion. Voice and piano lines relate flexibly with one another throughout, exchanging and sharing material (see the introduction and the first vocal phrase for an example).

Du bist die Ruh, Op. 7, No. 4*
(Friedrich Rückert)

You are Peace. 1839

This is a heartfelt but rather simple treatment of Rückert's intimate poem, which is better known in its setting by Franz Schubert. The first strophe features downward movement in the vocal phrases. Phrase shapes rise more hopefully in the second stanza. The ends of both stanzas match each other exactly. There is a brief codetta of a few measures. Notice the word painting and flexible phrase shapes at "Zur Wohnung hier" and "Von deinem Glanz."

*For a comparison setting, see Franz Schubert.

Die Mainacht, Op. 9, No. 6*
(Ludwig Hölty)

May Night. 1838

Hensel's setting features a serene vocal line over a gently moving accompaniment of broken chord figures, decorated at points with melodic fragments. Like Brahms's setting of this text, Hensel sets the last phrase of the stanza in an extended lyric line. Hers is an arching vocal line that descends on "traurig"—and in second strophe, "einsame." Brahms includes a fourth stanza which Hensel omits.

Some wide skips in the in vocal line seem not to be word painting but rather deep expressions of emotion: "über den Rasen streut" / "aber ich wende mich." The piano introduction features irregular phrase lengths, a hallmark of Fanny's musical style.

*An interesting comparison may be made of this song and the setting by Johannes Brahms.

Sehnsucht nach Italien
(Johann Wolfgang von Goethe)

Longing for Italy. 1822

This song divides Fanny Hensel's early songs from her more mature *Lieder*. Her experimental nature is clearly seen in this expressive but dramatic setting of Goethe's "Kennst du das Land" from Goethe's *Wilhelm Meister*.*

Fanny chose to set the poem in through-composed form, an unusual structure for her early works. Only the first stanza of the poem is used. The vocal line predominates, with flexible phrase shapes of Italian style; the accompaniment is a simple alternation of chord patterns. Dramatic tension builds to the climactic last section "Dahin, möcht ich mit Dir, o mein Geliebeter ziehn."

*See also settings by Schubert, Beethoven, Liszt, Schumann, Wolf, Tchaikovsky, and others.

Suleika
(Marianne von Wellemer)

Suleika. 1836

This poem, titled "Ach, um deine feuchten Schwingen," has been incorrectly attributed to Goethe. Its author was really Marianne von Wellemer.* Goethe ardently pursued the young woman, and they carried on an extensive correspondence in poetic form, taking the names Hatem and Suleika.**

Felix Mendelssohn, Franz Schubert ("Suleika II"), Karl Zelter, and Carl Banck also set this text. Fanny Hensel's composition, written in 1836, was her second setting of this poem (c. 1825 and 1836). She also composed a duet "Suleika und Hatem," published in 1827 under her brother Felix's name (Op. 8, No. 12). Fanny's musical setting captures the passionate mood of the text. Quarter rests in the opening vocal phrases convey Suleika's breathless plea to the West wind.

* See Schubert, "Suleika I."
**Suleika and Hatem were lovers in the Persian *Divan*, a collection of poems by Hafiz (ca. 1320-1389).

Extended Study List
Frühling • Bitte • Erwin • Morgenständchen • Im Herbst • Wanderlied • Dein ist mein Herz • Maienlied • Die frühen Gräber • Der Rosenkranz • Die Nonne • Der Maiabend • Warum sind denn du Rosen so blass

Selected Reading*
James R. Briscoe, ed., *Historical Anthology of Music by Women* (Bloomington: Indiana University Press, 1987). Contains biographies as well as musical examples of numerous women composers.
Marcia Citron, *The Letters of Fanny Hensel to Felix Mendelssohn* (Stuyvesant, N.Y.: Pendragon, 1987).
_____, "The Lieder of Fanny Mendelssohn Hensel." *The Musical Quarterly.* 1983, 69:570-593.
_____, "Felix Mendelssohn's Influence on Fanny Mendelssohn Hensel as a Professional Composer," *Curent Musicology* 37:38, 1984. 9-17.
Lorraine Gorrell, "Fanny Mendelssohn and Her Songs," *The NATS Journal* 42:5 (May/June 1986).
_____, *The Nineteenth-Century German Lied* (Portland, Oregon: Amadeus Press, 1993).
Sebastian Hensel. *The Mendelssohn Family* (1729-1847) *from Letters and Journals.* Trans. by Carl Klingemann. Second edition, 2 vols. (New York: Harper & Brothers [1881]).
John Glenn Paton, ed., *Sixteen Songs: Fanny Mendelssohn Hensel* (Van Nuys, CA: Alfred Publishing Co., 1995). Paton's preface contains interesting and valuable information on Hensel's song style, and her family background and personality. The sixteen *Lieder* are a varied selection from Hensel's output, well-edited and presented.
Carol Lynelle Quin, "Fanny Mendelssohn Hensel: Her Contributions to Nineteenth-Century Musical Life," D.M.A. diss., (Ann Arbor: University Microfilms International, 1981).
Victoria Sirota, "The Life and Works of Fanny Mendelssohn Hensel," D.M.A. thesis, Boston University, 1981.
Jürgen Thym, "Crosscurrents in Song: Five Distinctive Voices," in *German Lieder in the Nineteenth Century*, ed. Rufus Hallmark (New York: Schirmer Books, 1996), 153-185.
Françoise Tillard. *Fanny Mendelssohn.* Trans. by Camille Naish. (Portland, OR: Amadeus Press, 1996).
Nancy Walker, "Parallels between Fanny Mendelssohn Hensel and Clara Wieck Schumann: Their Lives and Their Songs," *The NATS Journal*, 50:4 (March/April 1994).

*Also refer to "Selected Reading" for Felix Mendelssohn.

Notes
1. Quoted in Marcia J. Citron, "The Lieder of Fanny Mendelssohn Hensel," *Musical Quarterly,* 68:4 (Fall 1993), 571.
2. Quoted in liner notes. *Fanny Mendelssohn Hensel Lieder.* Lauralyn Kolb, soprano; Arlene Shrut, pianist. Centaur Records compact disc CRC 2120, 1992, 3.
3. Judith Tick. Quoted in liner notes to *Lieder: Clara Schumann, Fanny Mendelssohn, Josephine Lang, Pauline Viardot-Garcia.* Katherine Ciesinski, John Ostendorf/Rudolph Palmer. Leonarda Records. Long playing recording LPI 107, 1981.

4. Quoted in liner notes. *Fanny Mendelssohn Hensel Lieder.* Centaur Records compact disc CRC 2120, 1992, 2.

5. Quoted in Marcia J. Citron, "Felix Mendelssohn's Influence on Fanny Mendelssohn Hensel as a Professional Composer," *Current Musicology* 37/38 (1984), 15.

6. Ibid., 16.

FELIX MENDELSSOHN (1809-1847)

It is bad enough that Felix has taken it into his head to be heard playing only boring accompaniments, but he now composes the type of pieces that nobody may see and that can hardly be performed. I consider such pieces stillborn children and I fear that he delves so deeply into this genre that nothing fresh, enjoyable, or lively comes forth any more...

—Lea Salomon Mendelssohn[1]

Felix Mendelssohn Bartholdy* was raised in an atmosphere of affluence and privilege. His family was wealthy, cultured, and respected. His father, Abraham Mendelssohn was a successful banker, the sixth child of the distinguished philosopher Moses Mendelssohn. His mother, Lea Salomon Mendelssohn, came from a wealthy family in which women were praised for their intellectual accomplishments. Lea Mendelssohn presided at the family's Sunday salons, which she named *Sonntagsmusiken* (Sunday musicales). The Mendelssohn children, Fanny and Felix, often performed at these gatherings.

Felix's early piano studies were with his mother, and in Berlin, piano and theory with Carl Zelter. There, Zelter introduced the twelve-year-old boy to the distinguished poet Goethe with whom he formed a warm friendship. Mendelssohn traveled abroad extensively, became municipal director of music at Düsseldorf in 1833, then moved to Leipzig as director of the Gewandhaus concerts in 1835, where he was instrumental in reviving interest in the music of Johann Sebastian Bach. In 1829, he conducted Bach's *St. Matthew Passion*, the first performance of the work since Bach's death in 1750.

Mendelssohn's songs do not achieve the level of his instrumental music; some consider that his overture to Shakespeare's *Midsummer Night's Dream*, composed at age seventeen, was never surpassed by his later creations. His catalogue lists seventy-nine *Lieder*; five of the early songs were by his sister Fanny. Charming and lyrical, his songs are chiefly characterized by a fine sense of melody and a vivid sense of poetic atmosphere. Texts cover a wide variety of moods and emotions. His accompaniments break no new ground; the piano does not reach an interactive partnership with the voice on any meaningful level. Song form is usually strophic, with simple harmonies. Melodies are rarely dramatic. Some of his most effective songs are his earliest. Mendelssohn's songs seem to emulate Schubert's song style more closely than other composers.

Hall suggests that Mendelssohn's privileged life probably influenced the general character of his music—graceful and melodious, written with solid workmanship and technique, their effect momentary.[2] As a group, his songs vary as to quality and do not stray far from conventional styles, but the best of them are appealing and lovely.

Mendelssohn was a gifted musician with a keen intellect. His personality and background—a classically structured upbringing combined with romantic disposition—caused his music to be regarded as restrained and somewhat superficial. His music has often been criticized for a lack of passion, but its craftsmanship, poetry and melodic invention have engendered new interest in his compositions. Among his best-known works: the oratorios *St. Paul* and *Elijah*; *Walpurgisnacht* for solo voices, choir and orchestra; incidental music to plays by Sophocles, Shakespeare, Racine, and Hugo; five symphonies; several concert overtures; a violin concerto; and numerous works for solo piano (including forty-eight *Songs without Words*).

*He added Bartholdy to his surname when he became a Protestant Christian.

Auf Flügeln des Gesanges, Op. 34, No. 2   **On Wings of Song. 1833-34**
(Heinrich Heine)

"Auf Flügeln des Gesanges" remains one of Mendelssohn's best-known, most popular songs. It is typical of Mendelssohn's graceful melodic style. A lovely lyric melody flows easily throughout the song, unhampered by rhythmic or harmonic variances. A "well-mannered" arpeggiated accompaniment supports the voice with gently changing harmonies. A lovely interlude divides the second and third stanzas. The final stanza contains some imaginative touches—"seligen Traum" (blissful dream) is echoed as a final statement to close the song. The overall atmosphere is one of effortless grace. When Heine heard this setting of his poems, he is supposed to have made the startling comment, "It has no melody."

Bei der Wiege, Op. 47, No. 6   **Beside the Cradle. 1839**
(C. Klingemann)

This lullaby, not hypnotic in mood, is a charming, quickly moving melody reminiscent of a simple folk tune. A happy little rhythmic pattern in the piano creates unity through this song; it is first heard in the introduction. The second stanza is more overtly lyric, emerging from the first stanza in an easy transition. "Bleibe nur fein geduldig!" (So just wait patiently!) is the last vocal phrase, sung to the opening pattern of the piano, and repeated again, creating a tidy little circular form.

Nachtlied, Op. 71, No. 6   **Night Song. 1846**
(Joseph von Eichendorff)

Mendelssohn wrote this *Lied*, one of his finest, shortly before his death. The text is an evening soliloquy with a reference to time moving through the night, taking many who did not expect to go—"So reist die Zeit die ganze Nacht/Nimmt manchen mit, der's nicht gedacht." There is great beauty and dignity in its brief form (AAB with a little codetta). The first two stanzas are set simply over a gently syncopated background in the piano, which sometimes doubles the vocal line. Mendelssohn varied the last stanza in an exultant dramatic fashion, with vocal phrases of greater breadth and expressiveness. The last two lines are repeated more solemnly at the very end, using the quiet mood of the opening.

Neue Liebe, Op. 19a, No. 4   **New Love. 1834**
(Heinrich Heine)

Moonlight revels of elves are recounted in this song. Heine's verses are full of vibrant images: riding, horns resounding, bells ringing. But a sinister suggestion lies beneath the fairylike gaiety. As the Queen rides by, the poet wonders if she is a sign of his new love, or a sign of death.

Light, fluttery figures in the piano introduce the elves riding through the woods. A nice mixture of mystery and gaiety is created by minor tonality and the dotted rhythm patterns in the staccato piano figures. Like the piano, the vocal line is full of prancing staccato articulations, which alternate with longer note values. Varied phrase lengths create interest (see especially the entry of the voice "Ihre Hörner hört' ich lingen"). Midway through the third verse, the whimsical texture fades and somber chords accompany the lines "Galt das meiner neuen Liebe?/Oder soll es Tod bedeuten?" The piano returns to its lively context, but a pall hangs over the concluding measures. Is it a warning of what is to come?

Extended Study List

Das erste Veilchen • An die Entfernte • Herbstlied • Hexenlied • Maienlied • Schilflied • Volkslied • Venezianisches Gondellied • Frühlingslied • Winterlied • Wanderlied • Der Blumenkranz • Erster Verlust

Selected Reading

John Michael Cooper, *Felix Mendelssohn Bartholdy: a guide to research, with an introduction to research concerning Fanny Hensel* (New York & London: Routledge, 2001).

Sebastian Hensel. *The Mendelssohn Family* (1729-1847) *from Letters and Journals.* Trans. by Carl Klingemann. Second edition, 2 vols. (New York: Harper & Brothers [1881]).

Felix Mendelssohn Bartholdy, *Letters from 1833-1847.* Edited by Paul Mendelssohn Bartholdy and Carl Mendelssohn Bartholdy. Trans. Lady Wallace (Boston: Oliver Ditson [1863]).

Michael Hurd, *Mendelssohn* (New York: T. Y. Crowell, 1970).

Herbert Kuperberg, *Felix Mendelssohn: his life, his family, his music* (New York: Charles Scribner's Sons, 1972).

Charles Rosen, *The Romantic Generation* (Cambridge: Harvard University Press, 1995).

R. Larry Todd, ed., *Mendelssohn and his world* (Princeton: Princeton University Press, 1991).

_____, ed., *Mendelssohn Studies* (Cambridge: Cambridge University Press, 1992).

Eric Werner, *Mendelssohn: a new image of the composer and his age,* trans. Dika Newlin (New York, Free Press, 1963).

Notes

1. Lea Salomon in a letter to to Carl Klingemann, young diplomat and friend of Mendelssohn's. Felix set a number of his song texts. Quoted in Eric Werner, *Mendelssohn: a new image of the composer and his age,* trans. Dika Newlin, 74.
2. James Husst Hall, *The Art Song,* 90.

ROBERT SCHUMANN (1810-1856)

My dear Clara, I am sending you a little song, to comfort you: sing it to
yourself softly, simply, like yourself..."
—Robert Schumann to Clara Wieck[1]

Although Schubert's treatment of the piano was unique for its time, it did not
venture far beyond suggesting atmosphere. With the songs of Robert Schumann,
the piano comes into its own as a full participant with the voice. Schumann transferred the expressive qualities found in his piano works into his songs. Before he
began to concentrate upon composing songs, he had written most of the large piano
works which brought him fame; *Davidbündlertänze, Toccata, Kreisleriana,
Fantasia in C, Arabeske, Humoreske, Kinderszenen, Novelletten, Nachtstücke,
Carnaval, Fantasiestücke, Papillons, Etudes symphoniques,* and his three piano
sonatas all preceded the "miraculous *Liederjahr*" (*Lieder* year) of 1840, the year of
his marriage to Clara Wieck.

The courtship and eventual marriage of Clara and Robert is a story that parallels that of Robert Browning and Elizabeth Barrett, who also struggled to finally overcome the bitter opposition of a dominant father-figure. After an extended
battle that ended in the courts, Clara and Robert were free to marry.

Prior to his marriage, Schumann had written only a few youthful songs. His
oft-quoted statement that he considered songs inferior to instrumental music is
amazing, when, a year later in 1840, he composed 138 songs, well over half his complete output! These included the cycles *Dichterliebe, Liederkreis, Frauenliebe und -
leben.* His total song output totals well over 200—thirty-three sets of solo songs.
For two years he devoted himself to songs, writing a minimum of one per day. He
was a skilled miniaturist, and songs proved to be a perfect medium for his talents.
He understood poetry intuitively and produced songs in which the style is condi-
tioned by poetic content. Schumann's songs demand considerable elegance of
phrasing, and a rubato that must remain within the frame of the rhythmic pulse.

His orientation as a pianist transferred naturally into his songs; the accompaniment takes on great significance. It is assigned melodic material that interre-
lates with the voice on an equal level; it is given a wide variety of figures and styles
reflecting Schumann's mastery as a piano composer. Schumann's *Lieder* make
extensive use of preludes, interludes, and postludes.

It is also natural that, as the son of a bookseller, Schumann's literary
background was highly developed. He was discriminating in his choice of texts, and
his experience as a writer on music and a critic greatly influenced his artistic
aesthetic. As the editor of the *Neue Zeitschrift für Musik*, Schumann's critical
writings had considerable influence on the musical life of his time. Many of his
literary contributions were signed "Florestan" or "Eusebius," autobiographical
alter egos of differing personalities (outgoing/dreamy) who also made their way
into his piano music. Occasionally he used the name "Raro," a name created from
linking Clara and Robert (ClaRARObert).

Many of Schumann's songs are cycles or collections devoted to poems of a single poet, an indication of his compulsion for organization. His verbal acuity and
need for order manifested itself in his life, which he recorded in a series of books:
a project-book, a day-book, a songbook, a correspondence-book, a cash-book, etc.
He and Clara kept a series of marriage diaries that reveal not only a myriad of
daily details but also chronicle their relationship in its many facets.

This obsession poured over into his songs and cycles, which were organized in carefully ordered key relationships, linked by motives, and loaded with extra-musical meanings. He made plentiful use of motives in his music, and his songs contain one in particular that spells the name of Clara (C-B-A-G-sharp-A), used numerous times and in numerous variations.

Schumann maintained close friendships with Felix Mendelssohn and Johannes Brahms, whom he promoted as the most important new composer of Europe. Brahms, Schumann, and Clara formed a fascinating triumvirate of talent and personalities. The relationship between Clara and Brahms has been the subject of much written speculation.

Schumann was a workaholic with tenuous mental stability. Throughout much of his life he suffered periods of deep depression and mood fluctuations. Several times he attempted suicide. In 1854, at his request, he was placed in an asylum where he died two years later.

Dichterliebe, Op. 48, Nos. 1-16   **A Poet's Love. 1840**
(Heinrich Heine)

Im wunderschönen Monat Mai (In the Marvelous Month of May) •
Aus meinen Tränen spriessen (From my Tears There Spring) •
Die Rose, die Lilie, die Taube, die Sonne (The Rose, the Lily, the
Dove, the Sun) • Wenn ich in deine Augen seh' (When I Gaze into Your
Eyes) • Ich will meine Seele tauchen (I Long to Sink My Soul) • Im Rhein,
im heiligen Strome (In the Rhine, the Holy River) • Ich grolle nicht
(I Do Not Complain) • Und wüssten's die Blumen (If Only the Flowers
Could Know) • Das ist ein Flöten und Geigen (There is Fluting and
Fiddling) • Hör' ich das Liedchen klingen (When I Hear the Sound of
the Song) • Ein Jüngling liebt ein Mädchen (A Lad Loved a Girl) •
Am leuchtenden Sommermorgen (On a Gleaming Morning in Summer) •
Ich hab' im Traum geweinet (I Wept in My Dreams) • Allnächtlich
im Traume (All Night in Dreams I See You) • Aus alten Märchen
(From Old Tales) • Die alte bösen Lieder (The Old and Evil Songs)

The following sources should be used to study this cycle in depth:

Arthur Komar, ed., *Schumann: Dichterliebe.* Norton Critical Scores (New York: W.W. Norton, 1971).

Gerald Moore, *Poet's Love: The Songs and Cycles of Robert Schumann* (New York: Taplinger, 1981).

Eric Sams, *The Songs of Robert Schumann* (London: Methuen, 1969).

For many, Schumann's *Dichterliebe* is the quintessential song cycle, an extraordinary synthesis of poetry and music. *Dichterliebe* and *Frauenliebe und -leben,* both composed within several months of one another, were the only two works that Schumann himself called "cycles." He titled his other song collections *Liederkreis* (circle of songs) or *Liederreihe* (row of songs). Both cycles have thematic links that run through the songs, and music from earlier songs appears at the end of both works.

The poems in *Dichterliebe* sketch a story of unhappy love, the betrayal of the poet by his lover. For his texts, Schumann chose poems from Heine's *Lyrisches Intermezzo* (1823), a collection of poems written after Heine's cousin Amalie had reportedly rejected him for another lover, whom she married. The principal theme running through Heine's work is unrequited love—often nostalgic, often bitter.

Schumann titled his cycle "Poet's Love." The original cycle had twenty songs, but four were excised before publication. (See Komar for the original ordering of the songs). Within what appears to be a rather simple theme—unrequited love—there is a wide variety of moods. The poems run the gamut from infatuation and ecstasy to anger, irony, bitterness, and finally, forgiveness. The first song speaks in the past tense, indicating that the lyrics that follow are a flashback. The poet's recollections of his lost relationship present the songs as a series of images, some dissolving into one another in the manner of a kaleidoscope.

It is an intimate poetic journey, psychological as well as emotional. A thread of inner tension runs throughout the poetry: despite the loss of his love and his renunciation of the relationship, the poet is still in love with his beloved. He cannot reject her, and allows his despair to overcome and begin to destroy him until the idea of forgiveness surfaces. Even as the cycle ends, we are not convinced that he has been able to rid himself of her memory, but has only learned to live with his grief.

The "Clara motive" (C-B-A-G-sharp-A) in various keys and permutations, is found throughout the cycle. "She" appears in the accompaniment of Song 2, in Song 4 ("Ich weine bitterlich"), in Song 7 (this time in retrograde), and in Song 9 in a veritable potpourri of forms. Imaginative piano figurations fill every song; with only a few exceptions, the songs in *Dichterliebe* are based on one accompaniment figure per song. Rosen observes that although Schumann's songs are separate from one another, several have endings "either so dissonant or inconclusive that they must be resolved by the opening of the following song"[2] (examples: Songs 1 and 2, Songs 2 and 3). Schumann's piano accompaniments are almost independent melodic entities within themselves. *Dichterliebe* makes extensive use of extended piano postludes (Songs 5, 6, 8, 9, 10, 11, 12, and 16). Chissell comments that many "have so much of the melody incorporated in the accompaniment that only a few alterations would be necessary to transform them into typically Schumannesque piano pieces."[3] In many instances, vocal melodies seem to derive from the song immediately preceding, creating a subtle sense of ongoing movement. Vocal phrases adhere closely to the inflections of the text, often focusing on one pitch. Additionally, several of the songs have melodies closely related in shape (examples: Songs 3, 4, and 5). Vocal articulation is predominantly a simple lyric recitative; even in "Ich grolle nicht," broad-lined lyric phrases are absent. There is no central tonal unity to the cycle, but instead, a sense of development from tonality to tonality, following the unfolding drama and emotional content of the poetry.

Song 1 features ambiguity of tonality and the inconclusive ending "fades" into the second song. Songs 2, 3, and 4, in closely related major keys (A, D, G), are declarations of love to the beloved; only in Song 4 do the "bitter tears" foretell the sorrow to come. Songs 5 and 6 are both in related minor keys (B minor, E minor). They do not address the beloved directly, but express intense memories of her kiss and her face. The poem of Song 6 makes reference to the Rhine River, to the city and cathedral of Köln, and the painting of the Madonna in the cathedral, whose likeness resembles the poet's beloved. Song 7 is the turning point in the cycle, a fierce and bitter song directed to the beloved. Schumann repeats "Ich grolle nicht" (I bear no grudge) six times during the song, in contrast to Heine's original two repetitions.

Songs 8, 9, and 10 are in related minor keys (A minor, D minor, G minor). Song 8 lashes out bitterly against his love. Song 9 recounts her marriage to another. In unwavering movement, the piano's running figures pile up sequentially, combined with sounds of the wedding festivities: flutes, violins, trumpets and drums, blare, roar and boom while the angels sob. Song 10 is the moment of deepest despair. Song 11 is humorous, although an undercurrent of agitation is still present. Song

12 introduces the healing idea of forgiveness. In Songs 13 and 14, the loved one is addressed for the last time—in dreams, her significance is diminished. Song 13 begins bereft of accompaniment, punctuated with chords that seem to replay the memory in his mind; the poet is suffused with weeping. Song 14 is a dream in which the beloved greets him warmly and offers a sprig of cypress. Fantasizing in Song 15, the poet describes a magical land where all is beautiful, and problems are nonexistent. He yearns to go there and be relieved of his sorrow.

In Song 16, he buries his love and desire, and with them, his pain. In the midst of the symbolic burial are touches of black comedy: the elaborate image and size of the coffin, the twelve giants who are pallbearers, and the choice of the largest grave possible—the Rhine. Here, his anger is repressed and tempered with wit. Schumann concludes the work with a long piano postlude taken from the end of Song 12, the point where forgiveness was introduced.

For Schumann the pianist, it is fitting that the piano resolves and completes the cycle. The luminous postlude affirms the eternal quality of the love just buried and provides a catharsis for the entire work. The theme moves through several keys and ends in C-sharp [D-flat], the dominant of the first song of the cycle, "Im wunderschönen Monat Mai." The circle has closed.

Frauenliebe und -leben, Op. 42   A Woman's Love and Life. 1840
(Adalbert von Chamisso)

Seit ich ihn gesehen (Since I First Saw Him) • Er, der Herrlichste
von Allen (He, the Noblest of All) • Ich kann's nicht fassen, nicht glauben
(I Can't Understand It, I Don't Believe It) • Du Ring an meinem Finger
(You, Ring on My Finger) • Helft mir, ihr Schwestern (Help Me, O Sisters) •
Süsser Freund (Sweet Friend) • An meinen Herzen, an meiner Brust
(At My Heart, at My Breast) • Nun hast du mir den ersten Schmerz getan
(Now You Have Hurt Me for the First Time)

Frauenliebe und -leben was the last cycle Schumann wrote before his marriage to Clara Wieck the following September. Like *Myrthen* (see below), it was intended as a wedding gift. Both cycles contain poems that attempt to mirror the emotional experiences of women at various stages of life. *Frauenliebe und -leben* narrates in a woman's words the progressive stages of her relationship with her husband from their first meeting until she sees him on his death bier.

As Charles Rosen observes, "a song cycle cannot tell a story directly—at best it can hint at one that remains untold. There is no narrative in *Frauenliebe und -leben,* although each song marks an important event in the typical life of an 'ideal' woman—ideal from the male point of view: the woman's life starts when she meets the man who will marry her and ends with his death, leaving her only with memories."[4]

The cycle has been criticized on several accounts. Chamisso's poetry is not of the highest quality and more importantly, when viewed in contemporary social light, the idea of a woman's entire being revolving only around her husband and her position as a wife goes against the grain for many.

Chamisso ended his collection of poems with a verse in which the woman, now advanced in age, finds comfort and peace in the continuity of life through her children and grandchildren. Schumann chose not to set this poem, finishing his cycle instead with a long postlude—a repetition of the first song—in which the widow reminisces over her lost happiness.

It is possible that in composing this cycle, Schumann was searching for a symbolic counterpart to his previous work, *Dichterliebe*, and Chamisso's poems offered him a view of love that provided a striking contrast with the bitter irony of Heine's verses.

SEIT ICH IHN GESEHEN. "Since I have seen him, I am blind to all else. Wherever I look I see only him." Chamisso's poem has two verses, full of longing. Schumann's simple strophic setting presents a clear picture of the young girl, unpretentious and appealing. For most of the song, the vocal phrases are doubled in the piano accompaniment, a technique that is important at the end of the cycle. Two measures of simple chords open the song, serve to link stanza to stanza, and close the song. They seem to suggest the young girl's simplicity as well as her uncertainty.

ER, DER HERRLICHSTE VON ALLEN. Here is an song of unabashed passion. Brimming with ardor, she extols the virtues of her sweetheart and vows that, even though her heart should break if she were not the chosen one, only the finest woman is worthy of his magnificence. Vocal phrases are ornamented with turns—often found in Schumann's vocal writing, and not surprising for a composer of piano works. A repeated chord accompaniment moves the song forward and perpetuates the ecstatic mood. The piano also echoes the initial vocal phrase in high and low registers; harmonic fluctuations mirror her uncertainty and changing emotions. A quiet postlude closes the song.

ICH KANN'S NICHT FASSEN, NICHT GLAUBEN. "I cannot believe it, cannot grasp it. He said 'I am yours forever.' Oh let me die, dreaming, cradled on his breast." This is a little C minor trio between two songs in E-flat major. It is composed of breathless vocal lines and chords in the accompaniment. Only near the end is there a small lyric interlude, reflective and almost awestruck. The opening vocal material concludes the song, reaching to a higher note for the word "glauben." The song ends quietly on a note of wonder.

DU RING AN MEINEM FINGER. This is a lovely legato setting, sober in mood when contrasted with the impulsive phrases of Song 3. As she gazes at his ring on her finger, she realizes that her life is changed. A fleeting reminiscence from Song 2 is heard ("hin selber mich geben und finden verklärt mich..."). The first phrase is heard three times in the song, varied slightly in the last repetition.

HELFT MIR, IHR SCHWESTERN. Bustling preparations for the wedding march bring forth a quick arpeggiated accompaniment, not unlike the one Schumann used for "Widmung." Her dream is about to be realized, and her vocal phrases rise and fall lyrically. Tiny melodic fragments from Songs 2 and 3 make their way into the texture at measures 27 and 30. The song's postlude is the wedding march, solemn but happy in its dotted rhythms. Its melodic material is a variant of the first vocal phrase.

SÜSSER FREUND. After five songs in flat keys, the tonality of G major is both fresh and striking, heralding a momentous announcement. It also is a turning point, dividing the cycle's first poems of girlish charm and youth with those of her maturity. In this song, she intimately tells her husband of her pregnancy. Schumann makes use of the same vocal phrase shape (which contains an augmented interval) for much of the song.

The song is in three sections. In the middle section she gathers her courage to confide her secret; there is a change of key and more resolute mood in an accompaniment pattern of repeated chords. The final words "dein Bildnis" (your image) are drawn from the previous phrase; the quiet repetition is set effectively and emotionally on the last chord resolution. Schumann uses a quotation from Beethoven's *An die ferne Geliebte*, a favorite reference for his love for Clara; it appears immediately following "geliebter Mann."

AN MEINEN HERZEN, AN MEINER BRUST. This song is not one of the most inspired in the cycle. A careful approach is required from singer and pianist in order to avoid a monochromatic mood. Instead of using a lullaby setting, Schumann chooses to express the young mother's ecstatic joy as she holds and rocks her baby with a quick tempo. Piano figures are arpeggiated until the last measures, which are accompanied by chords much in the same manner as Song 3. Vocal phrases are set syllabically and are rhythmically repetitive, in the fashion of "baby-talk." The postlude's last chords echo the last words of the previous song "dein Bildnis."

NUN HAST DU MIR DEN ERSTEN SCHMERZ GETAN. In striking contrast to the joy of the previous scene, a stark D minor triad opens this song. The first vocal phrase outlines that chord in heavily marked rhythms as the woman, newly widowed, gazes at her husband's body. This is an intensely dramatic song, unrelieved in mood until the final postlude. Schumann keeps the texture lean—only chords underline the singer's grief-stricken phrases. At "Es blicket die Verlassne vor sich hin, die Welt ist leer" (Left all alone, I stare at an empty world), the chords become more chromatic. Vocal phrases become lower in pitch, like a leaden recitative. She sings her last phrases: "Quietly I withdraw into myself; the curtain falls. There I have you and my lost happiness."

A quick transitory measure leads back to B-flat major and the music of the first song. The accompaniment of one entire stanza is reprised without alteration. In the first song, the piano doubles most of the vocal line, but at points the voice line exists on its own. Hearing only the accompaniment to this song causes the listener to supply and remember the singer's line, even as the widow is remembering it. It is a masterful musical device and a poignant emotional moment.

• From *Liederkreis*, Op. 39 (1840) •

"I have composed so much that it almost frightens me," Schumann wrote, "but I can't help it; I'm having to sing myself to death like a nightingale...The Eichendorff cycle is my most Romantic music ever, and contains much of you in it, dear Clara."[5] The twelve songs on poems of Eichendorff are inspired pieces of nature-romanticism. It is a collection rather than a cycle; the songs are bound together only by the their reference to nature, seasons, and times of day. Numerous variations can be found within these topics, and a wide variety of emotions and feelings can be attached to the poetic content. Each song is self-contained and loses nothing by being heard out of context, but taken as a group, the poems are carefully ordered by Schumann and the progress from one song to another is not haphazard. Almost all of the twelve poems makes reference to the sky and flight.

In der Fremde, Op. 39, No. 1   **In a Foreign Land.**
(Joseph von Eichendorff)

Schumann uses a through-composed setting for this first song of the collection. Its simplicity is deceiving, for it is full of subtle harmonic touches that reinforce the text. Melancholy chromaticism in the accompaniment illustrates the mood of the singer. His memories of home and parents—long gone—are coupled with a poignant desire to rest under the murmuring branches of the forest, where he too will be forgotten.

Several musical touches typical of Schumann's style are found in this lovely song: lyric melody, which is echoed or anticipated by the piano, and close-spaced arpeggios, which create unity. Material from the first phrase appears, subtly varied, at various points throughout the song.

Waldesgespräch, Op. 39, No. 3   **Dialogue in the Wood.**
(Joseph von Eichendorff)

This song is a chilling little scene: a wanderer on horseback, riding through the forest, is accosted by a lovely maiden whose beauty enchants him. Too late he recognizes her as the witch Lorelei. "You shall never leave this forest," she exults. The legendary Lorelei is a witch figure who sings siren songs from the cliffs above the sea, luring sailors and ships to destruction on the rocks. In this song she is found in the forest, away from "her castle on the Rhine" and, as Sams observes, assumes the mantle of Diana the huntress or of Nature itself.[6]

The young hunter is all eagerness and confidence; hunting horn calls and a strongly rhythmic riding motive accompany his entrance into the forest. As he sees the "schöne Braut" (fair bride), he offers to take her home, and, on the word "heim," without warning, the phrase cadences in another key. Even in this mysterious drama, it is a striking effect.

The beautiful maiden begins to speak with soothing arpeggios in the piano, weaving her spell. Once again the key changes and his accompaniment figure return, but now the stanza ends with his horrified realization that she is the witch Lorelei. Sweetly, she acknowledges her identity and her vocal phrases build lyrically to a triumphant climax, ending with her terrifying pronouncement, "nimmer mehr, nimmer mehr"—not unlike a witch's incantation—that he will never leave the wood. The piano postlude quietly brings the magic to an end with the horn call fading away in the chilly night air.

Mondnacht, Op. 39, No. 5   **Moonlit Night.**
(Joseph von Eichendorff)

"Mondnacht" is considered by many to be the most beautiful song in the *Liederkreis* and perhaps the loveliest of all of Schumann's songs. Schumann's opening bars are a blend of high and low registers, suggesting the romantic starry night and the union of earth and sky, which subtly mesh for the entrance of the voice. Repeated notes, intervals, and chords are combined with a gently moving bass line. The vocal line floats calmly above.

Schumann builds almost the entire song from one eight-bar phrase; it is repeated twice to form the first two stanzas and used again for the last two lines of the third stanza, for a total of five times. Its ethereal melody rises chromatically, and then is matched by a graceful answering phrase. The introduction is used again to separate the first and second verses.

Momentarily, at the words "Und meine Seele spannte/Weit ihre Flügel aus" (And my soul stretched its wings far abroad), the melody broadens and becomes more earthbound as the poet introduces himself into the poetic landscape his imagination has created. This slight change of mood is the only deviation from a scene of utter magic and profound stillness. Material from the piano introduction appears again, this time combined with the first two vocal phrases of this stanza, before the last repetition of the initial melody.

The formal structure of the song, then, is:

Introduction	6 bars
A melody	8 bars
A melody	8 bars
Introduction	6 bars
A melody	8 bars
A melody	8 bars
B melody w/intro	8 bars
A melody	8 bars
Coda (based on material from the Introduction material	

In spite of a formal scheme derived almost entirely from repetition, "Mondnacht" is a supreme example of the first lines of the poem, "It was as if the heaven had quietly kissed the earth."

From *Myrthen*, Op. 25 (Myrtles. 1840)

In February 1840, Schumann wrote to Clara from Leipzig: "Dear Clara; since early yesterday morning I have written nearly 27 pages of music (something new!) about which all I can tell you is that as I wrote it I laughed and wept for joy." [7] The music Schumann referred to was *Myrthen,* which was to be his wedding present to Clara. He had his publisher create a beautifully designed leather binding for the songs for presentation to his bride.

Not surprisingly, Schumann's love of puzzles and ciphers permeates this collection. There are twenty-six songs—the same number as the letters of the alphabet—and the "Clara theme" appears among them in various forms and disguises. Past joys and sorrows seem to form the theme of the poetry of *Myrthen*; Sams infers that within the selections are Schumann's ideas about the nature of man and woman and their relationship to one another.[8] The texts are a collection of various poets including Goethe, Heine and Robert Burns.

Widmung,* Op. 25, No. 1   **Dedication.**
(Friedrich Rückert)

The first song of the *Myrthen* cycle is an enthusiastic avowal of love and one of Schumann"s most popular songs. The title is his own, and provides a fitting opening for his wedding present to Clara. Not surprisingly, there are instances of the "Clara" motive through this song.

Song form is ABA', with the recapitulation lightly varied. The first section is an ardent pledge of love, set in rising vocal phrases that reach a high point at

"Wonne," then descend again, only to quickly climax on G-flat ("schwebe"). A rhythmic accompaniment pattern propels the song forward, in a burst of joy.

The middle section features a change of key and accompaniment pattern; a serene, almost religious atmosphere is produced by a chord pattern in triplets over which the vocal phrase floats. There are instances of two against three and an ornamental turn in the voice that refers to Schumann's piano works including *Novelletten* and *Arabeske*—a tribute to Clara.[9] The calm mood continues, concluding with a two measure transition to the return of the first section, achieved seamlessly in the vocal line by an enharmonic change at "du hebst mich *liebend* über mich..."/you lovingly raise me above myself)—one of the song's most intimate and tender moments.

*Franz Liszt transcribed this song for solo piano.

Die Lotosblume,* Op. 25, No. 7   **The Lotus-Flower.**
(Heinrich Heine)

This is another of Schumann's beautifully descriptive nature scenes, in a style somewhat reminiscent of Schubert. The lotus-flower, which blooms at night, avoids the sun, awaiting her lover, the moon. When his light wakes her, she blooms and glows and gleams with the pain of love.

A mood of calm and expectancy is produced by repeated chords in the accompaniment, coupled with a bass line in octaves. We are greeted in the first vocal phrase with the "Clara motive." Simple, melodic vocal lines use text-painting: as the lotus flower bows her head, the vocal line descends into the piano texture, waiting; a momentary change of key (C major to A-flat major) occurs without preparation at "Der Mond, der ist ihr Buhle" (The moon is her lover) for another effective moment. Here also the accompaniment chords migrate to the treble clef. From this point on, both accompaniment and voice gather intensity and seem to come alive as the flower turns her face to her lover, blossoming in ecstasy. Schumann repeats the last vocal phrase ("Vor Liebe und Liebesweh") as a little postscript.

*This text was also set by Robert Franz.

Der Nussbaum, Op. 25, No. 3   **The Walnut Tree.**
(Julius Mosen)

This lovely song is all charm and tenderness. Softly moving branches of a walnut tree whisper of a maiden who dreamed all day and night without knowing why. They murmur softly of the bridegroom who will come next year, and at their sound, the young girl smiles and drifts into sleep and dreams.

The rustling branches of the leaves are introduced by the piano in the first two measures. This melodic cell binds the song together; it punctuates the vocal phrases and, in tandem with the arpeggiated accompaniment, acts as a graceful agent of modulation. Vocal phrase endings have the same descending shape as this melodic cell for most of the song. Phrase shapes are flexible and delicate in both piano and voice; arpeggios in the piano are divided between both hands; vocal phrases are curved gracefully. Rhythms combine to produce a lovely lilting effect as the melodic material shifts back and forth from piano to voice. The vocal phrases are notable for their fragmented quality; the phrases seem unfinished until the piano motive completes them. They are of uneven length—two bars, then four.

Schumann's skillful transformation of an average poem into a extraordinary song is masterful. "Der Nussbaum" remains one of his best-known and most-performed songs, and deservedly so. It is a tiny masterpiece.

Die beiden Grenadiere,* Op. 49, No. 1   **The Two Grenadiers. 1840**
(Heinrich Heine)

This great dramatic song, with its incorporation of the French "Marseillaise" in the final measures, never fails to stir the listener. Heine was in Düsseldorf in 1816 and may have seen French soldiers returning from Russia. His poignant verses chronicle the dialogue of two soldiers, returning from imprisonment; they learn of the defeat of the Grand Army and of Napoleon's capture. They weep at the devastating news and wish they could die together, but one must return to his wife and children who need him. The other grenadier is mortally wounded; he extracts a promise from his comrade to take his body to France and bury him there, with his medals and sword. He will rest silently until the Emperor rides over his grave, then arise and defend him again.

Schumann sets the bleak scene with motives that suggest a halting march and a listless drum flourish. Sections of the song are seamlessly threaded together, following dramatic content rather than stanza divisions. The narrator begins; then the initial dialogue between the soldiers is heard, accompanied by somber chords. As the dying grenadier lists his wishes, there is a change of accompaniment; more agitated broken chords maintain forward movement and increasing intensity. His vocal line is declamatory but passionate. Finally there is a key change as his pent-up fervor explodes into the "Marseillaise," accompanied by renewed and vigorous martial figures, which include the opening drum flourish. But the effort is too much for him. The last vocal phrase resolves, but the harmonies continue, drooping and changing slowly as the soldier dies. In contrast to the stirring page of music that precedes it, this is a stunning, theatrical moment.

*Also see Richard Wagner's setting of this same text.

Die Kartenlegerin, Op. 31, No. 2   **The Fortuneteller. 1840**
(Chamisso, after Béranger)

Chamisso's text is a translation from the original French poem titled "Les Cartes, ou l'horoscope." Even in the German translation, it retains its Gallic wit and charm. In this sparkling little *scena*, a young girl tells her fortune, determined to find a love match for herself. As she turns the cards, numerous suitors and scenes appear, but a scolding old woman ruins her happiness—the cards don't lie. Her mother is awake, and the fortune telling comes to an end.

Schumann gives us a wonderful character sketch of the girl and her quicksilver mood changes as well as the dramatic action. She deals the cards with a practiced hand. The song is structured in little episodes; there are tiny sections of stop and go, as the cards are turned and read. Rests and fluctuations of tempo represent quick changes of mood. This girl is both merry and impatient; the turning cards produce reactions of instant joy or abject sorrow. These are mirrored in the music and the narrative vocal phrases. A vision of love triggers a more lyric declamation and a different mood in voice and piano; the king of diamonds brings visions of riches and luxury, but ominous descending figures with chromatic punctuations herald an enemy, and comforts disappear. In the midst of all the excitement a descriptive interlude (measures 122-131) provides a moment to think about what the cards have told her. A fermata at the end of this section leads into a change of tempo and mood. Mother has awakened. Hurriedly she clears the cards, sweeping them together in the piano's closing four bars.

Volksliedchen, Op. 51, No. 2   **Folk Song. 1840**
(Friedrich Rückert)

Schumann captures the charm of this fresh poem in a simple setting in three-part form, with a slightly varied *da capo*. Even in this unpretentious miniature, Schumann's innate elegance shows through. The uneasy thoughts of the second stanza are given a different accompaniment treatment, with subtle chromatic touches. The last vocal phrase is reiterated again, with a tiny little extension that emphasizes the girl's doubt. The piano postlude also vacillates before coming to an end. Hugo Wolf later used the same technique in the concluding measures of to end "Nun lass uns Frieden schliessen..." in his *Italian Songbook*.

Mit Myrthen und Rosen   **With Myrtles and Roses. 1840**
(Heinrich Heine) *Liederkreis*, **Op. 24**

Schumann composed another *Liederkreis* collection, Op. 24, on texts by Heine. This collection contains nine songs, unified by key structure and linking themes— among them, the "Clara theme."

Heine's poem contains, in capsule form, the events of the Robert-Clara relationship: past sorrow, present separation, future bliss, and the presentation of a book from which letters will leap into the beloved's eyes and whisper to her. Heine's text reads: "With myrtles and roses, fragrant cypress and gold foil I would decorate this book like a coffin and put my songs into it. There they would lie mute and dead but one day you will open the book and the songs' magic spell will break free and murmur to you in sad love-longing."

Schumann's marking is one of his favorites: *Innig* (heartfelt, warmly). Within the song's structure, there are many changes of tempo and mood, and different figures in the accompaniment. The exuberance of the opening is difficult to sustain through the changes, and the poem is certainly overtly sentimental, yet this song is among Schumann's best-known *Lieder*.

Heiss' mich nicht reden, Op. 98a, No. 5   **Bid Me Not speak. 1849**
(Johann Wolfgang von Goethe)

After years of constant reworking, Goethe finally completed his famous novel *Wilhelm Meister* in 1821, having first conceived the work in 1776. Drawn by the striking personalities of Goethe's characters, Schumann set nine songs drawn from the novel.

The child-waif Mignon is found by Wilhelm Meister in a traveling theater troupe. The songs she sings with the old mysterious Harper are a prominent feature of the novel. Neither is aware that Mignon is his daughter from an incestuous liaison with his own sister.

Mignon's songs ("Heiss' mich nicht reden," "Nur wer die Sehnsucht kennt," "Kennst du das land," and "So lasst mich scheinen, bis ich werde") are psychologically compelling, and their lyrics inspired dramatic settings from numerous composers,* including the best-known treatments by Schubert, Schumann, and Wolf. All the songs are filled with a sense of grief, secrecy, and a longing to return to her native Italy. Schumann employs a three-note theme in the Mignon lyrics (F-sharp, A-flat, G) in varying order. This cell appears in both melodic lines and as harmony.

Schumann's through-composed setting of this particular lyric seems to capture the intensity of Mignon's secrecy, beginning with a series of dramatic chords and a quasi-recitative vocal line. These give way in the third phrase ("Ich möchte dir...") to a lyric longing to share her inner thoughts—a romantically conceived vocal line accompanied by chordal harmonies. A modulation to the major key occurs at "Zur rechten Zeit" and remains in that key, although harmonic texture and vocal line fluctuate incessantly, illustrating Mignon's torment and uncertainty. Four measures of strongly declaimed chords form a transition back to the opening tonality. Here, Schumann interpolates the first text phrase, set in a murmuring low register, before concluding with the poem's last two lines.

*Mignon's lyrics have been set well over 150 times, most in the form of *lieder* for solo voice and piano. Ambroise Thomas's opera *Mignon* is also based on Goethe's novel.

Singet nicht in Trauertönen, Op. 98a, No. 7   **Sing Not in**
(Johann Wolfgang von Goethe)   **Tones of Sadness. 1849**

Philine is another character in *Wilhelm Meister*. She is an actress, a flirtatious charmer, and the antithesis of Mignon. Her music matches her personality—buoyantly melodic, flighty and fast-moving. Harmonic fluctuations point up her impulsive character. In seven stanzas she pours forth her credo of love and relationships—-"sing no sad songs about the night's solitude, it is made for companionship. Each day has its torment, each night its joy."*

Voice and accompaniment dance through key changes, counterpointing melodic fragments and finally arrive at Philine's last triumphant stanza that sounds like a little march. Now accompaniment and voice happily proclaim the text in rhythm together for four measures, then the rhythmic movement is restored. The piano is given the last word in a vivacious little postscript that suggests a flouncing little bow. Philine's dazzling little song is bewitching, and she herself is the epitome of the soubrette. She is surely the precursor of Zerbinetta in Strauss's *Ariadne auf Naxos*. Goethe's postlude to her song is found in Eric Sams's *The Songs of Hugo Wolf* and is worth quoting here also:

> She gave a little bow when she had finished, and Serlo (manager of the theatre company) gave her a loud "Bravo!" She skipped through the door and ran off laughing. They could hear her still singing and clattering with her heels as she went down the stairs.[10]

*Schumann discreetly omitted Goethe's original third stanza that celebrates the pleasures of making love. Wolf's setting of "Philine" should also be accessed for comparison.

Liebeslied, Op. 51, No. 5   Love Song. 1850 (?1840)
(Johann Wolfgang von Goethe)

This poem is taken from Goethe's *Der West-östliche Divan* (Divan of West and East), a collection that was later plumbed in some depth by Hugo Wolf. *Divan* (or *diwan*) is a term from Arabic literature indicating a collection of works by a single poet.[11] Goethe's immersion into the works of Hafiz, a Persian poet of the fourteenth century, yielded some 400 lyrics of widely varied emotional range.

"Liebeslied" is a neglected Schumann song. Its text is described by Sams as "gibberish and hopelessly unsuitable for a song text."[12] The words refer to the ability of lovers to communicate in private code by referencing a mutually agreed-upon text. Clara and Robert used codes in their letters and, given his love of mystery, puzzles and word games, it is not surprising this text held some appeal for Schumann. The date of composition is somewhat in doubt. Sams theorizes that it was likely composed for the couple's private pleasure and revised it later for publication in 1850.[13]

The setting is an exquisite lyric melody in which voice and piano overlap phrases that become more integrated and tightly knit as the song progresses. It is through-composed, and, in its effusive accompaniment and vocal writing, it seems the embodiment of romantic expression.

Mein schöner Stern!, Op. 101, No. 4   My Lovely Star! 1849
(Friedrich Rückert)

This song belongs to a short set of *Minnespiel* (love songs) from Rückert's *Liebesfrühling*, Op. 101. This was a dark period in Schumann's life, and no doubt this verse struck a responsive chord in him. "My lovely star! I beg you not to let your brightness fade by dark clouds in me, but let your light help my darkness shine." The two brief stanzas are almost prayer-like, and Schumann's setting reflects this, although the vocal line contains elements of dramatic intensity.

This song is designated for the tenor voice. Its arching vocal phrases reach upwards to the star addressed by the poet. An accompaniment pattern of repeated chords perpetuates the mood of solemnity in the starry night. Schumann sets Rückert's two stanzas strophically, and concludes with a postlude.

Extended Study List

Aufträge • An dem Mond • Jasminenstrauch • Schöne Wiege meiner Leiden • Zwielicht • Frühlingsnacht • Wehmut • Auf einer Burg • Lieb Liebchen, leg's Händchen • Mignon (Kennst du das land) • Lied der Suleika • Das verlassene Mägdlein • Lieder der Braut • Dein Angesicht • Aus den hebräischen Gesängen • Belsatzar • Stille Liebe • Er ist's • Die Soldatenbraut • Der Sandmann • Schneeglöckchen • Schöne Fremde • Stille Tränen • Tragödie • *Gedichte der Königen Maria Stuart* • Du bist wie eine blume •Venezianisches Lieder • Erstes Grün

Selected Reading

Gerald Abraham, ed., *Schumann: A Symposium* (Westport, Conn.: Greenwood Press, 1977).

Astra Desmond, *Schumann Songs* (Seattle: University of Washington Press, 1972). BBC Music Guides series, No. 22.

Rudolf Felber, "Schumann's Place in German Song," *The Musical Quarterly,* 1940. 26:340-354.

Dietrich Fischer-Dieskau, *Robert Schumann: Words and Music.* trans. Reinhard G. Pauly (Portland, Oregon: Amadeus Press, 1988). Treats the vocal compositions of Schumann.

Rufus E. Hallmark, "Robert Schumann: The Poet Sings," in *German Lieder in the Nineteenth Century,* ed. Rufus Hallmark (New York: Schirmer Books, 1996), 75-118.

Victoria Hart, "Equals in Love: *Frauenliebe und -leben* reconsidered." D.M.A. diss., University of California, Santa Barbara, 2004.

Arthur Komar, ed., *Schumann: Dichterliebe.* Norton Critical Scores (New York: W.W. Norton, 1971). Excellent source on this cycle. Score, historical background, essays in analysis.

Richard Miller, *Singing Schumann: an interpretive guide for performers* (New York: Oxford University Press, 1999).

Gerald Moore, *Poet's Love: The Songs and Cycles of Robert Schumann* (New York: Taplinger Publishing Co., 1981).

Gerd Nauhaus, ed., *The Marriage Diaries of Robert and Clara Schumann* (Boston: Northeastern University Press, 1993). A detailed account of the first four years of Clara and Robert Schumann's marriage.

Peter Ostwald, Schumann: *The Inner Voices of a Musical Genius* (Boston: Northeastern University Press, 1985).

Thilo Reinhard, ed., *The Singer's Schumann* (New York: Pelion Press, 1988). A collection of Schumann *Lieder.* Translations, IPA transcriptions, brief essays. Includes the complete song cycles as well as the most frequently performed songs.

Charles Rosen, *The Romantic Generation* (Cambridge: Harvard University Press, 1995).

Eric Sams, *The Songs of Robert Schumann,* 3rd edition (London: Methuen, 1993). An examination of 246 songs of Schumann, with English translations and excellent commentary.

Eugenie Schumann, *The Schumanns and Johannes Brahms: The Memoirs of Eugenie Schumann,* trans. Marie Busch (New York: The Dial Press, 1927).

Robert Schumann, *On Music and Musicians.* Ed. Konrad Wolff, trans. Paul Rosenfeld (New York: McGraw-Hill, 1946).

Stephen Walsh, *The Lieder of Schumann* (New York: Praeger, 1971).

Notes

1. Berthold Litzmann, ed., *Clara Schumann: An Artist's Life,* trans. Grace E. Hadow, 2 vols. (London: Macmillan. Orig. publ. in 3 vols., 1902-1908), 1:280.
2. Charles Rosen, *The Romantic Generation* (Harvard University Press, 1995), 207.
3. Joan Chissell, *Schumann* (London: J. M. Dent, 1970), 126.
4. Rosen, *The Romantic Generation,* 175.
5. Eric Sams, *The Songs of Robert Schumann,* 92.
6. Ibid., 95.
7. Ibid., 49.
8. Ibid., 50.
9. Ibid., 52.
10. Ibid., 190.
11. Michael Steinberg, liner notes to *Goethe Lieder: Schumann, Schubert, Wolf, Mozart.* Dawn Upshaw/Richard Goode. Electra Nonesuch Records compact disc 79317-2, 1994.
12. Sams, 231.
13. Ibid.

CLARA WIECK SCHUMANN (1819-1896)

> I once believed that I possessed creative talent, but I have given up this idea; a woman must not desire to compose—there has never yet been one able to do it. Should I expect to be the one?
>
> —Entry in Clara Schumann's diary, 1839[1]

These words from one of the most distinguished artists of her time are perhaps surprising, yet it drives home the mindset of the time concerning women as composers. Attitudes inherited from the eighteenth century died hard. Eminent eighteenth-century philosopher Jean-Jacques Rousseau had emphatically expressed his scathing perspective on female participation in artistic creation: "Women in general, possess no artistic sensibility...nor genius. They can acquire a knowledge...of anything through hard work. But the celestial fire that emblazons and ignites the soul, the inspiration that consumes and devours...these sublime ecstasies that reside in the depths of the heart are always lacking in women's writings." [2] With Rousseau's words ringing in the ears of nineteenth-century Europeans, it is small wonder that old ideas regarding women artists persisted.

As nineteenth-century Germany's middle class grew in numbers and cultural pursuits, young women began to pursue their talents as amateur musicians. In great part, their music making was confined to the home, and their drawing rooms became forums for new works and performances at evening concerts, though the music was rarely theirs. Those who were members of musical families achieved a high degree of musical education and sophistication; others were largely self-taught. The songs of Fanny Hensel, Clara Schumann, Josephine Lang, and Luise Reichardt are still being "discovered."

When Clara Wieck met Robert Schumann, she was already a distinguished piano virtuoso known throughout Europe. She had received a progressive musical education from her father, had performed solo concerts from a very early age, and was the first woman to achieve an international reputation as a concert pianist. After a stormy and bitter legal battle with her father-teacher-manager Frederich Wieck over her desire to wed Schumann, the couple was finally married in 1840.

Clara Wieck was a gifted, ambitious woman. Balancing domestic duties and a professional career was as difficult then as now, and much rarer. Clara continued to concertize and perform hundreds of concerts through eight pregnancies, and somehow found the time to continue her own composition. She became the principal champion and definitive interpreter of her husband's music, and for over sixty years sustained a career that reached legendary status.

In their "marriage diaries" one can read the effects of love and marriage on the creative state, the frustrations that both Robert and Clara felt while trying to achieve a balance between necessary solitude and the close relationship demanded by the marriage. Clara wrote in her diary: "Creative work is such a joy because one can take refuge from everyday cares in a tonal world for a little while."[3] Clara Schumann considered herself an artist first and a mother second, although this ordering neglected neither role.

Virtually forgotten is the fact that she was a fine composer in her own right, writing piano works, *Lieder*, and chamber music. Her songs were admired by her husband and by Brahms, Mendelssohn, and Liszt as well. Encouraged by her father, Clara began composing early, and, by the time of her marriage, had written numerous works for the piano. She continued to compose throughout her life; her published works included a piano concerto, string trio, various piano works and three collections of *Lieder*.

Clara composed twenty-eight *Lieder*, of which eighteen were published. Understandably, they have been eclipsed by Robert Schumann's larger and more visible body of songs. Her mature works reveal songs with beautifully shaped melodic lines and expressive accompaniments. Most of her *Lieder* were composed for special family occasions—Christmas, birthdays, etc. Robert encouraged Clara in her song writing, and she helped him select texts. A volume of both their songs was published in 1841, and contained one of their mutual favorites, Rückert's "Liebesfrühling."

Clara Schumann's songs, like those of her husband, make use of preludes and postludes. She employed chromaticism in relation to text and to evoke mood. Formal structures in her songs include strophic and strophic variation, ABA, and through-composed. Clara's mastery of the piano manifests itself in her interesting song accompaniments, which share the same expressive quality as those of the songs of her close friend of sixty years, Pauline Viardot. Clara Schumann's last songs have skilfully interwoven piano and vocal parts.

In 1878, at the age of fifty-nine, Clara accepted the position of principal piano teacher at the Hoch Conservatory in Frankfurt. Frau Kammervirtuosin Schumann taught until 1892 when she was almost seventy-three.

Liebst du um Schönheit,* Op. 12, No. 4   **If You Love for Beauty. 1841**
(Friedrich Rückert)

This song and the next were published as part of a collection of songs titled *Liebesfrühling* on Rückert poems by Robert and Clara. It is often designnated as Op. 37/12; it was Robert's Op. 37 and Clara's Op. 12. The publication did not designate the composers of each song. These were Clara's first published songs.

Clara composed this song during the first year of her marriage. Its melody and rhythms are simple, yet finely crafted; the intimacy of the poetry is captured beautifully. Inner voices in the piano accompaniment provide changing harmonic colors and rhythmic contrast under the simple, expressive vocal line. The same four-bar melody initiates the first phrase of every other poetic line: "Liebst du um Schönheit, o nicht mich liebe!; Liebst du um Jugend, o nicht mich liebe; Liebst du um Schätze, o nicht mich liebe!; Liebst du um Liebe, o ja mich liebe!" The consequent phrase which follows the first and third of these is identical; the answer to the second and fourth varies rhythmically and melodically. The final phrase is broadly emotional and extended "Liebe mich immer, dich lieb' ich immerdar!"

*See the setting of this poem by Gustav Mahler.

Er ist gekommen in Sturm und Regen, Op. 12, No. 2   **He came to me**
(Friedrich Rückert)   **in storm and rain.**
                                                                1836.

This is the most exciting of Clara's Op. 12 *Lieder*, its dominant component is a brilliant piano accompaniment. The vocal line, lyric in contrast to the vibrant accompaniment, is integrated skillfully into the texture. Two stanzas are cast in through-composed form; the range of the vocal line is enlarged for the second stanza. A driving rhythmic accompaniment depicting the "storm and rain," continues unabated throughout the piece, maintaining forward movement and dramatic tension. A dazzling piano introduction opens the song, and a short postlude concludes it with an equally sparkling flourish.

Lorelei
(Heinrich Heine)

Lorelei. 1843

Heine wrote his famous poem in 1823 and it was published in 1824. Its early title was Lore-Ley, but it also appears with the spellings Lorelei or Loreley. The story of the Lorelei is not an ancient legend, but dates from a ballad poem written by Clemens Brentano around the beginning of the nineteenth century. Loreley, or elfin rock, is the old name of a steep and dangerous rock in the Rhine River near St. Goarshausen, midway between Koblenz and Bingen. At that location, the river forms a dangerous narrows, and the rock produces an eerie echo.*
In his poem, Brentano transformed it into a woman's name, Loreley. She sits upon the rock high above the river, combing her long golden hair, and singing a song that lures sailors to their death.

In Robert Schumann's *Liederkreis,* Op. 39 (poetry by Eichendorff), the Lorelei is found in the forest (see "Waldesgespräch"), away from her Rhine castle. She appears to a huntsman, and pronounces his chilling fate—he will never leave the wood. There are five other settings of Heine's poem; the best known is probably that of Franz Liszt.

Vocal phrases are dramatic and breathless, underscored by a racing accompaniment pattern in triplets that urges the exciting story forward. Without pausing, the story unfolds in one exhilarating sweep to its *dénouement.*

*The rock is sometimes identified as the site where the Nibelungs hid their treasure under the Rhine.

Ihr Bildnis
(Heinrich Heine)

Her Picture. 1840-43

Heine's poem titled "Ich stand in dunkeln Träumen" has been set by six other composers, among them Edvard Grieg ("Ich stand in dunkeln Träumen"); Franz Schubert ("Ihr Bild"), and Hugo Wolf ("Ich stand in dunkeln Träumen"). "Ihr Bildnis" is Clara Schumann's first setting of this poem. She composed a later setting of the text, with the title "Ich stand in dunkeln Träumen," which appears in her *Sechs Lieder,* Op. 13 (No. 1), several measures shorter and with rhythmic variations in the vocal line. Most importantly, however, it lacks the astonishing unresolved ending in the vocal line and the tension of delayed resolution in the piano postlude of "Ihr Bildnis" that underscores the anguish of the text. "Ihr Bildnis" remained in the Schumann archive at Zwickau and was not published until 1992.

Extended Study List
Das Veilchen • Mein Stern • Der Mond kommt still gegangen • Das ist ein Tag der klingen mag • Warum willst du And're fragen? • Ich hab' in deinem Auge • Liebeszauber • Die stille Lotosblume • Was weinst du, Blümlein • An einem lichten Morgen• Geheimes Flüstern hier und dort • Auf einem grünen Hügel • Das ist ein Tag, der klingen mag • O Lust, o Lust

Selected Reading*

Jane Bowers and Judith Tick, editors. *Women Making Music* (Urbana, Illinois: University of Illinois Press, 1986).

James R. Briscoe, ed., *Historical Anthology of Music by Women* (Bloomington: Indiana University Press, 1987). Contains biographies of each composer as well as examples of their music.

Joan Chissell, *Clara Schumann: A Dedicated Spirit* (New York: Taplinger, 1983).

Berthold Litzmann, ed., *Clara Schumann: An Artist's Life.* Trans. Grace E. Hadow, 2 vols. (London: Macmillan. Orig. publ. in 3 vols., 1902-1908).

_____,ed., *Letters of Clara Schumann and Johannes Brahms,* 1853-1896. 2 vols. (London: Edward Arnold, 1927).

Kenneth Pennington, "Clara Schumann: Lieder Composer and Champion," *The NATS Journal* 47:2 (Nov/Dec 1990).

Nancy B. Reich, *Clara Schumann: The Artist and the Woman* (Ithaca, New York: Cornell University Press, 1985).

Pamela Susskind, "Clara Schumann as Pianist and Composer: A Study of Her Life and Works." Ph.D. diss., University of California, Berkeley, 1977.

Nancy Walker, "Parallels between Fanny Mendelssohn Hensel and Clara Wieck Schumann: Their Lives and Their Songs," *The NATS Journal,* 50:4 (March/April 1994).

*Also refer to "Suggested Reading" for Robert Schumann.

Notes

1. Nancy B. Reich, "Clara Schumann," in *Women Making Music*, Bowers and Tick, eds., 267.
2. "Women and the Lied, 1775-1850," in Jane Bowers and Judith Tick, *Women Making Music*, 225.
3. Kenneth Pennington, "Clara Schumann: Lieder Composer and Champion," *The NATS Journal*, 47:2 (Nov/Dec 1990), 8.

FRANZ LISZT (1811-1886)

The songs in their present form can stand on their own feet...and if some singers, neither coarse nor superficial, find the necessary courage to sing songs by the notorious non-composer Franz Liszt, then probably they too will find their public.

—Franz Liszt[1]

Franz (Ferencz) Liszt was born in Hungary, but quickly became a cosmopolitan citizen of Europe. Austria, France, Germany, and Italy could all claim him as a resident and part native. He received musical training in Vienna and Paris and became *the* piano virtuoso of his time, the object of adulation and fame—a nineteenth-century superstar. Famous throughout Europe as an interpreter of others' works as well as his own, Liszt spent most of his time on tour.

In 1848, he settled in Weimar with Princess Carolyne von Sayn-Wittgenstein, who had fallen in love with him during his tour of Russia and Poland. He was appointed honorary *Kappellmeister* to the Grand Ducal Court; there he conducted the opera and orchestra until 1861.

After his alliance with the Princess came the years of his *"vie trifurquée"* (three-fold life). In 1865, he became a secular priest. From 1869-1886, Lizst divided his time between Weimar, Budapest, and Rome. His music became bolder and more experimental; he was passionately concerned with the latest music of the French, German, and nationalist schools. In his Weimar classes he presided over a rising generation of of pianists; in Budapest he was instrumental in shaping the music and educational life that was the inheritance of Dohnányi, Bartók, and Kodály.[2] Liszt died at Bayreuth on a visit to his daughter Cosima, the wife of Richard Wagner.

In general, Liszt's songs have been eclipsed by his orchestral and keyboard music. They date from 1840, the year when he met Robert Schumann. Watson chronicles Lizst's songs as eighty-two in number: fifty-two German settings, fourteen French, five Italian, three Hungarian, one Russian and twelve English; there are several versions of some songs, which increases the overall number. Liszt revised thirty of the songs composed up to 1848, another four exist in three versions, and he made orchestral transcriptions of eight songs for voice and orchestra.[3] Additional vocal works include two oratorios and four masses. Nearly all the songs exist in other forms composed or arranged by Liszt himself, which indicates his desire to improve on his first efforts.

Liszt's songs contain a tremendous variety of melodic styles. His melodies are operatic in scope and contain vocal embellishments (an example: the early Petrarch settings). Derek Watson[4] divides "Lisztian melody" into several categories: lyrical, often ornamented, Romantic *bel canto* melodies; declamatory phrases that contain unusual intervals; monotone, recitative-like phrases with some melodic organization; short melodic fragments in the style of Beethoven; and melodies that are built primarily on descending intervals. Despite this wide range of melodic approaches, Liszt was often careless in setting words. In his late songs, however, he set his texts with great subtlety and fidelity to speech-rhythms.

Liszt made frequent use of rhythmic motives in his songs, often building an entire song around a motive; his use of short phrases anticipates Wolf. He preferred through-composed settings for his songs, probably because they offered a broader palette for his emotional, colorful compositional style. He made coloristic use of the piano in his song accompaniments; some are orchestral in texture.

The wide time span covered by Liszt's songs permit an overview of his harmonic development and experiments with the form. His early songs are generally simple in outline, with imaginative touches. As his song style developed, his harmonic experimentation increased, the fusion of poetry and musical setting became closer, and piano-voice textures became correspondingly integrated. In his later songs, he veered toward impressionism.

Oh! quand je dors   **Oh! While I Sleep. 1860**
(Victor Hugo)

This exquisite setting is Liszt's best known and probably most performed song. Noske calls it the "masterpiece of Liszt's French songs and...one of the most beautiful *mélodies* written before Duparc."[5] Liszt set fourteen French texts, including words of Victor Hugo, Alfred de Musset, and Alexandre Dumas. They contain few French stylistic traits, following instead the German *Lied* in overall conception. Noske refers to some of these *mélodies* as "French *Lieder*."

"Oh! quand je dors" is one of Liszt's early songs. Its first version was composed in 1844, close on the heels of the first version of the three *Petrarch Sonnets,* which he also revised just a year later than this *mélodie.*

It is Liszt's second version of this song that is usually performed. Its dramatic intensity lies just below the surface, only once rising in operatic fashion. Passion is mined through broad flowing vocal phrases—lyrically Italianate in style, and thoroughly sensual in atmosphere. Piano figures are equally romantic in concept.

Hugo's text is a reference to Petrarch and to Laura, the subject of Petrarch's own verses. Liszt takes the second poetic phrase "Comme à Pétrarque apparaissait Laura," and repeats it at the end of the *mélodie* in an exquisite nine-measure phrase. This ethereal ending is often cited as an example of masterful harmonic imagery. An arching vocal phrase is thrown into relief over a lean texture of three chords and two extended arpeggios, each subtly changing as the voice sustains a high G-sharp, in a suspended moment of rare beauty.

Three years later in 1847, Liszt transcribed the song for piano solo. Composer Peter Cornelius, Liszt's friend and pupil, made a German translation of the text ("O komm im Traum") and the song is sometimes sung in this version.

Es muss ein Wunderbares sein	**It Must Be a Wonderful Thing. 1852**
(Oscar von Redwitz)	

An intimate musical setting crowns the poet's wondering description of the love-union between two souls. Liszt repeats the last two lines "from the first kiss unto death, they speak only of love."

Within the murmuring vocal phrases are Liszt's characteristic drooping intervals. The lovely melodic line is derived from the accompaniment—a simple figure composed primarily of chords. There are two poetic stanzas, but they are set in through-composed form. Lizst's expressive musical treatment is in the manner of Schumann or Brahms in its quiet lyrical style. He composed this *Lied* between lunch and supper for Princess Augusta of Prussia at Ettersburg near Weimar.[6] Its simplicity of musical design sets it apart from Liszt's other *Lieder* and has won it a place on the list of his most-performed songs.

Freudvoll and leidvoll	**Joyful and Sorrowful. 1844**
(Johann von Goethe)	

This is one of the texts that Liszt set several times. The first version was composed in 1844, and subsequent settings were produced in 1848 and 1860. The 1848 version is more dramatic and agitated and uses a different melody; the first and third versions are flowing and lyrical.

The piano introduction contains arpeggiated chords of varying colors— E major, E minor, E diminished, E dominant seventh—to set the atmosphere for the "color" words of the poem: "joyful," "hopeful," "fearful," "sorrowful." The opening vocal phrase is one Liszt's wide-interval constructions, of descending major sixths: "Freudvoll und leidvoll, gedankenvoll sein..." Variants of the sixth also highlight "langen" (longing) and "bangen" (fearing).

Die drei Zigeuner	**The Three Gypsies. 1860**
(Nikolaus Lenau)	

In this *Lied* we find the Liszt of the *Hungarian Rhapsodies*. Lenau's long narrative ballad is used in its entirety. Lenau was a Hungarian poet, best remembered for his version of the Don Juan legend that inspired the tone poem of the young Richard Strauss. Liszt's famous "Mephisto Waltz" was the second of his *Two Episodes* from Lenau's "Faust." Strauss, Mahler, Wolf, Berg, and Pfitzner also set at least one of Lenau's verses.

An extended piano introduction sets the scene, its melodic writing free and unrestrained in the manner of a solo Gypsy violin. The singer begins the story in *parlando* style; Liszt uses syllabic test setting throughout, with some ornaments in the vocal line. A traveler happens upon three Gypsies; the character of each man exemplifies three ways of "facing the dark side of life—sleep it away, smoke it away, fiddle it away..." Formal structure is fluid (again, like Lizst's rhapsodies). There are three large sections in the song; each characterizes one of the Gypsies: the violinist who plays the *csárdás*; the reflective pipe-smoker, his head wreathed with curling smoke; and the unconcerned, sleeping Gypsy. Liszt gives each section its own dance rhythm refrain.

In addition to the Gypsy violin, Liszt uses other Hungarian elements in the song: the rhythms of the *csárdás* dance, Gypsy ornaments, and the Hungarian minor scale with its augmented-second interval.

This is one of Liszt's most dramatic settings, full of color and overtly theatrical. In addition to this version for voice and piano, Liszt wrote an orchestral accompaniment for this song. Four years later he reworked the piece as a fantasy for violin and piano, which in turn spawned a violin and orchestra verion in 1931. It is titled "Hungarian Rhapsody," but is unrelated to the *Hungarian Rhapsodies* for piano.

Ihr Glocken von Marling　　　　　　　　　　　**Bells of Marling. 1874**
(Emil Kuh)

"O bells of Marling, how brightly you ring; a holy song to swell around temporal sounds, as if to protect them." This is a mysterious, subtle song, impressionistic in both musical quality and effect. At this point in his life, Liszt had taken minor orders in the church. An atmosphere of religious mysticism permeates the song throughout until the final chord rings with an unusual inconclusive ending. The bells of the poem are heard in note clusters in the piano accompaniment, which is written almost entirely in the treble clef.

The poet Emil Kuh spent the last years of his life in Marling, southwest of Merano. Once a part of Austria, it is now in that disputed area of Italy, South Tyrol.[7] The church bells of Marling must have had not only a special sound but also a significant symbolism in Kuh's own experience. He attempts to invest the poetry with bell-sounds of differing resonances and vibrations: "Glocken," "Marling," "sänge," "Gesang," "Klang" are the deeper tones; "hell" and "Quell" are higher and lighter in sound.

This song is late in Liszt's song catalog and somewhat unique when contrasted with his other settings. The musical atmosphere is serene and tranquil, sustained by repeated clusters of eighth notes in the accompaniment. The text is set syllabically, with a few unaccompanied measures for the singer. Liszt employs unresolved 7th and 9th chords in the texture, but keeps the accompaniment simple and flowing throughout.

Extended Study List
Tre sonetti di Petrarca • Comment, disaient-ils • Kennst du das Land • S'il est un charmant gazon • Der König von Thule • Wanderers Nachtlied • Vergiftet sind meine Lieder • Du bist wie eine Blume • Das Veilchen

Selected Reading
John Douglas, "Franz Liszt as a Song Composer," *The NATS Journal*, 43:4 (March/April 1987).
Christopher Headington, "The Songs." Franz Liszt: The Man and His Music. Alan Walker, ed. (London: Barrie & Jenkins, 1976).
Stanley Irwin, "The Songs of Franz Liszt: A Survey and Catalogue, *The NATS Journal*, 49:3 (Jan/Feb 1993).

Charles Rosen, *The Romantic Generation* (Cambridge: Harvard University Press, 1995).
Alan Walker, ed., *Franz Liszt: The Man and His Music* (London: Barrie & Jenkins, 1970).
Derek Watson, *Liszt* (New York: Schirmer/Macmillan, 1989).

Notes

1. Quoted in Derek Watson, *Liszt*, 305.
2. Ibid., 181.
3. Ibid.,305.
4. Ibid., 181.
5. Noske, *French Song from Berlioz to Duparc*, 132.
6. Ibid., 308.
7. Elaine Brody and Robert Fowkes, *The German Lied and Its Poetry*, 223.

RICHARD WAGNER (1813-1883)

> Song composition for Wagner was not a routine or...everyday event. The Lied was one of those genres which were fairly remote from his thoughts. As a result, he wrote only a small number of songs and he usually had special concrete reasons for doing so.
>
> —Egon Voss[1]

> In this last decade of our century we are coming to see Wagner as a man who had influenced profoundly many aspects of contemporary thought and feeling.
>
> —M. Owen Lee[2]

Richard Wagner's interest in composing song was perfunctory; his musical style did not easily adapt to smaller forms. His complete songs fill an average-sized volume[*] and with the exception of the *Wesendonck Lieder*, they are not performed with much regularity. In addition to the Wesendonck songs, Wagner's most notable song is a setting of Heine's "Die beiden Grenadiere" in a French translation.

The majority of Wagner's songs are early works composed in Paris in 1839-40 during his first visit there. His brief stay was part of an attempt to persuade the French of his genius. At this time, Schubert's songs were highly popular and the salons were filled with performances of vocal works. As a means of bolstering his reputation and raising money, Wagner took advantage of the popularity of the *romance* and composed a number of songs on French texts, using French songs as models. Several factors mitigated against the success of these pieces: quality of texts, familiarity and ease with the French language, and inability to interest influential singers in performing and popularizing the songs. Not one to accept total defeat, Wagner incorporated material from some of these songs into his operas.

Despite his lack of interest in composing songs, Wagner derived inspiration from German *Lieder*; he was a great admirer of the ballads of Carl Loewe and pointed out that the entire opera *Der fliegende Holländer* was derived from the germ of Senta's ballad, an aria that clearly traces its influence to Loewe.[3]

In his book *Opera and Drama,* Wagner spelled out his beliefs regarding music theater: the words must share equally with the music in realizing the drama, the words should sound in alliterative clusters, the vocal line should derive directly from the rise and fall of the words, singers should give the impression of heightened speech when singing, and what sung words could not communicate, the orchestra should convey in ever-recurring musical "motifs of memory." He coined the word

Gesamkunstwerk (total work of art) to describe his music dramas, works in which music shared equally with poetry, drama, stage design, acting, and philosophy.

Wagner's musical and poetic principles exerted a profound effect on composers of his time, specifically Hugo Wolf and Gustav Mahler, and continued to influence composers and music for generations after. He was a musical visionary, a fascinating enigma, and the most influential of all nineteenth-century composers.

Sämtliche Lieder. Mainz: B. Schott, 1982. ED 7078.

Wesendonck Lieder   **Wesendonck Songs. 1857-58**
(Mathilde Wesendonck)

Der Engel (The Angel) • Stehe still! (Be Still!) • Im Treibhaus (In the
    Greenhouse) • Schmerzen (Torment) • Träume (Dreams)

The *Wesendonck Lieder* are by-products of a love affair; the set takes its name from Mathilde Wesendonck (1828-1902), the author of the poems. In 1854, Wagner was in exile in Switzerland. Mathilde and her husand Otto, a prominent Zürich silk merchant, were devoted supporters of Wagner. In 1857, the Wesendoncks rented Wagner and his wife Minna a small house adjoining the Wesendonck mansion. During the Wagners' stay, Wagner and Mathilde enjoyed an amorous liaison.

Wagner had been working on the libretto to *Tristan und Isolde* and finished it in 1857. He began to compose the opera, interrupting work to write five songs to poems by Mathilde, which proved to be exercises for the opera.

Tristan und Isolde displays the profound influence of Wagner's affair with Mathilde. In 1858 Wagner wrote to Mathilde: "A year ago I completed the text for 'Tristan,' and brought you the last act. You showed me to a chair, threw your arms around me, and said 'Now I have no wishes left!' On that day, at that hour, I was born again."[4]

Wagner designated two of the Wesendonck songs as studies for *Tristan und Isolde:* "Träume" (the second song, composed December 1957), and "Im Treibhaus" (the last song, May 1858). These songs anticipate the opera's style both harmonically and melodically; another of the songs, "Stehe still!", is reminiscent of *Tristan's* Act I.

The accompaniment to "Träume," built around a two-note motive, appears as part of the Act II love duet of *Tristan*. The poem presents dreams as the true reality that sustains lovers. Herein is the kernel of *Tristan and Isolde*—the ardently longed-for "love in death." "Im Treibhaus" contains extended passages that appear in the Prelude to Act III. These two songs are the most interesting of the set for their harmonic approach; the remaining songs defer too much to Mathilde's poetry, which was not on Wagner's level of musical invention.

Thematic undertones of *Tristan* are also present in Mathilde's poetry: pain and suffering are necessary for happiness. All five poems share the theme of the pleasures and pains of passionate love. Mathilde's occasional writings (poems, short stories, and plays) did not travel outside her immediate circle. For Mathilde, these songs must have symbolized a feeling that could not be displayed openly. Isolde's phrase "Mir erkoren—mir verloren!"[*] surely must have struck a responsive chord in Mathilde.

The *Wesendonck Lieder* are the only songs of Wagner's mature period; they are notable as settings of texts not his own (his Paris songs were the other exception).

Wagner's original title for the songs was *Five Poems by an Amateur Set to Music for a Woman's Voice by Richard Wagner*; in 1862 they were sent to the publisher as *Five Dilettante Poems*, suppressing the name of the poet, but indicating the poems were not his.[5]

In their original form, the songs are for voice and piano. Wagner orchestrated "Träume" as a birthday present for Mathilde; the remaining songs were orchestrated by Felix Mottl around 1880. Wagner and Mathilde's affair ended in 1858 and Wagner left for Venice where he completed *Tristan*.

*"Destined for me—lost to me."

Mignonne*   Beloved. 1839
(Pierre de Ronsard)

One of Ronsard's celebrated *Odes à Cassandre* ("Mignonne, allons voir si la rose") furnished Wagner with the text for this song, one of a small body of works produced during his first stay in Paris 1839-1840 (see Wagner biography). The songs are early in Wagner's career, and far afield from our perception of Wagnerian style. Unfortunately for Wagner, the French were having none of it, and his plans of doing well in Paris were unfulfilled.

"Mignonne" is cast in the mold of a salon *romance*, with a graceful vocal line over a broken-chord accompaniment—a style that might pass for Gounod. Wagner's penchant for drama in music is present even in these small forms. This song and "Les Deux Grenadiers" are striking examples of a Wagner not often heard.

One of Ronsard's favorite poetic themes appears in this ode: the transient quality of life, and the passionate need to seize pleasure from the moment.

*See also Cécile Chaminade.

Les deux Grenadiers   The Two Grenadiers. 1840
(François-Adolphe Loeve-Veimar, translated from the German of Heinrich Heine)

Heine and Wagner met shortly after the composer's arrival in Paris. Wagner composed this setting only a few months before Robert Schumann set Heine's powerful poem to music. The two versions should be compared, both for musical style and approach to the poem. Wagner quotes the "Marseillaise" in the piano accompaniment in the closing measures of the song; Schumann followed suit in his later setting, but gave the anthem melody to the voice instead.

With this poem, Wagner had a more compelling dramatic scene to work with than he did with "Mignonne." His extended setting maintains the forward motion of the drama with only a few flagging spots; nevertheless, the song is a fascinating study in Wagner's early vocal writing. Wagner himself paid for its publication, which included an expensive cover picture—a Parisian practice of the day.

Extended Study List
Dors mon enfant • Attente • Lied des Mephistopheles (*Sieben Kompositionen zu Goethes Faust*) • Gretchen am Spinnrade (*Sieben Kompositionen zu Goethes Faust*) • Adieux de Marie Stuart • Tout n'est qu'images fugitives

Selected Reading*

Peter Brubidge, and Richard Sutton, eds., *The Wagner Companion* (New York: Cambridge University Press, 1979).

Barry Millington, *Wagner* (New York: Vintage, 1987, originally published in 1984).

Ulrich Müller and Peter Wapnewski, eds., *Wagner Handbook,* trans. John Deathridge (Cambridge: Harvard University Press, 1992).

Michael Saffle, *Richard Wagner: A Guide to Research* (New York: Routledge, 2002).

Frederic Spotts, *Bayreuth: A History of the Wagner Festival* (New Haven: Yale University Press, 1994).

Cosima *Wagner's Diaries*, edited and annotated by Martin Gregor-Dellin and Dietrick Mack. Trans. and with an introduction by Geoffrey Skelton. v. 1-2 (New York: Harcourt Brace Jovanovich, 1978).

*According to M. Owen Lee "...books and articles on Wagner (22,000) are said to outnumber those on any other person known to history save only Jesus Christ, and possibly, Napoleon."[6]
The suggestions here barely scratch the surface of a rich and fascinating subject.

Notes

1. Egon Voss, Preface to *Richard Wagner: Sämtliche Lieder.* Mainz: B. Schott, 1982. ED 7078.
2. M. Owen Lee, *Wagner's Ring: Turning the Sky Round* (Summit Books, 1990), 12.
3. S. S. Prawer, *The Penguin Book of Lieder*, 89.
4. Quoted in Jonathan P. Ellis. Liner notes for *Wagner: Wesendonck-Lieder / Tristan und Isolde: Vorspiel, Liebestod.* Jessye Norman, Sir Colin Davis. Philips Records. Compact disc 412 655-2, 1975.
5. In *Wagner Handbook*, Ulrich Müller and Peter Wapnewski, eds., 66, 458.
6. M. Owen Lee, 99.

ROBERT FRANZ (1815-1892)

> The modern lyric demands a form as limited as possible, which dispenses with everything that is superfluous, thus leaving more to inference instead of expressing the flow of thoughts to the last drop.
>
> —Robert Franz[1]

Robert Franz was born in Halle into a manufacturing family. He was trained as an organist. His musical compositions include over 300 songs, church music, and choral compositions, but his reputation as a composer rests squarely on his *Lieder*. These are usually strophic in form and designed on a small scale. Overall, Franz's musical style is reminiscent of Robert Schumann's in its easy informality and in some of its musical traits.

Franz was highly respected by Schumann, Liszt, Mendelssohn, and Brahms. Schumann was instrumental in bringing Franz's music to the attention of the public. After receiving some of Franz's songs, Schumann had them published and reviewed them favorably in the *Neue Zeitschrift für Musik*; in 1872, Liszt published a biography of Franz.[2]

Franz wrote simple melodies in a moderate range, using German folk songs and hymns as his patterns. In general, his melodies are set syllabically and are structured around a rhythmic figure closely related to the poetic meter; Franz wrote, "The melody must be strictly in harmony with the words and the rhythm must only in very exceptional cases change."[3] Unfortunately, Franz's conservative approach and the lack of variety within his song structures hampered any real freedom of expression and limited his songs emotionally and expressively.

His key relationships are similarly unadventurous and predictable. He favored diatonic tonalities, with very few modulations. He was adamantly opposed to transposition of his songs; their range and tessitura make them most suited for performance by mezzo-sopranos and baritones.

Most of his songs are in strophic form, with piano accompaniments that double the vocal melody. Franz avoided dramatic poetry; his most successful songs are written to reflective texts. Unfortunately, Franz composed songs using a large number of poems that other composers had set before him, and his simplicity of style does not invite favorable comparison. His most memorable songs are settings by Heine and Möricke. Franz's gentle approach and late romantic charm do not lack appeal, but pall in comparison with the settings of his contemporaries. In 1848, Franz's hearing began to fail and he became totally deaf in 1867.

The late soprano Elisabeth Schumann was an enthusiastic supporter of Franz's songs, programming them regularly on her recitals. Since her death, Franz's *Lieder* rarely are heard in concert halls, but many serve as introductory German *Lieder* in teaching studios. Their charm, moderate musical demands, and inner warmth make them excellent literature for this purpose.

Es hat die Rose sich beklagt, Op. 42, No. 5   The Rose Complains. c. 1870
(Von Bodenstedt from the Persian of Mirza-Schaffy)

The rose complains her perfume will fade all too soon, but a poet assures her that through his verses her sweetness will last eternally. The passing of beauty is the essence of this poem, which has only six lines. Franz divides the poem into two stanzas of three lines and repeats them strophically. A piano phrase divides the poem neatly.

The rose was one symbol that epitomized the exotic orient (example: Fauré's "Les Roses d'Ispahan").

Widmung, Op. 14, No. 1   Dedication. c. 1860
(Müller)

"Widmung" is Franz's most beloved song. Its two stanzas are set like a hymn-tune; the accompaniment of simple chords doubles the vocal line throughout. Octave doublings in the accompaniment add texture and sonority to the setting. Vocal phrases are set syllabically in a simple melodic style. Simple alterations of chords are used for melodic color rather than for modulation. In spite of the simplicity of Franz's treatment, the overall effect of this song is heartfelt and charming.

Extended Study List
Ein Stündlein wohl vor Tag • Für Musik • Aus meinen grossen Schmerzen • Die Lotosblume • Die Rose, die Lilie • Im Herbst • Bitte • Gute Nacht! • Ja, du bist elend • Mädchen mit dem roten Mündchen • Selige Nacht • Auf dem Meer • Nachtlied • Kommt fein's Liebchen heut? • O säh ich auf der Heide dort

Selected Reading
Jürgen Thym, "Crosscurrents in Song: Five Distinctive Voices," in *German Lieder in the Nineteenth Century*, ed. Rufus Hallmark (New York: Schirmer Books, 1996), 153-185.

Notes
1. From an interesting extended excerpt from a letter from Franz to Sebastian B. Schlesinger (February 11, 1884) in which he holds forth at some length on his aesthetics of song. Quoted in Donald Ivey, *Song: Anatomy, Imagery, and Styles*, 218.
2. See Lorraine Gorrell, *The Nineteenth Century German Lied*, 232-236.
3. Ivey, 218.

JOHANNES BRAHMS (1833-1897)

> I want to publish my songs and should be so very much obliged if you
> could play them through beforehand and give me a word of advice about
> them...write and tell me which of them pleases you and whether you dis-
> like any of them...If possible write me a short comment on each. You need
> only give the opus or the number; for instance, Op. X, 5, bad; 6 outrageous;
> 7, ridiculous, and so on....

—Johannes Brahms to Clara Schumann, 24 April 1877[1]

Johannes Brahms's place as one of the great composers of the nineteenth century and one of the major German song composers is undisputed. It has been suggested that Brahms was a Janus who faced both the past and the future. He was a
diligent student and collector of old manuscripts, and his mastery of the musical
techniques and forms of the past allowed him to superimpose his own unique style
on them. His works are characterized by both strictness and freedom in form, line,
texture, and rhythm. He considered himself a self-taught composer. In his celebrated essay on Brahms, composer Arnold Schoenberg said that Brahms's music taught
him four important elements of style: musical asymmetry; elasticity of form ; sys-
tematic construction of movements; and economy, yet richness.[2]

Brahms composed approximately 380 songs for one, two, three, and four voices, including nearly 100 harmonizations/arrangements of folk songs and children's
songs. His fundamental interest in folk song and folk music permeated his musical aesthetic. His great respect and admiration for classical forms manifested itself
in musical symmetry, which is always found in his songs. This, coupled with his
strong lyric gift, gives his *Lieder* a high degree of emotional intensity and expressive impact.

Unlike Hugo Wolf, Brahms did not aim for a perfect synthesis of poem and
music in his songs. Although the musical totality is always related to the text, it is
the formal development of the music that takes center stage. Stein observes, "Once
the song is set in motion, the musical values become automatically more assertive
and determinant than the text; though there remains a very definite connection,
this relationship matters less."[3]

Brahms has been criticized for his seeming disinterest in choosing the best
poetry for his songs. Except for a few settings of Goethe, Heine and Tieck, his songs
'texts are drawn from lesser-known poets including Daumer, Groth, Lemcke,
Wenzig, Uhland, and Hölty. His only song cycle was Tieck's *Magelone Lieder.*

Brahms met Robert Schumann in 1853 and remained close to the family from
that time forward. The close relationship between Clara Schumann and Brahms
has remained both a cause for speculation and a maddening mystery. After
Schumann's death, Brahms became a source of strong support for Clara, and
MacDonald writes that "whatever the answer, in terms of what they *meant* to each
other, Brahms and Clara were certainly lovers."[4] In his music, Brahms, like
Schumann, used the musical theme-symbol "CLARA," and it is not far-fetched to
suppose that a significant number of his *Lieder* reflect his emotional involvement
and lifelong devotion to Clara Schumann.

Von ewiger Liebe, Op. 43, No. 1   Of Eternal Love. 1864
(From the Wendish by Josef Wenzig)

This song and the next belong to the same opus and are among the most frequently performed of Brahms's solo songs. They also share a similar mood and style in poetic atmosphere and intensity of musical treatment. An evening scene reveals a boy escorting his sweetheart home. He suggests that their relationship has brought her shame and offers to end it at once. She will have none of it, declaring their love is eternal, more enduring than iron or steel.

A typical Brahms bass line melody over broken chords is found in the opening bars; it anticipates the narrator's first vocal phrase ("Dunkel, wie dunkel in Wald und in Feld"). In the first two stanzas, the opening material is in B minor, inner phrases in D minor with a return to B minor, with only slight rhythmic changes to accommodate text.

The boy's dialogue makes up the third stanza. His vocal phrases are more insistent and dramatic, and the accompaniment pattern changes to triplet figures. This section is also in B minor, but the inner phrases are in F-sharp minor, returning to B minor.

Stanza four, the girl's reply, is the most extended of the four sections. Brahms switches meter from $\frac{3}{4}$ to $\frac{6}{8}$, and tonality from B minor to B major. Her vocal phrases are legato, less agitated, and more lyric. The overall texture is fuller and a small insistent motive is prominent. The repetition of the words "Unsere Liebe" calls forth a typical Brahms hemiola rhythm, which acts as a built-in *ritardando* and drives home the intense emotion of the girl's affirmation of love. The B major tonality is also a long-range resolution of the opening sections in B minor in which the couple discussed the uncertainty of lasting love.

Die Mainacht, Op. 43, No. 2   May Night. 1864
(Ludwig Christopher Heinrich Hölty)

In spite of the magical sounds and sights of a May night, a melancholy man wanders sadly in the woods. A scalding tear falls as he contemplates love, which is withheld from him. As he seeks the darker shadows, his solitary grief is thrown into relief as he shuns the beauty around him and hears the sounds of the nightingale and a pair of cooing doves.

This deeply reflective text struck a responsive chord in Brahms, whose favorite poetic themes included night, coupled with lament and loneliness. Hölty's original poem had four verses; Brahms omitted the second and used only three stanzas, setting them in a strophic design.

Brahms's skill at varying strophic form is clearly seen in "Die Mainacht." The second strophe is set apart by a change of key to B major (which modulates quickly back to the tonic of E-flat major) and a change of accompaniment pattern. This is enough to set it apart, but the vocal melody ("überhüllet vom Laub/girret ein Taubenpaar") is a variation of the initial vocal phrase ("Wann der silberne Mond durch die Gesträuche blinkt") and ends with one of the most beautiful and long-lined of Brahms's vocal phrases ("und die einsame Träne rinnt"). These four bars include many "fingerprints" of Brahms song style: expressive melody, dramatic harmonic progression, rich texture, and figuration. The final stanza returns to the opening material, but it is varied, and contains a repetition of the extended phrase from the second stanza, followed by one more long phrase that sums up the passion of the poet.

Hölty's text was also set in 1815 by Franz Schubert and in 1838 by Fanny Mendelssohn Hensel.

Botschaft, Op. 47, No. 1   **Message. 1868**
(Georg Friedrich Daumer, after Hafiz)

Brahms greatly admired Schubert's "Suleika I" and the mood of this song owes something to his respect; however, Brahms's setting presents the man who gives instructions to the breeze and not the girl who receives its message. "Blow gentle loving breeze about my beloved's cheek and in her hair. If she should ask how I am, say—his suffering was endless, but now he can hope because you, sweet one, are thinking of him."

There are three stanzas set in three sections of music. Brahms begins the recapitulation of the first stanza in the middle of the second, with a modulation at "sprich." The recapitulation is extremely varied and extended with longer note values, building to the final climax. In the accompaniment, broken chords in triplets run throughout the piece, creating unending motion. Vocal phrases are extremely flexible and light, changing to more relaxed, declamatory shapes in the middle section.

Vergebliches Ständchen, Op. 84, No. 4   **A Vain Serenade. 1881?**
(Lower Rhine folk song)

Brahms's setting of this folk-poem from the Lower Rhine sounds like a simple strophic song, but the accompaniment is varied for each verse. Titled "serenade in vain" or "useless serenade," it is really a dialogue song in four verses.

An ardent young man stands under his beloved's window, imploring her to let him in. Coyly she answers that her mother has warned her of the dire consequences of such an act. He replies that the icy wind and weather will freeze his love—and, not incidentally, him. After a switch to the minor mode for the third verse, the last stanza returns to the major and also gathers speed for the final humorous "go home to bed, then, good night, my lad!" The piano punctuates the last line, knowingly.

Feldeinsamkeit, Op. 86, No. 2   **Field Solitude. 1877**
(Hermann Allmers)

This is one of Brahms's most serene and beautiful songs. The poet lies in the high grass and feels that he is part of the texture of chirping crickets, blue sky and moving clouds overhead. Occasionally, Brahms used piano texture in his songs to illustrate nature, and this is a fine example. Register and rhythm of the piano accompaniment suggest clouds hanging suspended high above the earth—not only an illustration of the poetic setting, but also a creation of mood—all tranquillity and peace. Octave pedal points anchor the poem to the earth, while right-hand figures often float into higher realms. Vocal phrases arch upwards, then descend and finish with a graceful turn. There are two stanzas; for the second, Brahms retains phrase rhythms in voice and piano and varies the strophe harmonically, returning to the original tonality for the final phrase.

Sapphische Ode, Op. 94, No. 4   Sapphic Ode. 1884
(Hans Schmidt*)

Subtle harmonic nuances provide variety in this lovely legato song. The chordal accompaniment is syncopated, contrasting with the calm vocal line, fashioned of simple rhythms. There are two stanzas, set in strophic variation. Brahms compresses the musical meter for the shortened fourth line of each.

*The Baltic poet Schmidt was a friend of Brahms.

Der Tod, das ist die kühle Nacht, Op. 96, No. 1   Death is the Cool Night.
(Heinrich Heine)   1884

In mood, this song is linked to the third of the *Four Serious Songs*. Its atmosphere is subdued (Death is the cool night, Life is the sultry day). In an understated setting, Brahms captures the resigned melancholy and resignation of Heine's verse, as night draws near and the nightingale's song of love is heard in a peaceful dream. This song is perhaps the finest example of Brahms's fusion of text and music.

The syncopated rhythm in the accompaniment produces a lulling effect, giving way in the second stanza to arpeggio figures, embroidered with just a hint of the nightingale's song in the repeated top note of the chords. Even with a change of texture, Brahms retains the syncopated rhythm from the first stanza. The vocal line mirrors the mood of the piano; resigned and serene in the first verse, more lyrically expansive in the second stanza. Form is through-composed. A seven-bar postlude contains a tonic pedal point that gives a sense of finality and eternal rest.

Auf dem Kirchhofe, Op. 105, No. 4   At the Cemetery. 1886
(Detlev von Liliencron)

The scene is a churchyard during a rainstorm. Passing years have taken their toll on the grave markers, now hardly legible. The poet walks among them, surveying the ancient stones.

Many harmonic and rhythmic changes are found in this rather brief song: stormy opening music, harmonies that suggest crumbling old stones, a return to the storm, then a moment of peaceful reflection (almost like a sonata development section), and an unexpected Bach chorale texture in the major key in the concluding measures.

There are two distinct sections, each associated with natural elements and with emotional state. Both are ushered in by a turbulent four measures of arpeggios and heavy chords. Both begin with an identical first vocal phrase, but the first section is completed with shifting harmonies in the piano that suggest the decaying stones and crosses, finally coming to rest in a major key. Again the furious arpeggios are heard, and the second stanza modulates to the dominant of a restful

C major. Now a peaceful, chorale-like melody is heard, with longer legato phrases, as the poet sees the slumbering coffins marked with the word "Reborn." These tiny sections progress seamlessly, creating a striking contrast between the dramatic opening and the peaceful conclusion of the song.

This song bears some relation to the *Four Serious Songs,* which followed ten years later.

Immer leiser wird mein Schlummer*	**Ever Lighter Grows**
Opus 105, No. 2	**My Slumber. 1886**
(Hermann Lingg)	

In this melancholy text, a young girl is dying and wishes for her lover to come to her one last time. This song, like "Wie melodien zieht es," bears a tenuous relation to material in Brahms's *Violin Sonata No. 2* in A major.

The singer's physical state is illustrated by a vocal line of dotted rhythms and short phrases. Throughout the song the vocal line is doubled by the piano, either exactly or in some part of the melodic phrase. Dramatically this could be considered a poignant illustrative device, intensifying the singer's wishes, as well as bracing her physically. The last brief vocal phrases mount to an intensely-felt climax "Komme bald," before sinking back to a repeated, "komm, o komme bald!" (O come soon).

*This text was also set by Hans Pfitzner.

Wie Melodien zieht es, Op. 105, No. 1	**As Melodies a Feeling. 1886**
(Klaus Groth)	

The essence of Groth's poem deals with the elements of song: words and music and their power to arouse emotions. Melodies grow like flowers in the mind of the poet and float away like scent. Words likewise fade like mist, but the blend of tone and word brings tears to the eye.

Three subtly varied strophes comprise this lovely song; the last is the most intense. A romantic vocal line is accompanied by arpeggiated figures and is also doubled in thirds.

This is an excellent example of Brahms's melodic style. Brahms gives the singer only one beat before launching a broadly expressive vocal phrase (a device also used in "Meine liebe ist grün"). Brahms used material from this song in the first movement of his *Violin Sonata No. 2* in A major. The song was composed for Hermine Spies, a contralto for whom Brahms wrote many of his later songs.

Ständchen, Op. 106, No. 1   Serenade. 1886
(Franz Kugler)

"Ständchen" is the first of the five songs in Op. 106, published in 1889. Its mood is light and charming; its three verses are set with similar outer verses enclosing a contrasting middle stanza. A group of three students stand beneath a window, serenading a beautiful blond girl. Each has an instrument to accompany their song, which bursts into bloom in the piano interlude between verses in a rhapsodic lyric moment. At this point lengthened note values create a discrepancy in phrase lengths—a characteristic of Brahms. The plucked sound of the zither (or guitar) mentioned in the text is almost continuous in the left hand in the accompaniment; the flute and violin join in the middle section and particularly enhance the charming piano interlude before the last verse. This section illustrates, without the voice, the idea of "singen und spielen." Notice also the subtle rhythmic connections in some of the vocal phrases throughout the song.

Meine Liebe ist grün, Op. 63, No. 5   My Love is Green. 1874
(Felix Schumann)

Felix Schumann was the son of Clara and Robert Schumann; Brahms was his godfather. This poem was written when he was nineteen; its somewhat awkward verses are given a glorious setting by Brahms, who subtitled this song (with young Schumann's other verse "Wenn um den Hollunder") *Junge Lieder*. The mood is one of ardent, youthful emotion.

Harmonic fluctuations mark the two stanzas, which are set strophically. Brahms withholds the tonic until the close of the first stanza. He begins with a modulation into the tonic, arriving on the word "grün," and launches the first vocal phrase after one beat in the fast moving piano accompaniment. Submerged in its thick texture is a doubling of the vocal line. The songs of Op. 63 are on themes of youth and love, as well as old age recalling youthful emotions.

Zigeunerlieder,* Op. 103, Nos. 1-8   Gypsy Songs. 1887
(Hugo Conrat, after the Hungarian by Zoltán Nagy)

He, Zigeuner, greife in die Saiten ein! (Hey Gypsy, Sound
Your Strings!) • Hochgetürmte Rimaflut (Towering Rima at
Flood-Tide) • Wist ihr, wann mein Kindchen (Do You Know When My
Sweetheart...) • Lieber Gott, du weisst (Dear God, You Know...) •
Brauner Bursche (Swarthy Lad) • Röslein dreie in der Reihe
(Three Little Red Roses) • Kommt dir manchmal (Do You Sometimes
Recall...) • Rote Abendwolken (Rosy Evening Clouds)

Throughout his life Brahms was fascinated with the music of the Hungarian Gypsies. His *Hungarian Dances* date from the aftermath of the 1848 rebellion, when many Hungarian refugees emigrated to his native Hamburg. These songs are rearrangements from the eleven vocal quartets composed in 1887 as *Zigeunerlieder* for four voices. Texts were drawn from a German translation by

Hugo Conrat (a merchant friend of Brahms) of a collection of twenty-five Hungarian folksongs.

There are eight songs in the set, encompassing an array of emotions from exuberant joy to melancholy. Dance rhythms are found in the piano and also in the rhythms of the vocal lines of some of the songs. As does Dvořák in his Gypsy songs, Brahms begins and ends this set with strongly accented, broad-lined songs. In general, Brahms's settings are less involved and simpler than those of Dvořák in formal structure, texture, and approach to melodic line, but in spite of their simplicity, they do not lack for dramatic color and style.

Indigenous Hungarian vocal music lacks upbeats; all the words are accented on the first syllable. Brahms's settings preserve this quality; all the songs begin on the beat. All eight songs are in simple duple meter. Variety is created by use of syncopations, triplets, and dotted patterns. Gypsy *csárdás* rhythm is found in Song 3, with its two contrasting tempos.

*Brahms's Gypsy songs should be compared with those of Antonín Dvořák for musical style.

Vier ernste Gesänge, Op. 121, Nos. 1-4   **Four Serious Songs. 1896**
(Luther's translation of the Bible)

> Denn es gehet dem Menschen wie dem Vieh (For the fate of man is like the beast) • Ich wandte mich und sahe in alle (I turned and considered all those) • O Tod, wie bitter bist du (O Death, how bitter you are) • Wenn ich mit Menschen-und mit Engelszungen redete (Though I speak with the tongues of men and of angels)

After a hiatus of ten years without composing songs, Brahms created this set—perhaps his most expressive musical settings—a summation of his song style and his personal beliefs. He began their composition near the time Clara Schumann suffered a slight stroke, and completed them in the month of her death. He wrote to her daughters: "These songs concern you most seriously. I wrote them in the first week of May; I am often occupied with words of that kind, but I did not expect to hear worse news of your mother—but there is often something that speaks and works deep down in one, almost unconsciously, and at times it may well clothe itself in sound, as poetry or music...I ask you to regard them as really a funeral offering for your dear mother."[5]

Love, death, and resignation were themes Brahms had explored before, but nowhere are they more tellingly nor expressively joined than in these songs. It is important to notice that the texts of all four songs were adapted by Brahms from the Bible and, as such, are prose and not poetry. This results in total absence of clear metrical schemes and, therefore, greater rhythmic freedom.

In scope and style, the four songs are almost symphonic. A slow-fast-slow-fast pattern is found in the first song; the last song is a mirror structure of fast-slow-fast-slow. The two inner songs are tightly organized and relate to each other in the use of the falling melodic third, perhaps used as the symbol for death, or perhaps for weeping. This interval germinates from the beginning song, where it is found in both the first figure in the piano and the first vocal phrase. In the last section of "Ich wandte mich," (Song 2), minor tonality gives way to major and, under the vocal line "und des Bösen nicht inne wird" the piano outlines the falling third pattern that will become the opening vocal phrase of the next song, "O Tod, o Tod..." (Song 3). In this song, the falling thirds are inverted to rising sixths, illuminating another quality of death, that of benevolent rest. Major/minor contrast also exists in this song.

All four songs share a grandeur and nobility of mood, and there is a reminiscent bond between the set and Brahms's *German Requiem* in atmosphere and style.

DENN ES GEHET DEM MENSCHEN, WIE DEM VIEH (FOR THE FATE OF MAN IS LIKE THAT OF THE BEAST) ECCLESIASTES 3, 19-22.

"Death befalleth both the beasts and the sons of man. Man is not above the beast. All are dust and will return to dust. Therefore, I see there is no better thing than that a man be happy in his work, for that is his portion. For who will bring him to see what will be after him?"

ICH WANDTE MICH UND SAHE AN ALLE (I TURNED ABOUT AND CONSIDERED ALL THOSE...) ECCLESIASTES 4, 1-3.

"I turned and considered all that suffer oppression under the sun. And behold, there was weeping and wailing, and there was no one to comfort them because their oppressors had power. Then I praised the dead more than the living. And he who has not been born is better off than both for he knows not the evil that happens under the sun. "

O TOD, WIE BITTER BIST DU (O DEATH, HOW BITTER YOU ARE!) ECCLESIASTES 41, 1-2.

"O death how bitter you are to a man in the days of his prosperity, who lives without care, who is successful in all things and can still eat well! O death how welcome you are to the man in need who is weak and old, beset with every care and has nothing better to hope for, nothing more to expect!"

WENN ICH MIT MENSCHEN—UND MIT ENGELSZUNGEN REDETE (THOUGH I SPEAK WITH THE TONGUES OF MEN AND OF ANGELS) CORINTHIANS I, 3, 1-2 AND 12-13.

"Though I speak with the tongues of men or of angels, and have not love, then I am become as sounding brass. Though I have prophesy and understand all mysteries, and have not love, I am nothing. And now abideth faith, hope, love, these three; but the greatest of these is love.'"

Extended Study List

An die Nachtigall • An eine Aolsharfe • Erinnerung • Liebestreu • Wie bist du, meine Königen • O wüsst ich doch den Weg zürück • Dein blaues Auge • Sonntag • Wir wandelten • O liebliche Wangen • Therese • Verrat • Wenn du nur zuweilen lächelst • *Two Songs,* Op. 91 (voice/viola) • Der gang zum Liebchen • Der Schmied • Minnelied • Geheimnis • Komm bald • O kühler Wald • Wiegenlied • *Ophelia-Lieder*

Selected Reading

Max Friedländer, *Brahms' Lieder,* trans. C. Leonard Leese (New York: American Musicological Society Press, 1976).

Beaumont Glass, *Brahms' Complete Song Texts* (Geneseo, NY: Leyerle Publications, 2000).

Virginia Hancock, "Johannes Brahms: Volkslied/Kunstlied," in *Nineteenth Century German Lieder,* ed. Rufus Hallmark (New York: Schirmer Books, 1996), 119-152.

Max Harrison, *The Lieder of Brahms* (New York: Praeger Publishers, 1972). Critical discussion of Brahms's *Lieder* in context of historical and artistic developments of his time.

Berthold Litzmann, ed., *Letters of Clara Schumann and Johannes Brahms,* 1853-1896. 2 vols. (London: Edward Arnold, 1927).

Candace Magner, *Phonetic Readings of Brahms Lieder* (Metuchen, NJ: Scarecrow Press, 1987).

Eusebius Mandyczewski, ed., *The Complete Songs for Solo Voice and Piano by Johannes Brahms.* 4 vols. Trans. Stanley Appelbaum (New York: Dover, 1980).

Michael Musgrave, *The Music of Brahms* (London: Routledge & Kegan Paul, 1985). Chapter 6: Songs and Piano Music.

Arnold Schoenberg, "Brahms the Progressive," in *Style and Idea*, ed. L. Stein (London: Faber & Faber, 1975).

Eric Sams, *The Songs of Johannes Brahms* (New Haven, CT: Yale University Press, 2000). Excellent source on Brahms's *Lieder* and compositional style.

_____, *Brahms Songs* (Seattle: University of Washington Press, 1972). BBC Music Guides series No. 223.

Lucien Stark. *A Guide to the Solo Songs of Johannes Brahms* (Bloomington, IN: Indiana University Press, 1995).

Notes

1. Quoted in Malcolm MacDonald, *Brahms*, (New York: Schirmer Books, 1990), 245.
2. Arnold Schoenberg, "Brahms the Progressive," in *Style and Idea*, ed. L. Stein, 398-441.
3. Jack M. Stein, *Poem and Music in the German Lied from Gluck to Hugo Wolf*, 129.
4. Malcolm MacDonald, *Brahms*, 44.
5. Quoted in David Hamilton. "The Songs of Brahms," liner notes for *Brahms Songs*. Jan DeGaetani/Gilbert Kalish. Arabesque Recordings. Compact disc Z6141, 1983, 1989).

HUGO WOLF (1860-1903)

> There's something gruesome about the intimate fusion of poetry and music in which, actually, the gruesome role belongs only to the latter. Music has decidedly something of the vampire about it. It claims its victim relentlessly and sucks the last drop of blood from it.
>
> —Hugo Wolf[1]

> Wolf's songs have lived, and will live, because of their musical excellence...the music itself has a unique quality of intimate inter-relationship with words, with language, and with poetry.
>
> —Eric Sams[2]

Hugo Wolf's songs have been characterized as the "caviar of *Lieder* literature" because they exhibit a highly refined sense of style and intellectual concentration.[3] He has also been called the "Wagner of the *Lied*" and it is a fitting comparison only in the sense that he admired the musical techniques of Wagner and was able to incorporate them into his own style and into the more miniature form of song. With Wolf's songs, German song reached the ultimate synthesis of poem and music. Words and music are inextricably bound in Wolf's settings, to the point that it is extremely difficult to extract one from another. He referred to his songs as "poems for voice and piano," a telling description of the importance he placed on a complete fusion of music and text.

In the historical development of song, Hugo Wolf was at the right place at the right time. He had at his disposal all the lyric poetry of the century, he was on the cutting edge of new explorations in musical styles, and he could draw on the rich traditions of romantic *Lieder* as well. He was thoroughly grounded in the *Lieder* style of his predecessors, particularly Schubert, Schumann, and Loewe; he also understood the new declamatory style of Wagner, and was greatly influenced by it. He composed approximately 250 songs, each carefully crafted to extract the essence of the poetry.

Distinguished pianist-coach Martin Katz observes that:

> Wolf's name on a program strikes simultaneous chords of joy and terror in any accompanist. Joy, because of Wolf's ability to synthesize music and text in a way that allows both to emerge, not merely uncorrupted, but enhanced. Terror, because, if one is thorough, the technical execution of even his simplest measures is a formidable task...[4]

Self-taught, Wolf struggled for recognition all his life. He composed almost all his songs in an amazingly brief time span—around five years. The bulk of his *Lieder* were written between 1888 and 1891. He wrote in a frenzy of enthusiasm, often composing several songs a day, and volumes in a few weeks. During this period he completed over 200 songs—all the songbooks of Möricke, Eichendorff, Goethe, Geibel, Keller and Heyse. This frantic activity was followed by a two-year period of inactivity and depression. From 1895-1897, he completed his opera *Der Corregidor*, plus another thirty songs or so, and began another opera, which he left unfinished. Thus, his stature as a composer rests solely upon his legacy of song.

Wolf's *Lieder* includes the five great "songbooks" and over 100 other songs. The diversity of styles and expression encompassed in these collections is an astonishing fusion of musical materials and literary taste. Wolf's earliest songs show the influence of Robert Schumann, but the last great *Italian Songbook* contains tiny masterpieces of rare quality, unique to his overall output. Distinguished pianist-accompanist Gerald Moore said it best when he wrote "...Wolf inhabits a different world in each lyric, gives to each poet a different style."[5]

Wolf also composed a symphonic poem, the *Italian Serenade* for string quartet or chamber orchestra, and a small number of instrumental and choral works. His unfinished opera, *Manuel Venegas*, was to contain several songs from the *Spanish Songbook*: "Wer sein holdes Lieb verloren," "Wenn du zu den Blumen gehst," and "Bedeckt mich mit Blumen."

In 1897 Wolf manifested unmistakable signs of mental instability, spent a brief time in a sanitarium, and was discharged. A relapse made a second incarceration necessary and, during this hospitalization, Wolf died.

From the *Möricke Lieder*

Wolf set fifty-three songs on poems of Eduard Möricke (1804-1875) in quick succession between February and October of 1888—approximately one song per day in the quiet of his Perchtoldsdorf house on the outskirts of Vienna. The Möricke set was his first major collection. Its songs are a colorful kaleidoscope of moods and styles, giving it the broadest range of all of Wolf's collections. Möricke's poems offered Wolf a rich array of subjects. Wolf's custom of not setting poems his predecessors had used unless he felt he could set them better gave him the Möricke all to himself; Schumann had set only five poems, Brahms two, and Schubert had been too early for Möricke.

Möricke was a devout Protestant pastor, who has been called "a son of Horace out of a Swabian village-girl." His poetry is characterized by religious devotion, humor, realism, and imagination. Sams points out the quality of "goldenness" in Möricke's work—poems that use images from nature (sunlight, golden grapes, golden bell-notes) as well as those containing a contrasting darker side of demonic character.[6] The mood swings found in Möricke's verses must have struck a responsive chord in Wolf, whose personality and creative work patterns shared similar oppositions.

The Möricke songbook contains some of Wolf's best-known songs. The set is characterized by more melodic settings coupled with Wolf's imaginative thematic development and individual design. The poems treat a variety of subjects: nature scenes, character portraits, humorous texts, and love poems (both lyrical and erotic).

Das verlassene Mägdlein
(24 March 1888)

                                            The Abandoned Maidservant.

Of this song, Wolf wrote in a letter: "I let myself be suddenly taken captive by the magic of this poem, something outstandingly good has resulted, and I think that my composition can stand comparison with Schumann's."[7]

This song is a rare instance of Wolf setting a poem that was already set well by a composer he respected. There is really no introduction, only four bars that present the rhythm that glues the song together. The poem's mood is desolate and stark, compressing a complete miniature drama into a short song. A young, grief-stricken servant girl stares without seeing into the hearth-fire, recalling her dream of a faithless lover and wishing even as the day has begun that it would end soon. We are not given details—who the boy was or why he left—only that her grief is rekindled by the sudden sparks of fire from the hearth.

Wolf's setting is simplicity itself, a poignant picture in simple, transparent textures. Unity is created by a rhythmic motive that repeats throughout the song (quarter/eighth-eighth) maintaining a hypnotic effect and painting a striking portrait of the emotions of the young maid. A change of vocal color and mood cuts through her bleak mood at "Plötzlich, da kommt es mir," but returns to the despairing atmosphere of the opening. In fifty-two measures of music, Wolf has created a penetrating psychological portrait, a skill that culminated in the striking miniatures of the *Italian Songbook*.

Er ist's
(5 May 1888)

                                            Spring is Here.

The poet exuberantly welcomes the coming of spring. Wolf's setting is exhilarating: the sights, smells and sounds of spring are hailed in a jubilant nonstop tempo. Vocal phrases are brief and breathless. There is an extended and fiendishly difficult piano postlude.

Wolf binds the song together by using a quick-moving accompaniment pattern in triplets, a combination of arpeggios and broken chords, and by repeating several motives. Möricke's poem was also set by Schumann and Franz. These songs should be examined with Wolf's for an interesting comparison of what the poem meant to each composer. Their responses are markedly different.

Begegnung
(22 March 1888)

Encounter.

The "encounter" of the title takes place on the street as a boy and girl meet each other by chance, having spent a turbulent night together the evening before. The inexperienced couple eyes each other awkwardly. Captivated by her charm, he dreamily remembers her kisses, but she disappears around the corner.

A very quick accompaniment and a matching vocal line of equal breathless quality illustrate the storm of the night before—not only the weather, but the ardor of the young couple. Like a lightly moving whirlwind, piano figures rise and fall in chromatic syncopations. This two-bar pattern and its melodic variants unify the song. Phrase direction and agitated movement also suggest the emotions of the young couple. A switch of key from minor to major occurs as the girl comes into the view, and his memory replays the encounter of the evening before. Wolf uses the melodic material that accompanied the girl's entrance and converts it to exit music, whisking her like a breeze, around the corner and out of sight.

Nimmersatte Liebe
(24 February 1888)

Insatiable Love.

"You'll go wild with delight when you hear it," wrote Wolf to a friend after completing this song.[8] He explained one reason—he had inserted a rollicking student song at the end.

Syncopated suspensions in the piano immediately signal a sly, playful mood. Mörike's erotic texts embarrassed his contemporaries, but Wolf's musical treatment is discreet and delicate. The middle stanza is peppered with augmented triads, in a chordal accompaniment that is rhythmically syncopated against the vocal part. This begins in triads and develops in scope and range until at "Das Mädchen hielt in guter Ruh," the chords alternate every measure between treble to bass clef in an unrelenting search for new delights.

The final stanza begins as the first, but soon gives way to the student song. Wolf marks it "Mit Humor" and the happy tune cites the fact that King Solomon in all his wisdom never made love any other way. The last line of the poetry bears repeating, so Wolf obliges—the final allusion to the wisdom of Solomon is like the punch line, delivered with a knowing grin.

Der Gärtner
(7 March 1888)

The Gardener.

This fairy tale scene is almost child-like in its simplicity and charm, an example of a very tuneful Wolf song. Astride a great white horse, a princess rides by an adoring gardener who has scattered sand along the way she will pass, hoping for a feather from her gaily decorated hat.

Wolf's setting is fresh and as enchanting as the text. A dotted rhythmic figure in the accompaniment illustrates the prancing gait of her horse and ties the song's stanzas tightly together. Vocal phrases are gracefully lyric. Musical elements in the song seem to point only to the princess, not to her adoring servant, who is both subject and narrator of the poem. Only a slight pulling back on the words "Blüte" and "alle" in the last verse make his inner feelings really apparent.

Elfenlied   Elf-Song.
(7 March 1888)

An amusing little child's tale of a playful elf is the subject of this tiny bit of enchantment. Onomatopoeic effects abound in the poetry. An elf sleeping in the forest is awakened by the village watchman's cry: "Eleven!" Thinking he is being summoned (eleven=elf) the little sprite, still half-asleep, stumbles down through the wood and down to the village walls, lit by glowworms. Thinking the glistening lights are a party, he tries to look in and bumps his head against the hard stone.

Wolf highlights the text with brilliant details in dynamics, texture and key changes. A rising scale ponderously announces the watchman's cry "Elfe!", which falls an octave. As the story progresses the accompaniment patterns change, but the falling octave remains in the texture in varying note values, as the elf keeps hearing his name. His stumbling steps into town are attended by a glittering little "glowworm" figure of sixteenth notes. The vocal lines are set syllabically in small note values with only a few little two-note slurs. The poor elf's confusion is mocked by the call of "Gukuk!" (Cuckoo), probably to the delight of the children for whom Möricke wrote this poem.

Auf ein altes Bild   On an old painting.
(14 April 1888)

Möricke's profound poem contains only six lines. A beautiful painting of a summery green landscape greets the eye of the spectator. On the canvas, the Christ Child plays happily on the Virgin's lap. In the background of beautiful green forest grows the tree for the cross.

In character, the song resembles a miniature hymn. A calm introductory passage ushers the spectator to the painting; in fourths and thirds, it is tinged with modality in keeping with the religious subject of the art. Contrary motion in close intervals between voice and piano perpetuates a solemn, almost prayer-like mood. Only the stabbing dissonance at "Kreuzes Stamm!" interrupts the serenity, then is resolved quickly—a poignant moment that contrasts with the enjoyment of the painted scene.

Wolf wrote to Edmund Lang: "My last song, which I have just finished, is without a doubt the crown of all. I am still in the grip of the enchantment of the mood...everything is still shimmering in green all round me."[9]

Verborgenheit   Seclusion.
(13 March 1888)

Wolf composed this song on his twenty-eighth birthday, and it quickly gained popularity in his lifetime. It has remained one of his most famous songs—strange in a way, since it has none of the earmarks of Wolf's musical style save his deeply felt response to the poem. Its nobility of mood is achieved through broad vocal phrases and strongly supportive accompaniment figures. Although Wolf expressed annoyance at its popularity, the song text accurately expresses his personality and creative temperament. Möricke was supposedly a shy man; the poem's title can mean "secrecy" or "privacy" as well.

There are four stanzas; the fourth and first use the same words. Wolf sets them to the same music. Verses 2 and 3 are more agitated, as conflicting emotions are revealed in the text. The accompaniment changes as well, becoming an insistent chordal pattern, and the texture becomes thicker overall.

Despite the sentiment of the text, "Verborgenheit" remains a warm, tender expression of an introspective text, crafted with the same care Wolf lavished on all his songs.

From the *Goethe Lieder*

During the winter of 1888-89, Wolf composed fifty-one songs on poems by Johann Wolfgang von Goethe. With the exception of "Die Spröde," the Goethe collection was completed in less than four months.

The Goethe songs can be divided into groups: there are ten songs from *Wilhelm Meister*; four extended ballads, seventeen songs from the *West-östliche Divan* (one of the most renowned German poetic works on the Orient), and a collection of assorted texts drawn from other Goethe sources. In general, the Goethe songs exhibit a spaciousness of style not found in his other collections.

Not surprisingly, the songs manifest Wolf's intellectual response to the poems, and perhaps for that reason are not as lyrical as *Lieder* from other poem books. In particular, his settings from Goethe's *Wilhelm Meister* contain psychological elements as well as a close-knit fusion of tone and word. In these songs, some of Wolf's most-performed *Lieder*, Mignon and the Harper are fleshed-out emotionally as well as musically.

Harfenspieler I - Wer sich der Einsamkeit ergibt   **Who Gives Himself**
Gesänge des Harfners/The Harper's Songs   **to Loneliness.**
(27 October 1888)

There are three Harper's Songs; Wolf finished them in four days. Each is suffused with the blind harper's melancholy. Wolf's musical settings feature complex harmonies that maintain tension and illustrate the mental state of the Harper. All the songs are tied together by a descending chromatic figure.

In this, the first of the trilogy, the Harper reflects on his loneliness, without revealing that it is his overwhelming sense of guilt that is responsible for his torment and his desire for solitude. By day and night he is shadowed by pain and woe. His only escape will be in the grave, where he can truly be alone.

The Harper improvises the song for Wilhelm Meister, who has come to visit him. He plays in the key of G minor; Wolf uses strummed harp figures to accompany the first two stanzas. Harmonic progressions are the central element of this song, and in combination with vocal line and texture, maintain a disoriented mood. Painful chromatic touches suggest the grief of the singer.

Voice and piano operate independently of one another, coming together occasionally at a cadential points to relieve tension. Vocal phrases are declamatory in style. The end of the second stanza cadences, tenderly consonant, on the word "allein" (alone), and a new piano figure takes over—the Harper now plays broken chords, and some major harmonies.

The singer's last note is the tonic, but the piano finishes on an unresolved dominant chord. Brody and Fowkes cite this song out as setting the stage for Berg's *Sieben frühe Lieder*.[10] In terms of fusion of text and music, it must rank among Wolf's finest achievements.

Mignon (Kennst du das Land)   Do You Know the Land.
(17 December 1888)

Goethe's novel *Wilhelm Meister* contains memorable lyrics sung by the mysterious Harper and the child-waif Mignon. The Harper's songs are heavy with guilt and despair. Mignon's are full of secrecy, grief, and longing for her homeland. Their lyrics have fascinated numerous composers and produced some memorable song settings. Neither character knows that they are father and daughter—Mignon is the child of the Harper's incestuous liaison with his own sister. His sin has sent him wandering crazed through the world, far from his native Italy. Mignon, born in Italy but abducted by vagabonds and brought into Germany, is forced to sing and dance in a troupe of traveling entertainers.

In Goethe's novel, Mignon appears at Wilhelm's door and sings this song, accompanying herself on a zither. In its words, she recalls the beauty of her Italian homeland, the grandeur of her home and the mountain passes over which her captors brought her.

Wolf's memorable setting is basically strophic in form, although its musical texture is complex. Vocal phrases are subtly varied for each stanza and each stanza has a different accompaniment pattern. Rhapsodic piano interludes divide the stanzas, with the vocal line declaiming "Kennst du es wohl?", which then rises dramatically to Mignon's emotional cry "Dahin!"

Brody and Fowkes[11] diagram the structure of the first stanza (and the basic pattern for each verse) in this manner:

Section	Key	Meter	Length
Refrain (piano)	G-flat major	$\frac{3}{4}$	4 bars
Kennst du das Land (a)	G-flat, mod. E-flat	$\frac{3}{4}$	8 bars; 8 bars
Kennst du es wohl? (b)	F minor	$\frac{9}{8}$	11 bars
Dahin! (c)	B-flat minor mod. G-flat major	$\frac{9}{8}, \frac{3}{4}$	3 bars; 3 bars
Refrain (piano)		$\frac{3}{4}$	4 bars
			(includes a bar overlap with c)

Wolf's powerful setting, highly dramatic and tinged with the exotic, is unlike any of the previous treatments of this text by other composers. Its piano writing is reminiscent of Liszt, and its expansive lyric lines are quasi-operatic in style. Its complex texture is orchestral in concept, and, indeed, Wolf did compose an orchestral setting for this song. "Kennst du das Land" is among Wolf's masterpieces.

Der Rattenfänger   The Rat-Catcher.
(6 November 1888)

The old thirteenth-century folk fable of the rat-catcher, also known as the Pied Piper, is told here in the words of the piper himself. Wolf's setting is one of sparkling charm and good humor. There are three stanzas, set with a strong strophic feeling.

Buoyant rhythms and artful key shifts accompany the piper's dancing journey through the streets. His catchy vocal line is a brilliant *tarantella*, a smooth con-man's pitch as well as an introduction to his talents: he rids the town of mice and weasels, he also captivates children with his fairy tales, and he is irresistible to women. Wolf subtly varies the vocal line from one stanza to the next. The Piper's vocal line is as slippery as the scurrying rodents heard in the piano's opening measures.

Wolf's gay rhythmic setting easily obscures the dark underside of this text—the rat-catcher's reputation as a kidnapper and his demonic character. His magic powers that lure the mice away from towns also lure the children. The vocal line has considerable force and swiftness that masks evil. It is relentless in its forward motion, sweeping its victims with it.

At the song's finish, the story is not over, and we are left to fill in the conclusion based on our own evaluation of Goethe's text and Wolf's musical translation. The song is a dazzling *tour de force* for singer and pianist. Wolf later rescored this song for orchestral accompaniment.

Die Spröde   **The Coy Shepherdess.**
(21 October 1889)

A charming pastoral scene, complete with a lovely young shepherdess, is unveiled in this song. Her mood is carefree and as she walks, she sings "so la la!" and it rings across the fields. Thyrsis offers her one lamb for one kiss, three for three. She continues to smile and sing. Another suitor offers her ribbons, and the third one, his heart. She scorns all the offers.

This song is often paired with "Die Bekehrte" (The Repentant Shepherdess) in which the young girl is seduced by a young man playing the flute. Like Goethe's Gretchen, her peace is now lost. Both songs have some musical links to one another, although they were not written together.

There are three verses of "Die Spröde" and each ends with the shepherdess's song, a flexible vocal line that varies slightly with each verse, in response to the preceding text. Accompaniment figures are delicate arpeggios and lightly played chords. Sams categorizes the minor seconds in the piano prelude as Wolf's motive of "smallness," indicating he might have been thinking of the figure of a Dresden shepherdess. Sams also identifies other motives of mocking laughter and contentment.[12]

Anakreons Grab   **The Grave of Anacreon.**
(4 November 1888)

Anacreon was a Greek lyric poet of the sixth century B.C., well-known for his poems on love, nature, wine, and song. Born in Asia Minor about 550 B.C., he later went to Athens and died there at age eighty-five. Goethe's poem captures the classicism of his subject; Wolf's musical setting is notable for its simplicity and lyric feeling.

Delicate piano figures paint the natural beauty surrounding the grave of the poet: twining vines and roses, the silence of nature broken by chirping crickets, and the cooing of doves—a fitting place of rest for the laureate of nature.

A three-note cell heard in the piano introduction (right hand, first three notes—leading tone, tonic, supertonic) becomes the basis for the first vocal phrase. As the narrator draws nearer, the harmony becomes more complex and thicker in texture. His description of the grave is accompanied by fluctuating harmonies, serenely traveling via a beautiful arching vocal line (measures 7-10) to the magical phrase "Es ist...Anakreons Ruh." Wolf intensifies the wonder of the moment by breaking this phrase with a rest as the inscription is read. "Ruh" is set on the lowest pitch in all the song's melodic phrases. The textures in this middle section, as in many of Wolf's songs, suggest a string quartet.

It remains for the piano to close the piece serenely, as though the narrator is walking away, but he turns back to look again at the poet's resting place. This song has been described as "marvelous in its pagan calm and peace."

From the *Eichendorff Lieder*

The poetry of the great romantic writer Joseph von Eichendorff (1788-1857) furnished many composers with song texts, and Wolf was no exception. There are twenty *Lieder* in this collection and their overall mood is generally bright and cheerful. Wolf's settings are somewhat less ambitious in tone than in the Mörike songbook.

Robert Schumann set many of Eichendorff's poems, for the most part choosing texts that dealt with nature. Wolf's choices for his Eichendorff songs are smaller in number than his other song collections. He chose humorous, more lighthearted poems, dominated by character studies. Character portraits that are drawn from the words of the poem's speaker attracted Wolf (example: "Die Zigeunerin"); in the Eichendorff songs, a single poetic persona speaks directly. Youens observes that Wolf was particularly drawn to Eichendorff's "quirky" figures— mercenary soldiers, Gypsies, sailors—figures outside the establishment.[13] Romantic texts, such as "Verschwiegene Liebe," and "Nachtzauber" are also present in the collection.

Der Musikant   The Musician.

(22 September 1888)

One of the character sketches in the Eichendorff collection is the figure of the wandering minstrel. Wolf accompanies him on his journey with contrasting patterns in the piano; the left hand plays the minstrel's harp, and the right-hand figure resembles a restless fiddle tune. His melodic line is a jaunty folk-like tune which, like him, seems unable to rest.

Wolf's setting is a commentary on the musician's self-portrait. The four stanzas are half-humorous and half-bittersweet, as the minstrel reflects on his vagrant life. Wolf takes the opening rhythmic figures in the piano and uses them to accompany the first stanza, where they generally outline the vocal phrase. The opening introduction appears again between the first and second verse.

Now a new melody appears as the minstrel speaks of singing the "fine old songs" in the snow, never knowing where he will rest. The accompaniment becomes more chromatic and the interlude between verses remains bitter. The third verse is tinged with touches of harmonic "pity" from the young girl who sees the poor vagabond. The last verse (again introduced by the little fiddle tune) is a variant of the second stanza, but after two phrases, the music of the opening vocal material is heard again.

Verschwiegene Liebe   Silent Love.
(31 August 1888)

"Through the silent night, thoughts freely float—over the treetops, away into the light. If she could guess who has thought of her as the trees murmur and no one is awake but the clouds....my love is silent as the night."

The subtle sophistication of Eichendorff's poem is mirrored in Wolf's gorgeous setting. The meter is $\frac{12}{8}$; a soft melody is heard in the left hand of the piano, coupled with broken chord figures that rise dreamily. For most of the song, the accompaniment remains in the treble clef. Sustained vocal phrases in combination with the piano figures produce a lulling, nocturnal effect.

Wolf breaks the two stanzas into musical sections of four lines/three lines, punctuated by a bar of $\frac{6}{8}$. The form is strophic, but varied slightly in the last section. Wolf's skillful mix of harmonies and textures creates a vocal nocturne of striking imagery.

Nachtzauber   Night Magic.
(24 May 1887)

Much of the emotional intensity of this song comes from Wolf's masterful manipulation of texture and harmony. Eichendorff's nature texts are full of symbolism; this text is rich in imagery, real and implied. Wolf's setting is complex, yet structured.

Melodic contours in the voice are broadly lined. Contrasting movement in the piano is created by a repeated sixteenth note pattern in the right hand, combined with fragmented melodic material in the left hand. The softly flowing motion is hypnotic and intense. Phrase shapes are used in their entirety for text illustration; one notable example occurs at "komm zum stillen Grund" (come to the still valley) as the voice sinks into the piano texture.

In this song, Wolf's rapport with the poet is unmistakable.

Die Zigeunerin   The Gypsy Girl.
(19 March 1887)

This is one of the few examples of Wolf's bravura writing for the voice. Images of nomadic Gypsy life appear in Eichendorff's poem: the crossroads, campfires, barking dogs, forests, and the happy freedom of wandering. The Gypsy girl declares her sweetheart must be a brown-skinned, bearded Gypsy who loves to wander. The enigmatic text is difficult to understand. It is taken from Eichendorff's novel, *Dichter und ihre Gesellen*, and the verses are sung by two people, an actress performing a Gypsy dance and the hero who takes the second verse, comparing the woman to a cat.

Wolf's accompaniment provides a colorful background for the singer's narration. A tiny pattern, suggesting a tambourine, is coupled with a dancing rhythm; these run throughout the song. There is a change of key for the second stanza, as well as an exciting change of accompaniment patterns—slinking cat-figures and rifle-shots, followed by the singer's mocking laughter, echoed in the piano. "Die Zugeunerin" is unusual for Wolf's use of refrains: the singer's wordless "la-las" and her mocking melismatic laughter.

The initial rhythmic accompaniment returns for the last stanza, coupled with a return of the beginning tonality. The singer's dance-like refrain comprises the last eight measures, capped by an exciting descending chromatic scale in the vocal line.

From the *Spanisches Liederbuch*

The songs of the *Spanisches Liederbuch* are musical settings of translations of sixteenth-century and seventeenth-century Spanish and Portuguese poems by Paul Heyse*and Emanuel Geibel. The poems and their subjects divide into sacred texts (ten songs) and secular texts (thirty-four songs). Despite the title, these *Lieder* do not really sound Spanish, but have a color and flavor that sets them apart from Wolf's other collections.

The sacred settings have a gentle but intense fervor, while the secular songs are rhapsodic and overtly romantic. Romain Rolland aptly described the secular songs as "glorious, ardent, capricious, of incredible variety...each one of them has a different face, its own individual character drawn with powerful strokes. The entire work effervesces with life."[14]

With the exception of three gentle portraits of the Holy Family, the sacred settings in this collection are among some of Wolf's most disturbing songs, filled with tense melodies and dissonant accompaniments. The texts deal with spiritual and physical pain, religious ecstasy and guilt. The secular texts are of lighter quality, pictures of love in both its bitter and sweet aspects. Spanish flavor is evoked through dance rhythms and accompaniment patterns that attempt to emulate guitar effects and vocal displays.

*Heyse won the Nobel Prize for Literature in 1910. His poetry was also set by Brahms.

Nun wandre, Maria	You Must Journey On, Mary.
(4 November 1889)	

Joseph's words of encouragement to Mary on the journey to Bethlehem are the text for this song. The Holy Couple cling to one another, their plodding footsteps marked heavily in the piano accompaniment. Softly moving thirds provide continuous movement throughout the song. These intervals are combined with a left-hand accompaniment of octaves and fifths and open chords. The motion stops only momentarily as the word "Bethlehem" calls forth a fermata and the couple anticipates a resting place. Vocal phrases are soothing and small ranged; repeated notes create a reassuring mood. Phrases climb upward as Joseph senses the end of their journey is near. Chromatic harmonies underline Mary's failing strength "Wohl seh ich, Herrin, die Kraft dir schwinden" (Well I see, Lady, your strength is waning), but the journey resumes, harmonically more consonant, buoyed by Joseph's "Getrost!" (Take heart).

The weary couple resolutely wends their way toward the shelter of the little town; Joseph's last phrase "Komm! nah ist der Ort" (Come! shelter is near) is marked "as from a distance." The last few meaures in the piano are in E major (the tonic major) as the tiny caravan moves slowly and softly into the distance, toward welcome rest.

Herr, was trägt der Boden hier   Lord, What Grows in This Ground.
(24 November 1889)

A mere twenty-seven bars of music constitute the compass of this song, which is an intense and concentrated dialogue between Christ and the sinning believer. Wolf characterizes the words of the believer in rather timid questions, marked *piano*: "Lord, what grows in this ground that you water so bitterly?" Christ's replies are also subdued but authoritative: "Thorns, dear heart, for me, and for you the beautiful flowers."

Piercing dissonances are found throughout the song. Questions posed by the sinner are accompanied by an identical rhythmic pattern, sharply dissonant, repeated four times, then resolved. Solemn chords accompany Christ's answers—three times a question, three times an answer, the last response in dark dramatic octaves and a comforting, tender last phrase in simple chords.

In dem Schatten meiner Locken*   In the Shadow of My Tresses.
(17 November 1889)

"In the shadow of my tresses my lover has fallen asleep. Shall I wake him? Ah, no."

A fragment of *bolero* rhythm in the opening measures becomes the unifying rhythmic pattern throughout the song—an appealing character sketch of a young maiden and her thoughts as she watches her sleeping lover. She is torn between tender feelings for his peaceful rest, and a mischievous impulse to waken him. Her questioning thought "Weck ich ihn nun auf? Ach, nein!" is repeated three times, as an ending to each musical section. The first and last repetitions are identical, the middle one differs pitch-wise and triggers a modulation, although the pitch point of the phrase "Weck ich ihn nun auf?" remains steadfastly on the note C.

The mood is light and tender as her thoughts teasingly recount their relationship. Wolf's fluctuating harmonic centers suggest that their union is not always peaceful (she says he calls her a "little snake"). Veiled eroticism in the poem adds another dimension to her decision: They have made love a short time before; if she wakes him, the entire drama will be played out again. For the moment, he is ensnared in her beautiful tresses.

Wolf manipulates texture similarly. Her question is very cautious, lest she wake him. A single chord underlines the declamatory phrase each time and highlights the question. A tiny *piano* phrase underlines her moment of deliberation.

*This text was also set by Johannes Brahms, in the style of a folk song.

Bedeckt mich mit Blumen   Cover Me With Flowers.
(10 November 1889)

The poetic blend of death and flowers calls forth a sensuous setting from Wolf. In the accompaniment, soft cushioned chords suggest the bed of flowers wished for by the singer, who declares he is dying from love—life's sweetest pain. The first vocal phrase is intense and descends chromatically. The highest note in the voice part is reserved for the word "Liebe" which is the same pitch (F). Another languid melody is found in the piano, coupled with chordal accompaniment in an almost solo pianistic style (Sams calls it "Chopinesque"). At several points, the accompaniment shifts register from treble to bass. Vocal phrases are sensuous and chromatic, and thread in and out of the piano's melody. As Sams describes it, "The two intertwine continually a further floral tribute, this time to Wagner."[15]

Geh, Geliebter, geh jetzt	**Go Beloved, Go Now.**
(1 April 1890)	

This song is a fitting conclusion for the Spanish songs. It is a highly dramatic little scene: a young girl pleads with her lover to "Go, the morning is breaking...the town is beginning to stir...I'm afraid our neighbors will be scandalized. Flee from my arms! If you waste time, brief warmth may cost us long distress."

Wolf's setting is operatic in its vocal style and its piano accompaniment is orchestral in texture. This is a big dramatic song with intensely passionate vocal writing and equally romantic accompaniment. Sams observes that there are musical similarities between this song and Mignon's "Kennst du das Land"—parallelism in keys and key changes, their common $\frac{3}{4}$ - $\frac{9}{8}$ meter, and a feeling of impulsive movement in both songs.[16]

The song germinates from the first three bars of the piano prelude, which contains a unifying rhythm and a half-step melodic pattern. Wolf binds mood and texture together in the first section by an extended tonic pedal. "Geh, Geliebter, geh jetzt!" is interleaved between three descriptive stanzas: the bustling opening of the market and its morning sounds; the description of the sorrow his leaving will cause; and the consequences of his staying.

From the *Italienisches Liederbuch*

The *Italienisches Liederbuch* contains forty-six songs, translations from the Italian by Paul Heyse. Wolf composed the Italian songs in two books. Five years separated the composition of the two series. Wolf created the first twenty-two songs between September 1890 and December 1891; the second set of twenty-four songs was finished in a month's time between March and April of 1896.

The *Italian Songbook* contains the most skillfully crafted of all of Wolf's songs, and clearly exhibits his mastery in compressing musical and poetic materials. Each brief song is a highly distilled microcosm of emotion, with texts touching on all aspects of love and relationships. Piano and voice parts operate independently of one another, yet always maintain dialogue with overlapping motives and material. Tiny postludes often add a postscript to the text just heard. Wolf's manipulation of melody, harmony, and rhythm reaches its zenith in these exquisite miniatures.

All the songs are short, but there is great variety in formal structure, which derives from the poetry and the changing moods of the texts. With few exceptions, the songs are through-composed. Unity within the songs is achieved through pedal points, repeated rhythmic figures and accompaniment patterns. Texture is close-knit and often resembles a string quartet in style. Vocal writing in the songs is predominately declamatory, and lacks any sort of broad lyric quality. Most of the songs in the collection typically have two-measure phrases, patterned to conform to poetic form. Tonality in the Italian songs fluctuates and is often dissonant. There are many unprepared modulations, dictated by the text.

Heyse's verses are translations of Italian *rispetti*, (love songs of varying emotions with a verse form of eight lines), *velote* (the Venetian equivalent of the same form), *ritornelle* (songs in folk style), and Corsican songs and death laments.[17] Miniature character portraits are richly drawn in many of the songs, most especially in more humorous texts. Youens observes that over one third of the *Italian Songbook* texts are about women "who revile, dismiss, mock, or reproach their inconsiderate, faithless, and unsatisfactory lovers."[18] Orientation of the texts is split between male and female; some verses are without gender designation. When performed as a complete unit, the songs are generally divided between two singers, soprano and baritone.

Auch kleine Dinge...   **Even Small Things...**
(9 December 1891)

"Little things often delight us" is a fitting introduction to this collection of diminutive *lieder*, striking for their brevity and highly compressed musical style. Words that point up the value of tiny things are set with longer note values: "gern," "schwer," "klein."

An exquisite four-measure introduction in the piano contains the little four-note broken chord motive that remains a unifying constant throughout the song. Changing intervals subtly transform the little pattern until it becomes a chromatic staccato scale that neatly leads into the first vocal phrase.

Wolf even uses descending lines in the piano—some chromatic—to underscore the motivic pattern. Repeated notes in the vocal phrases impart a declamatory quality, but always retain delicate lyricism. Integration of voice and piano produces a close-knit texture of restraint but great expressiveness.

Nun lass uns Frieden schliessen...   **Let Us Make Peace...**
(14 November 1890)

"Let's now make peace, my dearest love; we've quarreled too long..." A rocking accompaniment rhythm creates a soothing atmosphere in which to offer the olive branch. Over-the-bar ties in vocal lines and piano accompaniment fall at different points and create a sustained texture, not unlike a lullaby. This serene mood remains unbroken to the end of the song.

A rock-steady bass line underneath the lilting rhythmic pattern in the right hand suggests that this relationship has been solid in the past. Questioning vocal phrases—"bekriegen?", "missraten?", "nicht vollbringt?"—end on a rising interval. The vocal line is questioning and somewhat hesitant in the last phrase, and the piano pattern repeats, turning around twice before finding a conclusive cadence.

Wie lange schon...   **How Long Have I Yearned...**
(4 December 1891)

The heroine of this song is comic in her yearning for the "ideal" lover—a musician! Now her wish has been granted and she describes her shy suitor; he approaches delicately, with downcast demeanor, playing the violin.

The meter is $\frac{2}{4}$. Unifying accompaniment patterns are pattern of three eighth notes in the right hand, initiated with an over-the-bar tie (these change register and also appear as octave figures), and a three-chord pattern (eighth-eighth-quarter) in the bass line. The rhythmic stresses of these two patterns, combined with a vocal line of displaced accents and repeated notes, create a character whose complaint verges on becoming ludicrous. Her announcement of her sweetheart's approach calls for a change in accompaniment texture, a hesitating little walking theme under her one-and-only really lyric phrase.

Wolf's postlude is probably his most brilliant comic writing. The ardent violinist plays his well-rehearsed piece. Marked "with great difficulty and hesitancy," it contains misplaced accents as he assiduously avoids that horror of horrors, a wrong note. Finally he triumphantly concludes with his "big finish," a slow trill. This match is probably made in rhythmic heaven—her vocal lines are peppered with syncopated stresses and over-the-bar accents.

The character in this song bears some resemblance to the young girl in "Ich esse nun mein Brot," whose humorous text is another wish for a lover—"a little old man aged, say, about fourteen years or so."

Mein Liebster singt...   **My Love Is Singing...**
(12 December 1891)

A rhapsodic, Chopin-like piano accompaniment takes center stage in this song; the vocal line is like a declamatory descant. A young girl yearningly listens as her lover sings beneath her window. As his song wafts upward, she turns away from her mother and weeps. Her tears blind her to whether it is still night or daybreak; she weeps with longing, tears of blood.

The piano takes the part of the lover; his passionate serenade is immediately recognized by the girl, whose first vocal phrase begins on the second beat. At several points, the serenader forlornly repeats a fragment of his melody. Wolf threads the vocal phrases through the luxurious accompaniment in brilliant fashion; both voice and piano retain their independence, and, although they overlap subtly, they never meet conclusively, just as the two young people
also remain separated.

Heut nacht erhob ich mich...   **Tonight I Rose at Midnight...**
(25 April 1896)

This song is an example of Wolf's "string quartet" sound. Linear orientation in the accompaniment produces a beautifully woven contrapuntal texture not unlike that found in chamber music. In only eighteen measures, Wolf captures an intimate avowal of love in a dialogue between a man and his heart. The musical essence of the song lies in Wolf's harmonic fluctuations, through which the melodic lines in the voice and those in the piano are subtly woven.

A two-measure introduction begins in what seems to be D minor, but resolves in the second measure to A major. Its calm pattern provides the material for the first vocal phrase. Wolf's subtle manipulation of sonorities produces a kind of musical *chiaroscuro* (distribution of light and dark). This is perhaps the most concise of all of Wolf's songs—a quiet nocturnal scene of great expressive power.

Ich hab in Penna...	I Have a Lover Who Lives in Penna...
(25 April 1896)	

This much-loved song presents a female counterpart of Don Giovanni, reveling in her conquests in a "catalogue aria" art song. As she reels off the list of her lovers, the breathless tempo never flags, nor does the machine-gun quickness of the vocal declamation. Piano and voice conspire to comment with one another as the phrases build cumulatively. An accompaniment pattern in thirds serves to remind us of Italian musical style and the strumming of a stringed instrument. Her teasing fickle character is seen in the spiky shapes and intervals of the vocal line. Her tirade continues toward the long held note which heralds her most triumphant achievement— "ten in Castiglione!" and the pianist is left to perform a brilliant virtuoso postlude whose structure leaves no doubt that this girl couldn't care less about any of it.

This song is a dazzling finish for the *Italienisches Liederbuch.*

Extended Study List

Morgentau • Mausfallen-Sprüchlein • Wiegenlied im Sommer • Fussreise (Möricke) • Der Tambour (Möricke) • Ein Stündlein wohl vor Tag (Möricke) • Der Knabe und das Immlein (Möricke) • An eine Aolsharfe (Möricke) • Agnes (Möricke) • Nixe Binsefuss (Möricke) • Gesang Weylas (Möricke) • Storchenbotschaft (Möricke) • Um Mitternacht (Möricke) • Zitronenfalter im April (Möricke) • Auf eine Christblume I and II (Möricke) • In der Frühe (Möricke) • Der Feuerreiter (Möricke) • Heimweh (Eichendorff) • Erwartung (Eichendorff) • Das Ständchen (Eichendorff) • Harfenspieler I, II, III (Goethe) • Cophtisches Lied I and I (Goethe) • Gleich und Gleich (Goethe) • Prometheus (Goethe) • Ganymed (Goethe) • Ach, des Knaben Augen...(*Spanisches Liederbuch*) • Mühvoll komm ich und beladen... (*Spanisches Liederbuch*) • Kling klinge, mein Pandero (*Spanisches Liederbuch*) • Wenn du zu den Blumen gehst (*Spanisches Liederbuch*) • Sagt, seid ihr es, feiner Herr... (*Spanisches Liederbuch*) • Mögen alle bösen Zungen...(*Spanisches Liederbuch*) • Trau nicht der Liebe...(*Spanisches Liederbuch*) • Sie blasen zum Abmarsch (*Spanisches Liederbuch*) • Wie glänzt der helle Mond (Keller Songs) • Wer rief dich denn... (*Italienisches Liederbuch*) • Nein, junger Herr... (*Italienisches Liederbuch*) • Ihr jungen Leute.. (*Italienisches Liederbuch*) • Mein Liebster ist so klein... (*Italienisches Liederbuch*) • Heb' auf dein blondes Haupt... (*Italienisches Liederbuch*) • Ich esse nun mein Brot... (*Italienisches Liederbuch*) • Mein Liebster hat zu Tische... (*Italienisches Liederbuch*) • Du sagst mir... (*Italienisches Liederbuch*) • Sterb' ich, so hüllt in Blumen... (*Italienisches Liederbuch*) • Wenn du mich mit den Augen streifst... (*Italienisches Liederbuch*) • Schweig einmal still... (*Italienisches Liederbuch)* • *The Michelangelo Songs*

Selected Reading

Mosco Carner, *Hugo Wolf Songs* (London: British Broadcasting Corporation, 1982).

Beaumont Glass, *Wolf's Complete Song Texts* (Geneseo, NY: Leyerle Publications, 2000).

William W. McIver, "The Declamation in Selected Songs from Hugo Wolf's *Italienisches Liederbuch,*" *The NATS Bulletin,* 34:2 (December 1977).

Timothy R. McKinney, "On the Value of Harmonic Analysis for Interpreting Hugo Wolf's Songs," *The NATS Journal,* 49:4 (March/April 1993).

Ernest Newman, *Hugo Wolf,* rev. ed. (New York: Dover Publications, 1966).

Henry Pleasants, ed. *The Music Criticism of Hugo Wolf* (New York: Holmes & Meier Publishers, 1979).

Eric Sams, *The Songs of Hugo Wolf.* Revised and enlarged edition. (London: Eulenburg Books, 1993). Classic reference to Wolf's compositional style in his songs.

Deborah J. Stein, *Hugo Wolf's Lieder and Extensions of Tonality* (Ann Arbor: UMI Research Press, 1985).

Louise McClelland Urban, English ed. and trans., *Hugo Wolf : Letters to Melanie Köchert.* Franz Grasberg, ed.(New York: Schirmer Books, 1991).

Allie Wise, "The Culmination of the Lied: Wolf's *Italienisches Liederbuch,*" *The NATS Bulletin,* 36:3 (Jan/Feb 1980).

Susan Youens, Hugo Wolf: *The Vocal Music* (Princeton: Princeton University Press, 1992). An examination of Wolf's songs, ranging from the beginning to the end of his creative career.

Notes

1. In a letter to Rosa Mayreder (the librettist of his opera *Der Corregidor*). Quoted in Harold C. Schonberg, *The Lives of the Great Composers*, 292.
2. Eric Sams, *The Songs of Hugo Wolf*, 2.
3. Elaine Brody and Robert Fowkes, *The German Lied and Its Poetry*, 260.
4. Martin Katz, foreward to *Hugo Wolf: Letters to Melanie Köchert*, ed. Franz Grasberg.English edition and trans. by Louise McClelland Urban
5. Gerald Moore, *Singer and Accompanist*, 217.
6. Sams, 59.
7. Quoted in Sams, 73. Schumann's setting (Op. 64, No. 2), is also titled "Das verlassene Mägdlein."
8. Sams, ibid., 76.
9. Ibid., 100.
10. Brody and Fowkes, *The German Lied and Its Poetry*, 290.
11. Ibid., 282.
12. Sams, 215.
13. Susan Youens, *Hugo Wolf: The Vocal Music*, 93.
14. Joachim Draheim. Liner notes to *Hugo Wolf: Spanisches Liederbuch / Manuel Venegas*. Mitsuko Shirai, mezzo-soprano, Hartmut Höll, pianist. Capriccio Recording. Compact disc 10-362, 1990.
15. Sams, 292.
16. Ibid., 302.
17. William W. McIver, "The Declamation in Selected Songs from Hugo Wolf's *Italienisches Liederbuch*," *The NATS Bulletin*, 34:2, 32-33.
18. Youens, *Hugo Wolf: The Vocal Music*, 75.

GUSTAV MAHLER (1860-1911)

> It is a funny thing, but when I am making music, all the answers I seek for in life seem to be there, in the music. Or rather, I should say, when I am making music, there are no questions and no need for answers.
>
> —Gustav Mahler[1]

Gustav Mahler was a brilliant composer and conductor. A man of quicksilver moods, he was by turns introverted and irascible, compassionate and generous, and frequently overwhelmed by his own genius and his unending search for perfection. He was viewed as tyrannical by musicians he conducted. His musical style was forged in prewar Vienna, which was then the center of the intellectual and artistic world. There he lived and worked with an extraordinary array of musicians, artists, and writers—among them composers Richard Strauss, Alexander Zemlinsky, Arnold Schoenberg, Alban Berg, Anton Webern, Gustave Charpentier, Antonín Dvořák, Hugo von Hofmannsthal, Richard Dehmel, and Gustav Klimt. Here too he met and married Alma Schindler, celebrated as "the most beautiful woman in Vienna."

As a composer and conductor, Mahler traveled throughout Europe—Germany, Russia, Holland, Poland, and Belgium—provoking adulation and controversy. In 1897 he occupied the post of the musical director of the Vienna Court Opera. He later accepted appointment at the Metropolitan Opera House in New York and also conducted the New York Philharmonic Society concerts. He died in Vienna in 1911.

With the exception of some early songs with piano, Mahler's songs are found in his major orchestral cycles. *Lieder eines fahrenden Gesellen* (Songs of a Wayfarer) is considered by many to be the first authentic orchestral song cycle.

In his early twenties Mahler discovered *Des Knaben Wunderhorn*, a famous collection of ballads and folk songs dating from about 1509, collected by Ludwig Archim von Arnim and Klemens Brentano and published during the first decade of the nineteenth century. The *Wunderhorn* anthology was to inspire Mahler with subject matter for both his symphonies and songs for the rest of his life.

There are twenty-four *Wunderhorn-Lieder.* Mahler's settings are not arrangements of folk songs nor do they have folk-tune quotations. Instead, he set the texts as though they belonged to the present moment. Mahler is said to have preferred a male voice for these songs.

Biographer Henry-Louis de la Grange observes that, in their epic style and dimensions, Mahler's *Wunderhorn* songs claim close kinship to the great ballads of Schubert and Loewe. "Mahler felt at home in the colorful, alive world of the Arnim-Brentano anthology. In it he found striking glimpses of man and his earthly destiny, both humorous and tragic, and reflections on the human condition which are often more vivid and profound than those conveyed by literary poetry."[2]

Both Mahler and Richard Strauss supplied orchestrations for many of their songs, removing the songs from the intimacy of a small performance space and into the more dramatic venue of the concert hall. Characteristics of solo song with piano are both reduced and enhanced by the larger "sound canvas" of orchestral instruments, and it remains for the listener to decide which version they prefer.

It is helpful to know the original performance medium for Mahler songs. In the case of the later *Wunderhorn* songs and the *Rückert-Lieder,* the original version is for orchestra and voice, and in performance with piano, some of these songs lose a great deal of impact and color.

The songs of Gustav Mahler number less than fifty, and seem to fall rather neatly into three main groups:

1880-1885	Three books of *Lieder und Gesänge aus der Jugendzeit* for voice and piano (including nine settings from *Des Knaben Wunderhorn*), *Lieder eines fahrenden Gesellen* (Songs of a Wayfarer) for voice and orchestra
1889-1899	Fourteen more settings of *Wunderhorn* poems (with orchestra)
1901-1904	*Kindertotenlieder* (Rückert) for voice and orchestra *Rückert-Lieder*

Mahler was primarily a lyricist, and all his songs display his melodic gift. His melodies are simple, but demanding, many have a folk-like character (*Ländler* dance tunes are incorporated into many songs). He frequently uses word painting in his *Lieder.*

Most of Mahler's songs are lengthy, and are written for heavy voices that have extensive range and dynamic facility. Mahler was quite specific in marking scores for tempo and symphonic style, and wrote accompaniments that continually comment on the text or heighten the emotional content of the words. Many of these songs feature two-part linear texture ion which vocal line and accompaniment interweave.

Mahler chose texts from later romantic poets, but avoided poetry that had already been set by other composers. His vocal lines contain expressive figures and careful attention to declamation and word stress.

Wer hat dies Liedlein erdacht?   **Who Thought Up This Song? 1892**
(**Lieder aus *Des Knaben Wunderhorn***)

This happy little song is one of Mahler's best-known. Its text comes from two *Wunderhorn* poems, "Wer hat dies Liedlein erdacht?" and "Wie Lieben erdacht." Mahler uses the first and last stanzas of the first poem but replaces the middle one with stanzas from the second poem (from the line "Mein Herzle ist wund" to "Macht

Kranke gesund"). The rhythm is a *Ländler* in $\frac{3}{8}$, *Mit heiterm Behagen* (With easy gaiety); *Gemächlich* (Moderate) for the middle stanza.

Mahler gives the singer two extended coloratura vocalises; the last ends the song with a triumphant flourish. The overall mood is good-humored; even the second section, which is more subdued and plaintive, has an underlying gaiety. The vocal line is tuneful and fresh. Unity is created by continuous movement in the accompaniment and some manipulation of motives. Mahler produces variety by inserting some dissonances against the charming diatonic melody in the voice—is this a little commentary?

Das irdische Leben   **Earthly Life. 1893**
(Lieder aus *Des Knaben Wunderhorn*)

This is surely one of song literature's most intense settings, a harsh indictment of the world's injustice. The meter is $\frac{2}{4}$, and Mahler's tempo markings in the piano version are: *Unheimlich bewegt* (Uncannily agitated) quarter note=104; *Nicht zu schnell, doch in stetig gleicher Bewegung* (not too fast, but always in the same tempo).

The text is a dialogue between a starving child and his mother, set with astonishing realism. The starving child's cries, which increase in desperation, are always in the minor key, while the mother's answers are in the relative major. As the tension mounts, Mahler varies the melodic lines; the child's pleas "Gib mir Brot" modulate until the final high G-flat, but the the mother's responses remain unyielding and repetitive—"Warte nur." Against this dialogue the unvarying monotony of the accompaniment figure (a sixteenth-note ostinato) perpetuates the horror of the scene.

Mahler commented about this song:

The text only suggests the deeper meaning, the treasure that must be searched for. Thus, I picture as a symbol of human life the child's cry for bread and the mother's attempt to console him with promises. I named the song "Das irdische Leben" for precisely that reason. What I wished to express is that the necessities for one's physical and spiritual growth are long delayed, and finally come too late, as they do for the dead child. I believe I have expressed this in a characteristic and frightening way...[3]

From the *Rückert-Lieder*

The next three songs belong to Mahler's *Rückert-Lieder*, composed between 1901 and 1904 , and unrelated to Mahler's folk influences. The Rückert songs have a lyricism and grace totally unique in Mahler's vocal works. Each song's form is determined by the poetic content. These songs were originally composed for orchestra and voice and first performed in Vienna in 1905. Each song is scored for a specific combination of instruments, which enhances the poetic mood and gives the songs a chamber-music transparency and intimate character; this makes transference to the voice-piano medium generally successful.

The songs form a collection rather than a cycle, and according to different sources, are often ordered differently. The poetry presents an array of subtle moods, all written in the first person, and obviously deeply personal to the poet. The

Rückert Lieder coincide in time frame with Mahler's composition of the *Kindertotenlieder*.

Ich atmet' einen linden Duft'
(Friedrich Rückert)

I Breathed a Sweet Scent. 1901

In shimmering accompaniment figures and delicate vocal lines, Mahler captures the delicacy of Rückert's verse—the scent of the lime branch placed on the poet's desk by his wife on his birthday. The text is full of the word play of "Linde" (lime-tree) and the adjective "lind" (mild, tender). The subtle perfume of the lime branch is synonymous with the scent of love.

The poem must have had personal connotations for Mahler as well. In a letter of 1879, he referred to a habit of climbing into the branches of a lime tree and looking "out on the world from my friendly tree-top."[4]

The orchestral version of this song is scored to create a transparent, evocative texture: single woodwind with a pair of bassoons, three horns, violins, violas, harp and celeste. The vocal line is submerged in this texture, with a layered and interactive accompaniment. This is less apparent in the piano-voice version.

Liebst du um Schönheit
(Friedrich Rückert)

If You Love for Beauty's Sake. 1902

In 1902 Mahler married Alma Schindler, and composed this tender love song for her shortly afterwards. Poetically, mood modulates with the poet's thoughts, culminating in the final melismatic climax, "dich lieb ich immerdar!" (I will always love you).

Dynamics remain intimate, scarcely rising above *piano* for the entire *Lied*. The key is C major with few modulations to speak of, but there are seventeen changes of meter in thirty-four bars. The tempo is *Innig, fliessend* (tender, flowing).

Mahler employs simple strophic form—three verses of six bars each and a fourth that is extended to nine bars for expressive purposes. Each verse is built of three ascending phrases followed by a fourthphrase, which descends. This order is changed in the last verse with the third phrase falling and the fourth rising to the last fervent "immerdar." The final phrase hangs suspended while the accompaniment resolves.

Although this song is quiet and lyrical, it is intensely passionate. Alma Mahler kept the autograph manuscript on her living room wall in New York.

Ich bin der Welt abhanden gekommen	I Have Become Lost
(Friedrich Rückert)	to the World. 1901

Generally conceded to be Mahler's greatest song, this *Lied* blends emotions from two planes of thought: nostalgia and regret on one hand; on the other, longing for inner completion and peace. The poet yearns for the internal world of art and love, reached through introspection and tranquillity.

Mahler set Rückert's poetry ten times and identified closely with its subtlety and delicate lyricism. The choice of through-composed form for this song seems fitting, for the poem and and music have a sense of arrested movement. There are three distinct sections, the second with a slightly faster tempo gradually accelerating to the third, which has been characterized as a long coda. Vocal phrases are sustained and lyric. Mahler's combination of musical elements gives the ending an effect of timelessness—patterns which in the prelude were ascending, now descend in the last section, ending with a long suspended fifth.

This song is the longest of all the *Rückert-Lieder*. It has been called autobiographical—during this time Mahler was embroiled in controversies with the Vienna Opera and the Philharmonic. It is certainly one of Mahler's finest and most deeply felt songs, which Charles Osborne has called the "quintessential Mahler *Lied* of farewell and withdrawal from the world."[5]

Extended Study List

Lieder eines fahrenden Gesellen • *Kindertotenlieder* • *Lieder aus Des Knaben Wunderhorn* • *Das Lied von der Erde* • Erinnerung • Hans und Grete • Ablösung im Sommer • Selbstgefühl • Scheiden und Meiden

Selected Reading

Elisabeth Mary Dargie, *Music and Poetry in the Songs of Gustav Mahler* (Peter Lang, Berne, 1981).

Henry-Louis de la Grange, *Gustav Mahler: Vienna, the years of challenge* (New York: Oxford University Press, 1995).

Michael Kennedy, *Mahler* (London: J. M. Dent, 1974). Master Musicians series.

Norman Lebrecht, *Mahler Remembered* (London: Faber & Faber, 1987).

Christopher Lewis, "Gustav Mahler: Romantic Culmination," in *German Lieder in the Nineteenth Century,* ed. Rufus Hallmark (New York: Schirmer Books, 1996), 218-249.

Donald Mitchell, *Gustav Mahler: The Wunderhorn Years* (Boulder, Colorado: Westview Press, 1976).

_____, *Gustav Mahler: Songs and Symphonies of Life and Death.* Vol. 3 (Berkeley: University of California Press, 1985).

Alma Mahler Werfel, *And the Bridge is Love* (New York: Harcourt & Brace, 1958).

_____, *Gustav Mahler: Memories and Letters,* ed. Donald Mitchell, trans. Basil Creighton (New York: Viking Press, 1969).

Notes

1. In a letter to Bruno Walter, quoted in *The NATS Journal* 33:3, 19.
2. Henry-Louis de la Grange, *Gustav Mahler: Vienna, the years of challenge*, 731.
3. Ibid., 742.
4. Quoted in Jack Diether, liner notes to *Dietrich Fischer-Dieskau / Leonard Bernstein in a Recital of Mahler Songs.* Columbia LP recording KM 30942.
5. Charles Osborne, *The Concert Song Companion*, 113.

RICHARD STRAUSS (1864-1949)

Where there is music, it must carry all before it; it must not come after the poetry.

—Richard Strauss[1]

Musical ideas, like young wine, should be put in storage and taken up again only after they have been allowed to ferment and ripen.

—Richard Strauss[2]

Richard Strauss's operas were his greatest contribution to vocal music, notably those written in collaboration with librettist Hugo von Hofmannsthal, one of Austria's greatest poets—*Elektra, Der Rosenkavalier, Ariadne auf Naxos, Die Frau ohne Schatten, Die Ägyptische Helena,* and *Arabella.* Strauss also composed over 100 *Lieder* for voice and piano, many of which he later orchestrated. He also composed a number of songs for voice and orchestra, including his valedictory work, *Vier letze Lieder* (Four Last Songs).

The inspiration for many of his songs was his wife, soprano Pauline de Ahna. They met in 1894 when Pauline sang the role of Elisabeth in Wagner's *Tannhäuser* at the Bayreuth Festival with Strauss conducting. A month later they were married; the union lasted over fifty years. De Ahna was known for her fiery temperament; Strauss's opera *Intermezzo* is an autobiographical work referencing their often-stormy marriage. Strauss and his wife also collaborated artistically for many years, which allowed them to travel together all over the world. Most of his *Lieder* were conceived for her voice.

For the most part, Strauss's songs were composed before 1900. During his most productive "song period" (1899-1901), he produced six different collections containing thirty-one songs. Nearly all of these (Op. 10 to Op. 49) were published within two years—and some within a few months—after they were written. All of the songs display his passionate lyricism and feature richly-textured accompaniments.

In addition to his operas, Strauss's dramatic ability is also seen in his vividly descriptive tone poems, among them: *Also sprach Zarathustra* (1895), *Don Quixote* (1897), *Tod und Verklärung* 1889, *Till Eulenspiegel's lustige Streiche* (1895), and *Don Juan* (1888).

Strauss did not experiment a great deal in his songs as he did in his works for instruments, although his orchestral compositions certainly influenced his *Lieder,* notably in matters of texture and color. His major contribution to the *Lied* was in his development of songs with orchestral accompaniment; in this practice, Strauss continued in the line of Berlioz and Mahler. Many of his songs originally written for voice and piano are more popular in their orchestrated versions.

During his lifetime, his compositions made him famous and wealthy; Strauss was the most publicized composer of the early twentieth century. His skillful, colorful orchestral style was a hallmark of his music, and through his instrumental works, he transformed the orchestra into a giant virtuoso ensemble.

Orchestral *Lieder*

As the century drew to its close, composers sought out a larger public than the song recital had been able to reach. Through orchestral *Lieder* they could manipulate a greater range of colors, textures and intensities than with the piano. Many critics opposed songs in this version, seeing total incompatibility between the intimacy of the *Lied* and its performance with orchestra. Rudolf Louis, the reactionary Munich composer-critic, wrote as late as 1909: "An orchestral accompaniment represents a danger for a purely lyrical text...There arises all too easily a disturbing inconguity between the intimate content of the text and demands for intensity made today upon [orchestral] media..."[3]

There were other reasons for orchestrating songs. In the early 1890s, Strauss set some of his songs orchestrally for his wife Pauline to sing at the many concerts he was invited to conduct. Strauss orchestrated twenty-seven of his *Lieder* and wrote fifteen others for voice and orchestra.

Zueignung, Op. 10, No. 1   **Dedication. 1882-83**
(Hermann von Gilm)

Op. 10 was Strauss's first collection of songs, composed at age eighteen. He expressly stated that he had the tenor voice in mind for this opus, although all voice types sing these songs with great pleasure.

"Zueignung" is one of his most familiar songs. The first two stanzas share identical opening phrases (four bars); the second verse is varied only slightly. The third stanza begins with the identical first phrase, then moves to an exultant high note climax (an example of word-painting on the word "Heilig"— holy) emphatically underscored with thick-texture repeated chords in the piano. Each stanza ends with the refrain "Habe Dank!" which was Gilm's original title for the poem.

The poet's solemn dedication to the loved one is set in broad vocal phrases, underlined with an accompaniment of octaves and triplets. Strauss retains the accompaniment of the first verse and uses it for the second, altering it only with one varied vocal phrase.

Die Nacht, Op. 10, No. 3   **Night. 1882-83**
(Hermann von Gilm)

This song quite early in Strauss's song output and is a fine example of his skill at intimate settings. Poetic mood is gentle, but tinged with the fear that the night, which steals beauty and light from the woods and town, will also steal the beloved.

Overall texture in this song is lean. The stealthy approach of night is announced by a single repeated note in the piano. With each measure it gathers weight, becoming thirds, chords, then a bass line with chords.

Strauss's manipulation of harmonic changes is subtle and beautifully integrated in the accompaniment—and with the voice, especially in the final measures. One of Strauss's style "fingerprints" is here in the last two phrases, in which he appends the first word of the last phrase ("O die Nacht, mir bangt, sie stehle/Dich") to the penultimate phrase.

Allerseelen, Op. 10, No. 8   **All Souls' Day. 1882-83**
(Hermann von Gilm)

All Souls' Day, November 2, is the day consecrated to the dead. Del Mar describes this poem as "a love song set against a background of graveside flower, and memories of May-time love." [7] The singer tries to use the day to his advantage and revive a love affair which has also died.

This is one of Strauss's early songs, verging on the too-sentimental, but saved by its glowing lyricism. The mood is intimate and tranquil. The piano introduction quotes melodic material from the vocal phrase that begins the last stanza "Es blüht und duftet heut auf jedem Grabe" (Today every grave is decked with fragrant blossoms). There is a vibrant climax reached at "Komm an mein Herz, dass ich dich wieder habe" (Come to my heart and let me hold you again). The piano ends with four measures of shifting harmonies that finally come to rest, but a little inconclusively, like the lover's question.

German composer and opera conductor Robert Heger orchestrated this song in 1932. Strauss liked the orchestral version and conducted it at his own concerts.

Ständchen, Op. 17, No. 2   **Serenade. 1885-87**
(Adolf Friedrich von Schack)

"Ständchen" is probably Strauss's most popular song—certainly one of his most familiar. It was orchestrated not by the composer, but by Felix Mottl, the Wagnerian conductor who also set four of Wagner's *Wesendonck Lieder* for orchestra and voice. Numerous arrangements of "Ständchen" exist for other combinations of instruments.

A feathery accompaniment of broken-chord arpeggio figures in the treble register wafts the serenade to the beloved's window. Vocal phrases are light and delicately shaped. In tandem with the piano figures, they create a sense of urgency and complete the ardent mood. "Open up, my love, but softly so that you wake no one...Treading soft as elves, fly lightly into the moonlit night, steal out to me in the garden..."

There are no real harmonic surprises in this song—all is buoyant melody. Strauss marks the tempo *Vivace e dolce,* in $\frac{6}{8}$ - $\frac{9}{8}$ time. There are three stanzas; the first two are identical; the third stanza changes mood and phrase shapes, and the piano pattern migrates to the bass register for several phrases. Unity is maintained through this piano pattern, which remains constant until the postlude. The final measures use melodic material from the last phrases of the first two stanzas.

Op. 17 consists of six songs for high voice, all to poems by Schack.

Morgen!, Op. 27, No. 4   **Morning. 1893-94**
(John Henry Mackay)*

Strauss completed Op. 27 when he was twenty-eight years old. It was also the year of his marriage to Pauline de Anha, and these songs were his wedding gift to her. Three were composed in May 1894 shortly before they left Weimar to return to Munich via Bayreuth; "Cäcilie" was added at the last minute on September 9. Strauss's dedication was: "To my beloved Pauline, 10 September 1894." Four *Lieder* constitute the set: "Ruhe, meine Seele," "Cäcilie," "Heimliche Aufforderung," and "Morgen!"

"Morgen!" has been described as "motionless ecstasy." The poem relates of the hope of two lovers that morning will see them close united, lost to the world in each other's eyes. Strauss's exquisite piano prelude seems suspended in time. It is sixteen bars long, almost half the song's total length, but it firmly establishes the atmosphere of wonder and deep rapture. The first entry of the voice emerges seamlessly from the piano and subsequent vocal phrases join the piano in an integrated texture. The manner in which the voice begins makes us believe it will only comment on the beauty of the scene, but it quickly establishes its own lyricism in the middle of the piano's textural range. Vocal phrases seem longer than they are due to varying rhythmic stress and phrasing over the bar lines.

Strauss chose a through-composed form for his setting. The flowing calm comes to an end in the last measures—a little coda—where the vocal line becomes chant-like and declamatory, ending poised on the leading tone. It remains for the piano to resolve the cadence, and add several measures of postlude, which brings the song to an end "that is no end"—a $\frac{6}{4}$ chord.

*Despite his name, John Henry Mackay was a German poet, born in Scotland of a Scottish father and a German mother. After the sudden death of his father, his mother and two-year-old Mackay returned to Germany where he grew up. In addition to "Morgen!" Strauss set another Mackay poem, "Heimliche Aufforderung."

Cäcilie, Op. 27, No. 2   **Cecily. 1892-93**
(Heinrich Hart)

"Cäcilie" is part of Strauss's popular Op. 27; this particular song was a last-minute composition, added to the group on the eve of his wedding. It features one of Strauss's passionate vocal lines, operatic in style with long-lined phrases and emotion to burn. The piano accompaniment is thick in texture and orchestral in feeling—indeed, Strauss orchestrated this song three years after its publication. There are three stanzas, marked "Very fast and lively" and most performers take this too much to heart; the tempo is quite difficult to sustain with control.

The middle section of the song is riddled with quick modulations. Much of rhythm of the vocal line and in the accompaniment is derived from the triplet rhythm of the words in the first phrase "*Wenn du es* wüsstest..." The constant rhythm helps the voice avoid being covered by the piano accompaniment. There is a bravura ending for both voice and piano. "Cäcilie" is distinctively Straussian in its effusive lyricism and passionate movement.

Befreit, Op. 39, No. 4   **Freed. 1897-98**
(Richard Dehmel)

This is one of Strauss's greatest songs. The essence of the poem is one of deep devotion which has "freed" the loving pair from suffering—a relationship that will soon be severed by death, but a bond that will remain eternal. The firm serenity of the music reflects the immortal quality of their love despite the poignant sorrow of the moment.

A theme, written in a chordal pattern in measure 9, recurs at various spots, but the true refrain lies in the bittersweet phrase "O Gluck" (O happiness), which crowns each verse of the song. Strauss extracted the melodic line that accompanies this and repeats it for each verse, in different keys. Marked *Langsam und innig,* the vocal phrases have considerable breadth and dramatic intensity. This song requires a mature singer both for the music and the poetry. "Befreit" was orchestrated in 1933.

Schlechtes Wetter, Op. 69, No. 5　　　　　　　　**Awful Weather. 1918-19**
(Heinrich Heine)

As the song begins, sheets of rain slap furiously against the windowpane, leaving no doubt as to the weather outside. Strauss's piano writing is brilliantly virtuosic, and the vocal phrases are quintessential Strauss—broadly lyric and flexible in shape. Angularity in the beginning vocal phrases point up the nasty weather beating against the pane.

Someone—a young girl?—sits at the window, staring into the darkness. From what she sees, she concocts an imagined story. It is a whimsical scene: a mother is in the street, gingerly making her way with a lantern. "She's probably buying flour eggs and butter for a cake to bake for her plump, golden-haired daughter who's at home dozing in front of a roaring fire." The character's description is punctuated by a little dissonances.

As her daydream unfolds, the strands of angry weather in the piano and angular phrases in the voice merge into a Straussian waltz, à la *Rosenkavalier*. In its romantic, sweeping melody, there is subtle humor. This story can't be real—it's a bit of fluff.

Continual use of diminutives ("Lichtchen," "Mütterchen," "Laternchen") in the poem is not only alliterative but creates an airy atmosphere that Strauss echoes in his setting.

Strauss's word-painting is subtle: the piano figures gradually melt into the waves of the maiden's golden hair, and the high little chirruping figures depict her blinking eyes. The piano continues the waltz fantasy as a little postlude, but it soon dissolves and reality returns instantly in the last measures as her frustration with the dismal weather continues.

This is one of Strauss's most delightful songs, well-known and frequently performed.

Extended Study List

Vier letzte Lieder (Four Last Songs - orchestra) • Ich trage meine Minne • Heimkehr • Ich wollt ein Sträusslein binden • Breit über mein Haupt • Du meines Herzens Krönelein • Meinem Kinde • *Ophelien Lieder* • Amor • Säusle, liebe Myrthe! • Wie sollten wir geheim sie halten • Traum durch die Dämmerung • Hat gesagt – bleibt's nicht dabei • Ruhe, meine Seele • Kling! • Die Zeitlose • Für fünfzehn Pfennige • Schlagende Herzen

Selected Reading

Norman Del Mar, *Richard Strauss: a critical commentary on his life and works* (Ithaca, NY: Cornell University Press, 1986). In three volumes. See Volume 3, Chapter 20: "A Lifetime of Lieder Writing."

Bryan Gilliam, ed., *Richard Strauss: New Perspectives on the Composer and His Work* (Durham, NC: Duke University Press, 1992).

Hanns Hammelmann and Ewald Osers, trans., *The Correspondence between Richard Strauss and Hugo von Hofmannsthal* (Cambrdige: Cambridge University Press, 1980).

Alan Jefferson, *The Lieder of Richard Strauss* (New York: Praeger, 1971). Detailed study of selected *Lieder,* with texts and translations, grouped by text subject.

Michael Kennedy, *Richard Strauss* (London: J. M. Dent, 1976). Master Musicians Series.

Barbara A. Petersen, *Ton und Wort: The Lieder of Richard Strauss* (Ann Arbor, Michigan: University Microfilm International Research Press, 1980).

_____, "Richard Struss: A Lifetime of Lied Composition," in *German Lieder in the Nineteenth Century*, ed. Rufus Hallmark (New York: Schirmer Brooks, 1996), 250-278.

Richard Strauss, Recollections and Reflections, ed. Willi Schuh. English trans. by L.J. Lawrence (Westport, Connecticut: Greenwood Press, 1977).

Notes

1. Quoted in Lorraine Gorrell, *The Nineteenth-Century German Lied*, 327.
2. Richard Strauss, "The Composer Speaks" in David Ewen, *The New Book of Modern Composers*, 3rd edition, 396.
3. Quoted in Henry-Louis de la Grange, *Gustav Mahler: Vienna, the years of challenge*, 734.
4. Norman Del Mar, *Richard Strauss: a critical commentary on his life and work* (Cornell University Press, 1986), 266.

HANS PFITZNER (1869-1949)

> The more the composer devotes himself to the word, the more he must cling to the word as a consequence of lack of musicality, so much more is the virtue of the song endangered...naturalness becomes "good declamation," characterization becomes word-painting, atmosphere becomes manipulation of the audience...
>
> —Hans Pfitzner[1]

Hans Pfitzner was an unconditional romantic in the tradition of Schumann, Brahms, and Wagner, and was well-known for his criticism of modern tendencies. His music is grounded in the harmonic style of the Romantic period, but filtered through his own individualism and subtle style.

Pfitzner was a composer and conductor. Early studies with his father, a violinist and music director at the Frankfurt Municipal Theater, and later studies at the Hoch Conservatory, led to teaching positions in Coblenz, Mainz, Berlin, and Strasbourg. In Strasbourg, he was director of the Conservatory and conducted the symphony orchestra. In 1910, he was made director of the opera as well; in 1914, he appointed Otto Klemperer as his deputy.

In Strasbourg, Pfitzner composed his most successful and important work, the musical legend *Palestrina*, written to his own libretto and conducted at its first performance by Bruno Walter. Production problems preclude many performances of this gargantuan work, although it has remained in the German repertory; *Palestrina* requires a large orchestra, lavish cast and huge production facilities. Pfitzner's work is not a tribute to the Palestrina as much as an exploration of the ideal realization of the artist's freedom both in self-determination and in responsibility to humanity.[2]

Pfitzner was professor of composition at the Munich Academy 1929-34. The Nazis upheld his music as in the best German tradition and contrasted it with the "degeneracy" of Strauss. After World War II, Pfitzner was found penniless in a Munich home for the aged by the president of the Vienna Philharmonic, who took him to Vienna where he was supported by the orchestra.[3]

Although Pfitzner composed choral works and operas, his crowning achievement in vocal writing is his large body of songs. Pfitzner composed one hundred *Lieder* for voice and piano and wrote fifteen orchestral songs. His early *Lieder* are influenced by Schumann and Brahms, and even in his more mature songs, he retained accompaniment styles from these early works. His music is romantic in a Wagner-Straussian style and, in particular, his songs are uniquely beautiful.

Pfitzner's songs are grouped in small collections, usually by poet. He was drawn to texts that portray the loneliness of nature. His preferred poet was Eichendorff, whose poems provided Pfitzner with twenty song settings and a cantata.

Tone-painting exists in Pfitzner's songs, motives are usually associated with bells and birdsongs, and play a large part in unifying structure. Most songs are densely chromatic, often combined with linear polyphony.

In addition to composing, Pfitzner was a man of great literary taste and culture, and a well-known writer on music.

Der Weckruf, Op. 40, No. 6   **Call to Rise. 1931**
(Joseph von Eichendorff)

Jaunty march rhythms open the song, accompanying the Almighty on his lonely nightly rounds, as he searches for believers but meets closed doors and closed hearts. Through the night only the forest offers company, but as morning dawns, the journey begins again and God knocks against doors of palaces and huts: "Wake up! The peaks are towering in flames."

Pfitzner's vocal melody is a simple tuneful walking song, almost folk-like in style, but laced with some irregular intervals. Stanza two paints the fruitless search, and the forest offers solace in a combination of low-register pitches and harmonic dissonances. Stanza three is a variation of the first strophe; the last stanza gathers thicker texture as it marches exultantly to the dramatic climax with expanded range in both piano and voice.

Die Einsame, Op. 9, No. 2   **The Solitary One. 1894-95**
(Joseph von Eichendorff)

A serenely lyric melody floats over an undulating accompaniment of broken chords and arpeggiated figures. Again, nature is the dominant theme here, and the singer seems to personify Nature herself, alone in her domain. Eichendorff's poem is full of nature images: stars, brooks, forest rustlings, the song of the nightingale. Solitude here is not threatening, but represents fulfillment.

This song is a beautiful example of Pfitzner's melodic gift. The first vocal phrase emerges from the first measures of the piano. Both voice and piano are tonally grounded, yet harmonies subtly shift to create variety and a feeling of serenity and peace. The nightingale's song is skillfully woven into the oscillating piano figures. The last stanza is slightly broader with a change of piano figures and vocal phrase lengths. Pfitzner uses the opening vocal material for the piano postlude.

Nachtwanderer,* Op. 7, No. 2   **Night Wanderer. 1888-89 and 1897-1900**
(Joseph von Eichendorff)

Joseph Eichendorff (1788-1857) was a favorite poet of Pfitzner, who composed a major cantata, *Von Deutscher Seele* (Of the German Soul) to twenty poems of Eichendorff, and used many more of his texts for song settings. For Pfitzner, Eichendorff was the most important German romantic poet of his generation.

"Nachtwanderer" presents, as do most of Eichendorff's nature texts, nature as a reflection of the spirit of the beholder. Here, Night rides through the land on a brown steed, plunging everything into darkness as he passes. There are four stanzas, underpinned with swiftly moving accompaniment figures depicting the wild horseback journey. Melodic material is repeated in the first three verses, each slightly varied as Night passes a fretful child, a young maiden, a river sprite. The last stanza is solemn and pontifical, as Night and Day struggle, and Night disappears into the grave that his horse has pawed out of the ground.

*For a comparison setting, see Erich Korngold.

Extended Study List
Naturfreiheit • Es fällt ein Stern herunter • Wiegenlied • Mein Herz ist wie die dunkle Nacht • Die Einsame • Abschied • Nachts • Herbsthauch • Wanderers Nachtlied • Ist der Himmel darum in Lenz so blau? • Immer leiser wird mein Schlummer • Das verlassene Mägdlein • Mailied • Die Nachtigallen • Neue Liebe

Selected Reading
Richard Mercier, *The Songs of Han Pfitzner: A Guide and Study* (Westport, CT: Greenwood Press, 1998). John Williamson, *The Music of Hans Pfitzner* (Oxford: Clarendon Press, 1992). Chapter 6: "Pfitzner and the Lied."

Notes
1. Quoted in Williamson, *The Music of Hans Pfitzner*, 213.
2. Helmut Wirth, "Hans Pfitzner," *The New Grove Dictionary of Music and Musicians*, ed. Stanley Sadie, v. 14, 613.
3. Michael Kennedy, editor, *The Oxford Dictionary of Music*, 2nd edition, 671.

ARNOLD SCHOENBERG (1874-1951)

If I am striving toward a goal that seems to me to be certain, nevertheless I already feel the opposition that I shall have to overcome...
—Arnold Schoenberg, writing after the composition of
Das Buch der hängenden Gärten[1]

Music without ideas is unthinkable, and people who are not willing to use their brains to understand music that cannot be fully grasped at the first hearing are simply lazy-minded. Every true work of art to be understood has to be thought about; otherwise it has no inherent life.
—Arnold Schoenberg[2]

Arnold Schoenberg was born in Vienna and studied as a pupil of Alexander Zemlinsky. He lived and taught in Berlin from 1901 to 1914, coming in contact with leading artists and writers of the expressionist movement.[3] Schoenberg's experiments with new forms of tonal organization evolved the "twelve-tone-row" concept, which formed the basis for most of his music from that time on. Twelve-tone music is based on a series of notes chosen from the twelve tones of the chromatic scale. Such a series, or "row" as it is called, serves as the germinating material for an entire composition.

Schoenberg's teaching and musical aesthetic had a profound influence on his pupils, notably Alban Berg (only eleven years his junior) and Anton Webern. Schoenberg fled Germany in 1933, emigrating to Paris and then the United States where he taught at the University of California at Los Angeles from 1936 to 1944.

Schoenberg's ground-breaking cycle *Das Buch der hängenden Gärten,* Op. 15 (The Book of the Hanging Gardens, 1908) charted new directions for twentieth-century vocal music. This cycle uses Stefan George's expressionist poems and exhibits the increasing complexity and independence of Schoenberg's vocal writing and musical textures. George's verses, a conscious departure from late-romantic poetry, were highly symbolic, elegant, and tinged with exoticism. They were perfectly suited to Schoenberg's developing atonal style and nonrealistic text treatment.

During this period in his career, Schoenberg composed two expressionist works for the theater, *Erwartung* (1909), an operatic monodrama and *Die glückliche Hand* (1913), the last work on a libretto by Schoenberg himself. Schoenberg's chamber work for voice and eight instruments, *Pierrot Lunaire* (1912), one of the most celebrated works of German expressionism—Stravinsky called it "the solar plexus as well as the mind of early twentieth-century music"—also belongs to this period.

Schoenberg's finest *Lieder* are found in the orchesteral *Gurrelieder* and *Opus 22 Orchestral Songs.* His preoccupation with song came to an end fairly soon. After *The Book of the Hanging Gardens*, Schoenberg's interest in works for voice and piano waned. *The Book of the Hanging Gardens* was so concentrated, with such complex musical, emotional, and psychological structure, Schoenberg had "said it all" and created a work that needed no follow-up. His last songs were *Opus 48* (1933).

Opus 2 Songs   **1899**

Erwartung (Expectation) *(Richard Dehmel)* •
Jesus Bettelt (Jesus Begs) *(Richard Dehmel)* •
Erhebung (Exaltation) *(Richard Dehmel)* •
Waldsonne (Forest Sun) *(Johannes Schlaf)*

These are Schoenberg's earliest published songs, still in the tradition of the German Romantic lyricism, but nonetheless containing characteristic musical elements found in Schoenberg's style: concentrated expressivity, rhythmic freedom, harmonic tension, and richness of invention. Schoenberg's early works owe much to Brahms and Wagner, and influences of both may be seen in *Opus 2.*

This set of songs is notable for manipulation of motives, thick textures, and vocal writing that begins to veer toward the dynamic shapes of Schoenberg's more mature vocal works. The songs are brief, presenting four disparate moods in effective settings.

The first three songs are on poems by Richard Dehmel and are intensely expressionistic. Sexual anticipation is the theme of Song 1: a man waits in the moonlight by "a sea-green pond near the red villa under the dead oak." Dehmel's poem is full of colors and, perhaps, conscious psychological associations for each. Schoenberg creates a "coloristic" chord, then manipulates it throughout the song. Song 2 is also a love song—to Mary Magdalene—and is similarly chromatic. Its vocal line is flexible and declamatory, somewhat in the style of Wagner. Song 3 is a simple love song in an expressive and appealing setting, the voice part submerged in a polyphonic texture. Song 4 seems not to belong to this group—and indeed, it was inserted to round out *Opus 2.* In comparison with the other three songs, it is a weaker but still attractive piece. It has a lilting lightness and a melodic simplicity not ordinarily thought of as part of Schoenberg's style.

Brettl-Lieder Cabaret Songs. 1901

Der genügsame Liebhaber (The Satisfied Lover) *(Hugo Salus)* •
Einfältiges Lied (Simple Song) *(Hugo Salus)* • Jedem das Seine
(To Each His Own) *(Colly)* • Mahnung (Warning) *(Gustav
Hochstetter)* • Galathea (Galathea) *(Frank Wedekind)* •
Gigerlette (Gigerlette) *(Otto Julius Bierbaum)* • Arie aus dem
Spiegel von Arcadien (Aria from *The Mirror of Arcady*) *(Emanuel
Schikaneder)* • Nachtwandler (Night Wanderer) *(Gustav Falke)*

Schoenberg's *Cabaret Songs* cannot be cited as characteristic of his musical style, but since their discovery and first recording in 1975 they have become recital favorites. Composed only two years later than his *Opus 2* songs, they are early works.

One of the types of German cabaret at the turn of the century was c alled *Brettl*. Here, poets of the day declaimed their verses to the accompaniment of music; casual, popular singing also took place in a setting that resembled a variety theater.

Schoenberg drew his texts from a wildly popular collection of light verse titled *Deutsche Chansons* (subtitled *Brettl-Lieder*) published in 1900. Ernst von Wolzogen, one of the contributors to the volume, founded a cabaret theater named Uberbrettl in Berlin in 1901 and toured the group to Vienna that spring. Wolzogen's goal was to change the structure of the existing cabaret to a more progressive, sophisticated format, with, above all, good music. After meeting Wolzogen and playing some of his songs for him, Schoenberg was invited to Berlin as conductor of the company's new house. Unfortunately, the company was short lived; the only record of a Schoenberg song performance is "Nachtwandler."[4]

All the cabaret songs are simple symmetrical forms with two and four-bar patterns supported by idiomatic accompaniments, although it must be said that all these accompaniments contain imaginative, witty harmonic touches and textures that elevate them above the popular song form. "Nachtwandler" is unique in the set for its tiny ensemble of piccolo, trumpet and side drum added to the piano accompaniment. Song texts vary widely; most are risque and suggestive, ranging from sexual innuendo ("Gigerlette") to Emanuel Schikaneder's hymn to women (Aria from *The Mirror of Arcady*).

Leonard Stein[5] surmises that these songs may have left their mark on later works, particularly *Pierrot Lunaire,* whose formal structures derive from popular dance forms.

Extended Study List
Das Buch der hängenden Gärten, Op. 15 • *Eight Songs for Voice and Piano*, Op. 6 • *Pierrot Lunaire*, Op. 21 • Die Aufgeregten, Op. 3, No. 2 • *Two Songs*, Op. 1 (Dank, Abschied) • Der verlorene Haufen, Op. 12, No. 2 • Ich darf nicht dankend, Op. 14, No. 1 • Mein Herz das ist ein tiefer Schacht • Waldesnacht • Gedenken • Nicht doch!

Selected Reading
Richard Lee Bunting, "Arnold Schoenberg's Songs With Piano Accompaniment: A Survey of Style Characteristics," *The NATS Bulletin*, 27:1 (October 1970).

David Ewen, *The New Book of Modern Composers*, 3rd edition (New York: Alfred A. Knopf, 1961).

Walter Frisch, *The Early Works of Arnold Schoenberg*, 1893-1908 (Berkeley: University of California Press, 1993). Chapter 4: "The Dehmel Settings of 1899."

Malcom MacDonald, *Schoenberg* (London: J. M. Dent, 1976). Master Musicians Series. Chapter 11: "The Songs."

Notes

1. Quoted in liner notes excerpted from Joseph Machlis in *Schoenberg: Complete Songs for Voice and Piano*, Volume 1. Columbia Masterworks LP31311.
2. Arnold Schoenberg, "The Composer Speaks," in David Ewen, *The New Book of Modern Composers*, 3rd edition, 339.
3. Expressionism, like Impressionism, began with painting and poetry: painters Kandinsky, Kokoschka, Klee and Marc, and poets Dehmel and George produced works that influenced Schoenberg. Expressionist artists and writers emphasized deep inner feelings. Expressionist composers distorted word accents to create tension; expressionistic music took as its point of departure the rejection of accepted beauty and the perpetuation of tension. Expressionism existed side by side with primitivism, dada, and futurism, roughly from 1908-1923.
4. Paul Griffiths, "The Fervent Pursuit of Expression." Liner notes to *Schoenberg: Erwartung / Brettl-Lieder*. Jessye Norman/James Levine. Philips Records. Compact disc 426 261-2, 1993.
5. Leonard Stein. Liner notes for *Schoenberg: Cabaret Songs; Nine Early Songs*. Marni Nixon/Leonard Stein. RCA Red Seal Records. ARL 1-1231, 1975.

JOSEPH MARX (1882-1964)

Marx's songs epitomize a period of high romanticism, emotional indulgence, and overt sensuality that characterized Vienna in the first quarter of this century...these songs are the musical equivalent of the stylized architecture of Otto Wagner, the elegant jewelry and objets d'art of Josef Hoffman, and decadently evocative paintings of Gustav Klimt.

—Gary Arvin[1]

Austrian composer Joseph Marx continued the tradition of Hugo Wolf and Richard Strauss in his 158 songs. His choice of texts ranged from traditional French poetry (Verlaine, Giraud, de Musset) to traditional verses in Japanese and Chinese, and German poems by Heine, Rückert, Möricke, Eichendorff, and Goethe. Interestingly, he created settings of the seventeen poems from Heyse's *Italienisches Liederbuch* that Hugo Wolf had not set.

Marx's other compositions include symphonic poems, choral works with orchestra, and chamber music. His music shares stylistic traits with his contemporaries: Wolf, Korngold, and Zemlinsky. Songs constitute the greatest part of his composed works, and their high quality has been compared to the *Lieder* of Hugo Wolf. Marx's songs are marked by thickly textured accompaniments that are at times orchestral in conception; and broad vocal phrases, that are often operatic in style.

Marx studied musicology at Graz University and was professor of theory at the Vienna Academy of Music from 1914 to 1922, serving as its director from 1922 to 1924. From 1924 to 1927 he served as Rector of the Vienna Hochschule für Musik and from 1931 to 1938 was music critic for the *Neues Wiener Journal*. After World War II, Marx wrote in the same capacity for the *Wiener Zeitung*. During the 1920s and early 1930s, Marx concentrated almost exclusively on composing orchestral works, followed by chamber music works. These compositions miss the stylistic synthesis he achieved in his songs. He published two books: a collection of his criticisms and essays and a book titled *Weltsprache Musik,* which deals with acoustics, tonality, aesthetics, and music philosophy. Marx returned to Graz to teach at the Graz University from 1947 to 1957 and died there in 1964.

Am Fenster At the Window. 1912
(from the *Italienisches Liederbuch* of Paul Heyse)

Marx set seventeen poems from Heyse's *Italienisches Liederbuch,* choosing the the texts that Hugo Wolf had not chosen for his *Italienisches Liederbuch* settings.

The song is in two sections: the first is lyric, the second, playful and somewhat faster as the lovely Italian maiden addresses the young man below her window. Here, the sweeping piano figures of the first section change to repeated chords with melodic patterns woven through. The first two measures of the accompaniment are used to separate sections and as material for the close.

Vocal phrases sound Straussian in the first section, declamatory in the style of Wolf in the second section. Marx's piano texture remains full throughout the song, and herein lies the greatest difference between Marx and Wolf's Italian settings. While Marx's Italian songs are leaner in style in comparison to the rest of his output, they still retain an opulence of sound and a sweeping lyricism that mark his overall style.

Nocturne Nocturne. 1911
(Otto Erich Hartleben)

Cast in ABA form, this song gives equal prominence to voice and piano. Of the forty bars of music, seventeen are for the piano alone, and twenty-three are shared.

This is a demanding song for both performers. The piano accompaniment is rhapsodic in style, with cascading arpeggios and scale passages reminiscent of a Chopin nocturne. Marx achieves an improvisatory, free feeling through surprising changes of mood and complex rhythms and harmonies.

Marx gives the singer broad lyric phrases that cover an overall melodic range of an eleventh. Emphasis on sustained lines with climaxes on high notes illustrates the poem's rapturous mood and its emotional intensity. Marx's style of writing for voice and piano emphasizes texture and mood more than relationship of melody to text. This exquisite song is like a miniature tone poem with words.

Regen Rain. 1910
(Anonymous German translation of Paul Verlaine's "Il pleure dans mon cœur")

Verlaine's delicate verse seems slightly overstuffed in this anonymous translation, but this is a fine song nonetheless. Verlaine's evocative verse must have captivated the unknown translator, who succeeded in transferring the general idea, but few details or nuances.

Marx's piano accompaniment is full of patterns suggesting rain and raindrops. Vocal phrases seem to signal a mood of intense passion and loneliness rather than the detached emotional atmosphere of the original French. Melodic phrases are dramatically conceived; a highly chromatic section of thicker texture appears with the third stanza. The last stanza is ushered in by the initial piano pattern, then returns to a leaner texture. Although the form is through-composed, Marx uses a variant of the first vocal phrase for the last vocal phrase.

Valse de Chopin   **Waltz in the Style of Chopin. 1909**
(from *Pierrot Lunaire* by Albert Giraud)

Marx set four poems* from Albert Giraud's *Pierrot Lunaire* three years before Schoenberg's groundbreaking chamber work.

Unity is achieved by the three motives in the accompaniment that reappear throughout the piece. Large arching intervals in the vocal line are built into extremely broad and flexible phrases. Unity in the vocal line is provided by rhythm; with few exceptions, the vocal line is built on the same rhythm throughout the song: half note–quarter note, which symbolizes the "fatal fascination" in the poetry.

The texture in the piano writing is highly Romantic. Piano techniques of Chopin and Liszt are recalled by octave figures, an extended prelude, interludes, and a postlude. There is some text painting in the bass line suggesting drops of blood (accented eighth notes). Abrupt modulations to other keys take place, but the tonality throughout remains grounded in F-sharp minor. Marx uses long pedal points as a further unifying device. Form is through-composed, although Marx utilizes phrase shapes as well as the recurring half note–quarter note rhythm in vocal phrases to create unity.

*"Valse de Chopin," "Pierrot Dandy," "Kolumbine," and "Die Violine."

Extended Study List

Schliesse mir die Augen beide • Wanderers Nachtlied • Bitte • Die Begegnung • Pierrot Dandy from *Pierrot Lunaire* • Jugend und Altger • Die Elfe • Hat dich die Liebe berührt • Selige Nacht Waldseligkeit • Marienlied • Ständchen • Maienblüten • Die Verslassene

Selected Reading

Gary Arvin, foreword to *Songs of Joseph Marx*. Songs in two volumes with companion CD of recorded performances (Milwaukee: Hal Leonard Corporation, 1992).

Notes

1. Gary Arvin, foreword to *Songs of Joseph Marx*.

ALBAN BERG (1885-1935)

The best music always results from ecstasies of logic.

—Alban Berg[1]

Alban Maria Johannes Berg was born of a German father and an Austrian mother. His talent for composition manifested itself early; he composed some seventy songs between ages fifteen and twenty. Musically self-taught, Berg worked in local government offices and immersed himself in the intellectual life of turn-of-the-century Vienna. His friendships with Zweig, Altenberg, Klimt and Kokoschka were to remain strong and influential throughout his life. In the first years of the century he met Arnold Schoenberg, eleven years his senior, and became his pupil.

Berg's early songs are in the tradition of Schumann; he chose texts from a wide variety of poets from Heine, Goethe and Möricke, to Hofmannsthal and Rilke. Musically these songs show influences of Debussy and Impressionism more than techniques of his teacher Schoenberg, whose aesthetic was to shape and influence Berg's development. Other composers who influenced Berg's musical style were

Gustav Mahler and Richard Strauss. Berg's love of literature was also important in determining his musical aesthetics.

Berg and Anton Webern became Schoenberg's most famous pupils. The impact of the "new Viennese school" (Schoenberg, Berg, Webern) was far-flung, affecting twentieth-century composition and composers in a highly influential way. Berg adopted Schoenberg's twelve-tone principles as the basis for his compositions, though he used the techniques less rigidly and with great imagination. Berg's approach to serialism was not always strict. Most of his rows have triadic outlines and tonal references. His serial techniques are easier to apprehend due to the lyricism and romantic expressiveness that are always present in his vocal writing.

Dense textures are a feature of Berg's music; he frequently used stacked harmonies and contrapuntal techniques in his accompaniments. Another feature of Berg's style is his use of constructive rhythms—patterns from which the structure could evolve. Berg was fond of using formal patterns from earlier musical styles (fugue and invention, variations, sonata, suite, passacaglia, etc.) as designs for his musical forms.

Berg's style effectively bridged the gap between the romantic past and the new atonal style. He was comfortable working in larger forms, which allowed his natural lyricism and dramatic expression to have free rein. Berg was a consummate musical dramatist. His operas are among his most important works: *Wozzeck* (1921) and *Lulu* (first performed 1937) are both still part of standard modern operatic repertory. Both operas have a large formal structure, and although it is not important that the listener know this, Berg worked them out carefully. For example, each act of *Wozzeck* is a large form: Act I - Exposition (Five character studies); Act II - Dramatic Development (Symphony in five movements); Act III - Catastrophe/Epilog (Six Inventions). Three vocal styles are employed in the opera: free lyric vocal declamation, *sprechstimme*, and spoken passages.

Nacht *(Sieben frühe Lieder*)*   **Night. 1907**
(Carl Hauptmann)

Hauptmann's poetry is full of illusory images of the night, sensual in their implications. "Nacht" is the most spectacular setting of the set, principally for its harmonic material, which features strong tonal progressions under whole-tone structures. Even in these early works, Berg's sense of formal symmetry is seen. The overall arrangement of "Nacht" is a *Bogenform,*** a favorite principle of Berg's in nearly all his subsequent works.[2] Berg links the outer sections of "Nacht" like a varied *da capo*; the opening vocal line is answered in the reprise by its own melodic inversion. Whole-tone harmonies pervade the first and last sections of "Nacht"; the two inner sections function like two stanzas, dominated by expressive use of chromaticism. A broad melodic vocal phrase—"Weites Wunderland ist aufgetan" (A broad wonderland is opened up)—ushers in the second section with a burst of lyricism. Thick textures are found in the piano accompaniment.

*Berg dedicated *Sieben frühe Lieder* (Seven Early Songs) to his wife Helene.

**Bogenform, from "bow" is an arch form in which the outer musical sections are related, then the next inner sections on either side, just inside the outer sections, then the next inner sections, and so on. (Examples: ABBA, ABCBA, etc.) One middle section usually forms the "keystone" of the arch. As in all formal structures, there are many variations possible.

Die Nachtigall *(Sieben frühe Lieder)*	The Nightingale. 1905-06
(Theodor Storm)	

"Passionately lyrical" might best describe this song, which is in three sections (ABA). A luxuriant piano texture supports a vocal line of broad lyric phrases. There is an expressive piano postlude that ends the song. Berg had been studying with Schoenberg two or three years when he wrote these early works, but this song shows none of Schoenberg's influence. It seems instead to look back to the Romantic *Lied* and Robert Schumann in particular. Its expressive vocalism makes it one of Berg's most appealing songs.

Vier Lieder, Op. 2	Four Songs, Op. 2. 1908-09

Schlafen, schlafen, nichts al Schlafen! (Friedrich Hebbel) •
Schlafend trägt man mich in mein Heimatland (Alfred Mombert) •
Nun ich der Riesen Stärkstein überwand... (Alfred Mombert) •
Warm die Lüfte (Alfred Mombert)

Op. 2 was a transitional work for Berg. He composed the songs in the summer of 1908 and published them at his own expense in 1910. At this time he was still a student of Arnold Schoenberg. The Op. 2 songs are slightly later than the *Seven Early Songs* and use texts by Hebbel, a nineteenth-century German poet, and by Mombert, who was Berg's contemporary. The poems are a blend of the mystical and the sensuous. Sleep and solitude are the principal themes: escape in sleep (1), return to homeland in sleep (2), a dream (3), and a daydream-image interpreted aloud (4).

In this song set Berg begins to move away from his early traditional style toward new style of vocalism that is closely tied to and based on speech rhythms. Vocal phrases have the rising and falling intervals of speech, with melodic fragments repeated alternately in the voice and piano.

Berg blurs tonality so that all three songs seem to progress naturally to the fourth song. Tenuous tonality is found in the first three songs, moving from a clearly defined D minor in the first song (but only in its use of the tonic triad to begin and end the song) to atonality in the fourth.

Song 1 (To Sleep, to Sleep) may be perceived as a shaped contour, a rising arch in which pitches expand from a tiny cell to broader and denser textures and then return again. Berg sets and sustains a somber mood with a rocking ostinato bass line, slow tempi, dark sonorities, and repetition and contraction of motives. Vocal phrases develop in a similar manner, beginning with a two-note ostinato figure (A-D), gradually expanding to broader contours of higher pitch and finally reaching a climax on F-natural on the word "fülle." At this point a general *ritardando* begins in both voice and piano, there is a gradual descent in pitch and the overall texture thins.

Song 2 (Sleeping I Am Carried) is a highly chromatic treatment of the strange, almost disembodied feeling of a return to homeland, captured in only eighteen bars of music. Although some feeling of E-flat is present, there is a general absence of strong tonality.

Song 3 (I Overcame the Strongest of Giants) is a heavily accented, thick-textured treatment of the text, which describes a dream of "overcoming the strongest of the giants" and finding the way home, guided by a "hand from a fairy-tale." Berg's vocal writing is angular and chromatic; the accompaniment derives from a descending interval in the right hand, mirrored in octaves in the left hand, and varied throughout the piece. Berg uses some material reminiscent of the first song (the descending A-D fifth and references to D minor tonality). Songs 2 and 3 share a similar formal shape, each featuring a return of opening materials in varied rhythm.

Song 4 (Warm the Breezes) is freer in the use of musical materials, especially in the vocal line, which closely parallels the dramatic development of the text. Text painting is present only in the piano accompaniment (the nightingale, the maiden in the grey dress). There are no musical references shared between voice and piano. Dynamics remain at a very quiet level (*piano*) until the girl speaks "He still isn't here. He made me wait..." Now the dynamic level changes suddenly and violently to *fortissimo*. Berg's formal structure may be divided into three brief sections: the first sets the mood; the second describes the mountain forest and the girl in the grey dress; the last functions as a sort of personal statement from the narrator/poet. For the first time, Berg does not indicate a key signature for this piece, which looks ahead to the musical language of his opera *Wozzeck*.[3]

Extended Study List

Schliesse mir die Augen beide (first setting) • An Leukon (Gleim) • *Five Songs*, Op. 4 (Altenberg Lieder) • Schliesse mir die Augen beide (dodecaphonic setting) • *Seven Early Songs* (arr. voice/orchestra, 1928) • *Der Wein* (voice and orchestra). 1929 • Operas: *Wozzeck, Lulu*

Selected Reading

Douglas Jarman, ed., *The Berg Companion* (Boston: Northeastern University Press, 1990).
Mary H. Wennerstom, "Pitch Relationships in Berg's Songs, Op. 2," *Indiana Theory Review,* 1:1, September 1977.

Notes:

1. Quoted in *The New York Times Magazine,* 1975. *A Dictionary of Musical Quotations*, compiled by Crofton and Fraser (London: Routledge, 1985), 18.
2. Douglas Jarman, ed., *The Berg Companion*, 42-43.
3. Mary H. Wennerstrom, "Pitch Relationships in Berg's Songs, Op. 2," 12.

ERICH KORNGOLD (1897-1957)

With regards to modern German music, my biggest hope lies with Erich Wolfgang Korngold. He is exceptionally talented, has a formidable technical knowledge and, most important of all, superb musical idas...he has so much talent that he could give half of it away and still have enough left for himself.

—Giacomo Puccini[1]

Erich Wolfgang Korngold was one of the most amazing child prodigies in history. His father Julius Korngold, was an influential, much-feared music critic in Vienna.

Erich's first composition was a song, written at age seven. At the age of eleven he had already composed for piano a ballet, *Der Schneemann (The Snowman)*. His teacher, Alexander Zemlinsky, orchestrated it, and it was premiered at the Viennese Court Opera in a command performance for the Emperor, Franz Josef. It created a sensation. Mahler, Strauss, and Puccini heard Korngold's works and were duly impressed by his talent. By age fourteen, Korngold had added an orchestral overture and numerous works for chamber groups to his catalog of compositions.

By the age of sixteen, Korngold had composed two short operas, *The Ring of Polykrates* and *Violanta*. His best-known opera, *Die tote Stadt* (1920), was premiered simultaneously in Cologne and Hamburg. Korngold was twenty-three. He later became a professor at the Vienna State Academy of Music.

Nicolas Slonimsky characterized Korngold's music as "the very last breath of the romantic spirit of Vienna."[2] Korngold left a legacy of around forty art songs, composed between 1911 and 1952. His song style derives from the great German romantic song tradition, but was especially influenced by Wolf, Strauss, Mahler, and Marx. Korngold's songs are characterized by freedom of form, sophistication of harmonic materials, and above all, by Korngold's melodic imagination and approach to poetic interpretation.

Korngold is probably best remembered as a composer of film music. In 1934, as anti-Semitism increased in Europe, Korngold accepted an invitation to Hollywood to arrange and conduct Felix Mendelssohn's music for a production of "A Midsummer Night's Dream." He signed a contract with Warner Brothers (one of the most generous ever offered a composer in Hollywood), and soon established himself as a major composer for films. His film scores, filled with broad adventure themes and tender romantic melodies, greatly influenced the development of film music. Korngold wrote twenty film scores and was awarded two Academy Awards. These works, unique in their integration of classical music and the film medium, include: Captain Blood, The Adventures of Robin Hood, The Sea Hawk, The Private Lives of Elizabeth and Essex, The Sea Wolf, and Anthony Adverse.

In the 1980s, Korngold's music began to be discovered again, and his major works were recorded. His songs are undiscovered treasures.

Nachtwanderer*, Op. 9, No. 2   **Night Wanderer. 1911**
(Joseph von Eichendorff)

In 1911, Korngold composed a set of twelve *Lieder*, all to texts of Eichendorff, as a birthday gift for his father. Only three were ever published—"Nachtwanderer," "Das Ständchen," and "Schneeglöckchen." Korngold designated them as part of Op. 9, published in 1916. At this time he had already composed two piano sonatas and a ballet, *Der Schneemann*, which had been performed to critical acclaim at the Vienna Court Opera.

The songs were probably first performed at a private salon in the home of Luise Von Fraenkel-Ehrenstein, former star of the Vienna Court Opera and a close friend of the Korngold family. Young Erich dedicated the Op. 9 songs to her in gratitude for her support.

Eichendorff's dramatic verse describes the Night, astride a charging horse, riding throughout the countryside until the cock crows at daybreak. Korngold opens the song with a somber accompaniment of bare, open fifths, like a tolling bell. As the ride progresses, the tempo relentlessly accelerates. Piano figures change and thicken, racing toward the final section, where, exhausted, the nighttime traveler sinks into the grave that his horse has pawed out for him.

Dissonances in the right hand of the accompaniment clash with the ostinato-like drone of open fifths in the left hand—a combination that creates an eerie, forbidding mood that complements Eichendorff's somber text. The harmonic texture is extremely inventive, subtly changing and developing throughout the song. At the final bars, Korngold combines B minor and B major as the rooster crows.

Brendan Carroll describes this song as "Korngold's "Erlkönig." [3]

*Also see the setting by Hans Pfitzner.

Das Ständchen, Op. 9, No. 3   The Serenade. 1911
(Joseph von Eichendorff)

Here is another serenade scene—a young student stands and sings beneath the window of his sweetheart. His lute is accompanied by sounds of evening, babbling streams and forest murmurs. The poet nostalgically recalls his youthful serenades—but sadly, his love passed away. He urges the young singer to sing on!

Korngold opens the song with an ardent, upward moving piano introduction, which he uses later to introduce the last section of the song. The opening vocal phrase, doubled by the piano, provides the rhythmic and melodic material on which the song is built. Intervals and phrase shapes derived from this opening melody are subtly altered, and appear in both voice and piano.

There are three sections in the song. The middle section, the poet's reminiscence, is notable for its change of tempo and mood. The opening piano introduction ushers in the final stanza, and a mood of buoyant optimism is restored. The influence of Richard Strauss can be heard in this setting.

Sommer, Op. 9, No. 6   Summer. 1916
(Siegfried Trebitsch)*

Korngold was sixteen years old when he composed "Sommer." It is a hymn to nature, richly flavored with the brashly romantic spirit of youth and the ambience of turn-of-the-century Vienna. The warbling blackbird in the text is introduced in the piano prelude, which features Mahler-like "nature" figures in the texture. Arpeggiated piano figures evoke the enthusiastic ardor of youth. The song concludes with an extended piano postlude.

*Trebitsch was a friend of the Korngold family. His translation of Rodenbach's novel *Bruges la Morte* formed the basis of Korngold's opera, Die *tote Stadt*.

Das Heldengrab am Pruth*, Op. 9, No. 5   The Hero's Grave at Pruth. 1916
(Heinrich Kipper)

Harmonic materials take center stage in this song. Korngold uses polytonality to create the detached, otherworldly feeling of the cemetery in the poet's garden. It is always springtime in the garden because the fallen hero rests there.

The piano introduction features triplet figures—eighth notes in the left hand, sixteenth notes in the right hand. The right hand figure alternates between C major and C minor; the left hand is in C-sharp minor. These piano figures whirl together in an eerie dance-like texture that reflects the text. This little section is used between the verses and as a postlude.

Vocal phrases are lyrical and romantic, above a piano accompaniment that is remains tonal, but with subtle and fleeting alterations (example: under the word "Pruth").

*The river Prut in Bukovina (now in Romania), was the scene of heavy Austrian losses in World War I.

Extended Study List
Four Shakespeare Songs, Op. 31 (Desdemona's Song; Under the greenwood tree; Blow, blow, thou winter wind; When birds do sing) • Was Du mir bist? • Nachts • *Songs of the Clown,* Op. 29 (Come away, death; O mistress mine; Adieu, good man devil; Hey Robin!; For the rain, it raineth every day) • Schneeglöckchen • Mond, so gehst du wieder auf • Die Geniale

Selected Reading
Brendan Carroll, *The Last Prodigy: A Biography of Erich Wolfgang Korngold* (Portland, OR: Amadeus Press, 1997).
Jessica Duchen, *Erich Wolfgang Korngold* (London: Phaidon Press, 1996).

Notes
1. Brendan G. Carroll, *The Last Prodigy,* 158. Quoted from an interview with Puccini published in the *Neue Freie Presse,* 12 September 1921.
2. Brendan G. Carroll, quoted in "Songs and Chamber Music of Erich Wolfgang Korngold," liner notes to *Rendezvous with Korngold.* Anne Sofie Von Otter, Bengt Forsberg & Friends. Deutsche-Grammophon 459 631-2, 1994.
3. Carroll, *The Last Prodigy,* 107.

KURT WEILL (1900-1950)

I have learned to make my music speak directly to the audience, to find the most immediate, the most direct way to say what I want to say, and to say it as simply as possible. That's why I think that, in the theatre at least, melody is such an important element because it speaks directly to the heart—and what good is music if it cannot move people.

—Kurt Weill[1]

Kurt Weill's persistent experimentation with hybrid forms of musical theater produced some of the most stimulating, expressive, and enduring works for the musical theater composed in this century. In a letter to Dr. Hans Heinsheimer (Universal-Edition, Vienna) Weill explained "I am the only creative musician who for years has worked consistently and uncompromisingly in the face of opposition from the snobs and the aesthetes toward the creation of fundamental forms of a new, simple, popular musical theater."[2]

Weill's early musical influences were from his father, a synagogue cantor. Weill studied piano, theory and composition in Dessau where he occasionally worked as coach and *répétiteur* at the city's Hoftheater. He was a regular member of Ferruccio Busoni's Berlin master classes for three years, and it is Busoni's influence that is most clearly seen in Weill's writings about opera.

With his wife, singer-actress Lotte Lenya, Weill fled Germany in 1933 after the Nazis banned his music and froze his bank accounts. His collaborative efforts in musical theater in Germany with Bertolt Brecht (including *Die Dreigroschenoper, Der Zar lässt sich photographieren, Aufstieg und Fall der Stadt Mahagonny, Der Silbersee* and *Happy End*), had been both successful and controversial. After the Weills' arrival in Paris, he composed incidental songs to *Marie Galante* and a larger work, *The Seven Deadly Sins.* The music for these works is laced with bitterness, but both are full of Weill's haunting melodies and characteristic dramatic energy.

In 1935 the Weills left Europe for the United States where they lived until his death in 1950. In America, Weill found a new career as a composer of works for the Broadway stage. He collaborated with the most distinguished librettists of the day. *Knickerbocker Holiday* (Maxwell Anderson); *One Touch of Venus* (Ogden Nash); *Lady in the Dark* and *The Firebrand of Florence* (Ira Gershwin) were among his works created during this period. In 1943 Weill became an American citizen. At the time of his death, Weill was working on a projected musical play, *Huckleberry Finn*, based on Mark Twain's novel, with book and lyrics by Maxwell Anderson.

Weill's works for the German theater and for the American Broadway stage yielded a rich body of songs that are regularly performed outside their original dramatic context. Outside the theater, Weill wrote very few songs for voice and piano or small ensemble. An early chamber work *Frauentanz* (Op. 10, 1932), *Ofrah's Lieder* (1916), a set of songs composed at age sixteen, and a group of songs of poems by Walt Whitman are several examples.

Performing Weill's vocal music demands dramatic flair and a sense of open communication. Some of the Weill-Brecht songs—biting, ascerbic, pessimistic, and full of murder, sex, and humanity taken to its lowest denominator— seem to fly in the face of artful interpretation. One critic has written "Weill-Brecht songs can indeed be done in a spoken-sung manner in which melody can be subservient to the thrust of the words...They also require style, dramatic depth and musical understanding...[It is] some of the finest theater music ever written."[3]

It is particularly striking that Weill's genius allowed him to adapt his musical style to three very diverse national cultures: German, French, and American. In each case, he was able to assimilate the social and musical environment and create works of great expressive and emotional impact.

Several Weill songs from stage productions are discussed here; Weill's career both in Germany and the United States warrants their inclusion as examples of his song style. Many of these are regularly programmed in recital in the voice/piano format, in the same way that selections from Bernstein's *Candide* and *Mass* are performed out of dramatic context.

In 1980, Lotte Lenya released a substantial number of unpublished Weill songs to soprano Teresa Stratas, who recorded them in in 1981. Lenya had guarded these works since Weill's death thirty years earlier; the texts are in German, French, and English. "Nanna's Lied," "Berlin im-Licht Song," and "Youkali" are songs from that collection.

Nanna's Lied   Nanna's Song. 1939
(Bertolt Brecht)

This was one of Lotte Lenya's favorite songs, written for her as a Christmas present. She never attempted to perform it publicly. Its three verses paint a poignant picture of a young prostitute. Brecht used an identical text in his play *Die Rundköpfe und die Spitzköpfe* (The Roundheads and the Peakheads), an allegorical work based on Shakespeare's *Measure for Measure*, which premiered in Copenhagen in 1936 with a musical score by Hanns Eisler. In the play, the song is sung by Nanna Callas, a Roundhead peasant's daughter who has resorted to prostitution.[4]

Formally, Weill's setting is strophic variations with refrain, which closely follows the poetic structure. The parenthetical last line of each stanza leading into the refrain, is spoken. The first two stanzas are identical, the third is varied in texture and Weill adds a countermelody in the accompaniment. Tonally, the song is a mixture of E-flat major and C minor. Brecht quotes from the poetry of François Villon in the refrain—"Where are the tears of last night...where are the snows from years gone by?"

"Nanna's Lied" is a touching, bitter verse whose style was perfect for the dramatic gifts of Lenya, who sang the song once for Brecht during a visit with the Weills in 1940. He termed the performance "absolutely unforgettable."

Berlin im Licht-Song   Berlin in Lights Song. 1928
(Kurt Weill)

"Berlin im Licht-Song" was commissioned as part of a festival organized by Berlin's utility industries to honor and promote the city of Berlin in 1928. The festivities were designed to demonstrate that, like New York or Paris, Berlin was also a "city of light." Historic landmarks and buildings were illuminated at night and there were firework displays and parades. People traveled into the city to view the spectacle and attend the cultural events that were part of the festival.

This song followed closely on the heels of the phenomenal success of *The Threepenny Opera* (premiered less than two months earlier) and might explain the style of setting Weill used—a wrong-note "slow fox trot" employed with great success in *Threepenny Opera*. Indeed, this song might have come from that score; its vocal style articulates the "song style" that Brecht and Weill established in *Threepenny Opera*.

Within its dance rhythms is an energy that underscores Weill's words: "Come on, turn on the lights so we can see what there is to see...Berlin in lights." According to one writer, Brecht may have collaborated on this text; underlying its light-hearted lines is a veiled darkness, perhaps implied by "the lady doth protest too much" delivery of the text. Weill's harmonies are riddled with subtle chromaticism that creates tension as well as color.

In his memorial tribute to Weill, Heinrich Strobel wrote: "Kurt Weill was a prophet of that wonderful unique cosmopolitan city of Berlin before Hitler that will never come back—indeed, in many respects he was its very incarnation."[5]

Youkali: Tango Habanera   Published 1935
(Roger Fernay)

This song with French text belongs to the period when Weill and Lenya were in Paris. After leaving Germany, Weill was working on the songs for Jacque Devel's play with music, *Marie Galante*. Encouraged by the success of two songs he had composed for cabaret singer Lys Gauty ("Complainte de la Seine" and "Je ne t'aime pas"), Weill wrote this single song. Its music is languid and nostalgic—a yearning for Youkali, "the land of our desires...where cares may be left behind...where love is shared...and promises are kept. Youkali is the hope in all human hearts, but only a dream...There is no Youkali."

"Youkali" is in strophic form—two stanzas with a long refrain, and contains Weill's trademark of major-minor alternation. Its narrative stanzas are set in a *tango* rhythm, but the *habanera* is used for the refrain. Weill's major-minor vacillation is used ironically here; the final phrases migrate to the major key, as hope for finding the Youkali dream is crushed.

Weill used materials for this song in *Der Kuhhandel* (1934) and *Johnny Johnson* (1936). Kowalke observes that the perceptive listener may find evidence in "Youkali" that *Carmen* was one of Weill's favorite operas.[6]

Surabaya Johnny *(Happy End)*   1929
(Bertolt Brecht)

Happy End is an uneven work, a kitschy story about the Chicago underworld and the Salvation Army locked in combat. Brecht and Weill contributed only the songs to this play; they are a mixture of cabaret, operetta, and popular dance music, blended at times into a complex harmonic idiom. The work is one of the most tuneful collaborations of Weill and Brecht.

"Surabaya Johnny" is a highlight of the score—an intense moment in which a young woman recounts her overwhelming passion for a man who only uses her. Deceptive in its simplicity, the song demands a wide range of emotional and dramatic expression from the performer. It is definitely a song for a singing actress, since Weill's vocal articulation blends sung phrases with a spoken line that ushers in the refrain (similar to "Nanna's Lied"), by turns rueful, bitter, angry, despairing.

My Ship *(Lady in the Dark)*   1940
(Ira Gershwin)

Lady in the Dark had a wildly successful initial run of 467 performances, surpassed only by Weill's other blockbuster Broadway hit, *One Touch of Venus* (1943), which William King, musical editor of the *New York Sun*, termed "one of the most delightful evenings in the theatre" he had ever had.[7]

Lady in the Dark is a spoof of psychoanalysis; Moss Hart wrote the play, lyrics were by Ira Gershwin. The musical starred Gertrude Lawrence as Liza, and the cast included a newcomer named Danny Kaye. The heroine of the story is Liza Elliott, editor of a successful fashion magazine, whose emotional turmoil about personal relationships has brought her to an analyst's couch. Much of the work is taken up by three large dream sequences.

"My Ship" belongs to parts of Liza's suppressed childhood and remains "in the dark," to be fully remembered only when she can fully assimilate and process and her repressed memories. Fragments of "My Ship" appear at various moments in the score during Liza's "dream sequences" but it is during her final session of psychoanalysis that Liza remembers the song in its entirety at the moment when she realizes she is in love with Charley Johnson.

"My Ship" is a beautiful ballad, cast in the normal thirty-two bar form of American popular songs. When performed apart from the score, it teeters on the brink of sweetness, but is saved by its lovely melody and any honest interpretation by a singer who can let the phrases speak for themselves.

Speak Low *(One Touch of Venus)*   1943
(Ogden Nash)

This haunting song belongs to the score of Weill's most successful American theater work (567 performances), *One Touch of Venus*. The work is listed as a musical comedy with book by S.J. Perelman and Ogden Nash with lyrics by Ogden Nash.* Its story: in a twentieth-century suburb named Ozone Heights, an unassuming barber named Rodney Hatch inadvertently performs a magic spell that brings a 3,000-year-old statue of the goddess Venus to life. Confronted by the passionate goddess, he falls in love. However, Venus's love for a mere mortal cools quickly when she sees the life of the suburban housewife. Rather than accept this fate, she returns to Mount Olympus.

In its original conception, Weill thought the plot and its role personalities lent itself to "a very entertaining and yet original kind of 'opéra comique' on the Offenbach line."[8] The part of Venus was written with Marlene Dietrich in mind, but the title role was created by Mary Martin. Venus's beguiling song "Speak Low," is the principal love duet of the score and became the hit of the show.

Weill's initial Offenbach conception turned instead into a sophisticated, witty and romantic score, thoroughly American in character. "Speak Low" is a *beguine* squarely in the Cole Porter vein, and in its style, a gentle parody of American popular song. Its curvaceous melodic line is memorable, and it is deservedly a classic on the list of American song standards.

*Five selections from *One Touch of Venus* are reprinted in *Kurt Weill in America* (Chappell): "Speak Low" "That's Him," "Foolish Heart," "The Trouble with Women," and "Westwind."

Lonely House *(Street Scene)*   1947
(Langston Hughes)

Weill's opera *Street Scene* (1947) is based on Elmer Rice's play of the same name. Rice adapted his play for Weill's work and wrote some lyrics, but the bulk of the song lyrics are by Langston Hughes.* Originally composed for Broadway, *Street Scene* chronicles one day in front of a poor midtown New York tenement in the 1930s. Its musical ensembles and arias are interleaved with dialogue. Weill wrote: "In *Street Scene* I achieved a real blending of drama and music, in which the singing continues naturally where the speaking stops and the spoken word as well as the dramatic action are embedded in the overall musical structure."[9] Early in the collaboration Weill had requested from Hughes that the opera should include humor, bitter commentary, and the emotional power of two love stories (Mrs. Maurrant's and Rose's).[10] The "two love stories" are both melodramatic; the characters are ethnic stereotypes. Themes range from domestic violence to striving for upward mobility and escape from poverty.

"Lonely House" is a moving soliloquy, sung by Sam Kaplan. In a quiet moment alone, Sam reflects his inner isolation and despair within the teeming subculture of his neighborhood. Sam's mood is established in the first two short vocal phrases, which have wide descending and ascending intervals on the word "lonely." Sam's arioso is a modern lament, a stylistic blend of the blues and real operatic vocalism. It is a blurred line between opera and musical theater that Weill explores throughout the numbers in *Street Scene's* score.

*Five selections from *Street Scene* are reprinted in the collection titled *Kurt Weill in America*: "Lonely House," "We'll Go Away Together," " What Good Would the Moon Be?", "A Boy Like You," and "Moon-Faced, Starry-Eyed."

Extended Study List

Je ne t'aime pas • Songs from *Marie Galante* (Les filles de Bordeaux, Le Roi d'Acquitaine, J'attends un navire, Le grand Lustucru) • Lost in the Stars (*Lost in the Stars*) • Somehow I Never Could Believe (Anna Maurrant's aria from *Street Scene*) • What Good Would the Moon Be? (*Street Scene*) • The Saga of Jenny (*Lady in the Dark*) • *Ofrah's Lieder* • Pirate Jenny (*Threepenny Opera*) • Ballad of Sexual Dependency (*Threepenny Opera*) • *Three Walt Whitman Songs* • Und was bekam des Soldaten Weib? • Complainte de la Seine • Sing Me Not a Ballad (*Firebrand of Florence*) • Stay Well (*Lost in the Stars*) • September Song (*Knickerbocker Holiday*) • Die Muschel von Margate • *Frauentanz*, Op. 10 (soprano, flute, viola, clarinet, horn, bassoon)

Selected Reading

Susan Harden Borwick, "Perspectives on Lenya: Through the Looking Glass," *The Opera Quarterly,* 5:4 (Winter 1987-88).

Kim H. Kowalke, *Kurt Weill in Europe* (Ann Arbor: UMI Research Press, 1979).

_____, ed., *A New Orpheus: essays on Kurt Weill* (New Haven: Yale University Press, 1986).

Ronald Sanders, *The Days Grow Short: The Life and Music of Kurt Weill* (Los Angeles: Silman-James Press, 1980).

Jürgen Schebera, *Kurt Weill: An Illustrated Life* (New Haven, CT: Yale University Press, 1995).

David Patrick Stearns, "The Americanization of Kurt Weill," *Opera News* 55 (November 1990).

Larry Stempel,"Street Scene and the Enigma of Broadway Opera," in *A New Orpheus: Essays on Kurt Weill*, ed. H. Kowalke (New Haven: Yale University Press, 1986). Chapter 17.

Lys Symonette and Kim H. Kowalke, eds. and trans. *Speak Low: The Letters of Kurt Weill and Lotte Lenya* (Berkeley: University of California Press, 1996).

Kurt Weill. Liner notes to original cast recording of *Street Scene,* made at time of the original run. Reissued as an LP record (Columbia Special Productions, COL 4139), 1973.

Notes

1. Kurt Weill, written a year before his death. Quoted in liner notes by Stephen Hinton, *Speak Low: Songs by Kurt Weill.* Anne Sofie Von Otter, John Eliot Gardner. Deutsche Grammophon CD 439 894-2. 1994.
2. Kurt Weill. Letter to Dr. Hans Heinsheimer, Univeral-Edition Vienna. *Kurt Weill Newsletter*, 3:1, Spring 1985. David Farneth, "Correspondence from the Archives," The Kurt Weill Foundation, 14.
3. Don Heckman, "Faithfull Takes Turn as Chanteuse," *Los Angeles Times.* Calendar Section, F9. Monday April 17, 1995.
4. Kim Kowalke. Liner notes to *Teresa Stratas: The Unknown Kurt Weill.* Nonesuch Records. LP recording D-73019, 1981.
5. Ibid.
6. Ibid.
7. In a letter from Weill to Ira Gershwin, *Kurt Weill Newsletter* 3:1, 13.
8. In a letter to Ira Gershwin. Quoted in Ronald Sanders, *The Days Grow Short: The Life and Music of Kurt Weill* (Los Angeles: Silman-James Press, 1980), 323.
9. Weill's notes about his approach to musical theater were in his liner notes to the original recording of the work. Quoted in Sanders, ibid., 359.
10. David D'Andre, "Street Scene Research Documents at Yale University and the Rubin Academy of Music and Dance," in *Kurt Weill Newsletter,* 12:1, Spring 1994, 14.

French Mélodie

The history of French *mélodie* spans about 130 years, from Berlioz to Poulenc. (The term *mélodie* is used to distinguish classical French song or art song, from popular song or folk song). The *mélodie* is descended from earlier French song forms, notably the eighteenth-century *romance*,* a song form characterized by its simplicity. The *mélodie* emerged as a distinct form in the middle of the nineteenth century due to several factors:

- the decline in the artistic level of the *romance*
- the introduction into France of Schubert's *Lieder*, which became very popular and widely published and disseminated.
- the new romantic poetry, which gave composers material that called for new compositional styles and techniques.

Hector Berlioz was the first composer to call his short vocal pieces *mélodies*. His earliest songs were no more than strophic pieces, still clinging to the unaffected style of the *romance*, but with *Les Nuits d'été* (1841), Berlioz created the first cycle of *mélodies*. In these five songs, he established a close synthesis between text and music using techniques from his orchestral compositions—manipulations of motives, descriptive accompaniment figures, interaction between voice and piano, and an expressive treatment of the text. It was clear that the *mélodie* had become a serious vocal form.

During the Romantic era, the *mélodie* continued to develop freer forms, more lyric vocal declamation, and increased expressiveness in the accompaniment. Composers such as Franz Liszt, Félicien David, Ernest Reyer, Henri Reber, Charles Gounod, Camille Saint-Saëns, Victor Massé, Georges Bizet, Léo Délibes, Jules Massenet, César Franck, and Edouard Lalo had texts of higher literary value at their disposal and wrote many significant songs. *Mélodies* gradually acquired greater unity of word and tone and a closer blend of style and refinement that was to culminate in the songs of Henri Duparc, Emmanuel Chabrier, Ernest Chausson, and the first collection of songs by Gabriel Fauré.

Early composers of French *mélodie* were inspired by the poetry of Théophile Gautier, Victor Hugo, and Charles Baudelaire. Composers also set poetry by the Parnassian poets, a group of writers inspired by the clarity of form and declamation found in Greek poetry. Gounod, Duparc, Chausson, and Fauré (in his early songs) used numerous texts from these poets for their songs.

Paul Verlaine's poetry was the great touchstone for French *mélodie* in the nineteenth century. Verlaine's interest in the musical resonances of words, the repetition of vowel sounds and alliteration, and his fascination with poetry as pure sensation produced texts that sparked some of the most beautiful and characteristic French *mélodies*, notably those of Fauré and Debussy—for example, Fauré's *La Bonne chanson* and *Cinq mélodies de Venise*, and Debussy's *Ariettes oubliées* and his two sets of *Fêtes galantes*.

Francis Poulenc was the dominant French composer of *mélodies* in the twentieth century. He added 150 songs to French song repertoire, each of lyric beauty and appealing character, embracing a wide range of dramatic and emotional moods. Poulenc was a member of a group of Parisian composers dubbed "Les Six" or the "Groupe des six" (Georges Auric, Louis Durey, Arthur Honegger, Darius Milhaud, Germaine Tailleferre, and Poulenc). These composers were greatly influenced by composer Erik Satie and writer Jean Cocteau. Their common reaction against over-inflated Romanticism and the vagueness of Impressionism led them to compose music that expressed clarity, precision, and simplicity. Despite their common beliefs about art, the musical styles of the composer of Les Six were quite diverse; they were more a group of friends than a musical trend. After Poulenc's death in 1963, the *mélodie* ceased to have any significant impact as a vocal form.

Erik Satie, Reynaldo Hahn, Maurice Ravel, Albert Roussel, and Jacques Leguerney are among the later French composers whose songs embody the clarity of expression and rich harmonic style that characterize the *mélodie*. Leguerney, a contemporary of Poulenc, wrote sixty-eight *mélodies* using almost all texts from Renaissance poets. His last song was composed in 1964, one year after Poulenc's death; his *mélodies* are the last substantial body of song in the great French tradition.

French *mélodie* has definite qualities and characteristics; Debussy wrote that "clarity of expression, precision, and concentration of form are qualities peculiar to the French genius."[1] Singers who want to perform French *mélodies* well need poetic sensibility, intelligence, taste and sensitivity to the clear inflection of syllables within long, flowing melodic lines. Distinguished French baritone and pedagogue Pierre Bernac described the art of the greatest French composers as an "art of suggestion, more often expressing moods and impressions than precise emotion."[2] In other words, French song blends precision with lyricism, and demands that the performer be able to communicate with both elegance and wit.

*The *romance* was the predominant form of French classical song in the early decades of the nineteenth century. It evolved from earlier French poetic/vocal forms and featured highly expressive, sentimental music. There was little or no musical-poetic interaction between voice and accompaniment. During the Revolution and the Empire the *romance* reached its zenith, embracing a wide range of emotional texts: sentimental, heroic, passionate, and dramatic. A famous example of a *romance* is Martini's "Plaisir d'amour."

Notes
1. Quoted in Pierre Bernac, *The Interpretation of French Song,* 33.
2. Ibid.

HECTOR BERLIOZ (1803-1869)

It is indeed a rare genius who can create works whose simplicity is in direct proportion to their size. Unfortunately, I am not one of them; I need ample resources to produce any effect.

—Hector Berlioz[1]

Hector Berlioz composed around fifty songs and it is with these songs that the important period of French *mélodie* began. He composed his earliest songs in the style of *romances,* the prevailing vocal form of the day. These early songs are strophic, each verse sung to the same music. Five collections of Berlioz's songs were published during his lifetime. Most notable was the group titled *Mélodies irlandaises,* afterwards reprinted as *Irlande,* on translated texts by Thomas Moore. Berlioz called these songs *mélodies,* and although their overall style is closer to the *romance* than the later French *mélodies,* they closely integrate the text and music with strong harmonies and beautifully shaped melodies. These youthful compositions are dedicated to Harriet Smithson, the great love of Berlioz's life.

Berlioz lacked interest in the traditional song form for piano and voice. He required orchestral instruments to achieve the musical effects that characterized his compositional style. He orchestrated more than half of his songs; as he did so, he made considerable revisions in most of them, each time changing them to accommodate more orchestral instruments. As a result, many songs appear in several versions.

Berlioz's most important vocal work is *Les Nuits d'été* (1841), which is the first great cycle in French *mélodie.* In this group of songs, Berlioz established a more complex and sophisticated level of sung poetry than had appeared in the early *romances,* and opened the door for further developments in *mélodie.* Berlioz was probably the first composer to consistently use the term *mélodie* in connection with his songs.

Melody was a primary element in Berlioz's style, although the main focus of the music is not always found in the melody itself, but in its relationship to the accompaniment. Berlioz wrote highly expressive melodies of extended phrases that were frequently open-ended and asymmetrical.

His harmonies are basically tonal; occasional passages of bitonality and polytonality appear in his larger works. He exploited diminished 7th chords to the limit, often using them in a series to highlight the poetry. He also sustained musical tension and dramatic intensity by chains of sequences.

Berlioz was deeply sensitive to poetry and insistent that the form of the music be dictated by the expressive content of the poetry. He numbered many poets among his friends (Alfred de Vigny, Auguste Barbier, Gérard de Nerval, Théophile Gautier, Alfred de Mussset), and they provided texts for many of his songs.

Les Nuits d'été	The Summer Nights. 1841
(Théophile Gautier)	1856 (orchestral version)

Villanelle • Le Spectre de la rose • Sur les lagunes (Lamento) • Absence • Au Cimetière (Clair de lune) • L'île inconnue

Les Nuits d'été was first published in 1841 with piano accompaniment and later with an orchestral accompaniment. The 1841 version for voice and piano was designed for mezzo-soprano or tenor, with No. 5 being assigned to the tenor. For the 1856 orchestral version, Berlioz revised the original score, probably to suit the dedicatees. He transposed Nos. 2 and 3 into lower keys and indicated a preference for male voices in Nos. 2 and 5.[2] If these indications are taken literally, four singers would be required for the orchestral version: soprano (Nos. 1, 4, 6), contralto (No. 2), baritone (No. 3), and tenor (No. 5). Instrumentation varies for each song.[3]

Modern performances of the complete work are most often done with one singer—an appropriate key is chosen from the piano or orchestral version, or transpositions are used as needed. The songs are more effective with orchestra; the piano accompaniment is awkward at times, and the character of these songs calls for the rich and varied colors that Berlioz draws from instrumental sources.

The work is symphonic in conception, and is, in general, operatically conceived for the voice. Each song suggests a miniature tone poem and has some unique element (an individual emotional mood or harmonic coloring) that sets it apart from the rest. All the songs share rich melodic passages.

Although the *mélodies* do not form a tight-knit homogenous group, they are all settings of one poet, Théophile Gautier. Each song treats some phase of love and the theme of longing, which further unifies the group. Songs 1 and 6 frame the group with an optimistic mood and lively tempi; the interior *mélodies* are more extreme expressions—laments for love lost.

VILLANELLE (VILLANELLE). A fresh spring song opens the set. Flowing rhythmic patterns and harmonic modulations embellish a simple but flexible melodic line. The form is strophic; three stanzas contain subtle musical variations that define the poetry. (Example: Compare the phrases "Que l'on voit au matin trembler" and "Pour parler de nos beaux amours." In the second phrase, Berlioz changes only two notes, a tiny alteration that highlights the text "to talk of our glorious love"). In the second and third stanzas, Berlioz uses figures from the vocal line in the piano accompaniment in imitative style, a lively exchange of material that creates a counterpoint-like texture and propels the *mélodie* to its close. Berlioz initiates imitative counterpoint between the voice and piano beginning at the third line of text. Figures derived from the vocal line are found in the piano accompaniment.

LE SPECTRE DE LA ROSE* (THE SPECTRE OF THE ROSE). Gautier's sensual poem reveals a romantic dramatic scene, the languorous aftermath of a ball. The ghost of a dying rose, pressed all evening against the bosom of a beautiful young girl, comes back to haunt her dreams. It will return every night to dance at her bedside; its fragrant perfume is its soul and it is from paradise. Its destiny was one to be envied, dying so beautiful a death; its tomb is her breast.

Berlioz sets these rich poetic images in an elaborate musical texture. The vocal line is operatic in scope. The form is through-composed, although the same melodic phrase initiates each of the three sections. Each section opens with *cantabile* passages that become more uneven and fragmented as the poetry builds to the climactic point of each section—verses one and two feature opulent soaring vocal phrases "Tu me promenas" and "J'arrive du paradis"; verse three ends quietly and poignantly, the melodic phrases dropping lower and lower ("Here lies a rose that every king will envy").

At the words "Mais ne crains rien, je ne réclame, Ni messe ni *De Profundis,*" Berlioz creates a stunning example of text painting: a series of descending diminished 7th chords vividly illustrates the flower's passion as its life's energy ebbs.

*Gautier's poem was also the basis for the ballet of the same name.

SUR LES LAGUNES [LAMENTO] (ON THE LAGOONS). This song is one of the laments of the set, a mournful narrative that matches No. 5 in mood. The two *mélodies* are also linked by a motive of a minor second that dominates both vocal line and piano accompaniment. Berlioz uses this tiny interval with several variations throughout the musical texture.

Vocal passages are *chant récitatif,* punctuated by a repeated refrain that is heard at the end of each verse. The emotional mood is one of intense despair.

The *mélodie* is through-composed in a languid $\frac{6}{8}$ meter.

*Gautier's poem was also set by Gounod ("Ma belle amie est morte") and Fauré ("Chanson du pêcheur").

ABSENCE (ABSENCE). This *mélodie* is generally the most admired of the set. Gautier's original poem has eight strophes. Berlioz chose to set only three, using the first as a recurring rondo, so that the form is A B A C A. Musical texture throughout this *mélodie* is classically sparse and restrained despite the passionate mood of the text.

Berlioz immediately establishes a mood of loneliness for an absent lover in the first vocal phrase, which repeats twice with verses two and three, and is used in phrases of free arioso. The mood of loneliness is further reinforced by an irregular resolution of the tritone in the third bar, a musical *faux-pas* that offended many critics.

AU CIMETIÈRE* [CLAIR DE LUNE] (IN THE CEMETERY [MOONLIGHT]). Like "Sur les lagunes" (No. 3), this *mélodie* is subtitled "Lamento," but this lament is much more lyrical. The poet stands in the moonlit cemetery listening to the mournful cooing of the dove, which he associates with the weeping of his dead beloved. The vocal line is legato and almost Italianate, with vocal material that repeats throughout the song. This is graceful melancholy indeed.

There are six verses in the poem, arranged in an A B A pattern of three large sections. Shifting harmonies, combined with stepwise vocal phrases and rigid rhythmic patterns, create a sense of anxiety and unrest.

*This text, in abbreviated form, was also set by Henri Duparc ("Lamento").

L'ÎLE INCONNUE (THE UNKNOWN ISLE). Berlioz concludes the group with this *mélodie* of delicate charm. The theme of the poetry is somewhat like Baudelaire's "L'Invitation au Voyage," set by Duparc—an invitation to a romantic voyage. Somewhat whimsically, a young man offers a pretty girl a voyage to anywhere she wants to go, describing the grandeur of his boat in fanciful terms. In response to his invitation, the young maid asks to be taken "to a safe shore where love lasts forever." He replies, "That shore, my dear, is quite unknown in the land of love."

Berlioz uses conventional rhythm patterns in a texture that matches the opening song. Compared with the other *mélodies* in the set, these vocal phrases are sweeping and flexible. Nautical allusions in the poetry and the subtitle "Barcarole" are complemented by $\frac{6}{8}$ meter and a tempo marked *Allegro spiritoso*.

Extended Study List

La Mort d'Ophélie • La Belle voyageuse • La Captive • Le Coucher du soleil • Elégie • Zaïde • Le Chasseur danois • Le Chant des Bretons • Le Roi de Thulé • Le Matin • Les Champs

Selected Reading

A. E. F. Dickinson, *The Music of Berlioz* (New York: St. Martin's Press, 1973).

D. Kern Holomon, *Berlioz* (Cambridge: Harvard University Press, 1989).

Jeffrey Langford and Jane Denker Graves, *Hector Berlioz: A Guide to Research* (New York: Garland Publishing Inc., 1989).

Brian Primmer, *The Berlioz Style (London:* Oxford University Press, 1973).
Julian Rushton, *"Les Nuits d'été:* cycle or collection?" in *Berlioz Studies,* ed. by Peter Bloom
(Cambridge: Cambridge University Press, 1992).
Sheri Moore Weiler, "Hector Berlioz's *Les Nuits d'été:* A Performer's Perspective," *Journal of Singing*
61:4 (March/April 2005), 359-370.

Notes

1. Quoted in Frits Noske, *French Song from Berlioz to Duparc* (New York: Dover, 1970), 92.
2. Julian Rushton, *"Les Nuits d'été*: cycle or collection?" in *Berlioz Studies*, 113.
3. Ibid., 132.

CHARLES GOUNOD (1818-1893)

The true founder of the *mélodie* in France was Charles Gounod.
—Maurice Ravel[1]

France is essentially the country of precision, neatness and taste, that is to
say the opposite of excess, portentousness, disproportion, long-windedness...
—Charles Gounod[2]

In addition to being the leading composer of French opera in the nineteenth
century, Charles Gounod is often referred to as the "father of the *mélodie.*"
Gounod's songs appeared when the French composers had declining interest in the
romance as a vocal form. The introduction of Schubert's *Lieder* into France had
stimulated French composers, and they became more interested in using the piano
to help interpret the text and in writing vocal lines with an increasing variety of
articulation. The *mélodie* began a new phase around 1850, developing into an independent, specifically French genre.

French poets began to write poetry of higher literary quality, with freer phrase
forms and meter that dictated freer musical structures, and French composers
began to vary song forms to accommodate the structure and pattern of the new
poetry. (Until then, song had been predominantly strophic.)

Gounod composed over 200 songs, choosing texts by prominent contemporary
poets; his first *mélodies*, composed in the 1840s and 1850s, used poetry by Victor
Hugo, Alfred de Musset, La Fontaine, and Théophile de Banville. Gounod set his
texts with careful attention to versification. Saint-Saëns commented on Gounod's
sense of prosody: "Not the least of his merits is that he guided us toward the great
tradition of the past, basing his vocal music on correctness of declamation."[3]

Gounod's songs are uneven in quality, but his *mélodies* reach a significant level
above what had been composed before. Although some songs retain prominent features of the *romance*, notably strophic form and simple accompaniments, their
overall style reflects the beginning of new directions for French *mélodie*. Many
were written for the French bourgeoisie, who were interested in taking French
song into their parlors along with Schubert's *Lieder*. Gounod's carefully crafted
songs established that French song could blend beautiful melodies, expressive
accompaniments, and fine poetry with the same results as the German *Lied*.
Although critics point to a lack of depth in many of his songs, some of them express
deeply felt emotion in a refined understated way.

Gounod's songs have *sensibilité** and fluid lyricism, which are hallmarks of his
compositional style. His *mélodies* are notable for their elegance and for their
French sense of proportion: small, well crafted, graceful—characteristics that were
to influence Fauré.

As a young man, Gounod studied in Italy after winning the Prix de Rome. The experience shaped his song composition and influenced his melodic lines, which display Italianate suppleness and charm. His three-year-long visit to England during the early 1870s yielded many songs of quality, set to English texts, including the song cycle *Biondina* (1871-72), a Tosti-like work geared to the tastes of the Victorian public. In keeping with his reputation as an international composer, he also set texts in Italian and Spanish. He also admired the works of Schubert, Chopin, Schumann and Mendelssohn; elements from their styles may be found in his *mélodies*, absorbed into his personal idiom and stamped with Gallic sensibility.

Gounod composed accompaniments that are almost always subordinated to the voice—simple, graceful figures coupled with small melodic or rhythmic motives. He was fond of using arpeggiated chords, broken chords, and repeated chords in his accompaniments to produce an expressive atmosphere and a feeling of calm. There are extended introductions and preludes in many Gounod songs.

In today's light, Gounod's *mélodies* may seem slightly faded or overly sentimental, but they contain the seeds from which French *mélodie* was to develop and flower. His position as an innovator in the development of French *mélodie* cannot be denied.

*Sensibilité is difficult to define exactly. It denotes a heightened expressive response to that which is beautiful. A person who has *sensibilité* has an innate sense of refined taste.

Sérénade   **Serenade. 1855**
(Victor Hugo)

An Italianate vocal line of *bel canto* purity is the prominent element in this well-known Gounod song. It is set over a rocking accompaniment figure, which provides a lulling but somewhat sensual atmosphere for the text. There are three poetic stanzas, set strophically. Gounod ends each with miniature coloratura vocal phrases.

Viens, les gazons sont verts   **Come, the Lawns are Green. 1875**
(Jules Barbier)

This charming but abbreviated *mélodie* has a text of two stanzas. The poet is Jules Barbier, one of Gounod's librettists for *Faust*. The mood is delightful and fresh, and the vocal passages are an excellent example of Gounod's skill as a melodist.

L'Absent   **The Absent One. 1876**
(Charles Gounod)

Gounod provided his own poetry for this *mélodie*, which is one of his best-known songs. It is said to have been written as an apology to his wife, a public mea culpa for his well-publicized liaison with Mrs. Georgina Weldon in London.[4]

Vocal passages of considerable breadth are legato and tranquil, set above a softly expressive arpeggiated accompaniment. Gounod uses the arpeggiated pattern for subtle harmonic modulations that continue through the *mélodie* and complement his verse with its heartfelt emotional plea ("Tell me...if my beloved, while I lie awake, Remembers the absent one"). It is altogether possible that Gounod's flexible harmonic progressions in this song could have influenced Fauré. Gounod closes with an extended piano postlude.

Venise   Venice. 1842
(Alfred de Musset)

"Venise" is one of Gounod's loveliest songs. A quickly moving piano introduction calls to mind the exciting sights and sounds of a sultry Venetian night. This bustling pattern quickly dissolves into a languid, rhythmic barcarole figure of arpeggios in the bass line, embroidered with graceful sixteenth-note figures. The voice enters with a supple melody, blending with the piano figures to evoke the rocking gondolas moored in the quiet water of Venice's lagoons, lit by dancing lights in the city. This is a secretive and mysterious Venice.

Gounod uses the barcarole pattern in the piano as the basis for flexible and subtle modulations. It also serves to unify the formal structure, as does the faster paced piano introduction used between sections.

O ma belle rebelle   O my beautiful rebel. 1855
(Jean-Antoine de Baïf)

Jean-Antoine de Baif was a member of the Pléiade, a group of seven poets led by Pierre Ronsard.* Baif's poetry is especially notable for its innovative metrical schemes. He was interested in unrhymed lines and the possibilities for setting them. The subject of "O ma belle rebelle" is Louise Labé, the most prolific French poetess of the sixteenth century, often called "la Sappho lyonnaise." One of her lovers was believed to be the poet Clément Marot. She appears in Marot's collection of poems titled *L'Adolescence Clémentine* (1532), where she is referred to as "La belle rebelle."

Gounod's setting is the height of understatement, a perfect example of the French style of lyricism and precision. Using strophic form and varying the vocal line only to accommodate word stress, Gounod shapes smooth and elegant vocal phrases that float above a simple accompaniment. The accompaniment features its own bass melody, which provides a link between verses. "O ma belle rebelle" resembles a stylish madrigal, accompanied by a lute or guitar, and in listening, one can hear the link to Fauré. Composer Jacques Leguerney said that this was one of his favorite French *mélodies*.**

*For more information on the Pléiade, see the section on Jacques Leguerney.
**In a conversation with the author.

Extended Study List
Au rossignol • Chanson de printemps • Mignon • Chant d'automne • Ce que je suis sans toi • Rêverie • Le Vallon • Où voulez-vouz aller? • Envoi de fleurs • Le temps des roses • *Biondina* • My true love hath my heart (Sir Philip Sidney) • The Fountain Mingles With The River (Percy Bysshe Shelley) • If thou art sleeping, maiden (Henry Longfellow)

Selected Reading

James Harding, *Gounod* (New York: Stein and Day, 1973.)

Brian Thompson, *The Disastrous Mrs. Weldon* (New York: Broadway Books, 2001). Chapter 6, "Gounod."

Notes

1. Quoted in Frits Noske, *French Song from Berlioz to Duparc*, 160.
2. Quoted in liner notes by Roger Vignoles, *Au jardin des aveux*, Virgin Records VC 7 991179-2, 1991.
3. Noske, 164.
4. Graham Johnson, "Charles Gounod and the French *Mélodie*," liner notes to *Songs by Gounod* (The Hyperion French Song Edition, Hyperion Records CDA 66801/2 1993). Mrs. Georgina Weldon was a celebrated eccentric of the Victorian age. She was a singer of questionable technique, believing that the secret of fine singing was to sing with clenched teeth and an immobile face.
5. In conversation with the author, 7 July 1991.

PAULINE VIARDOT (1821-1910)

> Viardot is the most gifted woman I have ever met in my life.
>
> —Clara Schumann[1]

Pauline Viardot's eighty-nine years spanned a tremendously colorful and vital life. An internationally famed singer, Viardot's extraordinary talents and superior intelligence made her a highly visible and important figure in the musical and literary affairs of her time. Viardot moved easily among the Parisian milieu of Chopin, Alfred de Musset, Berlioz, George Sand, Rossini, Eugène Delacroix, Liszt, Gustave Doré, and Gounod. She was loved by de Musset, Gounod, and Berlioz, and later by Russian poet Ivan Turgenev. One of the greatest singing actresses in operatic history, her friendship with composers, especially Meyerbeer and Berlioz, had an important influence on the music they produced for the stage.

Michelle Ferdinande Pauline Viardot (née Garcia) was a talented and complex woman. She came from a famous musical family: her father was Manuel Garcia, renowned singer, vocal teacher and impresario; her mother Joaquina, was an actress and singer; and younger sister Maria Malibran was a celebrated opera star. Pauline studied composition with Anton Reicha and piano with Franz Liszt.

In 1839, at the age of seventeen, she made her singing debut in Rossini's *Otello*. Soon after, she married French writer and critic Louis Viardot, twenty-one years her senior. Through her husband, she met the leading literary figures of the day—among them, Russian poet Ivan Turgenev, who became her lover and confidante. Viardot, her husband, and Turgenev maintained a subtle, complicated *ménage à trois* that lasted until 1883 when both men died, coincidentally in the same year.

Viardot was at her best performing roles that offered maximum possibilities to exploit her considerable dramatic talents. Gounod wrote the title role in his first opera *Sapho* for her and she created a sensation as Fidès in Meyerbeer's *Le Prophète,* but perhaps her finest role was Orphée in Berlioz's French version revival of Gluck's *Orfeo ed Euridice*. Not surprisingly, late in her career she made a specialty of Russian songs; Tchaikovsky composed "None but the lonely heart" for her. Saint-Saëns dedicated *Samson et Dalila* to her.

Viardot's songs mirror her forceful personality and colorful life. She composed over 100 vocal pieces, more than ninety of which were published during her lifetime. Far from being a collection of salon pieces of the day, Viardot's compositions encompass varying styles and have a theatricality and large dimension about them.

Viardot was an accomplished pianist. Her piano accompaniments are often complex and sometimes threaten to overwhelm the vocal line, but the songs are absorbing and, as one might imagine, well conceived for the singer. Most are in strophic or modified strophic form, with occasional modulations into distant keys.

She was fluent in five languages and her choice of texts reflects her wide knowledge of literature and her extensive travels. She used a variety of sources ranging from simple folk texts to the best poets of the day. Her settings of non-French texts are often laced with exoticism. She set a number of Pushkin texts in German translation, probably a by-product of her liaison with Turgenev. She also made vocal arrangements of instrumental works by other composers, setting four of Chopin's mazurkas as songs[*] and reworking Brahms's *Hungarian Dance* No. 7 as a duet.[**] In addition to her songs, she composed four operettas, three to texts by Ivan Turgenev.

[*] See "Extended Study List."
[**] Brahms composed his "Alto Rhapsody" for Viardot.

Aime-moi, (Mazurka Op. 33, No. 2 by Frédéric Chopin)   Love Me. 1848
(Text by Louis Pomey)

This *mélodie* is one of the Chopin piano mazurkas that Viardot arranged for voice and piano. The text is by Louis Pomey, Turgenev's stepbrother, who provided many texts for Viardot's songs.

Transcriptions were accepted as normal musical practice in the nineteenth century; Lizst's numerous transcriptions were highly popular. Chopin and Viardot were good friends and had high mutual regard for each other's artistry. Chopin was so pleased with the results of Viardot's "re-compositions" that he often accompanied her at the grand piano when she performed them. In transcribing these works, Viardot made some alterations in the originals to accommodate the vocal line, but skillfully retained Chopin's musical style. This particular mazurka is one of Chopin's showpieces; the vocal line requires considerable flexibility from the singer and is not for the fainthearted.

Bonjour mon cœur   Good Morning, My Heart. 1886
(Pierre de Ronsard)

This is a brief but charming song. It recalls a morning meeting of lovers; the text is laced with compliments for a young girl from her sweetheart. Viardot's sprightly piano accompaniment—broken chords and arpeggiated figures that underpin a simple, delicate vocal line—complements the Renaissance poetry of Pierre Ronsard, one of France's earliest and most renowned poets. Viardot's dramatic sense takes over in the final measures ("Good morning, my sweet rebel"), but the moment remains in keeping with the delicacy of the mood.

Le Chêne et le roseau	The Oak and the Reed.

Le Chêne et le roseau
(Poet unknown)

The Oak and the Reed.

An unknown poet tells a simple tale of a strong, proud oak and a modest reed growing nearby. Viardot must have seen the drama in the story; the vocal lines tend to sound operatic, alternating with piano figures that graphically paint the text. As the story unfolds, a storm threatens to uproot both tree and reed, but each holds fast through a blizzard of flying scales and a few short measures that are reminiscent of Gluck's aria "Divinités du Styx" from *Alceste*. Frédéric Chopin accompanied the first performance, which may explain its colorful, virtuoso piano accompaniment. Viardot dedicated the song to her husband, Louis Viardot.

Sérénade
(Théophile Gautier)

Serenade. 1884

This is a lively *mélodie* of Spanish flavor set to a Gautier poem. A $\frac{6}{8}$ dance rhythm begins in A minor, and migrates to A major for the end of the song. Viardot deftly integrates oriental elements into the piano accompaniment. Viardot's family background and her flair for the dramatic is revealed in this colorful setting.

Haï luli!
(Xavier de Maistre)

Ah, alas! 1880

Here is a French counterpart to Schubert's "Gretchen am Spinnrade." It is a poignant picture of a lonely village girl, seated at her spinning wheel. As she tries to spin, she thinks only of her lover, and worries that he will not come to her.

Viardot uses rhythms that suggest the spinning wheel. The short piano introduction and the first accompaniment figure create the image of the treadle. The vocal line is smoothly graceful and expressive, giving the impression of a folk song. There are three stanzas, each divided by a beautiful, limpid refrain ("Haï luli").

The "treadle motion" in the piano stops abruptly between the verse and refrain. A new piano figure is introduced to accompany "Haï luli." It is derived from the original pattern used for the verse, but it also incorporates rolled chords. This combination evokes the circling spinning wheel.

Viardot skillfully alters each repetition of stanza and verse, making subtle harmonic changes and modulations to accommodate dramatic mood and maintain variety.

"Haï luli!" is the fourth song in the collection *Six mélodies et une Havanaise variee a 2 voix*. It is an altogether beguiling *mélodie*.

Extended Study List

Der Jüngling und das Mädchen (Pushkin) • Berceuse cosaque (Lermontoff/Pomey) •_Madrid (de Musset) • Arrangements of Chopin's Mazurkas (texts: Louis Pomey). (Seize Ans, Op. 50:2; La Danse, Op. 50:1; L'Oiselet, Op. 68:2) • Adieu les beaux jours • L'Enfant et la mere • Rossignol, rossignolet • Die Soldatenbraut •Chanson de la pluie • Der Gärtner • Die Beschwörung

Selected Reading

Jane Blowers and Judith Tick, *Women Making Music* (Urbana, Illinois: University of Illinois Press, 1986).

James R. Briscoe, editor, *Historical Anthology of Music by Women* (Bloomington: Indiana University Press, 1987).

Rupert Christiansen, *Prima Donna: A History* (New York: Viking, 1984). Chapter 2: "Romantic Opera."

Susan C. Cook and Judy S. Tsou, ed. and introduction, *Anthology of Songs: Pauline Duchambge, Loïsa Puget, Pauline Viardot, Jane Vieu* (New York: DaCapo Press, 1988). Contains ten songs of Viardot, 32-84.

April Fitzlyon, *The Price of Genius: A Life of Pauline Viardot* (London: John Calder, 1974).

Henry Pleasants, *The Great Singers,* rev. ed. (New York: Simon and Schuster, 1981). Pages 216-223 deal with Viardot.

Notes

1. Quoted in liner notes by Eugen Ott, trans. Susan Marie Praeder. Liner notes to *Pauline Viardot-Garcia: Songs.* (Karin Ott, soprano, Christoph Keller, piano. CPO digital disc 999 044-2, 1989. West Germany).

CÉSAR FRANCK (1822-1890)

It is a matter of little importance whether the music is descriptive...what is of the first importance is that a composition should be musical, and emotional as well.

—César Franck[1]

César Franck wrote comparatively few songs, but his strong personality and unique style of composing led to the founding of a school of musical thought and style among his contemporaries. He taught organ at the Paris Conservatoire for many years, and was organist at the Church of Sainte-Clotilde. Through his friendships, he established a circle of important composers who not only shared his musical aesthetics but also helped to disseminate it.

As a mentor and teacher, he exercised an enormous influence on French music and especially on French song in the late nineteenth century. His most noted pupils were Duparc, Chausson, and d'Indy. After his death, Franck's ideas continued to be perpetuated by d'Indy at the Schola Cantorum. In 1872, with the aid of Saint-Saëns, Duparc, and Bussine, Franck founded the Société Nationale de Musique, whose object was to promote new French chamber music and to revive the habit of attending concerts rather than the opera.

Franck's songs are not representative of his overall compositional style. His early songs are overly romantic; his later songs reveal a mastery of fluid line and a more transparent style. Prominent characteristics in Franck songs are: strophic settings, chordal accompaniments in block, broken or arpeggiated figures; rather dense harmonic textures full of chromaticism; and simple vocal lines. He chose texts from famous poets such as Hugo, Musset, and Sully-Prudhomme, although he did not always set poems with regard for correct rhythmic accentuation.

The two *mélodies* noted here are generally considered Franck's most outstanding.

La Procession   The Procession. 1888
(Charles Brizieux)

This *mélodie* is deservedly well known. Franck originally composed it for voice and piano, and later scored it for orchestra. He also created a version for voice and organ.

Brizieux's poem describes the ceremony of blessing the crops, a procession in which the people carry the Host across the fields. The simple reverence of those in the procession is evoked in music of great strength, beauty, and religious grandeur. Pedal points, fugato, and a liturgical chant appear in the *mélodie*—musical devices common to church music.

The song is in two sections: the first is the procession; the second, a narrative reflection on the scene. Franck uses two themes in the first section. The first is solemn and religious in mood; the second is the *Lauda Sion*, a liturgical chant heard in the accompaniment with the vocal line singing over it. The vocal line in the first section is articulated in a quasi-recitative style, but becomes a much freer declamation in the second part of the song.

The music becomes intensely expressive moment at the words "Soleil! darde sur lui tes longs rayons couchant" (Sun! cast your long sunset beams upon it!) as the crowd kneels reverently around the monstrance containing the Host. Toward the end of the song, the two themes from the first section reappear: "Dieu s'avance à travers les champs" (God advances across the fields).

Nocturne   Nocturne. 1884
(Louis de Fourcaud)

Demuth says that "in the *Nocturne* we find the real Franck." The poet invokes the night to "give me your serenity, bring light to my troubled soul, pervade my thoughts, bring silence to my heart, and pour sleep into my eyes." Each stanza in turn describes the night as "fresh/transparent, lovely/ starry, saintly/taciturn, grand/solemn." The music for each stanza is varied to express the different moods and the words of the invocation.

Franck begins the song with a beautiful vocal melody, which is introduced by a descending chromatic line in the piano. The first three verses are in the minor key; the vocal material is the same for the second and third verses, except for slight modifications to suit the meaning of the poetry. The fourth verse is in the major key, with broader arpeggiated figures in the piano, which produce a feeling of spaciousness. The overall mood is one of nobility, depth of feeling, and, pervading all, the dark majesty of the night.

Composer Guy Ropartz, a member of Franck's circle, scored the song for orchestra.

Extended Study List
Le Mariage des roses • S'il est un charmant gazon • Lied • Mignonne • Roses et papillons

Selected Reading
Laurence Davies, *César Franck and His Circle* (London: Barrie & Jenkins, 1970).
_____, *Franck* (London: J. M. Dent and Sons, 1973). Master Musicians Series.
Léon Vallas, *César Franck*, trans. Hubert Foss (Westport, CT: Greenwood Press, 1976).

Notes
1. Quoted in Léon Vallas, *César Franck*, 245-6.

GEORGES BIZET (1838-1875)

Without form, no style; without style, no art.

—Georges Bizet[1]

Georges Bizet composed nearly fifty *mélodies*, most of which conform to the style of Gounod, his teacher at the Conservatoire. Although Gounod's influence can be seen immediately in Bizet's songs, Bizet's rhythmic style is more forceful and his keen dramatic sense goes far beyond Gounod's typical sentiment. Bizet did not often set texts in the most sensitive way; with the exception of Victor Hugo, the poets he chose were unremarkable.

Bizet wrote most of his songs before he was thirty. His leaning toward vocal music was no doubt influenced by his father, who taught singing. Bizet wrote *mélodies* that are extremely well suited for the voice. Accompaniments to his *mélodies* are filled with sensitive details, and colorful rhythmic patterns. He was an outstanding pianist, and the accompaniments to his songs are filled with sensitive details, and colorful rhythmic patterns.

According to Claire Croiza, Fauré used to say of Bizet: "Light, sensibility, and charm" and Saint-Saëns said "We differ in everything, following a different ideal, he searching above all for life and passion, and I running after the chimera of purity of style and perfection of form."[2]

Chanson d'avril   **Song of April. 1866**
(Louis Bouilhet)

Bizet composed this charming *mélodie* in 1866 in a style characteristic of Gounod. Its mood is youthful and fresh; the vocal line is graceful and the piano accompaniment adds to the overall mood but seems to share no meaningful interaction with the voice. Bizet sets the text syllabically and uses strophic form. Although no one component of style is particularly distinctive, the *mélodie* is an engaging example of Bizet's affinity for creating free-flowing melodies.

Adieux de l'hôtesse arabe   **The Farewell of the Arabian Hostess. 1866**
(Victor Hugo)

This is perhaps the best-known of Bizet's *mélodies*. It is a characteristic example of the fascination with oriental subjects that permeated the work of poets, musicians, and artists of this period.

Hugo's text, taken from *Orientales*, describes a scene in which a native Arab girl is being deserted by her lover, a young and handsome traveler. In an attempt to persuade him to stay, her "good-bye" is full of enticing and voluptuous images. Bizet's musical response to the dramatic situation and the imagery of the text results in vocal phrases that are freely undulating, dance-like, and intense. Musical material used here foreshadows the exoticism and obsessive rhythms that Bizet developed and used later in his opera *Carmen*. The seeds of Carmen's bewitching "Habanera" are embedded in Bizet's sensual vocal lines, and the incessant beating of a tabor in the piano accompaniment figures.

Bizet writes a melismatic phrase for the voice for the final "Souviens-toi!" It is a miniature coda of twelve bars, which he marks to be sung "in a voice broken by sobs."

Absence*   1872
(Théophile Gautier)

Bizet's response to Gautier's poem is markedly different from that of Hector Berlioz, who used the same text for a *mélodie* in *Les Nuits d'été*. Berlioz's setting is the better known of the two. Bizet set six of Gautier's eight verses, while Berlioz chose to set only three, using the first verse as a recurring refrain.

The most striking feature of Bizet's setting is the vocal writing. In contrast to Berlioz's majestic, static phrases, Bizet's vocal line is unabashedly and overtly romantic. Sweeping, flexible vocal phrases are complemented throughout the *mélodie* by equally broad melodic lines in the left hand of the piano accompaniment. These countermelodies in the piano texture are coupled with a pattern of repeated chords in triplets in the right hand of the piano. The give and take between voice and piano urges the song forward and reinforces the romantic drama of the text.

*For a comparison setting, see Hector Berlioz, *Les Nuits d'été*.

Guitare   Guitar. 1866
(Victor Hugo)

Bizet composed this colorful *mélodie* while he was writing his opera *La Jolie fille de Perth* (1867). He animates the accompaniment with an exuberant bolero rhythm, which he also used in his well-known *mélodie* "Ouvre ton cœur." Bizet added the "Tra-la-las" to the text; they not only lengthen the *mélodie*, but also help to underline the uninhibited personality of the protagonist. The leading lady of Bizet's masterpiece *Carmen* surely was born from this family tree. Hugo's poem, written in 1838, was titled "Autre guitare," and not "Guitare." This *mélodie* appeared in *Feuilles d'Album* (six songs to poems of Musset, Ronsard, Hugo, Millevoye and Lamartine).

*A number of other composers set this verse: Victor Massé ("Ramez, dormez, aimez!"), Saint-Saëns ("Guitare"), Liszt ("Comment disaient-ils") and Lalo. Bizet's version is the most famous.

Extended Study List
Ouvre ton cœur • Pastorale • Vieille chanson • Douce mer • La Chanson de la rose •Après l'hiver • Berceuse • La Chanson du fou • La Coccinelle • Le Grillon • L'Abandonnée • A une fleur • Adieux à Suzon

Selected Reading
Mina Curtiss, *Bizet and His World* (New York: Alfred A. Knopf, 1958).
Winton Dean, *Bizet* (New York: Collier Books, 1962, revised edition, London, 1975).

Notes
1. Bizet to his pupil Galabert. Quoted in Winton Dean, *Bizet*, 250.
2. Betty Bannerman, *The Singer as Interpreter: Claire Croiza's Master Classes*, 78.

EMMANUEL CHABRIER (1841-1894)

Chabrier is absolutely, typically French. He is the most gifted inventor of unimagined harmonies, of rare combinations of timbres, the most vigorous colourist and the most straightforward melodist.

—Henri Barraud[1]

Chabrier, I love him as one loves a father! An indulgent father, always merry, his pockets full of tasty tidbits. Chabrier's music is a treasure house you can never exhaust.

—Francis Poulenc[2]

Emmanuel Chabrier composed a small number of *mélodies*, all firmly rooted in the conventional *romance*. These songs are strophic in form, but Chabrier modified either the melody or harmony to conform to the words of the text. Chabrier's songs are full of wit, whimsy, and good humor. About Chabrier's *mélodies*, Claire Croiza commented: "There is a male quality that a woman singer can never give entirely. It must be a man who drinks well and eats well. There is a basic roundness and frankness [to the style]..."[3] Chabrier was very explicit in marking his scores for desired articulations and musical nuances.

L'île heureuse   **The Happy Isle. 1890**
(Ephraïm Mikhaël)

This *mélodie* is one of Chabrier's best-known songs. For this lightweight poem, Chabrier composes a melodic line of considerable flexibility and charm. He separates the stanzas of the poem with ritornello sections in the piano. Chabrier is very explicit in marking his scores for desired articulations and musical nuances.

Ballade des gros dindons   **Ballad of the Big Fat Turkeys. 1890**
(Edmond Rostand)

Chabrier's settings "animal songs" might be considered forerunners of Ravel's *Histoires naturelles* and Poulenc's *Le Bestiaire.* The animals and insects found in these songs display traits that are almost human. The poems are by Edmond Rostand and his wife Rosemond Gérard. Chabrier liked to call these *mélodies* his "Barnyard Suite."

Chabrier was living in the country when he composed these songs. His sense of humor and talent for musical characterization is readily apparent in these delightful, colorful settings, which were not meant as caricatures but as occasions for good-natured laughter. "Pastorale des cochons roses" (Pastorale of the Pink Pigs), which is not discussed here, is the fourth *mélodie* in this group of farmyard vignettes.

"Loudly and heavily" is Chabrier's indication for the piano, which introduces the pompous gait of the overweight birds. Heavy triplets in both voice and piano finally disintegrate into a comical piano ritornello, which separates each stanza. In this twelve-bar interlude, Mozart's serenade in *Don Giovanni* is slyly quoted by Chabrier—an amusing musical comment on the text, which states, "Love and its sweet songs are too futile a pastime" for these portly birds.

Villanelle des petits canards	Villanelle of the Little Ducks. 1890
(Rosemond Gérard)	

Little ducks waddle in a merry line along the bank of the river. The vocal line and piano accompaniment, embellished by grace notes, dip in off-balance rhythms to match the ducks' movements. Chabrier highlights the comical mood throughout the *mélodie* with phrases of staccato notes, which alternate from *ppp* to *f*, with plenty of *sforzandi* peppered throughout.

Les Cigales	The Cicadas. 1890
(Rosemond Gérard)	

"The cicadas, these tiny beasts, sing better than the violins!" observes the poet in this delightful paean to the tiny insects with the large sound. Chabrier composes a lyrical vocal line, and marks *dolce* at the recurring refrain, "Les cigales, Ces bestioles." Singing cicadas appear in the piano accompaniment, as rolled chordal patterns are transferred from register to register. These alternate with a sixteenth-note figure that suggests the incessant humming of the tiny insects. A final flourish of six bars in the piano reflects the brilliance of the hot French sun, and the last sounds of the cicadas fade away.

Extended Study

Pastorale des cochons roses • Lied• Chanson pour Jeanne • Romance de l'étoile • L'Invitation au voyage • Toutes les fleurs • Sérénade de Ruy Blas • Credo d'amour • Adieux à Suzon • Couplets de Mariette • Ronde gauloise • Chants d'oiseaux • Le pas d'armes du roi Jean

Selected Reading

Rollo Myers, *Emmanuel Chabrier and His Circle* (London: J. M. Dent and Songs, Ltd., 1969).
Francis Poulenc, *Chabrier* (Paris: La Palatine, 1961).

Notes

1. Quoted in Pierre Bernac, *The Interpretation of French Song*, 80.
2. To Stéphane Audel in conversation. Francis Poulenc, *My Friends and Myself*, trans. James Harding, 54.
3. Betty Bannerman, *The Singer as Interpreter: Claire Croiza's Master Classes,* 79.

HENRI DUPARC (1848-1933)

I live in the regret for what I have not done, without troubling about the little I have done.

-—Henri Duparc[1]

Henri Duparc composed only sixteen songs, but they are among the most beautiful in the French literature, full of melodic and harmonic subtleties. He was a perfectionist, and his severe self-criticism of his own work led him to continually revise and polish his compositions; he destroyed many songs, refusing to let them be published. His slim catalog of *mélodies* was composed in a period of seventeen years, but stands as a major contribution to French song.

Duparc's songs are characterized by skillful construction, broad but supple melodic lines, rich harmonic structure, and complex piano accompaniments that border at times on dense orchestral-like textures. He chose texts by living poets, all from the Parnassian school,[*] among them Lahor, Sully-Prudhomme, Baudelaire, Silvestre, and de Lisle.

Duparc had strong views about singers, the human voice, and his songs. He detested any sort of vocal exhibitionism. (Claire Croiza recounts that Duparc said to her: "If I had known what some singers do with them, I would never have put any *rallentandi* in my songs."[2]) For the most part, he composed for the type of voice he preferred, the "violin-voice, capable of fluent, flexible phrasing and a real intensity of tone.[3]

Duparc commented on his intricate accompaniments in 1914 in a personal letter to singer Claire Croiza, who had visited the composer and performed some of his songs for him: "Please thank your most charming friend [Ivana Meedintiano], and tell her that concerning her accompaniment about which she was very wrong to excuse herself, I regret I am not at all of her opinion: I find, on the contrary, that it was excellent; and I like immensely this expressive way of accompanying, that follows and envelops the voice like a garment, making one with it, that —in a word —is not pianistic, but orchestral, from the heart and the intelligence."[4]

With the exception of "Au pays où se fait la guerre" and "Testament," which were set for medium voice, and "La Vague et la cloche," which was set for low voice, the remainder of Duparc's *mélodies* were conceived for high voice. Transposing Duparc's songs poses problems; due to the extensive range of the songs, brilliance is sometimes sacrificed in lower keys. Two of the *mélodies*, "La vague et la cloche," and "La Vie antérieure" were originally scored for orchestra; Duparc later supplied a piano-voice version. A number of other songs were orchestrated at later dates, most by the composer.

Around 1885, Duparc was stricken with a nervous disease that had lain dormant since childhood, and his ability to compose ceased. He retired to the country and lived another forty-eight years in artistic silence. Despite his slim number of song compositions, Duparc provided French song with a legacy that firmly establishes his place in its history.

---

*The Parnassians were a group of French poets who adopted the ideals of the French Pléiade poets of the sixteenth century as their artistic credo. Essentially miniaturists, the Parnassians were more concerned with perfection of form than with feeling or emotion. Most of their poetry is elegant but highly impersonal in style.

Chanson triste   **Sorrowful Song. 1868**
(Jean Lahor)

This is Duparc's first *mélodie* and he marked it "with tender and intimate feeling." Its overall mood is one of loving consolation and hope. Its slightly sentimental musical qualities look back to the salon *romances* of Gounod.

Duparc dedicated this song to his brother-in-law, an amateur singer of considerable gifts; the vocal range extends over an octave and a sixth. "Chanson triste" contains stylistic features that became characteristic of Duparc: the vocal line pivots around the dominant; phrase lengths are spacious and flowing, buoyed by nonstop arpeggiated accompaniment figures that build and sustain harmonic intensity; and the melodic line and its contours are carefully conceived to illuminate the text.

Countermelodies appear in the piano at various points; the most important of these appears at "tête malade" and continues through "Et lui diras une ballade." Using fragments from the vocal line, Duparc creates a beautiful melody in the piano, then intertwines it with the vocal melody throughout the section—less than six measures, but crafted skillfully for maximum effect.

A brief postlude built on the vocal phrase "Et dans tes yeux pleins de tristesses" closes the *mélodie* quietly and nostalgically.

L'Invitation au voyage   **Invitation to a Journey. 1870**
(Charles Baudelaire)

This is one of Duparc's most famous songs. Shimmering textures describe the country of Holland as the poet invites his love on an imaginary journey to its flower-filled fields, hazy skies and peaceful canals. Duparc chose two stanzas of Baudelaire's poem for his setting, omitting the middle verse.

The *mélodie* is cast in modified strophic form. For the second verse, Duparc uses a slightly altered vocal line and adds a countermelody in the piano at "C'est pour assouvir/Ton moindre désir," alterations that build toward a shift in piano figures. Duparc uses piano figures to reinforce the mood throughout the song; two chords alternate in the first verse and change to glistening arpeggios in the second verse, evoking the luminous light that bathes the land in golden color. Midway through the last stanza the accompaniment reinforces the climax at "Dans une chaude lumière" with a change of register and a sudden fortissimo octave in the left hand. For the reprise of "La, tout n'est qu'ordre et beauté," Duparc uses melodic fragments in the piano, drawn from previous vocal lines. He assigns bold contours to the vocal line. Like all Duparc's songs, this one is difficult technically for both pianist and singer.

"L'Invitation au voyage" is superb because the nostalgia, veiled sensuousness, and dramatic impact of Baudelaire's poem are stunningly illustrated in the musical texture.

Lamento   **Lament. 1883**
(Théophile Gautier)

Duparc set only three stanzas of this lengthy poem by Gautier, which was also used by Hector Berlioz for his *mélodie* titled "Au cimetière." The scene is an isolated cemetery. The poet describes a white tomb surrounded by dark, velvety yew trees. In their branches a pale dove makes a plaintive sound. Soft vowels in the poem produce resonances that complement the mournful mood: *roucoulement, doucement, l'unison, tombe, l'ombre, colombe.*

The first section of the *mélodie* consists of two stanzas set to the same music, varied only by a few rhythmic changes in the vocal line. Intense grief is expressed by the calm legato of the vocal line, which moves gracefully in stepwise motion. A running figure in the accompaniment prepares an abrupt change of dramatic mood at the words "Ah! jamais plus..." The poet's outburst initiates the third stanza and a quicker tempo, which returns to the mood of hopelessness found in the beginning of the *mélodie* for a last brief vocal phrase. Accompaniment figures are predominantly chordal, changing only at the moment of *crescendo.*

Duparc opens the *mélodie* with a plaintive progression of four minor chords which he uses as a unifying motive, not only harmonically but melodically as well. The progression has a slow mournful character that produces an almost hypnotic effect. The progression appears three additional times in the song and is found in modified form in the faster section, blended into a new piano figure. Duparc takes the upper notes of the chords (D, C-sharp, C-natural, A) and uses them in the vocal line throughout the song, a total of five times. The motive appears for the last time in the final measures of the *mélodie*, this time extended in a last cadence.

Phidylé   Phidylé. 1882
(Leconte de Lisle)

A verdant countryside scene, warmed by the sun and fragrant with the odors of herbs and flowers, forms the setting for one of Duparc's longest *mélodies*. The poet watches over his beloved, asleep in this lovely spot, and tells her: "Rest, O Phidylé, for when the sun sets you will awake, and I will have my reward." The song's rhapsodic mood is passionate, the vocal phrases long lined, and the accompaniment is harmonically rich and complex.

Overall, the texture is quite thick and almost orchestral in its style to complement the voluptuous verse. Duparc skillfully builds the momentum of tempo, phrasing, and harmonic material to a tremendous and effective climax in the final stanza. Material from the extended introduction is used in the concluding postlude. Like "Extase," this song shows traces of Wagner's influence.

This *mélodie* calls for a substantial voice and an excellent pianist. Although women sing this song and have recorded it, the poem is so definitely a man's text that it presents problems for the female voice—both for the words and the vocal weight required for the ending stanza.

Le Manoir de Rosemonde   The Manor of Rosemonde. 1879
(Raymond de Bonnières)

This song is built on an agitated rhythmic figure in the piano, fashioned of octaves underscored by an ascending bass figure. Rugged and vigorous, this rhythm drives the song forward, accompanying the poet on his desperate search for someone or something unattainable –the "bleu manoir de Rosemonde." Is the "bleu manoir de Rosemonde" a perfect love, the meaning of life, eternal happiness? We are never told. Barbara Meister informs us that the phrase "blue manor of Rosemonde" probably refers to legends of two Rosemondes.[5] The first Rosemonde was a wife of a Lombard king (c. 570 A.D.), whose story was used in epic poems, one of which was written by the English poet Swinburne. The second Rosemonde, a mistress of Henry II of England, also inspired many romantic tales. But de Bonnière's poem is cryptic and tantalizing in its unanswered questions. It seems to imply a more mysterious meaning in the last lines of the poem: "I have traveled through this sad world, and thus have caused my own death / Far away, far away, without discovering / The blue manor of Rosemonde." Since the protagonist in the song goes through the world alone and wounded by love, without attaining his goal, we can attach our own psychological and emotional meanings to his words.

This is probably the most intensely dramatic of Duparc's *mélodies*, presenting a scene that is terrifying in its momentum. Texture, mood, and climactic moments recall classic melodrama. The vocal line is strongly declamatory, balanced by a lyric ending in the last stanza as the exhausted traveler finally reaches the end of his journey without having attained the object of his quest. At this point, the piano texture shifts to a quiet chordal accompaniment, finally concluding with a faint echo of the galloping opening figure.

Extase   **Ecstasy. 1878**

(Jean Lahor)

Duparc purposely patterned this *mélodie* on the style of Wagner's *Tristan und Isolde* in tribute to Wagner. Bernac calls this *mélodie* a "Wagnerian nocturne" for the piano.[6] Although the piano dominates the *mélodie* with a richly composed prelude, interlude, and postlude, the voice unfolds unhurriedly over its figurations, singing only six lines of text. The singer's last word , "mort" (death), ushers in the postlude, which contains material from previous vocal phrases, particularly "Mort exquise."

Duparc handles this slowly evolving texture skillfully, and the gradual buildup of intensity is stunning. Overall, the piece is brief in comparison to other Duparc songs, but it is crafted with care for the interaction between voice and piano, within a texture that pays homage to Wagner, yet is totally French in sentiment and style.

Extended Study List

La Vie antérieure • Au pays où se fait la guerre • Sérénade florentine • Soupir • La Vague et la cloche • Elégie • Le Galop • Testament • Romance de Mignon

Selected Reading

Laurence Davies, *The Gallic Muse* (New York: A.S. Barnes, 1967).

Sydney Northcote, *The Songs of Henri Duparc* (London: Dennis Dobson, 1959). A succinct but excellent discussion of all of Duparc's songs.

Rémy Stricker, *Les mélodies de Duparc* (Paris: Actes Sud, 1996).

Susan Youens, "Baudelaire in Music: Henri Duparc's Setting of 'L'Invitation au Voyage'," *The NATS Journal* 38:4 (March/April 1982), 9-13.

Notes

1. Sydney Northcote, *The Songs of Henri Duparc*, 41.
2. Betty Bannerman, *The Singer as Interpreter: Claire Croiza's Master Classes*, 95.
3. Northcote, 56.
4. Bannerman, 187-88.
5. Barbara Meister, *Nineteenth-Century French Song*, 257.
6. Pierre Bernac, *The Interpretation of French Song*, 63.

ERNEST CHAUSSON (1855-1899)

I believe firmly in the reality of expressed thoughts, and a thought can only be considered expressed when it is dressed in a sufficiently beautiful form.

—Ernest Chausson[1]

Ernest Chausson wrote close to fifty *mélodies*, spanning his entire compositional output (1877-1898). Chausson was first a pupil of Massenet, then of César Franck. He was one of Franck's best-known pupils and became an ardent disciple of the older composer. Chausson's salon on the Boulevard de Courcelles was often a meeting place for the Franckists.

Although he composed in other genres, Chausson seemed at ease when working with smaller forms. He was intensely subjective, and the smaller form of song seemed to suit his aesthetics most comfortably. His songs are elegant, subtle, refined, and personal. Chausson was one of the first French composers to fall under the spell of Richard Wagner, and Wagner's influence is evident in some of his songs. Henri Duparc, another pupil of Franck, was also influenced by Wagner, but his songs manifest Wagner's influence in breadth of line and texture, while Chausson's retain the elegance and subtlety of the French style.

Melody is an important element in his songs; he was fond of writing melodic lines that begin in the lower range and then ascend gracefully. His earliest songs have a certain detached quality; his later songs contain deeper, more expressive features. Elegiac texts seemed to inspire him to compose his richest songs. He often used altered scale degrees (flatted sixths and sevenths in major keys) to create a specific emotional mood.

He composed with a sense of classical balance and simplicity, and was fond of using ternary forms, although he altered their structure freely. He rarely mixed figures in his piano accompaniments; most songs have one unvarying pattern used throughout the piece.

Although Chausson set poems of Gautier, Lahor and Verlaine, he had a special taste for the poetry of Jean Richepin, Camille Mauclair, and a close friend, Maurice Bouchor. Bouchor's poems are tender and nostalgic; their simplicity seemed to complement Chausson's aesthetic preferences.

Chausson's tragic death from a bicycle accident cut short a promising career. With the exception of "Les Temps des lilas," the songs annotated here all belong to Op.2. These seven *mélodies* are early compositions, but nonetheless provide examples of his overall style.

Nanny   **Nanny. 1880**
(Leconte de Lisle)

"Nanny" was Chausson's first published song, and one of his earliest pieces for the voice. It is fluent, melodious, and light in texture. Chausson uses one of his favorite devices in the song, an unvarying pattern of sixteenth notes against triplets in the piano. The song opens with a chromatic phrase in the piano, which is then sung by the voice. Melodic lines feature descending passages, which illustrate the melancholy mood of the poem. The song is in modified ternary form.

Les Papillons   **Butterflies. 1880**
(Théophile Gautier)

This *mélodie* is a sparkling miniature song, with a texture as light and airy as the quicksilver flight of the butterflies described in the poem.

The vocal line is fluid and lyric, underlaid with a repeated piano figure that represents the fluttering flight of the butterflies. The nonstop piano figures launch the song and continue throughout until at last, without slowing down, the *mélodie* dissolves into thin air. Only at the words of the last phrase, "Fleur de mon âme, Et j'y mourrais," can the performers pause.

Hébé   Hébé. 1882
(Louise Ackermann)

Chausson subtitles this *mélodie* "Greek song in the Phrygian mode." The poem is derived from Greek mythology. Hébé is the cupbearer for the gods, and the symbol of eternal youth. The graceful young girl passes among the gods offering a golden draught of life-preserving liquid. A sobering thought underlies this scene: once Hébé has passed by with her cup of youth, we cannot recall her.

Chausson creates a transparent musical texture in which the piano and voice share melodic phrases that overlap one another. He uses modal harmonies to reinforce the simple mood. The overall musical effect is one of innocence. Man's vain attempt to recapture youth once it has passed is mirrored in the last vocal phrase, which ends without a feeling of complete closure, leaving the piano to conclude with a wistful and melancholy melody.

Le Charme   The Charm. 1879
(Armand Silvestre)

"Le Charme" is Chausson's most concise *mélodie*, and also one of his most touching. It is noteworthy for its simplicity and elegance, skillfully compressed into a brief twenty-eight measures.

Chausson sets the three stanzas strophically, but lengthens the last stanza by four bars. The song is intimate and direct, its emotion refined. There are no climactic moments and no overt displays. Chausson doubles the vocal line in the piano, which is unusual in his songs.

Le Colibri   The Hummingbird. 1882
(Leconte de Lisle)

This *mélodie*, one of Chausson's best-known songs, is one of his early efforts in the genre. De Lisle's poem describes the flight and death of a hummingbird, drawing an analogy between the tiny bird and the soul of the poet, a theme that presents nature as an allegory for erotic love. De Lisle's poetic imagery is unusually rich, and inspired Chausson to compose one of his most lyrical and overtly emotional songs.

Chausson's musical setting is sophisticated, set in $\frac{5}{4}$ meter. Chromatic passages and rich harmonic textures are prominent in the middle section. At the musical climax "Vers, la fleurs dorée," repeated chords in the accompaniment give way to rolled chords. Melodic material is shared between voice and piano; vocal passages are Italianate in feeling. Only at the end of the song does the poet become subjective, comparing his soul's wish to die from the kiss of his lover, just as the hummingbird dies upon drinking deeply of the flower's nectar.

Le Temps des lilas	**The Time of Lilacs. 1893**
(Maurice Bouchor)	

"Le Temps des lilas" is one of Chausson's subtlest songs, a classic example of his grace and delicacy. It belongs to a set of three songs for voice and piano titled *Poème de l'amour et de la mer*, Op. 19. Each of these three songs was composed separately, begun in the summer of 1882 and completed in 1890.

Literature and music in the 1880s had undergone vast changes as the romantic age waned and faded. Taking note of the era that was passing, poetry took as one of their themes reminiscences of things bygone. Bouchor's verse, "The time of lilacs and roses has passed" emphasizes loss, change, and nostalgia for the past.

Chausson unified these three songs with a short motive in D minor from this song. The motive appears prominently in the piano accompaniment in several places. It is a beautiful theme expressing deep personal grief for a lost love.

At return of the melody, there is a change of register and the tonality shifts from major to minor.

Extended Study List

La Dernière feuille • Sérénade italienne • La Chanson bien douce • Amour d'antan • Apaisement• Cantique à l'épouse • Dans la forêt du charme et de l'enchantement • Chanson perpétuelle (voice/string quartet, piano) • La Caravane

Selected Reading

Jean-Pierre Barricelli and Leo Weinstein, *Ernest Chausson: The Composer's Life and Works* (Norman: University of Oklahoma Press, 1955). Part II, Chapter 2, treats Chausson's *mélodies*.
Isabelle Bretaudeau, *Les mélodies de Chausson* (Paris: Actes Sud, 1999).
Ralph Scott Grover. *Ernest Chausson: The Man and His Music* (Lewisburg: Bucknell University Press, 1980). Chapter 2 deals with Chausson's *mélodies*.
George Newton, "Ernest Chausson and His Mélodies," *The NATS Journal,* 21:2, 1964.

Notes

1. In a letter to Raymond Bonheur. Quoted in Jean-Pierre Barricelli and Leo Weinstein, *Ernest Chausson: The Composer's Life and Works*, 55.

GABRIEL FAURÉ (1845-1924)

To come to Fauré in the history of French song is to enter the promised land.
—James Husst Hall[1]

It is truly in his songs that Fauré offers us the flower of his genius.
—Maurice Ravel[2]

Gabriel Urbain Fauré was one of the great composers of French song who, with Duparc and Debussy, perfected the *mélodie* as a true art song form. In his 100 *mélodies*, Fauré created an extraordinary range of songs—all original in conception, constantly developing in style, and pointing the way toward future works.

Fauré's *mélodies* express a broader range of emotion and a greater variety of musical textures than earlier *mélodies*, extending the musical parameters of French song and inspiring new techniques of song composition.

Fauré has been compared to a skillful watchmaker—with great precision, his *mélodies* overflow with subtle nuances and delicate detail. His approach is elegant and rational, and it deals with sentiment rather than literal sensation—a uniquely French characteristic. Emotion in Fauré is not overt, but emerges from his method of text setting; there is no attempt to literally interpret words. Careful study of his mature vocal works continually uncovers new musical discoveries, discreetly submerged in a skillfully constructed whole.

Music critic Louis Aguettant wrote that Fauré's music embodied the essence of classicism:

Fauré's music is the place for reconciling opposing forces: the normal and the unusual, refinement and simplicity, charm and power, sensual detail and organic unity. In this collection of balances we recognize the concept of classicism.[3]

Claire Croiza, one of Fauré's most devoted interpreters who sang the title role in his opera *Pénélope* many times, described Fauré's style to her master classes:

These songs…are tender, yet virile, never sentimental. They shine with a light that is spiritual as well as physical; they are perfectly balanced and aristocratic in the best French sense, discreet and serene, but full of underlying passion.[4]

Fauré himself wrote:

I want to suggest the great mysteries in the clearest language. To imagine consists in trying to formulate all that one would desire that is best, all that outruns [*dépasse*] reality—"volupte" has no merit if it does not make us perceive, through the mirage of physical things, an unutterable reality that is beyond the reach of our senses.[5]

Croiza knew Fauré well and performed his songs with him. She was emphatic about finding and keeping the tempo in Fauré songs, which have a characteristic "allant" (forward movement) while observing all his expression markings—according to Croiza, Fauré gave exact indications. Unlike Duparc, who wanted a "violin-voice," Fauré believed "the voice should not have the 'voluptuous' prestige of a solo instrument, but be a '*porte-verbe*' [mouthpiece], with an exquisite timbre."[6]

During rehearsals of his opera *Pénélope*, the conductor Edouard Risler told Fauré that the work would last but would take time to be accepted. In a letter to his wife, Fauré commented: "It is alas, perfectly probable; it is even certain, when you think of the mediocrities the public likes to indulge in, and *with which it is indulged.*[7] Unfortunately, this statement seems to have contemporary implications as well.

Fauré's songs contain a wealth of invention and variety of style. For the purposes of study and definition, they fall into three compositional periods. Selections from each have been annotated below.

Early Style 1860-65

Le Papillon et la fleur • Chanson du pêcheur • Chant d'automne •
Mai • Aubade • Hymne • Dans les ruines d'une abbaye •
Sylvie • La Rançon • Seule! • Rêve d'amour • Lydia •
Les Matelots • L'Absent • Barcarolle • Sérénade toscane •
Ici-bas • Au bord de l'eau •Après un rêve

Opuses 1-8 were published in 1865 when Fauré was twenty years old. His first *mélodie* was "Le Papillon et la fleur" composed "in the school dining hall amid the smells from the kitchen."

For these songs, Fauré drew heavily on poetry by the Parnassian school of poets,* among them Armand Silvestre, Sully-Prudhomme, and Leconte de Lisle. Leconte de Lisle was the Parnassian poet with whom Fauré collaborated most successfully. De Lisle's formal, objective poetry seemed to mesh easily with Fauré's aesthetic and style. He composed five *melodies* on verses by de Lisle: "Lydia," "Nell," "Les Roses d'Ispahan," "La Rose," and "Le Parfum impérissable."

Fauré's *mélodies* from this period retain the tuneful sentimentality of early French song, but begin to take on characteristics that look to his mature style. Most of these songs are in strophic form, with figures in the accompaniment built from scales and triads (which Fauré retained throughout his *mélodies*).

*Verlaine, Mallarmé, and Baudelaire, whose poems were set by French composers, were also Parnassians, but later rejected the style, and joined Rimbaud to create the symbolist school, a movement that attempted to blur boundaries between poetry and the other arts.

Lydia, Op. 4, No. 2   **Lydia. c. 1870**
(Leconte de Lisle)

"Lydia" contains many of the features typical of Fauré's early song style: a smooth vocal line constructed of narrow intervals; strophic form; and a mixture of tonality and modality in the harmony (F major and the Lydian mode). Its simplicity is austere and deliberately archaic. Its melody of Hellenic purity is set in two identical stanzas with a transparent chordal accompaniment. Its original key is F major; Fauré's musical pun (Lydian mode) is quite clear.

Après un rêve, Op. 7, No. 1   **After a Dream. 1878**
(Romain Bussine)

"Après un rêve" is a famous Fauré *mélodie* whose familiarity threatens to overwhelm its inherent beauty and quality. It is Italianate in conception and atmosphere; the piano accompaniment is definitely subordinate to the voice.* Fauré wrote long, lyric vocal lines, set over an accompaniment of repeated chords. The softly percussive accompaniment creates and perpetuates intensity and passion but never sacrifices elegance. "Après un rêve" is in A A B form. The popularity of this *mélodie* has occasioned many instrumental transcriptions.

*Other Italianate settings by Fauré include "Sérénade toscane," " Barcarolle," and "Chanson du pêcheur."

Au bord de l'eau, Op. 8, No. 1   **At the Water's Edge. 1875**
(Sully Prudhomme)

In Fauré's languid musical setting, the poet dreams of sitting on the riverbank, watching the flowing water and floating clouds with his beloved. It is a wistful atmosphere, suffused with the hope that love can keep everything intact.

The vocal line weaves long strands of melody of differing lengths over a simple chordal accompaniment, which, at times, echoes fragments of the vocal line. Throughout the *mélodie*, voice and piano phrases overlap momentarily.

Middle Style 1880-1904

Nell • Les Roses d'Ispahan • Larmes • Au cimetière •
Les Berceaux • Le Voyageur • Automne • Notre amour • Le Secret •
Chanson d'amour • La Fée aux chansons • Aurore • Fleur jetée •
Le Pays des rêves • Les Présents • Noël • La Rose • Le Parfum
impérissable • Arpège • Soir • Dans la forêt de septembre • La Fleur
qui va sur l'eau • Accompagnement • Le Ramier • Le Plus doux
chemin • En prière • Prison • Clair de lune • Spleen • Madrigal •
Chanson de Shylock • *Poème d'un jour:* Rencontre, Toujours,
Adieu • *Cinq mélodies de Venise:* Mandoline, En sourdine,
Green, A Clymène, C'est l'extase • *La Bonne chanson* (9 songs)

Fauré's second period of song may be roughly divided into two sections of seven years each. Although he continued to set the poetry of the Parnassians, Fauré discovered the work of symbolist poet Paul Verlaine, and Verlaine's poetry dominates this era of composition and defines his mature style with works such as *La Bonne chanson*, *Cinq mélodies de Venise*, and the exquisite "Clair de lune."[8]

Fauré's songs from this period contain the following characteristics: increased use of modality, subtler harmonic touches, use of motives as linking elements, and an expressive emotional scope only hinted at in his earlier *mélodies*. Texture and increasing musical complexity become important elements in Fauré's middle style; these two elements culminate in the cycle *La Bonne chanson*.

Also during this period, Fauré composed another miniature song set. In 1887 Fauré's engagement to Marianne Viardot (the daughter of Pauline Viardot) was announced, but the liaison was short lived and broken off in a matter of four months. Fauré's three-paneled triptych, *Poème d'un jour* (Poem of a Day), on texts by Charles Grandmougin, was in part a reaction to his emotional state at the time.

Nell, Op. 18, No. 1   Nell. 1880
(Leconte de Lisle)

Influences of Gounod and the *romance* linger in the melodious vocal phrases and fluid accompaniment of "Nell." This *mélodie* belongs to Opus 18, which Fauré wrote after a fifteen-year hiatus from song composition.

Fauré's pliant phrasing sustains the charm and flowing character of the poem throughout the four strophes of the song, which teeters on the edge of sentimentality. Its opulent vocalism is underpinned with an unvaried accompaniment figure of broken chord patterns in sixteenth notes. By imperceptibly changing the chords, Fauré subtly modulates the harmony throughout the song, creating interest and maintaining momentum. A beautiful singing bass line descends within the moving sixteenth-note figures in the accompaniment; its downward motion is pitted against the rising motion of the vocal phrases.

In its musical style, this *mélodie* resembles "Notre amour." Both songs have fresh, supple vocal lines, an accompaniment of repeating figures, and an abundance of charm.

Les Berceaux, Op. 23, No. 1   The Cradles. 1882
(Sully Prudhomme)

The verses of Sully-Prudhomme* inspired one of Fauré's most enduring, somber, and touching *mélodies*. "From cradle to grave" is the chilling parallel drawn by the poet: the women rock the next generation of sailors; the gently swelling water rocks the ships that take the men to distant seas, and perhaps to their deaths.

"Les Berceaux" is unified by a figure in the accompaniment—an undulating rocking pattern that suggests both the cradles (*berceaux*) rocked by the sailors' wives and the boats (*vaisseaux*) rocked by the waves. This pattern in the accompaniment is unvaried from beginning to end, and is almost hypnotic in its effect. From a gentle descriptive beginning, the song builds to a dramatic climax. The overall effect is one of strength and simplicity, achieved by tight construction.

*Sully-Prudhomme received the first Nobel Prize for poetry in 1901.

Les Roses d'Ispahan, Op. 39, No. 4   The Roses of Ispahan. 1884
(Leconte de Lisle)

In this exotic *mélodie,* Fauré has blended orientalism with classic symmetry of form. He shared the fascination for the Orient that was sweeping artists in Europe. Fauré's approach is sensual, but remains discreet, often bordering on becoming sweetly sentimental, but never stepping over the line. The rich and voluptuous harmonies and the cross-rhythms in the accompaniment are especially noteworthy.

Fauré shortens the original poem by two stanzas. The four four-line stanzas have symmetrical line endings: The first stanza's lines end with *mousse, oranger, douce, léger*, and the order is reversed for the second through fourth stanzas, which end with *léger, douce, oranger, mousse*.[9]

The *mélodie* is in A A B A form. Fauré uses the same music for the first and second verses, but varies the melody and rhythm to conform to the text. A two-measure transition leads into the third verse ("O Leilah!"); this stanza functions as a development section. Fauré skillfully blends chromatic harmonies and rich textures in this section, finally returning to the music of the opening for the last verse.

---

*Cinq mélodies de Venise,** Op. 58   Five Venetian Songs. 1891
(Paul Verlaine)

Mandoline • En Sourdine • Green • A Clymène • C'est l'extase

During a visit to Venice in 1891 at the Palazzo Vendramin, Fauré found inspiration for five "Venetian" songs on Verlaine texts drawn from *Fêtes galantes* and *Romances sans paroles*. The palazzo was then the home of the Princesse Edmund de Polignac,** a great patron of contemporary music and art, and the set of songs was dedicated to her.

There is nothing Italianate about Fauré's settings except a nod to Venice in the barcarole rhythm of "A Clymène"; the title of the set refers solely to the place where the songs were conceived. Only "Mandoline" was actually completed in Venice. Fauré finished the remaining songs in Paris.

Although the set has no overall tonal plan, there are stylistic factors that suggest Fauré organized the cycle on other levels. He uses a recurring three-note figure of falling thirds as a linking motive in "En Sourdine," "Green," and" C'est l'extase." In addition to repeating this motive, Fauré chose poems of similar mood and arranged them to create a progression of scenes and stages in the relationship of the lovers in the poems.

Nectoux notes that the Venetian songs are like a suite in five movements, alternating fast and slow tempos. Songs 1, 3, and 5 feature staccato articulation and brisk tempos; Songs 2 and 4 are composed of smoother figures and have a more serene mood.

Prelude	"Mandoline" (Allegretto moderato/G major).
First slow movement	"En Sourdine" (Andante moderato/E- flat major).
Scherzo	"Green" (Allegretto con moto/G-flat major).
Second slow movement	"A Clymène" (Andantino/E minor).
Finale	"C'est l'extase" (Adagio non troppo/D-flat major).[10]

* Debussy's settings of "Mandoline," "En Sourdine," "Green," and "C'est l'extase " should be studied for comparison.

**The Princesse was formerly Winnaretta "Winnie" Singer, the sewing-machine heiress. In 1893, she married the Prince Edmond de Polignac. An ardent supporter of the arts, she hosted one of the most elegant and influential salons in Paris. She was responsible for bringing Fauré and Verlaine together, and would later be a patron to Stravinsky and Kurt Weill.

MANDOLINE (MANDOLIN). Watteau's painting *L'Indifferent* might well serve as an illustration for this poem and for Fauré's musical treatment, in which he places a graceful figure in the accompaniment to suggest the mandolin player. Fauré's introduction of the characters—Tircis, Aminte, Clitandre, Damis—is understated, and lacks the delineation of Debussy's setting. Fauré uses melismas on the words "chanteuses" (singing [branches]) and "tender" (tender [verses]) and repeats the first stanza to close the song.

EN SOURDINE (MUTED). This song is an exquisite nocturne. In her master classes, Croiza observed that Fauré adored nature and life, but sought to evoke them instead of describe them in his music. "He searched for serenity in *'ravissement'* [ecstasy]."[11] This is a perfect description of "En Sourdine." Fauré creates a voluptuous mood with muted harmonies, a vocal line that builds in intensity but never loses its elegance, and a piano accompaniment of delicate arpeggios that continue throughout until the nightingale's final benediction.

GREEN (GREEN). Fauré sets the ardent lines of Verlaine's poem in a moving chordal accompaniment. With fresh morning dew still on his brow, the breathless young lover brings his beloved flowers, green branches, and, above all, his heart. Fauré sent this song to Winnaretta Singer, asking "Have I succeeded in transposing this wonderful canticle of adoration? I don't know. It's difficult to interpret: slow moving but agitated in feeling, happy and miserable, eager and discouraged! What a lot in thirty bars!"[12]

A CLYMÈNE (TO CLYMÈNE). This song is the least-known—and least-performed—of the Venetian *mélodies*. It functions as a transition song, providing a change of mood and style between Songs 3 and 5. Fauré illustrates this poem with a barcarole rhythm, reminiscent of Venice.

C'EST L'EXTASE (IT IS ECSTASY). In this setting, Fauré returns to the pulsating figures of "Green." In a letter to Winnaretta Singer, Fauré explained he had tried a new form with this song (and with Song 3), referring to the linking of material from "Green" ("O le frêle et frais murmure" refers back to "J'arrive tout couvert encore de rosée") and "En Sourdine" ("Cette âme qui se lamente" refers back to "Ferme tes yeux à-demi").[13]

La Bonne chanson, Op. 61   The Good Song. 1892-94
(Paul Verlaine)

> Une sainte en son auréole (A Saint in her Halo) • Puisque l'aube grandit… (Since Dawn Grew Bright) • La lune blanche luit dans les bois… (The White Moon Gleams in the Woods) • J'allais par des chemins perfides… (I Wandered on Treacherous Paths) • J'ai presque peur, en vérité… (I Am Almost Afraid, in Truth) • Avant que tu ne t'en ailles… (Before You Go) • Donc, ce sera par un clair jour d'été… (Thus It Will Be on a Clear Summer Day) • N'est-ce pas?… (Isn't It True?) • L'hiver a cessé… (Winter Is Over)

Fauré's experiments with literary and musical structure begun in the Venetian songs came to a dazzling climax in *La Bonne chanson,* regarded as his masterpiece in the genre. As he had done with the Venetian songs, Fauré structured the cycle on a literary level, carefully ordering the poems for mood and content, and on a musical level, unifying the songs through recurring themes. From Verlaine's twenty-one published poems, Fauré chose to set nine.[*] He arranged the poems so that they seem to be one long lyric poem. All but the ninth song were completed in 1892-3; Fauré procrastinated a long while over the last song, which he finally finished in 1894.

Musically and poetically, the cycle is a balance of exhilaration and intensity, a unique combination of religious and sensual emotions. Verlaine wrote the passionate poems in 1870 in an outburst of joy over his engagement to Mathilde Mauté. The marriage proved disastrous; Verlaine deserted her in 1872 for the boy-poet Arthur Rimbaud.

When Fauré composed this work he was also carried away by an infatuation—for Emma Bardac, his neighbor on his summer holidays in Bougival.[**] Fauré wrote *La Bonne chanson* for Emma, and dedicated it to her. Nectoux recounts the reminiscences of the composer's son, Emmanuel, who at the end of his life, related with emotion "the private performances Emma gave of *La Bonne chanson* during the warm summer evenings at Bourgival, with his father at the piano."[14]

La Bonne Chanson has five themes, most often found in the piano accompaniment. They have no poetic or dramatic connection, but function purely in a musical sense throughout the nine songs.

Theme A (Carlovingien).	First appearance: "Une sainte en son auréole" (Bars 15-16).
Theme B (Lydia).	First appearance: "La lune blanche luit dans les bois" (Bars 9-12)
Theme C (Que je vous aime).	First appearance: "J'ai presque peur" (Bars 65-69)
Theme D (Birdsong).	First appearance: "Avant que tu ne t'en ailles" (Bars 6-8)
Theme E (Sun theme).	First appearance: "Donc, ce sera… (Bar 4)

Themes A, B, and C are found most frequently through the cycle. Notice that theme B is drawn from the first phrase of "Lydia" and probably refers to Emma Bardac. All of the themes are found in the final song "L'hiver a cessé." Themes D and E are secondary; they are introduced late in the cycle and not reprised until the last song.

La Bonne chanson is a complex work on several levels: poetically, thematically, harmonically. In this work, Fauré achieved an extraordinary synthesis between voice and piano—so close it has been described as a "quasi-orchestral" texture. Within it, Fauré manipulated musical elements freely: rhythmic fluctuation, harmonic invention, free and varied vocal style all combine in a network of sound that creates a mood of unending energy and overwhelming joy. Although Fauré tinkered with other styles of unifying song cycle form, he never surpassed the integrated unity found in this radiant masterpiece.

Perhaps due to the "chamber music" texture of voice and piano throughout the work, Fauré was persuaded to score the cycle for string quartet and piano in 1898. This version of *La Bonne chanson* was first performed in London at a private concert in the home of Fauré's friend, Frank Schuster. Fauré wrote to his wife the following day saying he found the accompaniment "redundant" and preferred the original version for voice and piano.

*The songs of the cycle use the following poems: in order, Nos. 8, 4 (the first, fifth, and last verses), 6, 20, 15, 5, 19, 17 (the second, third, and last verses), and 21 (the second verse is omitted).

**Emma was married to a wealthy banker, Sigismund Bardac. She left him to run off with Claude Debussy, whom she later married. Debussy himself was a piano pupil of Mathilde Mauté's mother. It was for Emma's daughter, Dolly, that Fauré wrote his suite of piano pieces, as a present on her birthday.

Clair de lune*, Op. 46, No. 2   **Moonlight. 1887**
(Paul Verlaine)

"Clair de lune" was Fauré's first setting of Verlaine, and it is one of his finest songs. Vuillermoz referred to this song as a "spectral *menuet*." It is difficult to disagree with Maurice Ravel, who declared it one of the most beautiful songs in all of French music.

In this *mélodie* Fauré broke new ground by writing an independent solo piece for the piano—with its own distinctive melody and harmonic structure—and subtly weaving the vocal line into the texture without either entity losing its unique individuality. Vocal phrases are almost without repetition, but the piano makes extensive use of three motives, which appear and reappear, interleaved with short episodes. The first motive is bars 1-2, the second bars 5-6, and the third begins at "Jouant du luth et dansant." The voice floats above the accompaniment like a countermelody or a descant and seems to "accompany" the piano at times.

Fauré perfectly suggests the elegant atmosphere of Verlaine's verse. The last vocal phrase "parmi les marbres" captures the "jets d'eau" with a graceful arching shape that rises, then falls. For variety of texture and extension of expressive musical compass, this is an extraordinary song.

*See also Debussy's setting of this poem.

Arpège, Op. 76, No. 2   Arpeggio. 1897
(Albert Samain)

Fauré set three poems by Samain—"Arpège," "Soir," and "Accompagnement"—
and all are excellent examples of his fluid harmonic style. They are also memorable
for their sophisticated treatment of the piano.

Fauré's accompaniment is transparent and "very French"; its construction
calls to mind two instruments playing—a harp-like arpeggiated left hand and a
singing melodic line in the right hand—obviously personifying the "soul of the
flute" in the poem. To this he adds a third line, the voice, whose phrases are more
subdued in range, but create the effect of a conversation with the piano.

Fauré varies the combinations of patterns in voice and piano, gradually building to a thick section where the melodies intertwine in the piano. As a unifying element, the solo melody from the beginning measures is heard in the final piano
postlude.

Late Style 1906-22

La Chanson d'Eve (10 songs) • *Le Jardin clos* (8 songs) •
Mirages (4 songs) • *L'Horizon chimérique* (4 songs) •Chanson •
Vocalise • C'est la paix • Le Don silencieux

In 1905, at age sixty, Fauré assumed the directorship of the Paris
Conservatoire. By this time, he had composed three quarters of his total number of
songs. He wrote four song cycles in his last style period: *Mirages, Le Jardin clos, La
Chanson d'Eve*, and his last work for the voice, *L'Horizon chimérique*. He also composed his opera *Pénélope* during this period.

Fauré's late style is marked by lean, sparse textures, skillful harmonic manipulations, and a sense of tonal ambiguity. Listen and compare any of the works from this
period with the *mélodies* from his early period such as "Le Papillon et le fleur" or
"Dans le ruines d'une abbaye." The early *mélodies* have an ingenuous charm stamped
with Gounod's influence; the last songs are complex and introspective. At this point in
his life, he was becoming deaf. His inability to hear extremes of range must have
affected his last songs. Most of these works lie in the midrange of the voice.

L'Horizon chimérique, Op. 118   The Illusory Horizon. 1921
(Jean de la Ville de Mirmont)

La Mer est infinie… (The Sea Is Infinite…) • Je me suis embarqué…
(I Set Sail…) • Diane, Séléné… (Diana, Séléné…) • Vaisseaux,
nous vous aurons aimés… (Ships, We Have Loved You…)

Fauré was seventy-seven when he composed this work—his last cycle—
on poems of the young poet Jean de la Ville de Mirmont, who had been killed in the
war in 1914. Of his four late cycles, this one is less austere in texture and more
expansively lyrical. The poetry is simple and direct; its rhythmic inflections are
set perfectly in a flowing melodic style that is both declamatory and lyric at the
same time.

Unlike the Venetian songs, there are no musical links in this set. Instead, Fauré unifies the songs through the expressive musical setting of the words, and through rhythmic figures that evoke the sea. Songs 1 and 4 are in D major, surrounding the two inner songs which are in flat keys, D-flat major and E-flat major. With the exception of Song 1 (ABA), all the songs are through-composed.

The third song, "Diane, Séléné," provides a contrast to the other three seascapes. A starlight night with a brilliant moon illuminates the poet who muses in the moon's glow, perhaps on board ship (the sea is not mentioned in this poem). He invokes Diane and Séléné, goddesses of the moon, yearning for the moon's peaceful serenity for himself. The *mélodie* is a beautiful example of Fauré's skill in evoking a dream-like atmosphere by the simplest of means. The entire accompaniment is in four-part harmony. Poulenc achieved the same results sixteen years later in a similar setting, "Une herbe pauvre" *(Tel jour, telle nuit)*.

"Car j'ai de grand départs inassouvis en moi," the last line of the last song, is poignant both in its poetic context and as a valedictory of Fauré's career. It was the last vocal phrase he was to set: "For I have great departures unsatisfied in me." *L'Horizon chimérique* is dedicated to baritone Charles Panzéra, who recorded it several times during his distinguished career.

Extended Study List

Dans les ruines d'une abbaye • Dans la forêt de Septembre • La fleur qui va sur l'eau • Notre amour • Spleen • La Rose • Fleur jetée • Le Parfum impérissable • Prison • Le Secret • Automne • Au cimetière • Chanson d'amour • *Poème d'un jour* • *Mirages* • *Le Jardin clos* • *La Chanson d'Eve*

Selected Reading

Theodore Chanler, "Gabriel Fauré: A Reappraisal," in *Modern Music*, March-April 1945.

Laurence Davies, *The Gallic Muse* (New York: A.S. Barnes, 1967).

Jessica Duchen, *Gabriel Fauré* (London: Phaidon Press Ltd., 2000). 20th Century Composers series.

Robert Gartside, *Interpreting the Songs of Gabriel Fauré* (Geneseo, NY: Leyerle Publications, 1996).

Charles Koechlin, *Gabriel Fauré* (London: Dennis Dobson, 1976).

Jean-Michel Nectoux, *Gabriel Fauré: a musical life*. trans. by Roger Nichols (Cambridge: Cambridge University Press, 1991). Excellent source by a distinguished French scholar.

_____, *Gabriel Fauré. His Life Through His Letters*. Collected, ed. and introduced by Jean-Michel Nectoux, trans. J.A. Underwood (London: Marion Boyers, 1984).

Robert Orledge, *Gabriel Fauré* (London: Eulenburg Books, 1979).

Robin Tait, *The Musical Language of Gabriel Fauré* (New York: Garland Publishing, 1989).

Emile Vuillermoz, *Gabriel Fauré* , trans. Kenneth Schapin (Philadelphia: Chilton Book Company, 1969). Excellent biography of Fauré. Contains interesting material on his songs.

Susan Youens, "Gabriel Fauré's 'Clair de lune,' Op. 46, No. 2." *The NATS Journal* 37:1 (Sept/Oct 1980), 32-34.

Notes

1. James Husst Hall, *The Art Song*, 147.
2. Arbie Orenstein, *A Ravel Reader*, 387.
3. Quoted in Emile Vuillermoz, *Gabriel Fauré*, 96.
4. Claire Croiza, in *The Singer as Interpreter,* ed. and trans. Betty Bannerman, 79.
5. Ibid., 80.
6. Ibid., 81.
7. Quoted in Jean Michel-Nectoux. Liner notes for *Fauré: Pénélope*. Orchestre Philharmonique de Monte-Carlo, conducted by Charles Dutoit. (Erato Disques. Compact disc recording 2292-45405-2, 1982), 64.
8. For an excellent discussion of Fauré's settings of Verlaine in greater depth, see Jean-Michel Nectoux, *Gabriel Fauré: A Musical Life*, "The Verlaine Years."
9. See Barbara Meister, *Nineteenth-Century French Song*, 62-63.
10. Nectoux, *Fauré: A Musical Life*, 180.
11. Croiza, *The Singer as Interpreter*, 81.
12. Nectoux, *Fauré: a musical life,* 178-79.
13. *Gabriel Fauré: his life through his letters,* ed. Nectoux, Letter 99.
14. Nectoux, *Fauré: a musical life,* 181.
15. Vuillermoz, *Gabriel Fauré,* 80.

CLAUDE DEBUSSY (1862-1918)

Musicians who don't understand anything about poetry ought not to set it to music. They can only ruin it...

—Claude Debussy[1]

Music and poetry are the only two arts that move in space.

—Claude Debussy[2]

Claude Debussy composed a total of eighty-seven songs, including two that are unfinished, and some that exist in preliminary sketches or are unpublished. He wrote expertly for the voice and was keenly responsive to translating poetic nuance into musical expression. Possibly no other French composer was as attuned to blending poetry and music.

Composer Henri Sauguet, writing in the *Revue Musicale*, stated:

With Debussy, music does not travel along its own path, along-side, below or even above the poem: it is entirely moved by the poem itself; it is no longer a matter of accompaniment, but a play of light and shade which neither superposes or juxtaposes itself onto the text, but rather creates around it a mood, a landscape, like the reflection of a landscape or of a mood; it is more than a commentary or a setting, which cannot take the place of the text, merely emphasize it and extend it. And above this inner music, as vibrant as a series of waves emanating from the word, there is a singing line so sinuous, so close to this word, that it seems to be its profound, its very articulation.[3]

Debussy was scrupulous in marking his scores—every accent, dynamic shading, and tempo is noted on the page. Because tonal color plays such an important part in Debussy's overall song style, transposition should not be attempted except in the very early *mélodies*.

Debussy's literary tastes were highly refined. He maintained a visible and active role in the literary and artistic circles of his time. His extensive experience as a music critic gave him the ability to express himself on musical matters in writing as well as through his compositions.

Debussy chose to set poetry of his contemporaries, notably Verlaine and Mallarmé. Verlaine's verse with its inherent musical qualities provided Debussy with poetry for eighteen *mélodies*. Toward the end of his life, Debussy turned to the literature of France's past, setting texts by François Villon and Charles d'Orléans.

Between 1892-1902, Debussy achieved full mastery of the musical techniques and style with which he is most closely identified—Impressionism. Musical works from this period include the *String Quartet*, *Prélude à l'après-midi d'un faune*, *Chansons de Bilitis*, and *Pelléas et Mélisande*.

Debussy may be thought of as the French counterpart of Hugo Wolf. The song styles of both reflect a complete synthesis of poetry and music, with poetry *as poetry* the paramount determinant of the musical texture. Debussy's ability to divine the essence of the poetry and perfectly transform it into musical expression makes his *mélodies* unique in the history of French song.

Beau soir
(Paul Bourget)

Beautiful Evening. 1877-78

Paul Bourget provided the texts for several of Debussy's early songs. "Beau Soir" has been variously dated between 1878 and 1880, but Cobb suggests that 1883 is a more likely date.[4] It is perhaps the most best-known example of Debussy's early impressionistic style, a quiet scene washed with the setting sun and the warm evening breeze. Phrasing in voice and piano is extremely lyric in the style of Massenet and earlier French song, but this *mélodie* already exhibits Debussy's gift for blending text and musical material.

Pierrot
(Théodore de Banville)

Pierrot. 1881

This *mélodie* is published in a set of four early songs titled *Quatre Chansons de jeunesse*. The set includes "Pantomime," an early version of "Clair de lune," and "Apparition." With the exception of the last song, "Apparition," all the *mélodies* deal with characters or situations found in the Italian *commedia dell'arte*.

The *mélodies* were written for Marie-Blanche Vasnier, a singer with whom the young Debussy was infatuated. Debussy composed thirteen songs for her, known as "The Vasnier Songbook." They include early versions of several Verlaine texts, which he set again later. He also dedicated numerous other *mélodies*, published and unpublished, to Mme. Vasnier. Debussy's attempts to approximate speech in his vocal writing can be seen in these youthful transitional songs.

"Pierrot" furnishes a good idea of what Mme. Vasnier's voice was like: extremely high, light, and flexible. The poetic scene is late evening. Actor Jean Gaspard Debureau* leaves a just-finished performance at the theater. As he walks down the moonlit street, he is approached by a flirtatious girl. A bright moon looks askance at the scene.

Debussy weaves the famous folk tune "Au clair de la lune" ("Au clair de la lune, mon ami Pierrot") into the piano accompaniment throughout. The *mélodie* concludes with a coloratura-like coda in the voice as the actor disappears around the corner. Is it the laughter of the young seductress?

*Debureau was a famous French mime who created the role of Pierrot.

Mandoline*
(Paul Verlaine)

Mandoline. 1882

Elegant lyricism characterizes this *mélodie*, composed when Debussy was barely twenty-one years old. It is his first setting of Verlaine, and demonstrates his gift for divining the inner life of a poem. Although its text is taken from Verlaine's *Fêtes galantes*, Debussy did not include it in either of his two song sets from this work, but published it separately. It is one of the most popular of the early songs set to Verlaine's poems.

"Mandoline" is a light amorous serenade tinged with irony. Debussy initiates the airy mood immediately as the piano imitates the sound of the mandolin tuning up in open fifths, repeated an octave higher. The "sound pattern" of the mandolin serves as a unifying device throughout the *mélodie*.

The scene is reminiscent of a Watteau painting. We are detached observers of a not-quite-real landscape, full of sensuous energy, sustained by the ever-present strumming of the mandolin in the piano accompaniment. Verlaine's troupe of characters are drawn from the pastoral tradition: Tircis, Aminta, Clitandre, and Damis. Debussy comments on their characters through subtle nuances in the curve and articulation of the vocal phrase, which accompanies the introduction of each. Their idle chatter mixes with the rustling sounds of the branches; transparent blue shadows mix with the rose and gray of the moon.

Manipulation of texture is an important element in this song; Debussy is explicit in differentiating legato and staccato in the vocal line, which creates an almost pointillistic contrast with the delicate piano figures. Subtle examples of text painting may be found in the piano accompaniment and vocal line—for example: "Sous les ramures chanteuses." Debussy adds his own wordless refrain of "la-la's" as a miniature coda.

"Mandoline" is dedicated to Mme. Vasnier.

*Gabriel Fauré's setting of the same text, composed eight years later, should be studied for a comparison of musical style and poetic treatment. Also see Reynaldo Hahn's "Fêtes galantes."

Ariettes oubliées   **Forgotten Airs. 1885-87**
(Paul Verlaine)

> C'est l'extase• Il pleure dans mon cœur • L'Ombre des arbres •
> Chevaux des bois (Paysages belges) • Green (Aquarelles) •
> Spleen (Aquarelles)

This group of six songs on poems of Paul Verlaine is Debussy's first important set of *mélodies*. It predates both sets of *Fêtes galantes*. In the *Ariettes oubliées*, Debussy's mature style began to crystallize. The *mélodies* contain subtle musical responses to poetic elements and a distillation of harmonies and vocal writing that closely blend text and music.

Three poems in the set are from *Romances sans paroles*, two from *Aquarelles* and one from *Paysages belges*. Originally titled *Ariettes*, the title was changed to *Ariettes oubliées* fifteen years later when the set was reprinted after the critical acclaim accorded *Pelléas et Mélisande*. Debussy dedicated the set of songs to Mary Garden : "unforgettable Mélisande, this music (already somewhat old-fashioned) in affectionate and grateful homage."

C'EST L'EXTASE (IT IS ECSTASY). This *mélodie* is a stunning example of Debussy's skill in fusing poetry and musical sound. Verlaine's poem is intimate and sensual, a portrait of two lovers at one with nature—and with each other. The opening bars mirror the physicality of the text—the languorous fatigue of afterlove. Debussy's setting is richly evocative; the accompaniment is highly chromatic.

With this set of songs Debussy's unique vocal style begins to emerge clearly. The text is always underscored and highlighted by the music. Debussy uses the melody to coordinate the harmony, accompaniment, and rhythmic materials. He uses small intervals and a narrow-range melody to create an intimate, confidential atmosphere, and uses larger intervals at points of extreme emotion (see the high sustained climax at "et la tienne"). Note Debussy's text painting of the rustling grass ("Cela ressemble au cri doux que l'herbe agitée expire") and the muted rolling of the pebbles under the water ("Le roulis sourd des cailloux").

IL PLEURE DANS MON CŒUR (IT WEEPS IN MY HEART). A line from a poem by Rimbaud prefaces this *mélodie*: "Il pleut doucement sur la ville." (It rains softly on the town). Debussy marks this *mélodie* "sad and monotonous." The piano accompaniment seems listless but also restless, consisting of forty repetitions of two-bar phrases that perpetuate the mood of ennui. Poetic alliteration (*pleuvoir*—to rain; *pleurer*—to cry) helps illustrate the wistful melancholy of the poet as he listens to the falling rain.

Midway in the third stanza a tiny moment of recitative appears: "Quoi! nulle trahison?" freely sung, but without overt drama. An arching octave leap at "Ce deuil (et sans raison)" disturbs the stillness of the moment and provides a beautiful transition back to the original G-sharp minor tonality and its whole-tone melody.

L'OMBRE DES ARBRES (IN THE SHADOW OF THE TREES). Debussy prefaced this *mélodie* with a quotation from Rostand's *Cyrano de Bergerac:* "The nightingale sits on a branch of a tall tree thinking she is drowning in her reflection in the water beneath." The poet's hopes, weeping in the high branches of the tree, are drowned as he sees his reflection in the pallid landscape.

Many mirror images in Verlaine's poem are intricately structured to confuse object, image and symbol.[5] Additionally, its two stanzas share the same rhyme scheme.

Debussy subtly constructs musical reflections as well: the second half of the song employs the accompaniment from the first half, in varied fashion. Debussy also makes use of the tritone in voice and piano —an interval which "mirrors" itself even when inverted—and a recurring E-sharp octave, which is perhaps identified in some way with the traveler's shattered hopes.

CHEVAUX DES BOIS (MERRY-GO-ROUND). A Belgian country fair with a rustic merry-go-round is the scene for this poem. A hand-turned crank emits boisterous music, which accompanies the whirling wooden horses. In an attempt to lessen his boredom, the poet rides the merry-go-round with an empty stomach and an aching head. People at the fair are described musically: the children eager for candy and a good time, the sly pickpocket who works the milling crowd. At last evening falls, the merry-go-round turns more slowly, and the sky is dotted with stars.

The piano accompaniment begins unevenly, a toccata-like pattern of repeated melodic and rhythmic figures. Harmony varies for each verse, but always returns to the original chords, even as the little merry-go-round comes round again. Vocal phrases also mirror the spinning motion ("Tournez cent tours, tournez mille tours") of the revolving platform and then return to the original starting place.

"Tournez, tournez" functions as a rondo-like refrain, unifying the song. A beautiful contrast between the opening of the *mélodie* and the ending section occurs as the same melodic material is used, basically unchanged, but at a tempo twice as slow, as the little carousel winds down and the first stars appear.

GREEN (*AQUARELLES* I). Verlaine gave English titles to several of his poems: "Spleen," "Green," and "Nevermore" (not set by Debussy). "Green" and "Spleen" are subtitled "Aquarelles" (Watercolors). Verlaine viewed his poetry in terms of music, writing in *Art poétique*: "De la musique avant toute chose, Pas la couleur, rien que la Nuance!"

An ardent youth—not unlike Mozart's Cherubino—is the protagonist of this song of youthful passion. He dashes impulsively through the early morning dew to his beloved—"Voici des fruits, des fleurs, des feuilles et des branches"— in a burst of freshness, enthusiasm, and tenderness.

Octaves and cascading arpeggiated figures in the accompaniment suggest whole-tone harmonies and point up the breathlessness of the poetic content. As the youth recalls the passion just passed, vocal phrases end downward on the words *fatigue, reposée, délasseront*. The final verse echoes the music of the opening, slowed considerably to a more intimate, sensual expression as he seeks cool repose in the arms of his beloved.

The song's form is a rather straightforward ABA.

SPLEEN (*AQUARELLES* II). As in "Il pleure dans mon coeur," the poet's state is one of ennui—an intentional avoidance and disdain of almost everything except his loved one. This song has two tempi: slow and fast, depicting the mood swings of the poet. Debussy again employs the tritone in this song and delays a firm feeling of tonic key until the end of the piece.

The opening vocal phrases set the mood of emptiness and lassitude by repeating a single pitch eleven times with little variance in rhythm—a musical expression of spleen, the organ once thought to be the cause of ill temper and melancholy as well as erratic mood swings.

Fêtes galantes I   1892
(Paul Verlaine)

En sourdine • Fantoches • Clair de lune

Paul Verlaine published *Les Fêtes galantes* in 1869. It is a collection of poems inspired by the graceful paintings of Watteau, depicting elegant ladies and gallant cavaliers exchanging courtly pleasures in exquisitely manicured parks. The scenes beautifully symbolize the French style of restraint and taste.

Debussy composed two sets of songs titled *Fêtes galantes,* as well as other songs taken from Verlaine's collection. *Fêtes galantes* I was completed in 1892. It is a triptych of three unrelated panels, unified only by the Watteau-like scenes and the fanciful and flirtatious moods that run through each.

EN SOURDINE* (MUTED). Nature as a refuge from worldly suffering is the principal theme of this poem. It is dusk, not quite day nor yet night. Nature is embodied through a series of veiled images: branches create a refuge and shield for the lovers, the wind ruffles the grasses at their feet, and the song of the nightingale mirrors their despair.** The lover commands his beloved to abandon herself to nature, using a list of verbs: *pénétrons, fondons, ferme, croise, chasse, laissons*.[6]

Debussy's setting is near-hypnotic; vocal phrases are declamatory and murmuring, widening only occasionally in scope, and never rising above the dynamic level of *mf.* Melodic material is based largely on the "black-note" pentatonic scale. The piano accompaniment sustains the same muted sensuous mood with delicately colored harmonies and triplet figures, which imitate poetic images of the rustling grass and rocking breeze.

*This languorous and evocative poem also inspired musical settings by Fauré, Hahn, and Laparra.

**The nightingale, symbol of disillusioned love, figures prominently in the poetry and is evoked musically in a figure that Debussy reprises in "Colloque sentimental," the last song of the second set of *Fêtes galantes.*

FANTOCHES (MARIONETTES). Verlaine's poem paints a witty scene awash with characters from the Italian *commedia dell'arte*: the Doctor from Bologna, Scaramouche, Pulcinella, and the pirate and a young maiden—is it the Captain and Colombine? Scaramouche and Pulcinella are the two puppeteers, "united by an evil design." Shadowy black in the moonlight, they gesture grotesquely, symbolically directing the action. Despite their devious intrigue, the overall mood is gay and spontaneous, as if to establish that this is a pantomime play.

There is no discernible plot. The characters seem motivated by desire, apparent pawns in the hands of the two dark figures. The "excellent Doctor" from Bologna leisurely gathers herbs in the cool meadow, while his half-naked daughter glides through the fields in search of her handsome Spanish pirate on whose behalf a nightingale screams in distress. Wenk calls attention to the highlighting of the word "détresse" to indicate the pirate's sexual desire, the "stage prop nightingale" that screams raucously on the pirate's behalf, and the expressions *avec lenteur* (with slowness) and "à tue-tête" (at the top of its voice).[7]

"Fantoches" calls for supple phrasing from the singer. Staccato and legato are constantly juxtaposed throughout the vocal part. The Doctor's daughter receives the most musical attention. She is etched in evocative vocal shapes that match her demeanor, mood, and actions ("piquant minois," "sous la charmille," "se glisse"), capped by a lascivious "la-la" as a final comment after the word "demi-nue" (half-naked).

Accompaniment figures are based throughout on a constant sixteenth-note rhythm. A short three-note motive, introduced at the beginning of the song, functions as a unifying device. It reappears in several variations in the description of every character and for the final time in the last vocal phrase. The colorful Spanish pirate is suggested by rhythmic patterns reminiscent of a habanera and the Spanish guitar.

A final flourish ends the song as the three-note motive appears twice in the last vocal measures as the voice sings "la-la," as if to accompany the exit of the puppeteers, each disappearing in turn.

CLAIR DE LUNE (MOONLIGHT). Debussy captures the luminous atmosphere of Verlaine's poem in his second setting of "Clair de lune." He wrote the first setting as part of the Vasnier Songbook and also used the title for his well-known piano piece from the *Suite bergamasque*.

"Your soul is a chosen landscape" begins this famous poem by Verlaine, which was also set by Gabriel Fauré. The entire *mélodie* is permeated by the calm of the moonlit panorama, evoked in an expressive tranquil setting.

Poetic images include fountains, music, dancing, softly swaying branches and overall, the calm moonlight, which is both beautiful and melancholy. Fanciful figures play upon the "chosen landscape"—the soul or imagination. But their happiness is only imagined—as fictitious as the masks that hide their identities.

Debussy illustrates the scene with a short piano prelude, which contains a motive that is based on the pentatonic scale. Sustained vocal passages, which are similar in style to those found in Song 1, are accompanied by unexpected harmonic transitions and modality. Debussy highlights selected words by subtle musical means: *mode mineur, bonheur, chanson, sangloter d'extase, tristes*. Small motives linked to poetic images may be found scattered throughout the accompaniment texture.

Fêtes galantes II   1904
(Paul Verlaine)
Les Ingénus • Le Faune • Colloque sentimental

The second set of *Fêtes galantes*, composed in 1904, has sparser textures, freer tonalities, and a more concentrated compositional style than the first set. None of the Watteau-like scenes of the first set are found here; instead, these three poems are focused on the disenchantment of love and the passing of youth.

Debussy's personal life was in turmoil during this time; these compositions coincided with his liaison with Emma Bardac and his final break with his first wife. *Fêtes galantes II* is dedicated to Emma, Debussy's second wife, the singer for whom Gabriel Fauré composed *La Bonne chanson*.

LES INGÉNUS (THE INNOCENTS). Verlaine's nostalgic verse is tinged with the sweet pain of youthful uncertainty. A naive and simple scene reveals lovely young girls in formal dress, their youthful escorts eager to catch forbidden glimpses of flashing ankles or graceful white necks. As evening falls, the young women lean dreamily on the gentlemen's arms, whispering beguiling and perplexing words. Suspended within the moment, they retain a discreet, otherworldly charm.

Tonal ambiguity characterizes this *mélodie*. Debussy's free-floating harmonies are carefully contrived to complement the uncertain emotions and repressed sensations of the youths in the poem. Debussy uses the whole-tone scale in the second section of the song and subtly repeats motives and figures in the piano accompaniment throughout the *mélodie*. The last section of the *mélodie* sustains the mysterious unfulfilled mood with chromatic harmonies that avoid a tonal closure. The song ends with an augmented A-flat chord.

LE FAUNE (THE FAUN). Time images abound in this poem: time past, time present, time fleeting. The incessant beating of the *tambourin* (small drum) in the piano accompaniment acts as a unifying ostinato throughout this *mélodie*. This rhythmic pattern also imparts exotic and mysterious overtones to the poetic scene: a neatly ordered bowling lawn, presided over by a somewhat menacing statue of a terra-cotta faun. The "melancholy pilgrims" of the poem are attracted to the old statue whose silent laughter foretells less happy moments ahead.

No doubt the faun indicates Pan. His flute pipe is present in the *mélodie*. Debussy begins by giving the piano a solo line to be played "like a flute," then introduces the monotonous figuration of the drumbeat in the piano, weaving rich harmonies around the constant rhythm. Verlaine's poetic rhyme scheme uses two like-sounding word patterns (*cuite, suite, conduite, fuite/ boulingrins, sereins, pélerins, tambourins*), creating rhythmic intensity in the poetry that is reinforced by the repeated rhythms of the piano accompaniment.

COLLOQUE SENTIMENTAL (SENTIMENTAL COLLOQUY). "Colloque sentimental," the last of the twenty-two poems in Verlaine's *Fêtes galantes,* provides a chilling climax to the series of poems. Its blended themes of despair, death and disillusion inspired one of Debussy's most skillfully crafted songs.

In this extraordinary *mélodie,* the ghosts of two lovers meet in a wintry park frozen with ice. As they speak of their former love, their dialogue matches the setting: glacial and detached from feeling. The poem is structured in rhymed couplets, the emotional tone is somber, the vocal line is narrow in range and recitative in style throughout.

Debussy uses the musical texture as a tool to illustrate the poetic content and musical mood. Texture ranges at its barest from a single vocal or piano line to a ten-note piano chord accompanying the voice. The vocal range extends an octave and a sixth but the piano part ranges over nearly six octaves.[8] Debussy employs whole-tone melodies and open fifths to evoke the barren park and the emotional emptiness of the exchange.

The two ghosts are characterized by different piano accompaniments: the first with a sparse chordal style, the second with richer textured harmonies. The narrator who begins and ends the song is given a simple linear melody to accompany his brief account of the scene.

At the word "specters," we hear a C-natural in the accompaniment, and we hear it in some part of the texture during all of the uncommunicative conversation between the two ghosts. The longest pedal point to be found in any of Debussy's compositions also appears in the section containing the dialogue between the two spirits.[9] Debussy repeats the pitch A without interruption for thirty-two measures, producing a musical tension that matches the tense, monotonous, non-inflected speech of the ghostly couple.

Several times during the *mélodie*, Debussy tellingly quotes the nightingale's song ("voix de notre désespoir") from "En Sourdine," the first song of the first series of *Fêtes galantes*. Thus, the bird that personifies love's despair ties the two sets of songs together symbolically and musically, forecasting the disenchantment of love found in the last song of the series and unifying the two sets by a subtle musical component.

Chansons de Bilitis   **Songs of Bilitis. 1897-98**
(Pierre Louÿs)

La Flûte de Pan • La Chevelure • Le Tombeau des naïades

Chansons de Bilitis is generally conceded to be the most perfect example of Debussy's ability to merge musical and poetical elements. Debussy composed the Bilitis songs while he was working on his opera *Pelléas et Mélisande,* which he completed in 1902.

The *naissance* of these exquisite songs was based on a celebrated literary hoax perpetrated by Debussy's close friend Pierre Louÿs, who claimed to have discovered a collection of poems written by Bilitis, an ancient unknown Greek poetess, etched on the walls of her tomb. No doubt Louÿs's verses, full of veiled eroticism, gained a certain respectability from being dated as ancient historic verses.

For the songs of Bilitis, Debussy couched the simple but sensuous poetry in harmonies and melodic material of antique flavor and classical style, mixing modality, chromaticism, and a melodic but fragmented vocal approach. The three songs form a triptych of panels illustrating three seasons of love: wondering young love, sensuous mature love, and the fading retreat of dimmed passion.

Six months after the premiere of the *Chansons de Bilitis*, Debussy composed incidental music for a recitation/pantomime of twelve other poems from the "Bilitis" collection. The short work was scored for two flutes, two harps, and celeste.

LA FLÛTE DE PAN (THE FLUTE OF PAN). Louÿs's poem, titled "La Syrinx," reflects the hidden eroticism of the myth of Pan, who transforms Syrinx into a reed flute and plays upon her, converting his sexual desires into art.[10] The flute is prominent in the poem and the music. Debussy launches the scene with a sinuous ascending line in the flute (piano) that employs the whole-tone scale.

Bilitis describes her awakening to love. She sits on the lap of her lover while he teaches her to play the flute. Imitative phrases of teacher and student are heard in vocal passages and piano figures; ultimately, their lips join on the flute and the songs of both intertwine.

Curved phrase contours predominate in melodic material for both voice and piano. Modal harmonies evoke ancient Greece, and the naïveté and freshness of the young Bilitis is mirrored in her murmuring vocal lines.

This song and the next contain textbook examples of Debussy's mature style: manipulation of the whole-tone scale, recitative-like phrases built on one note or very small scale intervals, duple versus triple rhythms, and exotic chord progressions.

LA CHEVELURE (TRESSES). Symbols of union permeate the second song. Bilitis describes a vivid, erotic dream told to her by her lover. Her story begins with shy restraint and eventually flowers into a passionate curving phrase "Par la même chevelure la bouche sur la bouche." This is underlaid with pulsing syncopated piano figures that finally come to rest at the climatic moment that concludes the section, "ou que tu entrais en moi comme mon songe." The tower scene from *Pelléas* is recalled as the lover twines Bilitis's hair around his neck.

The last five measures are intimate and revealing. Both parties are shaken by the intensity of passion just recounted. Debussy was adamant that this passage not be overemphasized. His famous statement "Above all, no *frisson!*" should be quoted here.

LE TOMBEAU DES NAÏADES (THE TOMB OF THE NAIADS). "The third *Chansons de Bilitis* contains all the music for which I am beholden to my well-organized nature," Debussy wrote to Louÿs in December 1897.[11] Piano figures act as a cohesive element throughout the song; they are built with various sixteenth-note patterns, underlining the inexorable and unchanging mood that underlies the narrative. The tension in the opening bars, produced by the recitative-like vocal lines and the unvarying accompaniment pattern, is vivid and easily felt.

Bilitis finds herself in an icy forest, following her lover. Images that illustrate the dimming of passion between the couple are scattered throughout the frozen landscape of the text: the frost-covered wood, Bilitis's hair spangled with icicles, her sandals packed with snow, the icy spring, and the broken ice sheets raised to the sky.

Love between the couple has dimmed; the journey is a search for an unattainable goal. Heavy chords in the piano accompany Bilitis's stress-laden footsteps; she realizes his distance from her. Debussy then introduces a new figuration depicting hoof marks in the snow.

One of the most marvelous moments in all of Debussy's *mélodies* occurs as the man breaks the ice of the frozen spring with his spade—the spring where the naiades had laughed. The singer approaches this climactic point through a whole-tone melodic line "Et avec le fer de sa houe," which gathers energy, seesawing back and forth on one interval as he chips away at the frozen ice. Finally, the climactic point "riaient les naïades" erupts from the melodic tension like the ice breaking, underscored by high-pitched joyous piano figures that frolic like the voices of the water nymphs.

Ballades de François Villon   **Ballads of François Villon. 1910**

Ballade de Villon à s'amye • Ballade que Villon feit à la requeste de sa mère pour prier Nostre-Dame • Ballade des femmes de Paris

In an article in *Musica* (March 1911) Debussy wrote:

Oh, lately, I've set to music, I don't know why, three ballades by Villon. . .Yes, I do know: because I've wanted to for a long time. Well, it's difficult to follow, to "strike" the right meter and still retain some inspiration. If you're just putting things together, content to juxtapose, of course it's not difficult, but then it's not worth the trouble either. Classic poetry has a life of its own, an "inner dynamism," as the Germans would say, which has nothing to do with us.[12]

Debussy's Villon songs stand out for their directness of musical expression and leaner, more hard-edged vocal passages. Villon's three poems have different subjects, earthy in style and passionate in declamation. In setting them, Debussy captures the fifteenth-century atmosphere in which Villon lived and wrote.

BALLADE DE VILLON À S'AMYE (BALLAD OF VILLON TO HIS BELOVED). Even as Villon sings of the treachery and falseness of his love, he begs for pity. Debussy's opening indication is "with an expression of anguish and regret." Chromatic figures and transparent textures underpin vocal passages that are predominantly recitative in style. Debussy opens the *mélodie* with a little rhythmic cell consisting of a thirty-second note followed by a double-dotted eighth note; subtle variations of this cell continue to appear in the piano throughout the song. This pattern is strongly reminiscent of the rhythm used throughout the first *mélodie* of *Le Promenoir des deux amants*. This song contains one of the few passages in Debussy's songs which he marked *forte*: "Or, buvez fort, tan que ru peut courir" (Now drink deep e'er the spring runs dry).

BALLADE QUE VILLON FEIT À LA REQUESTE DE SA MÈRE POUR PRIER NOSTRE-DAME (BALLAD MADE AT THE REQUEST OF HIS MOTHER, FOR A PRAYER TO OUR LADY). Responding to a request of his aged mother, Villon writes a prayer for her to the Virgin Mary. His plea reveals her humility and abiding faith.

Debussy expresses this in strong but simple vocal contours. Open fifths, parallel triads, and modal elements in piano and voice impart a medieval, church-like atmosphere.

The tonality migrates from A minor to C major. Each refrain concludes with a phrase of strong affirmation: "In this faith I wish to live and die." The first two refrains close with a deceptive cadence; the last repetition ends decisively in C major.

BALLADE DES FEMMES DE PARIS (BALLAD OF THE WOMEN OF PARIS). In this poem Villon extols the chattering women of Paris, capturing their babble, gossip, and good-natured bantering in a nonstop, colorful narrative. His account is one of infectious zest; Parisian women carry off all prizes when it comes to the gift of glib conversation. Both piano and voice follow the jet-propelled momentum of Villon's malicious litany of female talkers.

This is probably the most robust *mélodie* in all of Debussy's songs. It contains the zest for life inherent in Villon's verse and in his subjects, the diverse and vivid array of Parisiennes. "But for the gift of gab, give me the women of Paris," Villon exclaims in decisive last phrase that ends the group with a colorful flourish.

Extended Study List

Cinq poèmes des Charles Baudelaire • Romance • Les Cloches • Voici que le printemps • Apparition • Pantomime • L'Échlonnement des haies • *Proses lyriques* • *Deux Rondels de Charles d'Orléans* • *Le Promenoir des deux amants* • *Trois poèmes de Stéphane Mallarmé*

Selected Reading

Jane Bathori, "Les Musiciens que j'ai connus" (The Musicians I Have Known). The Mayer Lectures. trans. Felix Aprahamian in *Recorded Sound*, No. 1, II (1962). "Debussy."

Jane Bathori, *On the Interpretation of the Mélodies of Claude Debussy,* trans. and with an introduction by Linda Laurent (Stuyvesant, NY: Pendragon Press, 1998).

Margaret Cobb, *The Poetic Debussy* (Boston: Northeastern University Press, 1982). A collection of the song texts with translations, dates of composition, location of original manuscripts. Also contains selected letters.

Laurence Davies, *The Gallic Muse* (New York: A.S. Barnes, 1967).

François Lesure, *Debussy on Music,* trans. and ed. Richard Langham Smith. (London: Secker & Warburg, 1977). Critical writings of Claude Debussy.

Edward Lockspeiser, *Debussy* (New York: McGraw Hill, 1972). Chapter 12 discusses the *mélodies.*

Roger Nichols, ed., *Debussy Remembered* (London: Faber & Faber,1992).

Marie Claire Rohinsky, ed., *The Singer's Debussy* (New York: Pelion Press, 1987). Brief notes on each of Debussy's songs. Translations and IPA phonetic transcriptions.

Arthur B. Wenk, *Claude Debussy and the Poets* (Berkeley: University of California Press, 1976). Scholarly discussion of Debussy's settings of Banville, Verlaine, Baudelaire, Mallarmé, Louÿs.

Susan Youens, "Debussy's Song Cycles," *The NATS Journal,* 43:1 (Sept/Oct 1986), 13-15.

_____, "Debussy's *Le Promenoir des deux amants* of 1910," *The NATS Journal,* 43:2 (Nov/Dec 1986), 22-25.

Notes

1. Quoted in *Debussy on Music,* François Lesure, 250.
2. Margaret Cobb, *The Poetic Debussy,* xiii.
3. Quoted in liner notes to *Debussy: The Complete Songs* by Stefan Jarocinski. (EMI France C 165-16371/,24.
4. Cobb, 61.
5. Arthur B. Wenk, *Claude Debussy and the Poets*, 106.
6. Ibid., 36-37.
7. Ibid., 28-29.
8. Ibid., 239.
9. Ibid.
10. Ibid., 180.
11. Cobb, 139.
12. Quoted in Cobb, 171.

CÉCILE CHAMINADE (1857-1944)

Chaminade's music speaks with an altogether personal voice: good-humoured, *charmant,* with a seemingly spontanesous, almost careless elegance.

—Bengt Forsberg[1]

Cécile Louise Stéphanie Chaminade was born in a suburb of Paris to a middle class family that valued the arts. Both her parents were amateur musicians. As a child, Cécile displayed an astounding ear for music, and her mother taught her piano. In 1865, the family moved to Vésinet where the little girl made the acquaintance of composer Georges Bizet who called her his "little Mozart." Bizet recommended her parents enroll Cécile in the Paris Conservatoire, but Monsieur Chaminade refused: "...girls of the bourgeoisie were intended to become wives and mothers." Nonetheless, Bizet saw to it that Cécile had a private education that paralleled that of the conservatory. She studied piano with LeCouppey, harmony with Savard and composition with Benjamin Godard. Her family hosted a regular musical salon in their home, attended by such composers as Ambroise Thomas, Gounod, Massenet, Saint-Saëns and Chabrier.

After her father's death, Cécile concentrated on her career as a pianist. Her programs frequently included her own compositions. She concertized throughout Europe, and made a successful tour of the United States. Here she gave twenty-five concerts in the 1907-08 season, and these launched her immense popularity in the States. From 1892, she performed regularly in England; one of her enthusiastic supporters was Queen Victoria, who invited her to Windsor on a regular basis. In 1913, the French government awarded Chaminade the prestigious Legion of Honor—the first female composer to be so honored.

An extremely prolific composer, Cécile Chaminade wrote approximately 400 compositions: works for piano, an opera, a ballet, a concerto for piano and orchestra, and well over 100 songs. Nearly all of her works were published and were staples in the elegant salon concerts during the turn of the century. Among the most popular today is the *Concertino for Flute and Orchestra* (1905). As the twentieth century progressed, her music fell out of vogue, perhaps due to reaction against post-romantic French music, but also attributable to the social and aesthetic conditions which influenced women and their music.

Mignonne*   **Beloved. 1894**
(Pierre Ronsard)

The text for this *mélodie* is one of Pierre de Ronsard's best-known odes,"Mignonne, allons voir si rose." First published in 1553, it contains Ronsard's most prevalent poetic themes: the passage of time, the fragility of life, and the invitation to live in the moment.

The poet draws a parallel between the rose and his youthful love. Just as the rose's opening blossoms anticipate their death in the same moment, so also will physical beauty fade and die.[2] The destructive nature of time is embodied in the poet's persuasive last lines "Comme à ceste fleur la vieillesse/Fera ternir vostre beauté" (For, just as this flower has faded/Old age will wither your beauty).

Chaminade's setting complements Ronsard's rich poetic lyricism with an graceful vocal line. Figures in the piano are based primarily on the opening measures. The piano often doubles the vocal line, or accompanies it in thirds. The overall texture is extremely lyric and elegant.

*Richard Wagner and Jean de Castro also set this text.

L'anneau d'argent   **The Silver Ring. 1891**
(Rosemond Gérard)

"L'anneau d'argent" is one of Chaminade's most popular and successful songs. In an interview with the *New York Herald*, Chaminade spoke about writing the *mélodie*:

> I found myself in a mood of vague sorrow about nothing in particular, simply a *tristesse des choses*. I picked up a book of verses by Rosemond Gérard, a very brilliant woman...I came across the poem of "L'anneau d'argent." It fitted with my sad mood. The melody just came to me. I sat

in my chair with the book in my lap, and sang the melody as it welled to my lips, and I wept as I sang it. Later, I wrote it down just that way and added the accompaniment I seemed to hear. It had made me weep, and that is why it made others weep.[3]

There is quiet passion in the text, in which the singer contemplates the silver ring her lover has given to her. She derives comfort from the memories it brings back, and declares she will wear it on her finger to the grave.

Forward motion is maintained throughout the song by a series of arpeggiated chords in the piano accompaniment . This figure also illustrates the delicate pattern on the ring, a circlet of twined flowers. There are three stanzas; the form is ABA'.

A number of Gérard's poems, and those of her husband Edmond Rostand, were set by Emmanuel Chabrier.* Chaminade set four other poems by Rosemond Gérard.

*See "Les Cigales" and "Villanelle des petits canards." Rostand was a French playwright whose greatest success was *Cyrano de Bergerac.*

Écrin   Jewel-case. 1902
(René Niverd)

This delightful *mélodie* sounds as though it might have come from an operetta—and indeed, its dedication to Mlle. Jeanne Leclerc, de l'Opéra-Comique, would seem to indicate it was written for a singer of lighter theatrical fare. Chaminade was not unfamiliar with operetta; she composed an opéra-comique titled *La Sévillane*, which she accompanied in private performance. It was later presented at both the Salle Erard and the Salle Pleyel.

"Écrin" is a charming example of Chaminade's lyric style. It has light, flirtatious vocal phrases, and teasing, playful rhythm patterns. Niverd's poetry is hardly significant literature, but it is a good example of the lighter, more theatrical verse of the period.

There are three stanzas, set in ABA form. The words celebrate the beloved's "mischievous eyes," and "satin lips," before declaring that her soul is the jewel in his crown, and the perfume that drives him mad.

Extended Study List
Mots d'amour • Fleur jetée • Ronde d'amour • Ma première lettre • Menuet • Espoir • Chanson triste • L'été • L'Amour captif • L'Absente • Amoroso • Amour d'Automne • Invocation • Tu me dirais

Selected Reading
Cécile Chaminade, "How to Sing and Play My Compositions," *Ladies' Home Journal* 22 (Nov. 1905), 19.
Marcia J. Citron, *Cécile Chaminade: A Bio-Bibliography* (New York: Greenwood Press, 1988).
Rupert Hughes, "Mme. Chaminade and John Philip Sousa Talk About Music," *The New York Herald. Magazine* (Nov. 15, 1908): 9-10.
Candace A. Magner, "The Songs of Cécile Chaminade," *Journal of Singing* 57:4 (March/April 2001).
Cécile Tardif, *Portrait de Cécile Chaminade* (Montreal: Courteau, 1993).

Notes
1. Bengt Forsberg, preface to liner notes "Mots d'amour: Cécile Chaminade *Mélodies*." Anne Sofie von Otter, mezzo-soprano; Bengt Forsberg, piano. Deutsche-Grammophon CD 289 471 331-2, 2001.
2. Mary Dibbern, Carol Kimball, and Patrick Choukroun, *The Songs of Jacques Leguerney* (Hilldale, NY: Pendragon Press, 2001), 61.
3. Quoted in Candace A. Magner, "The Songs of Cécile Chaminade," *Journal of Singing* 57:4, 26.

ERIK SATIE (1866-1925)

The musician is perhaps the most modest of all animals, but he is also the proudest. It is he who invented the sublime art of ruining poetry.

—Erik Satie[1]

I came into this world very young, at a very old time.

—Erik Satie[2]

Erik Satie and his music had a great influence on the works of his contemporaries. Unconventional and seemingly irreverent, Satie became a kind of father-figure for the avant-garde French composers, writers, and artists of the day. He enjoyed the friendship and admiration of Debussy, Stravinsky, Picasso, Roussel, Koechlin, Cocteau, Milhaud, Honegger and many others.

He was a curious personality of eccentric habits whose sense of the absurd and whimsical permeated both his life and his music. He had a taste for the bizarre and the inventive and hated pretentiousness in life and in art, bestowing amusing titles on many of his works, notably his piano pieces. Beneath the jokes and droll behavior he hid a sensitive, serious nature.

Satie's list of *mélodies* is slim, but they merit inclusion in any study of French song. Their style ranges from the jaunty rhythms of the dance-hall to the childlike innocence of fairy-tale subjects.

Ludions
(Léon-Paul Fargue)   1923

Air du rat (The Rat's Air) • Spleen (Spleen) • La Grenoùille américaine (The American Frog) • Air du poète (The Poet's Air) • Chanson du chat (Song of the Cat)

"Ludions" translates as "bottle imps,"* and provides a clue to the nature of the texts by Léon-Paul Fargue. The poems are so riddled with puns and illogical phrases that translating them is quite difficult. Fargue sometimes wrote in baby talk, his poems full of unrelated phrases garnered from the scenes that whizzed by his taxi-cab window on his infamous and constant cab rides through Paris.

Ludions, the last of Satie's purely vocal works, was composed two years before his death. The work is perhaps the finest of Satie's song groups. Fargue's nonsensical verse complements Satie's aesthetic, as the two friends' personalities closely matched one another. Both men were the objects of picturesque legends of Parisian artistic life.

All the *mélodies* in *Ludions* are quite short, like vignettes. Satie combines a popular music hall style for "Air du rat," "La Grenoùille américaine," and "Chanson du chat," with a mock-serious "tongue-in-cheek" treatment for "Spleen" and "Air du poète."

The first performance of *Ludions* was in December 1923 with the composer accompanying Jane Bathori in a concert of his music at the Salle des Agriculteurs.

---

*A *ludion* is a little figure suspended in a hollow ball, which descends or rises in a vase filled with water when one presses down on the elastic membrane covering the mouth of the vase.

Trois mélodies 1916

La Statue de bronze (Léon-Paul Fargue) • Daphénéo (Mimi Godebska) •
Le Chapelier (René Chalupt)

These three *mélodies*, to texts by three different poets, are charmingly diverse.
Satie did not compose them as a set, but they were published as such by Salabert
under the title *Trois mélodies*. Their subtle humor is vintage Satie—full of irony,
parody, and witty style.

LA STATUE DE BRONZE (THE BRONZE STATUE). The scene is a garden game—the
"jeu de tonneau." A bronze frog perches atop a cabinet with numbered chambers,
as players throw metal disks that fall into the compartments to score points.
Hitting the frog's mouth represents the highest tally. The bored frog dreams of
being liberated from her pedestal, able to use her wide-open mouth to utter "the
word." She wants to be free to join the other frogs hunched near the rust-colored
washhouse "blowing musical bubbles from the soapy moonlight."

Satie assigns detached figures to the accompaniment, whose jaunty lilt is reminiscent of a cakewalk; it is easy to picture the metal disks bumping down the
chutes to the compartments. Only when the frog voices her desires does the
texture become lighter. In the last measures of the song, with an oscillating
piano figure and a droning repeated note in the vocal line, Satie illustrates the
insects that sleep in the frog's mouth at night.

Satie dedicated this *mélodie* to soprano Jane Bathori who first recorded the
group in the early phonograph era.

DAPHÉNÉO (DAPHÉNÉO). Mimi Godebska, the sixteen-year-old daughter of
close friends of Satie's, wrote this little verse; Satie granted her anonymity
under the pseudonym M. God. Her poem is a nonsensical conversation
between Chrysaline and Daphénéo; their communication is one of straight-
faced innocence. Their dialogue is a play on words involving the sounds of
"un noisetier"—a hazel-tree—and the liaison that makes "un oisetier"—a
nonexistent word which would mean "bird-tree"—sound the same. Even at the
conclusion of this confused miniature exchange, Chrysaline is still not sure she
understands—nor are we.

LE CHAPELIER (THE MAD HATTER). Satie was fascinated by Lewis Carroll's
story *Alice in Wonderland*, which he once thought of turning into a ballet.
René Chalupt is the poet for the song, and the poem is based on the familiar
tea party scene. Satie uses this crazy occasion to poke fun at French opera by
indicating *Allegretto (genre Gounod)* and lifting in its entirety the "Chanson de
Magali" from Gounod's *Mireille* to serve as the vocal part. Since Gounod had
adapted this from an old Provençal folk song, Satie's treatment is a pastiche of
a pastiche! It is not known whether Satie was aware of the true origin of
Gounod's melody.

Despite the musical pun, the *mélodie* is gracefully conceived. The Hatter's
frantic posturings encompass a range of two octaves. His painstaking care to
grease his watch with "butter of the best quality" is set in a vocal phrase that

slides down in slippery sequences for an octave and a third. Satie dedicated this song to Igor Stravinsky.

La Diva de l'Empire	The Diva of the Empire. 1904
(Dominque Bonnaud and Numa Blès)	

The "Diva de l'Empire," one of Satie's café-concert songs,[*] was written for and performed by Paulette Darty, dubbed "la reine de la valse lente."[**] Satie also wrote "Je te veux," another slow waltz in the same lilting style, for her. Between verses and at the end of her numbers, she danced around the stage in graceful circles. Darty kept this song in her repertoire for many years.

This little cakewalk is strophic. It describes a seductive beauty, interspersing English words with French: "la grande chapeau *Greenaway, baby* étonné, *little girl* aux yeux veloutés," and so on. The British femme fatale enchants all who see her. The piano provides a snappy strutting rhythm throughout; the humor of the song is dependent on the play of words and sounds as well as the inserted English expressions.

[*]Café-concerts were one form of popular entertainment in Paris in the late nineteenth and early twentieth century. All-musical programs were often held outside; French popular singers presented repertoire that catered to lower and middle class audiences who came to talk, eat, drink and observe the long informal programs.

[**]The queen of the slow waltz.

Extended Study
Je te veux • *Trois mélodies de 1886* (Les Anges, Élégie, Sylvie) • L'Omnibus automobile • Tendrement • *Trois mélodies sans paroles* (Rambouillet, Les Oiseaux, Marienbad) • Allons-y Chochotte, • Chez le docteur • *Trois Poèmes d'amour* (Ne suis que grain de sable, Suis chauve de naissance, Ta parure est secrete) • *Quatre petites mélodies* (Élégie, Danseuse, Chanson, Adieu)

Selected Reading
Laurence Davies, *The Gallic Muse* (New York: A.S. Barnes, 1967).
Alan M. Gillmore, *Erik Satie* (Boston: Twayne Publishers, 1988).
James Harding, *ErikSatie* (London: Secker & Warburg, 1975).
Rollo H. Myers, *Erik Satie* (New York; Dover Publications, Inc., 1968).
Robert Orledge, *Satie the composer* (Cambridge: Cambridge University Press, 1990).
_____, *Satie Remembered.* trans. Roger Nichols (Portland, OR: Amadeus Press, 1995).
Nancy Perloff, *Art and the Everyday: Popular Entertainment and the Circle of Erik Satie* (New York: Oxford University Press, 1991).
Pierre-Daniel Templier. *Erik Satie,* trans. Elena L. French and David S. French (Cambridge: The MIT Press, 1969).
Ornella Volta. *Satie Seen Through His Letters,* trans. Michael Bullock (London: Marion Boyars, 1988).
Stephen Moore Whiting, *Satie the Bohemian: From Cabaret to Concert Hall* (Oxford University Press, 1999).

Notes
1. Part of the fragmentary writing found in Satie's room, written along the margins of notebooks or on pieces of old envelopes. Quoted in Pierre-Daniel Templier, *Erik Satie* (Cambridge: MIT Press, 1969), 64.
2. Quoted in liner notes. *The Irreverent Inspirations of Erik Satie.* Angel Records S-36713.

ALBERT ROUSSEL (1869-1937)

> My sole aim has been to serve my art, by giving clear expression to my thoughts. I hope that I have succeeded in this, for that is the only reward I desire.
>
> —Albert Roussel[1]

Albert Roussel composed almost forty *mélodies* as well as chamber music, ballets, and operas. In 1894 he left a highly successful career as a naval officer to pursue music. After completing his studies, he became professor of counterpoint at the Schola Cantorum in Paris. Satie and Varèse were among his pupils.

His love for the sea was an almost spiritual attraction that guided his personal development.[2] Roussel wrote that "to contrive to evoke [in music] all the feelings which lie hidden in the sea—the sense of power and of infinity, of charm, anger and gentleness—this must be the greatest joy that could be given in the world to an artist in the domain of his art."[3] Roussel's career in the navy perhaps contributed to his love for distant places. He took an extended tour of southeast Asia in 1909, which had tremendous influence on his composition, notably his opera-ballet *Padmâvatî* (1923). His attraction for the Orient is also shown in several song settings of Chinese lyrics.

Roussel's musical style is eclectic, but highly individual. His early works show the influence of Vincent d'Indy; works that date from 1910 to 1920 show Impressionistic features and, after 1925, more neoclassic features. His contemporaries, Debussy and Ravel, influenced his music, most particularly his songs. During the 1930s Roussel was generally acknowledged to be among the greatest of the living French composers.

Although Roussel abhorred programmatic compositions and descriptive symphonic poems, his affinity for fine literature and song led him to compose in this genre throughout most of his career. Roussel's *mélodies* are distinctive for their original treatment of harmony and their highly developed rhythms, which aid in creating striking musical effects. His songs are sensitively crafted and always have at their heart the expressive transference of the poetry.

Le Jardin mouillé　　　　　　　　　　　　　**Garden in the Rain. 1903**
(Henri de Régnier)

This lovely *mélodie* belongs to Op. 3, a set of early Roussel songs using texts by Henri de Régnier. Although this is an early song of Roussel, it clearly shows his skill in writing expressively for both voice and piano. The poem is interior and very subjective. It is a delicately etched picture of a sleeping garden that awakens leaf by leaf as a soft rain shower falls upon it.

Piano figures subtly suggest the raindrops hitting the leaves, the gravel paths, and the lawn. There are continuous changes of tempo throughout the song. Vocal passages are legato and beautifully calm, suggesting the subdued melancholy of the text, culminating in the poet's last words that compare his emotional state to that of the scene he views from his window ("I listen with closed eyes...to the wet garden dripping gently, In the darkness I have made inside me").

Réponse d'une épouse sage	Reply of a Wise Wife. 1927

(Chinese poem adapted by H. P. Roché)

His personal affinity for the Orient led Roussel to compose "The Reply of a Virtuous Wife," one of several Chinese texts in his catalog of songs. The words to this *mélodie* date from the eighth century and are actually French translations of English translations from the original Chinese.

A dignified and elegant Chinese lady speaks to a would-be suitor, proclaiming the sanctity of her married state, but at the same time letting him know that she wishes she were free. Her narrative is moving but very calm. Dramatically, the text fuses intense emotion with the restraint and ceremony ingrained in the oriental culture.

Roussel sets the poem delicately, suggesting an oriental atmosphere by using altered scales; he uses subtle variations in the vocal line as well. He notes dynamics precisely and changes accompaniment to balance the dramatic shifts in the text. Roussel maintains a subtle interplay between voice and piano throughout this expressive and very beautiful song.

Le Bachelier de Salamanque	The Bachelor of Salamanca. 1919

(René Chalupt)

Roussel set four poems of René Chalupt; this *mélodie* and "Sarabande" are listed as Op. 20. Chalupt's text is tongue-in-cheek and presents the picture of a frustrated Spanish serenader, determined to deliver his serenade after the curfew has sounded. In order to escape detection, he has disguised himself in a cloak and black hat. Furtively, he makes his way to the window of his longed-for beloved, the admiral's daughter.

Roussel has underscored this amusing scene with a striking pastiche of Spanish music; the piano imitates the universal instrument of serenaders, the guitar. The lively mood is mirrored in the vocal passages.

Sarabande	Saraband. 1919

(René Chalupt)

This is an exquisite example of Roussel's compositional craft, a song that perfectly captures a lovely spring night. A young lover walks with his beloved in a beautiful garden filled with marble fountains and stocked with white turtle doves. The atmosphere is hushed and mysterious, underlaid with sensual undertones.

The piano evokes the "slender sarabande" of the fountains and the gentle splashing of the falling droplets of water with several broken-chord figures. There are four distinct sections in the *mélodie*; in each section, the tonality and accompaniment figures change. Subtle harmonies match the subdued but voluptuous images in the text: the slow dripping of the fountains, feathers from the doves falling softly into the water, and the gentle drift of chestnut blossoms onto bare flesh. Roussel's integration of poem and music is wonderfully realized in this *mélodie*.

Cœur en péril
(René Chalupt)

Heart in Danger. 1933

Chalupt's flirtatious text is a narrative of a young man who is eager to convince his lady love of his fidelity. He reels off a list of royal beauties, extolling their virtues and personal attributes, but assures her that it is she who is the love of his life. His vocal phrases are tuneful, accompanied by a spirited accompaniment of Iberian flavor. Suddenly, his lively recitation of ladies and their attractions gives way to a quiet and intimate last section. Roussel's final measures of the song leave no doubt as to the sincerity of the young lover's feelings.

Jazz dans la nuit
(René Dommange)

Jazz in the Night. 1928

This *mélodie* has no counterpart in Roussel's other songs. It is full of imagination, wit, and musical variety. "Jazz dans la nuit" reflects Roussel's fascination with jazz, a style that appealed to many composers of that time, including Ravel.

Drowsy rhythms, chromatic harmonies and a languid, angular vocal line complement the picture of an outdoor park ablaze with multicolor lights. Vivid images are presented slowly and deliberately in kaleidoscopic fashion: gaudy lights, frenzied tangos, a wailing saxophone, and a discarded handkerchief stained with lipstick.

Roussel freely shifts tonality under the vibrant images in the poetry. He uses syncopation and some altered harmonies in an attempt to suggest a "jazzy" atmosphere within the context of art song form. Instead of becoming a blatant parody of another idiom, these musical elements are integrated into the composer's own personal style, and the *mélodie* becomes an animated musical commentary.

Extended Study List

Ode à un jeune gentilhomme • Amoureux séparés • Light • Flammes • *Deux poèmes de Ronsard* (soprano/ flute) • A Flower given to my daughter • Les Fleurs font une broderie • Voeu • Le Départ • Nuit d'automne • Adieux

Selected Reading

Jane Bathori, "Les musiciens que j'ai connus" (The Musicians I Have Known). The Mayer Lectures. Trans, from the French by Felix Aprahamian in *Recorded Sound* I, No. 5 (1961).
Basil Deane, *Albert Roussel* (London: Barrie and Rockliff, 1961).
Norman Demuth, *Albert Roussel* (London: United Music Publishers, 1947).
Marc Pincherle, *Albert Roussel* (Geneva: René Kister, 1957).

Notes

1. Quoted in Basil Deane, *Albert Roussel*, 158.
2. Ibid., 5.
3. Ibid.

REYNALDO HAHN (1874-1947)

La voix ! La voix humaine, c'est plus beau que tout!

—Reynaldo Hahn[1]

Reynaldo Hahn was Venezuelan by birth, but made a brilliant career in France, where, in addition to his career as a composer and singer, he was director of the Paris Opéra, music critic for the newspaper *Figaro*, and conductor of the Salzburg Festival. He maintained close friendships throughout his life with actress Sarah Bernhardt and writer Marcel Proust and was enough of a scholar to edit some of the works of Rameau.

Hahn wrote approximately ninety-five works for solo voice: eighty-four *mélodies*, five English songs (to texts of Robert Louis Stevenson), and six Italian songs in Venetian dialect.[2] Hahn's songs are often criticized for their "salon" style. Indeed, Hahn was a habitué of the most fashionable salons in Paris, where he was in demand as a performer. On these occasions, he often sang and played his own compositions.

When he began writing songs, French *mélodie* was at its height of development, an integral part of that kaleidoscopic artistic ferment known as *la belle époque*. The majority of his songs were written and published before 1912, after which Hahn turned to larger musical forms such as opera, operetta, and film music. Hahn loved the singing voice and sang constantly. The majority of his works were for the voice.

His biographer, Bernard Gavoty, described his singing voice:

> I heard him only once, in Annales, too little to speak of him at length, enough to be entranced. Was it beautiful? No, it was unforgettable. The voice was nothing exceptional...a fine baritone voice, not very large, flexible as grass, ruled with a marvelous intelligence, a reflective divination. An interminable cigarette dangled from the line of his lip, not as a "pose" but out of habit. He sang as we breathe, out of necessity.[3]

During 1913 and 1914, Hahn gave a series of lectures defining his beliefs about interpretation, style, and taste in singing. These lectures were later edited into a book titled *Du chant*.

Hahn's songs are models of French restraint—devoid of overt display, with lovely melodies in a modest vocal range. They reflect the style of his teacher, Massenet. No doubt Hahn fashioned most of them for his own voice, which was average in scope and size. He was sensitive to the demands of the text, and set words with intelligence. Hahn was drawn to poetry that complemented his intimate, rather calm musical style. Vocal lines in his songs are speech-like, but move freely. Piano accompaniments make use of ostinato figures, usually one or two measures in length.

Hahn shunned unusual compositional techniques and broke no new ground in his songs. Overall, his songs are attractive, simple and unpretentious. They are squarely within the romantic tradition of Gounod and Massenet, but accurately reflect the prevailing spirit of their time.

Si mes vers avaient des ailes   **If My Verses Had Wings. 1888**
(Victor Hugo)

This well-known *mélodie* is one of Hahn's earliest efforts, composed when he was about fifteen years old. Even at this tender age, Hahn's melodic gift and considerable technical skill in managing musical materials is evident. Hahn set the text in strophic form, with a tuneful melody over a sweeping accompaniment of arpeggiated chords.

L'Heure exquise *(Chansons grises)*   The Exquisite Hour. 1891-92
(Paul Verlaine)

Hahn was only eighteen years old when he composed *Chansons grises*, based on poems of Paul Verlaine. Hahn's empathy with Verlaine's poetry is evident in this set of songs. His teacher Jules Massenet introduced him to the publisher, Heugel, who published Hahn's song collection.

"L'Heure exquise" is the most familiar *mélodie* of this set and one of Hahn's best-known songs. It is marked *infinement doux et calme, délicatement,* and *discret.* Dynamically, the song ranges from *ppp* to *p.* Hahn's treatment of the text is intimate, with declamatory phrases of small range, moving toward an ecstatic wider-range melodic skip, "O, bien-aimée," and the final expressive phrase, "C'est l'heure exquise." The filigree accompaniment of arpeggiated chords is based on a pattern that rarely changes. Hahn's writing for both voice and piano produces a quasi-hypnotic effect and emphasizes the hushed atmosphere of Verlaine's text, a moment suspended in time.

D'une prison*   From Prison. 1894
(Paul Verlaine)

Hahn's treatment of Verlaine's poignant text is deceptively simple, but effective. He titled his setting "D'une prison" and repeated the first lines of the poem to conclude the *mélodie*. Hahn uses an ostinato figure over a pedal point in the piano, coupled with open parallel fifths to illustrate the bleak existence of the poet, gazing out his prison window.

*Compare Hahn's setting with that of Fauré ("Prison"), Delius ("Le Ciel est par-dessus le toit"), and Vaughan Willilams ("The Sky Above the Roof").

A Chloris   To Chloris. 1916
(Théophile de Viau)

"A Chloris" is an elegant setting that matches the archaic dignity of Théophile de Viau's seventeenth-century verse. Hahn gives the piano its own melody, ornamented with Baroque turns over a chaconne-like bass line. Vocal phrases are a mixture of short fragment, which capture the natural speech cadences of the breathless lover, and longer lyric lines. The combination of voice and piano creates a charming pastiche of Baroque style.[4]

Extended Study

Chansons grises (Chanson d'automne, Tous deux, L'allée sans fin, En sourdine, L'heure exquise, Paysage triste, La Bonne chanson) • Offrande • Tyndaris • Les fontaines • Infidelité • L'Incrédule • La Chère blessure •Fêtes galantes • Rêverie • Quand je fus pris au pavillon • Je me metz en vostre mercy • Le Rossignol des lilas • L'Automne • L'Enamourée • Venezia

Selected Reading

Bernard Gavoty, *Reynaldo Hahn: le musicien de la belle époque* (Paris, 1976).

Lorraine Gorrell, "Reynaldo Hahn: Composer of Song, Mirror of an Era," in *The Music Review*, 46:4, November 1985.

Reynaldo Hahn, *On Singers and Singing (Du Chant)*, trans. Leopold Simoneau (Portland, Oregon: Amadeus Press, 1990).

_____, *Thèmes variès* (Paris: Janin).

Debra Spurgeon, "The Mélodies and Songs of Reynaldo Hahn," *The NATS Journal*, 47:4, March/April 1991.

Notes

1. Hahn, in a letter to his close friend Edouard Risler, a concert pianist. Quoted in Bernard Gavoty, *Reynaldo Hahn: le musicien de la belle époque*, 186.
2. Debra Spurgeon, "The Mélodies and Songs of Reynaldo Hahn," 4.
3. Quoted in Lorraine Gorrell, "Reynaldo Hahn: Composer of Song, Mirror of an Era," 288.
4. Hahn edited some works of Rameau; he drew on his familiarity with this style in several of his *mélodies*.

MAURICE RAVEL (1875-1937)

Even when Ravel hits you over the head, he does it with overwhelming style and finesse.

—Eric Salzman[1]

Maurice Ravel's song represent a transition between the mature *mélodies* of Claude Debussy and vocal literature that follows, notably the songs of Les Six. Ravel's songs have a sense of flow and evenness of rhythmic structure that call for scrupulous execution. Like Debussy, Ravel insisted on technical accuracy from pianist and singer; his indications of dynamics, tempo, and phrasing are exact and precisely noted. Polish and refinement were prominent qualities in his personal life as well as in his musical compositions.

Ravel once commented that he did not want his music to be interpreted, but merely performed. The amalgamation of music and text—the arrangement of musical elements into a logical whole—was of utmost importance to him. In answer to charges that his music avoided any overt display of emotion, Ravel cited passages from *Histoires naturelles* where he had deliberately attempted emotional expression: "Le Martin-Pêcheur" and the ending of "Le Grillon."

Ravel was fastidious in his text setting. Tristan Klingsor, poet of *Shéhérazade*, wrote "For Ravel, setting a poem meant transforming it into expressive recitative, to exalt the inflexions of speech to the state of song, to exalt all the possibilities of the word, but not to subjugate it. Ravel made himself the servant of the poet."[2] Ravel chose a wide range of poetic styles for his songs, from Verlaine to Mallarmé, whom he considered France's greatest poet. He was drawn to colorful texts of travel and adventure, and a glance at his song titles confirms this fascination.

Ravel wrote elegant and subtle melodies, using classical phrase structure. Some melodies have a folk-like quality, others border on romanticism. His declamatory setting of the prose texts of *Histoires naturelles* caused a scandal at the work's premiere (see below). Ravel believed that free verse was preferable to metered poetry: "If the musician wishes to set regular verse, his music will simply underline the poem and sustain it, but will be unable to interpret it or add anything to it."[3]

Ravel's approach to harmony was rich and complex. His biographer, Arbie Orenstein, comments that "he extended tonality to the breaking point." Crisp, dissonant harmonies are a hallmark of Ravel's song style, which he derived basically from nineteenth-century masters. He also had an affinity for medieval and exotic music and these influences may be found in his songs as well. He frequently used tertian chord structures (9ths, 11ths, 13ths) in his music, as well augmented triads, unresolved dissonances, and pandiatonicism.

Driving rhythms are an important feature of Ravel's songs; he used dance rhythms (primarily from Spain) in many songs, notably the *Don Quichotte* set. His songs have very regular metric organization. He makes frequent use of dominant-tonic (V-I) motion in the bass. He composed difficult, virtuosic piano accompaniments and often gave the piano the main musical interest of his *mélodies*.

Sainte   **Saint. 1896**
(Stéphane Mallarmé)

Mallarmé described "Sainte" as a "short melodic poem." Its original title was "Saint Cécile jouant sur l'aile d'un chérubin" (Saint Cecilia Playing on the Wing of a Cherub).

This is Ravel's earliest published song and is Impressionistic in style. Viol in hand, St. Cecilia, the patron saint of musicians, looks down from a stained glass window. Ravel's setting is modal; a slow-moving chordal texture sustains the liturgical mood. A calm vocal line stands out simply from the arpeggiated chordal accompaniment, creating a fitting musical portrait of the serene "musicienne du silence."

Histoires naturelles   **Natural Histories. 1906**
(Jules Renard)

Le Paon • Le Grillon • Le Cygne • Le Martin-Pêcheur • La Pintade

The texts for the *Histoires naturelles* are written in prose—vignettes of the peacock, the cricket, the swan, the kingfisher, and the guinea-fowl—and are skillfully etched in both voice and piano. Ravel uses a highly individualized vocal style to capture the clarity and directness of the prose. "Prose is sometimes very pleasant to set to music, and there are circumstances in which it is marvelously appropriate to the subject. Thus, I selected several of Jules Renard's *Histoires naturelles*; they are delicate and rhythmic, but rhythmic in a completely different way from classical verses."[4]

Renard pokes gentle fun at the personal qualities indigenous not only to birds and insects, but also to humans. Written from an observer's point of view, the words have a sense of detached amusement about them, containing moments of irony, humor, and a little sarcasm.

Ravel's musical treatment of the text caused a scandal when *Histoires naturelles* was first performed by singer Jane Bathori and the composer in 1907. In an attempt to capture the precise declamation of the French language, Ravel ignored setting the mute *e*. For example, Ravel set the phrase "La fiancée n'arrive pas" (in "Le Paon") with only six notes: La—fian—cée—n'a—rrive—pas. The traditional setting would have used nine notes: La—fi—an—cé—e—n'a—rriv—e—pas.

Ravel explained that "the text itself demanded a particular kind of musical declamation from me, closely related to the inflections of the French language."[5]

As a result, a conversational vocal style emerged that captured the natural, light character of Renard's words. The audience gave the work a hostile reception (Bathori described it as "a bit stormy"), both in reaction to the text and to the musical setting. Debussy declared that Ravel was "acting like a conjurer, a fakir, a snake-charmer, who can make flowers grow around a chair." Fauré was astonished that "such things should be set to music."[6]

Indeed, a large part of the vocal writing in this cycle can be characterized as melodic recitative, but this is in perfect keeping with the nature of prose texts. Vocal phrases have precision and clarity, and are coupled with figures in the piano that always underline the visual images in Renard's prose, which is already quite musical in itself.

LE PAON (THE PEACOCK). After a long piano prelude—humorous with its exaggerated dotted rhythms that recall the French Baroque overture—the majestic peacock appears, beautiful, but stupidly pompous. It is his wedding day, but he waits in vain for his bride. The singer observes the scene, commenting on the posturing bird. The piano accompaniment underlines the peacock's strutting gait and, near the conclusion, the spreading of his brilliantly colored tail.

LE GRILLON (THE CRICKET). In this song, the singer does not see the tiny cricket busily cleaning his little house, but relies on the sounds he hears to imagine the little insect's activities.

Ravel vividly translates the motions of the small insect into piano figurations: raking sand by its door, filing down a tall blade of grass, winding up a tiny watch, turning a key in the lock, and lowering himself slowly into the ground.

To match the cricket's size, Ravel keeps the dynamic range of this *mélodie* between *p* and *pppp*. The vocal line features crisp declamation throughout, concluding with a calm legato section ("Dans la campagne muette les peupliers se dressent comme des doigts en l'air et désignent la lune") as the bustling activities of the cricket give way to the solemn quiet of the country evening. At this point, the accompaniment expands to chordal figures of fuller texture.

LE CYGNE (THE SWAN). The beautiful cello solo in Camille Saint-Saëns's *Carnival of the Animals* suggests the perfect image for the beginning of "Le Cygne." In this beautifully lyrical *mélodie*, the swan serenely cuts through the placid water, riding on a luxurious arpeggiated accompaniment. Ravel complements the lovely image with unhurried, calm vocal phrases.

Near the end of the *mélodie*, the romantic reverie is abruptly shattered by everyday reality. Searching in the rich mud for food, the swan breaks the water with his beak and comes up with a fat worm. The calm illusion is destroyed, leaving instead an ironic and humorous thought.

LE MARTIN-PÊCHEUR (THE KINGFISHER). This *mélodie* is generally conceded to be the gem of the collection. The singer is sitting quietly, fishing on a riverbank when a brilliantly-hued kingfisher perches momentarily on his fishing rod. The awestruck angler remains motionless, hardly daring to breathe, entranced by the loveliness of the bright blue bird, who finally flies away.

Ravel illustrates this suspended moment perfectly with a vocal line of melodic recitative, a subdued dynamic range, and harmonies of extended tertian chords, densely stacked.

LA PINTADE (THE GUINEA-HEN). The calm aftermath of the preceding song is rudely disturbed by blaring discordant 7th chords announcing the loud, angry guinea-hen, who threatens the order of the barnyard. The piano accompaniment is wide in dynamic range, from *ff* to *pppp,* and contains several changes of tempo. The rowdy guinea-hen is vividly evoked in both piano and vocal parts, a truly ferocious but comic figure.

Sur l'herbe   **On the Grass. 1907**
(Paul Verlaine)

This *mélodie* is Ravel's only setting of Verlaine. He suggests an eighteenth-century atmosphere with an accompaniment in triple meter that calls to mind a minuet.

Verlaine's poem is wry and cynical. The scene depicts an abbé, slightly worse for a bit too much Cyprian wine, exchanging a few disconnected gallantries at a party, especially with the ladies—innocent conversations on the surface, but licentious in undertone. Ravel writes angular but very flexible vocal phrases, in keeping with the abbé's intoxicated state.

Cinq mélodies populaires grecques   **Five Popular Greek Songs. 1907**
(M. D. Calvocoressi)

Le réveil de la mariée • Là-bas, vers l'église • Quel galant! •
Chanson des cueilleuses de lentisques • Tout gai!

Ravel did not compose this group of songs, which are in reality folk songs gathered by his friend, M.D. Calvocoressi, during a trip to the Greek islands. Calvocoressi, a Greek, translated them into French. Ravel harmonized the tunes, keeping their folk-like qualities intact. Ravel's musical settings capture the colorful and exuberant scenes of Greek peasant life. The texts are also vibrant and varied; an earthy combination of "props" found in Songs 1, 3, and 5 (ribbons, pistols and crockery) makes an effective contrast with the poetic elements found in Songs 2 and 4.

Ravel orchestrated the first and last songs; the remainder were scored for orchestra by his close friend, Manuel Rosenthal.

LE RÉVEIL DE LA MARIÉE. (THE AWAKENING OF THE BRIDE). A young Greek peasant calls out to awaken his bride on their wedding day. He has brought her a gift—a golden ribbon for her hair. Buoyant halo-like figures, underpinned by a pedal point on the note G, reflect the sunny happiness of the scene.

LÀ-BAS, VERS L'ÉGLISE (YONDER, NEAR THE CHURCH). As this *mélodie* begins, a procession is heard in the distance (*pp*) making its way towards an ancient church where many heroes lie buried. As it draws nearer, Ravel increases the dynamics bit by bit. The piano accompaniment mirrors the stately tread of the procession, and is almost hypnotic in its unvarying rhythm.

QUEL GALANT! (WHAT GALLANT CAN COMPARE WITH ME?). Energetic rhythm and an assertive vocal line, recitative in style, characterize the singer—a virile young man, eager to impress his lady love.

CHANSON DES CUEILLEUSES DE LENTISQUES (SONG OF THE LENTISK GATHERERS). This song, sung by women working in the fields, is marked by a beautiful legato line reminiscent of an ancient melody.

TOUT GAI! (ALL GAY!). The last song of the set is a vivacious dance composed mainly of "tra-la-las." It has a certain "devil-may-care" feeling throughout. A rhythmic piano accompaniment in $\frac{2}{4}$ sustains the folk-like quality of the nonstop dance. Sprinkled through this very short song are measures in $\frac{3}{4}$ that give the dancers a chance to catch their breath.

Don Quichotte à Dulcinée	Don Quixote to Dulcinea. 1932
(Paul Morand)	

Chanson romanesque • Chanson épique • Chanson à boire

Cervante's epic story of *Don Quixote de la Mancha* presents the conflict between ideals and reality. This miniature cycle was the Ravel's last vocal work. He composed it for a film version of Cervantes's *Don Quixote* in which the distinguished Russian bass, Feodor Chaliapin, was to play the leading role. Five composers had been selected by the film's producer to write the songs for the project. Ravel was late in submitting his work and in the end, Jacques Ibert's songs were chosen.

Ravel's musical portrait of the gallant knight, Don Quixote, is embodied in three *mélodies*, all based on characteristic Spanish dance rhythms: (1), the *guajira*, alternating $\frac{6}{8}$ and $\frac{3}{4}$ meter; (2) the *zorzica*, a Basque dance in quintuple meter; and (3) the *jota*, a lively triple-metered Spanish dance.

Baritone Martial Singher, who sang the first performance of the orchestral version in 1934, remembers that Ravel offered to dedicate the songs to him. When he protested he was unworthy of such an honor, Ravel asked him to choose one song from the set. Singher chose the second song; Ravel then commented that he had chosen the right one.[7]

CHANSON ROMANESQUE (ROMANESQUE SONG). The first song introduces the cultivated and intellectual Don Quixote, who seeks to impose the highest ideals on a materialistic world by sheer force of his will and creative imagination. Yet, for the lady Dulcinea, he would risk everything he holds dear.

CHANSON ÉPIQUE (EPIC SONG). Quixote's prayer to St. Michael and St. George is a reverent plea for them to bless his sword and his Lady. His vocal line is composed of sustained legato passages of noble character over a simple accompaniment.

CHANSON À BOIRE (DRINKING SONG). The set concludes with a drinking song. Although Quixote's tippling has made him overly boisterous, the *mélodie* never oversteps the bounds of his noble bearing. His robust laughter is heard in the piano accompaniment and even a hiccup intrudes between "lorsque j'ai" and "lorsque j'ai bu."

Extended Study List
Shéhérazade (voice, orchestra) • Vocalise en forme de habanera • *Chansons Madécasses* (voice, flute, violoncello, piano) • *Deux mélodies Hébraïques* • *Trois poèmes de Stéphane Mallarmé* (voice, piano, quartet, 2 flutes, 2 clarinets) • *Deux épigrammes de Clément Marot*

Selected Reading
Jane Bathori, "Les Musiciens que j'ai connus" (The Musicians I Have Known). The Mayer Lectures. Trans. Felix Aprahamian in *Journal of the British Institute of Recorded Sound*. Part I, 1961.
Laurence Davies, *The Gallic Muse* (New York: A.S. Barnes, 1967).
Basil Deane, "Renard, Ravel, and the 'Histoires naturelles' " in *Australian Journal of French Studies*, 12, (1964).
Norman Demuth, *Ravel* (London: J. M. Dent and Sons, 1956).
Robert Gartside, *Interpreting the Songs of Maurice Ravel* (Geneseo, NY: Leyerle Publications, 1992).
Roger Nichols, *Ravel Remembered* (New York: W. W. Norton & Company, 1987). Firsthand descriptions and anecdotes of Ravel by friends and associates.
Gerald Larner, *Maurice Ravel* (London: Phaidon Press Ltd., 1996). 20th Century Composers series.
Rollo H. Myers, *Ravel: Life and Works* (New York: Thomas Yoseloff, 1960).
Arbie Orenstein, ed., *A Ravel Reader: Correspondence, Articles, Interviews* (New York: Columbia University Press, 1990).
_____, *Ravel: Man and Musician* (New York: Columbia University Press, 1975). Includes Ravel's song output, catalog of works, historical recordings.
_____, "The Vocal Works of Maurice Ravel." Ph.D. diss., Columbia University, 1968.

Notes
1. Arbie Orenstein, *Ravel: Man and Musician*, 117.
2. Klingsor, after Ravel's death in 1937, speaking of Ravel's attitude toward composing songs.
3. Arbie Orenstein, ed., *A Ravel Reader: Correspondence, Articles, Interviews,* 339.
4. Ibid.
5. Ibid., 31.
6. Arbie Orenstein, *Ravel: Man and Musician*, 53.
7. Interview with the author, 22 January, 1985. Also recounted in Orenstein, *A Ravel Reader*, 507.

JACQUES IBERT (1890-1962)

Using a very eclectic style which was both exact and elegant, he knew how to express his imaginative ideas.

—David Cox[1]

Jacques Ibert was a younger contemporary of Maurice Ravel. His vocal writing is largely confined to operas, but his set of Don Quixote songs, written in 1932 for a film project, have become justly famous. Although Ravel's group of Don Quixote songs is perhaps better known, Ibert's settings provide a fascinating comparison study.

The history of the Don Quixote songs is somewhat bizarre. Film director Georg Pabst had made plans to produce a film on Don Quixote and had engaged the celebrated Russian bass Feodor Chaliapin for the title role. The film company secretly arranged a competition among five composers to provide songs for the film: Marcel Delannoy, Manuel de Falla, Jacques Ibert, Darius Milhaud, and Maurice Ravel. It was a messy situation; none of the composers was aware that the identical offer had been made to the others. Ravel was late in submitting his settings, and Ibert's songs were chosen, much to Ibert's embarrassment, as he was a devoted admirer of the older composer. Ravel considered bringing legal action against the film company but dropped the idea when the project's producers fled with the film's bankroll.

Chansons de Don Quichotte	Songs of Don Quixote
(Pierre Ronsard/Alexandre Arnoux)	

Chanson du départ (Song of Parting) • Chanson à Dulcinée
(Song to Dulcinea) • Chanson du Duc (The Duke's Song) •
Chanson de la mort de Don Quichotte (Song of Don Quixote's Death)

Ibert had studied drama before turning to music, and he had a keen sense of the theater. While Ravel chose poems of Paul Morand for his Quixote settings, Ibert used poetry of Alexandre Arnoux and one text by sixteenth-century poet Pierre Ronsard. In his musical realizations of these poems, Ibert captured a distinct idiomatic Spanish flavor. The set is dedicated to Chaliapin and the vocal line was written to flatter the strengths of the famous bass.

The first song, "Chanson de départ," is the only Ronsard text in the group. Ibert produces an improvised effect with a recitative-like vocal line ornamented at phrase endings and a piano accompaniment that evokes guitar figures. A piano ritornello containing guitar-like staccato figures introduces each vocal section; this alternates with rolled chords that accompany the free vocal sections. Ibert's blend of musical elements produces a distinctly Moorish atmosphere.

The second song, "Chanson à Dulcinée," also features free vocalism. Ibert uses the same text three times to introduce each section of the song. Staccato figures reminiscent of guitar strumming dominate in the piano writing. The *mélodie* closes on a soft high note, in deference to Chaliapin's remarkable vocal ability.

The third song, "Chanson du Duc," is a paean to Dulcinea. Ibert chooses a somewhat different texture, highlighting the vocal line, by including only accompaniment figures in the piano. He employs modality in the harmonic scheme of this song as well as in the last song.

The final song, "Chanson de la mort de Don Quichotte," is the account of Quixote's death. Ibert uses a slow habanera rhythm to accompany a simple, expressive vocal line. Quixote's eloquent last sigh on a high note ends this effective song.

Notes

1. David Cox, "Jacques Ibert," in *The New Grove Dictionary of Music and Musicians*, ed. Stanley Sadie, 1989. Volume 9, 1-2.

DARIUS MILHAUD (1892-1974)

> On his musical palette Milhaud possesses all the colors and the power of expressing the most varied feelings. His tenderness is equal to his force, and his very southern aggressiveness drenches [his] works with sun and frank gaiety.
>
> —Jane Bathori *(Les Musiciens que j'ai connus)*[1]

Darius Milhaud was a member of Les Six[*], six young talented composers of postwar Paris. Dubbed the "Groupe de Six" by critic Henri Collet, the group was unified principally by camaraderie rather than a single musical style, functioning as a dynamic social structure in miniature rather than a musical "school." Championed by influential writer Jean Cocteau and composer Erik Satie, the group members often presented their works at the same concerts and met regularly as friends. Louis Durey wrote: "Every Saturday, invariably, we gathered at Darius Milhaud's to make music, try our latest efforts, exchange our ideas. And it is without a doubt this great diversity within unity, the function of our six very different natures...which gave to the group its richness, permitted its development, and assured its renown beyond French borders."[2]

Milhaud was a native of Aix-en-Provence, and his compositions are filled with reflections of his love for his native Provence. In his autobiography *Notes Without Music*, Milhaud described himself as "a Frenchman from Provence, and by religion a Jew." Despite this simple description portrait, Milhaud was extremely cosmopolitan, well-traveled in his youth and influenced by the music he heard in Brazil and New York City.

Milhaud, with his wife and son, left France for the United States in 1940 and broke all contact with their homeland until the liberation of 1944. The Milhauds settled in California, where he taught on the faculty at Mills College in Oakland, California; Madeleine Milhaud taught French classes and directed plays in French. The Milhauds spent thirty-odd years in the United States; during that time Darius Milhaud became a spokesman for French culture and music.

Milhaud produced a tremendous number of musical compositions during his career. Although they were not uniform in quality, each exhibits Milhaud's careful and skillful craftsmanship. His prolific output includes works in almost all genres: symphonies, sonatas, concertos, string quartets, chamber works for various instruments, operas, songs, choral works, music for films, radio, and television. His music can be tender or dynamic, but whatever its mood, Milhaud's deep sense of humanity seems to underlie all his work.

Milhaud's vocal compositions are in keeping with the rest of his massive compositional output. He composed at astonishing speed; there are 265 songs (sixty-four different opus numbers). Milhaud's poetic preferences were for contemporary poets; he set poetry and prose of his friends Léo Latil and Armand Lunel, as well as Jean Cocteau, Francis Jammes, Paul Claudel, René Chalupt, Maurice Carême and André Gide.

Melodically, Milhaud's songs are like lyric fragments; his vocal lines are often small in range and almost recitative in quality. Milhaud creates textures between voice and piano that are chamber-like in quality—neither really predominates and interaction between the two is rare. His is a sparse lyricism, one of emotional mood rather than overt melody.

Milhaud often uses ostinati in the piano accompaniments and polytonality is present as a general rule. In general, most Milhaud's songs exemplify characteristics of the style termed *dépouillé* (stripped to the essentials).

*The *Groupe de Six* consisted of Francis Poulenc, Germaine Tailleferre, Georges Auric, Louis Durey, Arthur Honegger, and Milhaud.

Six chants populaires hébraïques, Op. 96   **Six Popular Hebrew Songs.**
1925

La Séparation (The Separation) • Le Chant du veilleur
(Watchman's Song) • Chant de deliverance (Song of Deliverance) •
Berceuse (Lullaby) • Gloire à Dieu (Glory to God) •
Chant hassidique (Hassidic Song)

Milhaud had deep-rooted religious sentiment and many of his vocal pieces specifically deal with his Jewish faith. He composed these six songs on melodies derived from the traditions of Polish or Ukranian Jewry and reworked in them in his individual style. In an interview with Claude Rostand, Milhaud stated that merely harmonizing folk melodies was not in his nature: "If one goes back to ancient popular themes, it is indeed to bring them back to life, to give them new strength, to actualize them...One must make these themes into one's own music!"[3]

Jane Bathori stated that the popular style of these songs "sometimes attains a moving grandeur."[4] They are passionate in style, brief in length, and varied in mood. Melodically, they are similar in their use of small range lyric phrases, sprinkled with solo cantilenas and moments of monodic chant.

Madeleine Grey sang the premiere performance of the set in Paris in 1925 with the composer at the piano. Baritone Martial Singher, also accompanied by Milhaud, recorded the set in 1932. Milhaud also composed an orchestral version of these songs.

Les Soirées de Pétrograd, Op. 55   1919
(René Chalupt)

L'Ancien Régime (The Old Regime): L'Orgueilleuse; La Révoltée; La Martiale; L'Infidèle; La Perverse; L'Irrésolue (The Haughty One; The Rebel; The Soldier; The Disloyal; The Perverse; The Wavering).

La Révolution (The Revolution): La Grand'mère de la revolution; Les Journées d'août; Monsieur Protopopoff; Le Convive; La Limousine; Le Colonel Romanoff (Grandmother of the Revolution; The Battles of August; Mr. Protopopof; The Guest; The Cloak; Colonel Romanoff)

After he returned from Brazil in 1919, Milhaud composed *Les Soirées de Pétrograd,* using poems by Réne Chalupt. Chalupt's verses picture Russia under the Tsars, then under the Revolution. There are twelve songs, divided evenly; each is a tiny miniature portrait of people and events. Collaer calls them "a series of snapshots...the shivering grandmother and the monk surrounded by his tolling bells..."[5]

Milhaud's vocal writing in this set has the terse intensity of Mussorgsky and his rich piano accompaniments are varied beautifully to enhance the poetic mood. The brevity of the songs compounds the tension of the poems.

Jane Bathori described the first performance of the little suite: "I sang them immediately after he had finished them at a session organized by Larionov and Gontcharov, celebrated designers of the Russian Ballet at the Galerie Barbazange;

but the Russians did not really appreciate the irony that the French are accustomed to applying to political events."[6]

Six chansons de théâtre, Op. 151b   Six Theatre Songs. 1936

> La Bohèmienne la main m'a pris... • Un petit pas, deux petits pas... •
> Mes amis les cygnes • Blancs sont les jours d'été • Je suis dans le filet •
> Chacun son tour, les animaux

Milhaud composed a number of pieces of incidental music for stage works. As a rule, these were used with plays to provide moments of lyric relief rather than to comment on the dramatic action.

Milhaud composed these six songs, of varying moods and lengths as incidental music for three stage works. Like most Milhaud songs, they are miniatures, illustrating various people and scenes. Since they are excerpts from three different plays, the songs contain no real musical links.

TWO SONGS. (excerpted from *Tu ne m'échapperas jamais / You shall never escape* by Georges Pitoeff): La Bohèmienne la main m'a pris... (The Gypsy took my hand...); Un petit pas, deux petits pas... (One little step, two little steps...).

A Gypsy fortune-teller's exaggerated warning about a bad boy is punctuated by ominous piano chords. As the old gypsy repeats her prediction, the piano crazily segues into a charming waltz. The second song is reminiscent of a bedtime story read to a child. Its sing-song melody describes a little dog, briskly trotting down the road, leaping over a stream, encountering the night and going to sleep. Both *mélodies* are extremely simple in vocal style and accompaniment.

TWO SONGS. (excerpted from *La Folle du ciel / The Mad Woman from Heaven* by René Lenormand): Mes amis les cygnes (My friends, the swans); Blancs sont les jours d'été (White are summer days).

"My friends the swans" is so short (only eleven measures) that it almost qualifies as a song fragment. It is a little *gymnopédie* with charming motion and a questioning quality. "White are summer days" maintains a feeling of movement and delicacy. Of the six songs in the set, these two *mélodies* are Impressionistic in mood and style.

TWO SONGS. (excerpted from *La Première famille / The First Family)* by Jules Supervielle): Je suis dans le filet (I am in the net); Chacun son tour, les animaux (Each in turn, animals).

The first of these two *mélodies* is a passionate cry of a woman whose personal feelings threaten to suffocate her. Rhythmic chord patterns dominate the piano accompaniment throughout; Milhaud sets the vocal line syllabically to maintain the melancholy mood. In spite of its somewhat intense text, the song is still charmin —a little like a languid Gershwin blues tune. The form is ABA, but the final measure lacks a conclusive finish.

The last song is an out-and-out jazzy little ragtime ditty, enumerating what to give animals (cow, horse, lion, snake, elephant, bird) to cure their ills.

Chansons de Ronsard, Op. 223   **Songs of Ronsard. 1940-41**

A une fontaine • A Cupidon • Tais-toi, babillarde! • Dieu vous garde

Although this work was originally composed for voice and orchestra, it is heard most often in its reduction for voice and piano. Milhaud composed it for coloratura soprano Lily Pons, and is one of his most popular vocal compositions. The set is a wonderful showpiece for soprano voice, fashioned with Pons's high-flying coloratura in mind.

Extended Study List
Trois Chansons de Negresse • *Poèmes juifs* • *Quatre poèmes de Léo Latil* • *Deux petits airs* (Mallarmé) • *Catalogue de fleurs* • *Machines agricoles* • Poème du Gitanjali • *Quatre poèmes de Paul Claudel* • *Trois poèmes de Jean Cocteau* • *Rêves* • *Deux poèmes d'amour* • *Petites legends* • *Tristesses* • *Voyage d'été*

Selected Reading
Jane Bathori, "Les Musiciens que J'ai connus. "The Mayer Lectures. Trans. Felix Aprahamian in *Journal of the British Institute of Recorded Sound*, Part III, XV, 1964, 238-45.

William Bolcom, "Reminiscences of Darius Milhaud." *Musical Newsletter* 7 (Summer 1977): 3-11.

Henry Brietrose, "Conversation with Milhaud.' *Music Educators Journal* 56 (March 1970): 55-56.

Paul Collaer, *Darius Milhaud*. Trans. and ed. Jane Hohfeld Galante (San Francisco: San Francisco Press, Inc., 1988). With a definitive catalogue of works compiled from the composer's own notebooks by Madeleine Milhaud and revised by Jane Hohfeld Galante.

Linda Laurent, "The Performer as Catalyst: The Role of the Singer Jane Bathori in the Careers of Debussy, Ravel, "Les Six," and their Contemporaries in Paris 1904-1926." Ph.D. diss., New York University, 1982.

Liner notes to *Darius Milhaud: Enregistrements historiques* 1928-1948. Archives de la Phonothèque Nationale (Paris: SACEM 150-122. The Classical Collector, 1992).

Darius Milhaud, *Notes Without Music* (New York: Alfred A. Knopf, 1953).

Claude Rostand, *Milhaud: Entretiens avec Claude Rostand* (Paris: Julliard, 1952).

Notes
1. Jane Bathori, "Les Musiciens que j'ai connus," Mayer Lectures, III, 1964, 241.
2. Linda Laurent, *The Performer as Catalyst*, 83.
3. Quoted in liner notes to *Darius Milhaud: Enregistrements historiques*, 1928-1948. Archives de la Phonothèque Nationale, 49.
4. Bathori, *Musiciens*, 241.
5. Paul Collaer, *Darius Milhaud*, 169.
6. Bathori, *Musiciens*, 241.

LILI BOULANGER (1893-1918)

Her talent was of a rare quality, all delicacy and poetry.
—Théodore Lindenlaub[1]

Lili (Marie-Juliette Olga) Boulanger grew up in the Paris of Fauré, Debussy and Stravinsky. As a child, she survived a life-threatening case of bronchial pneumonia and remained a semi-invalid through her pitifully short life. Despite this, she accomplished a great deal musically. Her musical talent was encouraged and supported by her older sister, Nadia*, who guided her early musical education. Nadia and Lili made an extraordinary impact on French musical life.

Both girls grew up in a musical home; their father and grandfather taught at the Paris Conservatory, and their mother had been a professional singer. At the age of six, Lili could sing songs by Gabriel Fauré, with Fauré at the piano. Fauré was a family friend of the Boulangers, and influenced Lili's musical development.

She began taking lessons in harmony, counterpoint, and composition, learning in months what normally took years of work. Lili's delicate health prevented her from attending school regularly; she studied with her sister Nadia and with Paul Vidal and Georges Caussade.

In 1913, Lili won the coveted Prix de Rome for her cantata *Faust et Hélène*. She was barely twenty years old and the first woman to be accorded this honor. She became an international celebrity almost immediately. Her friends and colleagues agreed that she had a brilliant career in composition ahead of her. Lili, however, must have had a premonition that her life was to be short. Her compositions are marked by a quiet quality and a solemnity of mood. Her harmonic language remained squarely descended from the Impressionist school.

Her best-known composition is the song cycle *Clairières dans le ciel*, written in 1914 during her residency for the Prix de Rome. The cycle of thirteen songs for tenor and piano was later orchestrated. Lili Boulanger died four years after writing this cycle. These years were her most productive as a composer; she wrote some fifty works during this span of time.

Her last work, *Pie Jésu* (for voice, harp, organ, and string quartet), was dictated note by note to her sister Nadia. On March 15, 1918, Lili Boulanger passed away at the age of twenty-four, a victim of Crohn's disease. Nadia Boulanger, deeply affected by her sister's death, devoted her life to conducting and teaching. She became a tireless champion of her sister's musical legacy.

In her short compositional career, Lili Boulanger established her own musical voice. Her music is distinctive for its sound qualities, and her experimentation with form and style. It is fascinating to speculate what she might have created had she survived.

*Nadia (Juliette) Boulanger is best remembered as possibly the most influential music teacher of the twentieth century. Critic Harold Schoenberg credited her with single-handedly shaping the course of American music from 1920-1940. Some of the twentieth century's most influential composers studied with her, including Aaron Copland, Roy Harris, David Diamond, Elliott Carter, Virgil Thomson, Walter Piston, Philip Glass, Marc Blitzstein, and many others.

Clairières dans le ciel   **Clearings in the sky. 1914**
(Francis Jammes)

Elle était descendue au bas de la prairie (She had gone down to the
end of the meadow) • Elle est gravement gaie (Solemnly gay) •
Parfois, je suis triste (Sometimes I am sad) • Un poète disait…
(A poet said) • Au pied de mon lit (At the foot of my bed) •
Si tout ceci n'est qu'un pauvre rêve (If all this is but a poor dream) •
Nous nous aimerons tant (We will love each other so) • Vous m'avez
regardé avec toute votre âme (You looked on me with all your soul) •
Les lilas qui avaient fleuri (The lilacs which had flowered) • Deux ancolies
(Two colombines) • Par ce que j'ai souffert (From what I have
suffered) • Je garde une médaille d'elle (I keep a medallion of her) •
Demain fera un an (Tomorrow it will be a year)

Clairières dans le ciel is a cycle of thirteen songs chosen from the twenty-four poems in Francis Jammes's poetic cycle, *Tristesses.** Jammes (1868-1938) was a pastoral poet from the Pyrenees region of Franch. He brought a popular appeal into French poetry, following the stylized approach of the Symbolists.[2]

The poems in this work are written in the first person, and seem to call for a male singer. Graham Johnson characterizes the songs as "a heady mix of sensuality and *pudeur*" and observes that "they suggest something passionately religious and religiously passionate."[3]

We are not told who the heroine of the poems is, or how she suddenly disappeared from the poet's life. The poems express his feelings toward his lost love. These complex and varied emotions are triggered by various objects and events: a Madonna at the foot of his bed, the memory of last year's lilacs, two columbines swaying on the hillside, a medal she gave to him as a keepsake, and a sudden rainstorm.

Clairières dans le ciel is a haunting cycle of considerable length. Musically, the work is skillfully integrated as to tonality and thematic cross-references, employed to bind the songs together, in the same way that Fauré linked songs in *La Bonne chanson*. For this reason, the work should be performed as a unit.** Lili Boulanger never heard the cycle performed; she was dying as its first performance was presented.

Boulanger orchestrated eight of the thirteen songs of this cycle before her death; no doubt she would have completed orchestrating the entire work had she lived.

*Tristesses was set in 1956 by Darius Milhaud.

**For an excellent discussion of this cycle, see Léonie Rosenstiel, *The Life and Works of Lili Boulanger,* 172-189.

Reflets   **Reflections. 1911**
(Maurice Maeterlinck)

"Reflets" is found in Maeterlinck's collection of poems titled *Serres Chaudes*. The Symbolist text is highly atmospheric and descriptive. It is cast in three brief sections; the first two are bound together by an arpeggiated accompaniment of subtly changing, impressionistic harmonies. It is gently reminiscent of Fauré in style, but contains more complex harmonic language. In the final section, Boulanger changes accompaniment patterns, using several figures that provide text illustrations at the lines "Les fleurs s'effeuillent une à une" (The flowers shed their petals, one by one) and "Sur le reflet du firmament" (Lit by the reflection from the heavens).

Boulanger blends a warmly lyric vocal line, sophisticated harmonic materials, and varied rhythmic patterns into a musical texture that captures the lonely melancholy of Maeterlinck's reflective text. Dynamics in this *mélodie* never rise above *mf.*

"Reflets" is an early work of Lili Boulanger, but it contains the general characteristics of her musical style. Boulanger orchestrated "Reflets." It remains unpu lished. She also left an unfinished opera to a text by Maeterlinck.

Extended Study List

Psaume 129 (baritone/orchestra) • Dans l'immense tristesse • Pie Jesu (voice/string quartet/harp/organ) • Attente • Les Sirènes (mezzo/chorus/piano) • *Faust et Hélène* (tenor/baritone/chorus/orchestra. Also, piano reduction) • Soir sur la plaine (soprano/tenor/orchestra) • Le Retour

Selected Reading

Karin Pendle, ed. *Women and Music: A History* (Bloomington: Indiana University Press, 1991).
Léonie Rosenstiel, *The Life and Works of Lili Boulanger* (London: Associated University Presses, 1978). Excellent source on Boulanger, with a thorough discussion of *Clairières dans le ciel.*

Notes

1. Léonie Rosenstiel, *The Life and Works of Lili Boulanger*, 203.
2. Shirlee Emmons and Wilbur Watkins Lewis, *Researching the Song* (New York: Oxford University Press, 2006), 244.
3. Graham Johnson, *A French Song Companion* (New York: Oxford University Press, 2000), 40.

FRANCIS POULENC (1899-1963)

J'aime la voix humaine.

—Francis Poulenc[1]

Poulenc is regarded by many musicians and critics as the natural successor to the great composers of French art song and is considered by many to be the last great proponent of the genre. Certainly his abundant legacy of 150 *mélodies* forms the last great group of songs added to the repertoire in the twentieth century. His abundant song output is marked by a versatility that prompted composer Virgil Thomson to declare him "incontestably the greatest writer of *mélodies* in our time."[2] Francis Poulenc had an intuitive approach to song composition.

His vocal works were specifically linked with a number of poets, all his contemporaries—among them, Guillaume Apollinaire, Paul Eluard, Max Jacob, and Louise de Vilmorin. No matter whose text he set, Poulenc closely matched the music to the poet's particular style. Poulenc: "I turn almost always to the same poets. The reason is that I believe that one must translate into music not merely the literary meaning of the words but also everything that is written between the lines, if one is not to betray the poetry. Each, poetry and music, should evoke the other."[3]

Two-thirds of Poulenc's songs were composed for concerts given by the composer and baritone Pierre Bernac. Bernac played an instrumental role in the creation of many of Poulenc's *mélodies*, and his invaluable book *Francis Poulenc: The Man and His Songs* should be consulted as the definitive resource for performance of Poulenc's vocal music.

Le Bestiaire ou Cortège d'Orphée	The Book of Beasts
(Guillaume Apollinaire)	or the Procession of Orpheus.
	1918-19

Le Dromadaire • La Chèvre du Thibet • La Sauterelle •
Le Dauphin • L'Écrevisse • La Carpe

Le Bestiaire is the first collection of *mélodies* Poulenc wrote and his first setting of Guillaume Apollinaire, who was to become the first important poet for Poulenc's songs. Poulenc first composed *Le Bestiaire* for voice and chamber ensemble, but is rarely performed in this version. Composer Louis Durey, another member of Les Six, also set *Le Bestiaire,* but in its entirety. Poulenc originally composed twelve settings but kept only six, and dedicated them to Durey.

Apollinaire's voracious appetite for reading of all types introduced him to the bestiaries of the Middle Ages. These, with Picasso's early woodcuts of animals, inspired him to write a contemporary bestiary, a parade of animals characterized in poetic quatrains. Eighteen of the eventual thirty poems of *Le Bestiaire* were published in 1908. An illustrated edition of the poems with woodcuts by Raoul Dufy (his first published illustrations) appeared in 1911.

Apollinaire's four-line poems have a high degree of wit and charm, but Poulenc cautioned that they not be sung with irony or "knowingness." Each of the songs is bound together by rhythmic or melodic cells, usually in the piano, that function as ostinati or as unifying elements. These also point up the tight musical construction of the cycle.

LE DROMADAIRE (THE DROMEDARY). Here is a portrait of the Portuguese explorer, Don Pedro d'Alfaroubeira, painted with a rather broad brush. Poulenc writes a chromatic descending ostinato figure in the left hand of the piano, and ties it to a heavy plodding figure in the right hand, which combine to evoke the slow but inexorable progress of the macho Don and his four camels. A four-bar postlude of very different character adds a rather startling but charming little comment.

LA CHÈVRE DU THIBET (THE TIBETAN GOAT). This little nine-bar song has four vocal phrases which seem irregular because of their rhythmic organization. It is a love song in which the poet compares his love's hair to the golden fleece for which Jason searched.

LA SAUTERELLE (THE GRASSHOPPER). In only four bars, Poulenc paints a picture of a delicate grasshopper, the food that sustained Saint John. The last two measures share the same melodic pattern, seesawing on two-notes—reminiscent of the grasshopper's tiny wings.

LE DAUPHIN (THE DOLPHIN). Poulenc paints the playful dolphin by alternating dynamics every two bars, *forte* and *piano*, almost a little conversation. The *forte* measures are unexpected, like the dolphin breaking up through the water. Bernac suggests a slower tempo (quarter note=116) for this song.[4]

L'ÉCREVISSE (THE CRAYFISH). Each melodic phrase in this song rises to the same pitch (C-flat) and then wanders down, illustrating the crayfish, whose hesitant movements match the uncertainties of life. A downward *portamento* in the last two vocal phrases leaves no doubt as to the direction of the shellfish—it goes backwards. Bernac advises the last measures should be marked *beaucoup ralentir*.[5]

LA CARPE (THE CARP). Poulenc uses a two-measure cell as an ostinato throughout the song to evoke the watery home of the carp. He also asks the accompanist to employ two pedals, a marking that occurs frequently in his piano scores. Marked *Très triste, très lent*, the soft haze of sound produced by this effect is a "sound characteristic" of Poulenc.

Poulenc writes a declamatory vocal line of small range; the combination of melodic phrase and piano ostinato produces an "other-worldly," underwater feeling.

Tel jour, telle nuit   Like day, like night. 1937
(Paul Eluard)

> Bonne journée • Une ruine coquille vide • Le front comme un
> drapeau perdu • Une roulotte couverte en tuiles • A toutes brides •
> Une herbe pauvre• Je n'ai envie que de t'aimer • Figure de force
> brûlante et farouche • Nous avons fait la nuit

Poulenc's collaboration with poet Paul Eluard produced thirty-four solo songs. The discovery of Eluard's poetry furnished an outlet for the natural lyricism that was so much a part of Poulenc's compositional style. Poulenc was drawn to Eluard because "the whole of his work is musical vibration."[6] Poulenc was adept at translating Eluard's surreal images into musical settings, which both complemented and illuminated them.

Tel jour, telle nuit has been characterized as Poulenc's finest cycle; certainly Poulenc's mature song style coalesces in this work. The entire cycle must be performed as a unit; single songs should not be extracted for performance. Poulenc attached great importance to the placement of *mélodies* in a group; the nine songs are carefully ordered for dramatic and musical effect. Eluard's poems cover the span of a day—from dawn until the two lovers turn out the lights at night. Despite the variety of dramatic moods found in the nine songs, *Tel jour, telle nuit* is serenely lyrical overall.

The underlying theme of *Tel jour, telle nuit* is love as a transcending force, surpassing selfish sensuality and moving to an embracing and unselfish relationship. Vague and mysterious images, beautiful more through association than through literal meaning, permeate Eluard's verse. Eluard's themes of oppositions: day-night, good-evil, light-dark, love-death—are found throughout the poetry.

Three transitional songs (Nos. 3, 5, and 8) provide contrast and introduce the songs that follow them. Songs 1, 2, 6, 7, and 9 are linked by lyricism, both overt and intimate. The first and last songs share the same key and tempo and serve as dramatic opposites as well; Song 1 deals with day, Song 9 with night. An extended postlude closes the work .

BONNE JOURNÉE (A GOOD DAY). Happy optimism pervades this first song, although the poet's thoughts are tinged with melancholy. As his day progresses, he meets friends and happy people and his outlook remains reflective but cheerful. Poulenc underscores the positive, confident feeling with octave figures in the piano accompaniment. Poulenc specified this song should be sung with "very peaceful joy."[7]

This *mélodie* is dedicated to Pablo Picasso. Poulenc later used the same octave figurations in "Picasso" the first song in his cycle *Le Travail du peintre* (1957).

UNE RUINE COQUILLE VIDE (A RUIN AN EMPTY SHELL). Here, Eluard's poetic portrait of a ruined house blends (incongruously) with the image of children happily playing in its decayed shell. Carefree youth and decayed ruins are juxtaposed simultaneously in a "sense of complete unreality."[8] The piano remains *sempre pp* for the entire song while the vocal part assumes the changes in dynamics.

227

LE FRONT COMME UN DRAPEAU PERDU (MY BROW LIKE A DOOMED FLAG).
This poem introduces the first presence of the second party—the loved one.
Vocal lines are strongly articulated and non-legato. For a brief moment at
"Je ne veux pas les lâcher/Tes mains claires et compliquées," a tender mood is
introduced. These are the same hands the poet clasps in the final song.

UNE ROULOTTE COUVERTE EN TUILES (A GYPSY WAGON WITH A TILED ROOF).
Très lent et sinistre (Very slow and sinister) is Poulenc's marking for this song,
which is reminiscent of the lugubrious recitative of Musorgsky. Poulenc writes
declamatory vocal lines fashioned with triplets, fermatas and breath marks for
dramatic emphasis and punctuation. *Parlando* articulation is called for,
always well stressed, intense, and extremely legato.

Steady chromatic chords dominate the thick-textured accompaniment. The
last vocal utterance ("du cœur") is quasi-parlando, scooped and breathy, disappearing into nothingness.

A TOUTES BRIDES (AT FULL TILT). This song is transitional, underscoring the
change in mood from the sinister atmosphere of the preceding song and providing a heightened contrast to the still calmness of the next song. Its mood is
violent and aggressive in an extremely fast tempo, which demands facile diction from the singer. The violin in Eluard's text is heard tuning up in the
piano's opening measures, as Poulenc employs the notes G, D, A, and E (the
pitches of the violin's open strings) in alternating fifths.

UNE HERBE PAUVRE (SPARSE GRASS). "Quiet," "soft," and "transparent" are all
adjectives that might be applied to this short song. A blade of wild grass pokes
through the snow and its taste seems cleansing to the poet.

Poulenc's musical setting has a gentle, almost religious quality. Quiet chordal
figures accompany the extremely simple melodic line; overall texture is sparse
and clean, and the text is set syllabically.

JE N'AI ENVIE QUE DE T'AIMER (I JUST FEEL LIKE LOVING YOU). Inserted
between Song 6 and 8 is this brief song of contented love. Eluard's poem is a
strange mix of delicate sensuality and strong determination. It is marked *Très
allant et très souple* (Very flowing and supple). Poulenc's setting is graceful and
flowing, providing a wonderful contrast to the neighboring *mélodies*.

**FIGURE DE FORCE BRÛLANTE ET FAROUCHE (FACE OF BURNING AND SAVAGE
STRENGTH).** This song serves the same purpose as Song 5—it prepares the
silence of the opening of the last song. Gloom and dark figures dominate this
transitional song. Eluard's poem contains both vehemence and calm, which are
contrasted musically.

Poulenc uses the closely related keys of B-flat and F in contrast also; at "Aux
veines du tempes," material in B-flat is heard over an ostinato built on F. The
dynamic intensity of the last vocal phrase prepares the "long silence" before
the beginning of the last song.

NOUS AVONS FAIT LA NUIT (WE HAVE MADE NIGHT). Poulenc ends the cycle
with one of his most beautiful love songs. Song 9 is related to the opening song

of the cycle by key, mood, recurring motives, duple figures, and piano postlude. He uses octave figures in the opening bars to immediately recall and link this *mélodie* with the first song of the cycle.

Warm, full, and completely calm, Poulenc's musical setting is an excellent example of his most expressive lyricism. The opening vocal phrase built of smooth conjunct intervals immediately sets the tone of calm intimacy. Poulenc said the coda that ends the cycle was written to allow the listener to prolong the emotions generated by hearing the work, much as in Schumann's *Dichterliebe*.[9]

Fiançailles pour rire	**Engagement for Laughter. 1939**
(Louise de Vilmorin)	

La Dame d'André • Dans l'herbe• Il vole •
Mon cadavre est doux comme un gant • Violon • Fleurs

"Few people move me as much as Louise de Vilmorin."[10] wrote Poulenc, who composed *Fiançailles pour rire* at his country house in Noizay at the beginning of the war. The first performance of this set of songs was in 1942 in the Salle Gaveau with Poulenc accompanying soprano Geneviève Touraine (the sister of Gérard Souzay).

The *mélodies* in this set may be sung separately; they are bound together only by the title of Vilmorin's literary collection. Bernac points out that Poulenc was attempting to write a work for a woman's voice comparable to *Tel jour, telle nuit*.[11]

LA DAME D'ANDRÉ (ANDRE'S WOMAN). André was the name of one of Louise de Vilmorin's brothers, although this text is probably not biographical. The André of this poem seems lackadaisical and incapable of a real relationship. He wonders if the current lady in his life will last or be merely a passing fancy, but he seems resigned rather than driven to find the answer.

Each of the verses ends with a question. Even the piano introduction seems to lead questioningly into the first vocal phrase. Symbolism is also present in the poem: the "garden" seems to stand for the woman's life.

Poulenc's musical treatment is sunny, fresh and lyrical. He ends the song with an indecisive cadence that matches the doubting qualities of the text and leads neatly into the second song.

DANS L'HERBE (IN THE GRASS). This poem dwells on the connection between love and death. A young woman is the singer; her words indicate that a relationship is over. He is dead for her...their relationship is dead. Again, inner meanings are present in Vilmorin's verse; trees with titles that stand for character and personality ("sur l'arbre de la Loi,"[under the tree of the Law], "arbre d'enfance"{the tree of childhood]) pique our interest in this couple and their liaison.

A characteristic Poulenc-style climax occurs at "En appelant, en m'appelant" (calling, calling me), which is followed immediately by an *irréal* (unreal, otherworldly), *subito p* at "Mais comme j'étais loin de lui..." (But I was far from him…). Poulenc shifts the tonality throughout, never fully establishing a decisive tonal center—perhaps to mirror the poetic content of the relationship. There is great intensity in the calmness of this song, which is dedicated—perhaps tellingly—to the mother of Poulenc's daughter.

IL VOLE (HE FLIES). Poulenc dubbed "Il vole" as "one of my most difficult songs. It seems impossible to interpret it without serious work and numerous rehearsals." [12] Vilmorin's text is based on the double meaning of the title: "he steals" or "he flies." La Fontaine's fable of the fox and the crow is also alluded to in the text, which is a clever play on words. Poulenc composed this song in one of his nonstop rapid tempos, and it demands brilliant technique from both singer and pianist.

MON CADAVRE EST DOUX COMME UN GANT (MY CORPSE IS LIMP LIKE A GLOVE). Vilmorin's poem is veiled and slightly mysterious, a feature found in many of her verses. Is this woman literally deceased or merely dead to all feelings of the world? Another of Vilmorin's poetic heroines set by Poulenc ("Aux Officiers de la garde blanche") shares similar emotions. Here the woman seems to be pleading for her lover to remember her in the bloom of her youth rather than what she might become.

Poulenc's musical setting is subdued but lyrical, maintaining its tranquil pace from beginning to end. Musically, this *mélodie* is similar to "Dans l'herbe."

VIOLON (VIOLIN). "Violon" evokes Paris. An elegant Hungarian restaurant on the Champs-Elysées is the setting of the poem. A refined lady patron is entranced with the Gypsy violinist who serenades her. Vilmorin's poem and Poulenc's musical setting were probably inspired by a festive evening in a Hungarian restaurant with Louise de Vilmorin's husband, Count Palffy, who had engaged a Hungarian tzigane orchestra for the occasion. [13]

Poulenc sets the *mélodie* in a slow waltz rhythm that reinforces the drama of the scene. The violin (and the violinist) are characterized in the piano accompaniment, which is full of arpeggios, overt Gypsy flourishes, double-stops, and glissandi. Poulenc also exaggerates the vocal writing—the singer must also employ *portamenti* ("amoureux," "plaisent," "tendus," "inconnu") as she becomes increasingly more tipsy and more enamored of the violin and its player.

The night club atmosphere, like the Hungarian music, is only suggested. The characters remain elegant and refined throughout.

FLEURS (FLOWERS). An ineffable melancholy permeates this song. A woman burns souvenirs from a romance that is finished, but at the same time lovingly remembers the relationship. The moment is a microcosm—a world of memory, capsulized.

Poulenc uses a calm tempo and a stunning lyric vocal line to create a mood of quiet reflection and sensuality. Poulenc: "Whenever this song ["Fleurs"] is sung separately, always try to precede it with a song in a distant key ("Violon" if possible) or a song in A; this will safeguard the impression of a *sound that comes from far away.*"[14]

The piano accompaniment is a characteristic Poulenc "sound print" of stacked chords, reminiscent of "Dans l'herbe." Voice and piano are closely linked through the singer's melody, which appears simultaneously within the chords of the piano, creating a closely knit texture that is beautifully effective.

Bleuet   **Young Soldier. 1939**
(Guillaume Apollinaire)

Poulenc based this song on one of Apollinaire's wartime poems, written in Paris in convalescence after a head injury; both Apollinaire and Poulenc served in World War I.

Poulenc, deeply moved by Apollinaire's poem and its intense human overtones, cautioned against singing the *mélodie* in too solemn a fashion, admitting he should have used "intimately" as the initial expression marking for the song.[15] "Bleuet" is a quiet and private moment in which a twenty-year-old boy (*bleu* is colloquial for "young soldier"), who does not yet know all that life can be, is characterized—and addressed—by Apollinaire in a sweetly serious speech. Poulenc's musical setting of the young soldier facing a battle and possible death ("It is five o'clock and you would know how to die") is quietly dramatic.

This touching *mélodie* is wonderfully suited for a tenor voice.

Banalités   **Banalities. 1940**
(Guillaume Apollinaire)

Chanson d'Orkenise • Hôtel • Fagnes de Wallonie • Voyage à Paris • Sanglots

Like *Fiançailles pour rire*, *Banalités* is not a cycle, but a group of songs. The poems have no connection with each other, and there are no musical links binding any of the songs together; however, their order provides a well-constructed recital group.[16] The songs may may be performed separately.

CHANSON D'ORKENISE (SONG OF ORKENISE). "Briskly, in the style of a popular song" is the marking for this *mélodie*.

In the imaginary city of Orkenise* there are huge city gates, presided over by large moustached guards who question people entering and leaving—and incongruously, they knit! There is a word with a double meaning in the poem: "Grise" can be translated as "gray" or "tipsy." The merry folk-like quality of the song opens the group with gaiety and, if one plumbs the poetry more deeply, a little food for thought.

*There is a road in Autun leading to the Roman gate by the same name.

HÔTEL (HOTEL). The poet has no desire other than to be lazy, bask in the sun, enjoy the quiet of his hotel room, and smoke. Poulenc's vocal line curves easily, indolent as the poet; the piano accompaniment is fashioned of Poulenc's luxuriant chromatic harmonies, stacked as if to cushion the laziness of the singer. "Hôtel" captures the poetic moment vividly—it is a time to be idle and self-indulgent and revel in the feeling.

FAGNES DE WALLONIE (WALLOON UPLANDS). In 1899, Apollinaire spent his holidays in the high plateau country of the Belgian Ardennes. This wild terrain is marked by vast heaths, twisted trees, and peat bogs, and swept by winds of considerable force. The gloomy setting inspires melancholy in the poet as he tramps through its dismal landscape.

Poulenc's spiky musical setting is a whirlwind of eighth notes sweeping from beginning to end; the vocal line is similarly turbulent and calls for pointed articulation. Poulenc's final measures with the familiar marking "toujours sans ralentir," rush forward to a *crescendo-diminuendo* for the voice on the word "vent." This song is one that Bernac characterized as a "swoosh" *mélodie*—one that flies by in a hurry but nonetheless contains all of Poulenc's careful craftsmanship and skill.

VOYAGE À PARIS (TRIP TO PARIS). Sandwiched between Songs 3 and 5 is a tiny sweetmeat, a paean to Poulenc's beloved Paris. It provides a respite from the intensity of the previous song and a relaxation before the lengthy final song "Sanglots." (Poulenc wrote in his diary that he had chosen the poetry for Songs 3 and 5 long before he began to put together this cycle).

Poulenc composed "Voyage à Paris" in the style of a valse-musette—the piano accompaniment fluctuates wildly, ranging over the entire keyboard, and bringing to mind the gaiety of the Parisian music hall. Apollinaire's brief poetic lines speak of his elation at leaving a dull place for Paris "which love must have created." Poulenc peppers his charming setting with indications of "aimable" and "avec charme."

SANGLOTS (SOBS). "Sanglots" is a title that seems incongruous in a group titled "Banalities" but Poulenc's penchant for surprise holds forth here. Apollinaire's poem is difficult to understand because of the juxtaposition of the main declamatory narrative and the interior "asides," which in effect form a poem within a poem.[*]

Poulenc's musical setting is one of his most eloquent (although he wrote in his diary that certain points in the song would always trouble him). Its eloquent lyricism is reminiscent of his style in "Tu vois le feu du soir" and "Voyage" (*Calligrammes*). The song proceeds serenely and without dragging to a stunningly intense climax at the words "est mort d'amour ou c'est tout comme," followed by an equally dramatic echoing phrase. The ending lines of the song sustain the profoundly calm mood.

*See page 75 in Pierre Bernac's *Francis Poulenc: The Man and His Music*, where he places these "asides" in parentheses.

C   1943
(Louis Aragon)

"C" is one of Poulenc's most poignant songs. The title "C" refers to the bridges of Cé near Angers; the song recalls May 1940 when numerous French fled before the invading German army. Louis Aragon was among them; his poem recounts his memories in the style of a medieval ballad that flashes back from the contemporary scene. There are four verses and an added couplet; every line of the poem ends with the sound /se/, regardless of the word.

This song assumed the character of a song of French resistance. Bernac and Poulenc included it on all their recitals during the Occupation. Bernac related the story of the French audience who rose and stood silently at its conclusion, to the puzzlement of the Germans in the hall.[17]

Lyrically and harmonically, "C" is one of Poulenc's most ravishing songs. He uses minor tonality to complement the poem's reminiscent qualities. To emphasize its dramatic character, Poulenc specifies myriad changes of dynamics and tempo throughout the song, as text images change from present to past.

Its tone of extreme melancholy and intensely felt emotion reaches an exquisite climax at the line "O ma France, ô ma délaisée," which Poulenc achieves by combining high pitch and soft dynamics. An arching interval leap on "délaisée" is articulated *crescendo*, then is suddenly interrupted by a *pianissimo* marking at the point of highest emotional intensity—one of the most beautiful moments in all of Poulenc's songs.

La Fraîcheur et le feu   The Coolness and the Fire. 1950
(Paul Eluard)

 Rayon des yeux... • Le matin les branches attisent... • Tout disparut... •
  Dans les ténèbres du jardin... • Unis la fraîcheur et le feu... •
   Homme au sourire tendre... • La Grande rivière qui va...

Composed in the spring and early summer of 1950, Poulenc dubbed this cycle the most "concerted" or bound together group of songs he had written to date. Eluard's text is actually one single, long poem; the entire cycle numbers less than 170 measures and is divided into seven songs, following the printed divisions in the text. It is dedicated to Igor Stravinsky.

La Fraîcheur et le feu occupies a unique place in Poulenc's vocal output both for formal construction and treatment of text. Musically and poetically, the work is governed by the principle of contrast. The catalog of contrasting terms found in the poetry is captured through musical components, which serve as balances for one another, including tempi (slow-fast) and the juxtaposition of major and minor material.

Poetically, woman is portrayed as cool freshness; man is seen as fiery unrest. The poetry's dominant theme is man's quest for self-knowledge, a search fulfilled bythe partnership and love of man and woman. The love force that makes universal knowledge possible becomes the all-powerful liberating force in human life. The difficult imagery in Eluard's poetry is consistently polarized between coolness (water) and heat (fire, sun) and between woman and man, darkness and light, sky and earth.

 RAYON DES YEUX... (BEAMS OF EYES). The opening song reveals man alone in shadow, without light. Poulenc uses an extremely rapid tempo and percussive sixteenth note motion in the piano to complement the agitated quality of the poem. The accompaniment often doubles the vocal line. Unrelenting piano ostinato and undulating vocal contours maintain a mood of helplessness in the face of unstoppable motion.

Le matin les branches attisent... (In the morning the branches stir up). This song is a contrast between morning and evening (day-night, light-dark). Like the fourth song in the cycle, it is transitional in nature. Poulenc suggests the twittering birds and rustling trees in the piano by using rapid arpeggios, which contain a repeated rhythmic cell. An extremely disjunct vocal line reinforces the sense of unrest.

Tout disparut... (All disappeared). Stravinsky's *Serenade in A* provided Poulenc with the opening motive for this lullaby-like song. Night has evolved from the preceding *mélodie*; man is now singing himself to sleep. Eluard's nocturnal setting is complemented by clear, sparse musical textures. Rhythmically, nothing disturbs the calm mood; Poulenc sustains the subdued lullaby in the piano with an arpeggiated figure outlined in eighth-note triads. At the line "soeurs miroitières" (sisters mirroring my tears), the piano "mirrors" the voice note-for-note under the text. Poulenc uses the introductory material as a short postlude.

Dans les ténèbres du jardin... (In the darkness of the garden). This brief transitional song recounts a fantastic dream, hallucinatory in nature. The delicate shapes of invisible women in the garden are evoked by a rising disjunct vocal line. Sixteenth-note figures in the piano and an extremely rapid tempo effectively illustrate the fleeting images that dreams produce.

Unis la fraîcheur et le feu... (Unite the coolness and the fire). At this point in the poem, Eluard unites coolness and fire. This song marks the turning point in the cycle, and Poulenc illustrates it musically with an interesting blend of quasi-contrapuntal and homophonic style, each a small "mini-section" of two verse lines. These two distinct little sections are preceded by a five-measure piano introduction.

Eluard divides his verse dramatically after the phrase "Unis tes lèvres et tes yeux." At this point Poulenc produces a vivid text illustration by having the piano line intersect the voice in a unison on the note F.

Homme au sourire tendre... (Man of the tender smile). This section of the poem is in litany form, a favorite device of Eluard. The poem develops the unified man and woman, reiterating the human qualities of each and their relationship to one another. Man and woman combine as one now, in four-bar phrases.

Poulenc's musical approach to the poem emphasizes terraced dynamics by phrases, which balance the layered poetic elements. As the litany progresses, he writes begins to gradually thicken the chordal accompaniment to maintain the tension. At the end of the song, Poulenc returns to the simpler sound qualities of the song's beginning and quotes the opening measures again in the piano coda.

La grande rivière qui va... (The great river that flows). In a recall of the first *mélodie*, Poulenc launches the last song in a dizzying thrust forward. Man is on the river of life. His search for self-knowledge is over, fulfilled through love (light). Eluard poetically reprises words as motifs: "soleil" (Song 1), and the river "big" by day and "little" by night (Song 2). Man is no longer dependent upon lullabies (Song 3), darkness, or dreams (Song 4). He has achieved unity with everything through love (Songs 5 and 6). Now Poulenc uses the cycle's piano introduction as a postlude.

Le Travail du peintre	**The Work of the Painter. 1956**
(Paul Eluard)	

Pablo Picasso • Marc Chagall • Georges Braque • Juan Gris • Paul Klee • Joan Miró • Jacques Villon

Le Travail du peintre was composed in response to a commission from American soprano Alice Esty, who sang the premiere in 1959. Poulenc often likened his aesthetic to poetry and painting, commenting "You must compare my music to literature or a picture."[18] The set of seven songs falls chronologically between two of Poulenc's three operas: *Dialogues des Carmélites* (1956); and *La Voix humaine* (1958).

The cycle marked Poulenc's last settings of the poetry of Paul Eluard. Before Eluard's death, poet and composer had spoken about this project. Many of Eluard's published collections had been illustrated by Chagall, Braque, Picasso, Villon, and Miró. Eluard and Poulenc knew these artists as well.

This unusual work is a synthesis of three arts—music, poetry, and painting. The seven *mélodies* are bound together by the work of the artists themselves. *Le Travail du peintre* is like a collection of beautifully displayed paintings, each reflecting the artistic personalities of all its creators—poet, composer, and artist. To better understand and enjoy the interrelation of images in *Le Travail du peintre,* performers and listeners should become familiar with the work of the seven artists.

PABLO PICASSO. Poulenc illustrates the larger-than-life Picasso with heavy rhythmic stresses, coupled with a declamatory, mid-range vocal line. Thick textures in the piano give a broad, sweeping sense of power. Poulenc employs a dynamic range of *f* to *fff* for this *mélodie*. A *subito piano* at measure twenty-nine provides a brief moment of relaxation. The opening measures of the *melodie* are a transposition of Mother Marie's theme from Poulenc's opera, *Dialogues des Carmélites*. Like Picasso, Mother Marie represents a figure of great streangth.

MARC CHAGALL. To view a Chagall painting is to experience the same light-hearted happiness as the figures found there. Lyricism in Chagall's work has an impassioned quality that is expressed through color. Another feature of his work is the intermingling of dream and reality; figures from both spheres float blithely in a sea of color, bearing witness to the celebration of life. Some of Chagall's favorite motifs are found in Eluard's verse. Poulenc described his musical setting as a "kind of rambling scherzo," and specifies an exuberant tempo marking.[19] Chagall's transparent textures are reflected in Poulenc's angular vocal line. The dreamlike images in Eluard's final poetic line are interpreted musically by Poulenc, who pits duplets in the vocal phrase against groupings of three in the piano.

GEORGES BRAQUE. Eluard divides his poem into two sections: one deals with the bird in flight (a recurring image in Braque's work); and the second, with landscape figures—specifically trees and leaves. The soaring bird is illustrated melodically by a lyrical, undulating vocal line. A grace note figure in the piano reinforces the idea of suspension in space. Rhythmic unity is provided by continuous eighth-note motion. Poulenc described this song as the most subtle and detailed of the cycle.

JUAN GRIS. Poulenc admitted a preference for this song and for "Villon." Eluard used litany form for the texts for both *mélodies*—a characteristic structure that Poulenc loved. The word stress patterns made it possible for Poulenc to use a favorite melodic device—short one and two-measure phrases of closely similar patterns. These small-range melodic figures occur in the first lines of stanzas one, three four, and five, and produce a feeling of calm, serene melancholy. Poulenc uses simple linear texture in both voice and piano, and seesaws between major and minor tonalities to illustrate the duality of light and shadow found in Gris's work.

PAUL KLEE. This song functions as a transition between "Gris" and "Miró." Poulenc wrote: "I needed a presto here. It is a dry song that must go with a bang."[20] "Klee" is a skillful combination of drama and movement. A thick-textured piano figure thrusts the song into motion; the tempo marking is 144 to the quarter note, producing a powerful, almost savage, movement forward. Vocal lines constantly reiterate rhythmic patterns—an additive effect that maintains the velocity of motion, and illustrates Klee's artistic style of layering small motifs (signs) in his paintings.

JOAN MIRÓ. Miró loved pure, bright colors. He was fascinated with the firmament. Images dealing with space in Eluard's poem are the sun, sky, clouds, dawn, night and the dragonfly. Poulenc illustrates the vibrant, fluid images found in Miró's work with a dense piano texture of major-minor seventh chords, coupled with a driving, declamatory vocal line.

JACQUES VILLON. Villon's passion for life reveals itself in patterns of movement in his paintings. This movement is mirrored in Eluard's dramatic litany of words, with the recurring phrase "en dépit," and Poulenc's strong, assertive accompaniment figures. Poulenc heightens the alliteration at the poem's climax ("l'aube," l'horizon," "l'oiseau," "l'homme," "l'amour") with a subtle textural change, filling in the piano's stark octaves with harmonies that seem to cushion the words and relax the tension.

Extended Study List

Quatre poèmes de Guillaume Apollinaire • *Trois poèmes de Louise de Vilmorin* • *Trois poèmes de Louise Lalanne* • Tu vois le feu du soir • La Grenouillère • Priez pour paix • Montparnasse *Chansons gaillardes* • *Airs chantés* • *Chansons villageoises* • *Métamorphoses* • *Calligrammes* • Ce doux petit visage

Selected Reading

Pierre Bernac, *Francis Poulenc: The Man and His Songs* (New York: W.W. Norton, 1977). All texts and translations, plus definitive discussions of style and interpretation.

Sidney Buckland, ed. and trans., *Francis Poulenc 'Echo and Source': Selected Correspondence* 1915-1963 (London: Victor Gollancz, Ltd., 1991). Three hundred fifty letters to and from Poulenc, giving insight into his creative processes and compositions, personal relationships, and important events in his career.

_____, and Miriam Chimènes, *Francis Poulenc: Music, Art and Literature* (Brookfield, VT: Ashgate, 1999). Excellent collection of essays on Poulenc.

Keith W. Daniel, *Francis Poulenc: His Artistic Development and Musical Style* (Ann Arbor: UMI Research Press, 1982). Excellent reference. Chapter 11 deals with the *mélodies*.

Laurence Davies, *The Gallic Muse* (New York: A.S. Barnes, 1967). Biographical sketches and discussion of the songs of Fauré, Duparc, Debussy, Satie, Ravel, Poulenc.

Henri Hell, *Francis Poulenc* (London: John Calder, 1959). General overview of Poulenc and his works through 1959.

Benjamin Ivry, *Francis Poulenc* (London: Phaidon Press, Ltd., 1996). 20th Century Composers series.

Carol Kimball, "Poulenc's *Le Travail du Peintre:* A Synthesis of the Arts." *The NATS Journal* 44:2 (Nov/Dec 1987), 5-11.

_____, "Unity from Contrast: Poulenc's *La Fraicheur et le Feu.*" *The NATS Journal* 44:5 (May/June 1988), 5-9+.

Wilfrid Mellars, *Francis Poulenc* (Oxford: Oxford University Press, 1993). Oxford Studies of Composers series.

Bennie Middaugh, "Poulenc: Tel Jour, Telle Nuit...A Stylistic Analysis." *The NATS Bulletin* 25:2 (December 1968), 2-4+.

Martin Néron, "The Images of Éluard: Poulenc's Tel jour, telle nuit," *Journal of Singing* 61:4 (March/April 2005), 343-351.

Francis Poulenc, *A batons rompus: écrits radiophoniques* (Paris: Actes Sud, 1999). Compiled, presented, and annotated by Lucie Kayas. In French.

_____, *Diary of My Songs (Journal de mes mélodies).* Trans. Winifred Radford (London: Gollancz, Ltd., 1985). The composer's thoughts on all of his songs—origins, performance/interpretation—in diary form.

_____, *Entretiens avec Claude Rostand.* (Paris: R. Julliard, 1954). Radio interviews with the critic Rostand, 1954.

_____, *Francis Poulenc ou L'Invité de Touraine. Entretiens avec Claude Rostand.* INA/Radio France. Archives Sonores INA. Two compact discs. 1995.

Marion S. Weide, "Poulenc's *Banalités:* A Surrealist Song Cycle," *The NATS Bulletin* 35:3 (Jan/Feb 1979), 12-16.

Vivian Poates Wood, *Poulenc's Songs: An Analysis of Style* (Jackson: University Press of Mississippi, 1979). Analysis of text, melody, harmony, form, and the role of the piano in Poulenc's songs.

Notes

1. Francis Poulenc, *Correspondance* 1915-1963 (Paris: Editions du Seuil, 1967), 248.
2. Quoted in Pierre Bernac, "The Songs of Francis Poulenc," *The NATS Journal*, February 1965, 5.
3. Pierre Bernac, *Francis Poulenc: The Man and His Songs*, 39.
4. Pierre Bernac, *The Interpretation of French Song*, 279.
5. Pierre Bernac. Master Class. Blossom Festival. Kent State University, Summer 1970.
6. Quoted in Bernac, *Francis Poulenc: The Man and His Songs*, 93.
7. Francis Poulenc, *Diary of My Songs (Journal de mes mélodies)*. Trans. Winifred Radford. 35.
8. Ibid.
9. Francis Poulenc, *Entretiens avec Claude Rostand*, 63.
10. Poulenc, *Diary*, 37.
11. Bernac, *Francis Poulenc: The Man and His Songs*, 137.
12. Poulenc, *Diary*, 55.
13. Ibid.
14. Ibid., 57.
15. Ibid., 59.
16. In a thought-provoking article in *The NATS Bulletin* (35:3), Marion Weide suggests that the cycle is a series of tableaux of remembered dreams, paralleling the surreal quality of the time (the German Occupation) during which life went on under a daily mask of banalities.
17. Pierre Bernac. Master class. Blossom Festival, 1970.
18. Elizabeth F. Hardee, "The Solo Songs of Francis Poulenc," Masters thesis. University of North Carolina, 1952, 122.
19. Francis Poulenc, *Diary*, 103.
20. Ibid.

JACQUES LEGUERNEY (1906-1997)

> The best song is the one in which the poetry and music are inseparable.
> The best poems are the ones in which you cannot read the poetry alone
> without thinking at once about the music.
>
> — Jacques Leguerney[1]

Most of Jacques Leguerney's sixty-eight *mélodies* were composed and published from 1940 to 1964. Many were commissioned and premiered by French baritone Gérard Souzay and his sister, soprano Geneviève Touraine, and pianist Jacqueline Bonneau. After Leguerney stopped composing in 1964, his songs became neglected.

Leguerney's songs are characterized by their use of French Renaissance poems, notably those of Pierre Ronsard.* The songs have virtuoso piano accompaniments that employ the full range of the piano. They are often dramatic, and have an individual sense of harmonic style and color, so much so that Pierre Bernac reportedly described these songs as *"mélodies* de pianiste."[2]

Leguerney's early songs are comparable in mood and style with Ravel or Roussel (who encouraged Leguerney's composition); later songs have been compared to those of Poulenc. A study of the mature Leguerney style (1943-1964) reveals a definite individuality, with each song closely following the demands of the prosody. It is for this reason that a French critic called Leguerney "the French Hugo Wolf."[3]

Leguerney's *mélodies* are "vocal chamber music" in which voice and piano share an equally rich musical and psychological role. John Ardoin of the *Dallas Morning News* wrote: "Leguerney's lyrical world is one that is entered effortlessly, and one in which a listener is made to feel entirely comfortable. He crafts vocal lines that are at times exuberant and at others quietly sensual. But there is always variety and a sure knack for illuminating his chosen texts, most of which are drawn from French renaissance poetry."[4]

The quality of Leguerney's text setting, the lyrical beauty, and harmonic innovations, which are particularly evident in the later songs, all call for his *mélodies* to be better known and more widely performed. They may be thought of as the last in the great mainstream of twentieth-century French song.

---

*Ronsard used poetry to express the feelings and intellectual ferment of the Renaissance. He was the leader of a group of poets called the Pléiade, who took as inspiration the ancient Greeks—Pindar, Horace, Petrarch, and Anacreon. *Pléiade* comes from the name of a constellation made up of seven stars; the sixteenth-century Pléiade poets were du Bellay, Belleau, de Baïf, Desportes, Dorat, Jodelle, Ronsard and de Tyard.

La Caverne d'Echo   **Cavern of the Echo. 1954**
(*Poèmes de la Pléiade*, VII)
(Saint-Amant)

Saint-Amant wrote at a time when poetry and music were almost inextricably linked. His verses frequently describe sounds, which in turn introduce visual images. Leguerney translates these into actual sounds that ideally complement the text.

Saint-Amant was an accomplished musician, celebrated for his skill on the lute. The lute appears in this text, which is taken from his poem "La Solitude." The setting is a dark grotto, a sacred place, still and absolutely peaceful. It is the home of the nymph, Echo.

Leguerney illustrates the grotto's mysterious resonance using bitonality: the vocal line is in the key of E-flat minor, and the piano oscillates between E-flat and F-sharp minor. Piano figures depict the strumming of the lute. Saint-Amant's verse contains many sounds with the consonant /r/, a rolling speech sonority that recreates the cavern's resonance.[5] Leguerney's musical treatment highlights the sound of the singer's voice echoing eerily in the cavern; this is especially effective in the concluding bars of the song.

La Nuit*
(Saint-Amant)

The Night. 1951

> Paisible et solitaire nuit... (Peaceful and solitary night...) •
> Lugubre courrier de destin... (Dismal messenger of destiny...) •
> Tous ces vents qui soufflaient si fort... (All the winds
> that whistle so strongly...)

La Nuit should not be thought of as a cycle, but one song in three sections, with no large pauses in between. For this work, Leguerney chose three stanzas from an extended poem of the same title by Saint-Amant. Each section (song) ends with the indication *enchainez* (link together), which should be strictly observed. Although the music's title page specifies *voix moyenne*, Leguerney felt La Nuit should only be sung by a baritone or bass-baritone, because the second song is very heavy and dramatic. As is the case with all Leguerney's *mélodies*, La Nuit demands an excellent pianist.

In La Nuit, nature serves as a symbolic analogy of the lover's passionate state of mind—images of his beloved are compared with images of the night and darkness. In the first song, the mysterious night envelops the bashful lover and becomes his confidante; the second song is more menacing as the night assumes the guise of the dismal messenger of destiny; and the third song concludes serenely and lyrically as the lover's fear of unfaithfulness is eased. The second song functions as a linchpin between the first and last song, both in dramatic content and musical treatment. Leguerney called it "black and serious."[6] It relies heavily on recitative-like lines in the voice.

Leguerney adapts the accompaniment style to the tone of the poem: Song 1 contains the hushed sounds of night and a mood of intimacy; chromatic figures evoke the mental torments found in Song 2; and a motive of sixteenth notes in Song 3 calls to mind the fountains in the text, as well as the faraway tinkling of a guitar. A strong unifying element in the work is Leguerney's use of motivic figures, which permeate all three songs; the opening motive from Song 1 is employed in the final postlude.

*For an expanded discussion of this cycle, see *Interpreting the Songs of Jacques Leguerney* by Mary Dibbern, Carol Kimball, and Patrick Choukroun, pages 218-227.

Come away, Death*   **1964**
(Quatre Mélodies)
(William Shakespeare - *Twelfth Night*)

This song is Leguerney's first setting of an English text. It was first performed in 1964 at the Shakespeare Anniversary Festival in Stratford-on-Avon by Gérard Souzay and pianist Dalton Baldwin. Souzay commissioned two songs from Leguerney, but the composer could not find a second text that he wanted to set. "Come away" was to be the last song he wrote, but its expanded harmonic palette and evocative vocal writing indicates a composer strong in his mature aesthetic.

Leguerney highlights the words "death" and "breath" by setting them off the beat. The vocal line begins with a rhythmic figure, which is like the solemn beat of a funeral drum. There are two predominant accompaniment figures: one calls to mind an Elizabethan lute, and the other is a chromatic turn of thirty-second notes, like the heavy tread of a funeral procession. Leguerney opts for a simple ending, avoiding the usual vocal melisma on the word "weep." He closes instead with a single piano measure of stark, ascending quarter notes that fall like tears.

*Also see the settings by Quilter, Argento ("Dirge"), and Finzi.

Ma douce jouvence est passée   **My sweet youth is passed. 1943**
(Poèmes de la Pléiade, II)
(Pierre Ronsard)

This is one of Leguerney's more popular *mélodies*. He composed this song in one day and described it as "not complicated." Ronsard's poem captures the humor of old age as well as its melancholy and pathos, as he laments his white hair, his blackened teeth, passing time and approaching death.

In the piano accompaniment, Leguerney uses simple chords based on a modal scale. Vocal phrases are also unadorned, emphasizing the mood of heaviness and melancholy.[7] The overall mood is gentle, quiet, and almost religious. By blending musical elements into a uniformly simple musical texture, Leguerney creates a highly emotional musical setting that perfectly illustrates the text.

A son page *(Poèmes de la Pléiade, II)*   **To His Page. 1944**
(Pierre Ronsard)

"A son page" is one of Leguerney's masterpieces, a virile character portrait framed in an exhilarating musical setting. There are four characters in the poem: a nobleman much the worse for drink; his page; and two women, Jeanne and Barbe.[8]

Carpe diem is the theme here. The singer philosophizes on this idea while enjoying his wine and the tender companionship of the two beautiful women. Leguerney illustrates the singer's intoxication using jagged vocal lines, driving rhythms, irregular phrase lengths, and repeated words. He inserts subtle text illustrations into the musical texture: the lute, and Barbe's twisted braid of long hair.

The robust, almost frenetic mood is perpetuated by energetic linear progressions in both vocal and piano lines. In the nonstop race to the final measures, we are reminded of Don Giovanni's "champagne" aria, removed to a renaissance setting. Leguerney repeats the last line of the poem "Que l'amour et le vin n'abreuve" three times, then adds nonsense syllables ("pom-pom-pom") for the last phrase—a masterful stroke that gives the effect of being off balance and not knowing—or caring—what tomorrow might bring.[9]

Epipalinodie*   **1947**
(Poèmes de la Pléiade, II)
(Pierre Ronsard)

"Epipalinodie" is one of Leguerney's most striking and effective songs, intense and dramatic in a whirlwind tempo from start to finish. The poet suffers the burning torments and tortures of love, his pain set in a stormy, dense-textured piano accompaniment and an unsettling vocal line of erratic shapes that match the poetic images. Flying arpeggiated figures in the piano change suddenly to dancing staccato patterns at "La nuit/Les fantômes volants" to illustrate the clacking beaks of the night phantoms.

This poem is Ronsard's ode to one of his loves, Denise, who lived in his childhood village of Couture. She was considered to be a sorceress, and when Ronsard accused her of this, he was convinced she cast a spell on him. Denise was later condemned as a witch by the town authorities, publicly beaten, and banished from the village.

*A *palinodie* is an ancient poetic form in which the author contradicts a previous poem.

---

*Le Carnaval**   **1953**
(Saint-Amant)

Le Grotesque (The Grotesque One) • La Belle Brune
(Beautiful Brunette) • Le Carnaval (Carnaval)

Le Carnaval is Leguerney's last cycle. For two of the three songs he chose the grotesque verses of Saint-Amant, but turned again to the material from Saint-Amant's *La Nuit* for the middle *mélodie*.

In contrast to the musico-poetic structure of *La Nuit*, this cycle contains two dramatic, somewhat violent songs that frame a middle song of delicacy and romantic feeling. Leguerney composed this work for baritone voice.

Song 1 is turbulent and heavy, both in poetic mood as well as musical treatment. Leguerney uses syncopation throughout to express a series of bizarre and unrelated poetic images. The picture is one of spontaneous unbalanced actions.

Song 2 provides a romantic centerpiece for the cycle. The poet describes his mistress in sensuous melodic phrases; the mood is one of luxurious description. Voice and piano share musical material that illustrates the poet's attempts to enchant his love with his lute, poetry, and persuasive ardor.

Song 3 is similar in mood to the first, and, although it is rough and heavy, it is still vivacious. Dizzying movement described in the poetry is expressed in Leguerney's non-stop musical treatment. After the premiere, Leguerney revised this song, assigning the piano a more significant and integrated role.

Le Carnaval is a close-knit colorful cycle, typical of Leguerney's mature style. After examining the manuscript, Francis Poulenc wrote to Leguerney:

> Dear Jacques: In Paris I took a quick look at your *Carnaval.* Now, a quieter reading has confirmed my first impression, namely that it is among the *best* of Leguerney. Everything about it is lively, sensitive and vigorously handled. In any case, these are precisely the kind of songs that lend themselves to orchestration, of that I am *certain.* Pierre [Bernac] agrees with me...(26 May 1954).[10]

*For an expanded discussion of this cycle, see *Interpreting the Songs of Jacques Leguerney* by Mary Dibbern, Carol Kimball, and Patrick Choukroun, pages 243-255.

Sept poèmes de François Maynard   **1948-49**
(Francois Maynard)

Plaintes d'Orphée • Epigramme à un mauvais payeur • A Chloris •
D'une maigre dame • Dans la forêt • Secret amour •
Compliments à une duegne

These seven *mélodies* resemble a gallery of portraits—a colorful collection of very disparate characters, painted with wit, passion, and lyricism. Leguerney ordered the songs carefully, in a well-planned sequence. The character of each text determines its placement: the solemn, serious Orpheus; the bitter tirade to the stingy employer; the tender but ironic speech to Chloris; the naughty jibes to a skinny woman; the poetic hymn to the forest nightingale; the amorous address to Phyllis; and the scathing insults to Margaret.

The cycle is notable for the complexity of its piano accompaniments, which Leguerney said were "more detailed and had a role at least equal to that of the voice."[11] The work is dedicated to Gérard Souzay, who gave its first performance.

PLAINTES D'ORPHÉE (ORPHEUS'S LAMENT). Leguerney creates a sensitive, meditative setting for Maynard's text. A descending arpeggiated figure in the piano evokes the sound of Orpheus's fabled lyre. His eloquent soliloquy is a lament, which, according to mythology, was the ultimate musical creation to convey the deepest despair.

EPIGRAMME À UN MAUVAIS PAYEUR (POEM TO A STINGY EMPLOYER). *Legato* and *staccato* articulation alternate in the vocal phrases of this *mélodie.* Leguerney was specific in directing that the song be sung lightly and gaily. Piano figures maintain the energy of the text, which is a sarcastic speech to a rich man who does not pay his servants.

À CHLORIS (TO CHLORIS). Leguerney considered this text to be a discreet love poem, capturing its essential quality by mixing charm with intense lyricism. Chloris is so consumed by her sorrow that she has no time for the poet. Although his entreaties fall on deaf ears, he remains bewitched by her grief.

D'UNE MAIGRE DAME (ABOUT A SKINNY LADY). This is the shortest song in the Maynard collection. It is the center song, dividing the first three songs from the last three. The words paint a sarcastic portrait of a woman who is so thin that her lovers compare her prodding knees to a fencing foil. The piano accompaniment punctuates with text with a sly little "commentary" of major and minor seconds.

DANS LA FORÊT (IN THE FOREST). In the quiet nobility of the forest, a heartbroken lover shares his sadness with the nightingale, symbolic bird of disillusioned lovers.

SECRET AMOUR (SECRET LOVE). "Secret amour" is linked to the previous song by poetic mood and musical texture. Leguerney combines lyrical vocal lines with a transparent piano accompaniment to create a texture that is like chamber music.

COMPLIMENTS À UNE DUÈGNE (MESSAGE FOR A DUENNA). Leguerney sets this comic but malicious text in a highly energetic musical texture. Altered chords in the piano underline the viciousness of the words. Driving rhythms in the piano and vocal line call for dexterity of articulation from both performers.

Extended Study List

Je me lamente *(Poèmes de la Pléiade, I)* • A sa maîtresse *(Poèmes de la Pléiade, II)* • Au sommeil *(Poèmes de la Pléiade, I)* • Invocation *(Poèmes de la Pléiade, IV)* • Ah! Bel-Accueil *(Poèmes de la Pléiade, II)* • *Le Paysage ou La Description de Port-Royal des Champs* • Comme un qui s'est perdu *(Poèmes de la Pléiade, IV)* • Le Vallon *(Poèmes de la Pléiade, VII)* • Le Paresseux *(Poèmes de la Pléiade, VI)* • Sérénade d'un Barbon *(Poèmes de la Pléiade, VI)* • Le présent *(Quatre Mélodies)* • Je vous envoie *(Poèmes de la Pléiade, I)* • *La Solitude* • Sonnet pour Hélène *(Poèmes de la Pléiade, VI)*

Selected Reading

Patrick Choukroun, "Jacques Leguerney: The Celebration of French Song," trans. Mary Dibbern, *The Opera Journal* 30:4 (1997), 42-46.

_____, "Jacques Leguerney ou la celebration de la mélodie française." Unpublished doctoral thesis, 1996. Université de Paris, IV, Sorbonne, Paris.

Delmas, Evelyne. "La Puissance expressive et poetique de l'œuvre musicale de Jacques Leguerney à travers son écriture, son style et son esthetique." Unpublished doctoral thesis, 1993, Université de Paris, IV, Sorbonne, Paris.

Mary Dibbern, Carol Kimball, and Patrick Choukroun, *Interpreting the Songs of Jacques Leguerney: A Guide for Study and Performance* (Hillsdale, NY: Pendragon Press, 2001). Leguerney's biography and song style, plus texts, translations, IPA transcriptions, and interpretive notes for all the *mélodies*.

Carol Fuqua Lines, "An Introduction to Jacques Leguerney's Settings of the Poetry of Ronsard," D.M.A. diss., Louisiana State University, 2001.

Lawrence David Sannerud, "Three Song Cycles of Jacques Leguerney: examples of his significant contribution to the French mélodie tradition." D.M.A. diss., The University of Arizona, 2004.

_____, "Jacques Leguerney: Nearly Forgotten Contributor to the French Mélodie Tradition Worthy of Revival," *Ars Lyrica* (Journal of the Lyrica Society for Word-Music Relations), Vol. 14, 2004, 3.

Paula Woolfolk, "The Songs of Jacques Leguerney," *The NATS Journal,* 42:4 (March/April 1986).

Notes

1. Interview with Mary Dibbern. Paris, France. Used by permission.
2. Liner notes by Mary Dibbern. *Mélodies sur poèmes de la Renaissance* (Jacques Leguerney). Harmonia Mundi France. LP recording HMC 1171.
3. Article by Albert Pinto titled "Les Mélodies d'un honnête homme" in the French newspaper *Centre-Presse et la Montagne.* August 24, 1986.
4. John Ardoin, "Discs provide a fine introduction to little-known French composer." *The Dallas Morning News.* February 1, 1987. Reviewof Leguerney recordings Harmonia Mundi France HMC 1171 and 1172.
5. Mary Dibbern, Carol Kimball, and Patrick Choukroun, *The Songs of Jacques Leguerney,* 156.
6. Interview material from sessions with Leguerney, with the author and Mary Dibbern, March 1986.
7. Dibbern, Kimball, and Choukroun, *The Songs of Jacques Leguerney,* 99.
8. Ibid., 95.
9. Ibid.
10. Sidney Buckland, ed. and trans., *Francis Poulenc: 'Echo and Source': Selected Correspondence* 1915-1963, 219.
11. Quoted in Dibbern, Kimball, and Chouroun, *The Songs of Jacques Leguerney,* 185.

American Song

American classical song, like Topsy in Uncle Tom's Cabin, "just growed." Its history is as eclectic as the cultures that make up America's population. From the earliest parlor songs of Stephen Foster to the appealing melodies of Richard Hundley, American song has passed through a number of transformations, but its style continues to mirror the American credo of individualism above all. To hear the songs of Charles Ives, Charles Griffes, Samuel Barber, Ned Rorem, Virgil Thomson, John Duke, Paul Bowles, Lee Hoiby, Dominick Argento, and William Bolcom is to experience a kaleidoscope of sound and color, drama and emotion.

American song "style" defies description, since its development has been sporadic at best. American songs for the concert hall began to be written with regularity only after the middle of the nineteenth century. At that time, it was the custom for American composers to study in Germany, so American song, from the late nineteenth century and into the early part of the twentieth century, was still rooted in European traditions. Many songs composed during this time were more sentimental than expressive, and highly erratic in quality. The songs of Charles Ives—very advanced for their time—were largely unknown. Charles Griffes studied in Germany; almost half of his songs are composed to German texts and are redolent with German romanticism. Edward MacDowell, who studied in Germany and in France, was the first American composer to achieve an international reputation. George Chadwick, Charles Martin Loeffler, and Sidney Homer were among the composers who began to develop and shape American song tradition.

Later, American composers went to France to study with the formidable *maître* Nadia Boulanger, bringing back Gallic sensibilities which filtered into their music. Among Boulanger's pupils were Virgil Thomson, Aaron Copland, and Theodore Chanler. Chanler in particular was highly influenced by French style. Ned Rorem spent considerable time in France, and although his songs reflect his own individual style, they display a clarity and elegance that is quintessentially French. Paul Bowles, a citizen of the world, distilled rhythm and color from his travels into his music.

It took a while—almost half of the century—for American song to come into its own. Most composers were not interested in producing a great body of song literature—or even a small one. Writing songs was not financially rewarding, and American singers preferred European song literature, notably *Lieder*. Despite this, numerous American composers were drawn to song composition, and collectively they composed a fair-sized body of literature. Although the quality of song composition was still developing, the sentimentality of the turn of the century disappeared and American song acquired a richer, more expressive voice.

Ned Rorem was the first twentieth-century American composer to really champion song as a genre, and he is considered by many to be the foremost American song composer. His songs and his passionate interest in song literature led the way for a new resurgence of interest in song composition.

Recent American composers have shown greater interest in producing vocal works, but on the large scale of opera. Productions of American opera have proliferated and commissions for new works are growing. *The Voyage of Edgar Allen Poe, Dangerous Liaisons, Shining Brow, The Ghosts of Versailles, McTeague, A View from the Bridge, Little Women, A Streetcar Named Desire, Dead Man Walking,* and *The Great Gatsby* have recently joined the ranks of American works such as *Vanessa, The Mother of Us All,* and *Susannah.* Samuel Barber, Virgil Thomson, and Dominick Argento are among the American composers who have created not only opera but a substantial body of song literature as well.

The American composers of the new generation continue to be eclectic in their song style. We have almost come full circle, from the popular idioms of Stephen Foster's parlor songs to the integration of popular music idioms into the art songs of Ricky Ian Gordon, Richard Hundley, John Musto, Jake Heggie, and Ben Moore. Their songs are easily accessible for the listener and their musical styles are appealing to singers.

Singers are finally discovering the rich quantity and quality of American song, and contemporary composers are responding with greater numbers of songs for the recital platform. American poetry has also come of age, and offers a colorful and varied array of texts.

It is doubtful that a definite American art song style will coalesce; meanwhile, there is a vast legacy of literature waiting to be discovered, and the clock is still ticking.

STEPHEN COLLINS FOSTER (1826-1864)

> Mr. Foster possesses more than ordinary abilities as a composer, and we hope he will soon realize enough [income] from his Ethiopian melodies to enable him to afford to drop them and turn his attention to the production of a higher kind of music.
> —Letter to *The Musical World and New York Musical Times*[1]

Stephen Foster, composer of such hits as "Oh! Susanna," "Beautiful Dreamer," and "Jeanie with the Light Brown Hair," was wildly successful with the public both in the United States and abroad. From 1849 to 1860 (four years before his death) the income from his published songs averaged over $1,300 a year, a modest sum by today's standards, but a substantial, comfortable salary in Foster's time. His nearly 200 popular songs were sung all over the world during his lifetime. A half dozen of them still rank among the world's greatest ballads, and at least twenty-five have become American "folk songs."

Deems Taylor speculates that Foster's songs were popular in the United States because they were written during a time when the country was yearning for folk music of its own.[2] At that time, the "folk songs" that were sung in America were foreign, brought here by peoople migrating from other countries, representative of other cultures and other lifestyles. Eager for their own native music, Americans adopted the Negro spirituals and the songs of Stephen Foster as their own.

Though his songs are identified with a turbulent time in our nation's history, they have become an indelible part of our country's musical fabric. They are genuine expressions of the time in which he lived. Natural, spontaneous, and unaffected, they also reflect Foster's own character and temperament, his love of home and family.

His songs fell into two categories: "household" songs for the parlor and stage songs for the minstrel shows. Foster composed more "household" songs than stage songs, about 150 songs in all. These songs, sometimes called "parlor arias," straddle the line between art song and popular music; they were written with enough intelligence and complexity to be appreciated by knowledgeable and sophisticated music professionals, yet they were simple enough to be performed and enjoyed by average people who were not accomplished musicians. Their style was rooted in the gentility of British-American ballads. (Several composers wrote similar parlor arias. The earliest American composer of this type of song was Francis Hopkinson.)

Foster's stage songs were composed for the minstrel shows of the day, and trace their origins to the English ballad-opera composers of the eighteenth century and Anglo-Irish-American traditional songs. The singers wore blackface (soot rubbed over their faces) and sang in a crude dialect. "Oh! Susanna" was a prime example of Foster's stage songs, and, with its publication, Foster's reputation as a song-writer became firmly established. Within a year of its publication, "Oh! Susanna" became the signature song of the gold-rush miners and the slogan of the westward-bound pioneers.

Overall, Foster wrote melodies that might be termed "sentimental," yet his melodies are fresh and graceful. They were accompanied by simple, modest piano parts. For each song, the dynamic markings and tempo indications are clearly specified by Foster.

He composed effortlessly. Fresh new melodies seemed never far from the tip of his pen. In the last eighteen months or so before he died, Foster wrote at least twenty-one songs to words by George Cooper, a new young friend. Cooper's account of their "song factory," as given to Foster's biographer Harold V. Milligan, is vivid: "He wrote with great facility and without the aid of a piano. If no music-paper was handy, he would take whatever paper he could find, and ruling the lines on it, proceed without hesitation to write. He seemed never at a loss for a melody, and the simple accompaniment caused him no trouble. These first drafts were taken out and sold to a publisher or theatre manager, practically without correction.[3]

Despite the popularity of his songs and the income he earned from them, Stephen Foster died in poverty, the last years of his life spent in heavy drinking and a vagabond existence. After his death a small purse was found, containing bills and coins amounting to thirty-eight cents and a slip of paper with the penciled words "Dear friends and gentle hearts," no doubt his next song title.

Foster's songs should not be dismissed, for they were influential in shaping the solo vocal literature of the United States. His songs influenced the music of later American composers, including George Gershwin and Charles Ives. When shorn of the overblown arrangements in which they are often heard, and performed with Foster's original simple accompaniments, his songs shine as the fresh creations they are. They transcend their time, and merit inclusion here for that reason.

Jeanie With the Light Brown Hair*   1854
(Stephen Foster)

Foster probably wrote this lovely tune with his wife, Jane, in mind. He composed a number of songs in which he used some form of her name: "Jennie's Own Schottische," "Jenny's Coming O'er the Green," "Jenny June," and "Little Jenny Dow."

Foster married Jane Denny McDowell, better known as "Jennie," in 1850, temporarily separated from her in 1853, and later reconciled with her. He probably penned this song and his other "Jenny songs" during their separation. He published it soon after the family was together again.

Foster wrote this song with an easy flowing melody and heartfelt sentiment which were characteristic of his style. He composed this song at his career's peak, when his songs were widely popular and his relationship with his publishers was solid. In 1853 Foster wrote that his quarterly earnings were "over five hundred dollars...for the dullest season."[4]

Foster's pride, and that of his publishers, was evident in "Jeanie." An advertisement in the *Musical World* proclaimed:

> *Jeanie with the Light Brown Hair.* Ballad. Words and music by S.C. Foster, 38 [cents] Mr. Foster's popularity as THE SONG WRITER OF AMERICA is too firmly established to require particular mention of any of his compositions. The above song fully sustains his reputation.[5]

"Jeanie" was only moderately successful. In its initial two and a half years it earned $217.80—royalties of two cents each on 10,890 copies.[6] Today it is one of the titles that springs to mind when Foster's name is mentioned—a prime example of the originality, beauty and simplicity of his melodies.

*See Ned Rorem's arrangement of this beautiful Foster melody.

Beautiful Dreamer   **Copyrighted 1864**
(Stephen Foster)

The publisher proudly announced "Beautiful Dreamer" as "the last song ever written by Stephen Foster, composed but a few days previous to his death." In actuality, the copyright in the first edition reads 1862, which suggests the song was composed and prepared for printing nearly two years before his death. Altogether, twenty-odd Foster songs were published posthumously, each claiming to be the "last composed" by Foster, so no one really knows which song was the final one.

Foster's song heroines were either "asleep or dead" observes Richard Jackson in his notes to the *Stephen Foster Song Book*.[7] The list of doomed heroines is long: Annie, Cora Dean, Little Ella's an Angel, Jeanie, Laura Lee, Nelly Was a Lady, etc. Throughout history, song literature is full of sleeping beauties, and Foster's lovely dreamer deserves a place in their ranks.

"Beautiful Dreamer" is one of Foster's most sentimental melodies and a prime example of his natural melodic gift. It is set in simple $\frac{9}{8}$ rhythm with a transparent broken-chord accompaniment that allows the wistful melody to predominate.

Ah! May the Red Rose Live Alway!   **1850**
(Stephen Foster)

This is one of Foster's finest early songs, composed while he was courting Jane McDowell and published three months before their marriage. Its lyrics clearly reveal young Stephen's yearning and uncertainty as he courts Jane, who is also being wooed by a rival lover.

The themes in this song were popular topics in the poetry and song of mid-Victorian America—innocent beauty, sentimental longing, and mortality. Foster took these themes and used them regularly in his songs.

"Ah! May the Red Rose Live Alway!" is an example of how simple his songs are—three strophic verses in $\frac{6}{8}$ time. It was published in 1850 by F. D. Benteen of Baltimore. It did not enjoy great success; over a period of seven years it sold just over 400 copies and paid Foster royalties of $8.12.

Extended Study List

Come Where My Love Lies Dreaming • Why, No One to Love • My Old Kentucky Home, Good Night • Nelly Bly • Gentle Annie • Old Black Joe • That's What's the Matter • Oh! Susanna • Old Folks at Home • If You've Only Got a Moustache • My Wife Is a Most Knowing Woman

Selected Reading

William W. Austin, *"Susanna," "Jeanie," and "The Old Folks at Home": The Songs of Stephen C. Foster from His Time to Ours.*, 2nd edition (Urbana and Chicago: University of Illinois Press, 1987).
Calvin Elliker, *Stephen Collins Foster: A Guide to Research* (New York: Garland Publishing Inc., 1988).
A Treasury of Stephen Foster. Foreword by Deems Taylor. Historical notes by John Tasker Howard. (New York: Random House 1946). Fifty songs by Foster, with introductory annotations.
Stephen Foster Song Book. Original Sheet Music of 40 Songs by Stephen Collins Foster. Selected, with Introduction and Notes by Richard Jackson. (New York: Dover Publications, Inc., 1974).
John Tasker Howard, *Stephen Foster: America's Troubadour* (New York: Tudor Publishing Company, 1943).
Diane Root, "The 'Mythtory' of Stephen C. Foster or Why His True Story Remains Untold," *The American Music Research Center Journal*, Vol. 1, 1991, 20-36.

Notes

1. Quoted in John Tasker Howard, *Stephen Foster: America's Troubadour,* 213.
2. Deems Taylor. Foreword to *A Treasury of Stephen Foster,* 8.
3. Howard, 318.
4. Ibid., 250.
5. Quoted in William W. Austin, *"Susanna," "Jeannie," and "The Old Folks at Home": The Songs of Stephen C. Foster from His Time to Ours,* 2nd ed., 207.
6. *A Treasury of Stephen Foster,* 107.
7. Richard Jackson, notes to *Stephen Foster Song Book* ,175.

H.T. BURLEIGH (1866-1949)

He is given full credit in the world of music for having saved the now famous Negro folk songs and spirituals from oblivion.

Lucien White[1]
Music critic for the *New York Age*

I hope to make my greatest reputation as an arranger of Negro spirituals. In them my race has pure gold, and they should be taken as the Negro's contribution to artistic possessions. In them we show a spiritual security as old as the ages...America's only original and distinctive style of music is destined to be appreciated more and more.

H.T. Burleigh[2]

Harry Thacker Burleigh was an African-American composer and arranger. He was also an excellent singer and enjoyed a long career as a church and synagogue soloist in New York City. He was born in Erie, Pennsylvania. His mother was the daughter of a slave; his grandfather used to sing spirituals to Harry as he grew up.

After graduating from high school, he became well established as a singer in the Episcopal Church in Erie. He began studying in 1892 at the National

Conservatory of Music in New York, on a scholarship. He studied voice, harmony and counterpoint, and played double bass and timpani in the conservatory orchestra. At the conservatory, Burleigh's association with Czech composer Antonín Dvořák—the new director of the conservatory—had a profound influence on his career as a composer. Burleigh copied manuscripts for Dvořák, and also introduced Dvořák to the spiritual. He sang many spiritual melodies for Dvořák, who used one of them, "Swing, Low, Sweet Chariot," in his *Symphony No. 9, "From the New World."*

Burleigh auditioned and won a position as the baritone soloist at St. George's Episcopal Church in New York City, and remained in there for fifty-two years. In 1900,he joined the choir of Temple Emanu-El, where he sang for twenty-five years. From 1913-1949, Burleigh was a music editor at G. Ricordi.

His study of African-American spirituals, traditionally referred to as Negro spirituals, and his musical arrangements of them were unparalleled. Burleigh was the first to bring the spiritual to the concert stage, introducing this unexplored repertoire to the concert going public for the first time.

In 1916, Burleigh published a collection of spirituals he had arranged for solo vocal performance, titled *Jubilee Songs of the United States of America.* Dunn-Powell observes: "For the first time, spirituals set in the manner of art songs were available to concert singers. Black singers such as Roland Hayes, Paul Robeson, Marian Anderson and William Warfield established the practice of ending their recitals with a set of spirituals, a traditional perpetuated by African-American singers of succeeding generations."[3]

In addition to his spiritual arrangements, Burleigh composed almost 150 sacred and secular songs. These were sung by a number of famous artists of the day, including John McCormack.

Burleigh described spirituals as follows:

They are practically the only music in America that meets the scientific definition of Folk Song. The voice is not nearly as important as the spirit, and then the rhythm. Their worth is weakened unless they are done impressively, for through all of these songs there breathes a hope, a faith in the ultimate justice and brotherhood of man. The cadences of sorrow invariably turn to joy, and the message is ever manifest that eventually deliverance from all that hinders and oppresses the soul will come, and man—every man—will be free.[4]

Deep River   arr. 1917
(Spiritual)

Between 1917 and 1924 almost four dozen of Burleigh's solo arrangements of Negro spirituals were published by Ricordi. "Deep River" was one of his earliest arrangements, and proved to be his most famous work. It first appeared as a choral setting, and in 1917, Burleigh made the solo arrangement that caused a sensation with audiences and performers alike. "Deep River" and other of Burleigh's spiritual settings were sung widely by well-known singers of the day—John McCormack, Marcella Sembrich, Roland Hayes, and later, Marian Anderson. Burleigh often sang his own arrangements in recital, accompanying himself at the piano.

Burleigh's arrangement of "Deep River" is not sad, but profoundly inspirational. The spiritual consists of four lines of text, cast in ABA form. The A section is a deeply felt melody ("Deep river, my home is over Jordan/ Deep river, Lord,

I want to cross over into campground"); the B section is more joyful in spirit ("O don't you want to go to that gospel feast/ That promised land where all is peace?"). Burleigh doubles the rhythm of the vocal phrases in the piano accompaniment, but embellishes the setting with ornamental melodic fragments that add just enough motion to the texture.

Some spirituals were used as "signal" songs, expressing in their text a kind of coded conversation that had double meaning. "Deep river" could have been such a song, signaling crossing over the Ohio River on the underground railway, journeying to Canada and freedom.*

There have been countless transcriptions of "Deep River." It exists in settings for violin/piano, organ, string quartet, solo cello, solo violin, and concert band. An orchestral arrangement was made in 1923.

*Observation by Dr. Alfonse Anderson, voice faculty, UNLV.

Saracen Songs   **1914**
(Fred G, Bowles)

Almona • O, Night of Dream and Wonder • His Helmet's Blaze •
I hear his footsteps, music sweet • Thou art weary • This is Nirvana •
Ahmed's Song of Farewell

Saracen Songs was Burleigh's first song cycle, and its scope was ambitious. Its poetry, by Frank Bowles, has an Eastern theme, and involves four characters: Yussouf, Almona, Hassan, and Ahmed. Burleigh designed the work like a miniature opera scene. There is a subtitle for every song (except the last) that sets the scene and establishes the emotional and personal ties between the characters: "Almona" (Song of Hassan); "O, Night of Dream and Wonder" (Almona's Song); "His Helmet's Blaze" (Almona's song of Yussouf to Hassan); "I hear his footsteps, music sweet" (Almona's song of delight); "Thou art weary" (Almona's song to Yussouf); "This is Nirvana" (Yussouf's song to Almona); and "Ahmed's Song of Farewell."

Rhythmic patterns unify the songs and help sustain the dramatic content of the "story"—a *habanera* rhythm in "Almona," syncopated chords laced with chromaticism in "O, Night of Dream and Wonder," and gently undulating chords that suggest a strummed instrument in "This is Nirvana." Harmonic textures tinged with impressionism perpetuate the exotic atmosphere of the poetry. The seven songs are brief, totaling only nineteen pages.

The tessitura of the songs suits a high voice best. Because the texts' content alternates between male and female gender, it has been suggested that two singers could effectively perform the cycle. During Burleigh's lifetime the cycle was not frequently performed in its entirety, but more often, as separate songs.

Saracen Songs is an excellent example of the type of contemporary poetry in vogue during the early years of the twentieth century. Today, the text seems excessively sentimental, clichéd, and overly dramatic, but Burleigh's musical setting saves it from banality.

Extended Study
Five Sngs of Laurence Hope • *Passionale* • The Grey Wolf By the Pool at the Third Rosses • O, Perfect Love • The Soldier • Three Shadows • Little Mother of Mine • The Dove and the Lily • Finvara • Lovely Dark and Lonely One • Passing By • Arrangements of spirituals • Ethiopia Saluting the Colors

Selected Reading

Richard Newman, *Go Down Moses: A Celebration of the African-American Spiritual* (New York: Random House, 1998).

Lourin Plant, "Singing African-American Spirituals: A Reflection on Racial Barriers in Classical Vocal Music," *Journal of Singing* 61:5 (May/June 2005).

Rosephanye Dunn-Powell, "The African-American Spiritual: Preparation and Performance Considerations," *Journal of Singing* 61:5 (May/June 2005). Contains an informative discussion of using dialect in performing spirituals, and provides a helpful table of words often sung in dialect, with suggested pronunciation.

Anne Key Simpson, *Hard Trials: the life and music of Harry T. Burleigh* (Metuchen, NJ: The Scarecrow Press, 1990).

Eileen Southern, *The Music of Black Americans: A History,* 3rd edition (New York: W.W. Norton & Co., 1997).

Earl L. Stewart, *African American Music: An Introduction* (New York: Schirmer Books, 1998).

Notes

1. In a review of one of Burleigh's broadcasts, 1928. Quoted in Anne Key Simpson, *Hard Trials*, 287.
2. Ibid., 296. Quoted from an article by Lester A. Walton, "Harry T. Burleigh Honored Today at St. George's," reprinted in *The Black Perspective in Music*, Spring 1974, 2:1, 81.
3. H.T. Burleigh, Foreword (1917) to *The Spirituals of Harry T. Burleigh* (New York: Belwin-Mills, 1984).
4. Rosephanye Dunn-Powell, "The African-American Spiritual: Preparation and Performance Considerations," *Journal of Singing* 61:5 (May/June 2005), 469.

AMY MARCY CHENEY BEACH (1867-1944)

Study how best to develop all the possibilities of a small form.
A small gem may be just as brilliantly cut as one weighing many carats.
—Amy Beach[1]

Amy Cheney Beach (Mrs. H.H.A. Beach) could be called the dean of American women composers. She was the first woman composer in the United States to realize a successful career writing art music. At the time of her death, she had composed more than 300 musical works, including a piano concerto, a symphony, a one-act opera, numerous piano pieces, choral works, chamber music, and 117 songs. With few exceptions, all of her compositions were published, a situation almost unheard of at the time. She was the first American female composer to have written a symphony but she is perhaps best remembered for her songs. She chose texts by well-known poets—Shelley, Browning, Tennyson, Shakespeare, Victor Hugo, Robert Burns, Goethe, Heine, and Schiller—and also contemporary authors whom she knew personally. During her lifetime her music was featured by many ensembles, her symphony attained wide popularity, and leading opera stars sang her songs. Despite her successes as a composer, critical assessment of her music at that time dwelt on the fact that she was a woman, and therefore her music could not be compared to that of mainstream male composers. Happily, later generations have reassessed the quality of her music. Amy Beach was a heroine to many American women, and by example, a groundbreaker for coming generations of female composers.

Her musical talent appeared at a very early age; at age four, she played by ear any music she heard, and composed her first pieces for piano. After formal studies in piano, at fifteen she made her debut playing with a Boston orchestra. As a composer, she was virtually self-taught, having studied formally for only one year. She taught herself harmony, counterpoint, and languages. She was the first American woman musician to receive all of her training in the United States and to write in the larger musical forms.[2]

After her marriage at eighteen to Dr. Henry Harris Aubrey Beach, a distinguished Boston physician twenty-five years her senior, she insisted on being known as Mrs. H.H.A. Beach. Her social status brought her into contact with the leading figures in musical, literary, and political circles. After her marriage, she continued to compose prolifically but gave only occasional concerts. She resumed an active concert career after her husband's death, establishing a reputation as a pianist and composer, and promoting her music.

She composed 117 art songs. Musical material from some of these found their way into her larger instrumental works. Beach composed in a late-romantic style throughout her life; her songs never changed in their general musical style. They reflect the dominant artistic current of the time, in which art was seen as an expression of the highest idealism.[3]

Beach maintained that song writing was recreation for her, something she turned to after working on more difficult projects: "I just drop the larger work for the day and write a song. It freshens me up; I really consider that I have given myself a special treat when I have written a song."[4]

Three Browning Songs, Op. 44   1900
(Robert Browning)

The Year's at the Spring • Ah, Love, but a day! • I send my heart up to thee!

Three Browning Songs, Op. 44, is dedicated to the Browning Society of Boston. These have proven to be Beach's most popular and enduring songs. Noted soprano Emma Eames often performed them on her concerts. *Three Browning Songs* was also published with violin obbligato, as duets for soprano and alto, and reissued in choral arrangements.

The first song, "The Year's at the Spring," gained great popularity, and became a surefire encore piece. When the set is performed, this song is often sung last. Beach composed it in her head while on a train; the train wheels' persistent rhythm found its way into the piano accompaniment.[5] The combination of sequential patterns in the vocal line and the persistent drive of the triplet figure in the piano produces an astonishing dramatic arc. "Ah, Love, but a day!" features beautifully shaped vocal phrases that arc and build to another intensely dramatic finish. Perhaps the most intricate setting is "I send my heart up to thee" in which fluid modulations emphasize points of varying emotions in the text.

Extended Study List
Empress of Night •Ariette • Ecstasy • Nacht • In the Twilight • Shena Van • Hush, Baby Dear • Dearie • Far Awa' • *Three Shakespeare Songs* (O Mistress Mine, Take, O Take Those Lips Away, Fairy Lullaby) • Chanson d'amour • Je demande à l'oiseau • Canzonetta • Nähe des Geliebten • Forgotten • Springtime • Juni • Sweet Content • Ein altes Gebet

Selected Reading
Adrienne Fried Block, *Amy Beach, Passionate Victorian: the life and work of an American composer* (New York: Oxford University Press, 1998).

Jeanell Wise Brown, *Amy Beach and Her Chamber Music: biography, documents, style* (Metuchen, NJ: Scarecrow Press, 1994).

Walter S. Jenkins, ed. by John H. Baron, *The Remarkable Mrs. Beach, American Composer: a biographical account based on her diaries, letters, newspaper clippings, and personal reminiscences* (Michigan: Harmonie Park Press, 1994).

Mary K. Kelton, "The Songs of Mrs. H.H.A. Beach," D.M.A. diss., The University of Texas, Austin, 1992.

Notes

1. Mrs. H.H.A. Beach, "Music's Ten Commandments as Given for Young Composers," printed in Block, 310.
2. Katherine Kelton, liner notes to *Amy Beach Songs*, Katherine Kelton, mezzo-soprano; Catherine Bringerud, piano. Naxos 8.559191, 1999.
3. Ibid.
4. Adrienne Fried Block, *Amy Beach, Passionate Victorian* (New York: Oxford University Press, 1998), 58.
5. Ibid., 150.

ARTHUR FARWELL (1872-1952)

Beauty, above all, and the genuine reaching of the emotions are, I suppose, the things I am chiefly after.

—Arthur Farwell[1]

I wonder if I shall ever write any more songs; who ever sings serious American songs, anyway? I never see a song of Ayres, or of mine, on a program anywhere. Does anybody sing any of them? If not for the present, do they have any meaning for the future??? After all, I have faith in the future."

—Arthur Farwell[2]

Arthur Farwell was a musical pioneer, devoting his energies to crusading for a uniquely American musical style. He was a prolific composer, producing works in almost every musical form. Many of his compositions for orchestra, chamber ensembles, vocal ensembles and piano are based on American Indian melodies and folk songs of the South and West.

After hearing the Boston Symphony Orchestra in concert, Farwell forsook degree studies in electrical engineering at MIT to study composition. He began study with George Chadwick, then, like many American composers, traveled to Germany and France to work and study. Upon returning to the States, he began crusading for American music modeled not on European traditions, but on indigenous American sources—cowboy ballads, Indian music, and African-Amercian music.

To provide a publishing outlet for music of composers who shared his beliefs, he established the Wa-Wan Press in 1901 in Newton Center, Massachusetts. Named for an Omaha Indian peace ceremony, Wa-Wan (To Sing to Someone) printed—in periodical form—music by American composers and articles on new directions in American musical thought. Some of these articles were written by Farwell himself. To keep Wa-Wan going, Farwell presented lectures throughout the United States and founded the American Music Society, which featured concerts by American composers in its twenty centers nationwide. In 1912, Wa-Wan was sold to G. Schirmer, who let it fall into decline and finally closed it down.

After 1910 Farwell lived in numerous locations throughout the country while he continued to compose. From 1909 to 1918, he lived in New York City, where he served as Supervisor of Municipal Concerts and the chief critic of *Musical America*. He later taught theory on the faculties of Michigan State University and the University of California. As a teacher, he influenced a number of his students, several of whom became prominent composers—among them, Roy Harris, Dika Newlin, and Bernard Rogers.

Farwell's earliest songs reflect the influence of his studies with George Chadwick; like many songs composed at the turn of the century, they exhibit strong European musical characteristics. Farwell composed five songs to poems by Percy Bysshe Shelley, and a setting of Francis Thompson's famous poem "The Hound of Heaven" for baritone and orchestra in 1935, Op. 100.

In his songs, Farwell demonstrates a strong relationship between text and music. Nowhere does he display this relationship more clearly than in his settings of Emily Dickinson, his favorite poet. He was one of the earliest American composers to be drawn to her poetry and he considered his thirty-nine song settings of Dickinson, most composed when he was in his sixties and seventies, to be among his best works.[3] In these songs, he used colorful piano writing with a wide-ranging variety of moods and style. His settings also display his deep sensitivity to Dickinson's poetic style and imagery.

Tenor Paul Sperry has been a major force in getting Farwell's songs into print and back into the concert hall. After Farwell's death, his manuscripts were thought to be lost, but surfaced at a warehouse auction; they now reside at Oral Roberts University. The selections annotated here are chosen from *Thirty-Four Songs of Emily Dickinson* (published in 2 volumes), edited and introduced by Paul Sperry, Boosey & Hawkes 1983.

Safe in Their Alabaster Chambers, Op. 105, No. 2 (Volume 1)   1938-41
(Emily Dickinson)

The song begins without an introduction. A somber but lyrical melody marks this song, evoking images of the sleep of the dead. An ostinato rhythm in the piano perpetuates the unchanging finality of eternal slumber in anticipation of the resurrection. More motion invades the middle section of the song, revealing ongoing life outside the tomb—singing birds, babbling bees, and laughing breezes. The vocal line is quietly set. The final stanza depicts a broad view of the universe and inexorable passing of time, set grandly over solemn chords. The final measures reprise the beginning ostinato rhythm.

The Grass So Little Has To Do, Op. 112, No. 2 (Volume 2)   1949
(Emily Dickinson)*

In this song, Farwell marked the vocal passages with dotted rhythms, ushered in after one measure of introduction. He creates a scene that is fresh and pastoral, a buoyant setting laced with chromatics and nonharmonic tones. With an energetic rhythmic treatment, Farwell suggests skipping; the piano is written in $\frac{6}{8}$ meter, the voice in $\frac{4}{4}$. He unifies the song with another rhythm, ending seven phrases with a similar pattern (quarter note tied to an eighth note on beat 3). He precedes the voice's last phrase "I wish I were the hay!" with dramatic silence.

*See also Vincent Persichetti's setting of this poem.

The Level Bee, Op. 105, No. 1 (Volume 1)   **1940**
(Emily Dickinson)

Perpetual motion characterizes this tiny song—a portrait in sound of the busy bee. Nonstop sixteenth notes in the right hand of the piano continue throughout the song, chromatic and colorful. As the bee searches for other flowers to conquer, so the voice and piano pass quickly through many harmonies in search of the final cadence. Farwell has crafted this charming little song with skill; its delicacy seems artless and easily achieved.

Extended Study List

Two Songs on Poems of William Blake • Drake's Drum • *Love's Secret* • *Three Indian Songs* • From *Thirty-Four Songs on Poems of Emily Dickinson* (published in two volumes): Summer's Armies (v.1) • Tie the Strings to My Life (v.2) • Ample Make This Bed (v.2) • I'm Nobody (v.2) • These Saw Vision (v.1) • Presentiment (v.1) • And I'm a Rose! (v.2)

Selected Reading

Evelyn Davis Culbertson, *He Heard America Singing: Arthur Farwell, Composer and Crusading Music Educator* (Metuchen, New Jersey: Scarecrow Press, Inc., 1992). Composers of North America, No. 9.

Brice Farwell, *A Guide to the Music of Arthur Farwell and to the Microfilm Collection of his Work* (Briarcliff Manor, New York: 1972).

Paul Sperry, Liner notes to *Paul Sperry Sings Romantic American Songs*. Albany Records TROY 043, 1990.

Notes

1. Quoted in Evelyn Davis Culbertson, *He Heard America Singing*, 673.
2. Ibid., 426. In a letter to William Treat Upton to congratulate him on his *Art Song in America*, Farwell questioned Upton's use of "modernity" to describe his songs.
3. Ibid., 446. In a letter written several years before his death to his friend Noble Kreider, Farwell expressed concern over the fate of his songs. Schirmer was liquidating the songs they published. Farwell lamented his neglect in trying to interest singers in his work. He felt that in the long run the Dickinson songs would "prove a real contribution to American song literature."

CHARLES IVES (1874-1954)

There is a great Man living in this country—a composer. He has solved the problem of how to preserve one's self and to learn. He responds to negligence by contempt. He is not forced to accept praise or blame. His name is Ives.

—Arnold Schoenberg[1]

I have a rough voice, but I can make a noise on the right note at the right time and on the right interval—and, in spite of the piano, get the song going somewhere. Any singer can do the same thing if he makes up his mind to it, unless he is a congenital musical defective, or with about the same musical mentality that is sometimes the possession of famous operatic stars.

—Charles Ives, speaking about the "difficulty" of his songs.[2]

Charles Ives was an American original, never compromising his musical convictions. He believed music needed to say something, and to that end, the idea, text, and music were inextricably linked. But he was so innovative, experimental, and far ahead of his time that his contemporaries were unable to accept or appreciate his music. He paid a heavy price for his musical philosophy; he was considered a musical eccentric and during the major part of his life suffered artistic and critical isolation from the musical establishment. His music was largely ignored or dismissed as "unplayable," and Ives waited years for most of his works to be performed. When recognition finally came (he received a Pulitzer Prize for his *Third Symphony* in 1947), it was almost twenty years after he had completely stopped composing.

Ives deeply embraced the freedom to experiment with musical ideas, which resulted in many twentieth-century compositional techniques, ranging from cluster chords to polytonality. His groundbreaking musical features actually predate, by several decades, the later "avant-garde" works of Schoenberg, Prokofiev, and Stravinsky.

Ives was inspired by his native New England—its hymn tunes, village bands, personalities, color and history. The strongest influence on his compositions was his father, George Edward Ives (1845-94), a trained musician and expert band leader, who passed his own attitudes toward freely experimenting with music on to his son.

Ives's 151 songs clearly show his musical individuality. The majority of his songs may be found in *114 Songs*, one of three works Ives printed at his own expense and distributed free of charge to lists of prominent musicians and personal friends.* This extraordinary collection of songs vividly displays Ives's obsession with sound and its expressive qualities, and the collection includes a wide range of texts, topics, and musical styles.

Aaron Copland wrote about *114 Songs* in 1933:

> The first impression…is bound to be one of confusion. For there is no order here—either of chronology, style, or quality…Almost every kind of song imaginable can be found—delicate lyrics, dramatic poems, sentimental ballads, German, French, Italian songs, war songs, songs of religious sentiment, street songs, humorous songs, hymn tunes, folk tunes, encore songs; songs adapted from orchestral scores, piano works, and violin sonatas; intimate songs, cowboy songs and mass songs. Songs of every character and description, songs bristling with dissonances, tone clusters and 'elbow' chords next to songs of the most elementary harmonic simplicity.[3]

Ives wrote an extended postface to *114 Songs*, which is typical of Ives in its feeling and directness:

> Some have written a book for money; I have not. Some for fame; I have not. Some for love; I have not. Some for kindlings; I have not. I have not written a book for any of these reasons or for all of them together. In fact, gentle borrower, I have not written a book at all—I have merely cleaned house. All that is left is out on the clothes line,—but it's good for a man's vanity to have the neighbors see him—on the clothes line.[4]

Ives's concluding paragraph of the postface to *114 Songs* is characterized by Howard Boatright as "a sort of declaration of rights for a song," and "the best possible introduction to Ives's idea of a song's function."[5] quoted in part below:**

> A song has a few rights, the same as other ordinary citizen…If it feels like kicking over an ash can, a poet's castle, or the prosodic law, will you stop it? Must it always be a polite triad…a ribbon to match the voice? Should it not be free at times from the dominion of the thorax, the diaphragm, the ear, and other points of interest?…Should it not have a chance to sing to itself, if it can sing?…If it happens to feel like trying to fly where humans cannot fly, to sing what cannot be sung…who shall stop it?—in short, must a song always be a song![6]

*The other two publications were *The Concord Sonata* and *Essays Before a Sonata*. Ives's remaining songs were published at a later date by John Kirkpatrick.

**The reader is urged to read the postface in its entirety.

General William Booth Enters Into Heaven   1914
(Vachel Lindsay)

William Booth, the first commander of the Salvation Army, is celebrated in this powerful song. It is so broad and complex that it resembles a huge musical canvas upon which Ives paints the frenzy of a religious revival, which he referred to in his *Memos* as "a Glory trance."[7] He is able to translate all the drama of Vachel Lindsay's poem into a gripping musical setting by using an amazing array of compositional techniques: complex rhythmic organization, additive structures, use of quotation, harmonic dissonance, and vocal passages built on narrow-range, speech-like figures—all trademarks of Ives's musical style. It is considered by many to be Ives's greatest song.

The opening measures contain a piano line of clustered chords, imitating Booth banging his revivalist drum, which draws us in immediately. Like a preacher roaring fire-and-brimstone, Ives gives General Booth the persistent phrase "Are you washed in the blood of the lamb?", which is repeated throughout, creating the persuasive and intense atmosphere familiar to the tent-revival. The narrow-range vocal phrase "round and round" ("Booth saw not, but led his queer ones round and round") is repeated four times to a circling piano figure—another example of rich text painting and effective text repetition. Ives also embeds the hymn-tune "There Is a Fountain" in the piano part, breaking the phrase into fragments and weaving those fragments through the accompaniment. The tension does not let up throughout this long song, and continues to build until the final measures.

In the text, Lindsay's poems quotes the words of the Salvation Army hymn "Are you washed in the blood of the Lamb?" while in the music, Ives quotes Lowell Mason's revivalist hymn "There Is a Fountain" ("There is a fountain filled with blood, drawn from Immanuel's veins"). Ives uses this hymn phrase to link each new musical section and repeats it numerous times for dramatic effect. He also sprinkles musical allusions to "Oh, dem Golden Slippers," "Reveille," and the gospel tune "Onward, Upward," throughout the song, even adding a brief suggestion of Handel's "Hallelujah" chorus when that word appears in the text.

After the intense buildup, Ives ends this song quietly. Low-pitched drumbeats fade into the distance and we hear an off-key version of the hymn for the last time, over which he writes "as a band marching away"—leaving the listeners with an inconclusive ending, calling for them to reflect on their own connection with the previous dramatic moments.

The Housatonic at Stockbridge   1921
(Robert Underwood Johnson)

Ives wrote in his *Memos*, "'The Housatonic at Stockbridge' was suggested by a Sunday morning walk that Mrs. Ives and I took near Stockbridge, the summer after we were married. We walked in the meadows along the river, and heard the distant singing from the church across the river. The mist had not entirely left the river bed, and the colors, the running water, the banks and elm trees were something that one would always remember."[8]

Like several of his songs, Ives originally wrote "The Housatonic at Stockbridge" as an instrumental piece. In 1921, he arranged it for voice and piano and included it in the last movement of *Three Places in New England* (originally titled *First Orchestral Set*).

"The Housatonic at Stockbridge" is an extremely complex song. It is one of his transcendental "stream-of-consciousness" songs in which divergent ideas are expressed simultaneously and freely, and the water represents the passing of time. To express the free flow of multiple ideas, Ives juxtaposes different, independent layers of music—a layer of diatonic harmonies on top of a layer of chromatic harmony. The song's tension keeps building through the overlap of the music which, like the river, moves inexorably towards the song's climax: "Let me tomorrow thy companion be, By fall and shallow to the adventurous sea!" The piano line contains two figures: the left hand plays a series of chords, the top of which forms an oscillating half-note figure that rocks back and forth beneath the music that the right hand plays, which is the material given to the strings in the original orchestral version. When the voice enters, it adds yet another layer of sound to the several layers already in motion, creating an effect of gently swirling waters.

Ives wrote in the score: "The small notes in the R.H. may be omitted, but if played should be scarcely audible. This song was originally written as a movement in a set of pieces for orchestra, in which it was intended that the upper strings, muted, be listened to separately or sub-consciously, as a kind of distant background of mists seen through the trees over a river valley—their parts bearing little or no relation to the tonality, etc. of the tune. It is difficult to reproduce this effect with piano."[9]

As with many Ives songs, this one contains an open-ended final measure in which Ives gives specific directions for the pedal, revealing a carefully "submerged" chord (*ppp*). The effect that this quiet contrast produces after the bombastic final chord (*fff*) is extraordinary.

At the River   1916
(Robert Lowry)

Aaron Copland also set this venerable hymn by Reverend Robert Lowry in his *Old American Songs*, though the two settings are quite different: Copland's treatment is simple and dignified; Ives's, more quizzical.

Ives interrupts the familiar melody with unexpected rhythms, surprises the listener with altered chords, and irreverently cadences the music on a "blue-note" chord before the hymn's refrain appears. He modulates to another key before the song closes with a dislocated rhythm in the vocal line and adds a hesitant cadence that seems loathe to accept the invitation implicit in the text. This technique creates an unfinished quality, a suspension of mental flow for listeners that requires them to finish the phrase or "create" an ending—a device commonly used with the stream-of-consciousness technique.

Memories. A—Very Pleasant, B—Rather Sad   1897
(Charles Ives)

Ives's predilection for boyhood memories produced some of his most moving vocal works. In "Memories," "The Things Our Fathers Loved," "Tom Sails Away," and "The Circus Band," Ives recalls past experiences, usually from childhood. According to Starr, the texts Ives chose for these songs are written in the present tense, demonstrating that memories are a living part of the present.[10]

"Memories" consists of two contrasting sections, each a short song in itself. The first memory (Very Pleasant) pictures two children eagerly waiting for the curtain to rise in the "opera house." Its melody is jaunty, and excited, set to a nonstop "as fast as possible" tempo. The rapid movement conveys a sense of wide-eyed anticipation, impatience at having to wait, and nervous tension as the two children "whistle and hum and beat time with the drum." The song also includes a phrase for the singer to whistle.

The second song segment, marked *Adagio* (Rather Sad), paints a nostalgic picture of the singer's uncle who always hummed a little wordless tune as he went about his daily activities. The simple melody ("'twas a common little thing, and kind 'a sweet") is set over a piano figure of equal simplicity. Together the melody and accompaniment create a sweetly poignant character sketch.

The Things Our Fathers Loved   1917
(Charles Ives)

In this song, Ives fuses his recollections of childhood and his close relationship with his father, producing an intensely emotional, patriotic text. The song is rich in music quoted from other songs that are distinctly American. Fragments from "Dixie," "My Old Kentucky Home," "On the Banks of the Wabash," "Sweet Bye and Bye," and the hymn "Nettleton" appear at various places in the voice and piano lines.

Ives accompanies each new image in the text with melodic or rhythmic transitions in the piano and/or the vocal line; sprightly marching rhythms that herald the village cornet band, dotted vocal rhythms that recall the organ on Main Street, a melodic fragment in the piano that accompanies Aunt Sarah as she hums gospels on her front porch, and an excited buildup of texture, tempo, and pitch that occurs as the town decks itself out for a holiday celebration. Each of these changes seems extremely short but builds effectively to the song's climax, "Now, hear the songs!"

To build cohesion among the diverse song quotations, Ives uses the interval of a third, which predominates through the vocal line and is also found in the melody and harmony of the piano accompaniment.[11] This interval provides a strong sense of tonality that supports the various "tunes" as they are remembered.

Ives maintains an atmosphere of wonder in the song's concluding measures. Instead of following the song's climax with a broad, decisive ending phrase, he returns to the mood of the song's beginning—an unfinished, open-ended vocal and piano phrase, reminding us that memories are elusive.

Tom Sails Away   1917
(Charles Ives)

"Tom Sails Away" is the third song in a group titled *Three Songs of War,* a set that also contains "In Flanders Fields" and "He Is There!" Its genesis was a rejected sketch for Ives's *Third Violin Sonata.*[12] It is one of Ives's most poignant songs—a cluster of childhood memories, viewed retrospectively. It recalls a series of warm family memories clouded by the wrenching leave-taking of brother Tom for World War I.

In this song, Ives evolved a musical texture that invites a return to the past. He often layers sounds or writes overlapping figures to produce a quiet, nostalgic mood. Here he blurs rhythm in the beginning of the song, creating an atmosphere of misty recall ("Scenes from my childhood are with me"). Combined, the piano figures and a languid vocal line produce an impressionistic feeling of free-floating meter. As the texture dissolves into free polyrhythms and polyharmonies, it creates a meterless kind of musical impressionism reminding us of the flow of time.

Ives introduces a new section with a memory of "Mother," followed by "Daddy's" return home from the mill. These happy memories disperse as Tom leaves ("But today! In freedom's cause Tom sailed away"). Now Ives quotes from the war tune "Over There"—each repetition slower and more wistful than the one before, until, without our realizing it, the jaunty march tune becomes a variation of "Taps" and we become aware that Tom may not return home. In a masterful stroke, Ives integrates the quotation into the song's emotional fabric. A return to the beginning piano and vocal lines concludes the song.

The Circus Band   1894
(Charles Ives)*

Ives composed this song while at Yale University. It is a joyous boyhood memory of the day the circus came to town. This stirring march "in quickstep time" recalls the exhilaration of watching the circus parade down Main Street with all its color, noise, and excitement.

"Hear the trombones!" Ives marks under the octaves in the pianist's left hand as a little interlude builds up to the final refrain. Ives sprinkled many such comments throughout his songs, asking the pianist (or singer) to shout it out during the performance or guiding them to interpretation. The piano accompaniment is densely textured throughout; the vocal line is buoyant and rhythmically driven.

At the conclusion of the second verse, Ives pops an ending phrase out of rhythmic sync ("that golden hair is all her own"), giving us the impression that the marchers have fallen out of step. Ives also sprinkles some "wrong" notes liberally throughout the chords to remind us of the typical small town amateur band— always enthusiastic but seldom perfect. "Circus Band" is a lifelike panorama of small-town life in a bygone day.

---

*"The Circus Band" is the last in a set of five songs that Ives called *Five Street Pieces.* Other songs in the group are "Old Home Day," "In the Alley," " A Son of a Gambolier," and "Down East."

The Cage   1906
(Charles Ives)

"The Cage" is Ives's shortest song, and probably his most enigmatic. There is no indicated meter. The text consists of two narrative lines ushered in by a measure that is repeated "two or three times" before the voice begins. This musical pattern sets the stage for the pacing leopard, quietly padding in circles behind the bars of his cage. This section is marked "Evenly and mechanically, no ritard., descres., accel., etc.,"[13] by Ives.

Ives constructs a vocal line of unmetered eighth notes which imitates the leopard's unvarying tread, interrupted only occasionally by longer note values. Broadly spaced chords in the piano also advance with even speed, pausing only twice to punctuate the pace with a rolled chord. Variances in piano and vocal lines occur at different places, creating an unbalanced feeling.

Despite the absence of indicated meter, Ives's song is tightly constructed. The one-phrase vocal line consists of whole-tone scale segments, and the piano chords are stacked on perfect fourths (the cage). Each line proceeds on its own but they intersect at various points along the way. One last staccato eighth note in the vocal part hangs over at the end of the song. "Is life anything like that?" muses Ives.

Charlie Rutlage   1920-1921
(D.J. O'Malley)

This song has been called "the greatest country-and-western number never to be performed at the Grand Ole Opry."[14] It is a graphic description of a cowpuncher who meets his death during a spring roundup. The song's text came from the 1920 printing of *Cowboy Songs* collected by John A. Lomax.

Ives begins Charlie's story with a rhythmic, rugged western tune that is eventually interrupted by a section of rhythmic speech, an account of Charlie's demise. Ives notates the precise rhythms to be spoken, but without approximation of pitch. "The notes," writes Ives, "are indicated only approximately; the time of course, is the main point."[15]

As the narration begins, Ives writes above the piano part "Whoopee ti yi yo, git along little dogies, Whoopee ti yi yo, etc." Tempo and dynamics in the spoken section are carefully orchestrated by Ives: "a little slower," "fast again," "*ff*," "faster and faster," "louder and louder," until the accelerated tumult reaches *ffff* ("at that moment...his horse turned and fell with him..."). The pianist punctuates the moment with fists on chord clusters. After a brief moment of reflection on the horror of the scene, the rocking gait of the opening bars resumes and the song closes as Charlie (we hope) reaches the portals of the Golden Gate.

In "Charlie Rutlage," Ives has given us a little slice of what, for many, represents the flavor of the West. It even seems fitting for the singer to adopt a vocal "twang" when performing this rollicking cowboy ballad.

Extended Study List
The Children's Hour • The Camp Meeting • There is a Lane • A Christmas Carol • Chanson de Florian • Walking • In the Alley • His Exaltation • Serenity • Ann Street • Grantchester • Down East • The White Gulls • When Stars are in the Quiet Skies • West London • A Sea Dirge • Requiem • Two Little Flowers • I Travelled among Unknown Men • Feldeinsamkeit • Son of a Gambolier • The Side-Show • Mists • Like a Sick Eagle • Songs My Mother Taught Me • Thoreau • Kären • from "The Swimmers"

Selected Reading

Geoffrey Block, *Charles Ives: A Bio-Bibliography* (Westport, Connecticut: Greenwood Press, 1988).

Howard Boatwright, "The Songs," *Music Educator's Journal* 61:2 (October 1974); 42-47. Issue devoted to the Charles Ives Centennial.

J. Peter Burkholder. *All Made of Tunes: Charles Ives and His Use of Musical Borrowing* (New Haven: Yale UniversityPress, 1995).

Henry Cowell and Sidney Cowell, *Charles Ives and His Music* (New York: Oxford University Press, 1955).

Stuart Feder, *Charles Ives "My Father's Song." A Psychoanalytic Biography* (New Haven & London: Yale University Press, 1992). Focuses on the mental life of the artist, particularly the influence of his father on his work.

H. Wiley Hitchcock, *Ives* (London: Oxford University Press, 1977). Oxford Studies of Composers, No. 14.

Charles Ives, *Memos*, ed. John Kirkpatrick (New York: W. W. Norton & Co., Inc. 1991). Ives's writings catalogued. A valuable source for Ives's life as a musician.

___, "Postface," 114 *Songs* (West Redding, Connecticut: C. E. Ives, 1922).

Vivian Perlis, *Charles Ives Remembered: An Oral History* (New Haven: Yale University Press, 1974).

Rosalie Sandra Perry, *Charles Ives and the American Mind* (Kent, Ohio: The Kent State University Press, 1974).

Frank R. Rossiter, *Charles Ives and His America* (New York: Liveright, 1975).

Gayle Sherwood, *Charles Ives: a guide to research* (New York & London: Routledge, 2002).

Larry Starr, *A Union of Diversities: Style in the Music of Charles Ives* (New York: Schirmer Books, 1992). An examination of Ives's music using his songs as the medium of study and the means of addressing his musical thought processes. Excellent analytical material on the songs annotated above.

David Wooldridge, *From the Steeples and Mountains: A Study of Charles Ives* (New York: Alfred A. Knopf, 1974).

Notes

1. Schoenberg's widow found this note in his papers after his death. Quoted in *Music Educators Journal*, 61:2 (October, 1974), 62. This issue is devoted to the Ives Centennial.
2. Charles Ives, *Memos*, ed. John Kirkpatrick, 142.
3. Aaron Copland, "The Ives Case," in *The New Music: 1900-1960* (New York: W. W. Norton, 1968), 112.
4. Charles Ives, Postface to *114 Songs*.
5. Howard Boatright, "The Songs," *Music Educators Journal* 61:2, 74.
6. Ives, *Essays*, 130-31.
7. Ruth Friedberg, *American Art Song and American Poetry,* Vol. 1, 127.
8. Ives, *Memos*, 87.
9. Ives, *114 Songs*, 31.
10. Larry Starr, *A Union of Diversities: Style in the Music of Charles Ives*, 69.
11. Ibid., 64.
12. Ives, *Memos*, 171.
13. Ives, *114 Songs*, 114.
14. Starr, *A Union of Diversities,* 112.
15. Ives, *114 Songs*, 22.

CHARLES GRIFFES (1884-1920)

> Griffes's music is almost always elegant, exquisitely crafted, and controlled. He never overstates the obvious, nor does he allow pride of technique to enter the process.
>
> —Donna Anderson[1]

Charles Tomlinson Griffes was one of America's first important composers, creating a substantial body of work during his brief lifetime. The fine quality of his work was never disputed, but after his death, his popularity languished. Recently, scholarly interest in his compositions, new publications of his songs, and recorded performances of his works have brought Griffes to the public's attention once again.

The majority of Griffes's songs are written in German and English. Songs he wrote during his study in Germany (with Engelbert Humperdinck) show influences of German romantic style. Griffes's German songs did not break any new musical ground; they are most notable for assimilating the German Romantic *Lieder* tradition of Brahms and Strauss. Griffes's developing style began to appear in these songs. He was attracted by texts of nostalgia and sadness, and German poetry furnished him with many choices.

After 1911, when he began setting English texts, his songs began to veer towards the Impressionistic style. His English songs exhibit a wider range of mood and style than those with German texts. His list of songs includes twenty-five songs with German texts and thirty-four songs with English texts (including English translations of Chinese, Japanese and Romanian texts).

His instinctive sense of synthesizing word and tone, his gift for melody, and his sensitivity to harmony make his songs effective and appealing. Also, his under-standing of the human voice allowed him to write sympathetically for the voice. Griffes's vocal phrases are elegant and lyrical.

Griffes was a voracious reader and eclectic in his choice of texts. Fluent in German, French, and Italian, he preferred to read books in their original languages. His wide-ranging taste in literature and poetry is evident in the rich variety and scope of his songs. He was especially drawn to books whose authors used pictorial and descriptive language. Not surprisingly, Griffes was also an avid photographer.

Griffes produced original and creative music that we often categorize into differ-ent "styles"—romantic, impressionistic, oriental, and abstract. But in making neat "classifications" of Griffes's songs, we should remember that his songs sprang from his sensitivity to words and his desire to translate the essence of poetry into sound.

His catalogue of songs is modest in size but not in quality or significance. Griffes's songs represent a valuable contribution to American song literature. Distinguished music historian Gilbert Chase summed up his stature as a composer: "Griffes's major works are American classics; his songs are among the best we have."[2]

Lament of Ian the Proud, Op. 11, No. 1   1918
(*Three Poems by Fiona MacLeod**)

This three-song set ("Lament of Ian the Proud," "Thy Dark Eyes to Mine," and "The Rose of the Night") represents Griffes at the peak of his artistic and technical command. Each song features extraordinary melodic interaction between the voice and piano. Griffes orchestrated the songs around 1918, the form in which he had originally conceived the set. With the exceptions of these orchestrations written for the Fiona MacLeod songs, all of his songs are composed for voice and piano.

"The Lament of Ian the Proud" is a dramatic song that critics have called Griffes's finest and one of the great songs of the English language. Griffes created an extraordinary musical setting for Fiona MacLeod's poem, which was inspired by Gaelic legend, capturing its emotion and drama in a colorful sweep of sound in a through-composed setting. His writing for voice and piano is highly chromatic throughout the song.

Ian's tragic lament, "O blown whirling leaf, And the old grief, And wind crying to me who am old and blind," is portrayed by haunting music, opening with a small mysterious leitmotiv that Griffes uses throughout the song. It appears in the piano texture numerous times, often altered slightly. Griffes also begins several vocal phrases with its rhythm.

As the old Scot recalls his memories—especially the stone on the moor that marks the grave of his beloved ("she will return no more ")—Griffes builds intensi-ty toward the final emotional climax. These last eight measures are one of the unforgettable moments in any of Griffes's songs. Here melody, harmony, and rhythm combine to portray the anguish of Ian, who nonetheless squares his shoulders to proudly face the wind. Griffes closes this ballad-like story with one last recall of the leitmotiv that began the song.

*Fiona MacLeod was a pseudonym for Celtic poet William Sharp, who used the name primarily for his works about the mystical Celtic world.

Auf geheimem Waldespfade*   By a Lonely Forest Pathway. 1909
(Nikolaus Lenau, English version by Henry G. Chapman)

This song belongs to *Five German Poems* (1909), Griffes's first published songs. Griffes composed a substantial number of songs during his studies in Germany to texts by Heine, Lenau, Geibel, Mosen, and Eichendorff.

Lenau's poem is a forest scene, a familiar setting for German Romantic poets. A lonely lover wanders down a dark path, dreaming of his beloved, and imagines he hears her voice singing in the distance among the rustling leaves. Griffes was clearly influenced by German Romanticism in this song, which has been compared to the songs of Brahms and Strauss. Its expansive melodic line and richly textured accompaniment may have been induced by his German studies, but the song is uniquely Griffes in its expressive evocation of mood.

Griffes sets the scene in the piano with a sixteenth-note figure, which he changes to a triplet figure to introduce the second stanza. For the final stanza, he switches the meter to $\frac{6}{4}$ in a new tonality, and ends the song with a climactic vocal line that sweeps expressively from high to low, as the singing of the beloved dies away in the woods.

Often sung in English translation, this song probably remains one of Griffes's most familiar. In 1940, the song was arranged for three-part women's chorus with the title "By a Lonely Forest Pathway."

*For a comparison setting, see Robert Franz's musical interpretation of this poem.

Symphony in Yellow, Op. 3, No. 2   c. 1912
(Oscar Wilde)   **published in 1915**

Griffes's synthesizes impressionistic harmonies with Wilde's evocative text. His writing effectively sustains Wilde's mood of suspended animation expressed in the line "The thick fog hangs along the quay." A fluid vocal line above an accompaniment of block harmonies —7th, 9th, augmented, and diminished chords—gives the song a quality that is static but not monotonous. He also blurs the rhythmic flow—the vocal line is written in triple meter, but heard against the piano rhythms, it seems to be in two.

Wilde's line "crawls like a butterfly" is accompanied by an ostinato of four half-note chords, the first pair descending, and the second ascending. The swaying rhythm gently shifts accents with ties over the barline. Griffes adds tiny chromatic alterations to the chords in the accompaniment—just enough to make the B major tonality hazy; the vocal line stays within the key, moving in regular four-beat patterns. The combination of rhythms and harmonies in voice and piano produces a lazy, blurred effect, perfectly depicting the content of the poetry.

Extended Study List

Song of the Dagger • Pierrot • Auf ihrem Grab • The Half-Ring Moon • The Vale of Dreams • The Rose of the Night • Phantoms • Tears • Meeres Stille • Mein Herz ist wie die dunkle Nacht • Two Birds Flew into the Sunset Glow • Thy Dark Eyes to Mine • We'll to the Woods, and Gather May • The Fountain of the Acqua Paola

Selected Reading

Donna K. Anderson, *Charles T. Grifffes: A Life in Music* (Washington: Smithsonian Institution Press, 1993).

_____,*The Works of Charles T. Griffes: A Descriptive Catalogue* (Ann Arbor: UMI Research Press, 1983).

Marion Bauer, "Charles Griffes as I Remember Him," *Musical Quarterly* 29 (July 1943): 355-380.

Josepha Kennedy, "The Song Cycles of Charles Tomlinson Griffes," *Journal of Singing* 55 (Sept. 1998), 17.

Edward M. Maisel, *Charles T. Griffes: The Life of an American Composer* (New York: DaCapo Press, 1972, updated 1984).

John V. Moore and David M. Reeves, "The Published German Songs of Charles T. Griffes," *The NATS Journal,* 41:2 (Nov/Dec 1984).

William Treat Upton, "The Songs of Charles T. Griffes," *Musical Quarterly* 9 (1923): 314-328.

Notes

1. Donna K. Anderson, *Charles T. Griffes: A Life in Music*, 221.
2. Gilbert Chase, *America's Music*, 522.

VIRGIL THOMSON (1896-1989)

A good melody is not just a poem's new suit. It must be a new skin, inseparable.
—Virgil Thomson[1]

Virgil Thomson was one of the most significant composers of the twentieth century as well as one of its most perceptive music critics and authors. He composed over three hundred musical works, including three operas: *Four Saints in Three Acts, The Mother of Us All,* and *Lord Byron.* His overall catalog includes eighty-odd vocal works, most for piano and voice, others for voice and instrumental combinations.

Thomson was one of the many pupils of Nadia Boulanger. He spent part of his career in Paris (from September 1925 until 1940) with only brief periods away. In Paris, his circle of friends included Darius Milhaud, Erik Satie, Jean Cocteau, André Gide, Pablo Picasso, and F. Scott Fitzgerald. But the most important influence on his musical career was Gertrude Stein. Stein and Thomson were close friends throughout their lives. Thomson set several of Stein's texts as songs and she provided the libretti for two of his operas, *Four Saints in Three Acts* (1934) and *The Mother of Us All* (1946).

From 1940 to 1954, Thomson was the music critic for *The New York Herald Tribune*, where his insightful music commentaries established him as one of the major critics of the day. He also founded the New York Music Critics' Circle , which from 1941 to 1965 gave annual awards for excellence to works that premiered in New York.

During the course of his distinguished musical career, Thomson was the recipient of numerous awards and honors, including the Pulitzer Prize (1949), a Guggenheim Fellowship, and the Kennedy Center Lifetime Achievement Award.

Thomson's songs are characterized by a simple style devoid of musical "gimmicks." His style is rooted in his Missouri Baptist boyhood but flavored with the stimulating milieu of Paris in the early years of the twentieth century.

Thomson worked primarily within diatonic boundaries, displaying his classic sense of form. He integrated modern idioms into his own individual style, but his songs retain an expressive charm which is always easy to listen to. Speaking of style, Thomson said, "It is not something you do, style is something you have. And if you have it, you don't have to think about it."[2]

Thomson was fastidious in his prosody, his attention to declamation no doubt fueled by his literary talent. He usually wrote vocal lines in short phrases or units that communicate poetic meaning. Thomson discussed his approach to setting English words in *Music With Words:* "The transmission of thoughts or of feelings requires that the words be pronounced (or read) as word-groups. Word-groups and groups of word-groups...are where communication begins...They are the minimal transmission units of either speech or song."[3]

Thomson highlighted his texts with music that articulated the poetic framework: "A piece of vocal music is primarily music. The words are received much more slowly. No wonder they must be set with precision, articulated with love, and projected with a constant care. They are related to the musical idea that frames and explains them."[4]

He was eclectic in his choice of texts. He wrote songs to old English texts, Spanish texts, and Shakespeare. His poets included William Blake, John Donne, Tennyson, Kenneth Koch, Marianne Moore, Thomas Campion, and his good friend Gertrude Stein.

Despite the deceiving sense of simplicity in all his work, it is always spiced with Thomson's sophisticated sense of wit and satire. Author Edward Albee once described Thomson as "a man whose wisdom is offhand but whose wit is serious."[5]

Virgil Thomson seemed able to provide a musical equivalency for the voices of widely diverse poets: the whimsy of Marianne Moore, the bizarre humor of Gertrude Stein, the elegant charm of Thomas Campion, the complicated vernacular of Shakespeare. The songs vary widely in musical effect. His accompaniments are wide in range—stark contrapuntal figures, simple triadic arpeggios, and dense chordal textures. Thomson's nearly seventy songs display an amazing spectrum of mood and color, and a masterful style that blends simplicity and sophistication. His simplicity never loses its intelligence or its polish.

Sigh no more, ladies*   1957
(William Shakespeare, from *Much Ado About Nothing*)

Thomson's Shakespeare set contains four other songs: "Was This Fair Face the Cause?" (*All's Well That Ends Well*), "Tell Me Where is Fancy Bred" (Incidental music to *The Merchant of Venice*), "Pardon, Goddess of the Night" (Incidental music to *Much Ado About Nothing*) and "Take o take those lips away" (*Measure for Measure*).

This song, like "Take, o take those lips away," is intended for a male voice. The vocal line is playful and reminiscent of a dance, full of shifting word stresses. It is supported by a lively rhythmic accompaniment with a marked Spanish flavor.

"The song and its accompaniment recall the *fandango*, also the Spanish guitar, vastly popular during Elizabethan times," wrote Thomson. "There is no overt attempt to take us to Venice, though Spain, as the chief world power, was felt as strongly there as in England. The hey-nonny refrain is a pattern, probably of English origin."[6]

*For comparison settings, see Geoffrey Bush, Peter Warlock, and Mario Castelnuovo-Tedesco.

A Prayer to St. Catherine   1959
(Kenneth Koch)

This song is from *Mostly About Love,* a set of four songs on Kenneth Koch's poems. Originally titled *Songs for Alice Esty,* the group also includes "Love Song," "Down At the Docks," and "Let's Take a Walk."

"A Prayer to St. Catherine" is an innocent, heartfelt entreaty to St. Catherine of Siena to cure the singer of chronic shyness and heartache. The musical setting balances the devout naïveté of the singer with witty allusions to St. Nicholas and St. Joanna.

The vocal line is disarming in its simplicity; set in declamatory style, it is an earnest plea to the Saint of Siena which sounds more like a heart-to-heart conversation. The accompaniment contains simple chords that point up the confessional quality of the vocal line and evoke the sound of tolling church bells.

For all its charm, the song contains a deeper expressive quality. It is a perfect example of Thomson's ability to capture an emotional mood and atmosphere by the simplest means.

If Thou a Reason Dost Desire to Know   1955-58
(Sir Francis Kynaston)

Composer John Cage describes this as "a love song, the text intellectually conceived, for it concludes with a statement of the ultimate separation of body and soul."[7]

Thomson's setting begins in D major and ends in C major. The song opens with a vocal line counterpointed against a single melodic piano line. As the song progresses toward its climax, the texture thickens and the harmonic tension builds. En route, diatonic harmonies accompany the poet's description of physical pleasures and builds to a musically graphic climax. Here the accompaniment features whole-tone clusters which quickly unravel to return to the beginning figurations. The song concludes with an incomplete cadence in the voice, finished conclusively in the piano.

Take, o take those lips away*   1956
(William Shakespeare, from *Measure for Measure*)

A crystalline, haunting melody is the outstanding element in this song. Repeated twice, the melody is melting in its expressive simplicity and must be counted among Thomson's most lyrical creations. "The melody is arpeggiated, the accompaniment guitarlike. It also suggests the horn. According to Shakespeare, the events take place in Vienna, a locale long associated musically with the sound of hunting-horns."[8]

*For comparison settings, see Amy Beach and Peter Warlock.

Extended Study List

Four Songs of Thomas Campion • Preciosilla • The Tiger • English Usage • My Crow Pluto • *Five Songs from William Blake* • *La Belle en dormant* • *Praises and Prayers* • *Old English Songs* • Look, How the Floor of Heaven • Berceau de Gertrude Stein • At the Spring • Hot day at the seashore • Susie Asado

Selected Reading

Kathleen Hoover and John Cage, *Virgil Thomson: His Life and Music* (New York: Thomas Yoseloff, 1959).

Michael Meckna, *Virgil Thomson: A Bio-Bibliography* (New York: Greenwood Press, 1986). Bio-Bibliographies in Music Series, Number 4.

Tim Page and Vanessa Weeks Page, eds., *Selected Letters of Virgil Thomson* (New York: Summit Books, 1988).

Virgil Thomson, *Virgil Thomson* (London: Weidenfeld and Nicolson, 1962).

_____, *A Virgil Thomson Reader* (Boston: Houghton Mifflin Company, 1981). An extensive collection of Thomson's articles. Includes two conversations with Thomson.

_____, *Music With Words: A Composer's View* (New Haven: Yale University Press, 1989). Twelve essays on composing vocal music, described by Thomson as a "how-to book by a workman with experience in both writing and performing vocal music."

Notes

1. Virgil Thomson, *A Virgil Thomson Reader*. 356.
2. In an interview with Phillip Ramey, quoted in Michael Meckna, *Virgil Thomson: A Bio-Bibliography*, 136.
3. Virgil Thomson, *Music With Words: A Composer's View,* 17.
4. Ibid., 48.
5. Quoted in Meckna, 9.
6. *Music With Words*, 94.
7. Kathleen Hoover and John Cage, *Virgil Thomson: His Life and Music,* 240.
8. *Music With Words,* 92.

ERNST BACON (1898-1990)

> Music is feeling rather than fact. Its humanness, mystery, morality or exaltation remain implicit...The song brings this home, for it is nearer the source.
>
> —Ernst Bacon[1]

Ernst Bacon was a distinguished composer, pianist, conductor, and educator. A recipient of three Guggenheim fellowships and the Pulitzer Prize Award for his *Symphony in D minor*, his body of works includes symphonies, piano concertos, chamber music, ballets and more than 250 songs, as well as several books about music.

Born in Chicago in 1898, he was educated at Northwestern University, the University of Chicago, and the University of California. He studied piano with Alexander Raab and G.D. Dunn, composition with Ernest Bloch and Karl Weigl, and conducting with Eugene Goosens.

Bacon taught at the Eastman School, San Francisco Conservatory, Converse College, and at Syracuse University (1945-63, professor emeritus from 1964). During his long career, Bacon founded the Carmel Bach Festival, and was its first conductor.

His chief aim as a composer was to express the spirit of America in music as Whitman, Emerson, Melville and others did in literature. He was deeply interested in America's history and folklore; its indigenous music, poetry, folk songs, jazz rhythms and geography—as well as the landscape itself where he hiked, climbed, and also painted—all of these elements found their way into his music. Bacon composed a folk opera, *A Tree on the Plains*, which, according to some, was the inspiration for *Oklahoma!*[2]

The distinguished photographer Ansel Adams, a lifetime friend, whom he met in the 1920s, influenced Bacon's aesthetic. Other influences in his life included poet Carl Sandburg, author Thornton Wilder, and singer Roland Hayes. His song compositions were especially influenced by the texts of Emily Dickinson and Walt Whitman.

Bacon's songs have an easy lyricism about them—a flowing quality that is reminiscent of folk melodies. His excellent sense of prosody resulted in settings that capture the rhythm, weight, and color of words. An accomplished pianist, he composed accompaniments that are imaginative as well as supportive of the text. He enjoyed manipulating traditional harmonies, utilizing them in unusual ways in his piano accompaniments. His music has been characterized as graceful, yet unexpected. His sister, Madi Bacon, wrote that he had a wonderful sense of humor that gave his music an energy and vitality.[3]

Bacon's early songs are leaner in texture; his later songs are more complex, with a vastly expanded harmonic approach. These songs are notable for Bacon's mastery of formal structure and overall texture. For his songs, Bacon chose texts by Dickinson, Whitman, Blake, Brönte, Teasdale, Sandburg, Housman, and Shakespeare, among others.

It's All I Have to Bring* *(Five Poems of Emily Dickinson)*   c. 1944
(Emily Dickinson)

Ernst Bacon set sixty-seven of Emily Dickinson's poems.** His infatuation with her work produced lyrically imaginative miniatures which he often referred to as "water colors." Ellen Bacon, the composer's widow, writes:

> The discovery of Emily Dickinson's poems was a revelation to Bacon. In his words, she could "with an economy as great as the classical Chinese poets and painters, conjure ecstasy, poignancy, immensity, grief, passion, and intimacy with nature." Bacon...sometimes spoke of a "spiritual marriage" to her.[4]

In 1939, Bacon wrote to singer Marian Anderson:

> The poetry of Emily Dickinson has long seemed to me one of the great achievements of womankind. Her style of lyricism lends itself more perhaps than any other poetry of this country to musical setting, for it gives lyric expression to philosophical human thought without the latter being too apparent.[5]

"It's All I Have to Bring," is probably Bacon's best-known song. It is an uncomplicated setting with a warm, lyric vocal line and an accompaniment to match.

Dickinson's eight-line poem divides itself into two sections. To accommodate the flexible poetic meter, Bacon mixes duple and triple time.

---

*For a comparison setting, see Lori Laitman's "It's All I Have to Bring Today," from the collection *Fresh Patterns.*
**A special source for Bacon's Dickinson settings is the compact disc CRI American Masters series, *Songs of Charles Ives and Ernst Bacon*, CD 675, on which Bacon accompanies soprano Helen Boatwright in twenty-two of his Dickinson settings. These songs are divided into the following thematic categories: Love and Sentiment, Loss, Nature, and Time and Space.

To Make a Prairie *(Five Poems of Emily Dickinson)*   1944
(Emily Dickinson)

> *To make a prairie it takes a clover*
> *and one bee...*

This beguiling song is only twenty-five measures long. The industrious bee is heard in the piano accompaniment, darting from clover blossom to clover blossom, in playful dotted rhythms. Bacon builds the song around the interval of a minor third, which appears in the first vocal phrase and also in the bass line of the piano accompaniment. Accompaniment patterns are a simple example of late medieval hocket technique.[*]

Bacon illustrates the words "And revery" in the voice with a giddy little syncopated line that dances upward, accompanied by the playful bee's rhythm, and anchored by a waltz figure in the bass line. This is a sparkling miniature that one wants to hear again.

[*]Hocket: A medieval technique of staggering rests and short phrases between two or more voices to give a "hiccup" effect. Definition taken from Stanley Sadie, ed, with Alison Latham, *Stanley Sadie's Music Guide* (New York: Prentice-Hall, Inc., 1986), 536.

Fond Affection[*]
(Anonymous)

"Fond Affection" is a beautiful example of a melody that seems to "sing itself." The folk-like tune drifts over a simple, fluid accompaniment of broken chords, flavored with rhythmic syncopation. Harmonies in the accompaniment fluctuate gracefully, following the word stresses of the text. In the second section of the song, cross-rhythms, altered chords, dissonances, and unresolved harmonies are subtly blended into the piano lines, adding sophistication without compromising the simplicity and uncomplicated character of the overall texture.

There are three strophes, each differentiated by different piano figures After the third stanza, Bacon repeats the opening melody, this time sung by the singer as a wordless vocalise.

[*]The words are from Sandburg's *The Amercian Songbag*.

One Thought Ever at the Fore[*]   1930
(The Divine Ship)
(Walt Whitman)

> *One thought ever at the fore—*
> *That in the Divine Ship, the World, breasting Time and Space,*
> *All Peoples of the globe together sail, sail the same voyage,*
> *are bound to the same destination.*

The musical lyricism in Walt Whitman's poems inspired Bacon to compose some twenty songs to Whitman's texts.[**] Just as he had perfectly caught the spirit of Emily Dickinson's supple verses, Bacon also captured the breadth and vision of Whitman's words.

"One Thought Ever at the Fore" is a setting reminiscent of a church chorale. A

271

hymn-like vocal line contains echoes of the melodic shape of the doxology tune ("Praise God from Whom All Blessings Flow"). The melody is exalted but solemn, inexorably moving toward the final measures with unhurried dignity.

The organ-like piano accompaniment is a combination of chords, coupled with a moving line in the right hand that functions like an obbligato with the vocal line. The singer's static phrases float above, like a majestic descant.

---

*Whitman's poem, from *Old Age Echoes* (1891), is titled "One Thought Ever at the Fore." Bacon titled his song "The Divine Ship," although in an early publication it appears with Whitman's title.
**Over a thousand musical settings of Whitman's poems exist.

Omaha
(Carl Sandburg)

> *"A span of steel ties up the kin of Iowa and Nebraska*
> *Across the yellow big-hoofed Missouri River..."*

The Syracuse Post Standard reported: "Bacon, like Copland and Ives, wrote music whose breath smelled American."[6] Carl Sandburg was another favorite poet of Bacon. The two men became friends in the early 1920s. Sandburg's poetic realizations of America and his use of the dialect of the "common man" appealed to Bacon's desire to capture the spirit of the American people and culture in his music.

"Omaha" bursts with jazzy color and energy. Sandburg's poetry is packed with vibrant imagery. Bacon interprets the lusty humor of Sandburg's poem in a setting filled with syncopation, cross-rhythms, rhythmically articulated vocal writing, and colorful harmonies. Vocal lines are declamatory and rhythmically driven. Bacon uses several piano figurations that are underpinned with octaves, which add weight to the texture. One figure creates the illusion of a railroad train, roaring into Omaha, the city that "works to get the world its breakfast."

Extended Study List

Farewell to a Name and a Number • Is There Such a Thing as Day? • It's coming—the postponeless Creature • Brady • How Still the Bells • The Commonplace • Gentle Greeting • O Friend • The Red Rose • Schilflied • Wanderers Nachtlied • Velvet People • Stars • The Lamb • Ancient Carol • Alabaster Wool • The Snake • Grand Is the Seen • On This Wondrous Sea • Eternity • The Grass So Little Has To Do • Wild Nights • I'm Nobody • Lingering Last Drops

Selected Reading

Ernst Bacon, "A Re-Affirmation of Simplicity in Song Writing," *Journal of Singing,* 55:2, Nov/Dec. 1998, 17-20. With a foreword by Ellen Bacon.
John St. Edmunds, "The Songs of Ernst Bacon," "Ernst Bacon. Poetry in Search of Music." *Sewanee Review,* October 1941, 499-501.
Paul Horgan, "Ernst Bacon: A Contemporary Tribute," foreword to *Fifty Songs,* Dragon's Teeth Press, 1974.
Page Swift, "Ernst Bacon: The Man and His Songs." D.M.A. diss., Indiana University, 1982.

Notes

1. Ernst Bacon, "A Re-Affirmation of Simplicity in Song Writing," *Journal of Singing,* 55:2, 19. Also in liner notes to *Songs of Charles Ives and Ernst Bacon.* American Masters Series. Helen Boatwright, soprano; Ernst Bacon and John Kirkpatrick, pianists. Composers Rercording Inc., CD 675. 1994.
2. Ellen Bacon, copy from the Ernst Bacon Centennial flyer, advertising Bacon's centennial year. Published by the Ernst Bacon Society, Inc., 1998.
3. Madi Bacon, in a letter to the author. July 4, 1998.

4. Ellen Bacon, liner notes to *Fond Affection: Music of Ernst Bacon*, CRI, 2002.
5. Ernst Bacon, in a letter to Marian Anderson, 1939. Quoted in "Performances," *Emily Dickinson International Society Bulletin*, 7:1, May/June 1995, 7.
6. Quotation printed in the Ernst Bacon Centennial flyer, 1998.

JOHN DUKE (1899-1984)

Vocal utterance is at the basis of music's mystery. The thing that makes melody a concrete expression of feeling and not just a horizontal design in tones is its power to symbolize the pull, the tension of our feeling of duration.

It is the ability to feel how the text of a song is assimilated by the music which distinguishes the singer of real interpretative insight from the vocal virtuoso.

—John Duke[1-2]

John Duke produced nearly 265 songs, distinguished for their variety of style, skillful craftsmanship, and genuine expression. His songs are still not as well known as they should be—there are too few recordings of Duke's work, and singers tend to stick with the same selections rather than exploring the richness of his musical invention.

Duke began his musical education early in life with piano lessons. At age sixteen, he attended Peabody Conservatory in Baltimore as a scholarship student, studying piano and composition. After World War I, Duke settled in New York City, where he continued his musical studies and worked at the Ampico recording laboratories. In 1920 he presented his debut recital as a concert pianist.

Duke's first songs were published by G. Schirmer in 1923; that same year he joined the faculty at Smith College, where he taught until his retirement forty-four years later. During a year's sabbatical in 1929, he studied composition with Nadia Boulanger in Paris and piano with Arthur Schnabel in Berlin. He was named to the Henry Dike Sleeper Chair of Music in 1960 and given emeritus status. He continued to write songs until his death in 1984.

Duke's songs represent a major contribution to song literature of this century. No one was more surprised by this fact than Duke himself, who wrote in 1981: "I am still amazed at the way my musical career has turned out. In my early days, my ambition was to be great pianist, and I could not have believed anyone who told I was destined to be a song composer."[3]

The Mountains are Dancing   **1955**
(e. e. cummings)

The text is Number 67 from *XAIPE*,[*] a collection of poetry published in 1950. The title is Duke's. The poem's variations of sound and meaning pit love as "wishing, and having and giving" against "keeping and doubting." As in all of cummings's verse, rhythmic drive and alliteration are dominant factors.

Duke's setting is vivacious and outgoing, a joyous waltz in $\frac{3}{8}$ time. The vocal line is buoyant, dancing in steady eighth notes, its swinging steps broken only at the refrains by tied notes. Text illustration contrasts "wishing and having and giving" (rising lines) with "keeping and doubting" (descending lines). The high-note ending represents a last burst of energetic feeling in a wonderfully exciting and evocative song.

*A Greek word meaning "rejoice."

i carry your heart   1960
(e. e. cummings)

Duke marked his last setting of e.e. cummings with one of his most lyrical and romantic songs. He wrote flowing phrases for both voice and piano, blending them in a texture that moves freely through cumming's poetic complexities. Duke restructured the original word groupings so that, as the song progresses, they synthesize into a single thought.[4] At the coda, he recalls the primary vocal motive as well as the piano figures from the main body of the song.

Luke Havergal   1948
(Edwin Arlington Robinson)

Though Duke chose to omit one verse of the original poem, "Luke Havergal" is considered one of his finest songs. Duke set this song in ABA form, beginning with an extended piano prelude. The song's first and last sections are subdued as the mysterious messenger directs Luke Havergal to "the western gate."* The messenger's chilling description is found in the contrasting B section, in G-sharp minor.

Duke's musical treatment complements Robinson's mystical text. Piano figures combine to create a romantic texture that illustrates the drama and demonstrates Duke's masterful handling of the piano.

*"The western gate" is usually interpreted in this poem as a symbol for death.

Bells in the Rain   1946
(Elinor Wylie)

The sound of bells permeates the piano accompaniment throughout the entire song. The sound of tinkling wind chimes is created by a tiny motive of ascending sixteenth notes in the high register combined with fourths and fifths. Raindrops "ring like bells of glass." The vocal line is sustained and peacefully lyric against this unvaried accompaniment. This wonderful song is one of Duke's most effective atmospheric settings.

Loveliest of Trees   1928
(A.E. Housman)

This is one of Duke's finest and most popular songs. It belongs to his earliest group of song compositions, characterized by recurrent motivic piano figures. Duke's setting captures the fresh youthful atmosphere of Housman's verse perfectly.

A memorable melodic line is set over lilting piano figures, suggesting the swaying branches of the cherry tree. A charming little countermelody (developed from a rhythmic-melodic motive) in the piano complements and embellishes the vocal line. Both melodies are diatonic and based on triad outlines.

The center section of the song is delineated poetically by reflection on time passed, and musically by an enharmonic modulation to the minor key which expresses more intense emotion. The song closes with a modulation and variations of the music contained in the opening.

Extended Study List

Dirge • Stop All the Clocks • Acquainted With the Night • White in the moon the long road lies • To the Thawing Wind • The Last Word of a Bluebird • Miniver Cheevy • Rapunzel • Richard Cory • *Six Poems by Emily Dickinson* • Spring Thunder • Viennese Waltz • Little Elegy • Central Park at Dusk • There Will Be Stars

Selected Reading

John Duke, "Some Reflections on the Art Song in English," *The American Music Teacher,* 25:4.

____, "The Significance of Song," *Ars Lyrica* I (1981), 11-21.

____, "Words as Musical Elements," *The NATS Bulletin* (September 1954).

Ruth C. Friedberg, *American Art Song and American Poetry.* Vol. II. (Metuchen, NJ: The Scarecrow Press, 1984). Chapters 2 and 3 are devoted to Duke. Friedberg's writing on Duke is a rich source of information about his songs and musical style.

____, "The Songs of John Duke," *The NATS Bulletin,* 19:4 (1963). Excellent discussion of the songs to 1963, grouping them chronologically.

David Wheelock, liner notes, "Just-Spring: Art Songs of John Duke." Recorded Anthology of American Music, Inc. 80576-2, 2001.

Notes

1. Quoted in Friedberg, "The Songs of John Duke," *The NATS Bulletin,* 19:4 (1963), 8.
2. John Duke, "Words as Musical Elements," *The NATS Bulletin* (September, 1954), 5.
3. Quoted in Friedberg, *American Art Song and American Poetry,* Vol. II (Scarecrow Press, 1984), 45.
4. Friedberg, *American Art Song and American Poetry,* 115-116.

AARON COPLAND (1900-1990)

> Everything Aaron has written sounds as if it came out in a burst of joy.
> —Leo Smit[1]

For many, Aaron Copland is the quintessential American composer. In his music, he captures the openness of spirit embodied in America's landscape and evokes an emotional response consistent with American culture. He wrote with a fresh, direct style that quickly became symbolic of American values and ideals. He pioneered musical sound qualities that we immediately identify with Copland—qualities that are linked with a national, classic feeling of "populism." Works he composed during the 1930s and 40s most exemplify the "Copland sound": *Billy the Kid, Rodeo, Appalachian Spring, Lincoln Portrait, Fanfare for the Common Man.*

During his long career, Copland received numerous honors: among them, the Pulitzer Prize in 1945 (*Appalachian Spring*), a Guggenheim Fellowship, Kennedy Center Honors in 1979, and an Oscar for his film score for *The Heiress* (1949). Copland also wrote a number of books on music: *What to Listen for in Music* (1939), *Our New Music* (1941, revised in 1968 as *The New Music, 1900-1960*), *Music and Imagination,*(1952), and *Copland on Music,* (1963).

Apart from two sets of folk music arrangements (*Old American Songs*) and one song cycle (*Twelve Songs of Emily Dickinson*), Copland wrote only a handful of songs. He admitted that he never thought of himself as a vocal composer since his music really developed from essentially instrumental techniques.[2] Still, his two major vocal works continue to occupy a secure place in the American vocal repertoire.

Copland's songs are taut and direct; even within their lyricism, his songs contain the typical Copland precision. Copland's impact on American contemporary music is immense, far reaching and incalculable.

Old American Songs   1950, 1952

Set 1	Set 2
The Boatmen's Dance	The Little Horses
The Dodger	Zion's Walls
Long Time Ago	The Golden Willow Tree
Simple Gifts	At the River
I Bought Me A Cat	Ching-a-ring Chaw

Copland's *Old American Songs* is anarrangements of hymns, minstrel songs, and folk songs drawn from various sources. Copland's arrangements vary as to texture and mood and several contain sophisticated rhythmic and harmonic touches. The songs nonetheless retain the original flavor of the folk melodies and are effectively idiomatic in feeling and style.

Both sets of *Old American Songs* were originally composed for voice and piano and later scored for orchestra. Several of the songs are available in choral versions. Copland took a break from his work on *Twelve Poems of Emily Dickinson* to compose these sets: "I was finally up to number eleven, and I felt myself bogged down,"[3] Copland said.

The first set, premiered by Peter Pears and Benjamin Britten at the Aldeburgh Festival in June of 1950, consists of five songs from different rural areas in the United States. Encouraged by their success, Copland composed a second group of five songs especially for bass William Warfield who had sung the first American performance of the initial set. Copland completed the second set in 1952 and performed it with Warfield in July of 1953 at the Castle Hill Festival in Ipswich, Massachusetts.

First Set   1950

THE BOATMEN'S DANCE is a banjo melody by Dan D. Emmett (1815-1904), composer of the celebrated song hit "Dixie." This tune was published in 1843, the year Emmett began a tour of the British Isles with his Virginia Minstrels.

THE DODGER is a satire on the presidential campaign of 1884 in which James G. Laine ran against Grover Cleveland. The piano accompaniment imitates the sound of a minstrel show banjo.

LONG TIME AGO is an anonymous minstrel tune with words adapted by George Pope Morris (1802-1864) and musical setting by Charles Edward Horn (1786-1849), British composer and singer. Copland's arrangement of the somewhat sentimental melody is simple, yet romantic.

SIMPLE GIFTS is a popular Shaker hymn tune dating from the period 1837-47. The melody figures prominently in Copland's ballet *Appalachian Spring* (1944), where it provides the basis for the variations in that work. Copland sets the straightforward melodic line over simple hymn-like harmonies.

I BOUGHT ME A CAT is a children's nonsense song from Oklahoma. Its many animal characters contribute their particular "sound," building cumulatively to total confusion. The accompaniment imitates barnyard sounds in its figurations and harmony.

This song was a "leftover" from a canceled theater project of Copland and playwright Lynn Riggs. Riggs taught this ditty from his Oklahoma childhood to Copland. Copland always clapped his hands twice before the last line of each stanza, "my cat says fiddle-eye-fee."[4]

Second Set 1952

THE LITTLE HORSES is a children's lullaby from the southern states. It is based on a version found in J.A. and Alan Lomax's *Folk Song U.S.A.*

ZION'S WALLS is a revivalist song credited to John G. McCurry (1821-86), composer and compiler of tune books. Copland used this song in his opera *The Tender Land* (1954), where it appears in the finale of Act I. Copland wrote an original countermelody for the song's piano introduction.

THE GOLDEN WILLOW TREE is a variant on the Anglo-American ballad known as *The Golden Vanity*, a melody that was used by Benjamin Britten in his folk song settings. The piano accompaniment simulates the sound and figurations of a guitar.

AT THE RIVER is a popular evangelical hymn, with words and music written in 1865 by Rev. Robert Lowry. It has become a beloved and much-performed "sacred hit." The melody was also arranged by Charles Ives. Copland's stately treatment of this text recalls an organ accompaniment.

CHING-A-RING CHAW is a minstrel song published in 1833. The text was originally a humorous presentation of Haiti as an island paradise for blacks. Copland altered the words to avoid racist implications. He wrote a piano accompaniment reminiscent of a banjo for this jaunty tongue-twister. Copland also used this tune in *The Tender Land.*

---

*Twelve Poems of Emily Dickinson** 1949-50

Nature, the gentlest mother • There came a wind like a bugle •
Why do they shut me out of Heaven? • The world feels dusty • Heart, we will
forget him • Dear March, come in • Sleep is supposed to be •
When they come back • I felt a funeral in my brain • I've heard an organ
talk sometimes • Going to Heaven! • The Chariot

Emily Dickinson's poems have inspired musical settings by many composers. She was a prolific writer, yet only seven of her verses were published during her lifetime—and those were published anonymously. From the age of twenty-three, she lived as a recluse, a charming New England eccentric whose most daring act was writing poetry which she then put away, out of sight.

After Dickinson's death in 1886, her sister discovered a box containing some 900 of her poems. The poems were originally published with alterations—to appease the literary sensibilities of the Victorian times. Later publications presented the poems in their original unedited form.

Emily Dickinson's poetry has consistently tragic overtones. Themes of nature, death, life, and eternity run through her work. Her poetry displays a "lyrical expressive language" which Copland found "folklike, with irregular meters and stanzas and many unconventional devices. The songs center about no single theme, but they treat subject matter particularly close to Miss Dickinson...It was my hope...to create a musical counterpart to Emily Dickinson's unique personality."[5]

Twelve Songs of Emily Dickinson was Copland's first work for solo voice since 1928. Copland said that he "was accustomed to composing for piano, it was the vocal lines that were my real challenge. I followed the natural inflection of the words of the poems, particularly when they were conversational...The harmony is basically diatonic, with some chromaticism and polytonality, and much of the piano writing is contrapuntal."[6] Copland composed the cycle at Sneden's Landing, New York, between March 1949 and March 1950. He found the house and grounds lent themselves to the mood of the poetry he was setting: "...old-fashioned and romantic and somehow just right for the nineteenth-century New England poet with her love of nature."[7]

At twenty-eight minutes, the cycle is Copland's longest work for solo voice and poses significant technical and interpretive challenges for the performer. The twelve poems are ordered for emotional and dramatic impact. The songs are skillfully crafted and encompass a wide spectrum of musical expression. According to Copland, these settings are "intellectual and discreet." The songs are not linked in cyclical fashion by continuity of text or music; only two of the songs (the seventh and twelfth) are related musically. Each song stands alone and can be sung separately, but Copland preferred them to be performed as a cycle. Even though there is no series of connective elements linking the songs cyclically, when they are heard as a unit, they provide a cumulative emotional mood that propels the work forward.

Copland uses simple melodic material, which is marked by occasional outbursts of dissonance. Vocal lines contain wide, angular intervals; for example, all the songs have interval skips of a ninth up and a seventh down. Melodic patterns often repeat. Rhythmic patterns are simply constructed and often repeated. The piano accompaniment contains occasional word-painting. Frequent meter changes abound, sometimes from measure to measure. Prosody is not always fluid; at times musical ideas tend to overwhelm the texts. Word setting is generally syllabic with occasional melismas. The songs contain recurring fermatas. Copland provides explicit markings for dynamics, tempi, and nuance.

Soprano Phyllis Curtin was closely associated with the cycle and performed it often, with Copland at the piano. "It was Aaron who found the musical voice for Emily Dickinson, and the times when I sang them best, I had the feeling that she was speaking. . . I don't know that I think of them as cyclical, but I think of them as all part of Emily's life, as part of her personality, as part of her living in New England, so that they progress one to the other, but not in a story form."[8]

Copland's intuitive and spontaneous response to Dickinson's poetry inspired this work which ranks among the most important contributions to American art song.

NATURE, THE GENTLEST MOTHER. Transparent, clear textures in the piano evoke Nature's gentle concern for her children. The song's mood is pastoral. It contains word painting—an occasional birdcall, and fluttering grace notes in the introduction that imitate nature sounds. The key is E-flat major; the song is marked "Quite slow" and also "Crystalline."

THERE CAME A WIND LIKE A BUGLE. In dramatic contrast to the first song, Nature turns commanding and ominous. In this short song, the mood is fierce and musically dissonant, marked by jagged vocal lines and polytonality. Copland referred to the vocal melody as "bugle-like."[9]

WHY DO THEY SHUT ME OUT OF HEAVEN? Despite a charming mood of petulance, the poet is still filled with doubt. Vocal passages alternate between declamatory style and more lyric sections.

THE WORLD FEELS DUSTY. This song of love and death has a very slow tempo and an inconclusive final cadence. The radiant, expressive vocal line is typical of Copland's simple musical style.

HEART, WE WILL FORGET HIM. In this quiet love song, the poet addresses her heart, but doubts her own resolve. Marked "Very slowly," the music maintains a feeling of ambiguity mixed with undisguised and intense emotion.

DEAR MARCH, COME IN. Nervous elation over the coming spring is revealed in a flustered, chattering song. March and April are personified as exuberant but hesitant guests, each welcomed with a key change. The song is in $\frac{6}{8}$ meter. Repeated rhythms in the piano accompaniment perpetuate the bustling mood.

SLEEP IS SUPPOSED TO BE. In this song, Copland introduces the single thematic link in the cycle, the dotted-rhythm motive that appears in the closing song, "The Chariot." Copland's musical lines are reminiscent of his intstrumental style—wide-range passages for the voice and extended spacing in the piano accompaniment. The key signature of five flats remains constant, even when the voice ends in E major.

WHEN THEY COME BACK. When the blossoms come back will they remember to look the same? Will the poet be the same? Copland complements the poem's whimsical, wondering quality with canonic, imitative sections between voice and piano. The mood is delicate and hesitant. The vocal passages are reminiscent of Laurey's aria in *The Tender Land*, which Copland was also working on during this time.

I FELT A FUNERAL IN MY BRAIN. In this frightening scene, the poet imagines her own funeral—a dramatically charged emotional picture. The horror of the vision is accompanied with beating drums and tolling bells. The repeated rhythms become hypnotic and complement the poetic content.

I'VE HEARD AN ORGAN TALK SOMETIMES. Marked "Gently flowing," this song is musically simple and subtle in meaning. In it, the poet remembers church services she attended as a girl. Copland's accompaniment gently imitates the organ's stentorian tones in stately triadic harmonies.

GOING TO HEAVEN! This lively song is often sung separately from the larger work. A somewhat manic vocal line firmly proclaims the poet has doubts about the idea of going to heaven, although she confesses she is glad that others she knew believed in the idea. The piano accompaniment, full of imitative figures and staccato passages that seem to chuckle, provides a commentary on the promise of the title.

THE CHARIOT. Death courteously escorts the poet on a journey, the horses' heads set toward eternity. This song is one of Copland's most moving and effective. The song is marked "With quiet grace," and it chronicles the unhurried progress toward the finality of life. The song title is Copland's, and it fittingly renames the carriage that takes the two passengers to the "chariot," the mode of transportation most widely associated with heavenly journeys.

*Copland dedicated each of the twelve songs to a fellow composer. Dedicatees (in song order) are: David Diamond, Elliott Carter, Ingolf Dahl, Alexei Haieff, Marcelle de Manziarly, Juan Orrego-Salas, Irving Fine, Harold Shapero, Camargo Guarnieri, Alberto Ginastera, Lukas Foss, and Arthur Berger. Along with Alice Howland, Copland gave the first performance of the work at the McMillin Theater, Columbia University, New York, on May 18, 1950. Copland later orchestrated eight of the songs.

Extended Study List
Three Early Songs on Poems by Aaron Schaffer • Dirge in the Woods • Pastorale • Alone • Old Poem • Poet's Song • *As It Fell Upon a Day* (soprano with flute and clarinet) • Vocalise

Selected Reading
Robert Michael Daugherty, "An Analysis of Copland's *Twelve Poems of Emily Dickinson* [with]*Homage, a Score for Orchestra*," Ph.D. diss., The Ohio State University, 1980.
Peter Dickinson, "Ives and Copland," in *Heritage of Music Vol. IV* (Oxford and New York: Oxford University Press, 1989).
Sharon Cody Mabry, "*Twelve Poems of Emily Dickinson* by Aaron Copland: A Stylistic Analysis" (Ph.D. diss., George Peabody College for Teachers, 1977).
Vivian Perlis, *Copland: Volume 1. 1900-1942* (London and Boston: Faber and Faber, 1984).
_____, *Copland Since 1943* (New York: St. Martin's Press, 1989). Contains a discussion of Copland's vocal music by singers Alice Howland, Phyllis Curtin and William Warfield.
Marta Robertson and Robin Armstrong, *Aaron Copland: a guide to research* (New York & London: Routledge, 2001).
Joann Skowronski, *Aaron Copland: A Bio-Bibliography* (New York: Greenwood Press, 1985). Bio-Bibliographies in Music Series, No. 2.
Beverly Soll and Ann Dorr, "Cyclical implications in Aaron Copland's *Twelve Poems of Emily Dickinson*," College Music Symposium 32, 1992: 99-128.
Larry Starr, *The Dickinson Songs of Aaron Copland.* CMS Sourcebooks in American Music No. 1 (Hillsdale, NY: Pendragon Press, 2002).
Douglas Young, "Copland's Dickinson Songs." *Tempo* 103 (1972): 33-37.

Notes
1. Quoted in Vivian Perlis, 249. Perlis's second volume of Copland's biography provides interesting discussion on his vocal music from singers Alice Howland, Phyllis Curtin, William Warfield, and Copland himself.
2. Ibid., 157.
3. Ibid.
4. Ibid., 166.
5. Ibid., 158.

6. Ibid., 159.
7. Ibid., 157.
8. Ibid., 163, 165.
9. Ibid., 159.

THEODORE CHANLER (1902-1961)

He writes...with conscious sincerity and with unconscious distinction... There is a precision in the melodies without any harshness, and amplitude in the musical structure without any boasting...His songs have what is known in French manners as *tenue*.

—Virgil Thomson[1]

American composer and music critic Theodore Chanler studied composition in New York and then in Cleveland with Ernest Bloch; he continued his studies at Oxford, and then in Paris with Nadia Boulanger. In the mid-1930s, he returned to the United States where he continued to compose songs, setting a number of poems by his friend Father Leonard Feeney.

Chanler wrote in a style that is characterized by highly lyrical melodic lines and polytonality. He acknowledged Gabriel Fauré's influence on his compositions, especially his songs, and tried to apply Fauré's principles of song construction to his own music. He admired "the subtle simplicity of Fauré's thought, the unexpectedness that is yet always logical, and, most of all, how much he could say with few notes."[2]

Chanler's songs are marked by an unerring sense of prosody and lucid textures gleaned from his French training. They successfully integrate the French style with Chanler's lyricism and precise craftsmanship. Paul Sperry, distinguished researcher and champion of American art songs, describes Chanler's vocal style in the same breath with that of Paul Bowles: "Both enjoy filtering American popular music—jazz, ragtime, blues—through French-trained sensibilities."[3]

Chanler was inclined to compose small works; he composed approximately fifty songs, chamber music, and some piano pieces. He was especially fond of texts by Leonard Feeney and Walter de la Mare.

For a time, Chanler was the music critic for *The Boston Herald* and a regular contributor to the journal *Modern Music*. He taught at Peabody Conservatory from 1945 to 1947 and later at the Longy School of Music until he retired early, because of illness.

Eight Epitaphs
(Walter de la Mare)

1939

Alice Rodd • Susannah Fry • Three Sisters • Thomas Logge • A Midget •
No Voice to Scold • Ann Poverty • Be Very Quiet Now

This cycle is considered Chanler's masterpiece, and it is easily the best known of his thirty-odd published vocal compositions. The cycle consists of eight short songs on texts by Walter de la Mare, each an epitaph that offers a miniature picture of the departed. The songs contain varying expressions of grief, ranging from sweetly poignant to humorous and even sarcastic.

The three central songs call for a pianist with considerable technical facility. The vocal writing calls for a contralto or mezzo-soprano. The texture, register, and interaction between the piano and vocal lines is skillfully crafted. Rhythms and texture in the accompaniments illumine the texts: the rolling gait of a midget, the nervous twittering of three spinsters, the gentle hush that accompanies a sleeping child, the irregular motions of a colorful eccentric.

Each of the eight songs is an imaginary epitaph, taken from de la Mare's story "Benighted" in *Ding Dong Bell*. The scene is a graveyard at night. A couple sits on a low flat tombstone and wonders whether they shall forget or be forgotten after they pass. "The dark air was translucently clear, sprinkling its cold dew on all these stones and their overshadowing boughs." By the light of matches, they begin to inspect the stone markers, stooping side by side and reading together.

ALICE RODD. Here the deceased is an infant, Alice Rodd. Chanler's economy of means is beautifully realized: the opening piano theme is repeated, then expanded to usher in a new section, and the vocal line is derived from the piano theme, which is lyric and poignant.

SUSANNAH FRY. Susannah Fry's own voice etches her portrait "Here lie I, Susannah Fry...dreaming as I always did." Voice and accompaniment have different textures; the vocal line is recitative, punctuated three times by a melodic theme of descending, close-spaced chords in the piano. The combination of voice and piano lines produces a dreamy, otherworldly effect.

THREE SISTERS. This is a longer song than the two preceding it. It is a narrative of three spinster sisters, all laid to rest together. From the musical setting, we might guess that the trio was a nervous group. Chanler's setting is a study in perpetual motion, with running sixteenth-note patterns in the piano, accompanying a recitative-like vocal line. Fortuitously, the setting is in triple meter.

THOMAS LOGGE. *Allegro assai, alla burla* is the marking for "Thomas Logge," characterized in the text as a "rascally dogge." Rhythmic and metric fluctuations punctuate the humorous narrative as Logge's life is capsulized on his tombstone with considerable flair and bravado.

A MIDGET. Of all the songs in the cycle, this one most clearly shows the influence of French song style on Chanler's composition. The song is a study in expressive text setting and elegance. Dancing figures in the piano accompany playful vocal passages that characterize this little person.

NO VOICE TO SCOLD. Another infant grave is described in this epitaph. The song is written in a manner that does not call to mind a distinct personality, but a mood instead.

ANN POVERTY. At six measures, this song is the shortest in the cycle. It is simple in vocal declamation and accompaniment.

BE VERY QUIET NOW. The cycle concludes with another miniature song. There are only five vocal phrases, underpinned by harmonies of open fourths and fifths. Solemn chords in the piano mark the admonition of the epitaph, which warns the reader to "Be very quiet now: a child's asleep."

O Mistress Mine[*]   1936
(William Shakespeare from *Twelfth Night*)

Chanler's treatment of this popular Shakespeare text features a shimmering Fauréan accompaniment that embellishes the vocal line from beginning to end—elegant, delicate and buoyantly romantic. The setting is a fine example of Chanler's application of the French style in his composition.

*For comparison settings, see Roger Quilter, and Gerald Finzi.

Extended Study List
These My Ophelia • I Rise When You Enter • The Doves • Memory • The Flight • The Lamb • *The Children*

Selected Reading
Theodore Chanler, "Poetry and Music," *Modern Music* 18 (May/June 1941): 232-234.
_____, "Poetry, Music and Time," *Modern Music* 21 (Nov/Dec, 1943): 3-5.
Thomas Collins, "Theodore Ward Chanler: American Song Composer," *The NATS Bulletin* 30:2 (December 1973).
E.A. Nordgren, "An Analytical Study of the Songs of Theodore Chanler (1902-1961)," Doctoral diss., New York University, 1980.
Robert Tangman, "The Songs of Theodore Chanler," *Modern Music* 22 (May/June 1945): 227-233.

Notes
1. Virgil Thomson, The *Musical Scene*. Selected essays and reviews (New York: Greenwood Press, 1968). 213.
2. Theodore Chanler, "Gabriel Fauré: A Reappraisal," *Modern Music* 22 (March-April 1945).
3. Paul Sperry. Liner Notes. *Paul Sperry Sings Romantic American Songs*. Albany Records TROY043, 1990.

SAMUEL BARBER (1910-1981)

...if I'm writing music for words, then I immerse myself in those words, and I let the music flow out of them.

—Samuel Barber[1]

Samuel Barber (with Aaron Copland) was the most frequently performed American composer of his generation, from 1941 until the mid-60s. He enjoyed early fame and enduring acclaim as a composer, and he lived to see virtually all of his music recorded.

Of the 106 songs he composed for solo voice and piano, forty-eight are published.[2] He also composed two operas: *Antony and Cleopatra*, which opened the new Metropolitan Opera House in New York in 1966; and *Vanessa* (with librettist Gian Carlo Menotti), which many people still consider *the* American opera.

His music is characterized by typical American directness and simplicity, making it appealing and easy to understand. Though his music is very "American," it still reflects a musical style that retains and integrates many European traditions. Virgil Thomson commented on Barber's music: "Old wine in new bottles seems to be his aim."

Barber was a charter member of the first class at the Curtis Institute of Music. While at Curtis, he met Gian Carlo Menotti and they began a long-lasting friendship and professional collaboration. His friendship with Menotti, as well as the artistic orientation of the Curtis faculty no doubt influenced Barber's creative development and his inclinations toward European roots in his music.

His maternal aunt was contralto Louise Homer, of the Metropolitan Opera, a celebrated singer of her day; his uncle was well-known composer Sidney Homer. Both influenced his early musical experiences, and Barber's uncle remained a strong mentor until his death in 1953.

Barber's songs have a lyric grace that we immediately identify with his music. He was a careful craftsman; his songs are romantic and sophisticated in concept. When choosing texts, he was drawn to romantic poetry, which fit his musical style well. Barber felt that the poem was of primary importance in his songs: "I try...not to distort the natural rhythms of a poem, because if this happens the words will be distorted and so will the public's understanding of them. I very much want the words to be comprehensible. My songs, like *Lieder*, tend to highlight the texts." [3]

Barber's affinity for vocal composition developed as a natural outgrowth of his own vocal training, his flair for languages and his fondness for poetry. His songs are well conceived for the voice, exercising the singer's intellect as well as vocal technique. After his death, soprano Leontyne Price, preeminent interpreter of Barber's vocal music, wrote: "For a singer Barber's music is always a challenge; but the end product is so rewarding and so terribly vocal, you can't wait to pick up another piece of his. It also falls intellectually to the mind and beautifully on the ear, which is a rare combination."[4]

Sure on this Shining Night (*Four Songs*, Op. 13)   1938
(James Agee)

Barber's penchant for lyricism and his affinity for romantic texts found voice in this beautiful song, which has become one of his best loved and most performed. Barber's musical treatment of James Agee's poem captures the outstanding components of his song style in concentrated form: a romantic lyric line, carefully crafted interplay between voice and piano, and classically oriented formal organization. Agee's poem is a contemplative soliloquy, which celebrates both nature and the human heart's optimism for harmonious existence.

Vocal phrases are long and expressively lyric. Words are set with natural accents intact, producing flexible meters throughout the song. The rhythmic pattern of the first vocal phrase ("Sure on this shining night") repeats throughout the song in both voice and piano. At the beginning and ending of the song, melodic material is used in canonic form between voice and piano.

Barber assigns the piano an accompaniment of repeated chords. This persistent pattern throws the lyrical vocal writing into high relief and also maintains dramatic intensity throughout the song. In fact, this song has been called "Brahmsian," perhaps justified by Barber's use of melodies and harmonies which recall patterns found in Brahms songs such as "O kühler Wald" or "Liebstreu."

Rain has fallen (*Three Songs*, Op. 10)   **1935**
(James Joyce)

Op. 10 contains three of Barber's best-known songs on texts of James Joyce ("Rain has fallen," "Sleep Now," "I Hear an Army"). The set includes a tonal connection between the three songs: the first and last songs are in the same key (C minor for high voice, A minor for low voice), framing the center song, which lies a minor third below. Barber may have placed the poems in this order to produce a triptych, corresponding to a relationship that begins lyrically and ends in stormy dissolution.

Joyce's text is nostalgic—the plea of a lover to his beloved to remember their happiness. The musical mood is suffused with melancholy, intensified by the rain and the drooping trees heavy with water.

Piano figures introduce this song, serenely suggesting the falling rain, and continue throughout, embroidering the broadly lyric vocal passages. The initial vocal melody returns in varied form three more times during the course of the song, but the song's climax is found in the piano. The voice enters one last time with a final phrase that seems like a calm postscript to the piano's postlude. The piano accompaniment and the vocal line are a striking blend of chromaticism embedded within a lyric tonal framework and simple formal scheme.

I Hear An Army (*Three Songs*, Op. 10)   **1936**
(James Joyce)

Intensely dramatic in feeling, this song expresses the anguish of a lost love, realized in a horrible nightmare. The poem is harsh and full of stormy, agitated images—thundering horses, charioteers with fluttering whips, and fiery blows which stab the heart. This chaotic scene is reinforced by words that perpetuate the tension—"charging," "plunging," "fluttering," "clanging," "shaking," and "shouting."

Rhythmic figures dominate in the overall texture. These rhythmic figures are found predominately in the low range of the piano accompaniment. Vocal passages are angular in this song, a departure from Barber's usual lyric lines. A sense of ongoing motion is maintained until the voice is thrown into relief at the concluding phrase: "My love, why have you left me alone?" In the brief concluding measures, the piano returns to the figures and forceful mood found in the song's opening.

Hermit Songs, Op. 29   **1953**
(Irish texts, eighth-thirteenth centuries)

At Saint Patrick's Purgatory • Church Bell at Night • St. Ita's Vision •
The Heavenly Banquet • The Crucifixion • Sea-Snatch • Promiscuity •
The Monk and His Cat • The Praises of God • The Desire for Hermitage

Hermit Songs seems a logical outgrowth of two of Barber's personal predilections: his love of Irish literature and poetry, and his personal search for solitude in which to think and work—a pursuit which continued throughout his life.

For this cycle, Barber chose ten anonymous poems written by Irish monks and scholars, dating from the eighth to the thirteenth centuries. He chose texts that are wide-ranging in mood and length, encompassing thoughts that vary from intensely devout to ribald. Barber explained the origin and character of *Hermit Songs* in his notes:

> [*Hermit Songs*] are settings of anonymous, Irish texts of the eighth to thirteenth centuries written by monks and scholars, often on the margins of manuscripts they were copying or illuminating—perhaps not always meant to be seen by their Father Superiors. They are small and speak in straightforward, droll, and often surprisingly modern terms of the simple life these men led, close to nature, to animals, and to God.[5]

In order to accommodate the rhythmic irregularities of the poetry, Barber omits metrical signatures throughout the cycle. His extensive notes on the texts indicate his careful concern for the prosody; his supple vocal lines give the singer opportunity to project the text flexibly.

Hermit Songs contains a variety of forms and styles—through-composed, binary, ternary, strophic, recitative and aria forms.[6] The forms and styles are always dictated by the text and Barber uses them to create a unique ambience for this cycle.

Kreiling points out Barber's use of appoggiaturas and grace notes in the piano—ornaments which recall the sound of an old Irish harp and impart a distinctive Irish flavor to the work.[7] The medieval effect is further strengthened by liberal use of open fourths and fifths throughout.

Hermit Songs is one of Barber's most-performed vocal works; it ranks among the foremost song cycles of the twentieth century. It was first performed in 1953 by soprano Leontyne Price with the composer accompanying—an occasion which inaugurated a long professional collaboration and friendship between Barber and Price.

AT SAINT PATRICK'S PURGATORY. Strong, forceful rhythms mark the pilgrimage to Loch Derg. A steady *ostinato* figure in the piano accompanies the pilgrim's resolute steps.

CHURCH BELL AT NIGHT. The accompaniment evokes the sound of a bell, swinging backward and forward while the hermit sings (somewhat wistfully) that he would rather keep tryst with the bell than "be with a light and foolish woman."

ST. ITA'S VISION. This tender lullaby, preceded by a section of declamatory recitative, makes up a little miniature *scena*. St. Ita imagines that she is nursing the Christ Child; it is a moment of religious ecstasy blended with distinctly human desires. Accompanying triplet figures provide a rocking effect.

THE HEAVENLY BANQUET. This song describes an amiable feast for "Heaven's family." Vocal passages consist of eighth notes over a undulating rhythmic piano accompaniment. The droll whimsy of the singer who wishes for "a great lake of beer for the King of Kings" is tinged slightly with good-natured greed.

THE CRUCIFIXION. This song is one of the better known in *Hermit Songs*. Its stark fourths and fifths evoke the intense emotion of the crucifixion. A motive in the high register of the piano features a grace note. This "bird-like" motive is heard throughout the song ("At the cry of the first bird, they began to crucify Thee...").

SEA-SNATCH. The sea's fury is evoked in this song of tempest. The vocal line is harsh and angular while the accompaniment is reminiscent of surging waves.

PROMISCUITY. Barber uses conventional speech declamation as the basis for the vocal line in this miniature song that contains only two lines of text. The unadorned declamatory line gives greater impact to the sly text.

THE MONK AND HIS CAT. This song paints a happy picture of a scholar and his cat, a compatible pair. Each has his own work to do, but they provide good company for one another. The playful padding movements of the animal are heard in the delightful rhythmic patterns in the piano accompaniment. The scholar and cat are completely content to be "alone together."

THE PRAISES OF GOD. Melismatic vocal passages are found on the word "Laudation." The lilting pointillistic piano figurations happily celebrate the text.

THE DESIRE FOR HERMITAGE. The first section of this song, which is a passionate plea for solitude, is marked "Calm and sustained." The vocal line always returns to the central note initiated by the piano at the beginning of the song, just as the monk always returns to his cell, the center of his earthly existence. Within the song's meditative mood, there is fervent lyricism, especially in the B section. The song ends with a return to the quiet opening.

The Secrets of the Old (*Four Songs*, Op. 13)   1938
(W.B. Yeats)

This song is an affectionate reminiscence that celebrates the bonds of a lasting friendship in which gossip and story-telling are valued activities. The light and airy vocal line that decorates the text is as amusing as the knowing observer who reflects upon youthful love from the lofty vantage point of age. Vocal phrases seems to dance pointillistically as the little character sketch progresses. The overall mood and style of the song recalls "Monks and Raisins," another of Barber's playful rhythmic settings.

Rhythmic organization fluctuates to match word stress; the first twelve measures contain four metric signatures, $\frac{5}{8}$, $\frac{2}{4}$, $\frac{3}{8}$, and $\frac{5}{4}$, as well as nine rhythmic oscillations.[8] Through all the rhythmic changes, the eighth note remains triumphant, with piano figures gaily rooted in an "oom-pah" accompaniment. The song retains a playful, supple feeling throughout, with only a tinge of wistful mood in the final measures.

O boundless, boundless evening (*Three Songs*, Op. 45)   1972
(Georg Heym, trans. Christopher Middleton)

In the year 1972, Barber composed the last of his published songs—*Op. 45*, a set of three songs written for baritone Dietrich Fischer-Dieskau, commissioned for the singer by the Lincoln Center Chamber Music Society. In these three songs, Barber used harmonies that are more dissonant than his usual style.

"O boundless, boundless evening" is a text translated by Christopher Middleton from the German of Georg Heym. It contains a dusk-drenched pastoral scene, a tranquil landscape which recalls the lyrical mood and style of "Sure on this shining night," *Dover Beach*, and "Nocturne." Yet within this bucolic evening's beauty hides the darkness implicit with the coming night ("Yet in ravines between the hills already nests the night").

Barber the pianist creates a dense-textured piano accompaniment that still retains a serene effect. The accompaniment employs counterpoint, imitates vocal material, and at one point states the opening vocal phrase in a Chopinesque solo moment for the pianist. The final phrases of the voice announce the coming night and bring the undulating motion of the piano to a halt.

Vocal phrases are expansive and lyric, recalling the style used in Barber's other lyrical songs. The vocal phrases are diatonic in contrast to the highly chromatic piano accompaniment.

A Green Lowland of Pianos (*Three Songs,* Op. 45)   1972
(Jerzy Harasymowicz, trans. C. Milosz)

This poem, originally written in Polish, is full of humor and preposterous imagery. The outlandish text draws parallels between grand pianos and cows, and Barber sets it with considerable wit and flair.

Images in the text are surreal and poke subtle fun at concert hall performances and etiquette. Barber seems to have enjoyed the jest—the piano accompaniment is filled with text painting; glissandi and double trills appear to point up both the pianos and the gurgling frogs, luxuriant seventh chords are "chords of rapture." The vocal phrases contain humorous touches as well—an elongated stress on the first syllable of "moonish" is reminiscent of a mooing cow.

Extended Study List
The Daisies • Bessie Bobtail • With rue my heart is laden • Monks and Raisins • A Nun takes the veil • Sleep now • The Queen's face on the summery coin • Nocturne • *Mélodies passagères* • *Knoxville: Summer of 1915,* for soprano and orchestra • *Despite and Still,* Op. 41 • *Dover Beach,* Op. 31, for solo voice and string quartet

Selected Reading
John E. Albertson, "A Study of Stylistic Elements in Samuel Barber's *Hermit Songs* and Schubert's *Winterreise.*" D.M.A. thesis, University of Missouri, 1969.

Nathan Broder, *Samuel Barber* (New York: G. Schirmer, 1954).

Barbara B. Heyman, *Samuel Barber: The Composer and His Music* (New York: Oxford University Press, 1992).

Jean Louise Kreiling, "The Songs of Samuel Barber: A Study in Literary Taste and Text Setting." Ph.D. diss., University of North Carolina at Chapel Hill, 1986.

Victoria Etnier Villamil, *A Singer's Guide to the American Art Song,* 1870-1980 (Metuchen, NJ: The Scarecrow Press, 1993), 23-31.

Wayne C. Wentzel, *Samuel Barber: a guide to research* (New York & London: Routledge, 2001).

Notes
1. Jean Louise Kreiling, *The Songs of Samuel Barber: A Study in Literary Taste and Text Setting,* 325.
2. For a complete listing of published and unpublished songs see Barbara Heyman, *Samuel Barber: The Composer and His Music,* 519-521. Ten early songs are now available in published form and are included in the published song count. Heyman also lists two lost songs, and one incomplete manuscript.
3. Phillip Ramey, Interview with Barber quoted in liner notes. *Barber: Songs* Etcetera Recording KTC 1055, 1988.
4. Barbara B. Heyman, *Samuel Barber: The Composer and His Music,* 341.
5. Samuel Barber, Preface to *Hermit Songs* in *Barber: Collected Songs,* 74.
6. Heyman, 338.
7. Kreiling, 316.
8. James Hall, *The Art Song,* 290.

PAUL BOWLES (1910-1999)

Paul Bowles's songs are enchanting for their sweetness of mood, their lightness of texture, for in general their way of being wholly alive and right.

—Virgil Thomson[1]

If you were typical, it would be the end of our civilization. You're a manufactured savage.

—Gertrude Stein, in a letter to Paul Bowles[2]

Paul Bowles was a "loner." He led a multifaceted existence as a writer, composer, ethnomusicologist, and world traveler. He is better-known for his prolific literary works than his musical compositions.

Bowles composed not only a good-sized body of songs but also music for plays, films, ballet, orchestra, piano, chamber ensembles, and an opera written on a Guggenheim Fellowship. Bowles's songs are striking for their lyricism, economy of means, and natural fusion of text with music. About Bowles's songs, Virgil Thomson said: "The texts fit their tunes like a peach its skin."[3]

Composer and friend Ned Rorem describes Bowles's operas as "suites of songs." Rorem further describes Bowles's music in *The New Groves Dictionary of Music* as: "nostalgic and witty, evocative in its use of American jazz, Mexican dance and Moroccan rhythm and exclusively in short forms."[4] Bowles confessed in an interview that he enjoyed composing in smaller forms: "As a composer I find that I don't like 'big' music...Today, there isn't much room for little pieces, I suppose, but that doesn't make them any less valuable."[5]

His prose has a distinct rhythmic quality. Bowles acknowledged that his musical training probably influenced his literary style: "I've written a great many songs. Prosody, I think, has more to do with it than anything else—the value of the spaces between the words."[6]

He traveled during his early adulthood in the 1903s, journeying to Paris, Berlin, Morocco, and Mexico. He studied composition with Aaron Copland who, along with Virgil Thomson, influenced his music. In Paris, he also met Gertrude Stein, who became a friend, providing him with texts for vocal compositions.

Bowles was also a pioneer ethno-musicologist—his two-record set of Moroccan music was issued by the Library of Congress. He studied and collected music from all over the world, including tapings of folk music from North Africa, South and Central America, the Antilles, and Spain. Often he subtly integrated ethnic materials from some of the places he lived and visited around the world into his songs.

Bowles composed music for about fifteen years. Around 1940, he began writing music criticism for *Modern Music*, and was persuaded by Virgil Thomson, then music critic for the *New York Herald Tribune*, to join the staff as a music reviewer. After the publication of his highly successful first novel, *The Sheltering Sky* (1948), Bowles essentially abandoned composing for writing, producing a series of very successful novels. Ned Rorem comments: "His professional life has...been sliced cleanly in two, with no seeming connection between the pieces."[7] In the mid-1940s Bowles moved to Tangiers, where he lived until his death.

Blue Mountain Ballads   1946
(Tennessee Williams)

Heavenly Grass • Lonesome Man • Cabin • Sugar in the Cane

Blue Mountain Ballads is probably the best-known of Paul Bowles's songs. Dating from the mid-1940s, the settings of these four disparate Tennessee Williams texts represent scenes from an imaginary Mississippi town. Williams's poetry often uses rhymed couplets and images that spring from his rural southern childhood.

Bowles and Williams were good friends and colleagues. Williams's play *The Glass Menagerie* was presented with background music by Bowles, who then provided scores for other important Williams plays: *Summer and Smoke* (1948), *Sweet Bird of Youth* (1959), and *The Milk Train Doesn't Stop Here Anymore* (1963).

Bowles spoke of these songs in an interview with Mike Steen: "I remember in '46 Tennessee gave me some lyrics and asked me if I would like to use them to write songs. One was called 'Gold Tooth Woman,' I remember that. I didn't use that. But I did use four called *Blue Mountain Ballads*...They made a suite...They have gone into the repertory now."[8]

HEAVENLY GRASS. Williams describes the soul's journey from heaven to earth and back in a simple narrative that is preserved in a luminous musical setting by Bowles. The vocal line is in antecedent-consequent form: the question couched in $\frac{5}{4}$ meter in a modal setting, the answer in $\frac{4}{4}$ meter and major tonality. This pattern varies only once in the song. Modal elements maintain the setting's folk song quality and point up the simplicity of the text's mood.

LONESOME MAN. "Lonesome Man" is filled with syncopations in a ragtime accompaniment, a portrait of a loner, shunned by society ("nobody ever stops my way"). Bowles mixes metric fluctuation within the song's $\frac{4}{8}$ meter, as the old man's rocking chair keeps a steady movement going throughout the song, pausing only at two wistful recitative phrases that let us know he rues his isolation more than he lets on. This song is right on the mark—a colorful, sensitive snapshot of a Southern character.

CABIN. Bowles marks this story of seduction "Like a ballad." The song opens with a simple folk-like introduction of thirds accompanied by a broken chord-figure for the left hand of the piano. The poetry is highlighted with implied metaphors; the cabin surrounded by hollyhocks represents the woman's innocence, and the winter storm represents the passion that destroyed the lovers. The text is related by a narrator. The overall form is ABA; the middle section is set in the minor key, rising to a climax "where they kissed and sinned."

SUGAR IN THE CANE. Bowles gives an unabashed, jazzy treatment to this text, which is a young woman's litany of her considerable personal attributes, couched in exaggerated metaphors ("I'm red pepper in a shaker....I'm potatoes not yet mashed..."). His ease with musical theater idioms is evident in this song, which is drenched with rhythmic vitality throughout.

Once a Lady Was Here   1946
(Paul Bowles)

This is one of Bowles's most successful and frequently performed songs. The original tempo marking is "Slowly and easily." "Once a Lady Was Here" merges Bowles's keen harmonic and rhythmic sense with the musical theater idiom. The meter seesaws back and forth from $\frac{4}{8}$ to $\frac{5}{8}$, asymmetric but never losing an easy flow. A vibrant piano line is a fine example of the charm and freshness of Bowles's melodic style.

Bowles's text is a narrative written from the viewpoint of an observer. We can only witness the scene without personal involvement. The song is an interesting blend of Bowles's vibrant musical style and his guarded personality.

Three   1947
(Tennessee Williams)

Bowles used another text by Tennessee Williams for this short, poignant song. Speaking in the first person, the poet remembers three loves in a poem of three stanzas. In contrasting his three loves, the poet remembers that number three ("buried under frost") stayed forever in his heart.

The song's meter is in three, a diminutive *sarabande* that complements the text and recalls a small *gymnopédie*. Bowles's simple vocal line is fashioned like a miniature incantation, a fragmented "she loves me, she loves me not."

A Little Closer, Please (The Pitchman's Song)   1941
(William Saroyan)

During the period Bowles was involved in writing music for Broadway plays, he enjoyed collaborations with Tennessee Williams and William Saroyan. This song is a setting of the Pitchman's Song from William Saroyan's play *Love's Old Sweet Song*. It depicts the ubiquitous amiability of the salesman, who begins his pitch in small fragments of recitative. The song quickly accelerates into a dapper, yet sensual march, beginning with the title's words in a hypnotic swinging rhythm.

April Fool Baby   1935
(Gertrude Stein)

Bowles commented that Stein wasn't particularly interested in music (she considered it an inferior art), but that she had an ear for dissonance and consonance.[9] He set several of Stein's texts, including one titled "Letter to Freddie," her nickname for him (Frederic was his middle name).

"April Fool Baby" has the usual energetic, slightly off-center charm of a Stein text. Its eccentric wordplay is complemented by a piano part based on jazz idioms, showcased in several tiny interludes. The final measures contain a reflective, intimate moment that doesn't last long, but acts as a setup for a quick, buoyant *coup-de-grâce*.

Extended Study List

Secret Words • Letter to Freddy • *Scenes from the Door* • *Cuatro Canciones de Garcia Lorca* • *Three Pastoral Songs* • *Gothic Suite* • Voici la feuille • Ainsi parfois nos seuils • In the Platinum Forest • Sleeping Song (originally titled "Baby, Baby") • Night Without Sleep • Her Head Upon the Pillow • My Sister's Hand in Mine • On a Quiet Conscience • My Love was Light

Selected Reading

Paul Bowles Selected Songs. Researched, edited and produced by Peter Garland with the supervision of the composer (Santa Fe, N.M.: Soundings Press, 1984).

Paul Bowles, *Without Stopping: An Autobiography* (New York: Putnam, 1972).

_____, Timothy Mangan and Irene Herrmann, eds., *Paul Bowles on Music: Includes the Last Interview with Paul Bowles* (Berkeley: University of California Press, 2003).

Gena Dagel Caponi, ed., *Conversations with Paul Bowles* (Jackson, Mississippi: University Press of Mississippi, 1993). A collection of interviews with Bowles.

Cori Ellison, Liner notes. *William Sharp, baritone: Works by Thomson, Hundley, Hoiby, Klein, Bowles, Musto*. New World Records NW 369-2. 1989.

Peter Garland, "Paul Bowles and the Baptism of Solitude" in *Americas: Essays on American Music and Culture, 1973-80* (Santa Fe, N.M.: Soundings Press, 1982).

Jeffrey Miller, *Paul Bowles: A descriptive biography* (Santa Barbara: Black Sparrow Press, 1986).

Ned Rorem, "Come Back Paul Bowles," *New Republic* (April 22, 1972). Reprinted as "Paul Bowles," *Pure Contraption* (New York: Holt, Rinehart and Winston, 1974).

Notes

1. Virgil Thomson in the preface to *Paul Bowles: Selected Songs*.
2. Quoted in Peter Garland, "Paul Bowles and the Baptism of Solitude" in *Essays on American Music and Culture* 1973-80, 186.
3. Thomson, preface to *Selected Songs*.
4. Ned Rorem, "Paul Bowles" in *The New Grove Dictionary of Music and Musicians*.
5. In *Conversations with Paul Bowles*, Gena Dagel Caponi, ed., 8.
6. *Conversations*, 43.
7. Cori Ellison. Liner notes to *William Sharp, baritone. Works by Thomson, Hundley, Hoiby, Klein, Bowles, Musto*. New World Records NW 369-2, 1989, 5.
8. *Conversations*, 35.
9. Ibid., 9.

LEONARD BERNSTEIN (1918-1990)

> I am a serious composer trying to be a songwriter...I wrote a symphony before I ever wrote a popular song.
>
> —Leonard Bernstein, May 1954[1]

The songs of Leonard Bernstein defy homogenous grouping. They exist in many different contexts: Broadway shows, operetta, revues, incidental music, opera, musicals, theatre pieces, and finally, the songs or cycles for voice and piano. In fact, the number of songs written for voice and piano alone or in song cycles is quite small when compared to the numerous songs which exist in Bernstein scores for the musical theater, many of which have become American classics.

Leonard Bernstein was one of the most visible musicians on the American scene: a superstar composer, conductor, and teacher. Through his television lectures, Bernstein educated millions of viewers. He was gifted with the talent and ability to bring music to the general populace in an understandable way. Commercially, his music was wildly successful, his legacy of recordings abundant. His incredible energy and questioning spirit made him a sort of "Renaissance" man of music.

Although Bernstein enjoyed enormous success in his career, Gradenwitz observes that a recurrent theme in all his compositions, light or serious, is the element of loneliness, doubt and sorrow.[2] One of Bernstein's last vocal compositions was a song cycle for baritone and mezzo soprano titled *Arias and Barcarolles*, a set of songs that contains some of his most synthesized biographical musings.

Bernstein's best-known vocal compositions are found in his works for the American musical theater. His most famous work is probably *West Side Story*, an instant hit from its premiere in 1958. It broke new ground for the American musical stage and today remains an enduring classic, referred to in some camps as an "American opera." Composer Lukas Foss wrote of Bernstein: "His music has the rare quality of instant communication."[3]

Leonard Bernstein made a significant impact on twentieth-century music and its audiences. His legacy endures. In *Findings*, a book of Bernstein's personal writings and musing, he pinpointed his feelings about music:

Life without music is unthinkable,
Music without life is academic.
That is why my contact with music is a total embrace.[4]

La Bonne Cuisine   **1947**
(Emile Dumont, English trans. by Leonard Bernstein)

Plum Pudding (Plum Pudding) • Queues de boeuf (Ox-tails) • Tavouk Guenksis (Tavouk Guenksis) • Civet à toute vitesse (Rabbit at Top Speed)

La Bonne Cuisine is a witty cycle of four songs, settings of recipes from a French cookbook by Emile Dumont, published in 1899, titled *La Bonne Cuisine Française (Tout ce qui a Rapport a la Table, Manuel-Gide pour la Ville et la Campagne)*: "Fine French Cooking (Everything that has to do with the Table, Manual Guide for City and Country"). Bernstein translated the recipes himself, perfectly highlighting their humor; he even wrote a title that serves as a sly comment on the French *mélodie*.

Bernstein has carefully gauged song order according to musical pace and dramatic value; two lively songs begin and end the set, framing two slower songs in the middle.

The group of songs may be sung in the original French, or in the composer's English translation. The humor contained in the English translation is especially effective in performance. The singer needs excellent diction to perform these songs well.

PLUM PUDDING. "Plum Pudding" is a song that maintains a frenzied atmosphere from start to finish. An angular vocal line in eighth notes darts over a wide range, pausing only twice to break the pace (for the cook to consult the recipe?) before continuing headlong to the end.

The piano appears to assist the chef in his nonstop creation with a rhythmic chordal pattern that continues throughout the song.

OX-TAILS. Vacillating harmonies combine with a vocal line that swings between broad declamation and more lyric motives. A perfect character from which to generate a subtext is celebrated chef Julia Child whose down-to-earth culinary commentary would probably include the first line of text: "Are you too proud to serve your friends ox-tail stew?"

TAVOUK GUENKSIS. "Tavouk Guenksis" is a Turkish recipe featuring chicken. The singer pompously announces "Tavouk guenksis" and then comments "so Oriental" in a bluesy cadence. As the recipe is read, the piano plays in smoky, indolent rhythms to imitate the beating of a *tambour*. The vocal line is peppered with augmented intervals to evoke a proper eastern atmosphere. The chef gives only general directions; one must know the Arab way of doing things to have success with this recipe. The last vocal phrase echoes the beginning "Tavouk guenksis...a Turkish heaven," with the same bluesy cadence.

RABBIT AT TOP SPEED. "Rabbit at Top Speed" rounds out the group with a lively discourse on a quick way to prepare rabbit stew. With crazed enthusiasm, the chef whips up a recipe whose directions seem less than quick and whose portions seem more than substantial. The hectic pace slows briefly at mid-song for a lyrical moment of admiration for an essential ingredient: "a bottle and a half of rich claret." Vocal passages are short melodic segments, combined with the same skill that creating this recipe demands.

Two Love Songs   1949
(Rainer Maria Rilke)

Extinguish My Eyes • When My Soul Touches Yours

Bernstein set two poems by German poet Rainer Maria Rilke, and he dedicated them to mezzo-soprano Jennie Tourel, who gave the first performances of each. Both songs use ostinato motives in the piano and pedal points. Both settings are expressive interpretations of Rilke's poetry, which is both rich and delicate in feeling.

EXTINGUISH MY EYES is set in a polytonal texture. The intensely lyric vocal line combines with an accompaniment that uses ostinato rhythms and oscillating figures to intensify the text's passionate litany. The first section in $\frac{6}{8}$ begins in the treble clef in the piano; the second section in $\frac{5}{4}$ is over a pedal C marked *forte* and "with fire." The final section includes a return to the music of the beginning section, with the accompaniment repeated exactly and the vocal line partially altered. The final vocal phrase is hummed.

WHEN MY SOUL TOUCHES YOURS features a more declamatory approach in the vocal writing. The piano accompaniment is low-ranged for the first verse, a passionate avowal of love. In the second verse, a softer and more lyrical mood evolves, and the piano line shifts into higher realms.

A Simple Song *(Mass)*   1971
(Stephen Schwartz)

Bernstein subtitled *Mass* "A Theatre Piece for Singers, Players and Dancers." He took the text from the Liturgy of the Roman Mass. He composed *Mass* at the request of Mrs. John F. Kennedy for the opening of the John F. Kennedy Center for the Performing Arts, Washington, D.C. *Mass* was first performed there on September 8, 1971. Alvin Ailey was the choreographer.

The work has been characterized as Bernstein's closest synthesis between the concert hall and the Broadway stage, and also criticized as a hodgepodge of too many styles. It contains both religious and social elements and can be seen as indicative of the 1960s' spirit and thought.

In an interview discussing *Mass*, Bernstein said that for him, the Celebrant was "that element in every person without which you cannot live, without which you cannot get from day to day, cannot put one foot in front of the other. He represents the quality that makes you go on living. I suppose this can be defined partly by the word 'faith,' partly by the word 'hope,' partly by the word 'anticipation' "[5]

"Simple Song" is sung by the Celebrant to the accompaniment of an electric guitar. The opening din of a solo quartet singing the Antiphon ("Kyrie"), suddenly gives way to the quiet chords of the solo guitar accompaniment.

The song is aptly titled. It *is* simple—almost stark—in both text and accompaniment. It begins with a section of recitative-arioso accompanied by chords built in open fifths and octaves. A more organized accompaniment of swinging figures in a popular style underpins the second section; "I will sing the Lord a new song." It concludes with a coda and brief cadenza "Lauda, Lauda, Lau-day," with a jazzy inflection.

This is a hymn of praise to the Almighty, designed in simple terms even as the early psalmists must have sung their verses. Its simple mood captures the singer's childlike, humble faith. Like "Glitter and Be Gay," this song is often extracted for solo recitals.

Glitter and Be Gay *(Candide)*   1956 (1973)
(Lillian Hellmann)

Bernstein wrote the comic operetta *Candide* (1956), his third work written for the musical stage, in collaboration with playwright Lillian Hellmann. Using Voltaire's original work, Bernstein and Hellmann fashioned a charming work whose overall solemnity did not please the critics. Amazingly, Bernstein was working on *West Side Story* (which opened the following year) in tandem with *Candide* and some material was switched between the two works.[6]

Candide was overhauled in 1973 to enormous success; new lyrics were added by Stephen Sondheim and the work was directed by Hal Prince. The work is most often performed in this modified form, which still includes the sparkling overture from the original version, a delightful staple of symphonic programs.

Cunegonde's aria from *Candide* is often performed on the concert platform independent of the full operetta. It is a dazzling musical showpiece in which Cunegonde laments her fallen state, all the while exulting in the fine jewelry collection she has amassed through her transgressions. It is "mock operatic" and a tour-de-force for the performer. Cunegonde's vocal lines are full of whizzing scale passages and patterns reminiscent of Mozart's Queen of the Night.

I Hate Music! (A Cycle of Five Kid Songs)   **1943**

My name is Barbara • Jupiter has seven moons • I hate music! •
A big Indian and a little Indian (Riddle Song) • I'm a person too

I Hate Music! was Bernstein's first song cycle. He composed it two years after his graduation from Curtis Institute, and three years after he had studied conducting under Serge Koussevitzky at the Berkshire Music Center (now known as Tanglewood). The next year, he was to compose three of large works: *Fancy Free* (ballet), *On the Town* (musical), and *Symphony No. 1 (Jeremiah)*.

He dedicated the song cycle to his artist friend Edys Merrill, with whom he shared an apartment for a short time in the fall of 1942. She often shouted "I hate music!" when Bernstein was coaching singers, accompanying dancers, or entertaining friends.

There are five songs in the collection, sung by a ten-year-old girl named Barbara. The songs are ordered like a palindrome structure, not by their musical content, but by tempo and mood: Songs 1 and 5 are like "bookend" pieces, revealing Barbara's personality; Songs 2 and 4 are in faster tempo with uneven meters, flanking the center of the cycle, Song 3 ("I hate music!"). The light, satirical cycle is only seven minutes in length. Even in these small miniatures, Bernstein's skill with jazz idioms is readily apparent.

Barbara's vocal line has an ingenuous quality about it. At times it seems improvised, like a child's spontaneous singing. Barbara is quite candid about her likes and dislikes, and has strong opinions on most any subject. She loves riddles and despite her age, wants to be recognized as "a person too." Although he subtitled the cycle "Five Kid Songs," Bernstein writes these directions in the front of the score: "In the performance of these songs, coyness is to be assiduously avoided. The natural, unforced sweetness of child expressions can never be successfully gilded; rather will it come through the music in proportion to the dignity and sophisticated understanding of the singer."

Mezzo-soprano Jennie Tourel and Bernstein gave the first performance at the Public Library in Lenox, Massachusetts August 24, 1943.

Extended Study List

Songfest • *Arias and Barcarolles* (for Mezzo-Soprano, Baritone and Piano Four Hands) • Piccola Serenata • Four Songs from *Peter Pan* • So Pretty • Silhouette • Bernstein's works for the musical stage: *West Side Story, On the Town, Wonderful Town, Candide, 1600 Pennsylvania Avenue*

Selected Reading

Don Alan Andre, "Leonard Bernstein's *Mass* as Social and Political Commentary on the Sixties," D.M.A. diss., University of Washington, 1979.

Leonard Bernstein, *Findings* (New York: Simon and Schuster, 1982). Taken from Bernstein's letters, personal notes, and public lectures.

_____,"Leonard Bernstein Discusses his *Mass*," *Hi Fidelity and Musical America* 22: February 1972.

Humphrey Burton, *Leonard Bernstein* (New York: Doubleday, 1994).

Schuyler Chapin, *Leonard Bernstein: Notes from a Friend* (New York: Walker, 1992).

Jack Gottlieb, ed. *Bernstein on Broadway* (New York: Amberson, 1981). Introductory articles by George Abbott, Harold Prince, Jerome Robbins, Stephen Sondheim, Betty Comden and Adolph Green.

Peter Gradenwitz, *Leonard Bernstein: The Infinite Variety of a Musician* (New York: Oswald Wolff Books, Berg Publishers, 1986).

Paul R. Laird, *Leonard Bernstein: a guide to research* (New York & London: Routledge, 2002).

Notes

1. Quoted in Peter Gradenwitz, *Leonard Bernstein: The Infinite Variety of a Musician,* 131.
2. Ibid., 143.
3. Quoted in *Bernstein on Broadway,* Jack Gottlieb, ed., 5.
4. Leonard Bernstein, *Findings,* 266.
5. "Leonard Bernstein Discusses his *Mass*," 69.
6. See Humphrey Burton, *Leonard Bernstein,* 269.

VINCENT PERSICHETTI (1915-1987)

Persichetti's song settings are...eminently singable. They have certain recurring gestures that singers find grateful...always the line, and its shaping with words, is something that can be sung with vocal beauty.

—Paul Hume[1]

Vincent Persichetti's career in music was multi-faceted: composer, virtuoso pianist, teacher, administrator, author, critic, music editor, and governmental advisor. He composed in every genre, but his instrumental compositions are more familiar than his songs. Persichetti remarked that "people think they've heard my songs when they haven't."[2]

As a teacher and writer, Persichetti had a huge impact on American music. For twenty years, he headed the Theory and Composition Department at the Philadelphia Conservatory. In 1947, he joined the faculty at Juilliard, where he remained until he retired in 1987. He was the author of *Twentieth-Century Harmony,* a widely respected theory textbook. He also wrote innumerable articles, essays, and reviews on music during his long career.

Persichetti generally confined his composition to one medium at a time. His vocal compositions range from minuscule settings of Japanese *haiku* to *Harmonium,* an extended solo vocal work of sixty-five minutes, which is considered to be his major vocal composition. He wrote most of his songs in sets and cycles; almost half of his vocal output sets American poets. Some of Persichetti's songs remain unpublished.

Persichetti's fifty-nine songs date from the 1950s and are marked by musical economy and taste, an unerring sense of prosody, and sensitivity to poetic content. His vocal writing seldom poses huge technical problems. His accompaniments lean toward sparse textures but always express poetic mood. In addition to his songs, Persichetti composed numerous choral compositions and one chamber opera, *The Sibyl (A Parable of Chicken Little),* commissioned by the Pennsylvania Opera Theater.

Probably the best-known Persichetti songs are four settings of Emily Dickinson, Op. 77. Composed six years after *Harmonium,* this modest but charming set has remained an engaging favorite in the performing repertoire.

Emily Dickinson Songs, **Op. 77**   **1957**

The Grass • I'm Nobody • When the Hills Do • Out of the Morning

Persichetti's settings of these four poems are beautifully shaped. Musically, the songs are not difficult, and they work well as literature for beginning students. The vocal phrases are lyric and melodious, and piano accompaniments are almost transparent in texture. Each song realizes Dickinson's direct poetic style admirably, catching the emotional impact of the verses in brief but exquisite settings.

THE GRASS. Persichetti's unabashed lyricism overrides everything in this song, marked *Andante affettuoso*. A sparse rhythmic pattern for the piano creates a rocking figure that contrasts nicely with the vocal phrases. Persichetti's fresh, easily moving music captures the happy complacency of the poem.

I'M NOBODY. Dickinson's wit is parried by Persichetti's musical setting, which features syncopated material that is bandied back and forth between piano and voice.

WHEN THE HILLS DO. This beautiful setting of Dickinson's enigmatic declaration of love is based on sequential progressions in the piano. The voice enters on the topmost note of the last piano chord, a graceful coming together that creates a beautifully knit construction.

OUT OF THE MORNING. Wide-ranging piano arpeggios are pitted against vocal lines that descend stepwise, creating a synergy of sound. The piano figures are ascending and optimistic; the vocal lines are falling and doubtful.

Extended Study List
Harmonium, Op. 50 (1951) • *English Songs* (seventeenth century lyrics), Op. 49 (1951) • *e.e. cummings Songs*, Op. 26 (1945) • *Robert Frost Songs*, Op. 76 (1957) • *Carl Sandburg Songs*, Op. 73 (1957) • *A Net of Fireflies*, Op. 115 (1971) • *Two Chinese Songs*, Op. 29 (1945) • *Sara Teasdale Songs*, Op. 72 (1957) • *James Joyce Songs*, Op. 74. 1957 • *Hilaire Belloc Songs*, Op. 75 (1957)

Selected Reading
Donald L. Patterson and Janet L. Patterson, *Vincent Persichetti: A Bio-Bibliography* (New York: Greenwood Press, 1988). Bio-Bibliographies in Music Series, Number 16.

Roger Scanlan, "Spotlight on American Composers: Vincent Persichetti," *The NATS Bulletin*, 34:3, 42.

Notes
1. Review in *Washington Post*. Quoted in Patterson, *Vincent Persichetti: A Bio-Bibliography*, 177.
2. Persichetti in an interview with Ruth Friedberg. Quoted in Friedberg's *American Art Song and American Poetry*, Volume 3, 86. During this interview, he also made reference to the reticence of voice teachers to teach American art songs.

NED ROREM (b. 1923)

If you sing words as you would speak them, if you develop a viewpoint about the verse, if you care about the sense, then the music—or at least my music—will automatically fall into place around the poem like a velvet cloak around a naked form.

—Ned Rorem[1]

Ned Rorem is one of America's most distinguished composers and its most prolific composer of songs. Although his compositions are wide-ranging—works for chamber groups, orchestra, piano, and operas—it is his songs that are possibly his best musical portrait. In his compositions, Rorem blends his keen literary sensitivity and elegant lyric sense. He admits that he conceives all his compositions in terms of vocal expression: "I always think vocally. Even when writing for violin or timpani, it's the vocalist in me trying to get out. Music is, after all a sung expression, and any composer worthy of the name is intrinsically a singer whether he allows it or not."[2]

Rorem's catalog of art songs includes more than 500 works in the medium. They exhibit discriminating taste and an elegance of style—perhaps a result of seven years spent in Paris and his warm friendships with some of France's stellar composers and artists. His associations with members of the group Les Six, notably Francis Poulenc, influenced his musical thinking; Rorem interpolates Gallic style into his work in a highly individual way.

Rorem's first songs date from the 1930s; many are settings of poet Paul Goodman. His songs have considerable variety and versatility of style. The later songs are sophisticated and more complex in style. Many of his works were conceived for specific singers: Phyllis Curtin, Gianna D'Angelo, Regina Safarty, Charles Bressler, Beverly Wolff, Phyllis Bryn-Julson, Katherine Ciesinski, Rosalind Rees, and Donald Gramm.

A prolific author, Rorem has written numerous books and articles which chronicle his career as a composer, his life in general, and his observations about music and musicians. His writing is erudite, gossipy, often maddening, and thought provoking, but never dull. He writes sensitively and gracefully; he uses words to preach, teach, edify, and pique. To date, he has written eighteen books, among them: *Music from Inside Out* (1967); *The Paris Diary of Ned Rorem* (1967); *An Absolute Gift* (1978); *Setting the Tone* (1983); *Settling the Score* (1988); and *Knowing When to Stop* (1994); and *Other Entertainment* (1996). Among his numerous awards is the 1976 Pulitzer Prize for his orchestral suite *Air Music.*

In 1997, he produced a tour de force vocal work, *Evidence of Things Not Seen*, a cycle of thirty-six poems by twenty-three poets. It takes the listener on a quietly epic journey from innocence to experience and on to solitude and extinction—essentially, the entire span of a human life.

The Lordly Hudson   1947
(Paul Goodman)

In 1948, the Music Library Association declared "The Lordly Hudson" the best published song of the year, and it remains one of Rorem's best-known and most performed works. The song is both lyric and dramatic; the inexorable flow of the stately Hudson is evoked in supple melodic phrases underlaid with a strong rhythmic chordal accompaniment. Also implicit in Goodman's poem is the passionate pride in home (Manhattan), and a patriotic elation in things familiar. Rorem admitted being influenced by Poulenc's "C," employing some of the same arching intervals at points of high emotion.[3]

Early in the Morning   1958
(Robert Hillyer)

In this song, an American reminisces about a visit to Paris during his youth. Surely this song is a musical interpolation of Rorem's Parisian stay mixed with Hillyer's poem of rich images of recall. The song is set in a nostalgic waltz rhythm, redolent of the *valse-musette,* and evokes the ubiquitous Parisian accordion accompaniment associated with popular French songs. The vocal line is unashamedly melodic.

Rain in Spring   1949
(Paul Goodman)

Paying homage to Goodman, Rorem wrote that he never tired of setting Goodman's words to music: "He was my Goethe, my Blake, and my Apollinaire."[4] Rorem composed the song in one sitting and never revised it. It is dedicated to Henri Hell, biographer of Poulenc.

This charming song, the first music Rorem wrote after arriving in Paris, captures the freshly minted atmosphere of soft spring rain. The music is languid; a falling melody of double-dotted rhythms in the piano sets the mood. The texture and harmony are quintessentially French.

Visits to St. Elizabeths (Bedlam)   1957
(Elizabeth Bishop)

Rorem describes "Visits to St. Elizabeths" as "my most dramatic song. The mechanically shaped poem, like a solemn nursery rhyme, was written by Elizabeth Bishop after seeing her colleague, Ezra Pound, in St. Elizabeths hospital where Pound was incarcerated for treason after World War II."[5]

St. Elizabeths was an asylum for the insane ("This is the house of Bedlam/ This is the man that lies in the house of Bedlam…"). A percussive accompaniment propels this violent song forward in a tempo that remains constant throughout the song. The text is based on the nursery rhyme "This is the house that Jack built," with its cumulative verses. The combination of musical and dramatic tensions builds to a jolting finale with a litany of disturbing images of the asylum. The striking cover for the first publication of this song was drawn by Jean Cocteau in 1963.

O you whom I often and silently come   1957
(Walt Whitman)

In fourteen bars, this song with its intimate avowal of love flows quietly by. It was one of a number of songs that Rorem composed in 1957 in Hyères, a town in southern France. Other Whitman settings Rorem completed in Hyères that summer are "Sometimes with One I Love," and "Look Down, Fair Moon."

The song contains a gliding and sinuous vocal line (Rorem indicates "Supple" as a tempo marking) set in *parlando* fashion over a simply textured piano accompaniment. There is a subtle interchange between piano and voice in the last half of the song.

Alleluia   1946

"Alleluia," in $\frac{7}{8}$ meter, is a rhythmic tour-de-force for both singer and pianist. Full of infectious energy and color, it is an exciting romp from start to finish. The word "alleluia" is sung forty-one times in all manner of permutations, gathering momentum with each new repetition. A brief middle section in a more relaxed tempo provides the only moment of release before the headlong dash to an exhilarating climax—an unfettered shout of joy—"Alleluia!"

Rorem: "It makes a theatrical closing number, although its first performance, by Janet Fairbank, was as a rousing curtain-raiser. 'Alleluia' seems to be among my best-recalled songs, perhaps because the pianist as well as the soloist has a chance to show off."[6] Rorem dedicated the song to Jennie Tourel.

Love   1953
(Thomas Lodge)

The text for this song is by Thomas Lodge, an early sixteenth-century poet. Rorem composed the song during a stay at Hyères, a town near Toulon in the south of France (see annotations above) where he spent a great deal of time during the 1950s.

The song is built on two melodic-rhythmic patterns shared by the voice and the piano—three alternating quarter notes in thirds in the voice, and a repeated rhythmic pattern (half note, whole note) in the piano. The rhythmic patterns of the vocal phrases remain unvaried throughout the song. The piano texture changes at measure twelve, moving forward with two new rhythmic patterns, using its own quarter note motion in counterpoint with the vocal line. The intertwining of voice and piano lines creates a fluid rhythmic texture of question/answer that fits the poetic construction perfectly.

*For a comparison setting, see Daron Hagen.

Ferry Me Across the Water*   1978-79
(Christina Rossetti)

"Ferry Me Across the Water" is from Rorem's *Nantucket Songs*, a collection of nine songs on unrelated poems by Theodore Roethke, William Carlos Williams, Christina Rossetti, Edmund Waller, Walter Savage Landor, and John Ashbery. Rorem composed all the songs on Nantucket Island, hence the title. Although Rorem describes the collection as "entertaining," and "emotional rather than intellectual," these songs demand a high level of technical and interpretive skill from both singer and pianist.[7]

Rorem describes the song as a "languorous legato." Rosetti's poem is touching and folk-like; there are three stanzas. Rorem uses a rocking chordal figure in the piano accompaniment, which remains unvaried throughout the song. The vocal form is strophic, altered only in the final phrase. The singer's last note is a high G-sharp, creating a beautiful effect that adds just the right touch to this stunning setting. Rorem directs that it "should be floated effortlessly on a golden thread into the stratosphere."[8]

*For a comparison setting, see Daron Hagen.

Flight for Heaven   1950
(Robert Herrick)

To Music, to becalm his Fever • Cherrie-ripe • Upon Julia's Clothes •
To Daisies, not to shut so Soon • Epitaph upon a Child that died • Another
Epitaph • To the Willow-tree • Comfort to a Youth that had lost his Love •
To Anthea, who may command him Anything

Flight for Heaven, composed for bass Doda Conrad, was Rorem's first published song cycle*, one he says he is "not ashamed of."[9] It is a youthful work, but
one that firmly establishes Rorem's style: a fluid vocal line, musical textures that
highlight the text in the most elegant and economical way, accompaniments that
emphasize and support the vocal writing, and a skillful blend of lyricism and emotional content. Like many of Rorem's early works, it makes far fewer demands on
the voice than some of his later songs.

For his texts, Rorem chose nine poems by Robert Herrick (1591-1674), one of
England's greatest lyric poets. Herrick's poems celebrate the abundance of life's
pleasantries with sophisticated and subtle verses, which are often erotically frank
and joyful. Herrick's verses survive in part because of their lyrical quality—a concentration of sound and verbal richness. These features make them perfect foils for
Rorem's romantic settings. The overall structure of the cycle is carefully plotted for
musical variety and symmetry.

One of the most striking songs is "Upon Julia's Clothes," a text under laid with
sensuous feeling. Rorem sets the elegant, vibrant verse in a flowing accompaniment that highlights the lightness of Julia's "silken" movements, creating a shimmering image full of delicate suggestion.

The remaining settings are no less appealing: "To Music, to Becalm his Fever"
opens the cycle with the poet's fervent supplication to Music to sustain him until
death; "Cherrie-ripe" is lighthearted but not trivial; and "To Daisies, not to shut so
Soon" has the airy brightness of an English summer day. Nestled at the heart of
the cycle are two small songs, which total only twenty measures. These are touching epitaphs to children. Children's deaths were common, tragic events in the seventeenth century. Rorem's simple setting perfectly mirrors the gentle solemnity of
the verses, and provides a moment of reflection and calm within the cycle. "To the
Willow-Tree" is lyric and wistful; the matter-of-fact tone of "Comfort to a Youth" is
softened by Rorem's musical treatment. As this point in the cycle, Rorem inserts a
brief piano interlude, which contains musical material from the preceding songs.
It both summarizes what has gone before and introduces the final song. Herrick's
declaration of noble and idealized love, "To Anthea, who may command him
Anything," completes the cycle on a note of grandeur.

Now Sleeps the Crimson Petal*   1963
(Alfred, Lord Tennyson)

Rorem's setting of "Now Sleeps the Crimson Petal" is an exotic setting
featuring blurred tonalities and opulent harmonic materials. A short piano
introduction establishes a mood of luxurious calm and introduces a motive that
functions as a unifying device through the song. Unity is also created by repeating
melodic patterns from the vocal phrases at various times through the song.

Rorem sets all of Tennyson's poem.* There are two stanzas of four lines each, which open and close the poem. The interior section of the poem consists of three sets of duplets:

> Now droops the milk-white peacock like a ghost
> And like a ghost she glimmers on to me.
>
> Now lies the earth all Danaë to the stars
> And all thy heart lies open unto me.
>
> Now slides the silent meteor on, and leaves
> A shining furrow, as thy thoughts in me.

For this section, Rorem uses the same pattern for each vocal phrase, changing it only for the last set of duplets. There, a new melodic shape appears, with more movement and text painting on the words "slides" and "meteor." Melodic material from the opening stanza is reprised for the last verse ("Now folds the lily all her sweetness up.").

This is an atmospheric setting that is rather unique in Rorem's songs.

*For comparison settings, see Roger Quilter and H.T. Burleigh.

Jeanie With the Light Brown Hair   arr. 1982
(Stephen Foster, arr. Rorem)

In homage to Stephen Foster, and for baritone Alan Titus, Rorem composed an arrangement of one of Foster's loveliest melodies, "Jeanie With the Light Brown Hair."* In keeping with the character of the melody, Rorem sets its two verses simply, allowing the melody to remain center stage for the song. The first verse is underpinned with traditional harmonies, the second verse is embellished with newer, more evocative harmonies, clothing Jeanie in a different costume, without compromising her beautiful sincerity.

*Foster's original song can be found in the Stephen Foster section.

Extended Study List
Evidence of Things Not Seen • *Hearing*• *Poems of Love and the Rain* • *Poèmes pour la paix* • *The Santa Fe Songs* (chamber work for voice, violin, viola, cello, piano) • Pippa's Song • You the Young Rainbow • Are You the New Person • Such Beauty As Hurts to Behold • The Silver Swan • *Cycle of Holy Songs* • *Women's Voices* • I Am Rose • To You • From an Unknown Past • The Serpent • Ode • See How They Love Me • Sally's Smile • *The Nantucket Songs* • For Poulenc • Sally's Smile • I Never Knew

Selected Reading
M. R. Bloomquist, " Songs of Ned Rorem: Aspects of the Musical Setting of Songs in English for Solo Voice and Piano." Doctoral diss., University of Missouri, Kansas City, 1970.
Leslie M. Holmes, "A Conversation with Ned Rorem, Part 1." *Journal of Singing* 58:5 (May/June 2002), 443-447.
_____, "A Conversation with Ned Rorem, Part 2." *Journal of Singing* 59:2 (November/December 2002), 171-174.
Arlys L. McDonald, *Ned Rorem: A Bio-Bibliography* (New York: Greenwood Press, 1989).
Bennie Middaugh, "The Songs of Ned Rorem: Aspects of Musical Style," *The NATS Bulletin*, 24:4 (May 1968), 36-39.
Philip Lieson Miller, "The Songs of Ned Rorem," *Tempo*, 127 (December 1978), 25-31.
Ned Rorem, *Knowing When to Stop: A Memoir* (New York: Simon & Schuster, 1994).

_____, *A Ned Rorem Reader* (New Haven: Yale University Press, 2001).

_____, *The Paris and New York Diaries of Ned Rorem* 1951-1961 (San Francisco: North Point Press, 1983).

_____, "A Composer Offers Some Candid Thoughts on His Art." *New York Times* (May 1, 1983), sec 2, 21.

_____, "*The NATS Bulletin* Interviews Ned Rorem." *The NATS Bulletin*, 39:2 (December 1982).

_____, *Setting the Tone: Essays and a Diary* (New York: Coward-McCann, 1983). Articles on singing and song: "The American Art Song," "More Notes on Song," "Writing Songs," and "Song and Singer."

_____, *Settling the Score: Essays on Music.* (New York: Harcourt Brace Jovanovich, 1988). See: "Poetry of Music," "Some Singing in America," "Anatomy of Two Songs," "A Postscript on Whitman."

_____, "Some Notes (Mostly Sour) on Singing Songs." *New York Times,* April 20, 1975, sec. 1, page 1.

_____, *Pure Contraption: A Composer's Essays* (New York: Holt, Rinehart & Winston, 1974).

Notes

1. Rorem, in "*The NATS Bulletin* interviews Ned Rorem" (Nov./Dec. 1982).
2. Quoted in Philip Ramey, "Ned Rorem: Not Just a Song Composer," *Keynote* 4:3 (1980). In Arlys L. McDonald, *Ned Rorem: A Bio-Bibliography*, 14.
3. Quoted in Ruth C. Friedberg, *American Art Song and American Poetry*, v. 3, 214.
4. Quoted in McDonald, *Ned Rorem: A Bio-Bibliography*, 211.
5. Ned Rorem, introductory notes, *Ned Rorem. Songs Vol. 3* (Boosey & Hawkes, 1990).
6. Ibid.
7. Ibid.
8. Ibid.
9. Some commentary taken from Carol Kimball, liner notes to *Four Composers: One Voice*. Paul Kreider, baritone; Ned Rorem, David Del Tredici, Virko Baley, and Daron Hagen, pianists. Arsis CD 142, 2003.

LEE HOIBY (b. 1926)

I love words. I love language. I take special care that the words should be understood, and not only that, but the music should help them further, to elucidate the feeling, the meaning of the words, otherwise there's no reason to set it to music.

—Lee Hoiby[1]

Although Lee Hoiby has been characterized as a twentieth-century American neoromantic, he balks at the label, protesting: "There is nothing neo about me!"[2] For Hoiby, the most important reason to compose is to complement the meaning of the words with expressive and meaningful music. At Curtis, he studied composition with Gian Carlo Menotti, who influenced his style, and he acknowledges Samuel Barber as his "spiritual guide, my mentor musically in a way, just by osmosis."[3]

Hoiby's compositions are consistently natural, expressive, accessible, and always vocally rewarding for a singer. Hoiby's songs certainly reflect the dramatic flair of Menotti and the warm lyricism of Barber. They are marked by a classical character, always lyrical (Hoiby pays homage to Schubert as influencing his vocal writing). His texts range from joyful to serious, and blatant humor finds a place in his poetic settings as well.

He wrote his first songs in the 1950s when he was a student at the Curtis Institute; at present writing, he has composed over 100 songs and still counting. In addition to songs, Hoiby has composed piano concertos, chamber and orchestral music, and music for ballet, theater, television and film. But vocal music forms the largest portion of his compositions: operas, works for chorus and orchestra, an oratorio, and his many songs.

Where the Music Comes From
(Lee Hoiby)

1974, revised 1986

This is one of Hoiby's most familiar and instantly appealing songs. In it, Hoiby bases the piano accompaniment on a chordal motive, which he expands to provide a flowing rhythmic structure that propels the song from beginning to end. In its original version, Hoiby dedicated it to "The Guide," a support group he was involved with at one point in his life. In 1986 Hoiby revised the song, a practice he regularly employs with his vocal compositions. Its three stanzas are each highlighted by a modulation into a higher key, and the overall feeling is that of a gentle popular song.

Lady of the Harbor
(Emma Lazarus)

1985

Hoiby composed this song for the centenary of the Statue of Liberty. Using Emma Lazarus's poignant words inscribed at the base of the statue as his text, he wrote one of his most effective songs, filled with quiet passages and bravura moments.

The vocal line begins quietly, with the accompaniment suggesting the flow of water surrounding the "lady of the harbor." Eighth rests on a series of downbeats intensify the poetic line ("your poor...your huddled masses...yearning to breathe free"), building to a leap of a major ninth, highlighting the drama of Lazarus's words ("Send these...the homeless, tempest-toss'd to me"). A meter change from $\frac{9}{8}$ to $\frac{6}{8}$ at the word "lamp" emphasizes the word "lamp," and the singer's high note adds force to the musical climax. A steady pulse underpins the song, highlighting the solemnity of the text and creating tension throughout the piece.

Jabberwocky
(Lewis Carroll)

1986

Lewis Carroll's classic tale of the fantastic Jabberwock inspired one of Hoiby's most humorous and colorful settings. The story provides many opportunities for text painting, and the song contains many instances of this, particularly in the piano.

The piano accompaniment contains figures that evoke bouncy images of a child skipping, characterizing the carefree youth and providing a fitting introduction for the whimsical scene. This buoyant accompaniment continues throughout the song, providing continuity for the story.

Even as the bizarre tale unfolds, Hoiby's vocal line never loses its lyrical, elegant character. Only at the appearance of the Jabberwock do both piano and voice take on a dramatic character. Broad operatic lyricism paints the line "Come to my arms, my beamish boy!" The entire song is a miniature *scena*, whimsical and true to Carroll's fantastic text, ending as it began, with the same music.

There Came a Wind Like a Bugle   1987
(Emily Dickinson)

This is a large song, quite operatic in style. It is found in the collection *The Shining Place,* (formerly titled *Four Dickinson Songs)*. The piano accompaniment is technically demanding, increasing the tempo with a series of chromatic scale figures that give way to triplets. The triplets prepare a wonderful melisma for the voice when the word "flying [tidings]" converges with the piano figures to intensify the text. This example is one of the few in which Hoiby uses *fioritura* for the voice.

The Serpent*   1979
(Theodore Roethke)

Hoiby composed a set of six songs for soprano Leontyne Price, titled *Songs for Leontyne* ("The Doe," "In the Wand of the Wind," "Evening," "Autumn," "Winter Song," and "The Serpent"). "The Serpent," about a serpent so obsessed with singing that he is compelled to "give up serpenting," is a story that never fails to delight audiences. Roethke's comic story is filled with alliterative "hisses" that indulge Hoiby's sense of humor and provide many chances of text painting. Energetically rhythmic, the song contains coloratura figures in the wide-range vocal line (middle C to high B-flat) that call for considerable vocal flexibility. Like other Hoiby songs that "tell a story," this piece has the flavor of a tiny operatic scene.

*For a comparison setting, see Ned Rorem.

In the Wand of the Wind   1952
(John Fandel)

This is another setting from *Songs for Leontyne,* using John Fandel's evocative, visual poetry. Hoiby's setting flies by, quicksilver as the poetic images it illustrates ("This was a day the trees turned silver in the wand of the wind"). In spite of the quick tempo, the musical texture is substantial, and the vocal line has an almost bravura style as it joyfully welcomes springtime.

What if...   1986
(Samuel Taylor Coleridge)

Arpeggios and descending figures in the lower piano range introduce Coleridge's gentle, questioning text. Accompaniment figures seem open-ended and hazy, complementing the text, with veiled, almost mysterious, half-finished images of sleep. Allusions to sleep in the text produce lyrical, hushed vocal phrases that broaden only at the words "And what if when you awoke, you had the flower in your hand?" The final measures maintain the enigmatic mood; the final cadence is indecisive, ending with a single piano note.

Extended Study List

The Shining Place (formerly *Four Dickinson Songs*)• *Southern Voices* • *Songs of the Seasons* • *Four Whitman Songs* • *Night Songs* • *Songs for Leontyne* • *Three French Songs* • *O Florida* • Lied der Liebe • Always it's Spring • Go and Catch a Falling Star • An Immorality • The Lamb • Autumn • Sonnet 116 • *Three Ages of Woman* • *Bon Appetit!* (a miniature monodrama-text by Julia Child)

Selected Reading

Lori Ellefson Bade, "Lee Hoiby: The composer and his compositional style, his role in the history of American music, and his song output." Doctoral diss., *University of Texas, Austin*, 1994.

Dolores Fredrickson, "Lee Hoiby: Incurable Romantic." *Clavier*, 31 (January 1992): 16-19, 24.

Lee Hoiby, "Contemporary Art Music: Observations from Those Who Create It," *Music and Artists* 5 (June-July 1972): 13.

Robin Rice, "The Songs of Lee Hoiby" (Doctoral thesis. Cincinnati College-Conservatory of Music, 1993). Excerpts and quotations used by permission.

Liner notes. *Songs of American Composers.* Leonarda Records. 1984. Performances of "The Doe," "The Serpent," "In the Wand of the Wind," "Autumn," and "Winter Song" by Kristine Ciesinski, mezzo-soprano with Lee Hoiby, pianist.

Notes

1. Quoted in Robin Rice, *The Songs of Lee Hoiby*, 17. Unpublished doctoral thesis. Cincinnati College-Conservatory of Music, 1993, 17. Dr. Rice has graciously given the author permission to quote from his dissertation.
2. Ibid., 9.
3. Ibid., 11.

RICHARD FAITH (b. 1926)*

> Faith considers himself only to be a composer of the heart who relies on his musical gifts to bring joy to others.
>
> —William Lavonis[1]

For too long the songs of Richard Faith were known mostly to those inside the university music community. Now his songs receive attention from those outside the ivy-covered walls, thanks to their recent publication by Leyerle Publications. Faith's sixty-odd songs run the gamut from sophisticated concert pieces to simple miniatures. He composed his first songs around 1944 and continues to write today.

Faith developed an early interest in song literature largely because of his sister, Peggy Engstrom, and her gift for singing. Faith is eclectic in his selection of texts, choosing from a cross-section of excellent and often unexpected verse—Percy Bysshe Shelley, John Masefield, Edgar Allen Poe, Edward Lear, Conrad Aiken, Christina Rossetti, and William Shakespeare. He is fond of texts that provide images of nature. He treats poems imaginatively and intuitively, with an excellent sense of prosody. He groups many songs according to subject matter, and they may be sung separately or as a set. Faith encourages transposition to suit the needs of the individual singer.

Faith's general musical style might be termed neoromantic/impressionist. According to Lavonis, Faith's style is strongly influenced by Debussy, Ravel, and Rachmaninoff, with Brahms as a model for formal structure.[2] Faith's harmonic style is grounded in tonality but contains elements of modality and harmonic color that call to mind English song, specifically Vaughan Williams.

Faith is an especially gifted composer of expressive melodies. He is scrupulous in setting a poem's rhythm and often includes shifting meters that accommodate varying phrase lengths. Since Faith is himself a fine pianist, most of his songs have fairly sophisticated accompaniments which often contain figures derived from poetic rhythms.

Richard Faith is widely recognized for composing pedagogical works for the piano. From 1961 until his retirement in 1989, Faith was in residence at the University of Arizona as professor of piano. Since 1981 he has won awards from ASCAP for his compositions.

*Biographical material and annotations on the songs used by kind permission of the composer and Leyerle Publications, publishers of *The Songs of Richard Faith.*

Remembrances   1946-89

Music, when soft voices die • The keen stars were twinkling •
Remember me • Music I heard with you

Faith did not compose these songs as a group, but wrote them as individual pieces during the period 1946 and 1989. Because of their subject matter, Faith later decided to make them a set.

MUSIC, WHEN SOFT VOICES DIE (SHELLEY). This beautifully expressive setting is probably one of Faith's most frequently performed songs. A dark and somber mood pervades its first section, giving way to feelings of greater tenderness at the words "Rose leaves..."

Faith: "The principal *motif* in the introduction of this song is presented in its first measure. Measure 2 is a varied repetition of this motif. Measures 3-4 together are one unit as are measures 5 and 6. Within their confines, each of these segments must be played very legato and expressively."

THE KEEN STARS WERE TWINKLING (SHELLEY). Faith: "With tenderness of expression and inflection, sing this piece with a conversational quality. The mysterious romanticism of the poem is conveyed by the accompaniment. At the phrase, 'Though the sound overpowers,' I suggest a more powerful delivery, as if compelled by an inner force. This will create a strong contrast to the preceding and following sections."

REMEMBER ME (CHRISTINA ROSSETTI). Faith composed a simple, lyrical setting for this song. He directs it to be sung in the "plaintive manner of a folk song." Faith: "Although the words have a sentimental quality and the music makes flowing arches, it would be best to understate its romantic effusiveness. Strive for a clear, direct delivery; yet, the voice should sound as if it is coming from a distance."

MUSIC I HEARD WITH YOU (CONRAD AIKEN). Faith: "Emotional directness is a primary characteristic of this song. Singer and pianist may allow themselves to be overtly expressive. It is important that the singer not deliver a string of individual words but rather make the sentences come to live. For example: 'Music I heard with *you* was *more* than *music.*' The singer's part contains three *ossias*. In each case the higher note is preferred."

Christina Rossetti Songs   1991-92

Spring quiet • Echo • My heart is like a singing bird

For a more recent composition, Faith again turned to Christina Rossetti for poetic inspiration, as he had done in 1954 when he set her verse "Remember Me." This work was commissioned by mezzo-soprano Julie Simson and pianist Gary Arvin and is dedicated to them.

This set is typical of Faith's work in that he places considerable importance on song order for mood and drama. Faith: "Although 'Echo' was composed first, I decided to place it second in the set—after 'Spring Quiet' and before 'My heart is like a singing bird.' I felt that they were more effectively balanced with this arrangement."

SPRING QUIET. Faith: "Underlying the trills and warblings in the accompaniment are words that are full of reflective thought. First, we learn of the poet's longing for spring. Then, with the words, 'We spread no snare,' and, 'Here is heard an echo of the far sea,' it is apparent that this little poem has deeper meanings than we first thought. Thus, there are two states, or moods, that need to be fused into one; the feeling of lyrical rapture that spring has inspired and the musings of a religious mystic who has seen beyond mere outward beauty. At the words 'Here the sun shineth,' the voice should begin to soar with the idea of describing great distances. This allusion to far spaces quickly dissolves, however, as the music flows to its ending with murmurings of spring-like sounds."

ECHO. Faith: "This song begins in the piano with a slow, sad dance that the narrator perhaps heard long ago in the arms of her/his lover. When the singing begins, I envision it being performed *sotto voce* and *parlando*. The coda 'Come back to me in dreams' introduces a new melody. Although the vocal line is lower in *tessitura*, the expression of love is intensified."

MY HEART IS LIKE A SINGING BIRD. Faith: "In contrast to the preceding songs this one displays strong expressions of joy. Several shades of feeling are revealed about love: its wonder, its joy, victory, and even its humor. A contrasting mood is felt in the middle section with the words, 'Raise me a dais of silk and down,' in which the poet creates colorful words and pictures. All this should be performed without rhythmic interruption as the song moves rapturously to its final climax."

Four Elizabethan Songs   1982

To Celia • O, the month of May • Sonnet LIV • It was a lover and his lass

Unlike *Remembrances*, these songs *were* conceived as a set, although each song may be performed separately. Each song was composed in the order in which it stands in the group; Faith believes this order presents the best possible contrast and balance when the four songs are performed together.

Musically, the group contains balanced forms, traditional harmonies and sparser textures that capture the spirit of the texts. The set is dedicated to tenor Jerold Siena.

To Celia (Drink to me only with thine eyes...Letter 33 of Philostratus, translated by Ben Jonson). Faith: "In reading this poem one evening, I felt particularly dissatisfied with the traditional musical setting. I wanted to hear it with as much romantic intensity as the old Greek Philostratus projected and which Ben Jonson recreated so well in his translation. Optimistically, I began my own setting of the words, attempting to catch their passion while retaining a certain stateliness that seems inherent in the text.

"Ringing declaration of love is heard at the outset of the song. The second section beginning with 'I sent thee late a rosy wreath,' should be *quasi parlando*. By the time we reach 'since when it breathes and smells,' we have returned to the passionate feeling of the beginning. With the reiteration of the first melody on 'Drink to me,' however, the accompaniment creates a new mood, at once more intimate, yet dance-like. The feeling of total directness is now gone; we are existing as though through a veil of time. The closing is both tender and nostalgic."

O, the month of May (Thomas Decker). Faith: "Clear articulation and rhythmic precision are the prime requisites for performing this humorous song. While keeping a steady tempo throughout, the singer has the challenge of projecting three moods.

"The first section is carefree and gay. The section beginning with 'Now the nightingale' is more *legato*, more plaintive. With the words, 'But O, I spy the cuckoo,' there is a need for more dramatic intensity. When a woman sings 'O the month of May,' she may wish to substitute male names for 'Peg' and 'Peggy' and 'King' for 'Queen.'"

Sonnet LIV (Shakespeare). Faith: "This is one of Shakespeare's many sonnets in which he addresses a youth of noble rank who was probably Henry Wriothesley, Earl of Southampton, and also Shakespeare's patron. It is the poet's task to urge the Earl to marry and to become a father in order to preserve the grace and beauty of such noble lineage. The symbolism in this sonnet is not difficult to understand; the rose stands for marriage; and the canker-blooms, 'which die unto themselves,' represent the unmarried state.

"The mood here is one of restrained passion. The poet is using powerful means of persuasion but he also defers to the young man's beauty and high position. In performance these elements should all be present: beauty of tone; elegant diction; and controlled passion."

It was a lover and his lass (Shakespeare).* Faith develops the song from the rhythm of the opening line, using it in the piano introduction and then as a generative element in the accompaniment.[3] Faith: "Jocular, jerky, bouncy are to me the words that describe these lines and their musical setting. Bring out these characteristics within the framework of an ongoing rhythmic line."

*For comparison settings of this text, see Gerald Finzi, Geoffrey Bush, Peter Warlock, and Mario Castelnuovo-Tedesco.

Extended Study List

Sea Pieces • *Songs of Spring* • The Solitary Reaper • Dover Beach • Dark Hills • The Sun Has Set • Hymn of Praise (voice/organ) • The Wind Blows Out of the Gates of the Day • God Be in My Head • What Sweeter Music

Selected Reading

Richard Faith, Performance notes in *The Songs of Richard Faith:* Vol. 1, for voice and piano (Geneseo, N.Y.: Leyerle Publications, 1993).

William J. Lavonis, "The Songs of Richard Faith." Doctoral diss., University of Cincinnati, 1991.

_____, "The Songs of Richard Faith." *The NATS Journal* 51:1 (Sept/Oct 1994), 13-18,72.

Lori Laux Lovell, "The Solo Songs of Richard Faith: A General Survey of Style" D.M.A. diss., University of Nevada, Las Vegas, 2002).

Notes

1. William Lavonis, "The Songs of Richard Faith," *The NATS Journal* 51:1, 72.
2. Ibid., 13.
3. Ibid., 16.

DOMINICK ARGENTO (b. 1927)

The voice is not just another instrument. It is the instrument par excellence.
—Dominick Argento[1]

Songs represent the composer's purest utterance, his most private being, unadorned, uncluttered, devoid of posturing, spontaneous, distilled.
—Dominick Argento[2]

Dominick Argento is one of America's most distinguished contemporary composers, and certainly its leading composer of lyric opera. His operas have been performed in important opera houses in Europe and the United States, and his new operas now attract singers of international reputation. He has been honored with numerous awards, including the Pulitzer Prize for *The Diary of Virginia Woolf,* two Guggenheims grants, a Fulbright for study in Italy, three National Endowment for the Arts grants, and ASCAP awards.

The majority of Argento's compositions are vocal and demonstrate his tremendous knowledge of voice. His widely diverse works display his innate dramatic sense and have instant audience appeal. Although his style remains predominately tonal in context, his music freely combines tonality, atonality, and twelve-tone writing in a rich harmonic mix.

Argento's first song cycle was *songs about spring* (e.e. cummings), an early work completed during his undergraduate days at Peabody Conservatory. Many of his vocal compositions were influenced by his wife, soprano Carolyn Bailey.

His catalog of works is heavy with vocal works for the stage—operas, chamber operas, and monodramas, including *Postcard from Morocco, The Voyage of Edgar Allen Poe, Miss Havisham's Fire, Casanova's Homecoming, The Aspern Papers,* and his thirteenth work for the stage, *The Dream of Valentino,* was premiered in January 1994 by the Washington Opera.

With few exceptions, Argento chooses prose texts rather than poems for his song cycles: Elizabeth Barrett Browning's letters to her sister (*Casa Guidi*), the expedition journals of the ill-fated Swedish explorer Salomon August Andrée (*The Andrée Expedition*) and the diary of Virginia Woolf (*From the Diary of Virginia*

Woolf). Argento stated that "I've almost given up setting poetry, just because prose allows me more freedom musically, to make lines longer, to make them go in interesting directions. Poetry in a sense dictates the highs and lows, the duration, the rhythm. I find it liberating to work with prose."[3] Argento is also drawn to the element of personal self-discovery that exists in all these texts: "The common thread in all these texts—songs *and* operas—is that the principal speakers, for one reason or another, stop doing whatever it is they normally do...they stop looking out over the world and look inward, into their own hearts and discover something there they had been too distracted to notice before or too bound by convention to admit."[4]

From the Diary of Virginia Woolf   1974

The Diary. April, 1919 • Anxiety. October, 1920 • Fancy. February, 1927 •
Hardy's Funeral. January, 1928 • Rome. May, 1935 • War. June, 1940 •
Parents. December, 1940 • Last Entry. March, 1941

From the Diary of Virginia Woolf is a powerful work—intensely dramatic, memorable and unsettling. Commissioned by the Schubert Club of St. Paul, Minnesota, and first performed by mezzo-soprano Janet Baker and pianist Martin Isepp, this cycle won the 1975 Pulitzer Prize for music. It immediately became a part of the standard repertory.

When Argento learned that Baker would sing this cycle, he began searching for a text. "For me, the end result of anything I've written is the merging of my music with the persona of the singer who is singing it."[5] To display Baker's immense sensitivity, consummate artistry and interpretive skill, Argento wanted a text "rich yet subtle, something with a wide range of emotions yet whole and singular, something feminine but not the hackneyed sentiments so frequently ascribed to women by male authors."[6] He quickly chose a text by English novelist Virginia Woolf, whose novels he had recently been reading.

At first, Argento thought he might use several passages from Woolf's novel *The Waves,* describing the phases of a sunrise over the sea. While researching the novel, he also read Woolf's diary, published by her husband after her death. "No sooner had I read a few entries there than I realized this was the place to search, not the novels,"[7] he said.

The eight diary excerpts Argento finally chose for his cycle chronicle major events or emotional landmarks in Woolf's life from 1919, the beginning of the diary, to 1941, the last entry before her suicide. The entries document Woolf's journey of artistic self-discovery, and her dispassionate observations of her literary, emotional, social, and creative life.

"I decided on a sort of twentieth century *Frauenliebe und -leben* and even my last song's return to the musical material of the first is Schumannesque,"[8] Argento commented. Although Argento's work is complex, the music and text are connected throughout the cycle. The cycle begins with the first diary entry and ends with the last, giving the work a feeling of unity. The first song contains a statement of a twelve-tone row that forms the work's nucleus. Its structure is highly lyric and flexible. The last song contains wisps of themes and rhythmic fragments from the previous songs and repeats a section of the opening with almost identical notation. Thematic repetition is a central element to the cycle; themes are manipulated like *leitmotivs*. Piano and voice share motives and phrase fragments throughout.

From the Diary of Virginia Woolf is a tour de force for performers, with its operatic tone and a mood that flows continuously from one song to the next. Due to Argento's tight integration between the voice and accompaniment, these songs require a singer and pianist who have exceptional ensemble skills. The texts express a variety of moods: gaiety, reflection, solemnity and despair.

The songs contain moments of exquisite lyricism and even within their disparate moods and emotion, they retain an elegant style and feeling. The wide-ranging vocal line contains skips, leaps and intricate rhythms; its style is often highly chromatic and predominantly declamatory. The piano writing is complex, requiring an exceptional pianist with the dramatic and technical skill to control the metric and rhythmic pacing.

From the Diary of Virginia Woolf is an extraordinarily riveting work, immediately drawing the listener into Woolf's personal world. Listeners and performers alike comment on the cycle's strong emotional impact. Argento says "Of all my cycles, *Virginia Woolf* most directly addresses the issue of 'who am I, what do I really feel?' The strong concentration these texts focus on self-knowledge may have prompted me to write my most moving music."[9]

THE DIARY. Woolf muses on what form her diary should take. "I should like to come back after a year or two and find that the collection had coalesced....into a mold transparent enough to reflect the light of our life." This song introduces the modified tone row that Argento uses to symbolize the diary.

ANXIETY. Woolf describes her anxieties about life: happiness is always tempered by the feeling of "walking across a narrow strip of pavement over an abyss." As she expresses her thoughts, Woolf reveals her impending madness. Rapid skittering, nonstop eighth notes in the piano mirror Woolf's nervous tension and emotional apprehension: "Why is life so tragic; why, why, why?" The same tension propels the vocal passages—quick note values, rapid tempo, and syncopation, requiring machine-gun-like diction.

Argento uses a motive from Gay's *The Beggar's Opera* as Woolf's text speaks of attending a performance of the work.

FANCY. This song is a teasing self-conversation. Woolf begins: "Why not invent a new play?" Her mind game distills actions into the most streamlined form. She uses two-word phrases and "invents" two protagonists, male and female. Argento presents each miniature phrase in a different meter, and varies the piano figures for each. "Woman thinks. He does." He also divides the tone row equally between the genders—half for woman, half for man.

HARDY'S FUNERAL. Woolf writes a detailed description of Thomas Hardy's funeral—slightly melodramatic, often humorous, suffused with the sound s of a huge cathedral organ and tolling bells, and filled with the sense of fragile mortality. Argento's setting contains music that is reminiscent of swinging censers, liturgical chants ("Requiem Aeternam"), and the solemn tread of a funeral procession.

ROME. Woolf's words provide a sunny portrait of Rome—a composite of kaleidoscopic snapshots from her memories of the city. Argento begins the accompaniment with a mandolin tune and lets the musical texture grow thicker as

Woolf loses herself in a comfortable, rambling narrative. Argento includes a quotation from Puccini's *Tosca* —a musical reminiscence of Rome that complements Woolf's memories. This contracts back into the sparser texture of the opening section, as she writes of the prime minister's offer to recommend her for the Companion of Honour. "No, no, no," she demurs.

WAR. World War II was full blown in the last months of Virginia Woolf's life. German planes flew over her house daily, bombs fell so close they rattled the windows, and her London home was destroyed in an air raid.

Argento's setting contains the sounds of an air raid and machine guns; the song's style is recitative throughout, accompanied by machine-gun-like repeated high notes, alternating with a similar pattern of notes in the very low range. Piano figures barely overlap the unaccompanied vocal phrases at the beginning of the song and merge only near the song's end. Linked with the text, this musical effect is chilling. Woolf's line "I can't conceive that there will be a 27 June 1941" is prophetic.

PARENTS. Woolf's tranquil memories of her parents evoke some of the cycle's most lyrical moments for both voice and piano. Woolf's warm collection of remembrances gathers into a reverie, finally interrupted by the preceding song's insistent machine-gun motive, now acting as a psychological memory trigger. The vocal line's lyrical phrases disintegrate into terse recitative. Piano and voice try to recapture the serene memory by beginning a lyric phrase again, but it vanishes, unfinished.

LAST ENTRY. Four days before she died, Virginia Woolf wrote her last diary entry. She wrote things down, no matter how trivial, feeding her hope that all her "odds and ends" would blend into a coherent life pattern. What *does* coalesce from Woolf's diary is a profound human portrait of the author—intricate, poignant, fascinating—captured in Argento's skillful integration of text, mood, and music.

Argento introduces no new motives in this song: instead, he repeats music and text from the previous songs, as if searching for an ordered pattern to fit Woolf's need for an organized existence.

The piano reminds us of a clock tolling the time as the text expresses Woolf's thoughts: "And now with some pleasure I find that it's seven; and must cook dinner. Haddock and sausage meat. I think it is true that one gains a certain hold on sausage and haddock by writing them down."

Six Elizabethan Songs   1957

Spring • Sleep • Winter • Dirge • Diaphenia • Hymn

About this work, Argento writes:

These *Six Elizabethan Songs* exist in two versions: the first—with piano accompaniment, was composed in Florence during November and December of 1957 and is dedicated to the tenor Nicholas Di Virgilio, who premiered the work the following year; the second version, with baroque ensemble accompaniment, was written in 1962 for the soprano Carolyn Bailey, who premiered the cycle in Minneapolis with the University Baroque Ensemble.

The songs are called "Elizabethan" because the lyrics are drawn from that rich period in literature, while the music is in the spirit (if not the manner) of the great English composer-singer-lutenist, John Dowland. The main concern is the paramount importance of the poetry and the primacy of the vocal line over a relatively simple and supportive accompaniment. [10]

Argento's most popular and most performed cycle is *Six Elizabethan Songs,* his second song cycle. Argento acknowledges that he chose these texts for their convenience —to fulfill Di Virgilio's request for a recital cycle. Though Florence's bookstores offered limited choices for English poetry, Argento found a volume of Elizabethan lyrics which he decided to use.

The cycle is characterized by strong lyricism. The texts lend themselves to formal structures and are constructed in two and three-part sections, varied slightly. Piano and voice are integrated, but not to the extent found in *Virginia Woolf.* Accompaniments demand a pianist with great facility, and the vocal writing is extremely lyric with a number of sustained high notes and other passages requiring a singer with considerable flexibility.

SPRING (THOMAS NASH). The first song of the cycle is a charming tribute to the Spring—lyric and buoyant. The form is ABA'. The piano patterns suggest a lute or guitar accompaniment.

SLEEP (SAMUEL DANIEL)[*]. As in Song 1, the opening melody is repeated at the song's close. The lovely setting is characterized by long lyric lines accompanied by rich harmonies.

WINTER (WILLIAM SHAKESPEARE). Playful pointillistic vocal lines abound in this two-stanza text, set in a headlong tempo that calls for a singer with flexible diction and an articulate pianist. The driving rhythmic setting is characteristic of the English *gigue*, using points of imitation between voice and piano.[11]

DIRGE (WILLIAM SHAKESPEARE). "Come Away Death" is a favorite Elizabethan text for composers.[**] The two-stanza text contains bleak evocations of death which the piano accompanies with simple thirds in the right hand. Each stanza begins with vocal phrases that are exact replicas—an eerie echo-like device. Although the musical texture remains simple throughout, the harmony is varied and interesting.

DIAPHENIA (HENRY CONSTABLE). Constable pays ardent homage to his beloved. Argento uses a breathless tempo that beautifully captures the poet's quicksilver text. He interrupts this tempo at each stanza's conclusion by adding phrases with expanded note values and breadth of mood.

HYMN (BEN JONSON). This song is a majestic hymn of praise to Diana, goddess of the hunt. Argento marks his vocal writing with sensuous lyric phrases of considerable breadth. He uses the piano melody, played by the right hand, to double the vocal line in some sections. Each stanza ends with the phrase "Goddess, excellently bright" set with the same melody, varied and expanded in the final repetition.

*For comparison settings of this text, see Ivor Gurney and Peter Warlock.
**Also see settings by Quilter, Finzi, Leguerney, and Korngold.

Extended Study List

songs about spring • *The Andrée Expedition* • *Casa Guidi* • *Letters from Composers* (high voice, guitar) • *To Be Sung upon the water* (high voice, clarinet, piano) • *Miss Manners on Music* • Operas: *Postcard from Morocco, The Voyage of Edgar Allen Poe, Miss Havisham's Fire, Casanova's Homecoming, The Aspern Papers, The Dream of Valentino.*

Selected Reading

Dominick Argento, *Catalogue Raisonné as Memoir: A Composer's Life* (Minneapolis: University of Minnesota Press, 2004).

_____,"The Matter of Text," *The NATS Journal,* 44:4 (March/April 1988), 6-10. Reprint of his keynote address to the NATS national convention in San Antonio, 1987.

_____, " The Composer and the Singer," *The NATS Bulletin,* 33:3, (May 1977), 18-25. Reprint of his keynote address to the NATS national convention in Philadelphia, 1976.

_____, Liner Notes. *Argento: Six Elizabethan Songs.* American Contemporary Words and Music. CRI Recording. CRI 380 stereo LP. 1978.

Leslie Kandell, Liner notes. *Permit Me Voyage. Songs by American Composers.* Mary Ann Hart, mezzo-soprano; Dennis Helmrich, pianist. Albany Records. TROY 118. 1994.

Roger Pines, "Dominick Argento: Writing American Bel Canto," *Opera Monthly,* 1:8, December 1988, 20-25.

Roger Scanlan, "Spotlight on Contemporary American Composer," in *The NATS Bulletin* 22:3 (Feb/March 1976).

Notes

1. Quoted in *Boosey & Hawkes Newsletter* 15:1, May 1985.
2. Argento, "The Composer and the Singer." Keynote address. NATS national convention, 1976, 20.
3. Roger Pines, "Dominick Argento: Writing American Bel Canto," *Opera Monthly,* 1:8, 22.
4. Dominick Argento. Keynote address. NATS national convention, 1987.
5. Ibid., 9. The Argento commissioned cycle was originally slated for Beverly Sills and later Jessye Norman, but both singers were unable to schedule the performance. Argento had very different ideas about texts for each of the sopranos. When Baker accepted the assignment, Argento began searching for a text suitable for her artistic personality.
6. Argento, NATS Keynote address, 1976, 24.
7. Ibid.
8. Leslie Kandell. Liner notes. *Permit Me Voyage: Songs by American Composers.*Albany Records, CD TROY 118, 1994.
9. Argento. NATS Keynote address, 1987, 10.
10. Argento. Liner notes. *Six ElizabethanSongs.* CRI recording 380 stereo LP, 1978.
11. Roger Scanlan, Roger Scanlan, "Spotlight on Contemporary American Composer," *The NATS Bulletin,* 53.

RICHARD HUNDLEY (b. 1931)

He is an impassioned lyricist, who loves to caress the words with beguiling melody. Singers clearly love to sing these songs. They're a balm for weary throats and weary ears.

—Thor Eckert, *The Christian Science Monitor*[1]

Richard Hundley is at the forefront of active American song composers. Born in Cincinnati and raised in Kentucky, he now resides in New York City. He attended the Cincinnati Conservatory of Music and continued his musical studies in New York with Israel Citkowitz, William Flanagan and Virgil Thomson.

Hundley's numerous songs are now enjoying critical acclaim and are regularly performed on concert platforms. His songs have been sung and championed by several generations of famous and rising artists: among them, Arlene Auger, Teresa Stratas, Frederica von Stade, Anna Moffo, Judith Blegen, Rosalind Elias, Betty Allen, William Warfield, Giorgio Tozzi, Kenneth Riegel, John Cheek, and Paul Sperry.

Hundley is one of only twelve composers recognized as a "standard American composer for vocalists" by the International American Music Competition sponsored by Carnegie Hall and the Rockefeller Foundation. He shares this honor with the distinguished company of Dominick Argento, Samuel Barber, Paul Bowles, Aaron Copland, David Diamond, John Duke, William Flanagan, Charles Griffes, Charles Ives, and Virgil Thomson. Hundley has also been honored with three MacDowell Fellowships, and won ASCAP awards, and he receives numerous commissions from performers eager to sing his lyric, beautiful melodies.

Hundley's songs exhibit a return to romantic feeling, tonal harmony, and melody. About his music, Hundley says, "The chief source of inspiration in my songs are the words themselves, and I try to recreate the emotion I experienced on first reading the poems. My ultimate aim is to crystallize emotion."

Melody is the prime ingredient in Hundley's songs. "Hundley's songs could stand on their vocal lines alone," according to Virgil Thomson. James Keller, reviewing the premiere of Hundley's *Songs for Soprano, Flute and Piano* in 1992, wrote in *Musical America* that "this composer is a sort of American Poulenc, expert at creating characterful melodies and illuminating their corners with flashes of harmonic surprise."[2]

In addition to his many songs, Hundley has also composed choral works, chamber music, a piano sonata, and several songs with orchestra. Drawing on his personal experiences with many of the best- known American composers and international singers, Hundley is in demand for his lectures and master classes on American song literature in general, and his own music in particular. He gives an annual master class on his songs at the Juilliard School.

The Astronomers (An Epitaph)   1959
(Based on an inscription found in Allegheny, Pennsylvania)

Susan Campbell   *Brian Campbell*
1863-1910   *1862-1909*

Astronomers
We have loved the stars too deeply
To be afraid of the night.

A poignant epitaph provides the text for "Astronomers," one of Hundley's most beautiful and effective songs. The vocal line begins as a one-line recitative, accompanied by quiet chords. The texture expands beautifully as the singer finishes the names and dates, sings the word "astronomers," and begins the last extended "epitaph" phrase which arches into the night's void and disappears in a quiet *diminuendo*. An extended postlude provides a wonderful solo moment for the pianist and exquisitely captures the breadth and mystery of the starry night.

Sweet Suffolk Owl   1979
(Anonymous Elizabethan verse 1619)

Hundley balances the witty mood of this Elizabethan verse with a slightly pompous accompaniment of heavy chords that retains a buoyant feeling throughout this brief song. The vocal line features dotted rhythms and gentle syncopation. A miniature melisma on the word "rolls" provides a flash of text painting. The final measures reprise the two phrases of the owl's provocative cry, "Te whit, te whoo!"

Ballad on Queen Anne's Death   1962
(Anonymous)

Marked *Allegretto,* this charming song fluctuates between $\frac{3}{8}$, $\frac{5}{8}$, and $\frac{6}{8}$ time, with a piano accompaniment reminiscent of an Elizabethan lute. The song is a gentle paean to Queen Anne, lamenting her death by observing how the spring months (March, April, May) react in sympathy, having lost the "flower of flowers." The entire song has the feel of an improvised ballad, with fluctuating rhythms, varying stresses within the vocal phrases, and the piano's intimate, plucked accompaniment.

Some Sheep Are Loving
(Gertrude Stein, Lesson 12 from the *First Reader*)

Hundley composed this insouciant song for contralto Lili Chookasian who wanted a light, fast song to end her recitals and found such songs in short supply for her voice type in the early 1960s. Hundley acknowledges this was his "first experience at setting a long, wordy, abstract poem. Virgil Thomson suggested I set the words for clarity, and assured me that the meaning would take care of itself."[3] Hundley set Gertrude Stein's crazy play on words and word-sounds as a bouncy waltz with a pointillistic vocal line, perfectly in sync with the kaleidoscopic text.

Come Ready and See Me   1971
(James Purdy)

Hundley chose a poem by his close friend, James Purdy, as the text for one of his most popular songs. Hundley believes that the American musical theater has strongly influenced today's art song,[4] and he wrote "Come Ready and See Me" with such flowing style and beautiful melody that it seems to belong on the Broadway stage.

James Purdy's poem expresses longing for a love not yet experienced ("come ready and see me before it's too late...come before the years run out"). The arpeggio-filled accompaniment provides a graceful feeling of movement throughout.

Waterbird   1988
(James Purdy)

"Waterbird" began its life as part of a cantata Hundley composed in 1980 (*The Sea is Swimming Tonight*). Its beautiful melody so affected tenor Paul Sperry[*] that he commissioned a solo version.

Hundley created a strophic setting for the poem's two brief stanzas. He wrote a tiny piano interlude introducing the return of the beautiful melody, this time underpinned with a heavier, more insistent piano texture consisting of figures that evoke watery images. With the final coda, he reprises the poem's first line, and the closing measures express a questioning atmosphere.

*Sperry has recorded this and a number of other Hundley songs (see "Selected Reading"). He is recognized as an outstanding interpreter and passionate champion of American art song.

Moonlight's Watermelon   1993
(Jose Garcia Villa)

This song belongs to *Octaves and Sweet Sounds*, a collection of songs to poems by twentieth-century poets. The work was commissioned by Art Song Minnesota, a festival sponsored by the University of Minnesota. The songs were first performed by mezzo-soprano Glenda Maurice and pianist Ruth Palmer at St. Paul's McKnight Theatre in The Ordway in St. Paul during the summer of 1990. The songs may be sung as a set, or they can be performed individually by men or women.

Hundley's buoyant setting of this lighthearted text is akin in mood and style to "Some Sheep Are Loving." Hundley cast both songs as waltzes, and both songs use texts that play with the sound and sense of words.

This song's accompaniment figures occasionally recall a Joplinesque rag and a broader range of overall mood and texture. "Moonlight's Watermelon" is a charming romp, a playful setting of equally playful words.

Extended Study List

My Master Hath a Garden (Anonymous Elizabethan Verse) • Maiden Snow (Kenneth Patchen) • For Your Delight (Robert Louis Stevenson) • Evening Hours (James Purdy) • Spring (Shakespeare) • Isaac Greentree (An Epitaph) • *Octaves and Sweet Sounds* (1993): Strings in the Earth and Air (James Joyce); Seashore Girls (e.e. cummings); Moonlight's Watermelon (Jose Garcia Villa); Straightway Beauty On Me Waits (James Purdy); Well Welcome (Gertrude Stein, from *Stanzas in Meditation*) • Softly the Summer • Wild Plum • Sweet River

Selected Reading

Lisa A. Cellucci, "An Examination of Selected Songs by Richard Hundley." D.M.A. diss., University of Cincinnati, 2000.

Esther Jane Hardenbergh, "The Solo Vocal Repertoire of Richard Hundley: a pedagogical and performance guide to the published works" Ed.D. diss., Columbia University Teachers College, 1997.

Leslie Kandell, liner notes to *Permit Me Voyage,* Mary Ann Hart, mezzo-soprano and pianist Dennis Helmrich. Albany Records, TROY 118, 1994.

Paul Sperry, liner notes to *Paul Sperry Sings Romantic American Songs,* Paul Sperry, tenor and Irma Vallecillo, pianist. Albany Records, TROY 043-2.

Notes

1. Eckert's review in *The Christian Science Monitor* quoted by Paul Sperry in liner notes to *Paul Sperry Sings Romantic American Songs,* with Irma Vallecillo, piano.
2. Biographical material on Mr. Hundley taken from "The Songs of Richard Hundley," program notes from the New York Chapter of the National Association of Teachers of Singing. NATS Summer Workshop. New York City, 1993. Used by permission.

3. Leslie Kandell. Liner notes to *Permit Me Voyage.*

4. Ruth C. Friedberg, *American Art Song and American Poetry*, 249.

WILLIAM BOLCOM (b. 1938)

I hope to embrace an enormous emotional range in music: from the sublime to the ridiculous, often both at once, and everywhere in between.

—William Bolcom[1]

Bolcom composes music that audiences can like and critics can respect.

—John Rockwell[2]

William Bolcom's distinguished career includes study at the University of Washington, Mills College, Stanford University and the Paris Conservatory with Darius Milhaud and Olivier Messiaen.

In 1988, Bolcom received the Pulitzer Prize for his *12 New Etudes for Piano.* Among his recent major premieres are: his *Fifth Symphony*, commissioned and premiered by the Philadelphia Orchestra (1990), his *Fourth Symphony,* premiered and recorded by the Saint Louis Symphony (1988), which earned him a Grammy nomination for "Best Contemporary Composition"; and his *Fantasia Concertante,* premiered by the Vienna Philharmonic (1986).

Since 1973, William Bolcom has been a member of the faculty at the University of Michigan, Ann Arbor, where he is professor of composition. With Robert Kimball, he coauthored the book *Reminiscing with Sissle and Blake* (1973) and also edited the collected writings of composer George Rochberg, *The Aesthetics of Survival: a Composer's View of Twentieth-Century Music* (1984).

Bolcom is fluent in the techniques of classical and American popular idioms— jazz, rock, pop—and his music often contains characteristics from these styles. His own musical idiom is cosmopolitan and eclectic, freely blurring the boundaries between classical and popular styles in a uniquely communicative way. He acknowledges Charles Ives as the earliest and strongest influence on his music.

Bolcom composes in a wide range of forms: operas, symphonies, vocal works, chamber pieces, theater works, and concerti for various solo instruments. He produces vocal works that tend to fall into larger forms—operas, chamber works and theater pieces. His massive setting of William Blake's *Songs of Innocence and Experience* (1984), for soloists, chorus, and orchestra was recently recorded to great critical acclaim.

In 1992, his opera *McTeague*, commissioned by the Chicago Lyric Opera, received critical acclaim. Since that time, Bolcom has composed other operas: *A View from the Bridge* (1999), and *A Wedding* (2003).

His collaboration with author-lyricist Arnold Weinstein resulted in several works for the stage: *Dynamite Tonight* (1963), billed as "an opera for actors," *Greatshot* (1966), a "theater opera," and *Casino Paradise* (1991).

In addition to his busy career as a composer, Bolcom accompanies his wife, mezzo-soprano Joan Morris, in recitals of American popular songs. Among their numerous recordings are albums of songs by Kern, Gershwin, and Berlin as well as Bolcom's own *Cabaret Songs.*

Bolcom's music reaches out on many levels. It is original, accessible, expressive and brilliantly conceived.

Cabaret Songs
(Arnold Weinstein)

Volume 1
Over the Piano
Fur (Murray the Furrier)
He Tipped the Waiter
Waitin
Song of Black Max
(As told by the de Kooning boys)
Amor

Volume 2
Places to Live
Toothbrush Time
Surprise!
The Actor
Oh Close the Curtain
George

Bolcom has a keen sense of drama that carries over not only into his works for the stage, but his other music as well. *Cabaret Songs* is a song set based on texts by Arnold Weinstein, professor of English at Columbia University, who called it an "elusive form of theater-poetry-lieder-pop-tavernacular-prayer."[3] About this collection, Weinstein wrote: "The scene is the piano, the cast is the singer."[4] Bolcom composed this collection for his wife, mezzo-soprano Joan Morris.

Kurt Weill and Bertolt Brecht achieved great success with this style with cabaret style with such works as *The Threepenny Opera* and *Happy End.* The lure of cabaret also touched composers Arnold Schoenberg (*Brettl-Lieder*) and Benjamin Britten, who composed his *Cabaret Songs* to texts by W.H. Auden. American stage works born from cabaret style include Marc Blitzstein's *The Cradle Will Rock* and Weill's *Johnny Johnson.*

Bolcom's settings are unique—a deft blend of popular and classical idioms. They are highly entertaining—witty, irreverent, and occasionally erotic. The twelve compositions present a number of character portraits etched in song: the comings and goings of Black Max, a dapper Mafia-type ("Song of Black Max"); Uncle Murray, a retiree who now has no guilt eating greasy knishes ("Fur"); the cocktail pianist playing sad love songs ("Over the Piano") for a pretty customer—a situation slightly analogous to Poulenc's "Violon"; an insouciant girl whose good looks cause havoc wherever she goes, dancing through the song to the infectious rhythm of a *pachanga* ("Amor"); and George, an outrageous cross-dresser directly out of *La Cage aux folles* ("George") with a fondness for singing opera. The songs contain vivid scenes, including a wild cocktail party ("O Close the Curtain") and the disillusionment of the morning after ("Toothbrush Time"). There are also quieter, reflective moments, but always tinged with the cabaret's ambience. This collection is an elegant hybrid of the vernacular and the classical, measured and mixed in judicious portions.

Volume 3
The Total Stranger in the Garden
Love in the Thirties
Thius King of Orf
Miracle Song
Satisfaction
Radical Sally

Volume 4
Angels are the Highest Form of Virtue
Poet Pal of Mine
Can't Sleep
At the Last Lousy Moments of Love
Lady Luck
Blue

Volumes 3 and 4 of *Cabaret Songs* appeared in 1997, premiered by Bolcom and Morris. In these collections. Bolcom pays homage to his teacher Messiaen ("Angels are the Highest Form of Virtue"); Schoenberg ("Thius King of Orf"); expressionism ("The Total Stranger in the Garden"); and George Gershwin ("Blue"). Bolcom has written about Gershwin's ability to synthesize various styles into a "meaningful and enjoyable musical experience."[5] Bolcom has achieved the same thing with his four volumes of *Cabaret Songs*.

I Will Breathe a Mountain   1991
A song cycle from American Women poets

Pity Me Not Because the Light of Day (Edna St. Vincent Millay) • How to Swing Those Obbligatos Around (Alice Fulton) • The Crazy Woman (Gwendolyn Brooks) • Just Once (Anne Sexton) • Never More Will the Wind (H.D.) • The Sage (Denise Levertov) • O To Be A Dragon (Marianne Moore) • The Bustle in a House (Emily Dickinson) • I Saw Eternity (Louise Bogan) • Night Practice (May Swenson) • The Fish (Elizabeth Bishop)

I Will Breathe a Mountain was a commission from mezzo-soprano Marilyn Horne, who premiered the cycle in New York in the spring of 1991. The texts for these eleven songs were all written by women poets and chosen by Ms. Horne from a list submitted by Bolcom and poet Alice Fulton. Not surprisingly, the collection contains a colorful mélange of poetic moods and musical styles.

Bolcom also employs a wide range of vocal styles throughout the eleven songs, including rhythmic speech, lyric melody, *sprechstimme*, vocal glissandi, and a bit of everything in between. He uses complex rhythmic and harmonic treatments as well, and captures the essence of each poem with considerable skill.

"Just Once," is a manic musical setting, which represents an agitated search for truth. A dense, unyielding chromatic pattern creates a thick maze through which the vocal phrases sift and blend, finally emerging empty-handed, in a last vocal phrase without accompaniment—"only to find them…gone." "How to Swing Those Obbligatos Around" is peppered with hints of ragtime and jazzy coloratura text-painting on the word "swing." "Crazy Woman" is a brilliant and angry setting, translated in chord clusters and out-of-kilter vocal shapes. Emily Dickinson's "The Bustle in a House" has a simple setting befitting the poet's simple prose. Marianne Moore's "O To Be A Dragon" is freely theatrical and pontifically perfect. "Night Practice" is a highlight of the group with its powerfully expressive setting and a final last line that gives the cycle its title. "Night Practice" is printed in pictorial typography, in the shape of a mountain (see also Poulenc/Apollinaire: *Calligrammes*).

This collection is a welcome addition to American recital repertoire. The songs may be sung separately. Performance time: thirty minutes.

Extended Study List
Songs of Innocence and Experience (9 solo voices, 3 choruses, children's chorus, and orch., 1956-81) • *Open House* (tenor/chamber orch., 1975) • *Tillinghast Duo* • When We Built The Church (*Dynamite Tonite*) • *Songs to Dance* • *Symphony No. 4* (third movement "The Rose" on a text of Theodore Roethke, 1988) • *Three Irish Songs* (mezzo/baritone, ensemble, 1978) • *Three Donald Hall Songs* (mezzo/baritone, ensemble, 1979) • Night, Make My Day (*Casino Paradise*) • Lime Jello Marshmallow Cottage Cheese Surprise • The Digital Wonder Watch

Selected Reading

Austin Clarkson, "William Bolcom," in *The New Grove Dictionary of American Music,* H. Wiley Hitchcock and Stanley Sadie, eds. (London and New York: Macmillan, 1986).

Susan Elliott, "William Bolcom," *The New Grove Dictionary of Opera,* Stanley Sadie, ed. (New York: Grove's Dictionaries of Music, 1992), v. 1, 530.

John Rockwell, "Music, Every Which Way," *New York Times Magazine,* 16 August 1987.

Notes

1. Susan Feder. Liner notes to *William Bolcom: Symphony No. 4; Session I.* St. Louis Symphony Orchestra, Leonard Slatkin/Joan Morris. New World Records long playing digital recording NW 356, 1988 .

2. John Rockwell, "Music, Every Which Way," *New York Times Magazine*, 51.

3. Arnold Weinstein. "What is a Cabaret Song," introductory notes to *Cabaret Songs* Vols. 1 and 2 by William Bolcom/Arnold Weinstein.

4. Ibid.

5 Kristen Stauffer Todd, "Cabaret as Musical Montage: The Cabaret Songs of William Bolcom," liner notes to *Blue: the complete cabaret songs of William Bolcom and Arnold Weinstein.* Michelle Murray, soprano; David Murray, piano. Summit Records DCD 361, 2003.

THOMAS PASATIERI (b. 1945)

> Pasatieri's style seems to represent a firm re-establishment and expansion of the Romantic tradition.
>
> —Roger Scanlan[1]

Thomas Pasatieri is one of America's most prolific composers. He began as a precocious talent who wrote a generous number of compositions by age fifteen. Though he confined his composition almost exclusively to vocal music, by age thirty, he had composed twelve operas and 400 songs, as well as numerous works in other genres—film, theater, and ballet.

Before entering the Juilliard School, Pasatieri studied with Nadia Boulanger. At Juilliard he worked with Vittorio Giannini and at age nineteen was awarded the first doctorate in composition ever given by the school. After leaving Juilliard, he continued composition studies with Vincent Persichetti and Darius Milhaud.

In addition to his songs, Pasatieri has composed an impressive number of operas, selecting dramatic, well-known stories for his libretti. A partial listing of his operas includes *Washington Square, The Trial of Mary Lincoln, The Seagull,* and *The Three Sisters.* His operas have been produced at Lincoln Center, Kennedy Center, and many major opera houses in Europe. His song cycles have been sung by nationally and internationally known singers.

Pasatieri's vocal music is personal, distinctive, and suited to the dramatic intent of his texts. His music is often overtly emotional, especially in his operas. His sound palette runs to rich, thick-textured harmonies that function within a tonal framework. His musical style—melodic, highly theatrical, and readily accessible—has been described as "post-Puccini."

Pasatieri has taught at the Juilliard School, the Manhattan School of Music, and the Cincinnati College-Conservatory of Music. In 1984, he moved to California to work in films and television. His film orchestrations can be heard in *Road to Perdition, American Beauty, The Little Mermaid, The Shawshank Redemption, Fried Green Tomatoes, Scent of a Woman,* and *Finding Nemo,* among many others.

Three Poems of James Agee   **1973**

How Many Little Children Sleep • A Lullaby • Sonnet

These three poems of James Agee deal with a parent's realization that his child must mature, experience life's joys and sorrows, and ultimately die. With great warmth and lyricism, Pasatieri's settings express the themes of sadness, despair, and the inevitable loss of innocence that run through Agee's poems.

In these songs, Pasatieri displays his gift for melodic writing—lyrical and intimate. Pasatieri's vocal writing is rich, including melismatic phrases, recitative, speech rhythms, and broad lyric passages. The piano score is no less rich—predominantly chordal, but with highly ornamented sections that call for a pianist of considerable ability and dramatic flair. Although the piano and voice complement each other beautifully, Pasatieri's vocal line stands out—direct, expressive, and very Italianate in feeling.

About this set of songs, Pasatieri writes:

> In the summer of 1973, I began to read about the life of James Agee and to study his works. I was fascinated and moved by this multi-leveled, straightforward writing and chose three poems to set to music. In a way *Three Poems of James Agee* concerns the "loss of innocence." It passes through the fragile world of childhood and closes with strength and resolve, embracing maturity with the simple phrase "from now on." Shirley Verrett premiered the cycle in New York in 1974 in a performance that remains as one of the musical highlights of my life.[2]

HOW MANY LITTLE CHILDREN SLEEP. Pasatieri begins this song with winding vocal phrases accompanied by the same melody he used in the two-measure piano introduction. He employs this theme in various guises throughout the song, always writing in a lyric and romantic style.

LULLABY. The brief piano introduction contains musical figures that simulate a rocking lullaby. Rolling piano chords accompany the voice as it enters with a broad, sweeping phrase and joins the piano, sharing the same melody. The song's middle section contains a key and meter change and much more movement in both voice and piano. The final measures return to a quasi-recitative vocal line accompanied by single chords.

SONNET. The song opens with a dramatic recitation, then gathers momentum as the mood and musical texture intensify.

The Harp That Once Through Tara's Halls   **1977**
(Thomas Moore)

Pasatieri dedicated this setting of Thomas Moore's familiar verse to soprano Beverly Sills—and it is well suited for her voice. In general, the vocal range is high. The meter is $\frac{6}{8}$. The piano score contains harp-like figures and the accompaniment doubles the vocal line throughout. Vocal passages are written in a simple folk-like style, reminiscent of singing with an Irish harp.

Extended Study List

Three Sonnets from the Portuguese • Ophelia's Lament • These Are the Days • To Music, Bent is My Retired Mind • There Came A Day • *Three Poems by Kirstin Van Cleave* • Instead of Words • *Heloise and Abelard* (dramatic cantata for soprano, baritone, piano) • *Rites of Passage* (mezzo-soprano, chamber orchestra) • *Far from love* (soprano and 4 instruments) • *Three Married Songs* (voice and cello) • Alleluia • *Day of Love* • *Sieben Lehmannlieder* • *Windsongs* • Overweight, Overwrought Over You • *Two Shakespeare Songs* • *Three American Poems*

Selected Reading

Elise K. Kirk, "Thomas Pasatieri," *The New Grove Dictionary of Opera,* ed. Stanley Sadie (London: Macmillan Press, Ltd., 1992). Vol. 3, 898.

Thomas Pasatieri, "The American Singer: Gold Mine for Composers," *Music Journal* 32 (January 1974).

Roger Scanlan, "Spotlight on American Composers: Thomas Pasatieri," *The NATS Bulletin,* 31:2 (December 1974), 41.

Notes

1. Roger Scanlan, "Spotlight on American Composers: Thomas Pasatieri," *The NATS Bulletin*, 31:2, 1974, 41.
2. Thomas Pasatieri, liner notes for *Sharon Mabry Sings Rochberg, Pasatieri, Coe.* Owl Recordings, OWL-28.

JUDITH LANG ZAIMONT (b. 1945)

Judith Lang Zaimont has brought to her vocal solo music an interpretation of the texts that is fresh and individualistic.

—Linda McNeil[1]

Judith Lang Zaimont is internationally recognized for her distinctive style, characterized by expressive and vibrant energy. Zaimont's principal composition teachers were Hugo Weisgall, Jack Beeson and Otto Leuning. She also studied privately with Leo Kraft and André Jolivet.

Zaimont has received numerous awards for her compositions, including the Debussy Fellowship and Broadcast Music Awards, ASCAP awards, the gold medal in the Louis Moreau Gottschalk centenary competition, two Delius Competition prizes, a Guggenheim Foundation Fellowship in Composition, a Presser Foundation National Award, and fellowships in compositions from the Anton Seidl and Woodrow Wilson Foundations. Most of her compositions are the result of commissions; her works have been performed throughout the United States, England, France, Australia and Germany.

Her dramatic sense draws her to colorful texts that have many interpretive possibilities. She chooses texts that are wide-ranging, from e. e. cummings, to the French symbolists, to the ethnic-based texts of the Eskimos and American Indians.

A signifcant portion of Zaimont's compositions are vocal—solo and choral works. She writes skillfully and knowledgeably for the voice. Zaimont's vocal music has been described as evocative, dramatic, colorful, commanding, and imaginative.[2]

Zaimont's songs employ free musical techniques that reflect her personal response to the poetry. "Very often I will hear in my head a linear contour, a rhythmic setting—in short, the whole musical setting complete. I try to develop vocal lines independent of the instrumental parts and I pay particular attention to the rhythmic scansion."[3] Her harmonic approach reflects the poems' dramatic and emotional content through polytonality, atonality, or shifting sonorities.

Zaimont writes music that requires performers with great musical, interpretive, and technical skill. She is scrupulous about marking her scores with performance indications.

Because Zaimont is dedicated to women in music, she has had considerable involvement with women's music organizations. She is active in the League of Women Composers and has served as chief editor of two books about women composers: *Contemporary Concert Music by Women: A Directory of the Composers and Their Works*, and three volumes of *The Musical Woman: An International Perspective*.

Zaimont has taught on the faculties of Adelphi University, Queens College, and the Peabody Conservatory of Music. She is now retired and lives in Arizona.

Greyed Sonnets: Five Serious Songs   1975

Soliloquy (Millay) • Let It Be Forgotten (Sara Teasdale) • A Season's Song (Millay) • Love's Autumn (Millay) • Entreaty (C. Rossetti)

For this cycle, Zaimont chose texts that reflect her discerning taste in poetry. "I chose the poems of *Greyed Sonnets* after being introduced to the writings of Edna St. Vincent Millay. As a modern romantic, I felt akin to many of her sentiments."[4]

The premiere performance was reviewed by *The New York Times:* "The music is strongly emotional, suiting the texts, yet carefully constructed..."[5] A subsequent performance was reviewed by the same critic: "Miss Zaimont's avowed purpose...was to match the ambiguity of the poems she had set to music, a fine quintet by Edna St. Vincent Millay, Sara Teasdale and Christina Rossetti, and she did this successfully while creating an effective wide-ranging vocal line."[6]

New-fashioned Songs   1983

Fair Daffodils (Herrick) • When, Dearest (Suckling) • The Eagle (Tennyson) • It is a Beauteous Evening (Wordsworth) • The Host of the Air (Yeats)

This group of songs is written for low/medium voice and piano. The title *New-fashioned Songs* is particularly telling as it symbolizes Zaimont's characteristic quality of bringing a new dimension to poetic content. Zaimont's choice of poetry reflects her characteristic concern for texts that have "room for music."[7] The diverse images and moods in this group of texts lend themselves to Zaimont's search for multilevel, emotional poetry.

Extended Study List

Chansons nobles et sentimentales (Baudelaire, Verlaine, Rimbaud) • *Four Songs* (e.e. cummings) • *The Ages of Love* • *In the Theatre of Night: Dream Songs on Poems by Karl Shapiro* • *Will's Words* • *Vessels—Rhapsody for Mezzo and Piano* • *A solemn music* (cycle for baritone) • *Coronach* (cycle for soprano) • *A Woman of Valor* (mezzo, string quartet) • *Two Songs for Soprano and Harp* • *The Magic World* (bass baritone, piano, percussion) • *From the Great Land: Women's Songs* voice, clarinet, piano, Eskimo drum)

Selected Reading

Aaron I. Cohen, *International Encyclopedia of Women Composers* (New York: R. R. Bowker Company, 1981).

Diane Peacock Jezic, *Women Composers: The Lost Tradition Found* (New York: The Feminist Press 1988).

Jane Weiner LePage, *Women composers, conductors and musicians of the twentieth century.* (Metuchen, NJ: Scarecrow Press, 1983). Selected biographies, in two volumes.

Linda McNeil, "The Vocal Solo Works of Judith Lang Zaimont, *The NATS Journal,* 49:5 (May/June 1993), 5-10.
Susan Stern, *Women Composers: A Handbook* (Metuchen, N.J.: The Scarecrow Press, 1978).
Judith Lang Zaimont, Catherine Overhauser, and Janne Gottlieb, eds., *The Musical Woman: An International Perspective,* Volume I (New York: Greenwood Press, 1984).

Notes

1. Linda McNeil, "The Vocal Solo Works of Judith Lang Zaimont," *The NATS Journal,* 49:5, 1993, 5.
2. MacNeil, 5.
3. Jane Weiner LePage, *Women composers, conductors and musicians of the twentieth century,* 329.
4. Ibid., 328.
5. Raymond Ericson, reviewing *Greyed Sonnets. The New York Times,* 20 November 1975. Quoted in LePage, 328.
6. Ibid., 329.
7. McNeil, 5.

STEPHEN PAULUS* (b. 1949)

> Paulus's music...is marked by its appealing combination of tonality and accessibility [and] practically begs to be sung.
>
> —Bob Cartland[1]

Stephen Paulus is one of America's most prolific and accomplished composers. He has composed a wide range of works for the voice, including pieces for solo voice, chorus (in combination with chamber ensemble and large orchestra), and nine works for the dramatic stage. In addition to his vocal compositions, Paulus has a considerable catalogue for orchestra and chamber ensemble. His works have been performed by ensembles throughout the United States and have been featured abroad at the Edinburgh and Aldeburgh Festivals, and throughout Europe and the Soviet Union.

Paulus studied composition with Paul Fetler and Dominick Argento. He was a composer-in-residence between 1983 and 1987 with the Minnesota Orchestra under the direction of Sir Neville Marriner and also served in that capacity with the Atlanta Symphony Orchestra, working with both Robert Shaw and Yoel Levi. He has been a resident composer at the Tanglewood Festival, Santa Fe Chamber Music Festival, Aspen Music Festival, and the Oregon Bach Festival. He is a recipient of both Guggenheim and NEA Fellowships and is also on the board of directors of ASCAP. As cofounder of the Minnesota Composers Forum (with composer Libby Larsen), he has also been active in promoting his colleagues' works.

Paulus's songs display a wide variety of poetic content and musical expression. They exhibit his fine lyrical sense, dramatic flair and attention to detail, and keen sense of prosody. He writes in a musical language that has been characterized as "irresistible in kinetic energy and haunting in lyrical design."[2] His works have been commissioned by a distinguished list of artists, including Evelyn Lear, Thomas Hampson, Paul Sperry, Håkan Hagegård, Doc Severinsen, Leo Kottke, and Janet Bookspan. A number of orchestras, including the New York, Philadelphia, Los Angeles, Atlanta, St. Louis, Minnesota, St. Paul, and BBC symphonies, have also commissioned his works.

Paulus's operas have been performed by the Opera Theatre of St. Louis, Washington Opera, Greater Miami Opera, Minnesota Opera and many others. His second opera, *The Postman Always Rings Twice,* was the first American opera production ever to be presented at the Edinburgh Festival.

---

*Biographical notes and commentary on the cycles *Bittersuite* and *Artsongs* by Stephen Paulus in liner notes to Albany Records recording TROY 036-2. Used by permission of the composer.

Bittersuite   1987
(Four Poems of Ogden Nash for Baritone and Piano)

For a Good Dog • The Middle • Old Men • Time Marches On

These poems by Ogden Nash reveal the poet's dark side as he contemplates death and aging. Paulus's musical treatment of the texts, especially in the final song, reflects the "bittersweet" tone of the cycle's title.

Nicholas Nash commissioned *Bittersuite* in honor of his parents, Mr. and Mrs. Edgar V. Nash. Paulus comments: "When Nick Nash and I first discussed this cycle the idea of using the poetry of Ogden Nash was mentioned. Nick sent me a sampling of the light and often humorous poetry that Ogden Nash is known for and he also included another set of poems. These were the ones about aging and death. It was these poems that captured my imagination and resulted in the cycle."

Paulus describes the songs in the cycle:

> The first and third song—"For a Good Dog" and "Time Marches On" move very quickly with a persistent vocal line and an always active keyboard accompaniment. My intent was to capture the sometimes frantic and relentless quality of time that the poet speaks of when he says "Time up, time up!" and "The seconds splattering upon the roof!" In songs two and four I wanted to portray a different perception of time—the one in which the poet pauses to reflect and analyze—although in a very terse manner. The accompaniment for these last two is both spare and atmospheric.

Bittersuite was completed in April of 1987, and it was premiered by Håkan Hagegård and Warren Jones at The Schubert Club International Artists Series, Ordway Music Theatre in St. Paul, Minnesota, February 12, 1988.

Artsongs   1983

Archaic Torso of Apollo (Rainer Maria Rilke) • The Dance (William Carlos Williams) • Museum Piece (Richard Wilbur) • Seurat (Ira Sadoff) • On Seeing Larry Rivers' *Washington Crossing the Delaware* at the Museum of Modern Art (Frank O'Hara) • Moor Swan (John Logan) • Warrior With Shield (Michael Dennis Browne)

Paulus comments on the cycle:

> The idea of *Artsongs* originated with tenor Paul Sperry and also with Bruce Carlson, Executive Director of The Schubert Club in St. Paul, Minnesota. Paul Sperry also commissioned this work and his charge was to create a song cycle of poems about the visual arts. The final poem in the cycle, "Warrior With Shield" was commissioned especially from poet Michael Dennis Browne. I am grateful also for his invaluable assistance in helping to compile this set of seven poems.

The purpose in selecting these particular poems was two-fold. On the surface I wanted each poem to make a comment about a well-known work of art. Additionally, I wanted each poem to provide the listener with something to reflect upon. In some cases the result is a moment of humor or wit (as in Richard Wilbur's "Museum Piece"). In others, such as "Seurat," the painting serves only as a point of departure to provide the poet with an opportunity to delve into deeper thoughts and feelings.

Paul Sperry and Irma Vallecillo presented the premiere performance of *Artsongs* on May 11, 1983 at the St. Paul Hotel, St. Paul, Minnesota as part of The Schubert Club's 100th anniversary celebration.

Combining the arts of poetry and music to illustrate another (art) has been tried before by Poulenc (*Le Travail du peintre*, 1956), when he set Paul Eluard's poems on the cubists. In *Le Travail du peintre*, Poulenc uses poetry specifically about the artists' styles; in *Artsongs* Paulus uses poetry about specific art works, covering a broader spectrum of artistic styles and subjects and drawing the listener into the poetry and the artistic scene.

ARCHAIC TORSO OF APOLLO. The cycle opens with an intensely dramatic song. Thick textures in the piano direct our view to the headless torso of the god Apollo, and the accompaniment continues to comment on the text in rich harmonies throughout the song. Vocal articulation is closely tied to speech rhythms.

THE DANCE. Just as a Breughel canvas is filled with active figures of all sorts, so "The Dance" is filled with nonstop whirling figures. This musical illustration of Peter Breughel's great canvas *The Kermess*, vividly captures the painting's frantically joyous movement.

MUSEUM PIECE. Richard Wilbur's humorous characterization of museum guards ("the good gray guardians of art who patrol the halls on spongy shoes") is slyly clever, just irreverent enough to remind us that art isn't pompous, and that Edgar Degas once "purchased a fine El Greco which he kept against the wall beside his bed to hang his pants on."

SEURAT. Perhaps the most striking setting in the group is "Seurat," an extended piece of prose by Ira Sadoff which describes the sun-drenched Sunday afternoon captured in George Seurat's pointillist painting *Sunday Afternoon on the Island of La Grand Jatte*. The narrator—is it Seurat himself or simply one of the painting's impersonal characters?—describes the scene with cool detachment, perfectly suited to the surface tranquility of Seurat's works.

Just as Seurat's colors appear to change hues when juxtaposed with different colors on canvas, the music and text in "Seurat" also possess a chameleon-like quality, drawing the listener into a stream-of-consciousness experience and immersing him in the artistic scene.

ON SEEING LARRY RIVERS' *WASHINGTON CROSSING THE DELAWARE* AT THE MUSEUM OF MODERN ART. This setting expresses an energetic, patriotic fervor which masks the poem's underlying theme of emotional unrest. The setting is a dramatic, vibrant musical portrait, brimming with color. The strongly rhythmic, march-like accompaniment, designed in contemporary style, underpins the song.

MOOR SWAN. In a quiet and melancholy setting, piano arpeggios accompany the lyrical vocal line as it evokes images of the ugly moor swan. "When I am dead and gone think only of the beauty of my name," sings the homely bird, repeating her name three times with graceful melismas.

WARRIOR WITH SHIELD (HENRY MOORE, 1953). This dramatic song is ushered in by a warlike, percussive piano accompaniment. The complex poem compares the battered, incomplete warrior to the observer ("I am the icon of the incomplete you"). A variety of repetitive piano figures are used throughout the song, accompanying the strongly rhythmic vocal line.

Three Elizabethan Songs 1973

Fire, fire (Thomas Campion) • Come away, come sweet love (Anon.) •
Away with these self-loving lads (Fulke Greville)

At the heart of these three songs for soprano and piano is rhythmic vitality—intricate, extremely varied, and changing. Each song is quite brief. "Fire, fire" and "Away with these self-loving lads" are set in rapid tempos, framing the middle song "Come away, come sweet love," a more lyrical romantic setting complementing its ardent text.

Paulus integrates polytonality, polyrhythms, varying musical textures, and dramatic contrasts to create this musical setting. His notes for the cycle *Songs of Love and Longing* (1992) are applicable to these Shakespeare settings: "Always, the intent is to make the text intelligible and to support and embellish the message conveyed in the voice through the piano."

Extended Study List
All My Pretty Ones (soprano, piano) • *Mad Book, Shadow Book* (tenor, piano). 1976. • *Letters from Colette* (soprano, string quartet, piano, percussion). 1986. • *Night Speech* (baritone and orchestra). 1989. • *Songs of Love and Longing* (soprano, piano). 1992. • Operas: *The Postman Always Rings Twice* • *The Woodlanders* • *The Village Singer* • *The Three Hermits*

Selected Reading
E. Ruth Anderson, ed., *Contemporary American Composer: A Biographical Dictionary,* 2nd edition (Boston: G. K. Hall & Co., 1982).
Bob Cartland, "Stephen Paulus and His Postman," *Opera Monthly* 1:10 (February 1989), 24-32.
M. A. Feldman, "Triple Header," in *Opera Now* 49:17, 1985.

Notes
1. Bob Cartland, "Stephen Paulus and His Postman."
2. Review in the *Cleveland Plain Dealer*. Quoted on Stephen Paulus official website. stephenpaulus.com. Accessed 29 March, 2006.

LIBBY LARSEN (b. 1950)

Music exists in an infinity of sound. I think of all music as existing in the substance of the air itself. It is the composer's task to order and make sense of sound, in time and space, to communicate something about being alive through music.

Libby Larsen[1]

Libby Larsen is one of America's most prolific and most performed living composers. She has created a catalogue of over 200 works, spanning virtually every genre from intimate vocal and chamber music to massive orchestral and choral scores. Her music has been praised for its dynamic, deeply inspired, and vigorous contemporary American spirit. Constantly sought after for commissions and premieres by major artists, ensembles and orchestras around the world, Libby Larsen has established a permanent place for her works in the concert repertoire.

Raised in Minneapolis, Libby Larsen studied composition with Dominick Argento, Eric Stokes, and Paul Fetler. Larsen co-founded the influential Minnesota Composers Forum with composer Stephen Paulus, and served as one of its managing composers from 1973 to 1985. She has held residencies with the California Institute of the Arts, the Arnold Schoenberg Institute, the Philadelphia School of the Arts, the Cincinnati Conservatory, the Minnesota Orchestra, the Charlotte Symphony and the Colorado Symphony.

Larsen's keen sense of drama and strong interest in American popular music influences her musical style. Her music demonstrates her striking flair for combining traditional and contemporary musical elements. In some cases, she adds other elements to the mix; for example, in *Black Birds, Red Hills*, she integrates slides of Georgia O'Keefe's paintings into the musical presentation.

Like Dominick Argento, Larsen frequently uses prose texts instead of poetry. "While I set both poetry and prose, I am more drawn to prose because of its rhythmic freedom and honest emotion. Texts that reveal strong, colorful and fearless people, many times women, are especially attractive to me."[2] Larsen has set texts by Mary Cassatt, Belle Starr, Calamity Jane, Georgia O'Keefe, Eleanor Roosevelt, Queens of England, Elizabeth Barrett Browning, Brenda Ueland, and Willa Cather, among others, writing: "All of them decided to display their ideas widely and publicly and independently."[3]

Larsen cites Poulenc's *La Voix humaine*, Schoenberg's *Erwartung*, and Berg's *Wozzeck* as influences on her vocal writing. Larsen: "There are two things that these three works inspired in me. First, the composers' choice of texts, the texts being first personal, passionate and dramatic. Each text is exploring emotion, the emotion of desperation in *La Voix humaine,* the anticipation of disaster in *Erwartung* and the shared internal, expressionistic journey of Wozzeck and Marie. The second influence was the use of time, especially how fluid time becomes when one is inextricably embroiled in an emotional flow."[4]

Larson remains an active, articulate advocate for music of our time, and continues to add to the vocal repertory.

ME	1987
(Brenda Ueland)	

Why I Write This Book • Childhood • Adolescence • Greenwich Village •
Marriage...Divorce • Work • Art (Life is Love...) • The Present

This cycle was premiered in November 1987 by soprano Benita Valente in St.
Paul, Minnesota. Commissioned by the Schubert Club of St. Paul, the forty-one-
minute work is currently available through E.C. Schirmer.

Brenda Ueland's autobiography *ME: A Memoir* furnished the texts for the songs.
Ueland, a native of Minneapolis, is a local legend. She has been described as "Joan of
Arc, Robin Hood, Kathryn Hepburn, and a strolling minstrel all rolled into one."[5]

The cycle's eight songs are structured to build emotionally and chronologically through Ueland's autobiographical reminiscences. Songs I and VIII take place in
present time and serve as musical bookends, surrounding Ueland's memories
(Songs II through VII). The two songs are described by Harriett McCleary as
"structural pillars to the cycle, as the middle songs build chronologically, beginning
with childhood, and moving on to adolescence, coming of age in Greenwich Village,
marriage and divorce, and freelancing as a single parent."[6]

A unifying theme in the cycle is Ueland's reference to Goethe's motto *memento vivere* (remember to live), which became Ueland's credo, describing her determination to live life fully and face any adversity. Song VII, "Art (Life is Love)..."
provides the cycle's climactic point and contains "memento vivere," set in soaring
vocal phrases. Song VII connects the cycle thematically through its use of text, its
extended length (ten minutes), and its operatic vocalism. Song VIII concludes the
cycle in the present time, as Song I began it.

Sonnets from the Portuguese	1989
(Elizabeth Barrett Browning)	

I thought once how Theocritus had sung • My letters! •
With the same heart, I said, I'll answer thee • If I leave
all for thee • Oh, Yes! • How do I love thee?

Sonnets from the Portuguese, commissioned by the late soprano Arleen Auger,
is set for soprano, string quartet, bass, flute, oboe, clarinet, bassoon, two horns, percussion, and harp. The texts are six poems of Elizabeth Barrett Browning, chosen
by Larsen and Auger. The poems represent Browning's growth in mature love.
Larsen wrote: "She [Auger] admired the fact that within the stylized and romantic
language, lived a creative woman grappling with issues that seem still to engulf
modern women. What part of her voice must she sacrifice to the lover and the
world? Will the sacrifice be reciprocated? Can her essence survive?"[7]

The work is unabashedly lyrical in Larsen's uniquely individual style. The
cycle was previewed by Auger at the 1989 Aspen Music Festival with the Festival
Orchestra, Joel Revzen conducting. A revised version was later performed at the
Ordway Musical Theater with Revzen and members of the Saint Paul Chamber
Orchestra and the Minnesota Orchestra. Although a recording was planned,
Auger's illness prevented it, and the 1991 performance appears on the Grammy
Award-winning CD *The Art of Arleen Auger*. The work is also published in a version
for soprano and piano.

Love after 1950	**2000**

Boy's Lips (Rita Dove) • Blond Men (Julie Kane) • Big Sister Says
(Kathryn Daniels) • Empty Song (Liz Lochhead) •
I Make My Magic (Muriel Rukeyser)

Mezzo-soprano Susanne Mentzer commissioned this work and collaborated with Larsen in planning it. Larsen: "Each of the songs is an interior monologue about love. We chose a deliberate progression in the poetry, from the adolescent mystery of a first kiss through an affair, break-up, and reconciliation of sorts. This work, virtuosic in its performance, demands an understand[ing] of life, is no *Frauenliebe und –leben*, rather *Love after 1950* is the new woman's *Frau, Love 'em and Leave 'em.*"[8]

The poems, each with its own varied word rhythms, suggested a dance group to Larsen. She subtitled each song with a dance or musical style, and used it as a base for her musical approach. The five songs in *Love after 1950* are small slices of real life, each a snapshot in a photo album from a kinder, gentler era.

BOY'S LIPS (A BLUES). "Boy's lips are…are soft as baby skin…" Behind their grandmother's back porch, adolescent girls speak in awed whispers about the opposite sex. Vocal phrases are bluesy and languid, accompanied by piano figures of "lazy blue-third triplets and blue-third resolutions."[9] The languorous combination of tempo, vocal phrases, and piano accompaniment creates a totally organic texture of sound.

BLOND MEN (A TORCH SONG). "I think I ought to warn you that I hate blond men…" Larsen indicates "as a cocktail piano" in the score of this song, and creates an accompaniment of "piano-lounge gestures,"[10] to match the sensual atmosphere of the text. Voice and piano lines build gradually to a climactic point. The last three lines of text are a sexy postscript.

BIG SISTER SAYS, 1967 (A HONKY-TONK). At least one time in their "growing-up" years, girls of about eleven or twelve years old are told, "you have to suffer to be beautiful." Kathryn Daniels defines just what this means in her poem, which begins "Beauty hurts—big sister says." Big Sister's initiation ceremony into the world of grownup beauty is set to energetic, rhythm-driven vocal lines. The musical setting is a funny, delightful slice of the '50s, flavored with dashes of Jerry Lee Lewis, Bill Haley, and Elvis Presley. Both poem and music are right on the money.

EMPTY SONG (A TANGO). The end of an affair is chronicled in Liz Lochhead's poem, in which an empty shampoo bottle serves as an icon of what was. Its brand name is Spanish, and Larsen composes a "haunting tango of resignation"[11] to complement the text. Images in the poetry are concurrently colorful and poignant, set in a musical setting that matches perfectly.

I MAKE MY MAGIC (ISADORA'S DANCE). This setting has something of a *molto perpetuum* about it. It is a pulsating, forward-moving blend of voice and piano figures. There are small melismatic gestures in the vocal phrases and the piano texture is fashioned with figures of ongoing motion. A little piano gesture, like a flourish, is scattered throughout the accompaniment texture. The overall mood is one of being driven—driven to live, experience, and love.

Try Me, Good King: Last Words of the Wives of Henry VIII   2001
Katherine of Aragon • Anne Boleyn • Jane Seymour • Anne of Cleves • Katherine Howard

"Divorced, beheaded, died; divorced, beheaded, survived."
(This popular rhyme tells the fate of Henry VIII's six wives.)

Try Me, Good King is a cycle of five songs for soprano and piano, using for texts the letters and last words of five of the six wives[*] of Henry VIII, King of England from 1509-1547. Henry's wives ranged in age from seventeen to fifty-one, represented three different nationalities, had varied religious and educational backgrounds, and possessed vastly different levels of ambition and morality.[12]

Try Me, Good King is a fascinating work—musically absorbing and dramatically gripping. Larsen describes it as "a monodrama of anguish and power."[13] She captures the ambience of Tudor England by threading a lute song into the accompaniment of each song. All the lute songs, composed during the reign of Elizabeth I, are familiar examples of the genre. Each lute song is submerged in the texture of the song it "accompanies," creating, in Larsen's words, "a tapestry of unsung words, which comment on the real situation of each doomed queen."[14] There is also a bell-like motive that signals the emotional climax of each piece, functioning as a unifying device throughout the cycle.

Try Me, Good King has wonderful variety. In each song, Larsen has matched her musical approach to the mood of the text and the personality of each of the doomed and discarded queens.

KATHERINE OF ARAGON (KATHERINE OF ARAGON, FORMERLY QUEEN OF ENGLAND, TO KING HENRY VIII, 7 JANUARY 1536). LUTE SONG: JOHN DOWLAND'S "IN DARKNESS LET ME DWELL." As the devout Katherine of Aragon pleads for Henry's repentance and for his support of their daughter, Mary, relentless pedal tones within the accompaniment provide a sense of urgent pleading. The king had abandoned Katherine, as he pursued the alluring Anne Boleyn. When Katherine refused to grant him a divorce, Henry declared himself head of the church in England. He appointed an Archbishop of Canterbury who would grant him a divorce and marry him to Anne.

ANNE BOLEYN (LETTER FROM ANNE BOLEYN, QUEEN OF ENGLAND, TO HENRY VIII, 6 MAY 1536; EXCERPTS FROM TWO LETTERS FROM HENRY VIII TO ANNE BOLEYN; ANNE BOLEYN'S SPEECH AT HER EXECUTION, 19 MAY 1536). LUTE SONG: JOHN DOWLAND'S "IF MY COMPLAINTS." Anne Boleyn, mother of Elizabeth I, had been unable to provide Henry with a son, and was executed on false charges of witchcraft, incest, and adultery. Larsen captures Anne's high-strung personality in a musical setting of abruptly changing tempos and moods, and angular, declamatory vocal lines. Anne fiercely requests a fair trial, reminding the kind of his love for her, and of her faithfulness. Her defiant "Try me, good king" sections are linked by a slower middle section, its text, one of Henry's love letters to Anne. Anne's desperate pleadings return in the last section, each repetition of "Try me, good king" higher than the one preceding it. Larsen unifies the song with a repeated bell-like motive during the first and last sections. Following the tolling of the bell, Anne utters her final words in a halting, unaccompanied recitative: "I hear the executioner is good, and my neck is so little."

JANE SEYMOUR (JANE SEYMOUR, QUEEN OF ENGLAND, TO THE COUNCIL, 12 OCTOBER 1537; "TUDOR ROSE" [ANON.]). LUTE SONG: "TUDOR ROSE" (ANON.). This song is calm and composed, reflecting the personality of Jane Seymour herself. The serenely lyric melody reflects her gentleness and grace. The only queen to provide Henry with a son (Edward VI), the frail Jane died only twelve days after his birth. The Elizabethan song Larsen attaches to this song is "Tudor Rose." This flower references the family crest of the House of Tudor, and points up Jane's dedication to the monarchy.

ANNE OF CLEVES (ANNE OF CLEVES. QUEEN OF ENGLAND, TO HENRY VIII, 11 JULY 1540). LUTE SONG: THOMAS CAMPION'S "I CARE NOT FOR THESE LADIES." Anne of Cleves was chosen sight unseen as a wife for Henry. Their unconsummated marriage was very brief. The king found her unattractive, and the feeling was mutual. Anne happily consented to an annulment of the marriage. She remained in England for the rest of her life, and was known as the King's "most beloved sister." A strong and energetic chordal accompaniment swings under Anne's vocal lines, reflecting her delight at being able to dissolve the union, and her confidence as she agrees to the terms of the arrangement.

KATHERINE HOWARD (RECORDED AT HER EXECUTION BY AN UNKNOWN SPANIARD, 13 FEBRUARY 1541). LUTE SONG: JOHN DOWLAND'S "IN DARKNESS LET ME DWELL." Katherine Howard was known for her impulsive, emotional personality. She flirtatiously committed indiscretions in full sight of the court and the king. She was found guilty of committing adultery with Thomas Culpepper, and both of them were executed for treason. Her fear and desperation are reflected in the freely changing tempos throughout this song, as she pleads forgiveness from the crowd and the king. As her death approaches, her panic and mounting hysteria are illustrated in ascending vocal phrases.

*Katherine Parr, Henry's sixth wife, outlived the king. She earnestly tried to bring some appearance of domestic peace to the family.
**For a succinct, quick reference to Henry's queens, the reader is directed to "Tudor England: 1485-1603" http://englishhistory.net/tudor.html.

Extended Study List

Margaret Songs • *Beloved, Thou Hast Brought Me Many Flowers* (mezzo-soprano, cello, piano) • *Perineo* • *When I Am an Old Woman* • *Songs From Letters: Calamity Jane to her daughter Jane, 1880-1902* • *Black Birds, Red Hills* (soprano, clarinet, piano) • *Saints Without Tears* (soprano, flute, bassoon) • Jazz at the Intergalactic Nightclub • *Chanting to Paradise* • I love you through the daytimes • De toda la eternidad • The Apple's Song • *A Word from Your Jenny*

Selected Reading

E. Ruth Anderson, ed. *Contemporary American Composers: A Biographical Dictionary,* 2nd edition (Boston: G. K. Hall & Co., 1982).

Libby Larsen, "Music, Musicians, and the Art of Listening: Seven Truths About Music in the 21st Century," *Sigma Alpha Iota* Pan Pipes, 93:3 (Spring 2001), 8-9.

Jill Terharr Lewis, "Two Song Cycles by Libby Larsen: A Study of *Songs from Letters* and *Chanting to Paradise,*" Doctoral diss., University of Idaho, 2000.

Nancy Malitz, "Song of the Monster," *Opera News* 54:16, 1990. 44-46.

Harriet McCleary, "A Song Cycle by Libby Larsen: *ME* (Brenda Ueland)," *The NATS Journal,* 51:2, Nov/Dec 1994, 3-8.

Brian Morton and Pamela Collins, eds., *Contemporary Composers* (Chicago/London: St. James Press, 1992).

Eileen L. Strempel, "The Dramatization of Desire: Libby Larsen's Voice of Love in the *Sonnets from the Portuguese*," *Journal of Singing* 59:3 (January/February 2003), 221-227.

Laurel Ann Thoman, "A Study of Libby Larsen's *ME (Brenda Ueland)*: A Song Cycle for High Voice and Piano," Doctoral diss., University of Texas at Austin, 1994.

Ray Tuttle, "Composer Libby Larsen: Letting the Music Speak for Her," *Fanfare Magazine,* May, 2001.

Notes

1. Libby Larsen, on the home page of her official website.
2. Letter to the author. August 2, 1994.
3. Libby Larsen in e-mail correspondence to Juline Barol-Gilmore, July 30, 2004.
4. Quoted by permission of Oxford University Press.
5. Quoted in Harriet McLeary, "A Song Cycle by Libby Larsen: ME," *The NATS Journal* 51:2. Paul Johnson, a neighbor of Ueland, furnished this description of her.
6. Ibid.
7. Libby Larsen, liner notes to *The Art of Arleen Augér.* Koch International Classics CD recording 3-7248-2 H1, 1993.
8. _____, song description notes to *Love after 1950*, in *The Eternal Feminine.* Susanne Mentzer, mezzo-soprano, Craig Rutenberg, piano. Koch International Classics CD recording 3-7506-2 HI, 2001.
9. _____, Composer's notes, *Love after 1950* (Oxford University Press, 2001).
10. Ibid.
11. Ibid.
12. Deborah Silverberg, *Try Me Good King.* Poster paper presentation at the national convention of the National Association of Teachers of Singing, New Orleans, Louisiana, July 2004.
13. Libby Larsen, Composer's notes, *Try Me Good King* (Oxford University Press, 2002).
14. Ibid.

JOHN MUSTO (b. 1954)

John Musto is one of those rare composers who allows the qualities of a poem to emerge naturally through the music, just as a great sculptor releases the true contours of a figure.

—Mary Dibbern[1]

If there is a finer composer of song with piano alive and working in the world today, I would very much like to know his or her name.

—Graham Johnson[2]

John Musto was born in Brooklyn, New York, the son of a jazz guitarist. He attended the Manhattan School of Music as a piano major and studied with the late Paul Jacob. Musto's interest in improvisation eventually led him to composition. His music has been performed throughout the United States and Europe. *The London Times* characterized Musto's music as "[reveling] in the freedom which is characteristic of American music, the freedom to be conservative or radical or anything else, but above all to be one's self."[3]

Musto has been active in classical and popular music as both a composer and performer. His own compositions are marked with the same versatility. As an experienced contemporary music performer, Musto was chosen by composer William Bolcom to premiere *Etudes for Piano* on WNYC's nationally broadcast Americathon. Musto has recorded for Harmonia Mundi, Nonesuch, CRI and EMI recordings, and his own compositions have been recorded for Hyperion, Harmonia Mundi, MusicMasters, Albany Records, and New World Records, among others.

Musto's eclectic choice of song texts by Robert Frost, Langston Hughes, Eugene O'Neill, Dorothy Parker and several Elizabethan poets make his songs colorful and varied. In concerts that feature his songs, he often provides the accompaniment for his wife, soprano Amy Burton. Musto's music has been performed throughout America by such artists as William Sharp, Steven Blier, Amy Burton, Karen Holvik, Evelyn Petros, Sylvia Kahan, and Christopher Trakas.

Among his awards are two Emmys and two CINE Awards for his scores written for television. In 2000, he was awarded a Rockefeller Fellowship at Bellagio, Italy. He was a finalist for the 1996 Pulitzer Prize for his orchestral song cycle *Dove Sta Amore*. Musto's recent commissions include Carnegie Hall, Chanticleer, the Metropolitan Museum, the Vail Valley Music Festival and the Wolftrap Foundation.

John Musto has been a visiting professor at Brooklyn College and is a frequent guest lecturer at the Juilliard School and the Manhattan School of Music.

Recuerdo   **1987**

Echo • Recuerdo • A Last Song

Recuerdo is a cycle of three songs written for baritone William Sharp and pianist Steven Blier, who recorded it in a program of American song released after Sharp had won the 1987 Carnegie Hall International American Music Competition for Vocalists. The songs are unified by the Spanish title meaning "remembrance." Memories in different forms are at the heart of each poem. The middle poem, which is animated and upbeat, is framed by the solemn mood of the other two poems.

ECHO (CHRISTINA ROSSETTI). Rossetti's poem is suffused with mysticism that Musto sensitively captures in a subdued, low-key musical setting. The piano accompaniment is based on a rhythmic ostinato pattern that expands to broader-ranged, thicker-textured figures. Vocal passages are built in similar fashion, beginning softly and becoming more expansive at intensely emotional points. The song ends quietly and reflectively.

RECUERDO (EDNA ST. VINCENT MILLAY). Edna St. Vincent Millay's popular paean[*] to all-night revels in New York City features a young couple who has spent the night riding the Staten Island Ferry. The poem is a romantic vignette, set in a bluesy, ragtime style. Vocal lines demand flexibility and dramatic insight from the singer. "We were very tired, we were very merry, we had gone back and forth all night on the ferry" appears three times in the poem; with each reappearance, the theme descends another step, as the duo becomes increasingly weary. The accompaniment, which is involved and at times densely textured, holds the easy narrative together, grounded in figures reminiscent of a rinky-tink barroom piano.

*For a comparison setting of this poem, see Mario Castelnuovo-Tedesco.

A LAST SONG (LOUISE BOGAN). Musto subtitled this song "in memoriam Jeffery French." A softly lyrical introduction creates a beautiful elegiac mood, which continues throughout the song's first section. The musical mood is subdued but becomes increasingly intense as it builds to a climax ("Some things I overlooked, and some I could not find"). Dynamics, vocal range, and accompaniment texture all expand, then contract to a softer but still passionate feeling—a mood that remains throughout the song's final phrases.

Dove Sta Amore   **Where Lies Love. 1991**

Maybe • Sea Chest • The Hangman at Home •
How Many Little Children Sleep • Dove Sta Amore

Dove Sta Amore (1991) is a cycle of five songs for high voice and orchestra, commissioned by the Concert Artists Guild. The work was nominated for a Pulitzer Prize in 1996. The cycle consists of five songs on texts by twentieth-century poets. The poems are highly diverse in content; all deal with love in varying relationships. Musto sets the texts skillfully, employing innovative musical textures. The work calls for a high soprano voice of considerable range, agility, and musical accuracy, and an excellent pianist. *Dove Sta Amore* is also published in an edition for voice and piano.

MAYBE (CARL SANDBURG). The words of the poem are the whimsical musings of a woman who cannot make up her mind to get married or remain single. Touches of jazz are heard throughout the brief song in both the vocal line and the accompaniment. The vocal range is extremely large, covering slightly less than two octaves. The song should be sung with the utmost lyricism.

SEA CHEST (CARL SANDBURG). The singer realizes that her lover loves the sea as much as he loves her, and resigns herself to this inflexible relationship. The vocal line, in $\frac{3}{4}$ meter, has a folk-like quality. Musto stresses the folk style by repeating the first line of each stanza three times, each repetition slightly higher than the one before.

Musto manipulates rhythmic elements in a highly individual way. The accompaniment begins with a simple two-note pattern on beats two and three, the "missing" downbeat is provided by the vocal line after it enters. As the song progresses, the accompaniment figure is added to, and sustained by generous pedal indications in the piano (*molto pedale* is the marking in the score). The accompaniment texture becomes slightly blurred, creating a "watery" effect. Rhythmic tension builds until the last measures—perhaps predicting the unstable future in store.

THE HANGMAN AT HOME (CARL SANDBURG). "What does the hangman think about / When he goes home at night from work?" Sandburg's darkly humorous poem is coupled with an easy swinging piano accompaniment that softens the macabre text. Musto initiates the song with an introduction reminiscent of the piano patterns in of his song "Recuerdo." Tonalities are elusive and shift frequently. Vocal phrases are somewhat angular and rhythmically conversational. Rhythmic patterns in the accompaniment fluctuate freely, commenting on the words of the poem in a charming give-and-take.

HOW MANY LITTLE CHILDREN SLEEP (JAMES AGEE).[*] This is a lullaby in triple meter. The piano accompaniment is written in a simple rocking rhythm, coupled with a rambling melodic line in the right hand that intertwines with the fluid vocal phrases. The simplicity of patterns in both piano and voice allows the emotional text to be highlighted.

*For a comparison setting, see Thomas Pasatieri.

DOVE STA AMORE…(LAWRENCE FERLINGHETTI). Ferlinghetti's poem is full of word assonance ("love/dove"; "hillsong/willsong/plainsong/painsong"). This aural pulse propels this song from start to finish. Angular and melismatic vocal phrases are accompanied by piano figurations based on ostinato patterns. The mood of the poem and Musto's musical setting matches that of "Maybe," the first song of the set. The two songs are like a pair of cheery, energized bookends, enclosing three songs of more varied and serious poetic content.

Extended Study List

Triolet (Eugene O'Neill) • *Quiet Songs* • *Shadow of the Blues* (texts by Langston Hughes) • *Canzonettas* (three songs on anonymous poems) • Lament (Edna St. Vincent Millay) • *Two by Frost* (Nothing Gold Can Stay; The Rose Family–texts by Robert Frost) • *Enough Rope* (Social Note; Résumé; The Sea–texts by Dorothy Parker)

Notes

1. Mary Dibbern in conversation with the author. May, 1995. Ms. Dibbern is an accompanist/vocal coach who has been acquainted with Mr. Musto's music for a number of years.
2. Quoted on the website of Peer Music, Inc. http://www.peermusic.com, accessed 30 November, 2005.
3. Notes in *John Musto: Recuerdo*. (medium voice and piano). Peer-Southern Publishers, 1988. No author cited.

LORI LAITMAN (b. 1955)

She lets the texts inform her music, spinning lyrical neo-romantic vocal lines over shifting post-modern sonorities. It's a treat to hear contemporary art songs that showcase the voice as flatteringly as these, and which retain individuality and surprise without sacrificing accessibility.

—Joanne Sydney Lessner[1]
Opera News

Lori Laitman is clearly one of the most brilliant composers of the American genre.

—Adelaide Whitaker[2]

Lori Laitman has become one of America's prolific composers of art songs. Her works are enthusiastically received and frequently performed. Critics are enthusiastic in their praise of Laitman's songs, citing her taste for fine texts, and the nuance and color of her musical settings.

In an interview with Kathleen Watt, Laitman used three words to describe her music: "I would hope it's *timeless*. I think it's *beautiful*. And it's certainly *lyric*. Even in the funny songs there's a lyrical quality that is unmistakable." About her songs, she says, "I want my music to speak to all people, not just to singers."[3]

Laitman studied composition at the Yale School of Music, after graduating *magna cum laude* from Yale College. She has composed music for film, theatre, and various chamber ensembles, but since 1991 she has concentrated on composing for the voice. Laitman credits her friend, soprano Lauren Wagner, with introducing her to song composition. For Wagner, she composed her first song, "The Metropolitan Tower," a beautiful song that is still one of her best-known pieces. Laitman says: "I found my voice writing for the voice."

Dr. Adelaide Whitaker, who has commissioned seven works from Laitman, comments on Laitman's song style: "[The songs] utilize contemporary musical language that frees the expressive qualities of the poetry and the music: varying bar line lengths, free color associations, and an accompaniment that is a full partner in a complex, integrated web. Singers are thrilled to have songs that provide both joy and a challenge to prepare.[4]

Choosing texts is of paramount importance to Laitman, who affirms: "Everything I do, every melody that I write, is absolutely derived from the words."[5] It is clear Laitman has a remarkable gift for setting words to music. In this, her work embodies a continuation of the great art song traditions of the past.

Laitman draws her texts from many poetic styles. Some of her favorite poets are Emily Dickinson, Sara Teasdale, and Pulitzer Prize winner Mary Oliver. She has also been inspired to set the work of Elinor Wylie, Thomas Lux, Dana Gioia, and Christina Rossetti, among others. Laitman comments: "I respond differently to different poets. My Emily Dickinson songs have a certain flavor, whereas my Thomas Lux songs have another kind of flavor. But I think you can tell it's me."[6]

She enjoys the collaborative process of working directly with a poet when she can: "All my poets, every one, have been pleased so far. In fact, it has been revelatory—poets find that my work reveals aspects of their poems to them, and my singers reveal aspects of my own songs to me. It is wonderful to have these many layers going on." [7]

Recent performances of Lori Laitman's music in the United States have taken place at Weill Recital Hall, Merkin Hall and Alice Tully Hall (New York); Shriver Hall (Maryland); Benaroya Hall (Washington); The Cleveland Institute of Art (Ohio); and the U.S. Holocaust Memorial Museum, The Corcoran Gallery and The Kennedy Center (D.C.). In June 2004, The Cleveland Opera premiered Ms. Laitman's opera, *Come to Me in Dreams*.

Laitman has also composed a number of works for voice and one instrument: soprano/alto saxophone, soprano/clarinet, soprano/bassoon, soprano/trumpet, baritone/cello and baritone/double bass. In addition, she has written pieces for baritone/piano trio, baritone/cello and piano, and mezzo-soprano/piano trio.

Note: Biographical notes, the composer's commentary on the songs from published music and from her website, used by permission of Lori Laitman. Unless otherwise indicated, other quotations are taken from correspondence between the author and Ms. Laitman.

The Apple Orchard   2004
(Dana Gioia)

Laitman describes "The Apple Orchard" as "one of the most beautiful songs I have written." It is the first song she wrote for the tenor voice. Its simplicity of style is reminiscent of "The Metropolitan Tower," Laitman's very first song. Dana Gioia's poem is a modern day *carpe diem,* describing a path not taken, a love not claimed. The last lines of the poem poignantly frame the moment: "What more could I have wanted from that day? / Everything, of course. Perhaps that was the point— / To learn that what we will not grasp is lost." In the final measure, the last piano figure ascends, its closing note suspended in space, unfinished—poignantly mirroring the singer's last words.

Laitman comments:

The dramatic arc of the poem as well as the beautiful image of "Spring's ephemeral cathedral" drew me to "The Apple Orchard." This song is different than most of my other songs in that it begins and ends in the same key and uses the same rhythmic figuration throughout. Repeated arpeggiated chords create tension and a build-up to "pure desire" and the rhythmic anticipation of "nothing consumed" heightens the climax. The melodic cell of "nothing" repeats under the word "Everything," linking the two concepts together musically. The strings of the piano capture the last of the singer's sounds before restating the opening melody to end the song.[8]

"The Apple Orchard" is also available in a baritone version.

Echo   **1995**
(Christina Rossetti)

Rossetti's translucent verse prompted Laitman to create a fluid musical texture that matches the contemplative nature of the poem. The text is a theme of lost love. Laitman sets it in a simple ABA structure, utilizing a repetitive pattern of octaves in the right hand of the piano, combined with a pedal point in the left hand to draw the listener into the singer's reverie.[9]

This song is published in a number of keys for different voice types (Laitman has no problems with transpositions that work musically).

Pentecost (from *Becoming A Redwood*)   **2004**
(Dana Gioia)

Laitman considers "Pentecost" one of her most powerful and dramatic songs, commenting: "In many respects, the cycle it is from (*Becoming A Redwood*) is perhaps my most musically integrated."[10] Other songs in this cycle are: "The Song," "Curriculum Vitae," and "Becoming A Redwood." Poetic themes that run through the four poems are relationships, love, suffering, and healing through the passing of time. Laitman threads motivic material through the songs as well. The reader should access the entire cycle to trace the musical and dramatic use of these motives.

Laitman composed the cycle for her husband on the occasion of his fiftieth birthday. The first performance was given by soprano Barbara Quintiliani.

"Pentecost" is a poem by Dana Gioia, currently chairman of the National Endowment for the Arts. Its words are an anguished outpouring of grief, written following the death of Gioia's infant son. Laitman creates the unrelenting pain of memory through a left-hand ostinato in the piano, repeated for seventeen measures. Accompaniment shapes change and soften as grief subsides, and the song ends quietly with a hushed vocalise that recalls a melodic benediction. Vocal phrases are weaving and fluid, and suggest keening ("when memory/Repeats its prosecution"). The melodic and harmonic repetitions in voice and piano create enormous tension.

On the song's last page, Laitman writes: "This song should surge and ebb in its tempi—as indicated by 'push' and 'relax.' It should have a hypnotic and improvisational quality. It should 'breathe' and remain constantly expressive."

Laitman is orchestrating *Becoming A Redwood.*

Refrigerator, 1957 (from *Men With Small Heads*)   2002
(Thomas Lux)

Laitman's daughter, Diana, introduced her mother to the poetry of Thomas Lux (b. 1946). *Men With Small Heads* is a cycle composed of four of Lux's poems: "Men With Small Heads," "Refrigerator, 1957," "A Small Tin Parrot," and "Snake Lake."

Lux's poetry is deft and witty. Even when dealing with deep emotions, his poems retain a lightness of spirit that touches the heart. Lux has said of his poetry: "I want my audiences to have fun, enjoy it, be moved…and I want it to be understandable by dogs and cats—so that anyone who has never read poetry can relate to it."[11]

"Refrigerator, 1957" describes a foray into the old family refrigerator—we're not told by who or why. The handle is pulled, the door opened, and a checklist of the contents is made, itemized in fluid melodic phrases. Suddenly, the tempo shifts into high gear as the star item on the shelf is revealed—a jar of maraschino cherries! The jar of cherries is described in clever detail, and the protagonist wonders why it perhaps used once and then abandoned. Again, the imagined reasons are very funny, but in the final lines the poignant reason appears—"you do not eat that which rips your heart with joy."

Laitman describes this song as "a musical fantasy. Reminiscent of French songs, the opening veers into a $\frac{3}{4}$ section as the subject, "maraschino cherries," is introduced. A parody of Italian opera (combined with other humorous tidbits) leads to a lyric and touching close."[12]

"Refrigerator, 1957" is a contrast in tempos and in emotional mood. It is another example of Laitman's natural gift for setting humorous texts.

Last Night The Rain Spoke to Me (from *Early Snow*)   2003
(Mary Oliver)

"Last Night the Rain Spoke to Me" is the first song in Laitman's cycle *Early Snow*, commissioned by Dr. Adelaide Whitaker for soprano Jennifer Check. The three songs ("Last Night the Rain Spoke to Me," "Blue Iris," and "Early Snow"), are reflections on nature, written by Pulitzer Prize winning poet Mary Oliver. Oliver is a favorite poet of Laitman, who has written three song cycles on Oliver's verses: *Sunflowers* (1999), *One or Two Things* (2000), and *Early Snow* (2003). Laitman says "my Oliver settings are often my most complex musically."[13]

Poetic images in the text follow a sequence: the rain falls, joyfully returning to earth; the sky clears and stars appear; and the poet understands his spiritual unity with nature.

Gently falling rain is heard in the piano figures. Vocal lines are flowing and calm. Laitman comments: "The piece comes to a clearing in the middle, as the rhythm slows and the pedal sounds clear." At this point, two measures of unaccompanied text link the sections—"Then it was over/ The sky cleared…" Now the night sky is revealed, dotted with brilliant stars, heard in a grace note figure in the piano. The last vocal phrases are hushed—"Imagine! Imagine! the long and wondrous journeys still to be ours."

I Never Saw Another Butterfly[*] (soprano/alto saxophone) 1995-96
(Texts from poems by children killed in the Holocaust)

The Butterfly (Pavel Friedmann, 1942) • Yes, That's the Way Things Are (Koleba) • Birdsong (Anonymous 1941) • The Garden (Franta Bass) • Man Proposes, God Disposes (Koleba) • The Old House (Franta Bass)

On the suggestion of soprano Lauren Wagner, Laitman set poems from *I Never Saw Another Butterfly*, a collection of poetry written during World War II by children from the Terezin Concentration Camp. Wagner sang the first performance of the cycle with saxophonist Gary Louie in February 1996, at Johns Hopkins University, Baltimore, Maryland.

I Never Saw Another Butterfly is a powerful work. Laitman chose six poems that allowed her a variety of musical approaches in the songs. The six poems encompass a wide range of emotions; the words are full of hope, but are also heart-breakingly sad.

The idea of pairing of voice with saxophone came to Laitman as she read the texts: "I had planned on composing a piece for saxophonist Gary Louie, so, as I read these poems, the idea of the saxophone as the sole partner to the voice intrigued me..the sound of the saxophone itself could be haunting, soulful, and reminiscent of Klezmer[**] music."[14]

In June 2004, to honor what would have been Anne Frank's seventy-fifth birthday, the Cleveland Opera presented *Come to Me in Dreams*, a one-act opera fashioned of fifteen songs by Lori Laitman, joined together with a storyline by David Bamberger. The opera is the tale of a Holocaust survivor, and featured baritone Sanford Sylvan in the leading role. Laitman says "This unintended juxtaposition of staged songs adds new meanings to the original poems and to the emotional content of the music." Laitman has continued to set poems with a Holocaust theme.

[*]For a comparison setting, see *I Never Saw Another Butterfly* by Elwood Durr.
[**]Klezmer music is Jewish (Yiddish) folk music. Klezmorim were performing musicians in the German ghettos and many Jewish communities in eastern Europe. They entertained at social occasions such as weddings and circumcision feasts.

Over the Fence (from *Days and Nights*) 1994-95
(Emily Dickinson)

"Over the Fence" belongs to a collection of six songs titled *Days and Nights*, on poetry of Robert Browning, Emily Dickinson, Christina Rossetti, and Francis Bourdillon. Dickinson's exuberant poem inspired Laitman to craft a buoyant, witty, and altogether engaging musical setting.

Laitman marks the tempo as quarter note=132. She sets the dramatic mood with an extended piano introduction of playful rhythm in triplets, descending step-wise. The high energy in the musical texture is maintained by the accompaniment, which is laced with syncopation and changing figures that drive the song forward. Laitman comments: "The piano grows more intricate in the middle section—

employing hand crossing techniques reminiscent of Rameau's keyboard style—while the voice warbles above, attempting to capture the marvelous imagery of God, as a boy, jumping over the fence to eat berries."

Laitman divides the two sections of the song with an extended piano interlude, based loosely on the figures of the introduction. It features ascending chromatic scales that delightfully illustrate climbing the fence. "God would certainly <u>scold</u>," trills the singer on a single note—another amusing text painting detail.

"Over the Fence" provides a delightful glimpse of the composer's humor.

Little Elegy*   2002
(Elinor Wylie)

Laitman comments: "I wrote this song in memory of Reid Brecher, the oldest son of my friends Sande and Rick Brecher. Though Reid passed away from cancer at the age of twenty-three, he lived his brief life to the fullest. The harmonic direction at the end of this song is purposely unresolved."[15]

Laitman's setting contains irregular phrase lengths, and a tempo that fluctuates through the song. She assigns two figures to the piano that function as unifying devices. "Little Elegy" is a mere twenty-six measures long. In that brief space, Laitman has effectively captured the tenderness of the text in a microcosm of quiet beauty.

*For a comparison setting, see Ned Rorem.

Extended Study

Holocaust 1944 (baritone/double bass; baritone/cello) • *Long Pond Revisited* (baritone/cello) • *Fresh Patterns* • *Becoming A Redwood* • *Early Snow* • *One or Two Things* • *Daughters* • *The Throwback* • *Men with Small Heads* • *Four Dickinson Songs* • *Sunflowers* • *The Years* • Plums • The Ballad Singer • *The Love Poems of Marichiko* (soprano/cello) • *Armgart* • *Lines Written at the Falls* • *Mystery* • *Between the Bliss and Me* • *Fathers* (baritone/piano trio) • *Captivity* (soprano/trumpet) • *Living in the Body* (soprano/saxophone) • *One Bee and Revery* • *Swimmers on the Shore* (baritone/piano) • *On A Photograph* • *River of Horses* • *Orange Afternoon Lover* • *The Seed of Dream*

Selected Reading

Carol Fuqua Lines, "The Songs of Lori Laitman," *Journal of Singing,* 63:5 (May/June 2007).

Kathleen Watt, "An acclaimed art song composer takes the opera stage: Kathleen Watt speaks with composer Lori Laitman," *US Operaweb,* Online magazine devoted to American Opera. 2001-2004.

Notes

1. Quoted from "Biography, Lori Laitman" on artsongs.com, official website of Lori Laitman. Used by permission.
2. Adelaide Whitaker, "Thoughts of a Patron," on artsongs.com. Used by permission.
3. Kathleen Watt, "An acclaimed art song composer takes the opera stage: Kathleen Watt speaks with composer Lori Laitman." *US Operaweb,* an online magazine devoted to American opera, 2001-2004.
4. Whitaker, "Thoughts of a Patron."
5. Kathleen Watt, "Kathleen Watt speaks with composer Lori Laitman."
6. Ibid.
7. Ibid.
8. Lori Laitman, Composer's notes to "The Apple Orchard." Enchanted Knickers Music, BMI, 2004. Used by permission.
9. _____, liner notes to *Mystery: The Songs of Lori Laitman*. Lauren Wagner, soprano; William Sharp, baritone; Phyllis Bryn-Julson, soprano; Frederick Weldy, Lori Laitman, Seth Knopp, pianists; Thomas Kraines, cello, Gary Louie, saxophone. Albany Records TROY 393, 2000.
10. _____, in an e-mail to Carol Kimball, 12 January 2006.
11. Daina Savage, "Thomas Lux: Poetry for the people," An interview with Daina Savage. *Rambles: a cultural arts magazine,* January 1998. Accessed at http://www.rambles.net/lux_poetry.html

12. Lori Laitman, liner notes to *Dreaming: Songs of Lori Laitman*. Jennifer Check, soprano; Patricia Green, mezzo-soprano; Sari Gruber, soprano; Randall Scarlata, baritone; William Sharp, baritone; Gary Karr, double bass; Warren Jones and Lori Laitman, piano. Albany Records TROY 570, 2003.
13. _____, in an e-mail to Carol Kimball, 12 January 2006.
14. _____, liner notes to *Mystery: the Songs of Lori Laitman*. Albany Records, 2000.
15. _____, Composer's notes to "Little Elegy." Enchanted Knickers Music, BMI, 2002. Used by permission.

DARON ARIC HAGEN (b. 1961)

All music arises from the human voice—that's why art song to me is the most exquisite form.

—Daron Hagen[1]

To say that he is a remarkable musician is to underrate him.
Daron *is* music.

—Ned Rorem[2]

Daron Aric Hagen is a prolific and distinguished American composer. His compositions have been steadily commissioned and performed internationally by world-class orchestras, opera companies, chamber ensembles and soloists since his debut as a composer (Philadelphia Orchestra, 1983) and as a pianist (Denver Chamber Orchestra, 1986). The New York Philharmonic, Orpheus Chamber Orchestra, Brooklyn Philharmonic, Milwaukee Symphony Orchestra, National Symphony Orchestra, the American Composers Orchestra, the Buffalo Philharmonic, pianist Gary Graffman, the Kings Singers, Sara Sant'Ambrogio, and flautist Jeffrey Khaner are among those who have commissioned and premiered his music. He is the recipient of numerous prestigious awards and fellowships.

Hagen's commissions from major orchestras and performers between 1981 and 2005 include numerous orchestral works—three symphonies, seven concertos, several massive works for chorus and orchestra, two dozen choral works, ballet scores, concert overtures, and showpieces—as well as two brass quintets, two piano trios, a string quartet, an oboe quintet, a duo for violin and cello, solo works for piano, organ, violin, viola, and cello, and seventeen published cycles of art songs on poetry of over fifty poets. He has composed seven operas, including *Shining Brow* (1992), *Vera of Las Vegas* (1996), *Bandanna* (1998), *Broken Pieces* (2003) and *The Antient Concert* (2005), and is currently collaborating on *Amelia* with Gardner McFall and Stephen Wadsworth for the Seattle Opera.

In 2004, Hagen was elected President of the Lotte Lehmann Foundation, an international nonprofit organization dedicated to encouraging the performance and creation of art song. He is a passionate educator, ambassador of the arts, and advocate of young composers. He is a graduate of the Curtis Institute of Music and of the Juilliard School. Hagen's principal mentors were Leonard Bernstein, David Diamond, and Ned Rorem.

Hagen loves to write for singers, whom he considers some of the "most exquisite musicians."[3] Hagen says his songs require singers of particular skills: "[those who] respect the text, have excellent diction, and know how to act."[4] His choice of texts is wide-ranging, and includes many verses by Paul Muldoon; other poets include Whitman, Tennyson, Blake, Browning, and Dickinson.

He approaches text setting by reading poetry as prose, allowing the words to shine. Hagen says: "I do not repeat words. The poem already has a music of its own. It's my duty to find that music and cooperate with that structure and express it melodically and harmonically."[5] Using his gift for composing vocal lines, he produces songs that flow lyrically and illuminate texts with unerring musical and dramatic aim. His scores are full of extensive markings, requiring singers to use variety of tone color to achieve the emotions inherent in the texts.

Muldoon Songs   1989
(Paul Muldoon)

The Waking Father • Thrush • Blemish • Mink •
Bran • Vico • Holy Thursday

Hagen enjoys setting the poetry of Irish poet Paul Muldoon because of its high literary quality and vivid imagery. This set of songs for tenor voice and piano does not form a cycle, but rather a collection with a continuing subject. *Muldoon Songs* was commissioned by Paul Sperry, who gave the first performance. The songs extend over a range of two octaves, and are both lyrical and declamatory. Songs 3 and 4 are extremely brief and are the most limited in range. Performance time is approximately twenty minutes.

THE WAKING FATHER is a boyhood memory of a father and son fishing, by turn both exuberant and tender. The score calls for a singer who can perform many dynamic and dramatic variations. The piano accompaniment is fashioned of wide-spaced harmonic textures. The tempo is very fast throughout, with a brief pause for a moment of reflection midway through the song.

THRUSH is quite lyrical. Both voice and piano provide an interactive, conversational feeling throughout. Melodic vocal lines are step-wise and are repeated, extended, and varied throughout the song.

BLEMISH is a story about a girl with two different-colored eyes. The poem is only four lines long; Hagen sets it in a brief six bars, using bitonality[*] to complement the poetic subject, and specifies that the song be sung in one breath.

*Hagen: "My synesthetic reaction to B major is to hear blue, and when I hear E-flat major I see brown. Hence, the song is bitonal, with these two keys alternating hands every bar."[6]

MINK is a wry little poem set in eleven measures. The vocal line contains short, declamatory patterns peppered with syncopation. The piano holds forth throughout with an "oom-pah" rhythm. Hagen: " 'Mink' is about Captain Robert Nairac, who was abducted and murdered by the Irish Republican Army in 1977 and whose body was never found. While 'Blemish' disarms the listener, this song either slaps him—in Muldoon fashion, so long as the listener knows whom Nairac was—or passes by harmlessly if he doesn't."[7]

BRAN features a broad vocal line with many phrases initiated by a leap of a ninth or an octave. The tempo is a nostalgic waltz, complementing poetic content—another boyhood memory evoked by a present situation.

In VICO, Muldoon's alliterative poetry ends as it began—a poem of circular shape with no *real* ending. The frenzied accompaniment, that evokes a small gray "hand-wringing" squirrel on a treadmill, contains a steady stream of eighth notes that rises and falls unceasingly, matched by a vocal line of similar shape, with dotted quarters creating a rhythmic three-against-two. At times the two lines coincide, but both lines continue to move persistently until an interval of a major third finally signals the end of the journey. Hagen's rhythmic approach maintains tension and highlights the squirrel's monotonous effort. "Vico" continues without pause into the last song.

HOLY THURSDAY recounts the end of a relationship—in a restaurant, a couple lingers after a meal and watches the waiter as he eats. Piano textures are predominately chordal with many open fifths in the bass line that emphasize the emptiness of the moment. An expansive, lyric vocal line soars above the piano line.

Larkin Songs   2000
(Philip Larkin)

1a. Going	4a. 'Within the dream you said'
1b. Coming	4b. Talking in Bed
2. Interlude #1: Fiction and the Reading Public	5. Interlude #2: 'To write one song, you said'
3a. Counting	6a. 'Morning at last: there is snow'
3b. 'None of the books have time'	6b. The White Palace

Note: Daron Hagen's comments on *Larkin Songs* taken from a conversation with Carol Kimball, February 15, 2001. Used by permission.

For this cycle, Hagen chose ten poems by British poet Philip Larkin (1922-1985), whose provocative verse Hagen describes as being "like sherry as opposed to wine." Larkin's poetry, which fills one slim volume, has a singsong, chant-like quality about it.

Hagen says: "I wanted to find a poet obsessed with 'I, I, I' poetry to set to music. Then the singer can become the 'I' and you have a monologue, a *scena*. This cycle works very hard to be as simple as possible. The poems are like a portrait of a man looking back over the course of his life. The music gives you the interior material." The songs are ordered by the poems' chronology—from the late 1920s to the 1970s. As Larkin grows older, the poems take on a sense of isolation.

Larkin Songs is a haunting and intensely emotional collection in which words and music blend in sensitive, graceful phrases. Hagen classifies it as a song cycle: "It is unified by the recurring use of piano figures in a rather exposed linear texture. This is matched by a similar quality in the vocal writing." Hagen's delicate piano patterns, etched like snow pictures on a frosty window, create an effective and beautiful soundscape for Larkin's pensive verses. Several songs have repeated pedal notes that, like an insistent reminder, perpetuate the poet's lonely memories. The vocal writing is lyric but exposed (Song 4a is unaccompanied). Hagen's musical approach creates a close-knit, two-person chamber music texture, in which Larkin's poems, full of melancholy and reminiscence, are thrown into high relief. Hagen: "The longer that an art song composer can sustain a desired mood, the more exquisite the rendering of context, the more perfect a setting in which the listener can experience that text."

Larkin Songs was commissioned by the University of Nevada, Las Vegas Department of Music for baritone Paul Kreider. They were first performed by Kreider and Hagen at Ham Fine Arts Building, University of Nevada, Las Vegas, on February 18, 2001.

Love in a Life   **Songs arranged into a cycle in 1998.**

Love in a Life (Robert Browning) • Congedo (Nuar Alsadir) •
Ample Make This Bed (Emily Dickinson) • Stanzas for Music
(George Gordon, Lord Byron) • The Waking (Theodore Roethke) •
To You (Walt Whitman) • Love (Thomas Lodge)

Love in a Life* was compiled over the course of many years (1981-1998). All of the poems deal with love, and gather together its many and varied strands into a collection resembling pages in a photograph album—each picture with its own story.

*Hagen's quotations about these songs taken from: Daron Hagen, "Afterword," from *Daron Aric Hagen: Songbook* (New York: Carl Fischer, 2002), 168. Used by permission of the composer.

LOVE IN A LIFE (ROBERT BROWNING) NOVEMBER 2, 1981. This was the first song Hagen worked on as a student at the Curtis Institute. It "went through many drafts."

CONGEDO (NUAR ALSADIR) AUGUST 24, 1998. Hagen composed this song at Yaddo,* It is dedicated to the poet, Nuar Alsadir, who "gave me a manuscript of it early in the day and for whom I first played and sang my setting the same evening." Intensely lyric vocal lines lead this setting from the first unaccompanied phrase.

*Yaddo is an artists' community located on a 400-acre estate in Saratoga Springs, New York. Its mission is to nurture the creative process by providing an opportunity for artists to work without interruption in a supportive environment.

AMPLE MAKE THIS BED (EMILY DICKINSON) MARCH 13, 1989. This song was composed "in the course of an hour on a baby grand that had just been man-handled up five stories into the East Village garret on Saint Mark's Place in which I lived." Hagen's setting has none of the angst of his memory of his bruised piano; instead, it is a touchingly simple, almost hymn-like song.

STANZAS FOR MUSIC (GEORGE GORDON, LORD BYRON) DECEMBER 5, 1983. This song was composed in New York City and completed on December 5, 1983. It is dedicated to composer and pianist Craig Urquhart. Hagen chooses a linear texture in which rhythm and phrase shapes in voice and piano operate independently of one another. As the piano and voice lines intersect, they create a captivating structure in which the words resonate.

THE WAKING (THEODORE ROETHKE) SEPTEMBER 24, 1993. Hagen wrote this song "between composition lessons at Bard College in Annandale-on-Hudson, NY. (where for a decade I taught)." The vocal phrases are declamatory, but still have a mysterious weightlessness about them. The piano figures are chordal throughout, and gather dynamic intensity as they progress, like the tolling of bells.

To You (Walt Whitman) 1982. Hagen comments: "Both versions of 'To You' were composed in Philadelphia in 1982. The first setting views the encounter from one participant's perspective, the second from the other's. They should be performed without a break between them." The two settings are like a conversation; the first (song) is *Adagio*, the second song, *Allegretto*.

Love (Thomas Lodge)* October 30, 1981. "Love" was completed in Philadelphia on Oct. 30, 1981. Hagen marks it *Passionate, rueful (dotted quarter=116)*. In this rhythmically driven setting, changes of time signature occur every measure or every two measures. The changeable word stresses produced by these meter fluctuations, in tandem with varied articulations in the piano figures, create flexibility and buoyancy.

*For a comparison setting, see Ned Rorem.

Figments
(Alice Wirth Gray)

2000

Gravity • Why We Have Cats • The End of Daylight Savings Time •
Zoo Prepares to Adopt Metric System • Lines After Marianne Moore •
Deer in Mist and Almonds • The Poetry of Sausages: Morcilla

This cycle was commissioned by Paul Sperry, who sang the world premiere on April 22, 2002 at the Bruno Walter Auditorium at Lincoln Center, accompanied by the composer.

The wildly humorous—and ultimately touching—poems of Alice Wirth Gray inspired Hagen to write one of his wittiest cycles. All of the songs are pithy observations on the human condition.

Gravity opens with a pompous introduction of chords, followed by an equally pompous vocal proclamation. A lurching, tipsy waltz begins (marked "Loopy"), which accompanies a shocking account of the aftermath of the San Fernando earthquake—all of the Dostoyevsky fell off the bookshelves, but the Tolstoy stayed put!

Why We Have Cats is the vehement ranting of a woman who finds herself with five unwanted cats, which her neighbor abandoned.

The End of Daylight Savings Time is a mere eighteen measures long. Declamatory, unaccompanied vocal phrases alternate with vocal lines built in whole tones. A murky atmosphere is created when the vocal line is combined with chords of parallel fourths. The singer bemoans the scarcity of light—"the government's begun to ration it."

The singer is given only one pitch to sing in Zoo Prepares to Adopt Metric System, a tongue-in-cheek recounting of a request from the Ground Squirrel to the bureaucratic zoo administrators.

LINES AFTER MARIANNE MOORE and DEER IN MIST AND ALMONDS are settings that are less comical. Both have fluid vocal phrases and atmospheric piano figures. Piano figures in the $\frac{3}{4}$ sections of "Deer in Mist and Almonds" call to mind a Satie *gymnopédie*.

The final song THE POETRY OF SAUSAGES: MORCILLA, extols one of the great hedonistic pleasures—eating. Hagen creates an earthy, colorful setting, which he marks "Cooking Joyously," quarter note=160.

Extended Study List

Dear Youth (Civil War letters written from women to their husbands, for soprano/flute/piano) • *Echo's Songs* • *Rittenhouse Songs* (1981) • *Three Silent Things* (soprano/violin/viola/cello/piano) • *The Heart of the Stranger* • *Merrill Songs* • *Songs of Madness and Sorrow* • *Alive in a Moment* (baritone/string quartet) • *Phantoms of Myself* • Operas: *Shining Brow, Vera of Las Vegas, Bandanna*

Selected Reading

Francis Booth, "American Valhalla," *Opera News*, 57:15 (April 10, 1993), 24-29. An overview of Hagen's opera *Shining Brow*.

John Koopman, "Shining Brow, *Opera News* 58:5 (November 1993), 48-49. Review.

Paul Kreider, "Art songs of Daron Hagen: lyrical dramaticism and simplicity with an interpretive guide to *Rittenhouse Songs* and *Resuming Green*." D.M.A. diss., University of Arizona, 1999.

Russell Platt, "Artful Simplicity: the Art songs of Daron Hagen," *Journal of Singing*, 55:1 (September/October 1998), 3-11.

Jane McCalla Redding, "An introduction to American song composer Daron Aric Hagen (b. 1961) and his miniature folk opera: *Dear Youth*." D.M.A. diss., Louisiana State University, 2002.

Ned Rorem, "Learning With Daron," *Opera News*, 57:15 (April 10, 1993), 29.

Notes

1. Daron Hagen in conversation with Carol Kimball, November 2, 1994.
2. Ned Rorem, "Learning With Daron," *Opera News*, 29.
3. Hagen, in conversation with Carol Kimball, November 2, 1994.
4. Conversation with Carol Kimball, November 3, 1994.
5. Hagen, in conversation with Paul Kreider, November 1994. Used by permission.
6. Hagen's notes to "Muldoon Songs," on Hagen's official website.
7. Ibid.

British Song

British song has a history of peaks and valleys. Music flourished during the sixteenth and early seventeenth centuries, languished in the eighteenth and early nineteenth centuries, and regained its strength and quality in the twentieth century.

England's supremacy in music and poetry during the Elizabethan period was unchallenged. Early British solo song descended in a direct line from madrigals. Lute songs were the dominant song form of the sixteenth and the early seventeenth centuries. John Dowland, Thomas Campion, Henry Laws, Robert Jones, Philip Rosseter, and other Elizabethan composers wrote a wealth of songs, using the great poetry of that era, specifically that of William Shakespeare. Then, as now, Shakespeare's works have provided an abundance of subject matter for song composers of all nationalities. *The Shakespeare Music Catalogue* of Gooch and Thatcher (Oxford University Press) lists more than 20,000 items set to music.[1]

The seventeenth century was crowned by the vocal compositions of Henry Purcell (1659-1695), the last great English composer before the twentieth century. The editor of *Orpheus Britannicus*, the principal seventeenth-century collection of Purcell's songs, noted that Purcell had "a peculiar genius to express the energy of English words."[2] His one true opera, *Dido and Aeneas*, is the last great English opera until Benjamin Britten's operas.

Purcell's age was followed by the Georgian period (1720-1780), whose music was marked by formality and refinement. Composer Thomas Augustine Arne (1710-1778) was an important composer of this period. He wrote many songs— among them, "The Lass With the Delicate Air," which has served as a showpiece for many a neophyte soprano, and Britain's unofficial anthem, "Rule, Britannia!" Most eighteenth-century composers wrote prolifically for the theater; masques and ballad operas contained many lyric songs with simple melodies in strophic form. Private gatherings such as garden parties and outdoor concerts also demanded music, and songs were a part of the musical fare heard at these affairs.

The prevalent song form of the Victorian age was the drawing room or parlor ballad. These songs were typically sentimental, strophic in form, and had only a tenuous relationship between text and music; however, they were wildly popular and commercially profitable. Composers turned them out in great numbers and with seeming ease. As the nineteenth century progressed, parlor ballads became more sentimental and difficult to distinguish from one another. Composers often used the poetry of Tennyson and Kingsley and were influenced by Felix Mendelssohn, whose sojourn in London was influential in musical circles.

A group of early Edwardian song composers, known as the Frankfurt group,[3] included Roger Quilter (1877-1953), Percy Grainger (1882-1961), Henry Balfour Gardiner (1877-1950), and Cyril Scott (1879-1970). Their songs were tuneful but sentimental successors to the Victorian ballad.

Also in the nineteenth century, Hubert Parry (1848-1918) and Charles Villiers Stanford (1852-1924) were influential in British song, both as composers and as teachers. Their students were the next generation of English song composers. Stanford's pupils included John Ireland (1879-1962), Herbert Howells (1892-1983),

Gustav Holst (1874-1934), and Ralph Vaughan Williams (1872-1958). Their songs form the main core of twentieth-century British song and, in turn, influenced their contemporaries.

Stanford and Parry began a movement back to England's older poets, such as Blake, Herrick, Lovelace, and Shakespeare. Early twentieth-century composers set poetry by Alfred, Lord Tennyson; Robert Louis Stevenson; Thomas Hardy; Walter de la Mare; and Christina and Dante Gabriel Rossetti. Chief among the British poets of the twentieth century were Thomas Hardy and A.E. Housman. Housman's collection *A Shropshire Lad* became a magnet for English art song composers; its simplicity and musical lyricism was perfectly suited for song. Ralph Vaughan Williams, Ivor Gurney, John Ireland, Arnold Bax, George Butterworth, Cecil Armstrong Gibbs, Charles Orr, and E.J. Moeran were among the composers who set Housman's verse.

British art song experienced a resurgence in the twentieth century as numerous composers wrote songs in varied styles.[4] In the first half of the century, England dipped into its rich legacy of folk song and began to add its elements to art songs. Ralph Vaughan Williams's interest in British folk music motivated much of his song style. With Gustav Holst, Vaughan Williams plumbed England's own folk music for its distinctive melodic style and expressive qualities. He combined folk song and hymnody with European traditions of Bach, Handel, Debussy, and Ravel to create a style that is, for some, the national sound of British song.

As British song moved into the twentieth century, it reflected a variety of influences: German romanticism, French impressionism, neoclassicism, and modernism. British composers produced a highly diverse body of art song, mirroring their individual musical styles and backgrounds. Peter Warlock (1894-1930), Gerald Finzi (1901-1956), Frederick Delius (1862-1934), and George Butterworth (1885-1916) are composers whose songs reflect widely differing styles.

Benjamin Britten was the most prolific and famous English composer of the twentieth century. He is particularly distinguished for his vocal music; his operas revived the tradition of English theater music that had lain dormant since Purcell; his original and appealing songs to texts of the highest quality demand a singer of intelligence and musicianship. His excellent sense of prosody owes much to Purcell's word setting and melodic style; his melodies are integrated into a contemporary harmonic texture that is uniquely his.

Contemporary British composers such as Geoffrey Bush, Peter Dickinson, Madeleine Dring, Rebecca Clarke, and Robin Holloway continued the tradition of writing songs, but British art song is, in general, a sleeping giant awaiting another resurgence.

Notes

1. Two Hyperion CDs will provide the reader with an introduction to many art songs set to Shakespeare texts by British composers: *Songs to Shakespeare*, Anthony Rolfe Johnson, tenor/Graham Johnson, piano, 1991, Hyperion CDA66480, and Shakespeare's Kingdom, Sarah Walker, mezzo-soprano/Graham Johnson, piano, 1984, Hyperion CDA66136.
2. James Husst Hall, *The Art Song*, 231.
3. These composers, sometimes called "the Frankfurt Gang," all studied with Ivan Knorr at the Hoch'sche Konservatorium in Frankfurt-am-Main.
4. Four movements splintered from the ideals of the post-Victorians: Holst and Vaughan Williams supported a national style; the Frankfurt composers maintained a cosmopolitan aesthetic; Cyril Scott was highly influenced by the French style; and Arnold Bax and John Ireland defended a purely romantic outlook. (Robert Hansen, "The Legacy of the Twentieth-Century English Art Song." The NATS Journal 45:4, 6).

The Lutenists

What epigrams are in Poetrie, the same are Ayres in musicke, then in their chiefe perfection when they are short and well seasoned.
—Philip Rosseter[1]

Lute songs descended directly from the madrigal tradition. Although lute songs were not published in England until the end of the sixteenth century (Dowland's *First Booke of Songes or Ayres* in 1597), solo songs with lute were already well established on the continent. Lute songs were music of a simple and popular character, meant to be performed by solo singer (or as four-part ayres) and lute, often with a bass viol added. Not designed for public performance, they were intimate and personal in style. Many of the songs had added voice parts; the composer usually indicated whether the song could be performed by single voice and lute.

Lute songs usually followed a strophic format, with phrases cast in rhythmic units that corresponded to the poetic line. Few introductions (usually a chord sufficed) and interludes are found in these early songs. Harmonically, the songs exhibit some unsettled tonality, with vacillation between major and minor; melodically, the songs are tonal (favorite keys: C, F, G and D), still following madrigal practice. Polyphonic and contrapuntal treatment also carried over from madrigals. Popular poetry of the time, rich in contrasts—by turn, gentle, bawdy, earthy, and tender—provided the texts.

Elizabethan composers were highly successful in blending music and verse. For them, the inflection of the phrase was one of great subtlety and importance. Composers wrote music that followed the natural rhythmic stress of the words; these stresses sometimes fell on accented beats, but just as often on unaccented beats. Since the practice of accenting by bar lines was unknown in Elizabethan time, these "syncopated rhythms" are actually subtle musical renderings of the natural stress of the words. When these songs are performed with simplicity and accurate note values, the clarity and beauty of the writing becomes apparent.

Early lutes had six double strings of catgut and were plucked with the fingers. Later lutes had twelve strings; six were fretted and the others were used for bass notes and played with the thumb. Thomas Mace, an enthusiastic lute performer, published a work titled *Musicke's Monument* (1676) which provides us with much of the information we have concerning this instrument, and even a humorous account of how to store it:

...and that you may know how to shelter your Lute in the worst of ill weathers (which is moist), you shall do well ever when you lay it by in the day-time, to put it in a bed that is constantly used, between the rug and blanket (but never between the sheets, because they might be moist with sweat). A bed will secure from all these inconveniences, and keep your glew so hard as glass, and all safe and sure, only to be excepted that no person be so inconsiderate, as to tumble down upon the bed whilst the Lute is there; for I have known several good Lutes spoilt with such a trick.[2]

A list of distinguished composers of lute songs with representative literature follows:

WILLIAM BYRD (1543-1623)
I thought that love had been a boy • O mistress mine • My mind to me a kingdom is

ROBERT JONES (D. 1617)
What if I seek for love of thee • Go to bed, sweet muse • Sweet Kate

FRANCIS PILKINGTON (1582-1638)
Rest sweet nymphs • Underneath a cypress tree • Diaphenia

THOMAS MORLEY (1557-1603)
With my love my life was nestled • Mistress mine, well may you fare • It was a lover and his lass

TOBIAS HUME (D. 1648)
Fain would I change that note • Tobacco, tobacco

PHILIP ROSSETER (1575-1623)
When Laura smiles • If she forsake me • If I urge my kind desires

HENRY LAWES (1595-1662) 430 of his songs survive
I am confirmed a woman can • Beauty and love • Bid me but live

WILLIAM CORKINE (EARLY SEVENTEENTH CENTURY)
Sweete Cupid, ripen her desire • Dear, though your minde • Shall a smile or a guileful glance

HENRY CAREY (1690-1743)
The plausible lover • Divinest fair • Here's to thee, my boy

Two of the most representative composers of lute songs are Thomas Campion and John Dowland. Several lute songs of each are annotated below.

JOHN DOWLAND (1563-1626)

> He chose for musical setting some of the most perfect lyrics that have ever been written in the English language, yet never did he fail to re-create the full beauty of the poet's thought in music...no one has left us a musical legacy of more intrinsic loveliness than John Dowland.
>
> —Peter Warlock[3]

John Dowland, often considered the first great English song composer, was a virtuoso performer on the lute, gaining the patronage of King Christian IV of Denmark and later the Duke of Wolgast in Pomerania. Dowland traveled extensively throughout the continent, and his performances were highly acclaimed. His mastery as a performer on the lute is reflected in his musical settings. Through his travels and his many contacts, he developed a musical sophistication that he channeled into his compositions.

Dowland was a gifted melodist; his eighty-seven songs demonstrate his elegant style and blending of words with sound, as well as a wide range of emotion and technique. He created a unique style for the lute songs, and this style remained more or less unchanged for the life of the genre.

Dowland published four collections of songs: *The First Book of Songes or Ayres* (1597); *The Second Booke of Songs* (1600); *The Third and Last Booke of Songs* (1603); and *A Pilgrimes Solace* (1612). Also, three of his songs are included in *A Musicall Banquet* (1610), a collection of songs published by his son, Robert.

Come again, sweet love doth now invite   1597

Dowland did not use much text painting in his work, but relied instead on creating a general emotional mood or atmosphere to amplify and express the meaning of the text. He wrote this three-stanza song, one of his most familiar, as a lover's complaint. He establishes intense passion with a breathless reiteration of an ascending interval in the voice, echoed in the accompaniment—"to see, to hear, to touch, to kiss"—with a release of tension on a long climactic note "to die..." (an Elizabethan metaphor for making love).

Fine knacks for ladies   1609

This gay melody is a peddler's pitch at a country fair; however, it is also a metaphor for love. It is probably the most extroverted of all Dowland's lute song texts. It is characterized by clear-cut rhythms and simple harmonies.

In darkness let me dwell   1610

This song has been termed one of the great songs of English music, and it is included in the songs Dowland contributed to his son Robert's publication *A Musicall Banquet.*

In this song, Dowland creates a haunting atmosphere that expresses a sense of deep sorrow, unrelieved at first, and then finally broken with the passionate outburst "O let me living die." Dowland uses chromatic passages, dramatic vocal declamation, and colorful dissonances.

This song begins with a long introduction and contains many interludes. Dowland also uses an antiphonal section between the lute and the bass viol, pitting rhythms in the instruments against those in the vocal line to create a unique and effective contrapuntal texture.

Extended Study List
Dear, if you change • Who ever thinks or hopes of love • Flow not so fast, ye fountains • I saw my lady weep • A shepherd in a shade • Come away, come sweet love • Sorrow, stay • Flow, my tears • Weep you no more, sad fountains • What if I never speed?

THOMAS CAMPION (1567-1620)

> In these English ayres, I have chiefly aimed to couple my words and notes lovingly together, which will be much for him to do that hath not power over both.
>
> —Thomas Campion[4]

Thomas Campion was the most prolific of all the lutenists, composing no fewer than 118 ayres, published in five volumes (one with Philip Rosseter). All his songs are set to his own words and, although his poetic rhythms are fluid and charming, his musical treatment has been criticized as foursquare, lacking the musical variety or originality of Dowland. Many of his songs, however, overcome his too-direct approach; the best of them are excellent musical examples of lute song literature.

If thou longs't so much to learn   1617

An experienced young lady warns an innocent young man of the dangers of love; implicit in her warning is an invitation. Melodic phrases contain dance-like rhythms in keeping with the light-hearted mocking mood.

Oft have I sighed   1617

This is a slow, sad lament for an absent beloved. A beautiful limpid melody is embellished with some melodic turns; Campion takes the phrase "Oh, yet I languish still" and repeats it three times, each repetition descending chromatically.

When to her lute Corinna sings   1601

This is one of Campion's best songs, a delicious blend of words and music, with shifting rhythmic patterns to match the poetic stress.

Extended Study List

The cypress curtain of the night • Come, O come, my life's delight • Follow your saint • Never love unless you can • There is a garden in her face • To music bent is my retired mind • Jack and Joan • The peaceful western wind • Shall I come, sweet love, to thee? • Her rosy cheeks

Selected Reading

Lorraine Gorrell, "A Plaine and Easie Introduction to the Ayres of John Dowland," *The NATS Bulletin* 38:2 (Nov/Dec 1981).

C. Michael Hawn, "Baroque Corner: The Lute Songs of John Dowland," *The NATS Journal* 43:3 (Jan/Feb 1987).

Frederick Keel, preface to *Elizabethan Love Songs* (London: Boosey & Co., 1909). Keel's arrangements of lute songs are published in two volumes.

Carol MacClintock, ed., *The Solo Song*, 1580-1730 (New York: W. W. Norton, 1973).

Ian Spink, *English Song: Dowland to Purcell* (New York: Taplinger Publishing, 1986).

Peter Warlock (Philip Heseltine), *The English Ayre* (Westport, CT: Greenwood Press, 1970. First publication, Oxford University Press, 1926).

Notes

1. In his 1601 *Book of Ayres* (half of the songs were Thomas Campion's). Quoted in Ian Spink, *English Song: Dowland to Purcell*, 24.
2. Mace's writings also gave directions for choosing, repairing, tuning, keeping, and performing on the instrument.
3. Peter Warlock, *The English Ayre*, 51.
4. In his preface to *Two Books of Airs,* issued c. 1612. Quoted in Warlock, 102-103.

HENRY PURCELL (1659-1695)

The Author's extraordinary Talent in all sorts of Musick is sufficiently known, but he was especially admir'd for the Vocal, having a peculiar Genius to express the Energy of English Words, whereby he mov'd the Passions of all his Auditors.

—Henry Playford[1]

Purcell is to English sung what Shakespeare is to English spoken.

—H. Wendell Howard[2]

Henry Purcell was in the right place at the right time. When Charles II returned to England from exile in France, he was determined to recreate the splendor of the French court in his own country. Trained in the choir of the Chapel Royal, Purcell was appointed composer-in-ordinary to the King in 1677 and organist to Westminster Abbey in 1679. His principal duties were to provide anthems, birthday odes, and music for other royal ceremonies (including coronations) for the four monarchs he served: Charles II, James II, and William and Mary.

As composer to the Crown and the Abbey, he occupied a place of considerable musical eminence. He also composed in all musical genres of the day, although most of his works are connected with the court. After the accession of William and Mary, the Royal Musick was severely curtailed; Purcell and other composers were forced to supplement incomes by teaching, publishing, holding public concerts, and composing for the commercial stage. In 1690, Purcell became a full-time composer for the theatrical stage.

Many of his best-known and most-performed songs are found in his five operas, called "semi-operas,"[3] since the music is not continuous: *Dioclesian* (1690), *King Arthur* (1691), *The Fairy Queen* (1692), *The Indian Queen* (1695), and *The Tempest* (1695). Only *Dido and Aeneas* is an opera in the purest sense of the word since its music is continuous.

Purcell's songs endure as the cornerstone of British vocal music. During his brief lifetime he composed music to some fifty plays and single songs (Spink lists sixty-five strophic songs and 148 for theatrical productions)[4] He is also distinguished for his church music: full anthems, verse anthems, and cantata-anthems.

Purcell was known by the title of his first published volume of songs—"Orpheus Britannicus." His songs are natural and instinctively vocal—perhaps because he was himself a singer.* He is considered unsurpassed in setting the English language; his music has an unerring sense for depicting human emotions in a real and touching dramatic way, unparalleled for that time and rarely equaled since.

*Purcell was a countertenor.

Music for a while   *Oedipus.* 1692
(John Dryden)

This is one of two songs Purcell wrote for Dryden and Lee's play *Oedipus* (1692). The prophet Tiresias uses "Music for a while" to bring forth the ghost of the murdered Laius and discover the source of the curse on Thebes.

Text painting is liberal throughout the song: a caressing little turn on "beguile"; reiteration of the word "all" at various pitches; the insistent clashing half-step interval on "eternal"; and the "dropping" snakes in eighth notes punctuated by rests. Purcell uses his favorite musical device, the repeated ground bass, but departs from a strict treatment in the middle section, which modulates briefly to G minor and B-flat. Unity is maintained through the rhythm of the bass, which also propels the song forward. The combination of all these musical techniques creates extraordinary tension throughout the song. The opening section (both music and words) is repeated at the close of the piece. This song is considered to be one of Purcell's finest.

If music be the food of love   First setting. 1691
(Henry Heveningham)

Purcell set this text three times (1691, 1693, 1695). The first version is the simplest and perhaps the most tuneful—the last, perhaps the most passionately intense. Purcell's melodic line is urged along with sequences that build tension, which is released at the highest point of the phrase by a softer phrase shape. Notice the beautiful melismatic setting on the word "music" in the final vocal phrase.

I'll Sail Upon the Dog Star   1688
from D'Urfey's *A Fool's Preferment* staged in 1688

With this song, Purcell created one of the outstanding examples of English baroque song. It dates from the time he began to compose his operas; his theatrical treatment of this text is undeniable and marks his movement toward an ever-increasing Italian treatment of vocal phrases.

This song features word and phrase repetition and a developing manipulation of phrase length. Purcell's pictorial treatment of the word "pursue" is evident. Free canonic treatment is found throughout the song. Purcell assigns the word "chase" a sixteenth-note motive, which is freely imitated in the bass line; the same mirrored treatment occurs with the word "tear," which begins in the vocal line and races downward through the accompaniment.

Hark! Hark! the Echoing Air — A song in *The Fairy Queen*. 1692

"Hark! hark! the echoing air a triumph sings. / And all around, pleased Cupids clap their wings."

The Fairy-Queen, based on *A Midsummer Night's Dream*, was the most lavish of Purcell's semi-operas. It consisted of four masques associated with the fairy kingdom. Each masque is self-contained and captures the atmosphere of Shakespeare's original play in unique and associative ways, although Shakespeare's text is not used in any of the sections.

This song belongs to the elaborate Epithalamium* that ends the work. It is an outstanding example of the fresh energetic quality that characterizes Purcell's melodies. The voice is combined with Purcell's English adaptation of Italian trumpet aria style in the accompaniment. Purcell's text illustration is also present in the melody and rhythm ("clap their wings"). The vocal line is florid, with sequences of motives and phrase fragments that alternate with melismas on selected words.

*A wedding song or poem

Sweeter than Roses — *Pausanias*. 1695
(Richard Norton)

Pandora, Pausanias's unfaithful mistress, commands this song to be sung to heighten her anticipation as she awaits a visit from her newest lover. Purcell sets the song in three sections. The first is slow and ecstatic, featuring a languid melodic line of seduction. Melismatic text painting is used primarily on the words "cool" and "warm." Rising sequential motives on "dear kiss" are followed by more text illustration on the words "trembling" and "freeze." A short transition section "Then shot like fire all o'er" is characterized by a faster tempo and a rising vocal phrase (repeated sequentially) that literally "shoots" the words upward, ushering in a victorious final section which dances triumphantly to the end of the piece.

Extended Study List
We sing to Him • I Attempt from Love's Sickness to Fly • Fairest Isle • There's not a swain on the plain • What can we poor females do? • Bess of Bedlam (Mad Bess) • Let the dreadful engines • The Knotting Song • Ah, how sweet it is to love • The fatal hour comes on apace • One charming night • Since from my dear Astrea's sight • An Evening Hymn • Oh! Lead Me to Some Peaceful Gloom • The Blessed Virgin's Expostulation • Strike the viol

Selected Reading
Michael Burden, *Purcell Remembered* (Portland: Amadeus Press, 1996).
H. Wendell Howard, "The English Orpheus," *The NATS Bulletin* 29:2 (December 1972).
Robert Etherdige Moore, *Henry Purcell and the Restoration Theatre* (Cambridge: Cambridge University Press, 1961).
Ian Spink, *English Song: Dowland to Purcell* (New York: Taplinger Publishing, 1986).

Notes
1. Henry Playford, "Publisher to the Reader" in *Orpheus Britannicus*. Two volumes of Purcell's songs, published posthumously, appeared under this title in 1698 and 1702.
2. H. Wendell Howard, "The English Orpheus," *The NATS Bulletin,* 29:2, 26.
3. During the Restoration, English theater produced no real operas; dramatic music was integrated into spoken plays titled "masques," *divertissements* or other sung/danced episodes. Purcell had great success composing these "semi-operas" and numerous other incidental pieces for theatrical use.
4. Ian Spink, *English Song: Dowland to Purcell*, 208.

FREDERICK DELIUS (1862-1934)

> Music is an outburst of the soul. It is addressed and should appeal instantly to the soul of the listener.
>
> —Frederick Delius[1]

> There is only one real happiness in life, and that is the happiness of creating.
>
> —Frederick Delius[2]

Although Frederick Delius is an English composer, his song style can hardly be described as English in the sense of the sound quality of Vaughan Williams, Quilter, or other British composers of his era. Delius's sixty-five solo songs with piano accompaniment are notably cosmopolitan with a sophisticated musical approach and an eclectic choice of poetry. Most were composed before the turn of the century. In addition to solo songs with piano accompaniment, Delius's vocal works also include orchestral songs; choral music (unaccompanied and with orchestra), large choral works for soloists, chorus, and orchestra; and works for the stage.

In a sense, Delius's songs mirror his life and personality. He was born in Bradofr, Yorkshire, England, of German immigrant parents who were well-to-do wool merchants. He spent some time in the United States: in Florida, growing oranges (but concentrating on music), teaching music in Jacksonville and later in Virginia, and a brief sojourn in New York. In 1887, he went to the Leipzig Conservatory for further musical study. Delius eventually settled in France and married the artist Jelka Rosen. After the outbreak of World War I, Delius alternated living between England and France. The Deliuses made their home in France, Grez-sur-Loing, a quiet village on the edge of the Forest of Fontainebleau.

Both Delius and his wife spoke English, German, French, as well as some Scandinavian tongues. With the exception of his settings of Elizabethan texts and three settings of Shelley, he chose contemporary poetry for his songs in a number of languages: Norwegian, Danish, German, French, and English. In every instance, he had a unique gift for capturing the essence of the culture from which the text originated. His choice of texts was wide-ranging—from Elizabethan poetry, to Paul Verlaine, to Nietzsche. His love of Scandinavia and its literature was a powerful influence on his work; friendships with Grieg and Sinding were established during his years of study in Leipzig (1886-88). His earliest songs set Norwegian texts (*Five Songs*-1888 and *Seven Songs*-1889-90). Musical influences from Grieg are apparent in these sets, which are dedicated to Nina Grieg. Delius's settings of Norwegian and Danish poetry are found in German versions because he depended on their publication by German publishing firms. He composed songs throughout his career; they date from his earliest compositions until his last illness, and fall naturally into three periods.

Delius's style is basically that of a tone painter who followed no established form. His songs are characterized by his highly developed and personalized harmonic approach that influenced a new style of English song. His music has an improvisatory quality, an elegance of atmosphere, and a rich harmonic sense. Delius believed the essential elements in music were intensity of expression and emotion. In an article he wrote for *The Sackbut,* he expounded at length on what he felt was important in music: "Musical expression only begins to be significant where words and actions reach their uttermost limit of expression. Music should be concerned with the emotions, not with external events...It is only that which cannot be expressed otherwise that is worth expressing in music."[3]

Irmelin Rose   1897
(Jens Peter Jacobsen)

Written seven years later than Delius's opera of the same name,[*] this song belongs to a group of seven Danish songs, originally composed with orchestral accompaniment. Delius made singing English translations of the songs. Both opera and song are based on the same legend; the beautiful cold-hearted princess Irmelin turns away countless noble suitors, yet falls in love with a wandering troubadour.

The troubadour does not appear in the text of the song, but Delius evokes the archaic atmosphere in which the unattainable Irmelin dwells. An E-natural gives a modal tinge to the F-sharp tonality, and there are fleeting touches of other keys which give the song an improvisational, narrative quality. Delius sets the four strophes like an old ballad; stanzas one and four have varied music, stanzas two and three are exact repeats. A dotted rhythm in the accompaniment (dotted quarter/eighth/dotted quarter/eighth) ushers in the first vocal phrase over an F-sharp pedal—reminiscent of an early stringed instrument.

The inner stanzas two and three are higher pitched, expressing the optimism of Irmelin's suitors. The final stanza describes the cold unrelenting princess by a thinning of texture and more disjunct intervals in the vocal line.

In the song, as in the opera, the name "Irmelin" is always set musically as a descending major fourth, with the exception of the one time in the opera when she tells her own name, and it rises.[4]

*This song is sometimes known as "Irmelin." It is related to the opera *Irmelin* as well as to a much later, independent work, the *Irmelin Prelude.*

Twilight Fancies*   1889-1890
(Björnstjerne Björnsen)

This song is part of Delius's second Norwegian album (*Seven Songs from the Norwegian*) on texts by Bjørnson, Vinje, and Ibsen. Hutchings observes two Delian earmarks in these songs, composed early in Delius's career: use of echo-like refrains, especially at the ends of songs, and a leaning towards sentimental and popular-type settings.[5] Scandinavian verse, usually on themes of unrequited love, is characteristically full of narrative ballad style.

Another princess is found in the text of this song. Listening to the horn of a herd-boy below her window, she is stirred romantically and yearns for the unknown. A subdued vocal line, recitative in style, is set in a simple, rather transparent accompaniment texture. Delius's tranquil musical treatment is sustained and intense but retains the simplicity of a folktale. A recurring poetic refrain "When the sun goes down" establishes the refrain-form of the ballad, and poignantly on the last repetition—"And the sun went down"—is heard in the minor key.

* This song is also titled "The Princess" or "Evening Voices." The same poem was also set by Kjerulf and Grieg.

Love's Philosophy   1891
(Percy Bysshe Shelley)

Delius's settings of Shelley ("Indian Love Song," "Love's Philosophy," and "To the Queen of My Heart") are unique among his songs for their extroverted romantic sentiment. Shelley's ardent verse seems to call forth musical settings of romantic texture and broad long-lined vocalism.[*]

The meter is $\frac{4}{4}$; the accompaniment consists of running arpeggios in the left hand capped with chord patterns of quarter note/half note/quarter note. Vocal phrases are soaring, wide-ranged, and intensely lyric. These patterns change for the second stanza. Alternating sixteenth-note patterns occur here in both hands, and the vocal line is strongly declamatory. "And the sunlight clasps the earth" ushers back in the opening patterns which rush to the final measures. Delius repeats "If thou kiss not me" twice more after the initial statement.

*For a comparison setting, see Roger Quilter.

Il pleure dans mon cœur   1895
(Paul Verlaine)

Delius's Verlaine settings are considered by some to be the most perfect of all his songs. They are the only set not published with an English translation. Delius scored them for alternative piano or orchestral accompaniment.

The song is through-composed and in the minor key. The sound of raindrops permeates the accompaniment in an ostinato arpeggio figure overlaid with a tiny melodic fragment, continuing unchanged through the first two vocal phrases. Verlaine's mood of listlessness and unexplained melancholy is given voice by Delius in an accompaniment figure of moving eighth notes combined with vocal phrases that contain repeated notes. Many of the vocal phrases end with a falling interval (note especially "haine/peine" in the last two phrases) sustaining the despondent atmosphere.

In this song, Delius has captured a distinctly French mood and style. In comparison with Debussy's setting, this musical treatment seems sad and intense, rather than reflective and lyrical.

This piece was published in 1895 as *Two Verlaine Songs*—the other is "Le Ciel est par dessus le toit" (set as "Prison" by Fauré and Hahn, and as "The Sky Above the Roof" by Vaughan Williams). Other Verlaine settings by Delius are "La Lune blanche," "Chanson d'automne," and "Avant que tu ne t'en ailles."

Extended Study List
Young Venevil • To the Queen of My Heart • Indian Love Song • Dreamy Nights • It was a lover and his lass • Spring, the sweet spring • In the Seraglio Garden • The Homeward Way • Cradle Song • The Bird's Story • Black Roses • Beim Sonnenuntergang • *Sea Drift* (w/orchestra) • *Songs of Farewell* (w/orchestra) • *Songs of Sunset* (w/orchestra) • The Nightingale has a Lyre of Gold • *Cynara* (baritone w/orchestra)

Selected Reading

Anne Williams Allman, *The Songs of Frederick Delius: An Interpretive and Stylistic Analysis and Performance of Representative Compositions*. Ed.D. diss., Columbia University Teachers College, 1983. Examination of forty-four of Delius's sixty-five songs, with biographical background and analysis.

Trevor Hold, *Parry to Finzi: Twenty English Song-Composers* (Woodbridge: Boydell Press, 2002).

A. K. Holland, *The Songs of Delius* (London: Oxford University Press, 1951).

Arthur Hutchings, *Delius* (Westport, CT: Greenwood Press, 1970). Chapter 13: "Delius's Songs."

Edward Gilmore Hutchings, III. *The Published Solo Songs of Frederick Delius*. Unpublished D.M.A. dissertation. University of Miami, 1980.

Alan Jefferson, *Delius* (London: J. M. Dent and Sons, 1972). See especially Chapter 6: "Delius's Craft."

Christopher Redwood, editor, *A Delius Companion* (New York: Da Capo Press, 1977).

Notes

1. Frederick Delius, "The Composer Speaks," in David Ewen, *The New Book of Modern Composers*, 3rd edition, 152.
2. Ian Crofton and Donald Fraser, *A Dictionary of Musical Quotations*, 50.
3. Quoted in Harold C. Schonberg, *The Lives of the Great Composers*, 492.
4. Alan Jefferson, *Delius*, 89.
5. Arthur Hutchings, 158-59.

RALPH VAUGHAN WILLIAMS (1872-1958)

Words when sung are sometimes only the framework for sound.
—Ralph Vaughan Williams[1]

Ralph Vaughan Williams was one of the most important British composers of this century. He was a student of Hubert Parry and Charles Villiers Stanford, and also studied with Max Bruch in Berlin (1897) and with Maurice Ravel in Paris (1908). Although his initial musical style was strongly influenced by the German school, a radical transformation took place after his in-depth study of British folk songs.

One of Vaughan Williams's greatest life achievements was his work in reclaiming English folk music from extinction. Working with Cecil Sharp and others, Vaughan Williams's research[2] and compositions contributed to what became a "folk song movement" that influenced a generation of British composers as well as established a musical style whose sound quality is thought of as distinctly "British."

Vaughan Williams is rightly remembered as one of the great folk song collectors. Although he did not arrange these songs in new musical transcriptions, he combined the fruits of his study with his own strong musical personality, absorbing folk elements into his own style naturally.

His song style is simple but not ordinary. His earliest songs show the Victorian influence of Parry and Stanford; Parry's influence is seen most clearly in the cycles *The House of Life* and *Songs of Travel*. His mature songs contain melodies that are vigorous, but elegant; many contain modality and melismatic passages that soften the energy of his phrases.

The rugged strength of England's countryside inspired many of his rhythmic patterns as well. His accompaniments tend to be fairly simple in construction and style. His songs, like his folk song arrangements, have accompaniments in which the top notes of the harmonies double the vocal line. He had an ability to set words simply and correctly and his melodic lines generally outshine his accompaniments.

On Wenlock Edge, his cycle for tenor, string quartet, and piano, displays marked inspiration from his studies with Ravel combined with his study of folk song materials. A remarkably prolific composer, Vaughan Williams wrote songs throughout his creative life; the first extant song was composed in 1891 and the last not long before his death. These were the *Four Last Songs* (1954-58) on texts by his second wife, distinguished British poet Ursula Vaughan Williams.

In addition to art songs that total in excess of 150, he wrote arrangements, part-songs, unison songs, and hymn tunes. He composed five operas and left one unfinished; none have really survived in the repertory. Vaughan Williams was also distinguished as a symphonist and a composer of choral music and film music. From 1904 to 1906 he was responsible for the editing of the *English Hymnal* for use in the Church of England, and church bodies in Canada and the United States. In 1928 he collaborated with Martin Shaw, editing the famous *Oxford Book of Carols*.

Linden Lea - A Dorset Song   1901
(William Barnes)

Throughout Vaughan Williams's career "Linden Lea" remained one of his most popular songs and his biggest moneymaker. It was published in the first issue of *The Vocalist*, a new periodical that dealt with singing and singers.[3]

The subtitle "A Dorset Song" is misleading; it is not a folk song, but the melody is decidedly folk-like. Its three stanzas are set strophically; the overall sound quality is fresh and highly appealing. Both the poetry and Vaughan Williams's musical setting are quintessentially British, with a skillful combination of pastoral character, simple lyricism, natural harmonies, and heartfelt sentiment. One writer described its unforgettable melody as "a tune that would bear infinite repetition and not suffer from it, simply because its strength was its simplicity, and its simplicity its strength."[4]

Melody is foremost, accompanied by a flowing piano part that is equally lyric and warmly textured. Vaughan Williams maintains this free feeling by placing four syllables within a three-beat bar and varying the placement of the natural word stresses. Vaughan Williams is said to have composed this song in the course of a single afternoon.

Silent Noon*   1903
(Dante Gabriel Rossetti)
from the sonnet sequence "The House of Life" XIX.

The year after its composition, this song was incorporated into the cycle *The House of Life*. It is justly famous for its voluptuous atmosphere and textures. Like Debussy's "Green," this song celebrates a languid moment of after-love. Rossetti's verse is full of images that appeal to the senses. This setting reveals a sensual side of Vaughan Williams not always apparent in his other songs. Here he uses simple forms, investing them with rich lyricism and a vocal line that combine to evoke spaciousness and freedom. It is subtle romanticism, *par excellence*, with dynamics hovering around *piano* for most of the song.

A pulsating chordal accompaniment sets a luxuriant, peaceful atmosphere. At the key change, the chord figures (no longer syncopated in rhythm) are placed above a gentle arpeggiated bass line. Note the beautiful suspended moment "...the dragonfly/Hangs like a blue thread" that ushers in the phrase that turns again to the beginning material for the last section.

*For a comparison setting, see Charles Orr.

Songs of Travel   1904
(Robert Browning)

The Vagabond • Let Beauty Awake • The Roadside Fire •
Youth and Love • In Dreams • The Infinite Shining Heavens •
Whither Must I Wander? • Bright Is the Ring of Words •
I Have Trod the Upward and the Downward Slope

The first eight songs of this set were first sung in London in 1904 by Walter Creighton, baritone, with pianist Hamilton Harty. The history of the work is rather complicated. Although first performed as a complete cycle, the publishers refused to accept the songs as a whole group and divided them into two books: *Book 1:* "The Vagabond," "Bright Is the Ring of Words," "The Roadside Fire," published in 1905, reissued in 1907; and *Book 2:* "Let Beauty Awake," "Youth and Love," " In Dreams," and "The Infinite Shining Heavens," published in 1907. "Whither Must I Wander?", not a part of either published set, was added to the group as published later.

After the composer's death, the ninth song of the cycle, "I Have Trod the Upward and the Downward Slope," was discovered by his wife among his papers. This short song unifies the work thematically; it begins with a quotation from "The Vagabond," and quotes material from "Whither Must I Wander"; during the song and in the coda, material from "Bright Is the Ring of Words" is heard; and the song ends with the tramping rhythm of "The Vagabond." The complete cycle was reissued in 1907 by Boosey and Hawkes with the songs in the correct order (B&H 18741).

Songs of Travel has been termed an uneven work, some citing the failure of the accompaniments to do more than fill out harmonies in the vocal line rather than taking a more aggressive part in illustrating atmosphere or enhancing text. Rhythms throughout the cycle are conservative; it is in the melodic content that these songs reach their highest level. Melodies often cross the line into sentimentality, but are effective nonetheless.

THE VAGABOND. An "open-air quality" permeates the initial song and introduces us to the protagonist of the cycle, the wanderer. A mood of optimism prevails throughout, an affirmation of his unshakable belief in his chosen lifestyle. A striding bass line in octaves over chords accompanies a robust vocal line and maintains a sense of extroverted declamation, broken only at the section "White as meal the frosty field" which changes texture and mood but only for a brief moment. The opening material returns for the last section; the final measures fade into thin air as the wanderer disappears down the road.

LET BEAUTY AWAKE. Rich texture is created by an accompaniment of arpeggiated chords, joined at various spots by chords in the right hand that double the vocal line. There are two stanzas, set strophically, with only slight variations in the piano. Despite the romantic texture, the song seems to lack a strong conclusive ending.

The Roadside Fire. Staccato alternation of chords of thirds, fifths, and sixths accompany the first stanza of this song, repeated melodically in subsequent stanzas with slightly different piano figurations. Both voice and piano change direction for the last stanza, bursting into a broader melodic line accompanied by impressionistic arpeggios. The last phrase contains a bar of three beats to accommodate an illustrative melisma on the word "stretches" which tends to interrupt the flowing motion rather than highlight it.

Youth and Love. This song is one of the most beautiful and most skillfully crafted in the set. Brief quotations from "The Roadside Fire," "The Vagabond," and "Bright Is the Ring of Words" occur in this song. The accompaniment is an alternation of eighth-note chords and triplets, which remain in the treble clef for most of the song. These patterns move into bass and treble staves at the word "orchard (bloom)." A thickening of texture and widening of range is predictable at "Thick as stars at night..."; however, it is no less beautiful for the anticipation. Vocal phrases are both lyrical and broadly rhapsodic as well as declamatory.

In Dreams. Stevenson's melancholy text is musically interpreted by a highly chromatic vocal line and wandering tonality in the accompaniment. A softly syncopated inner line in the accompaniment reappears with regularity.

The Infinite Shining Heavens. A lyric vocal line wanders between $\frac{3}{2}$ and $\frac{2}{2}$ meter, underpinned by rolled chords. Triplets appear in the melodic line with regularity. This song somehow remains earthbound and, within the cycle as a whole, strangely ineffective.

Whither Must I Wander. Three stanzas set strophically, an affecting melody, and a simply conceived accompaniment that doubles the vocal line combine to make this song folk-like. Its text is poignant and with his simple musical setting the composer lets the words shine through. It's easy to pinpoint this song as not being part of the original published sets; its overall style and construction is distinctly different from the rest of the songs.

Bright Is the Ring of Words. Two moods alternate within this song: a vigorous open declamation and softer, more lyrical phrases. Accompaniment figures shift from block chords to broken chords with some arpeggios. Shifting meters also provide variety: $\frac{3}{4}$, $\frac{4}{4}$, and $\frac{5}{4}$ measures alternate in uneven patterns. Harmonic interest is created by the juxtaposition of distantly related chords and a thinning of texture at the phrase "Still they are carolled and said."

The second stanza is a strophic variation of the first, with rolled chord accompaniment in a high register. Several tonalities are touched on in the last several phrases, but the initial key of F major is finally reached in the last two measures—"And the maid *remembers*"—on the last word of the poem. The final cadence is also left dreaming, with the voice on the fifth of the scale and the piano on a wide-spaced chord in the second inversion.

I Have Trod the Upward and the Downward Slope. This song is a posthumous addition to the cycle, found by Ursula Vaughan Williams after the composer's death. Quotations from "The Vagabond," "Whither Must I Wander," and "Bright Is the Ring of Words" are found in the piano accompaniment , which is primarily chordal, with moving octaves in the bass. The vocal line opens with a declamatory measure marked *quasi recitative* and broadens to sustained phrases of reflective character that allow the piano accompaniment to dominate the overall texture.

Extended Study List

The House of Life • Orpheus With His Lute • The New Ghost • *On Wenlock Edge* (tenor and string quartet) • The Sky Above the Roof • The Water Mill • Dreamland • Claribel • If I Were a Queen • *Along the Field* • *Five Mystical Songs* • *Ten Blake Songs* (voice/oboe) • *Four Last Songs*

Selected Reading

William Mark Adams, "Ralph Vaughan Williams' *Songs of Travel:* A historical, theoretical, and performance practice investigation and analysis." D.M.A. diss., The University of Texas at Austin, 1999.

Stephen Banfield, *Sensibility and English Song: critical studies of the early 20th century* (Cambridge: Cambridge University Press, 1985). In two volumes. See Vol. 1, Chapter IV: "Three post-Victorians: Hurlstone, Bridge and Vaughan Williams."

Neil Butterworth, *Ralph Vaughan Williams: A Guide to Research* (New York: Garland Publishing Inc., 1990).

A.E.F. Dickinson, *Vaughan Williams* (London: Faber and Faber, 1963. Republished by Scholarly Press, Inc. 1970).

Hubert James Foss, *Ralph Vaughan Williams: a study* (Westport, CT: Greenwood Press, 1977).

Frank Howes, *The Music of Vaughan Williams* (New York: Oxford University Press, 1954). Chapter 3: The Songs.

Michael Kennedy, *The Works of Ralph Vaughan Williams,* revised edition (London: Oxford University Press, 1980).

Ursula Vaughan Williams, *Ralph Vaughan Williams* (New York: Oxford University Press, 1988).

Notes

1. Ralph Vaughan Williams, *The Making of Music*, 42.
2. During a decade of work, Vaughan Williams collected over 800 songs and variants.
3. Stephen Banfield. Liner notes, *On the Idle Hill of Summer.* Thomas Allen, baritone/Geoffrey Parsons, piano. Virgin Classics. Compact Disc VC 7-91105-2, 1990.
4. James Day, *Vaughan Williams*, 95.

ROGER QUILTER (1877-1953)

> If it were not for the songs of Roger Quilter, there would have been no Peter Warlock.
>
> —Peter Warlock[1]

The songs of Roger Quilter are marked by a distinctive melodic sense and a refined taste in the choice and setting of texts. His songs did not deviate from a conservative approach, and despite the "new paths" musical style was taking, Quilter held to his own comfortable aesthetic, producing 112 songs of generally uniform quality. Their melodic content and direct communicative appeal have kept them in the repertoire for many years. Many serve as excellent beginning literature for English song.

Quilter came from a privileged background—Eton, then music studies at the Hoch'sche Konservatorium in Frankfurt am Main, where he and four other Englishmen (Norman O'Neill, Balfour Gardiner, Cyril Scott and Australian Percy Grainger) became known as "The Frankfurt Gang."

In Gervase Elwes, Quilter found a singer to perform his songs and he wrote many works for Elwes's voice. There are some Quilter songs on an early Elwes recording (1912) and the composer dedicated the songs of Op. 3 and Op. 8 to Elwes, writing of him: "I could have never written in quite the same way if I had not known Gervase."[2] Quilter and Elwes collaborated professionally in many song recitals until Elwes's death in 1921.

Quilter loved English poetry; some of his best songs are settings of well-known poems by established poets: Shakespeare, the Elizabethans, Herrick, Blake, Shelley, Tennyson. He also set minor poets, with uneven results. His melodic expression seemed at its best when working with texts about love—a bittersweet gift for one to whom close relationships were threatening situations that became the cause for despair and eventual decline.

Melody is the primary ingredient in Quilter's song style; harmonic elements are skillfully integrated into the total texture, but they never become intrusive. His sense of prosody was excellent; his vocal writing not only stressed correct verbal accents, but intuitively highlighted the heart of the text with fresh melody and expressive harmony. His song cycle *To Julia* (Op. 8, on texts of Robert Herrick) was declared to be "the perfect English setting of perfect English words."[3]

His basic approach to song composition was established in Op. 3 and did not stray far from that point for nearly fifty years. Many of his best songs were composed before World War I, although he continued to write fine examples from the 1920s on. In his later life, he composed less, and no songs achieved the fame of his earlier works. Quilter's songs are products of the Edwardian era in which they were composed; there are a few that seem faded in today's brightest modern light, but they retain a grace of form and melodic beauty that still makes them appealing to both singers and audiences.

Love's Philosophy (*Three Songs,* Op. 3)*   1904-05
(Percy Bysshe Shelley)

Everything in nature combines, why not you and I? The natural mingling of nature's elements inspires a romantic rush of metaphor from the poet. Arpeggios prevail throughout the accompaniment in a toccata-like display—an ardent dash from beginning to end. Vocal phrases are sweeping and lyrical, with some small melismas ("rivers"/ "waves") for textual emphasis. Vocal material is echoed in the arpeggios and in the bass line. The mood is fresh, youthful and intense. Quilter builds to a bravura finish, and caps off the final climax with a brief piano postlude in the same vein.

Quilter was to set Shelley again in 1927—"Music, When Soft Voices Die."

*For comparison settings, see John Duke and Charles Gounod ("The fountains mingle with the river").

Now sleeps the crimson petal (*Three Songs,* Op. 3)*   1904
(Alfred, Lord Tennyson)

This is one of Quilter's best-known songs, and deservedly so; the lyricism of the vocal line is unmistakable. The overall style of this song and the others from this opus contain much of the essence of Quilter's songs. Tennyson's poem is not set in its entirety; Quilter cut six lines of poetry from the center of the original.

The text is set syllabically throughout; phrases are gracefully shaped. Quilter assigns a lovely melody to the piano as an introduction before the accompaniment becomes simple and doubles the vocal line for much of the song.

Quilter's musical setting hews to the poetic rhythm (iambic pentameter) without deviating, resulting in fifteen changes of metric signature in the song's twenty-seven measures. The introduction, interlude, and postlude are in $\frac{3}{4}$. The interlude and introduction are one and the same, transposed down an octave. Singer Gervase Elwes first sang this song and, impressed, took it to a publisher.

*For a comparison setting, see Ned Rorem.

Fair House of Joy (*Seven Elizabethan Lyrics*, Op. 12)   1907-08
(Anonymous)

This text comes from the lute song era (see Tobias Hume). The poet can sing of nothing but love which has ensnared him. Quilter seizes on the intensity of emotion in the text and sets it romantically. The texture is fairly thick throughout, created by chord figures with ample movement in the inner parts.

Vocal phrases are constructed of steps and simple skips, but great variety in the vocal line is achieved by varying metric stress of syllables within a three-beat bar. The second stanza lines up like the first until the final measures, which repeat the last phrase "And fall before thee," in a rather overt but highly effective ending. *Seven Elizabethan Lyrics* was one of Quilter's most successful song collections.

Go, Lovely Rose*   1922
(Edmund Waller)

Waller's gentle Edwardian verse produced one of Quilter's song masterpieces. Quilter is unashamedly sentimental in his setting and, in this particular case, it fits the poetry perfectly. The vocal line exhibits Quilter's gift of fluid melody; some vocal phrases are extended. The accompaniment is filled with gently moving harmonies, at times chromatic, with some metric variety of two-against-three. Song texture is rich overall. This song is a particularly good example of Quilter's song style.

*For a comparison setting, see Ned Rorem.

O Mistress Mine   1905
(William Shakespeare. *Twelfth Night*)

"O Mistress mine" belongs to a set of *Three Shakespeare Songs*, Op. 6. The songs, designed to be sung as a group, are "Come away, death," "O Mistress mine," and "Blow, blow, thou winter wind." *Carpe diem* is the overriding theme of the text, full of youthful ardor and impatience.

Quilter's piano accompaniment is structured with a dotted rhythm melody that serves as a brief introduction, followed by simple chords. The vocal line is equally uncomplicated, built with broken chords and simple rhythms and intervals. The first line of the text is repeated to complete the song, almost as a wistful afterthought.

Shakespeare's lighthearted text has prompted numerous musical settings, and despite its simplicity, Quilter's is among the most charming.

Extended Study List

Seven Elizabethan Lyrics: Weep you no more, sad fountains; My life's delight; Damask roses, The faithless shepherdess; Brown is my love; By a fountainside; Fair house of joy • *Five Shakespeare Songs:* Fear no more the heat of the sun; Under the greenwood tree; It was a lover and his lass; Take, O take those lips away; Hey, ho, the wind and the rain • *The Arnold Book of Old Songs* (arrangements of traditional folk songs) • *To Julia:* The bracelet; The maiden blush; To daisies; The night piece; Julia's hair; Cherry ripe • *Three Shakespeare Songs:* Come away, death; O mistress mine; Blow, blow, thou winter wind • *Three Songs of William Blake:* Dream Valley, The wild flower's song; Daybreak • The fuschia tree • The constant lover • I arise from dreams of thee • *Two Shakespeare Songs:* Orpheus with his lute; When icicles hang by the wall.

Selected Reading

Stephen Banfield, *Sensibility and English Song: critical studies of the early 20th century* (Cambridge: Cambridge University Press, 1985). In two volumes. See Vol. 1, Chapter 6: "The Edwardian Age (II)."

Scott Goddard, "The Art of Roger Quilter," Chesterian 94:47 (June 1925).

Trevor Hold, *Parry to Finzi: Twenty English Song-Composers* (Woodbridge: Boydell Press, 2002).

Michael Pilkington, *Gurney, Ireland, Quilter and Warlock* (Bloomington: Indiana University Press, 1989). English Solo Song Guides to the Repertoire.

Mark Raphael, "Roger Quilter, 1877-1953, the Man and His Songs," *Tempo* 30 (Winter 1953-54).

Joseph T. Rawlins, "Roger Quilter; The Singer's Composer," *The NATS Journal*, 48:5 (May/June 1992).

Notes

1. Warlock (pseudonym of Philip Heseltine) inscribed these sentiments on a song he sent to Quilter. Quoted in Mark Raphael, "Roger Quilter, the Man and His Songs," *Tempo* 30 (Winter 1953-54), 21.
2. Lewis Foreman. Liner notes, *Quilter Songs.* Benjamin Luxon, baritone/David Willison, pianist. Chandos Records. Compact disc CHAN 8782, 1989.
3. Ibid., 6.

JOHN IRELAND (1879-1962)

Nothing of Ireland's is shoddy or makeshift, and in his best work a firm structural sense is combined with a deeply personal poetry.

—Hugh Ottaway[1]

John Ireland wrote songs that are characterized by beautiful, inventive melodies, subtle harmonies, and a sensitively to poetry. In addition, he was a skilled craftsman and a master of form. However, he gave us a body of works which, when taken as a whole, reveal a certain inconsistency in quality. "While the best of [the songs] are among the finest by English composers this century, there are others in which a natural warmth of sentiment tends to spill over into sentimentality."[2]

Ireland's aesthetic sense was strongly influenced by writer Arthur Machen, who based his art almost entirely on symbolism and the power of suggestion. Ireland's songs do not aim to directly express images in the text, but rather to define musically the states of mind and feeling that they inspire.[3]

More than melody, it is Ireland's harmonic style that gives the text its clearest voice, underscoring and intensifying moods and images within the verse. He embellishes harmonies with chromaticism in a distinctive way—a way that is lyrical in its own right.

Composer Geoffrey Bush identifies the features of Ireland's song style as "beauty of line, subtlety of harmony, mastery of form, unfailing craftsmanship, sensitive response to poetry, and a thorough grasp of the potential of instruments either singly or in combination." He also lists abstract qualities inherent in Ireland's songs as "strength of purpose, empathy with nature, quirky humour, profound feeling, and an even profounder reticence."[4]

Like other English song composers in the early twentieth century, Ireland adopted a text-oriented style of composition, with a primarily syllabic approach to word-setting.* He generally let the natural form and meter of the verse determine the shape and rhythm of the melody. This style remained prevalent until it was broken by Benjamin Britten.

Ireland was the contemporary of English poets A.E. Housman and Thomas Hardy. Ireland composed two cycles to Housman's poems: *The Land of Lost Content* and *We'll To the Woods No More*. Both cycles capture the essence of Housman's words with extraordinary clarity. The second cycle, considered one of Ireland's finest works, contains two songs and a piano piece; it is such a poignant evocation of grief for the suffering of World War I that in later years the composer could not bear to listen to it.[5]

Ireland's nine song cycles include *Songs of a Wayfarer, The Land of Lost Content, We'll To the Woods No More, Songs Sacred and Profane, Five Poems of Thomas Hardy,* as well as some forty other songs.

*The late romantic *Lied*, the close-knit declamation of Debussy's *mélodies*, and the resurgence of the English folk song were potent influences on text setting in early twentieth-century English song.

I Have Twelve Oxen   1918
(Anonymous-Early English)

One of Ireland's best known songs, this piece is most appealing to performers and audiences for its energetic, boisterous emotion. It is often sung as the final song in a group because of its robust style and decisive finish.

Its setting is simple; the voice part uses simple rhythms and intervals, the accompaniment (for the most part, chordal) is supportive but does not interact meaningfully with vocal material. Each of the four stanzas has a slightly different rhythm in the accompaniment.

Spring Sorrow   1918
(Rupert Brooke)

This song has been termed Ireland's most perfect miniature; voice and piano lines are beautifully shaped to match the expressive quality of the poem.

As hawthorn buds signal the approach of spring, the poet's heart, frozen all winter, thaws and puts forth its own buds in the form of painful memories that have been suspended in winter frost.

The vocal line contains simple rhythms in a quiet folk-like melody. The piano accompaniment moves gently, doubling the vocal line in a chord texture of four or five parts. Ireland judiciously places a few chromatics in the line, but never detracts from the close-knit texture.

Sea Fever   1913
(John Masefield)

"Sea Fever" is Ireland's best-known song. Its text narrates an old sailor's desire to return to the sea. It is highly declamatory, but is not a recitative. The rhythms should be carefully articulated. The accompaniment is chordal with some chromatics.

"Sea Fever" was sung numerous times on radio broadcasts, where listeners voted it "the most popular of all British songs." Ireland told Gerald Moore that he considered this his best song, although he chafed at being identified as a composer on the strength of its popularity.[6]

Extended Study List
Land of Lost Content (A.E. Housman) • Love is a sickness • When I am dead, my dearest • *We'll To The Woods No More* (A.E. Housman) • When daffodils begin to peer • The three ravens • The merry month of May • If there were dreams to sell • The holy boy • If we must part • My true love hath my heart • *Five Poems by Thomas Hardy* • The Salley Gardens • The heart's desire

Selected Reading
Stephen Banfield, *Sensibility and English Song: critical studies of the early 20th century* (Cambridge: Cambridge University Press, 1985). In two volumes. See Vol. 1 Chapter 8: "Style and Personal symbolism in John Ireland."

Stewart R. Craggs, *John Ireland: A Catalogue, Discography, and Bibliography* (Oxford: Clarendon Press, 1993). With an introduction by Geoffrey Bush.

Trevor Hold, *Parry to Finzi: Twenty English Song-Composers* (Woodbridge: Boydell Press, 2002).

Michael Pilkington, *Gurney, Ireland, Quilter and Warlock* (Bloomington: Indiana University Press, 1989). English Solo Song Guides to the Repertoire.

Mark Alexander Whitmire, "Songs by John Ireland and Benjamin Britten to poems by Thomas Hardy." D.M.A. diss., University of Maryland College Park, 1991.

V. L. Yenne, *Three Twentieth Century English Song Composers: Peter Warlock, E. J. Moeran and John Ireland.* D.M.A. diss., University of Illinois, 1969.

Notes
1. Hugh Ottaway, "John Ireland," *The New Grove Dictionary of Music and Musicians* 1989, 326.
2. Ibid.
3. Stephen Banfield, *Sensibility and English Song,* v.1, 164-65.
4. Geoffrey Bush. Introduction to Stewart R. Craggs, *John Ireland: A Catalogue, Discography, and Bibliography,* xii.
5. Ibid., x-xi.
6. Ibid., 161-62.

GEORGE BUTTERWORTH (1885-1916)

> The songs...are further proof of the loss which British music sustained when Butterworth was killed in action in 1916...What might not have been? We can never know, but we can cherish what remains to us.
>
> Michael Kennedy[1]

The songs of George Butterworth show the influence of Ralph Vaughan Williams in their natural lyricism and use of musical materials. Butterworth declined to follow his father into a legal career, instead studying music at Eton and Trinity College, Oxford. He taught music at Radley and wrote music criticism for *The Times* of London. His close friendship with Vaughan Williams and Cecil Sharp led him to study and collect English folk songs and dances, which he integrated into some of his music.

Butterworth was a gifted miniaturist; his songs are carefully crafted and meticulous. His songs, together with those of Roger Quilter, seem inherently English in style and conception. Butterworth collected folk music, and his song style reflects his interest in the simplicity of folk materials. He incorporated various folk tunes in two of his orchestral works, *Two English Idylls* and *The Banks of Green Willow.*

Butterworth composed two song cycles to A.E. Housman's *A Shropshire Lad* (1911 and 1912). Although folk material is not directly quoted, these melodies have the distinctive flavor of folk songs, a characteristic simplicity and clarity that when coupled with Butterworth's simple accompaniments and forms, seem quintessentially English. Simplicity of style does not, however, denote a lack of quality or depth. Butterworth's songs are deceptive; they hide an abundance of subtle nuances. Influences of Debussy and Wagner are seen in his Housman settings, notably in "On the Idle Hill of Summer," in both harmonic treatment and use of melodic motives. He is best remembered for his two Housman cycles, *Eleven Folk Songs from Sussex,* and the song cycle *Love Blows as the Wind Blows* (1914).

Butterworth was often beset by a sense of purposelessness; he enlisted in the army at the outbreak of World War I, was sent to the front line in 1915, and was killed in France in 1916.

Selections from *A Shropshire Lad*   1911, 1912

(A.E. Housman)

Loveliest of Trees • When I was one-and-twenty •
The lads in their hundreds • Is my team ploughing?

LOVELIEST OF TREES.* Butterworth's piano accompaniment begins sparsely; a single melodic line evocative of softly falling blossoms twines with chords to produce a thicker texture—a picture of the cherry bough gently bending under the weight of the blossoms. Vocal phrases follow suit, simply lyric but moving toward an unaccompanied moment of reflection at "now of my threescore years and ten..." and turning back to longer phrases to conclude the song. The vocal line, still reflective, ends indecisively; the piano has the last commentary, ending the musings of the singer with a warmly decisive cadence.

*For comparison settings, see Ivor Gurney, John Duke, and Charles Orr.

WHEN I WAS ONE-AND-TWENTY. Melody dominates this setting, folk-like in mood. Butterworth sets Housman's two stanzas in modified strophic style, with only tiny changes at the conclusion of the second verse, and a restatement of the last " 'tis true" as a rueful postscript.

THE LADS IN THEIR HUNDREDS. Butterworth's setting seems perfect for Housman's verse—syllabic declamation that keeps moving forward, in vocal lines of even note values and uneven phrase length. Between verses, the piano is keeps the feeling of the country fair alive with little interludes that call to mind a rhythmic English country dance. Chords in the accompaniment punctuate the poet's description of the fresh-faced young men, moving inexorably toward the poem's poignant last line, "The lads that will die in their glory and never be old." In 1916 Butterworth was killed in combat at Pozières.

IS MY TEAM PLOUGHING? Housman's conversation between two men (one dead, one alive) is one of his most heartrending poems. The dead man's questions about his land, his old pastimes, his beloved, and his friend are set in a lethargic, hopeless line which is left rising in midair at the end of the last phrase; the triumph of the living man is unmistakable—robust and assertive, until the final ending phrase. Dynamics, pitch range, and tempo delineate the two speakers and although these contrasts are organized in a natural, simple way, the effects are chilling.

On the Idle Hill of Summer *(Bredon Hill and Other Songs)*　　　　1912
(A.E. Housman)

The beauty of the English countryside is marred for the poet, who sees only the devastation and waste of war. Butterworth's musical approach is lean, stripped to chord figures and a murmuring vocal line; both expand to slightly more animated figures in the last stanza. The last vocal phrase "I will rise" is set with an intensity uncharacteristic of Butterworth, and the harmonies used show the distinct influence of Debussy.

Extended Study List
Think no more, lad (*A Shropshire Lad*) • Look not in my eyes (*A Shropshire Lad*) • Bredon Hill • When the Lad for Longing Sighs • With Rue My Heart Is Laden • O Fair enough are Sky and Plain • A brisk young sailor • A blacksmith courted me • Roving in the dew • *Love Blows as the Wind Blows*

Selected Reading
Stephen Banfield, *Sensibility and English Song: critical studies of the early 20th century* (Cambridge: Cambridge University Press, 1985). In two volumes.
Robert Hansen, "The Legacy of the Twentieth-Century English Art Song," *The NATS Journal*, 45:4 (March/April 1989).
Trevor Hold, *Parry to Finzi: Twenty English Song-Composers* (Woodbridge: Boydell Press, 2002).
Christopher Palmer, "George Butterworth," *The New Grove Dictionary of Music and Musicians,* ed. Stanley Sadie (New York: Grove's Dictionaries of Music, 1989), Vol. 3.

Notes
1. Michael Kennedy. Liner notes to *British Composers: Vaughan Williams, Elgar, Butterworth.* EMI Classics. CDM 7 64631 2, 1984.

IVOR GURNEY (1890-1937)

The songs I had are withered/ Or vanished clean, / Yet there are bright tracks / Where I have been... And there grow flowers / For other's delight. / Think well, O singer, / Soon comes night.

—Ivor Gurney[1]

Ivor Gurney was a gifted poet and composer. Educated as a chorister in Gloucester Cathedral, he began to study on scholarship at the Royal College of

Music in 1911. His first mature vocal work, *Five Elizabethan Songs*, was composed in 1912.

Gurney also suffered from mental unbalance; from his early twenties, he was subject to breakdowns and once attempted suicide. Nonetheless, and despite poor eyesight, he enlisted in the military and served in France where he was wounded and gassed. Returned to England from the front, he spent time in several war hospitals. In 1922 he was placed in an asylum, where he remained until his death in 1937. Here he wrote some of his best poems. Only occasionally did his mental state intrude on the quality of his artistic work; his songs and his poetry have an appealing simplicity and the ability to immediately touch the heart. His poems number 1,700.

Gurney was an important English composer of songs, publishing eighty-two, the best of which were written between 1919 and 1922. Around 200 remain in manuscript and sketches. Gurney also composed six sonatas for violin and piano, five string quartets, one extended orchestral piece, and a number of smaller works. His songs may be divided into several categories that parallel his life: schooling, war, and mental breakdown. Gurney's songs from the war period are fairly small in number, but they are among his best and most innovative work.

As a poet, he was deeply sensitive to word setting and his love of English literature permeates his text choices. His musical approach has been termed "rhapsodic"; Gurney had an instinctive approach to composition and made few if any revisions to his work. His artistic instincts often produced some unevenness in his songs, but once Gurney's style is understood, the approach seems completely right. Biographer Michael Hurd writes: "Where [Gurney's] art is at its best…it is both distinctive and magical."[2]

In Flanders
(F.W. Harvey)   1915-17

Gurney, homesick for the Cotswolds, wrote the music for this song while in the trenches during World War I. The musical treatment is profoundly moving and intense. It is one of five songs he was known to have composed during combat—an incomprehensible activity. One song, "The Fiddler of Dooney," is gay and amiable; the rest of the songs use texts that deal with themes of the security and peace of home, and with the nature of death. The last of the serious "trench songs" sets Sir Walter Raleigh's farewell to life, "Even such is Time," penned the night before his execution. These songs are considered to be among Gurney's most outstanding works, and although they were not meant to be a cycle, they form a powerful group for performance.

The Fields are Full
(Edward Shanks)   1919

Gurney sets this short but lovely poem simply, with a lovely lyric melody in the voice and simple broken-chord patterns in the piano. There are two stanzas.

The second stanza begins like the first, but with the second phrase turns to new melodic material. A more reinforced, intense mood appears in both voice and piano as the pronouncement of the beauty of old age is heard. Gurney keeps this emotion in check; it does not become overblown, but remains a warmly romantic moment: "And loved with strength and loved with truth, In heavy age are beautiful."

Hawk and Buckle   **1920**
(John Doyle, pseudonym for Robert Graves)

Where is the landlord of old Hawk and Buckle? Where is the ostler of old Hawk and Buckle? Where is the daughter of old Hawk and Buckle? These are the questions asked in the three stanzas of this song. The answers: drinking, dozing, and trimming her hat.

Energetic folk song melody dominates the song, underpinned by a strongly accented chord accompaniment with few decorations. As we are told the whereabouts of Mistress Jenny, the last vocal phrases are subtly varied. The mood of the song is good humored in the best sense of an English folk song—not a usual Gurney characteristic.

From *Five Elizabethan Songs* (1912)

The next three songs are taken from *Five Elizabethan Songs,* published in 1920. In 1912, Gurney wrote to his friend F.W. Harvey as follows: "I have done five of the most delightful and beautiful songs you ever cast your beaming eyes upon. They are all Elizabethan—the words—and blister my kidneys, bisurate my magnesia if the music is not as English, as joyful, as tender as any lyric of all that noble host. Technique all right, and as to word setting—models."[3] Gurney's enthusiasm was not exaggerated.

SPRING (THOMAS NASHE). This is a dazzling setting of Nashe's famous paean to spring. Both piano and voice are given dance-like phrases of considerable flexibility. Gurney saturates the setting with a number of rhythmic-melodic figures that evoke birdcalls. These are introduced by the piano in the opening measures, a short two-note call that develops into faster, more agitated figures. The overall mood is one of brilliance and sparkle, a fine example of Gurney's response to Elizabethan poetry—spontaneous and fresh.

SLEEP (JOHN FLETCHER). This is one of Gurney's great songs and a fine example of his general song style.* An intense mood of repressed despair is maintained throughout the entire song, linked by rhythmic figures in the piano, altered notes in the vocal phrases, and very subtle text painting.

There is no strong sense of tonality throughout. Gurney's harmonic treatment is deliberately blurred, complementing the poetic content. The second stanza is accompanied by figures derived from the opening sixteenth-note motive, rhythmically altered. The vocal phrases are also subtle melodic variations of the first verse. Gurney repeats the last poetic phrase "O let my joys have some abiding."

*Gurney and Peter Warlock's settings of this poem should be compared. Both songs are outstanding examples of each composer's song style.

UNDER THE GREENWOOD TREE (WILLIAM SHAKESPEARE. *AS YOU LIKE IT*). A beautiful piano accompaniment provides rhythmic decoration and contrapuntal texture for the melodic vocal line of this fresh song. Text illustration is present in the phrase "But winter and rough weather," varied harmonically and rhythmically in verse two.

Gurney provides colorful variety in rhythm, harmony, and phrase construction, and maintains a sense of buoyancy throughout the song. The song ends with a twelve-bar postlude. Two tiny enigmatic phrases end the song; two descending staccato triads in the treble are answered by two rising open fifths in the bass, repeated at different pitch levels. Is this the cuckoo?

Extended Study List

Bread and Cherries • Tears • Black Stitchel • Cranham Woods • I Praise the Tender Flower • The Folly of Being Comforted • Down By The Salley Gardens • On the Downs • By a Bierside • The Fiddler of Dooney • Ha'nacker Mill • Carol of the Skiddaw Yowes • The Apple Orchard • The Twa' Corbies • Loveliest of trees • On the idle hill of summer • When I was one and twenty • Thou didst delight mine eyes

Selected Reading

Stephen Banfield, *Sensibility and English Song: critical studies of the early 20th century* (Cambridge: Cambridge University Press, 1985). In two volumes. See Vol. 1, Chapter 9: "The Music of Ivor Gurney."

Ivor Gurney, *Selected Poems,* ed. P.J. Kavanagh (New York: Oxford University Press, 1990).

David Warren Herendeen, "Lanes of Severn: Ivor Gurney, as illustrated by his war songs, 1915-1918." D.M.A. diss., The University of Arizona, 1993.

Trevor Hold, *Parry to Finzi: Twenty English Song-Composers* (Woodbridge: Boydell Press, 2002).

Michael Hurd, "Ivor Gurney," *The New Grove Dictionary of Music and Musicians,* ed. Stanley Sadie (New York: Grove's Dictionaries of Music, 1989), Volume 7.

_____. *The Ordeal of Ivor Gurney* (Cambridge: Oxford University Press, 1978).

Charles W. Moore, "Ivor Gurney: English Poet in Song," *The NATS Bulletin,* 20:3 (1964).

_____.*Maker and Lover of Beauty: Ivor Gurney, Poet and Songwriter* (Rickmansworth, Herts., 1976).

Michael Pilkington, *Gurney, Ireland, Quilter and Warlock* (Bloomington: Indiana University Press, 1989). English Solo Song Guides to the Repertoire.

Ralph Vaughan Williams and H. Howells, "Ivor Gurney: The Musician," *Music and Letters,* 29, 1938, 12.

Notes

1. "The Songs I Had," *Ivor Gurney: Selected Poems*, ed. P. J. Kavanagh, 86.
2. Michael Hurd, "Ivor Gurney," *The New Grove Dictionary of Music and Musicians*, 854.
3. Michael Pilkington, *Gurney, Ireland, Quilter and Warlock*, 31.

REBECCA CLARKE (1886-1979)

Her musical voice can be muted, or shy, but it can also be passionate, even brutal. Her craft includes a genuine commingling of delicacy and force, of familiar motions recast in new ways.

—Deborah Stein[1]

Rebecca Clarke's fascinating legacy of songs is just beginning to be known and appreciated, studied, and performed. Her songs are a treasure trove of astonishingly beautiful works, rich in musical invention and dramatic brilliance.

Although Clarke lived most of her life in the United States, she was born and educated in Great Britain. She studied the violin, and began to compose. Clarke was the first woman accepted to study with Sir Charles Stanford at the Royal College of Music in London. She worked with Stanford for three years, and on his advice, changed from violin to viola. She studied viola with the great Lionel Tertis, and was among the first women to join the Queen's Hall Orchestra. Clarke made her living primarily as a chamber violist.

She composed most of her music in the 1920s, an era that did not readily accept women as composers. However, the musical styles that existed during that time—impressionism, post-romanticism, and neo-classicism, shaped her musical aesthetic. Clarke wrote nearly 100 works—songs, chamber pieces, choral works, and music for solo piano, but no orchestral scores. Only about twenty pieces of her music were published during her lifetime, and at the time of her death (at age ninety-three), most of them had gone out of print.

Her *Sonata for Viola* (1919) has become the single most frequently performed work for that instrument, and it is the work by which she is best known today. She achieved what she called her "first whiff of fame" with this work, when it took second place—behind a sonata of Ernest Bloch—in a competition sponsored by Elizabeth Sprague Coolidge. Clarke had submitted the composition under a pseudonym; the jurors were astonished to discover a woman had composed the work

Fifty-three of her songs survive; the rest remain unpublished, and are the property of her estate. Clarke's vocal writing is expressive and varied; articulation in vocal phrases is always closely tied to the mood and drama of the text. Her harmonic approach is eclectic and inventive. She was fond of changing tempos, meters, and tonalities; she usually mixed modality, chromaticism, and open fourths and fifths into the texture to create a rich tapestry of sound

Clarke wrote a number of articles about music for *Cobbett's Cyclopedia of Chamber Music*. These may be found reproduced in *A Rebecca Clarke Reader*.

The Cloths of Heaven*   **c. 1912**
(W.B. Yeats)

This song was the one of the first of Clarke's songs to be published. She dedicated it to the famed English tenor Gervaise Elwes,** an early champion of her music. Clarke's response to Yeats's poetic images is a rich harmonic texture that includes modality, duple rhythms linked with triple rhythms, and planed chords. Debussy's musical influence is quite apparent in the setting.

A lovely moment occurs at the words "But I being poor, have only my dreams" as Clarke shifts tonality without preparation. The same rhythmic-melodic shapes used in the song's opening measures appear at the end of the song—this time, altered chromatically to illustrate the singer's plea, "Tread softly/Because you tread on my dreams."

*For a comparison setting, see Ivor Gurney.
**See section on Roger Quilter.

The Seal Man   **1922**
(John Masefield)

"The Seal Man" has been called "one of the most astonishing songs in the whole of the English repertoire."[2] Clarke composed the song in 1922, and always spoke of it as being one of her favorites.

Masefield's prose text belongs to his collection titled *A Mainsail Haul*. Its story is based on the Celtic myth of Selkies, or Silkies. These were shape-changing sea fairies, usually in the form of gray seals, that took on human form by casting off their sealskins. According to legend, they often came onto land in human form, sometimes to dance on the night of the full moon, but often to lure humans to their death. A male selkie, after assuming human form, had almost magical seductive powers over mortal women. "The Seal Man" is one of these beings—a seal in human form—that seduces a young woman and leads her into the sea to her death.

Clarke did not set the ending of Masefield's text, in which the seal man weeps over the body of the dead girl. By omitting this text, the girl becomes the focal point of the tragedy rather than the seal man's feelings of loss.[3]

Clarke sets Masefield's prose expertly, using a dramatic, declamatory style of vocal writing that gradually lets the chilling story unfold, gathering momentum and intensity as it goes. The piano accompaniment is sparse, consisting mainly of rolled chords that have the effect of a bardic harp, accompanying the storyteller's dramatic recitative. Clarke blurs tonality, using modal and pentatonic scales— there are measures of pitch centers rather than established tonalities—to achieve an atmospheric mood. There are constant shifts of meter throughout the song: $\frac{2}{4}$, $\frac{3}{4}$, $\frac{4}{4}$, and $\frac{5}{4}$.

"The Seal Man" is an extraordinary song, and one that lingers in the mind of the listener long after it is heard.

*For an interesting and thorough musical analysis of "The Seal Man," see Deborah Stein. "Dare Seize the Fire," in *A Rebecca Clarke Reader*.

Down by the Salley Gardens*   **1919**
(W.B. Yeats)

Composers use folk themes in different ways. Benjamin Britten's well-known arrangement of "Down by the Salley Gardens," offers the traditional Irish folk melody with words by W.B. Yeats in a setting that captures the melancholy of the text. Rebecca Clarke also set Yeats's nostalgic words using a simple accompaniment figure, but composed a new melodic line for the singer, coupling it with a musical texture that mixes folk elements with touches of impressionism. She marked it "flowingly, in folk-song style."

Rhythmically, Clarke pits two-against-three in voice and piano lines. Harmonically, she employs open fifths and pentatonic material in piano figures and vocal phrases. This mixture produces a Debussy-like sound quality that seems to characterize the illusory world of the lovers, yet within this sophisticated treatment, the overall quality of the song is simple and effortless.

Liane Curtis describes the dreamlike atmosphere of the accompaniment as "a wash of sound—a shimmering palette."[4] Their forward motion continues to the last line of each stanza, then stops abruptly. The Lover's remorseful confessional is unaccompanied, punctuated by a single wide-spaced chord under the word "young."

*For comparison settings see Benjamin Britten, John Ireland, and Ivor Gurney.

Extended Study List

Come, O Come my Life's Delight • Infant Joy • Cradle Song • Shy One • June Twilight • A Dream • Eight O'Clock • Greeting • *Three Old English Songs* (voice/violin) • Weep you no more sad fountains • Psalm 63 • The Aspidistra • *Three Irish Country Songs* (voice/violin) • The Cherry-Blossom Wand • Binnorie • Tiger, Tiger

Selected Reading

Liane Curtis, "Rebecca Clarke: A Case of Identity," *The Musical Times* (London) 137 (May 1996), 15-22.
_____, "Rebecca Clarke and the British Musical Renaissance," in *A Rebecca Clarke Reader,* ed. Liane Curtis (Waltham, MA: The Rebecca Clarke Society, 2005).
_____, ed., *A Rebecca Clarke Reader* (Waltham, MA: The Rebecca Clarke Society, 2005).
Deborah Stein, "Dare Seize the Fire: an introduction to the songs of Rebecca Clarke," in *A Rebecca Clarke Reader,* ed. Liane Curtis (Waltham, MA: Rebecca Clarke Society, 2005).

1. Deborah Stein, "Dare Seize the Fire," in *A Rebecca Clarke Reader*, 77.
2. Calum MacDonald, introduction to *Rebecca Clarke Song Album* (Boosey & Hawkes, 1995).
3. Deborah Stein, 53.
4. Liane Curtis, "Rebecca Clarke and the British Musical Renaissance" in *A Rebecca Clarke Reader*, 28.

CHARLES WILFRED ORR (1893-1976)

At eighty-two, one must be prepared for death in the fairly near future, but what does get me down is the terrible disappointment of never having, and never being likely to have any recognition outside a very small circle, as a song-writer.

—Charles Wilfred Orr[1]

Charles Wilfred Orr wrote only thirty-five songs. He came to music late, influenced by Delius's harmonic language, the tight musico-poetic structures of Hugo Wolf, and the poetry of A.E. Housman.

Orr felt he suffered "unjust neglect" because his compositions were not better known. He suffered from acute eczema and chose to remain isolated from many of his colleagues a great deal of the time, staying on the fringe for the sake of his health. Unable to travel internationally to promote his music, he spent his entire life in the village of Painswick in the Cotswolds, supporting himself from his song royalties and from his work as a critic for *The Music Review*.

His inability to travel and socialize certainly influenced the dissemination of his music; however, a more convincing reason might be attributed to taste and mindset of a British public steeped in the rediscovery movement of English folk song. Orr concentrated on the small form of song; he created few other musical works in other genres. This, plus the lack of support from fellow musicians, worked to keep Orr's music from being properly recognized.

Perhaps the musical intricacies found in Orr's songs have put off performers; it is a characteristic that does not give the songs immediate appeal for audiences. The quality of his musical style has also been debated, some pointing out that his unique musical approach nonetheless contains "English elements," while others proposing that "Orr was incapable of suggesting harmonic nuance and not coating with thick textural confectionery."[2] Orr's biography in Grove's *Dictionary* offers the following: "For all his slender output (thirty-five songs) Orr was one of the finest British songwriters of the century."

Two of Orr's supporters were composers Frederick Delius and Philip Heseltine (Peter Warlock); Orr sent manuscripts to Delius, who passed them on to Heseltine, who, at the time of his death, was in the process of trying to get some of the songs published.[3] Of Orr's songs, Heseltine wrote: "All the songs are beautifully made and show that your workmanship is at all times equal to the expression of your quite excellent ideas...the songs are a most remarkable achievement."[4]

Orr's songs are expertly crafted in a unique personal styled that combines some of the qualities of romantic German *Lieder* with English art song. He wrote extremely singable melodic phrases, which he composed independently of the piano accompaniment, then "fitted the piano part to them in such a way as to leave the voice paramount."[5] He set texts expressively and with great sensitivity. Orr avoided extreme registers in his songs, which lie for the most part in the medium range of the voice.

A number of his songs feature countermelodies or motives, used as interludes or hidden within the piano parts, in the style of Hugo Wolf. Another distinguishing feature of Orr's song style is the unexpected sonorities produced by the combination of his chromatic melodic lines and the striking harmonic progressions found in his piano accompaniments. Piano postludes appear in many of his songs.

Of his thirty-five songs, twenty-four are settings of A.E. Housman, of whose poetry Orr said: "Housman wrote verse that was (a) beautiful, (b) scanned, (c) rhymed, and (d) made sense; qualities that as far as I can see are very much to seek in present day poets. He is, I think, to English songwriters very much what Heine was to German and Verlaine to French composers..."[6]

Housman's poetry in *A Shropshire Lad* presents gentle images of English countryside scenes and a quiet contented patriotism. Linked to these idealized pictures are strong emotions of despair at the havoc war brings upon a country—psychological trauma of lives cruelly cut short and hopes shattered. Principal settings of poems from *A Shropshire Lad* were composed by Ralph Vaughan Williams, George Butterworth, Ivor Gurney, E.J. Moeran, and Charles Orr.

Is my team ploughing?* 1925
(A.E. Housman)

Housman believed this poem to be his best; it is certainly one of his most poignant verses, underlaid with an intensity that holds throughout until the last line. Melodic lines are set in a modal-diatonic framework, a mixture of Aeolian and Dorian modes, that recall folk song. The first section contains two verses set in modified strophic form, an alternation of the dialogue between the ghost and his living friend. The piano texture is starkly simple, with open intervals in the bass line, predominantly fifths and fourths. Orr's treatment of the phrase "I cheer a dead man's sweetheart" is set prominently, with great intensity.

*For a comparison setting, see George Butterworth.

With rue my heart is laden* 1924
(A.E. Housman)

Philip Heseltine (Peter Warlock) sent the manuscripts of a number of Orr's songs to the musical editor of the Oxford University Press, with a strong recommendation to publish them. Among them was this song, which Heseltine termed one of the loveliest songs any English composer had written: "It is perfectly beautiful, especially the last line—the emotion of 'where roses fade' could not be more completely realized or more perfectly expressed."[7]

Orr uses a rhythmic pattern from the opening vocal phrase as a unifying factor throughout the song.

*See also the settings by George Butterworth and Samuel Barber.

Extended Study List

In valleys green and still • Oh see how thick the goldcup flowers • The Carpenter's Son • When I was One-and-Twenty • The Isle of Portland • On Your Midnight Pallet Lying • Loveliest of Trees • Silent Noon • Bahnhofstrasse • Requiem • When Summer On Is Stealing • The lads in their hundreds • Oh, When I Was in Love with You • When the Lad for Longing Sighs

Selected Reading

Stephen Banfield, *Sensibility and English Song: critical studies of the early 20th century* (Cambridge: Cambridge University Press, 1985). In two volumes. See Vol.1. Chapter 14: "The uses and abuses of technique."

Philip T. Barford, "Five Songs from 'A Shropshire Lad,'" *Music Review,* 21:3, 1960, 260.

Ian A. Copley, "An English Songwriter, C.W. Orr," *Composer,* 1968, 13-14.

Trevor Hold, *Parry to Finzi: Twenty English Song-Composers* (Woodbridge: Boydell Press, 2002).

Sydney Northcote, "The Songs of C.W. Orr," *Music and Letters,* xviii (1937), 355.

Christopher Palmer, "C.W. Orr, An 80th Birthday Tribute," *Musical Times,* CXIV, 1973, p. 1565.

Joseph T. Rawlins, "Charles Wilfred Orr: A Neglected English Songwriter," *The NATS Journal,* 37:4, 15-18.

_____, "The Songs of Charles Wilfred Orr. Part II: The Songs" (concluded), *The NATS Bulletin,* 30:3, 32-37.

J. Wilson, *C.W. Orr: The Unknown Song Composer* (London, 1989).

Notes

1. Orr, in a letter to Eric Sams, a month before his death. Quoted in Stephen Banfield, *Sensibility and English Song,* v. 1, 301.
2. Stephen Banfield, *Sensibility and English Song,* v. 1, 304.
3. Joseph T. Rawlins, "Charles Wilfred Orr: A Neglected English Songwriter," 15.
4. Quoted in Barry Smith, *Peter Warlock: The Life of Philip Heseltine,* 204.
5. Quoted in Rawlins, "The Songs of Charles Wilfred Orr: Concepts, Influences, and Misconceptions," *The NATS Bulletin,* 30:2, 32.
6. Quoted in Stephen Cary, "A.E. Housman and the Renaissance of English Song," *The NATS Journal* 49:1, 18.
7. Quoted in Smith, *Peter Warlock: The Life of Philip Heseltine,* 204.

PETER WARLOCK (1894-1930)
(Philip Heseltine)

The poem must be re-created rather than interpreted.

—Peter Warlock[1]

I would rather spend my life trying to achieve one book of little songs that shall have a lasting fragrance than pile up tome upon tome on the dusty shelves of the British Museum.

—Peter Warlock[2]

Peter Warlock must be classified with the most gifted songwriters of the century. Lennox Berkeley once described him as "one of the most colorful talents in English 20th-century music."[3] Warlock was a strange mixture of gentleness and cruelty, sensitivity and self-criticism. His personality was brilliant, yet tormented. For most of his life, he rarely lived more than a few months at any address.

His musical compositions included some 119 solo songs, as well as some vocal chamber music, twenty-three choral works (some unaccompanied, some with keyboard, and others with orchestra), and a few works for orchestra or piano—all composed within a fourteen-year period. In addition, he was a distinguished editor and transcriber of early music (570 published items of Elizabethan and Jacobean music) and an author of nine books and seventy-three articles, as well as an editor and critic (51 reviews).[4] His musical style was influenced by his absorption of the music of Frederick Delius and Anglo-Dutch composer Bernard van Dieren (1887-1936), whom he met in 1917. From van Dieren, he learned to simplify his piano accompaniments and think contrapuntally.

He was often described as "an Elizabethan born out of his time," although Warlock was in many ways, ahead of his time. He came from a well-to-do family; his mother was Welsh and Warlock maintained strong ties with Wales throughout his life. He was educated at Eton; he was introduced to the music of Frederick Delius by his music teacher, and developed an all-consuming passion for Delius's music. He dropped out of Oxford after a disastrous year and moved to London, where he met Thomas Beecham, who promised him journalistic work.

As a composer, Warlock was virtually self-taught; any composition lessons were taken on in informal basis. His pseudonym (his real name was Phillip Heseltine) no doubt traces back to a period when he lived for a year in Ireland, dabbling in the occult. His biographer Cecil Gray claims this obsession caused him "certain psychological injuries from which...he never entirely recovered."[5]

In 1920 he was appointed editor of a new music journal , *The Sackbut*, which only published nine issues. He moved to the family home in Wales, completed a book on Delius and made arrangements of his music. He also composed large numbers of original songs, including his masterpiece song cycle *The Curlew*.

In 1924 he moved to rural Eynsford in Kent, where he shared a cottage with composer E.J. Moeran. Here he wrote *The English Ayre*, as well as a study on Gesualdo. He continued to compose, but with increasing depression. He eventually moved back to London to take part in the organization of the great Delius Festival in 1929. On December 17, 1930, he was found dead in his Chelsea flat, of gas poisoning. The coroner recorded an open verdict, and there are still arguments today as to whether or not he took his own life.

Numerous obituaries appeared after his death. Bernard van Dieren wrote of the musical works in the *Musical Times*: "In their finely-drawn melodic lines, their beautiful transparency and balanced structure, they show, as in everything Heseltine did, a consummate orderliness...if genuine emotion, infinite charm, and grace, can preserve a spirit as living reality for future generations...much of 'Warlock's' music will have become a national treasure when all that was ever said or written about it today will be forgotten."[6]

Pretty Ring Time   **1925**
(William Shakespeare. *As You Like It*)

"Pretty Ring Time" is Warlock's title for his setting of Shakespeare's "It was a lover and his lass."* The song is characterized by a buoyant approach to text setting, varied rhythmically for poetic stress. "Hey ding a ding ding" marks the words emphatically and decisively finishes each stanza. Text setting is syllabic note-for-note for the entire song, giving the effect of a patter song. There are variations in accompaniment textures between the verses; the accompaniment is thickest in the final verse, which is a strophic variation. Buried within the piano texture are several references to the sixteenth-century carol "Unto us is born a Son," presumably a hidden reference to "This carol they began that hour."[7] The singer is given a triumphant high G to end the song.

*For comparison settings, see Gerald Finzi, Geoffrey Bush, Frederick Delius, and Mario Castelnuovo-Tedesco.

Jillian of Berry   1926
(Beaumont & Fletcher. *The Knight of the Burning Pestle*)

A very quick tempo and pounding rhythms characterize this robust drinking song, peppered throughout with displaced accents. The piano accompaniment is chordal and wide-ranging, and contains many cross-rhythms. The vocal line, rugged and boisterous in the style of a folk song, is often in danger of being eclipsed by the thick-textured accompaniment. This extremely short song is often used to end a group, or as an effective encore.

Sleep   1922
(John Fletcher)

"Sleep" is one of Warlock's masterpieces—quite simply, a great song.[*] It was apparently intended for string quartet, and was set in this version in 1927. Warlock directed the voice part to "be sung as though unbarred, i.e. phrased according to the natural accentuation of the words, especially avoiding an accent on the first beat of the bar when no accent is demanded by the sense."[8]

Warlock writes long legato vocal lines in free speech rhythms; the piano texture is chromatic and contrapuntal. Subtle harmonic and rhythmic variations in vocal line and accompaniment at the text "Tho' but a shadow, but a sliding" is a highly effective moment of text illustration. Here Warlock uses the melodic material from the very first vocal phrase, varied only slightly and supported by an extremely chromatic texture in the piano.

A great intensity of longing is found in the concluding phrases of the two stanzas: "All my powers of care bereaving" and "O let my joys have some abiding," which use identical melodies, varied rhythmically. Each phrase is initiated by a tied note, the longest points of duration in the song.

[*]For a comparison, see the setting by Ivor Gurney.

Rest sweet nymphs   1922
(Anonymous)

This gentle lullaby—really a serenade—is sung to a group of young ladies. Wishing them pleasant dreams and joy, the poet plays his lute as he sings. Warlock uses a dotted note figure in the right hand reminiscent of the lute. The meter is $\frac{6}{8}$; a chain of second-inversion chords initiates a gently rocking accompaniment which continues throughout. Warlock employs his usual gentle dissonances in the chord structures; the piano accompaniment uses chord figures embellished with varied arpeggiations in the left hand, and a sparser texture of only a single-line figure above one chord in the bass.

The refrain "Lullaby, lullaby" is repeated at the conclusion of each verse. The voice ends its lullaby delicately on the fifth of the scale; it is left to the piano to provide the final soft cadence. Although Warlock later termed this song "rubbish," his setting is masterful.

My Own Country
(Hilaire Belloc)

1927

A wanderer's longing for home is a familiar theme of this song, one of Warlock's best-loved and most familiar. It is from a set titled *Three Belloc Songs* (the other two are "Ha'nacker Mill" and "The Night"). Belloc's country was Sussex, where the woods are deciduous and therefore have new leaves in spring; there are also striking groups of a few trees round ancient hill-forts such as Chanctonbury and Cissbury Rings.[9]

Warlock's setting has a folk song quality and a vocal line which moves quietly through the piece in eighth notes, set syllabically. Longer note values are found scattered throughout at the ends of phrases and to highlight words. The vocal writing reinforces a sense of wandering without haste or tension.

The first vocal phrase comes out of the piano introduction, then veers off on its own. The piano reinforces a sense of calm, in evenly moving chords throughout. Warlock employs some dissonances in chord structures. In the second verse, piano and voice switch ranges. The piano moves above the voice and the song modulates at this point ("and some stand few") to A major. At the words "all the woods are *new*," there is a sudden return to the tonic (F major).

Warlock uses modulation simply and effectively without intricate harmonies. The text is realized without overt sentimentality. The last vocal phrase begins softly ("And then I shall dream forever and all"), syncopated and with a slowly dissolving sense of tonality ("A good dream and deep"). Repeated bars of the prelude conclude the song. As with many poignant musical moments in Warlock's songs, this phrase might be construed as autobiographical in its emotional content.

Extended Study List
Take, O Take Those Lips Away • Spring • Twelve Oxen • The Bayly Berith the Bell Away • Captain Stratton's Fancy • Good ale • Bethlehem Down • Yarmouth Fair • Roister Doister • Mourn no Moe • Robin Goodfellow • Ha'nacker mill • The lover's maze • Sigh no more, ladies • Love for Love • The First Mercy • Piggésnie • Balulalow • *The Curlew* (cycle for tenor, flute, English horn, string quartet) • *Lilligay* • The contented lover • The Fox • The Wind from the West • As ever I saw • Sweet and twenty

Selected Reading
Kenneth Avery, "The Chronology of Warlock's Songs," *Music and Letters* 29, 398.
Stephen Banfield, *Sensibility and English Song: critical studies of the early 20th century* (Cambridge: Cambridge University Press, 1985). In two volumes.
Gerald Cockshott, "Peter Warlock: Some Notes on His Songs," *Music and Letters* 21 (1940), 246.
I.A. Copley, *The Music of Peter Warlock: A Critical Survey* (London: Dennis Dobson, 1979).
Cecil Gray, *Peter Warlock, a Memoir of Philip Heseltine* (London: Cape, 1934).
Trevor Hold, *Parry to Finzi: Twenty English Song-Composers* (Woodbridge: Boydell Press, 2002).
Michael Pilkington, *Gurney, Ireland, Quilter and Warlock* (Bloomington: Indiana University Press, 1989). English Solo Song Guides to the Repertoire.
Barry Smith, *Peter Warlock: The Life of Philip Heseltine* (Oxford: Oxford University Press, 1994).
Peter Warlock, *The English Ayre* (London: Oxford University Press, 1926).

Notes
1. Quoted in A. Copley, *The Music of Peter Warlock: A Critical Survey*, 53.
2. Warlock, in a letter to Bernard van Dieren, Anglo-Dutch composer. Quoted in Barry Smith, "Peter Warlock: a centenary tribute," *Gramophone*, 71:849 (February 1994), 26-27.
3. Quoted in Smith, ibid.
4. Statistics from F. Tomlinson, *A Peter Warlock Handbook,* Vol. 1 (London, 1974).
5. Copley, *The Music of Peter Warlock*, 101.

6. Quoted in Barry Smith, *Peter Warlock: The Life of Philip Heseltine*, 289.

7. Ibid., 235.

8. Ibid., 195-96.

9. Michael Pilkington, *Gurney, Ireland, Quilter and Warlock* (English Solo Song Guides to the Repertoire), 150.

MICHAEL HEAD (1900-1976)

Though his style is not strikingly individual, nor his concerns particularly penetrating, his music has charm and integrity and the solid backing of fastidious craftsmanship.

—Michael Hurd[1]

Michael Head was an English composer, singer, and pianist. His early studies were in mechanical engineering, which he abandoned to attend the Royal Academy of Music (1919-25) where he would become professor of piano. He was later made a Fellow at the Academy.

Head is known almost exclusively for his vocal music, which began to be published in 1917. Head's songs are quite appealing; they are harmonically conservative and melodically simple, "falling somewhere between the popular ballad and the art song proper."[2] He became his own best public relations man, giving numerous one-man recitals of his own music, touring widely, and making frequent broadcasts and several recordings.

Head's compositional style was eclectic, using a variety of approaches which obscured a sense of personal style in his songs: impressionism, romanticism, chordal and contrapuntal techniques, modality, and often an overly descriptive treatment that lacked depth or definition. His musical treatment in most of his songs scratches the emotional surface of the text and then moves on, leaving one with a feeling of incompleteness. Head was representative of the group of composers between the wars who were influenced by the harmonic language of Delius and responded to the lure of the abundant lyrical poetry of the day. These composers "made the most of their technical confidence and kept the market supplied with material for competitive festivals, singing lessons, broadcast recitals, and the occasional *soirée*."[3]

Head composed 122 art songs, written over a span of about fifty-eight years, from 1918 until his death in 1976.[4] Most of his songs were published quickly after their composition, and have remained in print. Despite his wide-ranging techniques, many of the songs in Head's large vocal output are worthwhile.

Lavender Pond (from *Six Sea Songs*)   **1949**

(C. Fox Smith)

The poem is subtitled "Surrey Commercial Docks." Its text describes the murky waters of Lavender Pond by London River, the battered barges that ride on the tide and the dank smells that pervade the area where swallows do not fly nor flowers grow. Compound meters— $\frac{12}{8}$, $\frac{9}{8}$, $\frac{6}{8}$ —provide a chance to use moving eighth notes in arpeggios for much of the accompaniment, which is generally heavy-textured throughout the song. There are awkward modulations in spots.

Vocal phrases are melodic and lyric bordering on the sentimental, in contrast to the somber verse.

A Piper
1923
(Seumas O'Sullivan)

A jaunty Irish piper's tune in the right hand of the piano begins the song, joined by chords in the left hand and finally, the voice. The meter is $\frac{9}{8}$, alternating with $\frac{6}{8}$ to fit the text stresses as needed. The tune continues in the piano; the vocal line is a simple rhythmic narrative line that acts as a sustained descant to the piano throughout. As the story continues, the accompaniment texture thickens slightly, reaching a climactic point with the voice at "And all the world went gay" (*allargando*). Just as quickly, the story ends, and the little piper's tune is heard in the piano, disappearing in the air.

Head also set another O'Sullivan text, "A Singer"—an unaccompanied piece that has a folk-tune quality in its melodic writing.

Sweet Chance
1929
(W.H. Davies)

This is a broadly lyric song whose first vocal phrase "Sweet Chance, that led my steps abroad" brings to mind Quilter's "Now sleeps the crimson petal." The accompaniment doubles the vocal line at times, and at others, harmonizes with it in thirds. Head's fluency with a number of styles of poetry can be seen in this song, which is not overblown but is instead a rather graceful setting of a somewhat prosaic verse.

Money-O!
(William Henry Davies)

"Money-O" is one of Head's most attractive and popular songs. This is a lusty song, folk-like in character, with a text meant for a man to sing. Head sets the words into a rugged vocal line, underpinned with a strongly rhythmic piano accompaniment. The opening section of the song is boisterous and swaggering; Head repeats it, slightly altered, at the conclusion of the song.

Extended Study List
Three Songs of Venice • *Over the Rim of the Moon* • *Three Songs of Fantasy* • *Songs of the Countryside* • *Three Cotswold Songs* • Dear Delight • Love's Lament • The Estuary • A Green Cornfield

Selected Reading
Stephen Banfield, *Sensibility and English Song: critical studies of the early 20th century* (Cambridge: Cambridge University Press, 1985). In two volumes. See Vol. 1, Chapter 14: "The uses and abuses of technique."

Elizabeth Loryn Frey, *The Songs of Michael Head: The Georgian Settings (and song catalogue)*. D.M.A. diss., Louisiana State University and Agricultural and Mechanical College, 1990.

Michael Hurd, "Michael Head," *The New Grove Dictionary of Music and Musicians,* ed. Stanley Sadie (New York: Grove's Dictionaries of Music, 1989), Vol. 8.

Notes

1. Michael Hurd, "Michael Head," *The New Grove Dictionary of Music and Musicians* (1989), 419.
2. Ibid.
3. Stephen Banfield, *Sensibility and English Song,* v. 1, 301.
4. Elizabeth Loryn Frey, *The Songs of Michael Head; The Georgian Settings.* D.M.A. diss., 1990. Abstract.

GERALD FINZI (1901-1956)

I don't think everyone realizes the difference between choosing a text and being chosen by one.

—Gerald Finzi[1]

Finzi unerringly found the live centre of his vocal texts, fusing vital declamation with a lyrical impulse in supple, poised lines.

—Diana McVeagh[2]

Gerald Finzi contributed a large body of song to early twentieth-century British literature. Of his more than 100 works, approximately two-thirds are for solo voice with accompaniment.

In general, Finzi's song style is solidly traditional. He wrote extremely lyrical melodies, unforced and natural, uncomplicated by embellishments, sentimentality or over-sophistication. Finzi's songs are characterized by skillful interaction between the voice and piano, in a sort of close imitative texture, a technique found in his shorter orchestral pieces. Occasionally these rhythmic-harmonic patterns have a monotonous quality, but in general are carefully crafted and manipulated to hold interest. Elgar and Vaughan Williams are often cited as influential in Finzi's melodic and harmonic approach.

Finzi's songs contain complex rhythmic patterns which frequently mask rather prosaic harmonic progressions. He does, however, make effective use of harmonies to highlight poetic atmosphere. Dissonance is skillfully integrated into the texture for effect, and chromatics often blur tonality to illustrate mood.

In addition to his songs, he produced choral works. Finzi worked slowly and fussily, sometimes putting away sketches for years without returning to them. He was highly self-critical. In 1951 Finzi was diagnosed with Hodgkin's disease and his feelings of time closing in became acute. Completing a musical work took on great significance. He wrote in 1938: "I should feel really suicidal if I didn't know that a song outlasts a dynasty."[3] Finzi's songs are published in sets. They cannot be properly designated as cycles, but are carefully ordered for poetic unity and balance. Only *A Young Man's Exhortation* might be termed a cycle.

Finzi loved poetry and had an extensive library; his songs use texts of uniformly high quality. Over fifty of his songs are set to texts by Thomas Hardy, whose poetic themes appealed to the pessimistic side of Finzi's personality and allowed him to express his despondency in musical terms. Both poet and composer shared and felt deeply the inexorable passing of time. Finzi's identification with Hardy's poetry was so strong that when he read a poem through, "certain lines would irresistibly call up music from him. In this way he collected scraps of songs...and put them aside, having to work hard and slowly to complete them."[4] After his death, a number of unfinished Hardy "fragments" were left. Among Finzi's cycles on Hardy poems: *A Young Man's Exhortation* (1933), *Earth and Air and Rain* (1936), and *Before and After Summer* (1949).

Although they never met, Finzi worked tirelessly for Ivor Gurney, and was a moving force behind the *Music and Letters* Gurney Number (1938) and the publication of his songs.

When Finzi completed his catalog of works in 1951, he wrote in the preface:

I like to think that in each generation may be found a few responsive minds, and for them I should still like the work to be available. To shake hands with a good friend over the centuries is a pleasant thing, and the affection which an individual retains after his departure is perhaps the only thing which guarantees an ultimate life to his works.[5]

Let Us Garlands Bring, Op. 18   1938-40
(William Shakespeare)

Come away, death • Who is Sylvia? • Fear no more the heat o' the sun •
O Mistress Mine • It was a lover and his lass

These five beautifully lyric treatments of some of Shakespeare's most familiar texts were created for baritone and piano and dedicated to Ralph Vaughan Williams on his birthday, October 12, 1942. The order of composition is as follows: Song 1 (1938); Songs 2 and 3 (1939); Song 4 (1942); and Song 5 (1940).

COME AWAY, DEATH.[*] Shakespeare's despairing lament is set in B minor, $\frac{2}{4}$ meter, peppered with some $\frac{3}{4}$ measures that create irregular phrase lengths as well as variety. A somber pattern of chords over a descending bass prepares the first vocal phrase; a variant of this pattern is found later in the accompaniment, led by the right hand. The vocal line ("Come away") is initiated by an ascending melodic fragment of three notes that reaches its point of stress on the unstressed half of the second beat—an effective sound quality against the heavy piano rhythms.

The form is in two sections, corresponding to the original text. Finzi sets the word "weep" in an arching six-measure melisma covering well over an octave in range. The last measures in the piano contain the opening melodic fragment ("Come away").

*For comparison settings, see Roger Quilter, Jacques Leguerney, Mario Castelnuovo-Tedesco, and Madeleine Dring.

WHO IS SYLVIA? Shakespeare's three stanzas are set in ABA form with a vivacious animated accompaniment. This is a happy tribute in a rollicking *allegro* tempo with plenty of rhythmic movement sustained throughout the entire piece. Brief interludes between the verses are constructed from the opening material.

*For a comparison setting, see Mervyn Horder.

FEAR NO MORE THE HEAT O' THE SUN.[*] Finzi sets this text with a stately melody of religious quality in $\frac{6}{4}$ time. Like the measured tread of a great funeral procession, the rhythm of the accompaniment and the vocal line keep pace with one another, with little or no movement in inner parts. Much of the time the bass line is in octaves. Texture overall is full and solemn. The last section—a benediction—is set in recitative chant style, finished by a reiteration of the opening phrase and another phrase as a closing valedictory.

O MISTRESS MINE.* A sprightly melody in the piano introduction sets the stage for this familiar verse. Vocal phrases are melodious as well, with some illustrative passages ("Trip no further pretty sweeting"). Phrases of similar shape unify the two stanzas, but there are enough differences to point up the poetic meaning ("Then come kiss me sweet and twenty / Youth's a stuff will not endure"). There is an eight-bar postlude that soberly ponders the last line.

*For a comparison setting, see Roger Quilter.

IT WAS A LOVER AND HIS LASS.* Shakespeare's delightful affirmation of young love is set in a spontaneous, fresh setting that is driven by juxtaposing different rhythm patterns in voice and piano.

The meter is $\frac{2}{4}$; the piano figure is syncopated (eighth/quarter/eighth), the vocal part is also syncopated. For each stanza, a $\frac{3}{4}$ bar is added to accommodate Finzi's setting of "ding a ding a ding" and provide more rhythmic variety. Several other bell-like patterns may be found throughout the piano texture. Unity is created through the use of the same music for the last poetic phrases of each stanza.

Stanzas 1, 2, and 4 share the same melodic structure. Stanza 3 seems slower as the accompaniment changes to gently moving thirds and sixths, then more somber half-note chords as the transience of life is contemplated. The interplay of rhythms in voice and piano combine to highlight the alliteration of the text and create a light pastoral atmosphere.

*For comparison settings, see Geoffrey Bush and Mario Castelnuovo-Tedesco.

Extended Study List

Before and After Summer (Thomas Hardy) • *Earth and Air and Rain* (Thomas Hardy) • *A Young Man's Exhortation* (Thomas Hardy) • *O fair to see* • *I Said to Love* (Thomas Hardy) • *Till Earth Outwears* (Thomas Hardy) • *To a Poet*

Selected Reading

Stephen Banfield, *Sensibility and English Song: critical studies of the early 20th century* (Cambridge: Cambridge University Press, 1985). In two volumes. See Vol. 1, Chapter 13: "Time and destiny: the Hardy songs of Gerald Finzi."

Arthur Bliss, "Gerald Finzi: An Appreciation," *Tempo* (Winter 1957-1958).

Trevor Hold, *Parry to Finzi: Twenty English Song-Composers* (Woodbridge: Boydell Press, 2002).

Diana McVeagh, "Gerald Finzi," *The New Grove Dictionary of Music and Musicians*, ed. Stanley Sadie (New York: Grove's Dictionaries of Music, 1989).

____, *Gerald Finzi: His Life and Music* (London: Boydell, 2005).

Burton B. Parker, "Textual-Musical Relationships in Selected Songs of Gerald Finzi," *The NATS Bulletin,* 30:4 (May/June 1974).

David Trent Schubert, "The relationship of text and music in Gerald Finzi's song set: 'I Said to Love.'" D.M.A. diss., The University of Oklahoma, 1993.

Notes

1. Quoted in Burton B. Parker, "Textual-Musical Relationships in Selected Songs of Gerald Finzi," *The NATS Bulletin*, 30:4, 12.
2. Diana McVeagh, "Gerald Finzi," *The New Grove Dictionary of Music and Musicians* (1989), 95.

3. Finzi, in a letter to William Busch, October 1938. Quoted in *Stephen Banfield, Sensibility and English Song*, v.1, 277.
4. Ibid., 287.
5. Quoted in Diana McVeagh. Liner notes to *Songs by Finzi and His Friends*. Hyperion Records, CDA 66015, 1981.

BENJAMIN BRITTEN (1913-1976)

> Britten has been for me the most purely musical person I have ever met and I have ever known. It always seemed to me that music sprang out of his fingers when he played the piano, as it did out of his mind when he composed.
>
> —Michael Tippett[1]

Benjamin Britten was the 20th century's most distinguished and significant British composer. Gifted and prolific, his compositions included piano pieces, symphonic works, concertos, chamber music, and particularly impressive contributions to vocal music.

In the great English tradition of Purcell, Britten had a special affinity for words and wrote extensively for the voice in all forms: opera, choral works, cycles for voice and instruments, and solo song. His operas in particular are the most important British contribution to that genre in this century. Britten explained his approach to texts and word setting:

> One of my chief aims is to try to restore to the musical setting of the English language brilliance, freedom, and vitality that have been curiously rare since the death of Purcell...Good recitative should transform the natural intonations and rhythms of everyday speech into memorable musical phrases (as with Purcell) but in more stylized music the composer should not deliberately avoid unnatural stresses if the prosody of the poem and the emotional situation demand them, nor be afraid of a high-minded treatment of words which may need prolongation far beyond their common speech length, or a speed of delivery that would be impossible in conversation.[2]

Thus, his style of word setting was not text-oriented, but a conscious attempt to capture in music the essence of the poem the poet had created in verse.

His long-standing liaison with tenor Peter Pears led him to create many vocal works and operatic roles for Pears's voice. No doubt much of his knowledge of writing for the voice was influenced by his close association with Pears as well as many of the other fine singers of his time. Britten's output of songs is extensive and his mastery of vocal writing developed and matured with each vocal work. Most of his songs are in sets and cycles. Among his most popular vocal music are his arrangements of British and French folk songs.

In 1947 Britten returned to his roots, purchasing a house in the tiny fishing village of Aldeburgh in Suffolk, 100 miles northeast of London. Britten lived and worked there until his death. In 1948 the Aldeburgh Festival of Music and the Arts was founded by Britten, Pears, and Eric Crozier to showcase the music of British artists. It quickly became world famous for the quality of its performers, concerts, and staged productions. Eight of Britten's operas were premiered at the festival, held annually in June and July. In 1969 a fire destroyed the concert hall, known as Snape Maltings, a converted old malt brewery barn. The new hall, completely rebuilt and dedicated by Queen Elizabeth II, is acclaimed for its acoustics and has been called the finest concert hall in Europe. A Britten-Pears School was also established at Snape Maltings. Benjamin Britten is buried in the Aldeburgh churchyard.

In 1965 he was awarded the Order of Merit, the highest honor that the English can receive in their own country.

A Charm of Lullabies, Op. 41   1947

A Cradle Song (William Blake) • The Highland Balou (Robert Burns) •
Sephestia's Lullaby (Robert Greene) • A Charm (Thomas Randolph) •
The Nurse's Song (John Philip)

Britten composed this cycle for Nancy Evans, who created the role of Nancy (named for her) in *Albert Herring* and sang Lucretia in *The Rape of Lucretia* at Glyndebourne in 1946.[3] It is Britten's only vocal work between 1940 and 1965 not written for the voice of Peter Pears.

All the songs are lullabies of one sort or another, greatly varied in musical style and dramatic situation and unconventional in their reflections of meanings and moods not usually thought of as related to cradlesongs. A subsidiary meaning of the word *charm* is "to put to sleep" and its derivation is from *carmen*—song. Britten's eclectic choice of poems reflects the range of his literary taste. *A Charm of Lullabies* is also a prime example of his ability to complement the words with music, whether the text is in formal poetic structure or only a simple dialogue. Britten captures the essence of each poem with a musical atmosphere that seems a perfect fit for the declamation and yet surprises us with unpredictable twists in melodic, harmonic, and rhythmic elements. In its clarity and directness, this work is a turning point toward his later vocal style.

A CRADLE SONG. A linear piano accompaniment sets the lullaby atmosphere. Rocking rhythm is established in the left hand of the piano. Its ostinato-like quarter-note pattern underpins a wandering melody in the right hand, constructed of varying combinations of eighth and sixteenth notes. Its close-range construction is varied only occasionally by slightly scrambling the rhythmic units. The combination of the two lines maintains a feeling of forward motion and a hypnotic, sleep-inducing atmosphere. The vocal line is also calm and generally small-ranged. *Parlando* is the marking above a one-note recitative phrase "O, the cunning wiles that creep in thy little heart asleep," although the piano loses its calm feeling as it expands in range. One more recitative phrase leads to the lovely climactic passage "Then the dreadful lightnings break." The song ends quietly, as it began.

THE HIGHLAND BALOU. This setting was most likely influenced by Britten's memories of Scottish songs heard in Lowestoft in his childhood. Scottish elements are found in the song, the Scotch "snap" and a bagpipe drone. "Sweet wee Donald" is lulled to sleep even though the even rhythmic flow in $\frac{4}{4}$ is temporarily displaced by measures of $\frac{5}{4}$ and $\frac{3}{4}$. The poem is by the great Scottish poet Robert Burns.

SEPHESTIA'S LULLABY. This lullaby, like the next, is constructed of two alternating sections (ABABA). "Weep not my wanton, smile upon my knee; When thou art old there's grief enough for thee" appears three times, varied slightly in its last appearance at the cadence. Word stress and mood dictate a faster tempo (*Doppio movimento-allegretto*) for the second section. Britten unifies the two sections by using pitches from the first section as grace notes in the second. This is the lament of a single mother, probably unwed, abandoned by the father of her child. Peter Pears wrote, "one sees the rickety tot as clear as day."[4]

A CHARM. This lullaby is menacing in tone, obviously the efforts of a frustrated nurse to coerce the child into dreamland. "Quiet, sleep! or I will make..." is followed by a litany of threats which will befall the unfortunate infant if he doesn't go to sleep. The song is an alternation of slow and fast tempi. The list of horrors promised as punishment for staying awake is set in $\frac{7}{4}$ meter, to be performed *prestissimo furioso*; the interjections of "Quiet, sleep!" are *largamente, ad libitum* in $\frac{4}{4}$, set over rolled harmonies and chord tremolos.

THE NURSE'S SONG. The atmosphere of the concluding song is that of a garden-variety lullaby, beginning with three short unaccompanied vocal phrases. The fourth phrase is joined by the piano in rocking figures, punctuated periodically by short arpeggios at various points along the way. Britten makes brief excursions into several tonalities through the song. A circular form is achieved as the last measures repeat the beginning unaccompanied phrases of the opening, and end simply and quietly—in the Land of Dreams.

Seven Sonnets of Michelangelo, **Op. 22**   **1940**
(Michelangelo Buonarroti)

Si come nella penna e nell' inchiostro (XVI) • A che più debb'io mai l'intensa voglia (XXXI) • Veggio co' bei vostri occhi un dolce lume (XXX) • Tu sa' ch'io so, signior mie, che ti sai (LV) • Rendeta a gli occhi miei (XXXVIII) • S'un casto amor, s'una pietà superna (XXXII) • Spirto ben nato, in cui si specchia e vede (XXIV)

Britten's first really important group of songs was composed during his self-imposed exile in the United States during the first years of World War II. Completed in 1940, the *Michelangelo Sonnets* cycle was premiered in public performance in London, September, 1942, by Britten and tenor Peter Pears. Edward Sackville-West, writing in the *New Statesman* called the Michelangelo cycle "indescribably moving...the finest chamber songs England has had to show since the seventeenth century."[5]

The *Michelangelo Sonnets* was the first cycle composed for tenor Peter Pears, with whom Britten shared his life and for whom he created most of his vocal works, including the leading roles in his operas. The work has been called a declaration of love between Britten and Pears. Pianist Graham Johnson describes the work as "a garland of songs to celebrate a marriage of minds and hearts."[6] Pears said of all the music that Britten composed "...this [group] had a very special meaning."[7]

Britten invested Michelangelo's texts with flowing Italianate vocal lines, lyric in the best sense of *bel canto,* but expressed in twentieth-century musical terms. The seven sonnets encompass a wide variety of moods with subtly disguised Italian dance-rhythms. For one performance in 1945, it may have been Pears who supplied subtitles for each, referring to "love's scope, impatience, serenity, uncertainty, confidence and nobility."[8]

Britten's skill in working with the Italian language is impressive, as was his aptitude for French in *Les Illuminations.* In both these works he was able to achieve a unique European stylization. The vocal writing is both intimate and exuberant, quasi-operatic and elegantly lyric. It is worth noting that the sonnets are in one form and in the same meter, which would normally pose problems in lyric settings, yet Britten's melodic treatment is varied and expressive. In keeping with all his cycles, the work is carefully planned as to key sequence, vocal style, and contrasts of rhythms and dynamics. Within this group of texts, Britten is able to achieve extraordinary contrasts.

Titles and translations are given below:

1. Si come nella penna e nell' inchiostro — Just as there is a high, a low, and a middle style
2. A che più debb'io mai l'intensa voglia — Why must I go on venting my ardent desire
3. Veggio co' bei vostri occhi un dolce lume — With your lovely eyes I see a sweet light
4. Tu sa' ch'io so, signior mie, che ti sai — Thou know'st, beloved, that I know thou know'st
5. Rendeta a gli occhi miei — Give back to my eyes
6. S'un casto amor, s'una pietà superna — If love be chaste, if pity heavenly
7. Spirto ben nato, in cui si specchia e vede — Noble soul, in whose chaste and dear limbs

---

Winter Words, **Op. 52**   **1953**
(Thomas Hardy)

At day-close in November • Midnight on the Great Western •
Wagtail and Baby • The Little Old Table • The Choirmaster's Burial • Proud
Songsters • At the Railway Station, Upway • Before Life and After

Winter Words is the only vocal work Britten composed between his operas *Gloriana* and *The Turn of the Screw.* It is one of the masterpieces of contemporary English song and stands chronologically at the midpoint of Britten's vocal works. Britten's musical response to Hardy's verse is profoundly expressive and captures the bittersweet emotion as well as the irony of these poems. Poetic content in the set is widely varied. Hardy's images are clear and moving. Banfield observes that nearly all the songs in this cycle seem to be primarily motivated by visual stimuli.[9]

This group of songs is described as "lyrics and ballads" and not a cycle. Hardy's poetry focuses on the loss of innocence that accompanies age and experience, and the transience of life. Themes that run throughout Britten's music are the struggle between good and evil, and the corruption of youth and lost innocence; therefore, it is hardly surprising that Hardy's poetry would attract him.

Britten's ordering of the poems and their musical setting produces an arch-form. The first and last songs are in D minor and D major and share a mood of emotional reflection. Songs 2 and 7 are in C minor and C major and both texts deal with railroads. Songs 3 and 6 depict birds and nature, and both settings are lighter in mood. At the heart of the group are Songs 4 and 5, both descriptive of personal experience. Song 5, the largest and most complex of the group, is preceded and followed by songs of faster tempo.

The songs are unified within themselves by small motives descriptive of poetic elements: train whistle triads in "Midnight on the Great Western," violin figures in "At the Railway Station-Upway," ascending and descending figures that picture the gamboling wagtail in "Wagtail and Baby," creaky off-beat clusters for "The Little Old Table," and birdsong flutterings in "Proud Songsters."

AT DAY-CLOSE IN NOVEMBER. Britten's eight-bar introduction contains all twelve notes of the chromatic scale, perhaps prefiguring his work on his chamber opera *The Turn of the Screw* (1954) in which each scene is linked to the one preceding by the statement or variation of a twelve-note theme whose intervals rotate like the turning of a screw. Additionally, the entire vocal line is structured from a three-note cell, varied in numerous ways throughout the song.

Wind-like figures in the piano permeate Britten's waltz. Only in the last verse does the movement even out as the children walk through the trees and "conceive that there never was a time...when no tall trees grew here."

MIDNIGHT ON THE GREAT WESTERN ("JOURNEYING BOY"). A child is pictured traveling alone on a train. Unexpressed danger seems imminent; the accompaniment maintains a constant motion as the train rocks towards an unnamed destination ("toward a world unknown"). Tremolos combined with staccato figures and syncopated rhythms create a feeling of unrest. Train whistles punctuate the texture at various points. The first line of each stanza refers to the "journeying" boy; Britten sets this word with the same vocal melisma, a touching and expressive articulation, as well as a unifying device.

WAGTAIL AND BABY ("A SATIRE"). Britten sets this little allegory as a light-hearted barcarole. A wagtail* sits in a stream, unconcerned when several fierce animals come to drink from the water. A baby observes the scene. At last, the wagtail flies away in fright when a perfect gentleman approaches. The baby is left thinking. The baby and the wagtail are illustrated by repeated chords in the left hand combined with ascending and descending chromatic figures in the right hand.

*A migrant bird with a long tail, which it grooms carefully.

THE LITTLE OLD TABLE. Hardy's work table brought forth this nostalgic poem which Britten sets in E minor with excursions into E major. The creaking table is pictured in both accompaniment and vocal phrases. A rhythmic ostinato of alternating pitches is punctuated with little melodic fragments which are repeated by the voice. In the second stanza it is the piano which seems to chase the vocal line. Figures in the piano alternate with one another to underscore the creaking of the table.

THE CHOIRMASTER'S BURIAL ("THE TENOR MAN'S STORY"). This song is one of Britten's best, and stands at the center of the group, like a miniature play or a brief *scena*. A narrator relates the tale of an industrious choirmaster who is laid to rest without benefit of any music, although he had requested a specific hymn be played. At midnight the vicar looks out on the graveyard to see a band of angels thronged round the grave, playing and singing.

Vocal phrases are plain, prayer-like recitative and melismas, underscored with simple chord harmonies for the first stanza. More animated figures illustrate the vicar's commentary in the second verse, and angelic arpeggios accompany the heavenly choir in the last section. Britten uses "Mount Ephraim," the hymn tune referred to in the text and forbidden by the vicar, in the accompaniment in the first and last sections.

PROUD SONGSTERS ("THRUSHES, FINCHES, AND NIGHTINGALES"). Fluttering figures in the piano depict the birds (repeated triplet figures, trills, and note clusters). The quick tempo of this song breaks the mood of the slower songs that precede and follow. Chromatic dissonances are peppered throughout the setting; the birds' constant movement gives them no time to ponder the fleeting quality of life.

AT THE RAILWAY STATION, UPWAY ("THE CONVICT AND BOY WITH THE VIOLIN"). This is another miniature scene. A handcuffed convict and his accompanying constable wait at the train station for the train that will carry him to prison. A little boy with a violin takes pity on the man and offers to play his fiddle for him. Violin figures make up the sparsely textured accompaniment: open strings, double-stops, flourishes and strums, spiccato, détaché bowing, and a final harmonic. The vocal line is recitative throughout; the only departure is the convict's peculiar utterance "This life so free / Is the thing for me"—a tuneful little melodic fragment.

BEFORE LIFE AND AFTER. This song, one of Britten's most beautiful, gathers together the poetic themes in this group. It is an emotional song, but its intensity is calm and quietly felt: life's pain could be eased by returning to an earlier gentler time, or by stepping ahead into another world.

A simple accompaniment of repeated chords with octaves buoys up a vocal line of gently turning shapes whose material is found periodically in the pianist's right hand. More chromaticism is added as the text reflects "the disease of feeling germed and primal rightness took the tinct of wrong," building to an intensely felt climax "How long?" and fading into nothingness.

Extended Study List

On This Island • *Folk Song Arrangements:* Vols. 1, 3, 5—British Isles, Vol. 2—France, Vol. 4—Moore's Irish Melodies, Vol. 6—England • *Beware* (3 early songs) • *Cabaret Songs* (texts by W.H. Auden) • *Canticle II: Abraham and Isaac* (mezzo-soprano and tenor) • *Les Illuminations* • *Quatre Chansons Françaises* • *Songs and Proverbs of William Blake* • *The Holy Sonnets of John Donne* • *Four Burns Songs*, Op. 92 • *Tit for Tat* (on poems by Walter de la Mare) • *Fancie* • *The Poet's Echo*, Op. 76 (6 poems by Pushkin) • *Phaedra*, Op. 93 (dramatic cantata for mezzo and small orchestra)

Selected Reading

Stephen Banfield, *Sensibility and English Song: critical studies of the early 20th century* (Cambridge: Cambridge University Press, 1985). Two vols. See Vol. 2, "Rethinking the Voice (II): Britten and his period."

Robert Gene Brewster, "The Relationship Between Poetry and Music in the Original Solo-Vocal Works of Benjamin Britten through 1965." Ph.D. diss., Washington University, 1967.

Humphrey Carpenter, *Benjamin Britten: a biography* (New York: Charles Scribner's Sons, 1992).

Eric Crozier and Nancy Evans, "After Long Pursuit: Nancy's Story," *The Opera Quarterly*, 11:1, 1994.

Peter Evans, *The Music of Benjamin Britten* (Minneapolis: University of Minnesota Press, 1979). Chapters 3 and 15.

Thomas Goleeke, "The Canticles of Benjamin Britten: A Consideration of Texts," *The NATS Journal*, 49:5 (March/April 1993).

Christopher Headington. Liner notes for *Composers in Person: Francis Poulenc/Benjamin Britten* (EMI Classics compact disc CDC 7 54605 2, 1993). Recorded in 1936 and 1947, Poulenc and Britten accompany Pierre Bernac and Peter Pears in their vocal compositions. Britten's *Seven Sonnets of Michelangelo* and *Holy Sonnets of John Donne* are found on this recording.

Christopher Palmer, ed., *The Britten Companion* (Cambridge: Cambridge University Press, 1984). See especially Chapter 26: Composer and Poet, and Chapter 27: Voice and Piano.

Donald Mitchell and Hans Keller, eds., *Benjamin Britten: A Commentary on his works from a group of specialists* (Westport, CT: Greenwood Press, 1972). Reprint of 1952 original edition by Rockliff Publishing Corporation, London. See especially Peter Pears, "The Vocal Music."

Donald Mitchell, ed., *Letters from a life: the selected letters and diaries of Benjamin Britten, 1913-1976*. Three vols. (Berkeley: University of California Press, 1991).

George Richard Tibbetts, "An analysis of the text-music relationship in selected songs of Benjamin Britten and its implications for the interpretation of his solo song literature." Doctoral diss., Columbia University Teachers College, 1984.

Mark Alexander Whitmire, "Songs by John Ireland and Benjamin Britten to poems by Thomas Hardy." D.M.A. diss., University of Maryland College Park, 1991.

A. W. Whittall, "Tonality in Britten's Song Cycles," *Tempo* 96, Spring 1971.

Notes

1. From Britten's obituary in the *Listener*. Quoted in John L. Holmes, *Composers on Composers* (New York: Greenwood Press, 1990), 39.
2. Benjamin Britten, "The Composer Speaks," in David Ewen, *The New Book of Modern Composers*, 3rd edition, 101. Britten used these words in the preface to his opera *Peter Grimes*.
3. Nancy Evans also sang in other Britten operas. She later became director of singing-studies at the Britten-Pears School in Aldeburgh. Her husband, Eric Crozier, librettist for Britten's operas *Billy Budd* and *Albert Herring*, was one of the co-founders of the Aldeburgh Festival.
4. Quoted in John Amis. Liner notes. *Britten: A Charm of Lullabies, Op. 41 and Folk Song Arrangements*. Bernadette Greevy, mezzo-soprano; Paul Hamburger, pianist. London Records STS 15166. Long playing record, 1970.
5. Humphrey Carpenter, *Benjamin Britten: a biography*, 177.
6. Graham Johnson, "Voice and Piano," in *The Britten Companion*, ed. Christopher Palmer, 290.
7. Christopher Headington, Britten (New York: Homes and Meier, 1982), 52.
8. _____, liner notes to *Composers in Person: Francis Poulenc and Benjamin Britten*.
9. Stephen Banfield, *Sensibility and English Song*, v. 2, 385.

MERVYN HORDER (1910-1997)

Mervyn Horder was born in London in 1910, son of the late Lord Horder, physician to King George V and King George VI. He was educated at Winchester College, Trinity College Cambridge, and the Guildhall School of Music. The ninety-odd songs of Mervyn Horder might be termed neoromantic in approach. Stylistically, they integrate a feeling of the English music hall with the classical recital platform. Texts set are far-ranging: Shakespeare, Housman, de la Mare, Belloc, Hardy, Betjeman, Auden, Herrick, Dorothy Parker, and his own verses, as well as others.

Horder's gift for natural lyricism and an infectious sense of melody crafts tunes that are immediately appealing and difficult to forget. In addition to his songs, his published music includes works for piano and editions and arrangements of books of carols.

Who is Sylvia?*
(William Shakespeare. *The Two Gentlemen of Verona*)

An introductory theme in the piano is important to the structure of this song, for it appears in the voice at the end of the first two strophes, and in varied form at the end of the third.

Horder interrupts the even vocal phrase lengths at the end of each stanza, taking the ecstatic theme from the piano introduction and giving it to the singer to end the first two verses ("That she might admired be," "And being help'd, inhabits there"). As the poem increases in excited praise of Sylvia, Horder concludes the last verse ("To her let us garlands bring") with a more elaborate variant of the melisma which ended the previous stanzas. Melodic material is also varied for this last stanza, and the accompaniment becomes fuller and richer in texture.

*For a comparison setting, see Gerald Finzi.

Under the greenwood tree*
(William Shakespeare. *As You Like It*)

This is a wonderfully evocative, tongue-in-cheek setting of this suggestive text. Horder uses tango rhythm in the accompaniment and voice. He fashions an extended phrase mid-stanza ("And turn his merry note, Unto the sweet bird's throat," and "Seeking the food he eats, And pleased with what he gets") and sets it in syncopation. Altered chords in the piano slyly punctuate "no enemy" (with "enemy" repeated). It is a highly effective, pleasing setting; one wishes for more than two stanzas.

*For comparison settings, see Madeleine Dring and Ivor Gurney.

Extended Study List
Where the Bee Sucks • Sigh no more, ladies • Caprice • O mistress mine • I love all beauteous things • To Electra • Loveliest of Trees • A Shropshire Lad • When I was one-and-twenty • Unfortunate Coincidence • Black Diamonds • When Music Sounds

GEOFFREY BUSH (1920-1998)

> For me, the chief problem in writing songs is to discover the right words.
> —Geoffrey Bush[1]

Geoffrey Bush, composer, pianist, lecturer, and broadcaster, was born in London in 1920. Bush's catalog of compositions includes four operas, solo songs, and works for orchestra and chamber groups. He had a scholarly interest in nineteenth-century British music, and edited volumes of nineteenth-century song. As a broadcaster, Bush was one of the most wide-ranging and sympathetic commentators on the British musical scene, his infectious enthusiasm thoroughly grounded in sound scholarship and a keen sense of perspective.

As a composer, Bush was largely self-taught; he decided to become a composer at the age of ten, while a chorister at Salisbury Cathedral. During school holidays he studied informally with John Ireland. He was educated at Salisbury Cathedral Choir School, Lancing College, and Balliol College, Oxford. In 1946, he became an extramural music lecturer at Oxford University and London University; and from 1969 he was a visiting professor at King's College, London.

Although he composed works in numerous genres, the essence of his style is rooted firmly in British vocal tradition. Bush credited his early years at Salisbury as having influenced his love of vocal music, his understanding of the voice and its capabilities, and his desire to compose for the voice.[2] He had this to say about writing songs:

> From the worldly point of view writing songs is an even more futile occupation than writing symphonies; the amateur singer is practically extinct, and those professional singers who are not obsessed with "Das Lied" get precious few opportunities to give a recital of songs of their own choice. Consequently they are hardly ever on the look-out for new songs; and it is distinctly discouraging for a composer who has written (as I have) nearly a dozen cycles to find, far from having sung them, most singers do not even know that they exist.[3]

Nonetheless, Bush confessed to being "addicted" to song writing. Although some critics find traces of Britten's influence in Bush's songs, he traced his style instead to "a common source—Henry Purcell, the model *par excellence* for anyone attempting to set the English language to music."[4] Bush's musical style is appealing and lyrical, firmly rooted in tonality. His works are skillfully crafted with economy of means. The discovery of Prokofiev's music influenced Bush's own composition, and a catalog of the qualities of the former—clarity of texture, mastery of form, love of harmonic "sidesteps," unending melodic invention, driving energy, humor—could serve as descriptors of Bush's music.

For his texts, Bush seemed to explore one area of lyrics at a time; he set poems from the sixteenth and seventeenth centuries, works by contemporary poet Kathleen Raine, children's rhymes and "poems from the past...whose modernity of feeling made them in a very real sense timeless."[5] Among the texts in this category are the traditional children's rhymes found in *Songs of Wonder* and idiomatic translations from a Greek anthology compiled by American scholar and poet, Dudley Fitts.

It was a lover and his lass*   **1947**
(William Shakespeare. *As You Like It*)

Bush's musical treatment of Shakespeare's familiar text is highly energized and dance-like. Three stanzas are set strophically in a strongly rhythmic setting that features repetition of phrases "hey and a ho," "hey," followed by a gaily descending melismatic passage on the word "[sweet lovers] love [the spring]" echoed in the piano. Its robust mood is reminiscent of a rustic country dance.

*For comparison settings, see Gerald Finzi, Roger Quilter, and Madeleine Dring.

Sigh no more, ladies *(Three Elizabethan Songs)*   **1947**
(William Shakespeare. *Much Ado About Nothing*)

In contrast to Virgil Thomson's robust, earthy setting of the same text, Bush's musical treatment is suave and elegant. It is set as a courtly waltz, whose refined steps are jostled out of kilter rhythmically at the words "To one thing constant never" and in the second verse "Since summer first was leavy." Bush elongates "Hey nonny nonny" into a little quasi-operatic ending. As is usual, a lyrical melodic line is accorded the singer.

I had a little nut-tree *(Songs of Wonder)*   **1962**
(Traditional words)

Bush originally created this set of songs for high voice and string orchestra in 1959, using seven songs to texts from a collection of traditional children's rhymes. He later made an alternative version with piano accompaniment, using five songs only ("Here comes a lusty wooer," "Polly Pillicote," "The wonder of wonders," "Old Abram Brown," and "I had a little nut tree").

This brief but charming setting features a bouncy melodic vocal line, in a rather elegant singsong style of the children's rhyme it sets. Displaced rhythmic accented are created by mixed meters. The piano accompaniment is in "oom-pah-pah" style, but takes up the vocal melody for a short interlude before the last two lines of poetry are repeated. The last word is given to the piano, which trails off into a questioning conclusion.

Bush commented about this group of songs, "Their surface simplicity conceals a wealth of mysterious and imaginative meanings."[6]

Three Songs of Ben Jonson   **1952**
Echo's Lament for Narcissus • The Kiss • A Rebuke

This work belongs to Bush's earliest song cycles, in which he explores texts from the sixteenth and seventeenth centuries, concentrating on a single poet or single unifying theme. Song 1 is a flowing lyric melody set over an undulating accompaniment fashioned of alternating thirds; Song 2 is an ingratiating waltz that utilizes several figurations, including the alternating figure heard in Song 1; Song 3 is driven by rhythmic figures in the piano, with just a hint of the accompaniment figure from Song 1 appearing fleetingly.

Extended Study List

Five Spring Songs (1944) • Fire, Fire! *(Three Elizabethan Songs)* • *The End of Love* (baritone, piano), 1954 • *Songs of Wonder* (S/T, string orchestra) 1959; S/T, piano, 1962 • *A Lover's Progress* (tenor, oboe, clarinet, bassoon), 1961 • *A Little Love Music* (S, T), 1976 • *Greek Love Songs* (1964) • Cuisine provençale • *Old Rhymes Re-set* (1987) • *Zodiac*

Selected Reading

Geoffrey Bush, *Left, Right and Centre: reflections on composers and composing* (London: Thames Publishing, 1983).

Notes

1. Geoffrey Bush. Liner notes to *A Little Love Music: Songs by Geoffrey Bush.* Chandos Records. CHAN 8830, 1991.
2. Telephone interview with the author. Phoenix, Arizona. 29 April 1995.
3. Geoffrey Bush, *Left, Right and Centre,* 130.
4. Bush, liner notes, *A Little Love Music.*
5. Geoffrey Bush, *Left, Right and Centre,* 126.
6. Bush, liner notes. *A Little Love Music.*

MADELEINE DRING (1923-1977)

Joy is something so special because it makes us young again, removing, if only for a few moments, all that unnecessary luggage we normally carry about.

—Madeleine Dring[1]

Her songs have the lyricism of Roger Quilter, the art of Herbert Howells, and the personality of Francis Poulenc.

—Wanda Brister[2]

Madeleine Winefride Isabelle Dring was a woman of many talents—pianist, violinist, composer, actress, singer, writer, and artist. At age ten she was admitted to the Royal College of Music Junior Department on a violin and piano scholarship. During World War II, Dring continued her work at the R.C.M. as a regular student. Her composition teachers included Sir Percy Buck, Herbert Howells, Ralph Vaughan Williams, and Gordon Jacob; however, her first piano teacher, Leslie Fly, was essentially her first teacher of composition during her formative years in the junior department.

In 1947, Dring married Roger Lord, whom she had met at the R.C.M. when they were fellow students. Lord was appointed principal oboist with the London Philharmonic Orchestra in 1949, and London was their home for nearly thirty years.

Dring composed more than sixty art songs—she called them "serious songs"— and a substantial amount of material for the intimate revues with which she was involved in the 1950s as an actress/singer. Since she was a talented singer and pianist, it is not surprising that Dring was attracted to song composition. Most of her songs were written with her own voice in mind; she often performed her songs at informal concerts, accompanying herself. The wide range and high tessitura of these songs indicates she had considerable vocal agility.

All of her songs are set to English texts, many by the Elizabethan poets— Shakespeare, Herrick, and Dryden. She also set contemporary poets such as Sir John Betjeman and her friends, D.F. Aiken, Joseph Ellison, and Michael Armstrong.

Her compositional style is difficult to pin down. Her music is delightfully eclectic, borrowing compositional devices from many historical periods. Hancock-Child described Dring's approach to composition as "pot-pourri—both irresistible and infuriating."[3]

Textures in Dring's songs are extremely inventive, and display her versatility in working with words and harmonic materials. Vocal phrases are crafted from and dictated by the harmony, and therefore are varied in shape and range. They are often more reminiscent of an instrumental line than a vocal melody. Dring's vocal writing has a unique lyricism of its own.

She had a playful nature and an optimistic personality; she was also known to have a fey sense of humor as well. Because she was a performer, she loved theatricality and drama.

Dring was also intensely interested in parapsychology, and wrote to a friend that she believed her compositional girls must have been "brought through the memory" of composing in a former life.[4]

Dring continued to compose songs throughout her life. She also composed works for solo piano, two pianos, and small instrumental chamber ensembles, as well as incidental music and songs for plays and revues. At the time of her death in 1977, only four of her songs had been published. Since that time, her music has become better known, largely through the efforts of Roger Lord, and writers and scholars who have discovered her delightful legacy of songs.

Blow, blow thou winter wind*   c. 1944
(William Shakespeare, from *Twelfth Night*)

Three Shakespeare Songs ("Under the greenwood tree," "Come away, death," and "Blow, blow thou winter wind") was the only song set published during Dring's lifetime.

Dring's musical approach is swift and forceful. Biting cold winter weather is established immediately by a two-measure introduction, peppered with chromaticism. Images of the winter wind are heard in the accompaniment, in arpeggiated figures that add commentary after the two poetic lines preceding the refrain "Heigh-ho! sing heigh-ho."

There are many sequential passages in the song; Dring was fond of using this formal organization in her songs. Hancock-Child observes that these segments gave Dring's music "an appealing air of organized chaos: What key are we going to now? Where will this phrase end up? Whatever next? Who knows! She always leaves her musical options wide open, ever ready to take an unexpected turn and startle, tease or shock."[5]

*For comparison settings, see Roger Quilter, Mario Castelnuovo-Tedesco, and Erich Korngold.

Business Girls *(Five Betjeman Songs)*   1976
(John Betjeman)

"Business Girls" and "Song of a Nightclub Proprietress" are part of *Five Betjeman Songs*, Dring's settings of the poetry of Sir John Betjeman (1906-1984). Knighted in 1969, Betjeman was named Poet Laureate of England in 1972. Stephen Banville describes the *Five Betjeman Songs* as "classic encapsulations of the poet's observations of the British and their surroundings."[6] Other songs in the Betjeman collection are "A Bay in Anglesey," "Undenominational," and "Upper Lambourne."

The scene is early morning in Camden.* As the commuter trains churn through the town, countless "business women" draw their baths in preparation for another workday. Broken-chord figures in the piano perpetuate their sense of boredom and serve to illustrate their routine, unvarying schedules. Dring highlights the melancholy that lies beneath their morning patterns, slipping subtle harmonic variations into the vocal line and the accompaniment. These girls realize they are likely to remain single forever, repeating the same ritual morning after morning.

Text painting takes over in the two measures after "Flying clouds and railway smoke," as Dring uses vocal material from the beginning of the song, playing with it harmonically. At the words "Rest you there, poor unbelov'd ones," the piano's broken chord figures change to block chords, but only for a moment—probably just long enough for that last gulp of coffee. As the ladies leave to face their workday grind, the broken chord motion begins again, and the autumn wind whirls around the girls' ankles as they run for the trolleybus.

*Camden was the town in which French poet Paul Verlaine wrote his famous poem "Il pleure dans mon cœur."

Song of a Nightclub Proprietress *(Five Betjeman Songs)*   1976
(John Betjeman)

"Song of a Nightclub Proprietress" is one of Dring's best known and most popular songs. It is often used as a recital encore, and has been recorded a number of times.

The scene is a British nightclub, reeking with all the attendant "morning after" smells—a blend of the bar, stale cigarettes, and the occasional piece of food on the floor. To a languid, jazzy piano accompaniment, we are introduced to the proprietress, who has arrived to clean up. She is both a comic and poignant figure. The text of the song is her soliloquy, in which she describes the scene at hand, reminisces about her "glory days," and reveals her touching, frightened insecurities.

Some of the words in the text need an explanation. Kummel was a very sweet, sticky German liqueur ("There was Kummel on the handle of the door"). "Pollies" is short for Apollinaris Water, a bottled thirst-quencher sold in Britain in the 1920s. It was usually found in fashionable, upper-class drinking establishments. It was non-alcoholic, and good for heartburn ("A box of baby 'pollies by the beer").[7]

Extended Study List
Four Night Songs • To the Willow Tree • Sister, awake • Mélisande • It was a lover and his lass • Take, O take those lips away • To Music • Under the greenwood tree • To the Virgins—to Make Much of Time • Come away, death • My proper Bess • The Cuckoo • The Reconcilement • *Love and Time* • Crabbed Age and Youth • Weep you no more, sad fountains

Suggested Reading
Stephen Banfield, "Madeleine Dring," *New Grove Dictionary of Women Composers,* ed. Julie Anne Sadie and Rhian Samuel (New York: Macmillan, 1994).

Wanda Brister, "The Songs of Madeleine Dring: Organizing a Posthumous Legacy," D.M.A. diss., The University of Nevada, Las Vegas, 2004.

Ro Hancock-Child, *Madeleine Dring: Her Music, Her Life* (Tetbury: Micropress, 2000). Out of print. The author is grateful to Dr. Wanda Brister for sharing this material from her personal library.

Alistair Fisher, "The Songs of Madeleine Dring and the evolution of her compositional style," Thesis, University of Hull, 2000.

Victoria Twigg, "Madeleine Dring," Thesis, Trinity College, London, 1982.

Sara Wharton, "Madeleine Dring (1923-1977), profile of a miniaturist," Diss., Royal College of Music, 1977.

Notes
1. Ro Hancock-Child, *Madeleine Dring: Her Music, Her Life,* 15. Quoted from one of the lectures Dring presented at the Centre for Spiritual and Psychological Studies, London, 1975.
2. Wanda Brister, "The Songs of Madeleine Dring: Organizing a Posthumous Legacy," 99.
3. Ro Hancock-Child, 55.
4. Ibid., 27. Dring in a letter to Eugene Hemmer, an American musician with whom she maintained a lively correspondence for the last decade of her life.
5. Ibid., 56.
6. Stephen Banfield, *New Grove Dictionary of Music and Musicians,* 2nd ed.
7. Wanda Brister, "The Songs of Madeleine Dring: Organizing a Posthumous Legacy." In a letter from Roger Lord to Brister, 47.

PETER DICKINSON (b. 1934)

Dickinson is an unusual composer.

—Anthony Payne[1]

Peter Dickinson, composer and teacher, organist, pianist and harpsichordist, conductor, critic and writer, was born in Lancashire from a musical family. His father, the contact lens pioneer Frank Dickinson, was a versatile pianist and church organist, and his sister is the well-known mezzo-soprano Meriel Dickinson. He was Organ Scholar of Queens' College and subsequently spent three years in the United States, including postgraduate studies at the Juilliard School. During this period he met and was influenced by Cage, Cowell and Varèse, and worked as a pianist with the New York City Ballet and as a critic and lecturer.

Dickinson's compositions include orchestral works, chamber music, music for wind and brass, choral music, keyboard works, and songs. His music has been performed worldwide and has been heard regularly on broadcasts and recordings. Dickinson's songs are characterized by a wonderful sense of rhythmic energy and inherent humor. Many of them incorporate jazz idioms. With his sister Meriel Dickinson, he has presented numerous series of successful recitals, broadcasts, and recordings. He is a contributor to *The New Grove Dictionary of American Music*, as well as many other books and periodicals. He gives regular talks for the BBC on a variety of musical topics.

Within the academic world Dickinson founded the Music Department at Keele University, Staffordshire, along with its Centre for American Music, one of the most important centers for the study of American music outside the United States. As first professor and head of the department from 1974 to 1984, he directed graduate and undergraduate programs of teaching and research—unique outside the United State—in popular music and jazz. He is currently Professor Emeritus of Keele University and lives in London.

Three Comic Songs   1972, rev.
(W.H. Auden)

My Second Thoughts • Happy Ending • Over the Heather

These songs are not at all cyclic. They are notable for their very sophisticated humor. Basically tonal, they contain some jazz idioms, especially in the accompaniment of Song 3. The work was first performed by Ian and Jennifer Partridge in a BBC recital broadcast in February 1977, for the 70th anniversary of Auden's birth. The duration of the set is eight minutes.

Extended Study List

Four Poems of Alan Porter (countertenor, harpsichord) • *A Dylan Thomas Song Cycle* (baritone, piano) • *An e. e. cummings Song Cycle* (mezzo-soprano, piano) • *Extravaganzas* (medium voice, piano) • *Surrealist Landscape* (high voice, piano, tape) • *Reminiscences* (mezzo-soprano, piano) • *Schubert in Blue* (mezzo-soprano, piano). Arrangements of Schubert's three Shakespeare songs in jazz style, commissioned for Meriel Dickinson and Christine Croshaw for the 150th anniversary of Schubert's death. First performed at the Wigmore Hall, February, 1978.

Selected Reading

Hugo Cole, "Peter Dickinson," *The New Grove Dictionary of Music and Musicians,* ed. Stanley Sadie (New York: Grove's Dictionaries of Music, 1989).

Roger Norrington, "Peter Dickinson," *Musical Times,* 106:1965, 109.

Anthony Payne, "Peter Dickinson," *Musical Times,* 112:1971, 755.

Notes

1. Anthony Payne, "Peter Dickinson," *Musical Times*, 112: 1971, 755.

ROBIN HOLLOWAY (b. 1943)

I feel a certain vampirism towards the works of art that touch upon my own aesthetic and moral preoccupations.

—Robin Holloway[1]

Robin Holloway has composed numerous song cycles and groups for the voice, the earliest published dating from 1968. In addition, he has written works for small orchestra, chorus and orchestra, concerti for solo instruments, and music for instrumental combinations of all sorts. Composer, librettist, teacher and writer, Holloway is currently Lecturer in Music at Cambridge University. He was educated at King's College, Cambridge, and New College, Oxford.

His early music was predominantly motoric; since 1970, he has tended to mix romantic and modernistic procedures, "laced with a generous range of musical quotations, varying proportions according to genre."[2] To critics of his style of composition, he writes:

I think there's a wonderful thrill about finding that I too can have a go at these things, that they aren't forbidden, that they are possible. Therefore I don't think my composition is imitation or pastiche. It's like the excitement of stumbling upon an old Roman road, and realizing that this was the way across this landscape that used to be used, that everyone understood it, and everyone went that way. And now I can go this way too.[3]

As an author, Holloway is equally prolific. His dissertation was published as *Debussy and Wagner* (London: Eulenburg Books, 1979), and he has contributed numerous articles on opera to books and periodicals, notably on Wagner, Strauss, Berg, and Britten.

Holloway's keen sense of the theatrical has produced several compositions associated with plays and drama. His opera *Clarissa* was finally staged in 1990, fourteen years after its composition. He plans more operatic composition in future, particularly in the comic vein. A partial list of his extensive works for solo voice is found below.

Extended Study List

Four Housman Fragments (soprano, piano) • *Banal Sojourn* (high voice, piano) • *Seven poems of Wallace Stevens* • *Five Little Songs about Death* (unaccomp. soprano). Poems by Stevie Smith • *The Noon's Repose* (tenor, harp). Three songs on poems by Eliot • *The Lovers' Well* (bass-baritone, piano). Poems by Geoffrey Hill • *Wherever We May Be* (soprano, piano). Five poems of Robert Graves • Willow Cycle (tenor, harp). Texts by Shakespeare, Raleigh, and traditional

Selected Reading

Robin Holloway, "Why I Write Music," *Tempo,* 129 (June 1979). Holloway issue.

Bayan Northcott, "Robin (Greville) Holloway," *The New Grove Dictionary of Opera,* ed. Stanley Sadie (New York: Grove's Dictionaries of Music, 1992). Volume 2.

Notes

1. Robin Holloway, "Why I Write Music," *Tempo*, 129 (June 1979).
2. Bayan Northcott, "Robin (Greville) Holloway," *The New Grove Dictionary of Opera*, 2:740.
3. _____, from an interview on BBC Radio 3 "Music Weekly" program, July, 1985. Quoted in "Holloway on Holloway," Boosey & Hawkes composers' brochure.

Italian Song

Italian life and culture is inextricably linked with singing. Opera was born in Italy around 1600, and is still a pervasive part of the Italian spirit. Italians are passionate about opera and about good singing. Pictures of composers appear on national stamps, and streets in every town are named for musicians. Almost every small town has its own lyric theater, and opera is programmed regularly on Italian radio and television.

Early composers wrote for the theater. Accompanied solo song could hardly compete with the grandeur of opera, and so held little interest as a musical form. With few exceptions, art song lay dormant from 1725 to around 1850.

As nationalism blossomed in the mid-nineteenth century, Italian composers began to write folk-like songs with sentimental tunes ("Neapolitan" songs), which became quite popular, but opera continued to dominate the vocal scene with the works of Belllini, Donizetti, Rossini, and Verdi.

In the twentieth century, Italian composers turned again to song composition as part of their music *œuvre*; however, this body of song is highly diverse and reflects widely differing musical approaches. Early in the century composers wrote songs based on traditions inherited from French impressionism, Italian verismo, and German chromaticism.[1] As the century progressed, song composition developed new characteristics, based on Italianate style. Renewed interest in Italian literature and cultural traditions generated new compositions, and composers sought to establish an Italian school of musical composition. Unfortunately, this has not happened, although there are many beautiful Italian art songs worthy of study and performance.

Notes

1. Ruth C. Lakeway and Robert C. White, Jr. *Italian Art Song*, 21.

EARLY ITALIAN SONG

Italian art songs of the seventeenth and eighteenth centuries were showcases for the voice, exploiting its sonorities and technical capabilities. For that reason, these songs show little blend of poetic/musical elements, but are instead skewed toward the voice as the primary performance medium. With rare exceptions, the accompaniment provides support and little more, although it is difficult to make anything but generalized judgments since modern editions are realizations from a figured bass.

Early Italian songs, most from the seventeenth and eighteenth centuries, are frequently used for beginning vocal study as well as on the recital platform. With the exception of Barbara Strozzi, the next group of composers concentrated primarily on opera, and the solo songs we hear most often are excerpted from their longer dramatic works. In the versions generally published for students, both accompaniment and vocal line are often romanticized, thereby losing the essence of the historical period in which these songs were created. The issue is further clouded by the accompaniments, which are realizations or arrangements for the piano keyboard derived from the figured bass. It is important to choose the most authentic published version available.

The term *aria* was first used at the end of the fifteenth century, and in the sixteenth century took on the meaning of *solo song*. In the 1800s, Alessandro Parisotti (1835-1913) researched and edited many vocal works from the seventeenth and eighteenth centuries, publishing them in three volumes arranged for voice and piano titled *Arie Antiche*.* In his preface to the collection, Parisotti described the stylistic characteristics of these works: "The music which composers in the seventeenth and eighteenth centuries wrote was informed above all by structural purity and simplicity, great emotion and a flavor of the sweetest serenity that influenced the entire piece. The music of today is quite the opposite: neurotic, jerky, and full of violent contrasts."

Despite his pronouncements, many nineteenth-century arrangements made of early Italian songs were "editorialized" to suit "modern" (nineteenth century) tastes: harmonies were altered, vocal embellishments were changed or eliminated, tempo markings were adjusted, and accompaniments were "updated" into a romanticized pianistic style.

Arie Antiche has now become a term to define the songs that predate the nineteenth century.

Selected Reading

Carol MacClintock, editor, *The Solo Song,* 1580-1730 (New York: W. W. Norton, 1973).

GIULIO CACCINI (c. 1546-1618)

This art admitteth no mediocrity...

—Giulio Caccini[1]

I believe that he who has a natural bent for singing will perhaps achieve that goal especially desirable in song: to give pleasure.

—Giulio Caccini[2]

Giulio Caccini was a singer, composer, voice teacher, and instrumentalist. He was probably a salaried court musician in Florence and, as such, was an active participant in the theatrical productions held at the Medici court. The Medicis, who were the Dukes of Tuscany, were noted patrons of art. Caccini was a renowned tenor; he often accompanied his performances on the arch lute.

Caccini was also a member of the Camerata of Giovanni de' Bardi, a group of intellectuals, professional artists, and high-ranking amateurs whose meetings influenced sweeping changes in the vocal music of the day. As a member of the Florentine Camerata, Caccini played an active part in formulating the *stile rappresentativo*[3] and the opera. He composed the music to *Euridice*, the first opera appear in print. Caccini also applied the Camerata's new style to the composition of solo vocal music, monodic songs with basso continuo. *Le Nuove Musiche,* published by Caccini in 1602, was the first collection of monodic songs (arias and madrigals) in the new style. In his foreword to this publication, Caccini codified the ornamentation to be used in performing vocal music. His writings greatly influenced the music of the forthcoming monodic period.

Caccini's wife and children were also professional singers. His daughter, Francesca Caccini, respected in her day as a composer, was the first woman to compose opera.

Amarilli, mia bella	Amarilli, my dear one. 1601
(Guarini)	

"Amarilli" is the best-known example from the celebrated collection *Le Nuove Musiche* (1602), the earliest surviving collection of solo song in the new Florentine monodic style. Caccini titled it a *madrigale*, a through-composed piece with uneven phrase lengths. Caccini's preface to this group of songs sets forth the tenets of the new style, including the ornamentation *(gorgia)* used in its performance.[4]

"Amarilli" has an expressive vocal line; each repetition of the beloved's name is set with varying ornamentation. Its form is ABCBC/codetta. It must be numbered as one of the great early art songs.

Tu ch'hai le penne, Amore	O Love, you have wings.
(? Ottavio Rinuccini)	

Ottavio Rinuccini provided libretti to both Jacopo Peri for the first opera, *Dafne* (1597)*, and Monteverdi for his opera *Arianna* (see "Lasciatemi morire").

The text is the ardent plea of a lover to Cupid, imploring him to fly to the breast of his beloved and pledge his heart and soul to her. There are three stanzas of text in this song, set in triple time. Vocal phrases have strong rhythmic word stresses. Some recordings of this song feature a *ritornello* between verses, which helps provide variety of form.

*The score for this work has been lost.

Al fonte, al prato	To the spring, to the meadow.
(Francesco Cini)	

Caccini was himself a virtuoso singer. He fashioned this delightful song in four strophes, giving the voice plenty of chance to embellish the text at key points, using ornamentations set forth in his preface to *Le Nuove Musiche*. Cini's poetry depicts a pastoral scene. The vocal lines are spirited and flexible. Modern performances usually feature a ritornello between verses.

Extended Study List
Belle rose purpurine • Occhi' immortale • O, che felice giorno • Aur' amorosa • Ohimè, se tant' amato • Sfogava con le stele • Udite, amanti

Selected Reading
Barbara R. Hanning, Suzanne G. Cusick, and Susan Parisi, "Caccini: Giulio, Francesca, Settimia," in *The New Grove Dictionary of Opera*, ed. Stanley Sadie (New York: Grove's Dictionaries of Music, 1992). Volume 1.

Carol MacClintock, ed., *The Solo Song 1580-1730* (New York: W. W. Norton, 1973). "To the Performer," and Part I.

George Newton, "*Le Nuove Musiche*—Caccini," *The NATS Bulletin*, 19:2 (December 1962).

Notes

1. Excerpted from Giulio Caccini, Foreword to *Le Nuove Musiche* (1602), in *Source Readings in Music History : The Baroque Era*, selected and annotated by Oliver Strunk (New York: W. W. Norton, 1965), 21.
2. Foreword to *Le nuove musiche e nuova maniera di scriverle* (*Le Nuove Musiche*, second book, 1614).
3. *Stile rappresentativo* (theatrical style) was a term applied to early seventeenth-century theatrical works; the style employed a declamatory rhythm over a slow harmonic motion. The term appeared in print for the first time on the title page of Caccini's opera *Euridice* (1600).

   There is some confusion about the differences between *stile recitativo*, *stile espressivo*, and *stile rappresentativo*. The differences remain, but in general the last term was used for the stage; *recitativo* approximates today's recitative, and *espressivo* seems to have denoted pieces with heightened emotional content (for example, Monteverdi's *Lamento d'Arianna*). *Stile rapprensentativo* seems to be the term of choice to denote the general qualities of the new vocal style with its heightened emotional and dramatic qualities.
4. Caccini's *gorgia accento* (accent), an apoggiatura on a strong beat for emotional effect; *cascata* (fall), running included the ornamental passages, usually with a range of an octave; *passaggi*, the "filling in" of notes between intervallic skips; *gruppo*, which resembles the modern trill, using adjacent notes; *trillo*, a rapid repetition of one note, a "beating" of the throat; *esclamazione*, a crescendo on a long note; and *crescere e scemare della voce*, a crescendo-descrescendo (also known as *messa di voce*).

CLAUDIO MONTEVERDI (1567-1643)

It was opera's good fortune that there should appear so soon a composer whose outlook was essentially dramatic.

—Gustav Kobbé[1]

Let the word be master of the melody, not its slave.

—Claudio Monteverdi[2]

Monteverdi's operas are the earliest example of the genre still performed regularly. Utilizing the new expressive recitative, Monteverdi created a sophisticated melodic treatment that emphasized dramatic and emotional content as well as correct accentuation of the text. He effectively combined the theatrical and compositional techniques of the Renaissance with the new techniques of the *stile rappresentativo*, drawing on his madrigals and dance forms, synthesizing them in a highly theatrical way.

Monteverdi served in the Mantuan court and in Venice, as the Maestro di Capella of San Marco and a composer for the theatre. In Mantua, he wrote three of his twenty-one works for the theatre. His works may be considered the culmination of a great period of change in vocal music. *Orfeo* is generally regarded as the first masterpiece in the history of opera, and, in effect, Monteverdi founded a new school of opera; the remainder of Monteverdi's surviving operas are remarkable for their exploration of human personalities and emotions.

Lasciatemi morire
Lamento d'Arianna from *Arianna*. 1608
(Ottavio Rinuccini)

Let me die.

Arianna was Monteverdi's second opera, composed one year after *Orfeo*. The complete score of *Arianna* is lost; of all the music for *Arianna*, we know only the heroine's lament, which Monteverdi later called "the most essential part of the work."[3]

According to Grout, "This song was probably the most celebrated monodic composition of the early seventeenth century and was declared by Gagliano to be a living modern example of the power of ancient (that is, Greek) music, since it was said to have moved the audience to tears."[4] The lament was widely circulated, published in several forms by the composer—solo song, five-part madrigal and, later, a sacred monody with the title *Pianto della Madonna*. Its success helped to establish laments as a regular feature of later operas.[5]

Monteverdi's penchant for natural declamation is seen clearly in the vocal lines—grave and sustained, but held with dissonances against the accompaniment for tension and dramatic passion. True to his statement about the paramount importance of the word, the significance of the words dictates the melodic line. High and low pitches are employed for dramatic effect in the first two short vocal phrases. The structural and musical innovations of Monteverdi's early works became staples for the development of opera.

Con che soavità, labbra odorate   **With what delight, o fragrant lips. 1619**
(Guarini)

Around 1570, the professional solo singer began to emerge as an important part of musical life. This piece is designated as *Concertato* a una voce e 9 instrumenti*.[6] In its original form there were three groups of instruments accompanying the voice at various times.

Monteverdi composed this work twelve years after his opera *La Favola* d'*Orfeo* (1607). It is an example of his skill in integrating music with text. The vocal writing is a mixture of recitative and arioso styles. Like the solo madrigal, single or short phrases are repeated and used to build to a climax through sequences. ("Con che soavità"; "Ma se godo un piacer," etc.). Monteverdi employs changes of tempo and rhythmic structure throughout, as well as suspensions, dotted rhythms, and short imitative motives.

*Concertato was a term used occasionally in the early seventeenth century in connection with various musical works based on the principle of "contrast" or "rivalry."

Extended Study List

Ahi, troppo è duro • Interrotte speranze • Illustratevi, o cieli (*Il Ritorna d'Ulisse in Patria*) • Disprezzata Regina (*L'Incoronazione di Poppea*) • Quel sguardo sdegnosetta • Tempro la Cetra • Partenza amorosa • Se i languidi miei sguardi • Sento un certo non so che • Ecco di dolci raggi • Eri già tutta mia

Selected Reading

Denis Arnold, *Monteverdi* (London: Dent, 1963).
Paolo Fabbri, *Monteverdi*, trans. Tim Carter (Cambridge: Cambridge University Press, 1994). Originally published in Italian as *Monteverdi* (E.D.T. Edizioni di Torino, Turin, 1985).

Notes

1. Gustav Kobbé, *The Definitive Kobbé's Opera Book*, ed., revised and updated by The Earl of Harewood, 3.
2. Quoted in *Composers on Music*, ed. by Sam Morgenstern, 19.
3. Quoted in Paolo Fabbri, *Monteverdi*, trans.Tim Carter, 93.
4. Donald Jay Grout, *A Short History of Opera*, 3rd ed., 65-66.
5. John Whenham, "Claudio Monteverdi," *The New Grove Dictionary of Opera*, ed. Stanley Sadie, 1992, v.3, 448.
6. G. Francesco Malipiero, ed., *Complete Works of Claudio Monteverdi*, v. 7 (Vienna: Universal Editions, 1926-1942).

BARBARA STROZZI (1619-1664)

> I must reverently consecrate this first work, which as a woman I publish
> all too boldly, to the Most August Name of Your Highness so that, under
> an oak of gold it may rest secure against the lightning bolts of slander
> prepared for it.
>
> —Barbara Strozzi, in the dedication to Op. 1
> for the grand duchess of Tuscany[1]

Barbara Strozzi was one of the most prolific and gifted composers of secular
vocal music in her century. Strozzi, the daughter (probably illegitimate) of poet-
librettist Giulio Strozzi, was adopted by him at age nine, lived with him all her life,
and was his sole heir. She was encouraged in her musical career by her father, who
had collaborated with Monteverdi and other established Venetian musicians. Giulio
Strozzi created the "Academia degli Unisoni" (the group of similar thinkers) which
met regularly at his house, its membership composed of poets, historians, philoso-
phers, and writers of the day. Barbara had the advantage of built-in audiences for her
compositions, which she performed, accompanying herself on the lute. During her
lifetime, over 100 of her compositions were published between 1644 and 1664.

There is speculation in printed sources (principally anonymous satires of that
time) as to Strozzi's morals; Venetian traditions often linked music-making and
courtesans. Strozzi is one of the few women of her period to have pursued a career
as a composer and achieved public recognition for her efforts; the preservation of
her music is highly unusual and gives credence to her work. Francesca Caccini
(1589-c. 1640), daughter of composer Giulio Caccini, was the only other woman
singer-composer of that time to have some measure of fame.

At that time, Venice was the operatic capital of Italy; the first public opera
house opened there in 1637, and the demand for new works never abated. Claudio
Monteverdi, Antonio Cesti, and Pier Francesco Cavalli were working there. Strozzi
tutored privately with Cavalli, but wrote no operas; her compositions are essentially secular arias and cantatas, designed for performance in private drawing rooms
for an elite, intelligent audience. Her arias are usually brief and in strophic form
or variations; the cantatas are longer and highly contrasted in form and vocal
articulations. Cantata format permitted a variety of dramatic expression and
musical contrasts; composers of the seventeenth century, including Strozzi, used it
with increasing frequency as the century progressed.

Strozzi's vocal works are marked by theatrical temperament and somewhat
virtuosic treatment of the voice; Strozzi herself was a highly accomplished singer.
Her scores are carefully marked with performance indications: tempo, dynamics,
and ornamentation. She chose lyrical poetry that often dealt with the theme of
unrequited love, setting texts in free forms. Strozzi's songs are marked by text
painting and skillful—often novel—handling of form. Her songs employed the *stile
concitato*, a style of heightened excitement and passion.

Amor, non dormir più   **Love, do not sleep anymore.**

Alternation between refrain and verse marks the form of this aria. The singer
makes a somewhat disgusted plea to love (Cupid?) to awake and satisfy her longing.

Non pavento io non di te — I am not afraid of you.

This is a multi-sectioned *da capo aria*, with free recitative sections interleaved between the opening refrain. Strozzi employs characteristic word painting in the line "La mia fe costante" (my constant faith); "Arma, arma" (arm yourself) is set in emphatic *concitato* style. Like many of Strozzi's texts, this one was probably written especially for her. This cantata is dedicated to one Giovanni Antonio Forni; the words might contain a hidden message from Strozzi to Forni.

Tradimento! — Betrayal! 1659
(Giovanni Tani)

This aria an excellent example of the *stile concitato*. Its vivid opening features a one-word refrain, "Tradimento!" that appears again before the second stanza and also concludes the work. The accompaniment is varied with each repetition. The poem has three stanzas, each with different emotional content. The last stanza uses a motive from the opening refrain ("Tradimento!").

Strozzi uses text painting on the words *legarmi* (to tie me), *incaterarmi* (to imprison me), and *lusinga* (entices).

Spesso per entro al petto — Often a little something passes through my heart.
(Cicognini)

There are three stanzas in this delightful strophic song; the text describes the pangs of love. Strozzi set the teasing verses with a vocal line featuring melismas leading to the key word in each stanza. The melismas curve through displaced stresses and land on the targeted word—*martire* (pain), *tormenta* (torments), and *furor* (madness)—a rhythmic treatment illustrative of the sensual torments of love. Each verse ends with a staccato refrain to a couplet of text: "Sarebbe pur da ridere/che fossse il mal d'amor" (How laughable it would be/If this were the sickness of love).

Extended Study List
Amore è bandito • Lagrime mie • Che si può fare? • Voglio morire • Soccorrete, luci avare • Gite, o giorni dolente • Rissolvetevi pensieri • Chi brama in amore • Luci belle, deh, ditemi perchè • A donna bella e crudele • Amor non si fugge • La fanciulletta semplice

Selected Reading
Jane Berdes, "The Women Musicians of Venice," in *Eighteenth-Century Women and the Arts,* ed. Frederick M. Kenner and Susan Lorsch. Contributions in Women's Studies No. 98 (New York: Greenwood Press, 1988).

Jane Bowers, "Women Composers in Italy, 1566-1700," in *Women Making Music,* ed. Jane Bowers and Judith Tick (Chicago: University of Illinois Press, 1986).

Candace Magner, "Barbara Strozzi: A Documentary Perspective, A Catalog of Works," in *Journal of Singing,* 58:5 (May/June 2002), 393-403.

Carol Plantamura and Jürgen Hübscher. Liner notes for *La Musica,* LP recording (Leonarda Records, LP 123, 1985). This recording features Strozzi, Francesca Caccini, Settimia Caccini, Sigismondo d'India, Alessandro Piccinini, Francesca Campana, Fabritio Coros, and Giovanni Kapsperger.

Ellen Rosand, "Barbara Strozzi, *virtuosissima cantatrice:* The Composer's Voice," in *Journal of the American Musicological Society* 31:2, 1978, 241-281.

_____, "The Voice of Barbara Strozzi," *Women Making Music,* ed. Jane Bowers and Judith Tick (Chicago: University of Illinois Press, 1986).

Glenda Simpson. Liner notes to *Glenda Simpson Sings Barbara Strozzi* (Hyperion Records Ltd. compact disc CDA 66303, 1989).

Notes

1. Quoted in Ellen Rosand, "The Voice of Barbara Strozzi," *Women Making Music*, ed. Jane Bowers and Judith Tick, 174.

ALESSANDRO SCARLATTI (1660-1725)

His own happy combination of strength and sweetness, of passion and humor, was not to be heard again in music until the time of Mozart.

—Donald Jay Grout[1]

Alessandro Scarlatti is credited with the creation of Neapolitan opera, a style that supplanted Venetian opera as the dominant form of the genre toward the end of the seventeenth century; however, research has shown that this assessment is somewhat overblown, and that Scarlatti is more correctly one of the last masters of older traditions rather than the intiator of a new style. His son, Domenico (1685-1757), composed over 600 harpsichord sonatas.

Scarlatti was able to pull together all the principles of the prevailing vocal style and mesh them into his own musical aesthetic. He turned his primary efforts toward composing for the stage, where the glamour of theater and drama with music, coupled with the public's fondness for virtuosity and display, attracted composers' major efforts.

Scarlatti composed about eighty-five operas. In them, comic roles appeared with regularity, and comic scenes featured realistic dialogue and local dialect. The new Italian overture firmly established itself in these works, which also featured greater emphasis on vocal ensembles, a larger orchestra with increased musical involvement in the drama, and the development of accompanied recitative. High Baroque aria style featured repetitive texts, motivic development, challenging vocalization, *da capo* construction, and tonal unity.[2]

Emphasis upon theatrical elements in opera spilled over into song composition. Musical and dramatic expression took precedence over fidelity to the text. The lyric beauty of the voice was paramount. Scarlatti's songs number around 200 and are among the best of the genre of that period. In addition to the prevalent characteristics of vocal music, he added a sweetness and fluidity of melody that sets his songs apart.

O cessate di piagarmi (*Pompeo.* 1683)   **O cease to wound me.**
(Nicola Minato)

There are two strophes to this plaintive lament ("O cease to wound me, or allow me to die"). The second is to be sung more slowly than the first. The melodic line moves stepwise, veering into larger intervals to color selected words ("lasciatemi/sorde"). The accompaniment (as realized by Parisotti) is a swaying barcarole of divided chords, with an insistent bass line. The constant movement of the accompaniment figures and the tension of the closely pitched vocal line sustains the mood of despair.

Pompeo was an early opera of Scarlatti. Its plot, like most of his operatic libretti, was based on ancient Roman history.

Le Violette (*Pirro e Demetrio.* 1694)   **The violets.**
(Adriano Morselli)

"Le Violette" is fresh, charming, and pastoral in mood. The words "violette" and "graziose" are repeated numerous times, in light staccato descending melodic sequences. Scarlatti's melody is simple and almost folk-like; melodic material from the vocal line is echoed by the accompaniment throughout in playful repetition.

Pirro e Demetrio was one of Scarlatti's most successful operas, composed in Naples during his appointment as musical director to the Spanish viceroy there.

Già il sole dal Gange (*L'Honestà negli amori.* 1680)   **The Sun on the Ganges.**
(Felice Parnasso)

The words to this *canzonetta* celebrate the dethroning of the night by the glory of the sun, sparkling on the river Ganges. The opera from which this piece is derived is set in Algeria in North Africa. John Glenn Paton observes that "dal Gange" is merely a figure of speech meaning the east.[3] Scarlatti composed this opera (his second) at age nineteen. This is one of Scarlatti's best-known and much-performed arias. Its strongly rhythmic, spirited melody is set in two strophes, which are tiny ABA forms.

Extended Study List
Toglietemi la vita ancor • Sento nel core • Chi vuole innamorarsi • Se Florindo è fedele • All' acquisto di gloria • Su, venite a consiglio • Son tutta duolo • Spesso vibra per suo gioco

Notes
1. Donald Jay Grout, *A Short History of Opera,* 3rd edition, 181.
2. Donald Ivey, *Song: Anatomy, Imagery, and Styles,* 161.
3. In the opera, the aria is sung by a page boy, Saldino, who is admiring the sunrise. John Glenn Paton, ed. *Twenty-Six Italian Songs and Arias,* 34.

ANTONIO VIVALDI (1676-1741)

One of his most important assets as an instrumental composer was his sense of the dramatic—something clearly apparent from his operatic scores.

—Eric Cross [1]

Venetian composer Antonio Vivaldi was one of the most important musical figures of his day. His fame as a composer was international and he was also acclaimed as a solo violinist. He was an extremely prolific composer, writing quantities of church music and operas, and over 450 concertos for various instruments. He composed sixty-three operas.

Vivaldi was extremely inventive with the *ritornello* sections in his concertos, as Handel would prove to be with the *da capo* aria form. Vivaldi's music is strongly diatonic, structured on tonic-dominant progressions, but he employed chromaticism—particularly diminished 7ths and Neapolitan and augmented 6th chords—for dramatic purposes.

His operas were produced throughout Italy—in Venice, Florence, Mantua, Milan, and Rome—as well as in Europe in Vienna and Prague. Vivaldi was an important figure in the formation of preclassical and classical style.

Agitata da due venti (*Griselda*. 1735)	**Buffeted by two winds.**
(Apostolo Zeno, adapted by Carlo Goldoni)	

Zeno's libretto *Griselda* was one of the most popular of all eighteenth-century librettos, and was set by numerous composers, among them, Alessandro Scarlatti. Vivaldi wrote the leading role for a contralto; it was sung by Anna Girò (see "Qual favellar?..."Anderò, volerò, griderò"). Griselda's arias are stunning vocal display pieces, filled with nonstop coloratura passages, large interval leaps, and vocal calisthenics of all types. The emotional state of the character was embodied in these vocal acrobatics. Vivaldi's operas contain a number of "storm" arias of this type, in which the stormy sea is illustrated in the vocal writing as well as by agitated orchestral figures. With its two-octave range, wide interval leaps, and quicksilver *passaggi* for the voice, this aria is a tour de force for the singer. It is a wonderful example of the vocal style of the Baroque period.

The combination of lightness of tone and fullness of sound gave the *bel canto* technique its characteristic sound of *chiaroscuro* (literally, light/dark) or *impasto* (paste). This indicated a full sound, but always with a brightness or "point" to the tone, which could execute all ornaments clearly and flexibly. A term used during Vivaldi and Handel's day was "folding up the voice with lightness."[2]

Qual favellar?...Anderò, volerò, griderò	**What has he said?...**
(***Orlando finto pazzo***. 1714)	**I shall go, I shall fly, I shall shout.**
(Grazio Bracciolo)	

This aria is notable for the recitative that precedes it, in which Origille finds the lifeless bodies of her beloved Grifone and of Tigrinda—killed by the sorceress Ersilla. Vivaldi's recitative contains mercurial changes of emotion that build naturally to the aria. The aria, "Anderò, volerò, griderò," is a whirlwind *Presto*, accompanied by a pulsating orchestral accompaniment. It is an excellent example of the declamatory style of vocal writing that Vivaldi used in many of his operas, notably those written for the voice of Anna Girò.[3]

Anna Girò was an Italian contralto who, from 1726 onward, created leading roles in Vivaldi's operas. There was speculation that she became Vivaldi's mistress, but this was never proved. Her dramatic ability was highly praised, but some contemporary accounts of her singing characterized it as rather weak.

Dite, oimè (*La fida ninfa*. 1732)   **Tell me, alas.**
(Scipione Maffei)

This aria and the one that follows are from *La fida ninfa,* an opera based on the libretto of a Veronese nobleman, Scipione Maffei. Vivaldi was invited to Verona to compose the opera, which was presented at the new Teatro Filarmonico, designed by the famous architect Francesco Bibiena.

This aria reveals Vivaldi's gentle lyricism. Accompanied by only a simple bass continuo, the beautiful lament features a vocal line that might have come from one of the slow movements of one of Vivaldi's concertos.

Alma oppressa (*La fida ninfa*. 1732)   **A soul weighed down.**
(Scipione Maffei)

This is a *da capo* aria (ABA). After the opening orchestral *ritornello*, the A section begins with the voice sustaining a single note *messa di voce**, on the fifth note of the scale, and then descending by steps to the tonic note ("Alma oppressa"). The aria proper then begins in a lively tempo, with florid vocal phrases that highlight important words in the text. Orchestral figures maintain forward motion and dramatic mood.

In the B section, Vivaldi employs text painting on the word *catene* (chains) in the form of syncopated interval leaps in the vocal line. The return of the A section is preceded by the ritornello and the opening vocal phrase "Alma oppressa," but both are now varied slightly for interest.

*Messa di voce evolved from the *esclamazione* of Caccini. It was the ability to *crescendo* and *diminuendo* on one note in any part of the range.

Extended Study List

Cessate, omai cessate • Sventurata navicella • Gelido in ogni vena • Di trombe guerriere • Dopo un'orrida procella • Di due rai languir costante • Zeffiretti, che sussurrate • O di tua man mi svena • Filli di gioia vuoi farmi morir • Piango, gemo • Ingrata si mi svena • Pur ch'a te grata

Selected Reading

H. Robbins Landon, *Vivaldi, Voice of the Baroque* (New York: Thames and Hudson, 1993).
Michael Talbot, *Vivaldi* (New York: Oxford University Press, 2000). Master Musicians Series, ed. Stanley Sadie.

Notes

1. Eric Cross, "Antonio Vivaldi," in *The New Grove Dictionary of Opera*, ed. Stanley Sadie, vol. 4, 1026.
2. In Andrew Stewart, liner notes *Cecilia Bartoli-Live in Italy*, London Records 289 455 981-2 LH, 1998.
3. Claudio Oesele, trans. Andrew Huth, liner notes to *The Vivaldi Album*, trans. Andrew Huth. Cecilia Bartoli, mezzo-soprano; Il Giardino Armonico, Giovanni Antonini, conductor. Decca 289 466 569-2 DH, 1999.

FRANCESCO DURANTE (1684-1755)

Francesco Durante was an eminent composer of the eighteenth century and the head of the Neapolitan school. Durante, a pupil of Alessandro Scarlatti, was in turn the teacher of Giovanni Pergolesi and many other musician-composers. He replaced Porpora as professor at the Conservatory of Loreto and succeeded Scarlatti as professor at the Conservatory of San Onofrio. He was well known for his liturgical compositions and for his writings on music. His compositions, while not as inspired as those of his teacher Scarlatti, are nonetheless well constructed and have graceful melodies. Durante wrote no operas.

Danza, danza fanciulla gentile   **Dance, dance gentle maiden.**
(Lorenzo Pagans)

Gently moving vocal phrases evoke the graceful movements of the dancing girl, as well as the soft rhythms of the sea by which she dances. Vocal phrases are full of ascending and descending scale patterns in sequences and melismas, all perpetuating the feeling of dance steps. This song is often performed with too vigorous a style; it should never lose its sense of graceful charm.

This melody appears without text in *Solfèges d'Italie* (No. 113), a collection of *solfeggi* composed for use as exercises by Italian singing teachers of the seventeenth and eighteenth centuries. Words were often added later.[1]

Extended Study List
Vergin, tutto amor

Notes
1. John Glenn Paton quotes this collection as the source for this song and also for Durante's "Vergin tutto amor." A copy of the first edition is in the Boston Public Library. The text appeared in a collection of verse titled *Echos d'Italie*, Lorenzo Pagans, ed. In *Twenty-Six Italian Songs and Arias*, John Glenn Paton ed. (Van Nuys, CA: Alfred Publishing, 1991), 104, 100.

GEORGE FRIDERIC HANDEL (1685-1759)

He did not revolutionize operatic form but he brought the novelty of his genius to the genre as he found it.

—The Oxford Dictionary of Music[1]

George Frideric Handel was one of the most prolific composers in the history of music. In his lifetime, he was the outstanding composer of opera in Europe. He cannot be called a composer of art songs (although he did write a small number), but he wrote nearly 1,000 solos in his operas, oratorios, and cantatas.[2] Many of these arias have entered the recital repertory and the voice studio as staples of vocal literature apart from their operatic settings. Sergius Kagen observed that Handel's adroit manner of writing for the voice makes his arias interchangeable between voice types; for example, tenor to soprano, bass and baritone to mezzo-soprano, and vice versa.[3]

Handel had an acute sense of theatricality and an exceptional—almost intuitive—understanding of the voice. He composed arias of extraordinary beauty, using the *da capo* aria form for many of them. Within the *da capo* structure, Handel devised a variety of modifications, which added interest and variety. He employed other aria forms as well: through-composed arias; arias in *rondo* form; arias in two-part (AB) form; and arias based on dance rhythms.

Working within the *opera seria* form, Handel developed the large dramatic scene which combined recitatives, arias, and often orchestral preludes, into one unified whole. He used the *da capo* form (ABA) for the majority of his arias, but within this structure, he devised a variety of modifications, that added interest and variety.

In the past fifty years, Handel operas have been produced more frequently on the opera stages of the world. A performance of a Handel opera is an evening of almost inexhaustible melody, miraculously scored and full of individuality.

Ombra mai fu (*Serse.* 1738)   **Never was shade so beloved.**
(Librettist unknown)
(After S. Stampiglia, Rome, 1694, based on N. Minato).

Serse was one of Handel's last operas. It was not successful in his lifetime, and closed after five performances. It is best remembered for its beautiful opening aria, "Ombra mai fu," but its score offers many other musical delights as well. *Serse* is an interesting blend of satire and passion. Lighter in style than some of Handel's other operas, it is somewhat unique in his operatic output.

As Act I begins, the Persian king Serse (Xerxes) is revealed in a magnificent garden with a summerhouse on the side. In his opening aria, he addresses his beloved and magnificent plane tree, admiring its beauty and luxuriant shade.

The form of the aria is through-composed, featuring melting vocal lines. This is one of the most famous of Handel's melodies, and is often performed as an instrumental piece with the title "Largo from *Xerxes.*"

Lusinghe più care (*Alessandro.* 1726)   **Sweetest flattery.**
(Libretto by Paolo Antonio Rolli,
based on Ortensio Mauro's *La superbia*)

*Alessandro** was the ninth opera that Handel wrote for the Royal Academy of Music. It was also the first work he wrote for the voices of rival sopranos Francesca Cuzzoni and Faustina Bordoni. Handel composed five operas in which the leading roles were taken by these "dueling sopranos."

During the Baroque period, the love for decoration produced a profusion of ornaments in vocal music. *Da capo* aria structure invited the use of ornaments. Scales, trills, repeated notes, octave leaps, and syncopation were all clichés in virtuoso singing. "Lusinghe più care" is a bravura aria, designed to display the singer's range and agility and to indulge the singer's powers of vocal display.

*The Alexander of the opera's title refers to Alexander the Great.

| Ah! mio cor (*Alcina.* 1728) | Ah! my heart. |

(Librettist unknown. After *L'isola de Alcina*, based on Ariosto, *Orlando furioso*)

Alcina was one of the greatest and most popular of Handel's later operas. It had eighteen performances during the period 1735-1737. This opera was influenced by French opera; its music is light, graceful, and less dramatic than Handel's usual style. *Alcina* was notable for its onstage spectacle, featuring impressive scenic transformations.

The sorceress Alcina lures heroes to her enchanted island and transforms them into trees, rocks, streams, or wild beasts. The knight Ruggiero is her latest conquest, but is not yet transformed. Ruggiero, in his bewitched passion for Alcina, forgets duty and his love for Bradamante, his wife. Disguised, Bradamante comes in search of Ruggiero. In the course of the opera, Ruggiero's eyes are opened; he breaks free from Alcina, and with the aid of superior magic, destroys her spells and the island, and rescues all prisoners.

In the aria "Ah! mio cor," Alcina confesses her love for Ruggiero. The vocal phrases are short, broken fragments, illustrating heartbeats or teardrops, accompanied by halting figures in the orchestra. In a spirited B section, Alcina remembers that she has power to punish Ruggiero.

| Verdi prati (*Alcina.* 1728) | Verdant meadows. |

(Librettist unknown. After *L'isola de Alcina*, based on Ariosto, *Orlando furioso*)

Ruggiero has been rescued by Bradamante, but he cannot help feeling a pang of regret as he looks back at the verdant green meadows and charming woods that will soon be lost. Ruggiero bids farewell to Alcina's magic island (see "Ah! mio cor") in this well-known *cantabile* aria of great beauty and lyricism.

"Verdi prati" is in *rondo* form (Orchestral *ritornello*/ABACA/*Ritornello* repeated), using the alternating sections to illustrate Ruggiero's changing emotions. The aria is constructed in *saraband* rhythm. Vocal phrases are simple and stunningly beautiful; the voice is doubled by the strings throughout, highlighting the melody. Carestimi, the castrato who first sang Ruggiero, initially rejected this aria because of its simplicity.

| Lascia ch'io pianga (*Rinaldo.* 1711, rev. 1717, 1731) | Leave me to weep. |

(Giacomo Rossi, trans. by A. Hill
Based on Tasso, *La Gerusalemme liberata*)

Rinaldo was Handel's first opera for London. He had two librettists for this opera, one Italian, the other English. The Italian Giacomo Rossi, wrote the first text, and Aaron Hill (Manager of the Queen's Theatre) translated and adapted it. Hill's translation incorporated English stage traditions and the conventions of British semi-operas (see Purcell). Two-thirds of Handel's music for this opera derives from his earlier Italian works.

Hill was also interested in enhancing the role of stage machinery, providing the type of effects associated with the style of the English masque. *Rinaldo* succeeded due to its onstage spectacles. These included dragons belching fire, and thunder and lightning. The most spectacular effect involved releasing cages of live sparrows into the theater. Joseph Addison, in his commentary in *A Spectator*, wrote about the tiny birds:

> There have been so many flights...let loose in this Opera, that it is feared the House will never get rid of them, and that in other Plays they may make their Entrance in very wrong and improper Scenes...besides the inconveniences which the Heads of the Audience may sometimes suffer from them.[4]

In this famous aria, Almirena laments her captivity. It is composed in a slow *saraband* dance rhythm (triple time with a secondary accent on the second beat). This rhythm lends a nobility and grace to the vocal phrases.

Laments were often the musical highlight of the opera, with the most organized formal structure. Handel borrowed this air from his opera *Almira* (1705), but fits it neatly into its new dramatic slot.

Extended Study

In *La flora*, vol. 3: (Dammi pace • Deh! Lasciatemi • Scorta rea • Sorge nel petto • Alma, sospira • Un momento di contento) • V'adoro, pupille (*Giulio Cesare*) • Svegliatevi nel core (*Giulio Cesare*) • Care selve (*Atalanta*) • Ritorna, o caro (*Rodelinda*) • Và godendo vezzoso e bello (*Serse*) • Si tra i ceppi (*Berenice*) • Furibondo spira il vento (*Partenope*) • Del minacciar del vento (*Ottone*) • Alma mia (*Floridante*)

Selected Reading

Donald Burrows, *Handel* (Oxford: Oxford University Press, 1994).
_____, *The Cambridge Companion to Handel* (Cambridge: Cambridge University Press, 1997).
Winton Dean, *The New Grove Handel* (New York: Norton, 1983).
_____, and J. Merrill Knapp, *Handel's Operas, 1704-1726* (New York: Oxford University Press, 1987).
Jonathan Keates, *Handel: The Man and His Music* (London: Victor Gollancz, 1992).
Paul Henry Lang, *George Frederic Handel* (New York: W.W. Norton, 1966).
Mary Ann Parker-Hale, *G.F. Handel: A Guide to Research* (New York: Garland, 1988).
Carol Schaub, "A Guide to Handel's London." *Choral Journal* 28:2 (1987): 32-40.

Notes

1. Michael Kennedy, *The Oxford Dictionary of Music*, 2nd edition (New York: Oxford University Press, 1994), 383.
2. Berton Coffin, *Singer's Repertoire, Vol. 5* (Metuchen, NJ: Scarecrow Press, 1962), 62.
3. Sergius Kagen, *Music for the Voice*, rev. ed. (Bloomington: Indiana University Press, 1968), 179.
4. Quoted in Anthony Hicks, liner notes to *Handel: Rinaldo*. Decca 289 467 087-2, 2000.

GIOVANNI BATTISTA PERGOLESI (1710-1736)

The truthful declamation of his songs is as indestructible as nature.
—André Grétry[1]

Giovanni Battista Pergolesi lived a scant twenty-six years. His initial efforts in composing for the stage produced only modest successes and the discouraged Pergolesi abandoned opera to enter the service of the Prince of Stigliano Colonna, for whom he composed thirty-odd sonatas for two violins and bass. In 1732, he turned again to opera, composing a comic work in the Neapolitan dialect, *Lo frate innamorato*, which was an immediate success. The twenty-three-year-old composer followed this with a serious opera, *Il prigioniero superbo,* for which he composed two *intermezzi* titled *La serva padrona*. *La serva padrona* was Pergolesi's masterpiece. Its highly compressed style helped clarify and synthesize the emerging form of *opera buffa*, and its fame ignited one of opera history's most famous wars—the celebrated *Querelle des bouffons*. The tiny work continues to be performed today, over 250 years after its first performance. Its arias are excellent examples of Pergolesi's gift for composing sparkling melodies in a fresh style.

There is continuing controversy about whether the song annotated here is the work of Pergolesi.[2] Nonetheless, it is one of the most widely performed of the *arie antiche*.

Se tu m'ami, se sospiri	**If you love me, if you sigh for me.**
(Paolo Antonio Rolli)	

This *arietta* is a charming example of Pergolesi's melodic style. Its vocal lines are graceful and simple. Tonality in the ABA form begins in the minor; the B section is in the major key, migrating back to the minor for the *da capo*. The four-measure passage that introduces the repeat of A uses a variant figure drawn from a vocal phrase in the first section ("Ma se pensi..."). The playful text describes the hapless suit of a shepherd who is told by his lady love that he is by no means alone in his pursuit of her favors, and that she does not intend to change.

Extended Study List

Nina (often titled "Tre giorni," this song is attributed to Vincenzo Ciampi [1719-1762]) • Stizzoso, mio stizzoso (*La serva padrona*) • A Serpina penserete (*La serva padrona*) • Confusa, smarrita, spiegar-ti vorrei (*Catone*) • Sempre in contrasti (*La serva padrona*) • Mentre dormi, amor fomenti • Ogni pena più spietata • Gemo in un punto e fremo (*L'Olimpiade*)

Selected Reading

Marvin E. Paymer and Hermine W. Williams, *Giovanni Battista Pergolesi: A Guide to Research* (New York: Garland Publishing Co., 1989).

Notes

1. Quoted in Marvin E. Paymer and Hermine W. Williams, *Giovanni Battista Pergolesi: A Guide to Research*, xii.
2. This song is now termed spurious, composed by Alessandro Parisotti, who attributed it to Pergolesi.

CHRISTOPH WILLIBALD GLUCK (1714-1787)*

> I have striven to restrict music to its true office of serving poetry...
> —Christoph Willibald Gluck[1]

Christoph Willibald Gluck, like Handel and Mozart, was an internationally renowned composer of his time. He was a German of Bohemian heritage, although he composed few works in German. He was educated in Italy, lived most of his life in Vienna, and created many of his greatest works in Paris. He has been called "the father of German opera,"[2] though his operas are written primarily to Italian and French texts. His song output is slender—nine odes of Friedrich Gottlieb Kopstock.

Essentially a dramatist, Gluck's musical career was centered in opera. His great historical importance was his role in the "reform" of operatic style of the day. With the opera *Orfeo ed Euridice*, Gluck and his librettist Ranieri de' Calzabigi established a new balance between music and drama and helped to purge opera of unrestricted practices and overblown productions, which had grown so excessive they threatened to submerge musical elements completely. Dramatic truth was sacrificed willy-nilly to florid vocal style and the whims and egos of singers who sought only to show their vocal prowess.[3]

In his quest for dramatic naturalness, declamation was supremely important, and Gluck's great gift for melody transformed arias into dramatically powerful utterances. Characterizations became human, plot lines were simpler, and music was stripped of unnecessary frills. Chorus, dance, and scenic effects were all turned towards one goal, integrated dramatic clarity. Gluck managed to bring together Italian melodic grace, German solemnity, and the elegant magnificence of the French operatic style.

Gluck composed over fifty lyrical dramas, but is primarily known for his reform operas: *Orfeo ed Euridice, Alceste, Paride ed Elena, Iphigénie en Aulide.* The aria below is from one of these, *Paride ed Elena,* and has become a standard of eighteenth-century song literature collections.

*Although Gluck's nationality would place him on the list of German composers, his song "O del mio dolce ardor" has become a classic among early Italian songs. For that reason it appears in this group of songs.

O del mio dolce ardor *(Paride ed Elena)*   **O you, my own true love. 1769**
(Ranieri de' Calzabigi)

Paride ed Elena was the third of the so-called reform operas and marked Gluck's last collaboration with librettist Ranieri de' Calzabigi. It was performed in Vienna in 1769, but met with little favor there, possibly due to its longwinded plot. Like his second reform opera, *Alceste, Paride ed Elena* also contained a dedicatory preface outlining the composer's and librettist's intentions vis-a-vis dramatic-musical structure and style.

This beautiful cantilena melody is a fine example of dramatic fervor within an elegant, lyric line. It has become a standard in all the early collections of Italian song. An uninterrupted chordal accompaniment maintains an atmosphere of intense, restrained passion throughout. The form is ABA.

Extended Study List

Spiagge amate • Die Neigung • Ode an den Tod • Der Jüngling • Die frühen Gräber • Die Sommernacht • Arias from *Alceste, Armide, Iphigénie en Aulide, Iphigénie en Tauride, Paride ed Elena*

Selected Reading

Donald Jay Grout, *A Short History of Opera,* 3rd edition (New York: Columbia University Press, 1988), Chapter 14.

Jeremy Hayes, Bruce Alan Brown, Max Loppert, and Winton Dean, "Christoph Willibald Gluck" in *The New Grove Dictionary of Opera,* ed. Stanley Sadie (New York: Grove's Dictionaries of Music, 1992). Volume 2.

Patricia Howard, *Christoph Willibald Gluck: a Guide to Research,* 2nd edition (New York & London: Routledge, 2003).

Notes

1. A fragment from Gluck's dedicatory preface to his opera *Alceste*, published in Vienna in 1769. Quoted in Donald Jay Grout, *A Short History of Opera*, 269.
2. Richard Boldrey, "Musical Perspective: Gli sguardi trattieni," *Singers'Edition: Soubrette* (Dallas: Pst...Inc., 1992), 42.
3. In eighteenth-century opera, castrati singers were the reigning "superstars," and comprised 70 percent of all male opera singers of that time. For a description of their personalities and the general milieu of opera houses and performances of that day, read the famous satire *Il teatro alla moda* by Marcello.

VINCENZO RIGHINI (1756-1812)

A thorough evaluation of Righini's work is still lacking, especially of his numerous songs...in these the composer by no means followed the usual paths, as his songs with variations prove.

—Gudrun Becker-Weidmann[1]

Righini and Mozart share the same birth year, 1756. Born in Bologna, Righini was trained as a singer, but retired from the stage after vocal misuse put an end to his performing career. He then turned to composition; his opera *Il convitato di Pietra* (1776)—yet another setting of the story of the stone guest—launched his career as a composer. His operas were acclaimed in their time for their combination of Italian vocal style and German craftsmanship.

In 1780, he went to Vienna at the Emperor's invitation to serve as Director of the Italian Opera and singing teacher to Princess Elizabeth of Württemberg. Righini had a distinguished career as a voice teacher; his studio included many professional singers in Vienna and Berlin. He composed around 200 songs in Italian, German, and French; many enjoyed popularity in their day. The two examples annotated here are from *Ariettas,* Op. 7, smaller in scope and less elaborate than arias, but no less demanding.

Affetti, non turbate, Op. 7, No. 5　　　　　　　　**Feelings, do not disturb.**

A dramatic piano introduction opens this song, illustrating the singer's mood of unrest and anxiety. Vocal phrases are operatic in style; the word "perchè" initiates numerous phrases that begin with a large descending interval. There are two stanzas, the second is expanded through the use of the last two lines of the verse ("Perchè non vi cangiate se avete libertà?"/Why do you not change if you are free?) in extended repetitions. The piano postlude is derived from the material of the introduction, but is expanded and altered in range and harmonic function.

Placido zeffiretto, Op. 7, No. 1　　　　　　　　**Gentle little zephyr.**

The singer implores the little breeze and the murmuring brook to find her beloved and tell him that someone is sighing and weeping for him. Undulating piano figures illustrate the gentle zephyrs of this song's title, in eighth- and sixteenth-note figures. Sixteenth notes in thirds create a soft ostinato in the right hand of the accompaniment; this same sort of figure was employed by Mozart in

"Soave il vento" in *Così fan tutte*, and serves well to evoke murmuring breezes. There is a key change (A minor) when the singer addresses the brook; this section is more dramatic in tone and dynamically enforced.

The song begins in D major; the second section in A minor, with a return to D major, this time varied and extended with a codetta. For the most part, vocal phrases are static and elegant; only in the final codetta is a phrase with sweeping range and graceful shape added.

Extended Study List
Io lo so che il bel sembiante • D'un genio che m'accende • Aure amiche, ah! non spirate • Vorrei di te fidarmi • Se amor l'abbandona • T'intendo, si, mio cor • Mi lagnerò tacendo

Selected Reading
Gudrum Becker-Weidmann, "Vincenzo Righini," *The New Grove Dictionary of Opera,* ed. Stanley Sadie (New York: Grove's Dictionaries of Music, 1992). Volume 3, 1326-7.

Edwin Penhorwood, ed. *Vincenzo Righini: Twelve Ariettas* (San Antonio, TX: Southern Music Co., 1991). Performance indications by Costanza Cuccaro and preface by Edwin Penhorwood. This collection is an excellent introduction to the music of Righini and serves as one of the few sources of information about this composer.

Notes
1. Gudrum Becker-Weidmann, "Vincenzo Righini," *The New Grove Dictionary of Opera*, 1992, Vol. 3, 1327.

REPRESENTATIVE COLLECTIONS OF EARLY ITALIAN SONGS

The following collections may be referenced for a more complete survey of songs from this historical period:

Italian Songs of the Seventeenth and Eighteenth Centuries. 2 vols. ed. Luigi Dallapiccola. Publisher: New York, International Music Co. One of the most reliable and accurate editions available.

Anthology of Italian Song of the Seventeenth and Eighteenth Centuries, 2 vols. ed. by Parisotti. Publisher: New York, G. Schirmer. Widely circulated performing edition of this literature, although the keyboard realizations are definitely nineteenth-century in style.

Alte Meister des Bel Canto, 2 vols. ed. by Ludwig Landshoff. Publisher: Frankfurt, F. Peters Corporation.

Arie antiche, 2 vols. Publisher: G. Ricordi.

La Flora, arie & antiche italiane, 3 vols. ed. Knud Jeppesen. Publisher: Copenhagen, Wilhelm Hansen. One of the most accurate and reliable editions available, it surveys the music of the *bel canto* period from 1600-1750. Contains many pieces not found in other editions.

Canzone scordate. An Anthology of Early Songs and Arias, arr. Arne Dørumsgaard. Volume 2: *Ten Early Italian Songs* (1600-1640), medium;

Volume 3: *Five Early Italian Songs* (1640-1700), high; Volume IV: *Five Early Italian Songs* (1640-1700), low; Volume V: *Six Early Italian Arias* (1620-1750), high; Volume VI: *Five Scarlatti Arias* (1660-1725), high. Available from Recital Publications, P. O. Box 1697, Huntsville, TX, 77342-1697.

Twenty-Six Italian Songs and Arias, ed. John Glenn Paton. Publisher: Alfred Publishing Co.

Italian Arias of the Baroque and Classical Eras, ed. John Glenn Paton. Published by Alfred Publishing Co. These are the most recent editions of early Italian songs. They include complete translations (including IPA), dramatic analysis of the text, and relevant background material about poet, and composer. Every effort has been made to research original sources, correct errors prevalent in earlier editions, and restore these songs to their authentic form.

NINETEENTH-CENTURY ITALIAN SONG

In addition to their works for the operatic stage, the most noted Italian opera composers of the nineteenth century—Rossini, Donizetti, Bellini, and Verdi—also turned their hand to composing a few *romanze da camera* (listed in modern editions as *composizioni da camera*). Designed for the amateur singer, these songs were written for the purpose of providing vocal entertainment at musicales in private homes, not unlike the early *mélodies* that served the same purpose in Parisian salons. Most of these songs retain operatic elements and are comparable to miniature arias, with fluid, graceful melodies and even cadenzas and embellishments. Because they were created for a specific arena of performance, there was little thought of fusion of poem and musical elements beyond a certain point.

Art songs composers in the latter part of the century retained this opera-centered style. Luigi Denza, Pietro Tosti, Luigi Arditi, Franco Alfano, Stefano Donaudy, and others wrote songs that were popular and vocally "showy." These were regularly programmed in the recitals of famous singers such as Nellie Melba, Claudia Muzio, and Enrico Caruso.

In the early twentieth century, a new group of composers emerged who turned to the past for inspiration and classic forms, blending them with modern approaches to song composition: Ottorino Respighi, Alfredo Casella, Ildebrando Pizzetti, Gian-Francesco Malipiero, Mario Castelnuovo-Tedesco, and Luigi Dallapiccola composed songs in a newer Italian style. However, Italian song has never regained the primacy in song that it relinquished after the Baroque period.

VINCENZO BELLINI (1801-1835)

Bellini's music comes from the heart, and it is intimately bound up with the text.

—Richard Wagner[1]

Vincenzo Bellini produced nearly a dozen operas during his short working life of appxoximately ten years. He also composed songs that reveal his mastery of expressive cantilena. Seemingly simplistic, the songs are filled with emotion.

Bellini's vocal writing always shows a close relationship between music and text—his contemporaries called his music *filosofica*.[2] He composed songs notable for their beautiful *bel canto* melodies, which emphasize the beauty of the voice, but still set the text precisely with respect for correct prosody. Bellini's songs are termed *arietti* (small "arias"), smaller in scale than those found in his operas, but no less demanding. The songs annotated here are from the collection *Sei ariette,* published in 1829.

Vaga luna, che inargenti *(Sei ariette)*   **Lovely moon. 1829**

In this delicate song, the poet implores the silvery moon to carry his declaration of love to his beloved. The piano introduction contains the beginning of a lovely *cantilena* melody taken up by the voice. A simple broken-chord accompaniment allows the vocal line to dominate throughout. There are two verses, set in strophic form. This song, written early in Bellini's compositional career, looks ahead to the aria "Casta Diva" in his opera *Norma*.

Vanne, o rosa fortunata *(Sei ariette)*   **Go, fortunate rose. 1829**

Here is another typically appealing Bellini melody, which is like a barcarole. The singer expresses his jealousy toward the rose, placed in the bosom of his beloved, although the flower is dying with despair at her beauty. His agitation is mirrored in the figures of the piano accompaniment, which maintains tension and forward movement.

Ma rendi pur contento *(Sei ariette)*   **O love, bring contentment. 1829**
(Pietro Metastasio)

Metastasio's verse is as smooth and elegant as one of his opera librettos. The words are a lover's declaration: "Bring contentment to her heart and I shall forgive you if my own heart is heavy...I live more in her than in myself." In setting this text, Bellini crafts an elegant and limpid *bel canto* line. Bellini's vocal writing was always passionately lyric, and this is an excellent example of his skill.

Almen se non poss'io *(Sei ariette)*   **If I cannot follow... 1829**
(Pietro Metastasio)

Bellini's songs display strong links with his operas. His shapely vocal phrases have been characterized as "unfolding melody." This song is full of phrases, broad-lined and filled with elegant ornamentation. The accompaniment is a series of simple broken chords, highlighting the exquisite *bel canto* vocal phrases. This song is a striking example of Bellini's *cantabile* melodic writing.

There are two sections AB. The B section is extended by florid ornamentation ("per voi, non è.")

Malinconia, ninfa gentile *(Sei ariette)* **Melancholy, gentle nymph. 1829**
(Ippolito Pindemonte)

This is a song filled with short but buoyant vocal phrases—a breathless, emotional pledge to the gentle nymph of love. Bellini sets the vocal line over a broken chord accompaniment, marked *Allegro agitato*. Its whirlwind motion urges the vocal phrases forward without stopping, to the end of this exciting, dramatic song.

Extended Study List
Il fervido desiderio • Dolente immagine di Fille mia • L'abbandono • Torna, vezzosa Fillide • La farfalletta • La Ricordanza • Bella Nice, che d'amore • Per pietà, bell'idol mio • T'intendo, sì, mio cor

Selected Reading
Leslie Orrey, *Bellini* (London: J. M. Dent, 1969).
John Rosselli, *The Life of Bellini* (New York: Cambridge University Press, 1996).
Herbert Weinstock, *Vincenzo Bellini: his life and his operas* (New York: Alfred A. Knopf, 1971).

Notes
1. Quoted in Friedrich Lippmann, "Vincenzo Bellini," *The New Grove Dictionary of Opera*, ed. Stanley Sadie, 1992, Volume 1, 391.
2. Ibid.

GIOACHINO ROSSINI (1792-1868)

Delight must be the basis and aim of this art. Simple melody—clear rhythm!

—Gioachino Rossini[1]

Most of Gioachino Rossini's songs were produced after he had reached the end of his career as an opera composer in 1829 with *Guillaume Tell*. Collections titled *Soirées musicales* and *Péchés de vieillesse* contain some of his best songs. *Péchés de vieillesse* (Sins of Old Age) consists of several volumes of an amazing variety of songs, many so brief they are all but musical exercises. Countless others were composed for Rossini's personal enjoyment, to be performed at private parties at his villa at Passy, or at the requests of singers. Rossini's songs feature his penchant for beautiful melody; many of the accompaniments are of the simple broken-chord variety, used in various combinations.

With the exception of the *Venetian Regatta*, the literature annotated here is drawn from a set of twelve drawing room songs published in 1835 under the title *Soirées musicales*, the name Rossini gave to his weekly gatherings for his colleagues and friends. He composed music for these occasions and the domestic music-making was of high quality.

La pastorella delle Alpi **The Alpine shepherdess. 1835**
(Conte Carlo Pepoli)

Rossini sets this text as a charming Alpine waltz. Tyrolean vocal acrobatics are heard in an angular vocal line and in the coloratura vocal refrain.

La danza	**The dance. c. 1830-35**

(Conte Carlo Pepoli)

"La danza" is probably the most famous classical Neapolitan *tarantella* around. The high-spirited tune is immediately recognizable; its perpetual motion is maintained through two verses. A high level of excitement is also sustained by the rapid-fire diction demanded of the singer.

---

*La regata veneziana**	**The Venetian Regatta. 1878**

Anzoleta avanti la regata • Anzoleta co passa la regata •
Anzoleta dopo la regata

This group of three songs forms a triptych that illustrates the Venetian boat races from the standpoint of an onlooker. Anzoleta is pictured on the banks of the Grand Canal, cheering for her gondolier lover as he takes part in the annual regatta. The three songs provide a running commentary on the race as well as the emotional state of Anzoleta. The first song features a charming flowing melodic line; the second is composed of short melodic fragments, mirroring a feeling of urgency and excitement; the third describes the excited elation of the couple. Accompaniment figures throughout the three songs are simple, a combination of broken-chord figures of all types; melodic interest and dramatic effect reside solely in the vocal line. The texts were originally written in Venetian dialect; Italian texts are also supplied in the published edition.

ANZOLETA BEFORE THE REGATTA. The pennants are waving as the regatta begins, and Venice has turned out to watch the race. Anzoleta instructs her lover: "See that you win it. Don't lag…drive your gondola, make it fly…your love is waiting for you. Bring me the winner's pennant tonight."

ANZOLETA AS THE REGATTA PASSES. Anzoleta looks over the parapet watching the boatman ply their oars against the wind. She anxiously looks for Momolo in the crowd of participants. He is in second place. Her heart pounding, she loudly urges him on. He sees her cheering him to victory.

ANZOLETA AFTER THE REGATTA. Momolo has won the regatta, and Anzoleta rewards her lover with a shower of kisses. As she wipes away his perspiration, she assures him that all Venice hails him the victor.

*Rossini also composed a duet by the same name which is part of *Soirées Musicales*.

Il rimprovero	**The reproach.**

(Pietro Metastasio)

"Mi lagnerò tacendo" (I shall lament in silence) reads the first line of this poem. Rossini set this familiar text dozens of times—from full-blown songs to brief sketches, to autograph measures inscribed for friends' albums, and in varying styles and moods. There are six versions in the 1857 volume of *Péchés de viellesse* (titled *Musique anondine)*.

Extended Study List

La gita in gondola • La serenata • La Francesca da Rimini • La pesca • La partenza • Quai voci, quae note• La separazione • Il trovatore • A Grenade (Ariette espagnole) • Tirana alla spagnola • Beltà crudele • L'invito • Se il vuol la molinara

Selected Reading

Denise Gallo, *Gioachino Rossini: A Guide to Research* (New York & London: Routledge, 2002).
James Harding, *Rossini* (New York: T. Y. Crowell, 1972).
Richard Osborne, *Rossini* (London: J. M. Dent, 1986).
Stendhal, *Life of Rossini,* trans. Richard N. Coe (New York: Criterion Books, 1957).
Nicholas Till, *Rossini, his life and times* (New York: Hippocrene Books, 1983).
Francis Toye, *Rossini: The Man and His Music* (New York: Dover Publishing, 1987. Reprint of *Rossini, a study in Tragi-Comedy*).
Herbert Weinstock, *Rossini: A Biography* (New York: Alfred A. Knopf, 1968).

Notes

1. Nat Shapiro, *An Encyclopedia of Quotations About Music,* 37.

GAETANO DONIZETTI (1797-1848)

If you want to know if a certain piece of music is good, play the melody without the accompaniment.

—Gaetano Donizetti[1]

Gaetano Donizetti's songs are, for the most part, not among his memorable vocal works. Although he produced more than 250 examples in the genre, many remain unpublished. A number of Donizetti's songs are in Neapolitan dialect. They tend toward bland accompaniments, and simple melodies that border on the predictable. Without the aid of really fine poetry, they lack the dramatic interest of his operas. Nonetheless, judicious choices in the hands of a fine interpreter can produce effective results.

Ah! rammenta, o bella Irene	**Ah! remember, o beautiful Irene.**
(Pietro Metastasio)	**Milan, 1830 or 1831.**

Eighteenth-century librettist and poet Pietro Metastasio was for many musicians, the poet *par excellence*. Bellini and Rossini also set verses by Metastasio, as did Mozart, Haydn, Schubert, and Beethoven.

This song resembles a miniature aria. Its vocal lines are spun-out lyrically in the best *bel canto* tradition. It is subtitled "Cavatina"; the opening tempo is marked *Larghetto*, but the second section is *Allegretto*, indicating a *cavatina-cabaletta* aria form. Even when writing songs, Donizetti could not help reverting back to the opera stage. Donizetti gave the piano texture more interest than usual in this piece.

Il barcaiolo
(L. Tarantini)

The boatman. 1836

Donizetti published *Nuits d'été à Pausilippe*, a collection of six songs, in 1836. The town of Posillipo, a picturesque suburb of Naples, is located in southern Italy. It sits on a volcanic ridge that projects into the northern part of the Bay of Naples. Posillipo is the location of many interesting ruins of Roman villas.

There are three verses in this song, depicting the calm sea on which the lovers row peacefully. However, should a storm arise, they would happily go to their death together.

A gentle *barcarole* rhythm is maintained through the first stanza. A florid melisma leads into the second section. As the imagined storm approaches, the musical texture thickens. Tremolo octaves in the piano accompany declamatory, dramatic vocal phrases. The charming opening material, embellished now by ornaments, is used to close the song.

Me voglio fà na casa
(Canzone napoletana)

I want to build a house. 1836

A young lover sings of his desire to build a house of peacock feathers and precious stones, surrounded by the sea. When his Nennella looks out her balcony, all will say—"Now the sun has come out!"

There are three short stanzas. Each is followed by a "tra la la" refrain of bubbling vocal phrases. In this song, Donizetti used the Neapolitan dialect, and it is full of sunlight.

Extended Study List

L'amor mio • La chanson de l'abeille • A mezzanotte • Le crépuscule • Romanza moresca • Amore e morte • Lu trademiento • La ninna nanna • Il sospiro • La zingara • L'ultima notte di un novizio • La conocchia

Selected Reading

William Ashbrook, *Donizetti* (London: Cassell, 1965).
Herbert Weinstock, *Donizetti and the World of Opera in Italy, Paris and Vienna in the First Half of the Nineteenth Century* (New York: Pantheon Books, 1963).

Notes

1. Robert Markow, "Looney Tunes," *Opera News*, 58 (January 22, 1994), 17.

GIUSEPPE VERDI (1813-1901)

> Others have composed music more graceful, less obvious, or more beautiful; but few have equalled the sheer vitality of Verdi's music.
>
> —George Martin[1]

> So-called vocal perfection concerns me little; I like to have roles sung as I wish, but I am unable to provide the voice, the soul, that certain something which should be called the spark—it is usually described by the Italian phrase 'to have the Devil on your back.'
>
> —Giuseppe Verdi[2]

Giuseppe Verdi's songs number less than twenty-five, yet his first published work (1838) was a set of six songs. Their publication anticipated his first opera, *Oberto*, by a year. The style of the songs is hardly what we think of as "Verdian"; instead, they share more musical characteristics with Bellini or Donizetti. At this point in his career, Verdi had not yet acquired the technical mastery or rich musical vocabulary of his mature compositions, although even in these early works, his keen dramatic sense shines through. Seventeen of Verdi's songs are published by Ricordi under the title *Composizioni da camera.*

The songs are interesting in their own right, but they also challenge Verdi "tune detectives" as being reminiscent of melodies in Verdi's operas. Indeed, melodies from some songs are developed or transformed and appear later in operatic works.

Composer Luciano Berio, who composed orchestral transcriptions for eight *romances* by Verdi, writes: "It is my belief that these eight *romances*...can be considered as true studies, in embryonic form, for *scene*, arias and cabalettas of Verdi operas. In fact, they contain echoes of *Nabucco, La forza del destino, Don Carlo,* and even an entire phrase, "Tacea la notte placida," from *Il trovatore.*"[3]

Perduta ho la pace   **My peace is lost. 1838**
(Luigi Balestri, translated from the German of Johann Wolfgang von Goethe)

Here is an Italian Gretchen at the spinning wheel, a translation by Verdi's friend Luigi Balestri of Margarete's lament from Goethe's *Faust* ("Meine ruh ist hin..."). Verdi's operatic vocal approach is unmistakable. A section of two vocal phrases (eight measures) beginning "Perduta ho la pace," returns between contrasting sections, which develop Margarete's emotional state. This recurring section is strongly punctuated with unvarying chord figures in the piano.

Strong rhythms are also found in the vocal line. Each new section broadens in melodic scope with increased activity in the piano figures, changing with her thoughts and climaxing at the ecstatic memory of her lover's look, the touch of his hand, and his kiss.

This song and the next appear in an album of six songs (*Sei romanze*, 1838), Verdi's first published work. He was twenty-five years old.

Deh pietoso, oh addolorata   O merciful mother of sorrows. 1838
(Luigi Balestri, translated from the German of Johann Wolfgang von Goethe)

This song, also from Goethe's *Faust*, forms a little companion piece to the preceding song. Here, Margarete prays to the Virgin to have pity on her and ease her overwhelming sense of guilt. In these two songs, Verdi lays the groundwork for his operatic heroines to come, who pour out their innermost emotions in impassioned arias. Typical Verdian melodic patterns, rhythms and approaches to word setting are found in both pieces.

The accompaniment is consistently simple throughout; Verdi's broad vocal phrases are prominent. A favorite Verdi technique can be seen in the vocal line: a short dotted-note anacrusis into a long high note. The vocal material in this song most likely served as derivative material for the second act finale of *Nabucco*, composed three years later.[4]

Lo spazzacamino   The chimney sweep. 1845
(S.M. Maggioni)

Verdi's second album of six songs, published in 1845, consisted entirely of settings of contemporary Italian poets. This is the song of a little chimney sweep, gaily touting his services. His unaccompanied street cry of "Lo spazzacamin!" precedes each of the three stanzas. Verdi's characteristic rhythmic melody is emphatically present, in alternating sections: Allegro $\frac{2}{4}$, and a lilting waltz refrain ("Ladies and gentlemen, for only a few pennies, I'll save you from fire!"). The character and mood of this song—one of of Verdi's most popular—brings to mind the character of Oscar in *Un ballo in maschera,* full of mischief and fun, and thoroughly ingratiating.

Extended Study List
Stornello • In solitaria stanza • L'Abandonée • Nell'orror di notte oscura • Non t'accostare all'urna • Il tramonto • La zingara • L'esule • Il poveretto • Ad una stella • Il mistero • Brindisi I & II • La seduzione

Selected Reading
Marcello Conati, *Interviews and Encounters with Verdi,* trans. Richard Stokes (London: Victor Gollancz, Ltd., 1984).
George Martin, *Aspects of Verdi* (New York: Limelight Editions, 1993).
_____, *Verdi: His Music, Life and Times* (New York: Limelight Editions, 1992).
Mary Jane Phillips-Matz, *Verdi* (New York: Oxford University Press, 1993).
William Weaver and Martin Chusid, eds., *The Verdi Companion* (New York: W.W. Norton, 1979).

Notes
1. George Martin, *Verdi: His Life, Music and Times*, 481.
2. In a letter to Giulio Ricordi from his home at Sant'Agata, 1871. In *Composers on Music*, ed. Sam Morgenstern, 188.
3. Luciano Berio, "Verdi: Eight Romances," trans. James Chater. Liner notes for *Verdi / Falla: Songs.* José Carreras, Luciano Berio conducting the English Chamber Orchestra. Philips compact disc 432 889-2. 1991.
4. Charles Osborne, *The Concert Song Companion*, 209.

FRANCESCO PAOLO TOSTI (1846-1916)

> He had a flair for...melody, less elegant than that of his bel canto predecessors, more plebian in style, and owing a great deal to popular Neapolitan song.
>
> —Charles Osborne[1]

Sunny Neapolitan melodies and intense emotionalism color the songs of Paolo Tosti, whose song style defines for many the ultimate "Italian song" sound—Italianate melody with a generous dash of Neapolitan popular song.

Tosti was a popular song composer of the late Victorian and Edwardian period; his songs number in the hundreds. He was well acquainted with leading composers of the day: Verdi, Puccini, Mascagni, Leoncavallo, and Boito, among others.[2] Tosti knew how to write engaging, flowing melodies that displayed the voice, and while these *romanze da camera* were not always of the highest artistic quality, they had an immediate appeal and were included in the concerts of the best-known opera stars of the period. Great singers of that day, Caruso and Melba among them, programmed Tosti songs and helped disseminate Tosti's work to a wide and highly appreciative audience.

Tosti composed over 350 songs, in Italian, English, French, and the Neapolitan dialect. He had an excellent knowledge of vocal technique, and was an accomplished singer and pianist. Many of his songs were probably written with his own voice in mind.*

Tosti moved to London in 1875, and became the singing teacher to Queen Victoria's children. He was also in charge of planning the Queen's private vocal concerts. He taught at the Royal College of Music and the Royal Academy of Music. He became a British citizen in 1906, and was knighted in 1908.

---

*Tosti was a lyric tenor.

La serenata   **The serenade. 1888**
(Giovanni Alfredo Cesareo)

Like "Goodbye," this song has always retained its appeal. Its lyrical melody is characteristic of Tosti's skill as a tunesmith. It is a passionate (somewhat extroverted) serenade, underpinned with strong arpeggiated figures that propel the lover's words to the window of his beloved. There are two verses.

Malìa   **Enchantment. 1887**
(Emanuele Pagliara)

"What was in that flower? Maybe a love potion...a mysterious power?" A bemused and totally enchanted lover recalls the charms of the beloved: her delicate movements, which cause the air to quiver; her magical words; her compelling glance.

The song is set strophically in two stanzas. Tosti chooses an ardent waltz rhythm for the poem, but keeps the melody delicate and tuneful. There are two mini-sections in each stanza, both dominated by sequential phrases. The first section builds to the second through rising patterns, the second uses descending sequences (Tosti knew what worked) to reach the final measures. Emotional tension is sustained throughout by this construction.

Ideale	**The ideal one. 1882**
(Carmelo Errico)	

"Ideale" is another much-performed Tosti song. A dream of the ideal one is recalled in this poem: "Return my sweet ideal, come back! Come back!" Tosti excelled at composing songs of operatic scope on texts about love, and this song fits neatly into that category.

Extended Study List

L'ultima canzone • Luna d'estate • 'A vucchella • Aprile • Ave Maria • Serenata d'un Angelo • Non mi guardere • Ha da venir! • Lamento d'amore • Addio! (better known by its English title, "Goodbye") • Penso! • Primavera • Ricordati di me • Tormento • Sogno • Vorrei • Rosa • Nella notte d'avril • Mattinata • E morto Pulcinella

Notes

1. Charles Osborne, *The Concert Song Companion*, 211.
2. From "Biography," in *Francesco Paolo Tosti: Thirty Songs*. (Ricordi, dist. Hal Leonard, 2002).

ERMANNO WOLF-FERRARI (1876-1948)

It's better not to compose lies, if only because it takes so many notes.
—Ermanno Wolf-Ferrari[1]

Ermanno Wolf[*] was born in Venice. He was attracted to music at an early age, but studied art, ostensibly to follow in his father's footsteps.[2] He studied art at the Academia di Belle Arti, Rome, and worked at music in his spare time.

In 1892, he moved to Munich to continue his art studies, and entered the Munich Akademie der Tonkunst, studying counterpoint with Rheinberger. He also spent time in Milan as a protégé of Boito. He met publisher Giulio Ricordi, who did not accept his works for publication.

Wolf-Ferrari served as composer-director of the Liceo Benedetto Marcello in Venice from 1903 to 1909. After resigning the post, he moved to Germany and devoted himself entirely to composing, dividing his time between Munich and Venice. The majority of his success as a composer was experienced not in Italy, but in Germany. In 1939, he was appointed professor of composition at the Salzburg Mozarteum. He moved to Zürich in 1946, returning to Venice for the last year of his life.

Wolf-Ferrari enjoyed his greatest successes with a series of comic operas, most composed to libretti of eighteenth-century comedies by Goldoni and Molière. These seemed to fit his musical style perfectly. The most successful included *I quattro rusteghi* (1906); *Il segreto di Susanna* (1909); *L'amore medico* (1913); *La vedova scaltra* (1931); and *Il campiello* (1936). His operas reveal his special flair for mixing eighteenth-century idioms with his own musical style, which is clearly eclectic and somewhat elusive. Predominantly diatonic harmonies are laced with Wagnerian chromaticism and Wolf-Ferrari's own expressive (and often far-flung) lyricism.

*He added his mother's maiden name, Ferrari, to his surname around 1895.

Quattro rispetti, Op. 11   1902

> Un verde praticello senza piante (A green lawn without trees) •
> Jo del saluti ve nel mando mille (I send you a thousand greetings) •
> E tanto c'è pericol ch'io ti lasci (And there is as much
> danger of my leaving you) • O si che non sapevo sospirare
> (O yes, I didn't used to know how to sigh)

A *rispetto* is an Italian verse form of eight lines. The first four lines rhyme alternately and the last four lines rhyme in pairs. The source of these four simple verses is unknown. The songs are not titled separately and should probably be performed as a group. Musically, the settings are markedly lyrical and display clear ties to nineteenth-century Germany. Only occasionally does Wolf-Ferrari employ more contemporary harmonic progressions or resolutions.

SONG 1. A folk-like melodic line in A minor is accompanied by simple chords throughout. Poetic images from nature are used as descriptors for the beloved, and ornamented turns in the melody decorate key words throughout (*piante*/trees; *amante*/lover; *riva*/shore; *viva*/image, etc.). The last three lines of poetry call forth a more dramatic mood which returns to the gentle opening phrase to conclude the song.

SONG 2. This song is more dramatic, accompanied by chordal figures, repeated at various points for emotional emphasis. Piano accompaniment is simple and chordal, often doubling the vocal line. The form is a modified ABA.

SONG 3. Melodically, this song seems more Italianate than the two preceding it. An emotional avowal of love, it is underscored by arpeggiated figures and features a graceful vocal line, which becomes increasingly expansive for the last three phrases.

SONG 4. The final song is in gay *tarantella* rhythm; the metronome marking is *presto*. Vocal phrases demand facile articulation; the accompaniment is vigorous with staccato articulation. Phrases are short; there are two uneven phrase rhythms that interrupt the brisk pace, but only fleetingly. This song provides an exuberant ending to this charming group.

Selected Reading
John C.G. Waterhouse, "Ermanno Wolf-Ferrari," in *The New Grove Dictionary of Opera,* ed. Stanley Sadie (New York: Grove's Dictionaries of Music, 1992), Vol. 4, 1171-72.

Notes
1. In a letter to Hans Gál, 6 September 1934. In *An Encyclopedia of Quotations About Music*, ed. Nat Shapiro, 245.
2. His father, August Wolf, was a well-known Bavarian painter of Jewish extraction.

OTTORINO RESPIGHI (1879-1936)

The romanticism of yesterday will again be the romanticism of tomorrow.
—Ottorino Respighi[1]

Ottorino Respighi composed more than sixty songs, most written between 1906 and 1933. His fondness for the voice led him to produce many effective and appealing vocal works. These include songs for voice and piano as well as vocal chamber works and larger choral compositions. Respighi's songs contain warm sentiment, and a feeling of calm serenity that pervades most of his work.

In 1900 Respighi went to Russia and played principal viola in the Imperial Opera Orchestra in St. Petersburg. There he studied with Rimsky-Korsakov, whose influence can be seen in Respighi's orchestral works with their coloristic effects and rich harmonies. His two symphonic poems (*I pini di Roma* and *Le fontane di Roma /* The Pines of Rome and The Fountains of Rome) brought him his greatest recognition. Although his operas won critical acclaim, none remain in the standard repertory.

In 1913 he joined the faculty at Rome's Liceo (later Conservatorio) di Santa Cecilia, and in 1924 was appointed its director. After his resignation in 1929, he continued to teach one class in advanced composition. He devoted himself to composing and conducting, and made two tours to the United States as a pianist and conductor.

His music displays a strong feeling for classical structure as well as classical serenity, although his style is emphatically his own—subjective and romantic. His feeling for the musical forms of Italy's past is seen in some of the titles of his song sets: *Cinque canti alla antica*, and *Arie antica*. Respighi's songs treat the voice as an instrument, submerging the vocal line into the accompaniment texture in order to capture the essence of the poem. "The poetic meter and meaning of individual words are not permitted to change the concept of the phrase line as a musical entity."[2]

There is a great variety of style and treatment in Respighi's songs; he was a linguist, and felt comfortable with either French or Italian texts. His songs have a subdued lyricism, elegant but often lacking rhythmic thrust. His earliest songs seem to be the most enduring. Respighi's songs are published as groups, but the individual songs are not connected cyclically.

Nebbie   **Mists. 1906**

(Ada Negri)

An inexorable rising vocal line sustains dramatic intensity through this song and musically illustrates the melancholy text, which pictures mists over moorlands, black-winged ravens floating above, and a wandering, despairing soul. Respighi evokes the hazy mists with a slowly rising scale that gathers intensity in its ascent.

Vocal phrases are submerged into the overall texture, giving the impression of great length and the effect of a faraway, transparent sound. The piano accompaniment is chordal and richly textured. A hidden tonic pedal is present in all but eight chords, and the moment of strongest rhythmic tension is based on octave swings of the same tonic.[3]

The music to this song was composed before the text was added. Respighi, suffering from acute melancholy, had stopped composing for a time. An irresistible urge to compose caused him to quickly fill four pages with music. A friend arrived with a volume of Negri's poems; upon reading "Nebbie," Respighi immediately thought of the music he had just composed. He sang the verses to the music, and they fit perfectly, as if composed simultaneously.[4]

Notte   **Night. 1905**
(Ada Negri)
from *Sei liriche* (Seconda serie)

This song is a fine example of Respighi's mature style. The approaching night is described in a song of ethereal atmosphere; poetic images include a fantastic garden scented with fragrant roses, mournful darkness and supreme quiet, light dew on the flowers, and the night weeping tears. The song features sustained legato lines in fairly high tessitura. Impressionistic influences are present in Respighi's musical approach to this poem. The formal structural scheme is ABA plus a Coda. The coda is given over principally to the piano, the voice intoning a long phrase on one note.

Extended Study List
Ballata • Bella porta di rubini • Scherzo • Contrasto • Invito alla danza • Nevicata • Io sono la Madre • La mamma è come il pane caldo • Mattinata • No, non e morto il figlio tuo • Mattino di luce • Piogga • Stornellatrice • *Il tramonto* (mezzo-soprano/string quartet)

Selected Reading
Pierluigi Alvera, *Respighi,* trans. Raymond Rosenthal (New York: Treves Publishing , 1986).
Raymond Jones, Jr., "A comprehensive catalog of the published art songs of Ottorino Respighi." PhD. diss., Washington University, 1988.

Notes
1. Quoted in James Husst Hall, *The Art Song,* 19.
2. Ruth C. Lakeway and Robert C. White Jr., *Italian Art Song,* 59.
3. Hall, *The Art Song,* 20.
4. Recounted in Elsa Respighi's biography of her husband, *Ottorino Respighi: His Life Story,* trans. Gwen Morris.

STEFANO DONAUDY (1879-1925)

> Donaudy's ingratiating melodies are so much like the *canzoni* of the eighteenth century that had he chosen he might have fooled his public...for many years with his "transcriptions."
>
> —James Husst Hall[1]

Stefano Donaudy's reputation as a song composer rests solely on thirty-six songs, titled *Arie di stile antico,* published in two volumes (1918 and 1922) by Ricordi Publishers (Milan). These charming songs emulate the *bel canto* style, and contain beautiful *cantabile* melodies as well as more spirited songs (example: "Spirate, pur spirate"). For years they have provided voice teachers and students with fine introductory Italian literature, and have served as excellent supplements to the usual fare of Italian songs from the seventeenth and eighteenth centuries. The published series do not contain translations.[2]

In composing his songs, Donaudy drew on various "ancient" song types such as *arie, arietta, ballatella, canzone, canzonetta, frottola, madrigal, maggiolata,* and *villanella.*

O del mio amato ben   **O, the lost enchantment.**

Subtitled "aria," this is one of Donaudy's most-performed songs. It is in strophic form; the two-stanza text is an impassioned lament for a lost love. The vocal line is a beautiful *cantabile* melody that demands excellent legato from the singer. A four-measure piano introduction is repeated between verses. The accompaniment begins calmly, supporting the broad lyric vocal phrase, then takes on a more passionate tone and slightly denser texture as the stanza progresses.

Freschi luoghi, prati aulenti   **Cool places, fragrant meadows.**

This *canzone* is light and fresh in mood, in keeping with its text about spring and nature. The opening vocal phrase derives from the delicate piano introduction; subsequent phrases are structured through sequences and graceful lyric fragments that rise to a climactic note, then fall sequentially. There are two stanzas, repeated exactly in strophic form.

Extended Study List
Spirate, pur spirate • Vaghissima sembianza • Luoghi sereni e cari • Amor mi fa cantare... • Quando ti rivedrò • Perduta ho la speranza • Amor s'apprende • Perchè dolce, caro bene

Notes
1. James Husst Hall, *The Art Song,* 19.
2. Donaudy's 36 *Arie di stile antico* were translated and analyzed as to musical form in a 1985 doctoral dissertation. See Frank John Aiello, "English Translations and Analyzation of Musical Forms of *36 Arie di stile antico* by Stefano Donaudy (1879-1925)." D.M.A. diss., The University of Oklahoma, 1985.

ILDEBRANDO PIZZETTI (1880-1968)

> Melody is emotion translated into musical sounds. Nor does the translation require an elaborate vocal line, so long as it sings true.
> —Ildebrando Pizzetti[1]

Ildebrando Pizzetti was a distinguished teacher as well as a composer. He taught composition at the Parma Conservatory (1907) and harmony and counterpoint at the Istituto Musicale (later Conservatory) of Florence (1908). He was appointed the conservatory's director in 1917. In 1936, he succeeded Respighi as teacher of advanced composition at the Academia di St. Cecilia in Rome; he later served as its president from 1947 to 1952. He retired in 1958 but remained active as a composer well into the 1960s. His students included composers Luigi Dallapiccola, Mario Castelnuovo-Tedesco, and Gian Francesco Malipiero. He composed some forty-five songs, including several vocalises, which span a period from 1902 to 1960. He is best known for his twelve operas.*

Throughout his compositional career (which included symphonic and choral works and chamber music, as well as songs and operas), Pizzetti remained basically conservative. Rather than adopting any of the musical approaches prevalent at the turn of the century, he turned to the music of the past as the basis for his works. He used tonalities and textures from early music in his early compositions, and characteristics drawn from early music appear in later works as well.

Pizzetti's songs exhibit a particularly sensitive approach to setting Italian poetry; he set contemporary poets and Italian poetry from the Renaissance as well as ancient Greek and Biblical texts. In his songs, these archaic influences combined with more contemporary elements (Musorgsky and Debussy were favorite models). Many of his songs are unified by a recurring phrase that often serves as an originating point for the formal structure.

*All Pizzetti's operas were premiered at La Scala (Milan) and other major Italian opera houses.

I pastori (*Cinque liriche,* No. 1)　　　　　　　　　**The shepherds. 1908**
(Gabriele d'Annunzio)

"I pastori" is Pizzetti's most famous song, called a *lirica*. It is pastoral in mood, with freely structured vocal phrases that give a feeling of unbarred meter. It is through-composed in several sections, each with its own particular texture or identifying motive. The introductory melody in the piano sets the pastoral atmosphere for D'Annunzio's poem, which describes the migration of shepherds from the mountains to the sea. The text contains symbolic references; the vocal writing is clearly influenced by Pizzetti's interest in early music. Pomfret observes that "Pizzetti's treatment of the vocal line is reminiscent of plainchant...generally syllabic, with short melismas at the ends of phrases."[2]

Pizzetti and D'Annunzio enjoyed a close friendship; composer Mario Castelnuovo-Tedesco, one of Pizzetti's most illustrious students, termed this song "...the most beautiful concert song of the last fifty years, and the most perfect musical expression of D'Annunzio's poetry."[3]

Quel rosignuol che sì soave piagne*　　　　**That nightingale that so softly cries.**
(Frescesco Petrarca)

The call of the nightingale opens this song—a single piano line based on a falling second (G-natural/F-natural) expands into a graceful arpeggiated trill and returns again to the slow falling second, now G-sharp/F-sharp. The first vocal phrase borrows the falling second interval as part of its pattern and uses it as a tiny motif to point up important words or stresses through the song.

A subdued atmosphere pervades the piece. Pizzetti directs that soft pedal be used throughout. There is a certain recitative-like spontaneity in the melodic lines of this work. Accompaniment figures are evocative of the bird: free, fluttering, and light; harmonies that are both joyous and sweet as well as plaintive and melancholy. The final line "Come nulla quaggiù diletta e dura" (how nothing in this life pleases and endures) is set to highlight the word "nulla." The final measures echo the major-minor alternation that has continued through the song.

*This song is the second in a set of three sonnets of Petrarch "On the Death of Madonna Laura" (*Tre sonetti del Petrarca: In morte di Madonna Laura*).

Extended Study List
La madre al figlio lontano (*Cinque liriche*, No. 2) • San Basilio (*Cinque liriche*, No. 3) • Il clefta prigione (*Cinque liriche*, No. 4) • Passeggiata (*Cinque liriche*, No. 5) • *Tre sonetti del Petrarca: In morte di Madonna Laura*• *Tre canti grece* (Three Greek Songs) • *Tre canzoni*

Selected Reading
Mario Castelnuovo-Tedesco, "Pizzetti," in *The New Book of Modern Composers,* ed. David Ewen (New York: Alfred A. Knopf, 1961).
Rachel Jensen, "The Songs of Ildebrando Pizzetti." D.M.A. diss., The University of Illinois at Champaign-Urbana, 2001.
Bonnie Pomfret, "Songs of Ildebrando Pizzetti," *The NATS Journal* 50:2 (Nov/Dec. 1993).

Notes
1. Ildebrando Pizzetti, "The Composer Speaks," in David Ewen, *The New Book of Modern Composers*, 3rd edition, 282.
2. Bonnie Pomfret, "Songs of Ildebrando Pizzetti," *The NATS Journal* 50:2, 14.
3. Hall, *The Art Song,* 21-22.

FRANCESCO SANTOLIQUIDO (1883-1971)

Francesco Santoliquido studied at the Liceo di Santa Cecilia in Rome. After graduating in 1908 he moved to Hammamet, a village in Tunisia, and divided his time between there and Rome. In Tunisia, he founded a concert society and in 1927, a music school that later became a conservatory. From 1923 until his death, he lived in Anacapri.

He was also an author, publishing books of poetry and short stories in English. His third wife was pianist/teacher Ornella (née Puliti), who trained with Casella and Cortot and taught at the Rome Conservatory.

Santoliquido's musical style can be termed neoromantic. His early works are expressive and sensitive but are not outstanding musically; they owe much in style to Wagner and Debussy. In his later compositions, Wagner's influence is less discernible and Debussian elements are merged with some dissonance and expressive elements reminiscent of Messaien.

His residence in Tunisia also impacted his musical style. He was drawn to exotic and colorful sound qualities; many of his works contain melodic elements of Arabian popular music. His works for voice include settings of Persian and Japanese poetry. He composed four operas and a ballet, as well as numerous works for orchestra and chamber ensembles. The group of songs annotated here is an excellent example of the quality of songs to be found within the *liriche da camera* (art song) tradition.

Tre poesie persiane   **Three Persian Poems. 1954**

Quando le domandai (Negi de Kamare) • Io mi levai dal centro
della terra (Omar Khayyam) • Le domandai (Abu-Said)

These songs are beautifully evocative of the atmosphere of the Middle East: languorous, mysterious, exotic. Vocal writing and harmonic color are similar in all three settings: vocal articulation is declamatory and quasi-recitative, and piano textures are sparse. The songs form a set: "While not cyclical, in the sense of shared melodic material, they are key related (the keys ascend in major thirds), and they progress logically in tempi and dynamics to create a strong program group."[1]

Song 1 begins with a three-note melodic motive in the piano, which reappears numerous times in various registers. There are three free-flowing sections constituting a total of twenty-four measures. Lakeway comments that "the song could be conceived as one long elastic phrase with fluctuations in tempo related to the emotion of the text."[2]

Allegretto bizzaro (lively and bizarre) is the tempo marking for Song 2, a setting that complements Omar Khayyam's enigmatic text. The vocal line is highly declamatory, using few pitches. A transparent texture in the piano changes frequently, providing commentary on the text. There is some text painting in the vocal line and dynamics.

The vocal line dominates Song 3 (the longest song in the set), although it remains declamatory with little melodic shape. An arpeggiated accompaniment is sustained throughout the song. The opening tempo marking reinforces the ethereal and mysterious mood: *Andante mistico (lentamente)*.

This group is published by Forlivesi (10803/10804/10805).

Extended Study List

Petits poëmes japonais • Tristezza crepuscolare • Riflessi • Alba di luna sul bosco • Nel giardino • Melancolie

Selected Reading

Ruth C. Lakeway and Robert C. White, Jr., *Italian Art Song* (Bloomington: Indiana University Press, 1989). Part Three.

Nicholas Slominsky, *Baker's Biographical Dictionary of Musicians.* 8th edition (New York: Schirmer Books/Macmillan, 1992), 870.

Notes

1. Ruth C. Lakeway and Robert C. White, Jr. *Italian Art Song*, 360.
2. Ibid.

PIETRO CIMARA (1887-1967)

Pietro Cimara, Italian conductor and composer, was born in Rome in 1887 and died in Milan in 1967. He was educated at the Academia di Santa Cecilia in Rome, where he was a student of Respighi. He made his conducting debut in Rome in 1916. He conducted at Santa Cecilia until 1927. In 1928, he joined the staff of the Metropolitan Opera and remained there thirty years, primarily as an assistant conductor, conducting special concerts and student performances and occasionally substituting at regular performances.

He composed numerous songs, which were published in Italy and in America.

Fiocca la neve   **Snow is Falling.**
(Giovanni Pascoli)

This is Cimara's most familiar song, a lullaby in which falling snow serves as a metaphor for a gently rocking cradle. An old woman, chin in hand, sings a fretful child to sleep. Cimara's atmospheric setting uses $\frac{6}{8}$ time and minor tonality. The form is ABA, the second section changing to a major tonality. Poetic nuances are mirrored simply in the vocal line; the piano accompaniment sits above the voice for much of the song, imaging the falling snow and the quiet scene. A slow *rallentando* begins in the final phrases at the words "lenta, lenta, lenta," (slowly, slowly, slowly) and is stretched to the end of the song.

Stornello
(Arnaldo Frateili)

The *stornello* was a popular verse that originated in Tuscany. Cimara invests these two stanzas, set strophically, with a beautiful melodic line; the piano introduction uses a simple folk-like tune in thirds in the right hand, coupled with a simple arpeggiated figure in the left hand. Simple chords accompany the entrance of the voice; at midpoint of the verse, the chords expand to combine all the figures into a warmer, lyric texture. A brief coda of two poetic lines concludes the song.

Extended Study List
Scherzo • A una rosa • Melodia autumnale • Non più • Paesaggio • Stornellata marinara • Ondina

Selected Reading
Ruth C. Lakeway and Robert C. White, Jr., *Italian Art Song* (Bloomington: Indiana University Press, 1989). Part Three.

Nicolas Slonimsky, *Bakers Biographical Dictionary of Musicians* (New York: Schirmer/Macmillan,1992).

MARIO CASTELNUOVO-TEDESCO (1895-1968)

> One of my ambitions has always been to wed my music with the pursest
> and highest poetry in the form of the song for voice and piano.
> —Mario Castelnuovo-Tedesco[1]

Mario Castelnuovo-Tedesco, an Italian-American composer, was known internationally for the delicate refinement of his style. He was a prolific and polished craftsman; his style tended toward neoclassicism. Lakeway and White cite four major influences on his work: a passion for Shakespeare, early Jewish music, his affection for the Tuscan countryside, and his devotion to his adopted country, the United States.[2]

Early fame enabled him to stay in his native Florence as a free-lance composer/pianist during the period between the world wars. As a Jew, he thought it sensible to leave Italy in the 1930s, and in 1939 he settled in southern California. In 1946, he became an American citizen and joined the faculty of the Los Angeles Conservatory as a teacher of composition. During the 1940s and 1950s, he composed film music (often under a pseudonym), and was a major influence on composers in this field—André Previn, Jerry Goldsmith, and Henry Mancini were among his students.

Castelnuovo-Tedesco composed prolifically in every medium—operas, oratorios, ballets, orchestral works, chamber compositions, film scores, and songs—some 210 works of evenly crafted quality. Much of his work remains unpublished. His Spanish origins and love for Spain contributed to his abilities to write music on Spanish subjects. He combined guitar with voice(s) in several works.

There is extraordinary variety and uniformly high quality in his songs. They show a great sensitivity to poetic imagery. Some of his finest vocal writing, *Thirty-three Shakespeare Songs,* springs from his enthusiasm for Shakespeare, who provided inspiration for an opera as well (*The Merchant of Venice*, 1961). He also set the poetry of Milton, Byron, Shelley, Elizabeth Barrett Browning, Edna St. Vincent Millay, Walt Whitman and others—some seventy-odd songs in Italian, German, English, and French. Most are arranged and published in sets.

Although the two selections annotated here are not in Italian, they are representative of Castelnuovo-Tedesco's style. They are also among the most performed of his songs.

Recuerdo* **Remembrance.**
(Edna St. Vincent Millay)

This setting demands an accomplished pianist. The recurring poetic refrain "We were very tired, we were very merry/We had gone back and forth all night on the ferry" is set in a rocking rhythm that complements the lassitude of the young travelers and the lapping of the water against the ferry. This melody is reprised as the poetic line is repeated. Accompaniment, tempi, and mood change with the sections of the poem. The musical treatment is markedly melodic and appealing.

*This setting should be compared with American composer John Musto's musical interpretation of the same poem.

Springtime*
(William Shakespeare. *As You Like It***)**

The text for this song is none other than the ubiquitous "It was a lover and his lass." Shakespeare's merry verse has enchanted numerous composers, and inspired many musical settings.

Castelnuovo-Tedesco's setting pays festive tribute to the spring. The first vocal phrase acknowledges the origin of the text with a little modal color. The phrase "in springtime" is set exuberantly, and is echoed by the piano, which also contains the sound of bird trills, harbingers of the season. The song is set strophically in an animated, lively tempo that requires facile diction from the singer.

*Also see settings by Thomas Morley, Peter Warlock, Gerald Finzi, Roger Quilter, and Geoffrey Bush.

Extended Study List
Twelve Shakespeare Songs • *Coplas* • *Three Sephardic Songs* (voice and harp) • Cadix • Stelle cadenti (popular Tuscan poetry) • Ninna nanna • La barba bianca • L'infinito • Tamburino • La ermita de San Simon

Selected Reading
Ruth C. Lakeway and Robert C. White, Jr., *Italian Art Song* (Bloomington: Indiana University Press, 1989). Part Two: The Second-Generation Composers.

Notes
1. Mario Castelnuovo-Tedesco, "The Composer Speaks," in David Ewen, *The New Book of Modern Composers*, 3rd edition, 111.
2. Ruth C. Lakeway and Robert C. White, Jr., *Italian Art Song*, 259-60.

LUCIANO BERIO (1925-2003)

> Luciano Berio has now firmly established his place as a great poetic musician.
> —Marcel Marneat[1]

Luciano Berio's music is inextricably linked with the voice. While he studied with Ghedini at the Milan Conservatory, he accompanied in the vocal studios and later became a conductor in provincial opera houses. He married singer Cathy Berberian in 1950. He studied serial techniques with composer Luigi Dallapiccola at Tanglewood. In 1955, Berio and Bruno Maderna founded the electronic studio at the RAI (Italian Radio), which was named the Studio di Fonologia Musicale. In 1963, he went to the United States and taught in California and at the Juillliard School, returning to Italy in 1972.

Berio's compositions contain serialism, electronic devices, and indeterminacy. His famous "Sequenza" series for various instruments, including voice, is largely aleatory. Many of his compositions feature "layers" of sound materials, which give his music a contrapuntal, linear quality.

Many of Berio's vocal compositions were created for his late wife, mezzo-soprano Cathy Berberian, whose willingness to explore all facets of vocal articulation offered Berio (and other contemporary composers) a "vocal palette of singular richness and wit."[2] With the exception of the *Sequenza III for Voice* (1966), most of

Berio's vocal works are for voice and chamber ensemble.

Berio's style includes diverse elements: imaginative use of timbral components, great directness, melodic expressiveness, use of extra-vocal effects, and a highly developed sense of the theatrical. The works Berio wrote for Berberian gave the twentieth century its most conspicuous body of new vocal writing and have generated other vocal compositions that use new techniques, notably the music of George Crumb and Bernard Rands.

Representative Listing of Berio's Works

Recital I for Cathy (mezzo-soprano and chamber ensemble)
Circles (female voice, violin, harp, 2 percussion), 1960.
Folk Songs (mezzo-soprano and chamber ensemble)
Sequenza for Voice III, 1966
Three Songs by Kurt Weill (arrangements for low voice and chamber ensemble), 1972.
Quattro canzoni popolari (voice/piano), 1946-47.
Chamber Music (female voice, violin, clarinet, harp, cello), 1953.

Notes

1. Liner notes to "Luciano Berio: Modern Music Series," Philips LP Recordiong 6500 631, 1970.
2. David Osmond-Smith, "Berio, Luciano" in *The New Grove Dictionary of Opera*, vol. 1, 423.

Russian Song

Russian classical song sprang from the chants of the Eastern Church and from its colorful heritage of folk music—a heady blend of oriental influences combined with imparted European influences.

Classical Russian song is called *romans*, from the French *romance*. One branch of Russian song, from Glinka to Tchaikovsky to Rakhmaninov, exhibits European features of form and style. Another school of Russian composers exhibits realism—songs that express the life of the people. The songs of Dargomyzhsky, Musorgsky, and even Shostakovich are examples of this style.

Whatever its roots or borrowings, Russian song wears its heart on its sleeve; it is highly emotional and demonstrative, generously drawing the listener into its colorful stories and music. Its melodies are rich and lyric, its poetic moods deeply felt.

The great tradition of Russian song was firmly established in the nineteenth century. Glinka and Dargomyzhsky, considered the first composers of classical Russian songs, dominated the first half of the nineteenth century, followed by the music of the "Moguchaya Kuchka" (or "Mighty Handful"): Borodin, Cui, Balakirev, Musorgsky, and Rimsky-Korsakov. This group of five composers wrote music that was highly nationalistic in style, composing 500 songs. Of the Mighty Handful, Musorgsky stands out as a composer whose vocal music existed (by his own admission) to reproduce in sound the qualities of human speech, which he believed to be strictly controlled by musical laws. Musorgsky's songs are highly dramatic and colorful, full of realistic characterizations.

The Mighty Handful were highly productive song composers, but when Russian song is mentioned, the names that come to mind most readily are Tchaikovsky and Rakhmaninov. Their songs, filled with sweeping lyric lines that often express melancholy, are highly appealing to performers and audiences.

Later Russian composers such as Medtner, Prokofiev, and Stravinsky continued the development of song. Medtner, although strongly influenced by German style, set exquisite songs to the poems of Pushkin. Prokofiev and Stravinsky infused their work with modern harmonies and rhythms. After the Russian Revolution, Stravinsky and Prokofiev, with other Russian artists, left Russia. Prokofiev returned later.

In 1932, the Central Committee of the Communist Party on literature and all the arts denounced all forms of "modernism" and "subjectivism." This effectively stifled the further development of solo song, notably the work of Shostakovich. Today, a variety of vocal music is being composed in the Russian states, but it is slow to filter far afield of its birthplace.

Sadly, singers have largely overlooked Russian song—perhaps through non-acquaintance with the Russian language, availability of published copies, or other cultural barriers. Only in the last decades, with publication of supporting reference books and recordings, has this rich source of literature begun to emerge in concerts, recitals, and recordings.

A note on Russian spellings:

It is often difficult to discern the correct spelling of Russian composers' names due to the spelling in their original Cyrillic alphabet. Confusion often arises when transliterating some Russian symbols into characters and sounds that do not exist in other languages or normally appear as two or three letter combinations. To compound the confusion, these sounds are often transliterated differently in English, French or German, due to spelling and pronunciation rules for each of these languages. These differences account for spellings such as Tschaikowsky, Tchaikovsky and Chaykovsky, Rachmaninoff and Rakhmaninov, or Moussorgsky and Musorgsky—each of which are spelled correctly for their country of origin. The spellings of Russian composers' names and song titles appearing in this book use the standard system of transliteration for the U.S. and U.K., and are consistent with the spellings found in *The New Grove Dictionary of Music and Musicians*.

MIKHAIL IVANOVICH GLINKA (1804-1857)

> Frequent encounters with singers and amateurs of singing gave me the practical acquaintance with [the] whimsical and difficult art necessary to manage the voice and dexterously write for it.
>
> —Mikhail Glinka[1]

Without Mikhail Glinka, Russian music would have taken a very different course. Glinka's musical style had a profound influence on all the important late nineteenth-century Russian composers—Balakirev, Musorgsky, Borodin, Rimsky-Korsakov, and Tchaikovsky. It was Glinka who, single-handedly, laid the foundation for a Russian musical tradition.[2] In his monograph outlining the development of the Russian romance, composer César Cui writes: "Mikhail Glinka should be considered both the father of the Russian romance and the founder of Russian opera."[3]

His musical education was haphazard, and he never developed a distinctive or consistent personal style of composition. As a child he had some lessons from the Irish pianist John Field. He studied composition seriously for six months in Berlin in 1834. The folk music of his childhood in St. Petersburg, and Italian *bel canto* opera were strong influences on his music. In his first important compositions, written in Berlin, he applied variation technique to Russian folk themes.

Glinka was inspired by the idea of creating a true Russian opera. He composed two operas, both of which reflect a synthesis of Russian melody with Western operatic form. His first opera *A Life for the Tsar*, first performed in 1836, was an immediate success, and established him as Russia's leading composer. For the first time, characteristic Russian music was heard on the operatic stage with stunning effect, particularly in the choral scenes. Glinka's writing of expressive Russian recitative no doubt influenced the work of Musorgsky.

Glinka's second opera, *Ruslan i Lyudmila* (1842), based on a fairytale by Aleksandr Pushkin, was less successful, but featured some strikingly original musical scenes, beautiful lyrical melodies, and colorful orchestrations. In this opera, Glinka created an absorbing blend of traditional and exotic musical styles. Although it did not enjoy popular success, *Ruslan i Lyudmila* was decisive in inspiring later works by Russian composers based on oriental and enchanted themes.

Glinka's orchestral works include the symphonic poem *Kamarinskaya*[4] and two overtures, *Jota Aragonesa* and *Summer Night in Madrid*, inspired by a visit to Spain.

Glinka's travels in Italy had given him a thorough knowledge of singing and writing for the voice. He was himself a competent singer and pianist, and was acknowledged to be a peerless performer of his own songs. Glinka composed nearly eighty *romances*, and one song cycle *Proshchanie s Peterburgom* (Farewell to St. Petersburg).

Glinka's songs are a combination of Russian character, lyric melody and sophisticated style. They are highly varied in content and character, and in them, one can observe a definite progression of greater freedom of form and mood. With them, Glinka created a new path for Russian art song.

Ya pomnyu chudnoye mgnoven'ye   **I remember that wonderful moment. 1840**
(Aleksandr Pushkin)

Some of Glinka's best songs are settings of Pushkin, and this one is perhaps the finest. It was composed four years after the premiere of *A Life for the Tsar*, a period during which Glinka produced some of his best *romances* .

It is an idealized *romance*, written in a sentimental style. One of the important components of this song is Glinka's compelling sense of phrasing. He writes broad-lined vocal phrases that often verge upon the operatic. With each successive verse, he varies the vocal line, pointing up the escalating drama and emotional momentum. Piano figures are also changed to complement text content and maintain dramatic intensity.

The influence of Bellini is clearly evident in this *romance*. Other romances that reveal Glinka's attraction for the *bel canto* style are twelve songs he composed to Italian texts.

V krovi gorit ogon' zhelan'ya   **The fire of longing burns in my heart. 1838**
(Aleksandr Pushkin)

Aleksandr Pushkin has no real rival for the romantic title of "national poet" of Russia. He was celebrated as such, even during his lifetime. This passionate text drew an equally ardent response from Glinka, who set the words in sumptuous vocal phrases.

Glinka's gift for writing expressive, winding melodies is an outstanding feature of this *romance*.There are two verses, set strophically. A swaying, strongly accented waltz in the piano accompaniment maintains the forward movement .

Somnenie   **Doubt. 1838**
(Nestor Kukol'nik)

Glinka composed this romance for Karolina Kolkovskaya, a fourteen-year-old singing pupil at the theatre school where he taught. Glinka's love of the Italian operatic style—notably that of Bellini, whom he met in 1831—is definitely reflected in the pliant vocal phrases.

Aleksandr Serov[*] recalls hearing this piece at a party in St. Petersburg, and impressed, wrote: "In the smooth, plastic, expressive melody [there was] a certain blending of Italian voluptuousness with a gloom, weariness, and sadness that was purely Slav."[5]

*Serov was a prominent music critic and composer of the day.

Extended Study List

Ne poy, kratsavitsa, pri mne (O never sing to me) • Gde nasha roza? (Where is our rose?) • Ya zdes', Inezil'ya (I am here, Inezilla) • Venetsianskaya noch' (Venetian night) • Zazdravny kubok (The toasting cup) • Adel' (Adèle) • Nochnoy zefir (Night zephyr) • Priznanie (Declaration) • Meri (Mary) • Pesn'ya Margarity (Gretchen at the Spinning Wheel) • Nochnoy smotr (The Night Watch) • Evreyskaya pesnya (Jewish Song) • Usnuli golubye (The Blue Waves are Sleeping) • Zhavoronok (The Lark)

Selected Reading

Gerald Abraham, "Glinka and his Achievement," *Studies in Russian Music* (London, 1935), 21.
David Brown, *Glinka: A Biographical and Critical Study* (London: Oxford University Press, 1974).
Mikhail Ivanovich Glinka, *Memoirs,* trans. by Richard B. Mudge (Norman: University of Oklahoma Press, 1963).

Notes

1. Glinka, writing about the three years he spent in Italy. From Mikhail Glinka, *Reminiscences*, trans. Mikhail Skorodyonok. Glinka's memoirs, first published in 1887, provide a remarkable self-portrait of the composer.
2. David Brown, *Glinka: A Biographical and Critical Study*, 1-2.
3. César Cui, *The Russian Romance: An Outline of Its Development*, published in St. Petersburg, 1896. Trans. James Walker. The author is indebted to Michael Cochran for sharing this material from his personal library.
4. Glinka's composition *Kamarinskaya* (1848), a kaleidoscopic array of orchestral variations, was said by Tchaikovsky to be the acorn from which the oak of later Russian symphonic music grew.
5. Brown., 139.

ALEKSANDR PORFIR'EVICH BORODIN (1833-1887)

> I am an incurable poet at heart, and I am cherishing the hope of one day getting to the end of my opera, though I can't help laughing sometimes.
> —Aleksandr Borodin[1]

Aleksandr Borodin belonged to the group of Russian nationalistic composers known as the Mighty Handful: Borodin, Cui, Balakirev, Musorgsky and Rimsky-Korsakov. The songs of Borodin and the Mighty Handful were all inspired by Dargomyzhsky.[2]

Borodin wrote his earliest compositions in the 1850s while he was a medical student at the Academy of Medicine and Surgery. In 1864, he became a professor of organic chemistry at the Academy of Medicine. He called himself "a Sunday composer," since the time he could devote to composition was limited.

Borodin's song list is slender—just sixteen songs. His three small sets of songs are varied in style and scope, reflecting his natural lyric gifts and refined eclectic taste. His songs, containing elements of romanticism, impressionism, and primitivism, blend a distinctly Russian sound with exotic colors and harmonies.[3] His songs have been described as emotional, but not sentimental in quality, with elegant and highly original piano accompaniments. Findeisen observes that the distinctive characteristic of Borodin's songs is the "spiciness of their harmonic combinations. They are replete with dissonances and chromaticism, imparting an exceptionally nervous quality to nearly all of his songs."[4]

Spyashchaya knyazhna   **The Sleeping Princess. 1867**
(A. Borodin)

Borodin's first published song is one of his best known, and is representative of his musical style. He wrote his own text and entitled it a "ballad." Evoking an image of an enchanted wood, "The Sleeping Princess" has a beautiful vocal line and a drowsy lyric atmosphere that complements the French fairytale *La Belle au bois dormant*. Like the fairytale, it is also mysterious and slightly ominous.

Borodin pays homage to French style by using a combination of impressionistic sound colors. The accompaniment contains a persistent syncopated interval of a second punctuated by an ominous tolling C (*sfz*) over an ostinato open fourth, producing a lulling, drowsy effect. The bass line contains whole-tone scales. The vocal line contains the repetitive refrain "sleep...sleep." This passage was so dissonant for its time that it created controversy among critics and branded Borodin as a musical radical.

Borodin dedicated "The Sleeping Princess" to Rimsky-Korsakov.

Pesnya temnogo lesa   **The Song of the Dark Forest. 1868**
(A. Borodin)

Although all Borodin's songs are lyrical, this one could be considered less so. Written in an epic, heroic manner, the setting evokes a feeling of a long-ago tale, told with breadth and power—by the forest itself. The forest tells the story of people who gathered together in the forest and then marched on a city, putting their enemies to death. According to some accounts, the song had difficulty getting past the censor who found it "seditious" and almost suppressed its publication.[5]

The vocal line is at times primitive in style (clearly influenced by Musorgsky) and contains irregularly barred phrases with meter changes every measure ($\frac{2}{4}$ – $\frac{5}{4}$ – $\frac{3}{4}$ – $\frac{7}{4}$), and the piano accompaniment is written in octaves, which creates a somber mood. The song contains irregular rhythms like those found in Russian folk music and suggests the natural speech patterns of a storyteller. "Song of the Dark Forest" has often been called Borodin's finest song.

Otravoy polny moi pesni   **My songs are poisoned. 1868**
(Heinrich Heine, "Vergiftet sind meine Lieder," trans. by Borodin)

Like several other early songs of Borodin, this song is based on texts by the German poet Heinrich Heine. It is brief, portraying the poet's hopeless desire for a woman who has poisoned his life with a "fatal venom." This song belongs to the same set (*Four Romances*) as the "Song of the Dark Forest," and both songs exhibit Borodin's mature musical style.

This song is full of passion and intensity, almost Chopinesque. The declamatory vocal line is fierce and bitter, accompanied by a piano that freely explores wide-ranging and dissonant harmonies. The same small lyric phrase in the piano that opens the song also closes it.

Extended Study List

Falshivaya nota (The False Note) • Morskaya tsarevna (The Sea Princess) • More (The Sea) • Iz slyoz moikh (From My Tears) • Razlyubella krasna devitsa (The Pretty Girl No Longer Loves me) • Shto tyh rahno, zoren'ka poblednela? (Why So Early, O Sunset?) • Dlya beregof otchizny dalney (For the Shores of a Distant Homeland) • Arabskaya melodiya (Arabian Melody) • Spes (The Arrogant One) • Chudny saht (The Magic Garden)

Selected Reading

Gerald Abraham, *Borodin: The Composer and His Music* (London: Wm. Reeves).

Serge Dianin, *Borodin*. Trans. Robert Lord (London: Oxford University Press, 1963). Chapter 9: "The Songs."

Notes

1. In a letter to L.I. Karmalina, 19 January 1877. Quoted in Dianin, *Borodin*, 97.
2. Linn Maxwell and Robert McCoy. Liner notes, *Romances of the Russian Masters* (Albany Records. Compact disc TROY 072, 1992).
3. The musical *Kismet* is based on themes from Borodin's music.
4. Nicolay Findeisen, *The Russian Art Song (Romance): An Essay on its Historical Development*. Published, 1905, trans. James Walker, 71. The author is indebted to Michael Cochran for sharing this material from his personal library.
5. Dianin, *Borodin*, 79.

CÉSAR ANTONOVICH CUI (1835-1918)

It contains charming things, but unfortunately it suffers from a certain insipidity...By nature Cui is more drawn towards light and piquantly rhythmic French music; but the demands of the "invincible band" which he has joined, compel him to do violence to his natural gifts and to follow those paths of would-be original harmony which do not suit him.

—Pyotr Tchaikovsky, commenting on Cui's opera William Ratcliffe (1869)[1]

César Cui was also one of the "Mighty Handful," and like the other members of the group, was passionate in his artistic nationalistic beliefs. Cui, a young officer in the Engineering Corps of the Russian Army,[2] was "recruited" into the group by Balakirev, who instructed him in music as well as his ideas for a new style of Russian art music based on the native music of the Russian people.

Cui composed more than 200 songs and eleven operas in addition to his orchestral and instrumental pieces. His music has been criticized as amateur in quality. He is best remembered as a music critic, writing on music from the Baroque to the Romantic periods, and including Russian compositions in his criticisms. His reviews, often pointedly frank, reflected his personal tastes and sympathies. Most importantly, they mirrored the national sentiments of Balakirev and his group and, through his publications, Cui became the spokesman for the group.

Cui's father was French and his mother Lithuanian. Not surprisingly, his music is probably the least "Russian" of the Mighty Handful. His compositions show influences of Western romanticism, and his musical style has often been characterized as a blend of Chopin and Schumann. The majority of his operas are from French sources; only three are based on Russian stories. He was comfortable composing in miniature forms, as witnessed by the large number of *romances* he wrote. His songs are elegant, graceful, and somewhat conservative. They are rarely animated or exuberant nor do they contain a Russian national flavor. For the most part, they seem more suited to the salon than the recital hall; however, the best of them are charming examples of the Russian *romance*.

Tsarskosel'skaya statuya   **The Statue at Tsarskoe-Selo.**
(Aleksandr Pushkin)

Cui's musical description of the statue on the fountain at Tsarskoe-Selo[*] is a representative example of his song style. The sculpture depicts a pensive young girl who sits holding the pieces of a broken water urn, through which the fountain's stream continues to flow. An unvarying arpeggiated accompaniment depicts the softly falling fountain water; the vocal line is charming but rather sentimental.

[*]Tsarskoe-Selo, also known as "Pushkin," is the town where Catherine the Great maintained her summer palace. Many artists, sculptors, poets and composers visited this small city to find solitude and inspiration.

Zdes' siren' tak bystro uvyadaet   **Here the Lilacs Quickly Wither. c.1890**
(Sully-Prudhomme, "Ici-bas," anon. translation)

In addition to his Russian songs, Cui composed songs on French texts by Victor Hugo, Jean Richepin, and Sully-Prudhomme—a curious trio of French poets to select from so many. Although Fauré's setting of "Ici-bas" is much better known, Cui's version is passionately intense in the style of Duparc and provides an interesting comparison of text setting. Cui also used another of Sully-Pruhomme's text for a setting titled "Solitude." This is the same poem that Duparc used for his *mélodie* "Soupir."

Sozhzhyonnoe pis'mo   **The Burnt Letter. 1825**
(Aleksandr Pushkin)

Here is a nineteenth-century text that deals with burning love letters.[*] The poet watches the letter burst into flame and turn to ashes, declaring that the ashes will remain with him forever, as his only consolation.

This *romance* is like a miniature dramatic *scena*. A solemn chordal flourish sets the drama in motion. The story begins with a recitative-like passage in the voice, which broadens into more melodic phrases. As the singer recalls the touching incident, piano figures change subtly, intensifying the dramatic mood. Oscillating piano figures outline the flames as the letters burn, the smoke from their fire curling upwards in the air. The final vocal phrases rise towards the ultimate cadence, but do not finish. Instead, the voice vanishes into the air, like the ashes of the burned letter. The piano brings down the curtain on this sad drama, using the same rhythmic chordal pattern with which the *romance* began.

[*]See Mozart's "Als die Luise," and Poulenc's "Fleurs" for eighteenth and twentieth-century examples.

Khristós voskrés   **Christ Has Risen.**
(Cui)

This lovely romance is classically conceived as to form. The poem heralds Easter and the coming of spring. There are three poetic stanzas; in the first, tolling bells announce Eastertide; in the second, nature responds as the ice breaks and the forests become green again; and in the last, the poet welcomes the joy that spring-time brings.

Cui's formal structure is simple but effective. The vocal phrases are identical for each verse. Each one ends with two exultant repetitions of "Khristós voskrés!", set in a higher register. The piano figures are varied for each verse, their rhythm and motion complementing the poetic content. These subtle variations in the structure provide just the right amount of variety in this beautiful song.

Extended Study List

Menisk (Mèniscus) • La Tombe et la rose (Victor Hugo) • Enfant, si j'étais Roi (Victor Hugo) • Solitude (Sully-Prudhomme) • Ya pomnyu vecher (I Remember an Evening) • Kosnylas' ya tsvetka (I Touched the Bloom Lightly) • Son (A Dream) • Moya balovnitsa (My Mischievous Girl) • Otchego eto, milaya? (Why is it, My Dear?) • Ne rozu Pafosskuyu (Not a Pathos Rose) • Zhelanie (Desire)

Selected Reading

James Bakst, *A History of Russian-Soviet Music* (Westport, CT: Greenwood Press, 1977).

Notes

1. Quoted in Richard Anthony Leonard, *A History of Russian Music* (London: Jarrolds, 1956), 83.
2. Cui's profession as a military engineer was a distinguished one. He was recognized as the greatest Russian authority on fortification.

MODEST PETROVICH MUSORGSKY (1839-1881)

> It is *the people* I want to depict; sleeping or waking, eating and drinking, I have them constantly in my mind's eye; again and again they rise before me all their reality—huge, unvarnished, with no tinsel.
>
> —Modest Musorgsky[1]

Modest Musorgsky stands out among the members of the Russian "Mighty Handful." He was innovative, controversial, creative, and rather obsessed with his unique vision of art and what it was supposed to be—a musical art that centered around realism that expressed the lives and experiences of common people realistically rather than symbolically. Russian writers of the day— Tolstoy and Pushkin are prime examples—were producing literary works that expressed realism, and Musorgsky was eager to embrace this new style in music. His goal was to use music to create realistic drama that would be popular with the masses.

With his opera *Boris Godunov,* Musorgsky pioneered the use of music to express dramatic action and psychological-emotional experiences. As such, *Boris Godunov* was a musical drama unique in its time. Musorgsky thought of the music not as mere tonal textures, but as an expression of the deep psychological essence of human life and experience. In *Boris Godunov,* he also perfected his genius for blending national elements into the music. These qualities are also reflected in his songs. He believed that every song was a small drama, its form created from dramatic tension, suspense, climax, and resolution.[2] His melodies also reflect realism. Rather than being sweeping and lyrical, they are almost speech-like, following the natural rhythms and inflections of the Russian language; they start and stop according to the expressiveness in dramatic speech (rather than to the bar line). Broken into short phrases like natural speech, these techniques create a sense of "pitched conversation."

Musorgsky composed about fifty *romances* in all. His songs reflect several influences: Russian folk songs and the musical styles of Berlioz, Liszt, and Schumann.

Pesni i plaski smerti	**Songs and Dances of Death. 1875-77**
(Count Golenishev-Kutuzov)	

Kolybel'naya (Lullaby) • Serenada (Serenade) • Trepak (Trepak)
Polkovodets (The Field Marshal)

These four songs successfully describe, with impressive dramatic force, the struggle between Man and Death. Death appears in assorted disguises throughout the cycle. With his insatiable need to consume human life, Death uses every means possible to destroy it—lies, hate, caresses, and even lullabies. Each song in this cycle is a different miniature drama complete with plot, characters and dialogue. The cycle is chilling in its dramatic realism.

Songs and Dances of Death was not published during Musorgsky's lifetime. He had planned to extend the cycle, including still more dramatic confrontations between Death and Man. He had even made sketches for several new songs, but he never finished the project. Musorgsky later used the theme of death to produce highly charged drama in his opera *Boris Godunov*.

KOLYBEL'NAYA (LULLABY). This song is perhaps the least "melodic" song in this cycle, and the most like "pitched expression." It is an excellent example of Musorgsky's ability to instantly create dramatic realism and characterization through simple musical means.

As morning's light begins to break, we see a distraught mother, weary from an all-night vigil near the cot of her dying child. She hears a knock at the door; Death enters and offers to watch over the child while she rests. Death speaks in quiet, chilling tones (not unlike Death in Schubert's "Der Tod und das Mädchen"). His words are laced with calm triplets, underpinned with simple chords in the piano—tempting, intense, and horrible. Death sings a repetitive "lullaby" phrase to calm the feverish baby, whom he finally claims for his own. The mother, in her deep anguish, sings brief phrases of angular and chromatic intervals accompanied by dissonant piano figures.

SERENADA (SERENADE). In this song, Death appears in his most menacing disguise—a lover. He stands beneath the window of an invalid maiden, seducing her with a voluptuous serenade. As the consumptive girl becomes increasingly caught up in the passionate music, she grows weaker and finally submits to the embrace of Death, who cries in a horrifying voice, "You are mine!" Musically, this song stands apart from the others in the cycle by virtue of its unabashed Romantic lyricism—almost Schumannesque or Lisztian in character.[3]

The serenade (the "A" section in the formal AABA pattern) consists of heavily accented, swaying lyric phrases that grow more intense and seductive with each repetition. The final measures contain Musorgsky's characteristic use of Russian speech patterns—a unique mix of declamation and fragmented melodies that builds to a terrifying dramatic climax as Death senses his victim's final vulnerability and takes her.

TREPAK (TREPAK). The title refers to the Russian folk dance of the same name, a strongly accented dance in two-beat rhythm. The story tells of a drunken old peasant lost in the forest during a howling winter blizzard. He is accompanied by Death, who celebrates with him, urging him to dance the *trepak*. Soon exhausted from his dance, the old man sinks to the ground, as Death exhorts the elements to tuck him into bed under a soft blanket of snow.

The song contains Russian folk elements—repetitive melodies and short vocal phrases of narrow range. The text and music are highly suggestive of the *trepak* folk dance. The *trepak* theme is repeated a dozen times, each time at the same pitch level, but with different accompaniments and harmonies, and small variations in melody, and rhythmic extensions. A short sixteenth-note figure in the piano is derived from the "Dies irae."

POLKOVODETS (THE FIELD MARSHAL). As the song begins, a fierce battle is underway, terrifying in its violence and cruelty. At the conclusion of the day-long struggle, Death, as the Field Marshal, appears astride his mighty war horse, and surveys the carnage, smiling. His bones gleaming in the moonlight, he commands the dead to rise and pass in review before him. After he counts his troops, Death assigns them to their graves, and then pounds down the earth overhead so that they can never rise.

Musorgsky uses the music to chillingly portray the battle's fury. Opening measures feature frantic, unceasing eighth-note triplets running in the piano and a series of small accented gestures that rise and fall in different octaves. Percussive effects in the piano portray the battle's fury. Flashing armor, thundering cannons, charging soldiers on horseback, and the falling of the wounded are illustrated in driving, thick-textured piano figures that seem to gain momentum as they progress. An arrogant martial theme represents Death and is also articulated in the vocal line with percussive dramatic force.

Detskaya   **The Nursery. 1868-72**
(Modest Musorgsky)

S nyaney (With Nanny) • V uglu (In the Corner) • Zhuk (The Beetle) •
S kukloy (With the Doll) • Na son gryadushchy (Prayer at Bedtime) •
Poyekhal na palochke (The Hobby-Horse) • Kot Matros (Sailor the Cat)

Musorgsky wrote the texts for these seven songs, which realistically capture the emotions and activities of a day in the nursery. It is a series of little scenes in a child's world, viewed through a child's eyes. *The Nursery* is not intended to be sung to children, but the childlike spirit is present throughout the cycle. Debussy called the cycle "a masterpiece" and wrote of Musorgsky: "No one has given utterance to the best within us in tone more gentle or profound; he is unique, and will remain so, because his art is spontaneous and free from arid formulas."[4]

Throughout the songs, the piano aids in telling the story. It depicts many characters and actions with vivid expressiveness, among them: a limping king and sneezing queen (Song 1); a mischievous child unwinding the Nurse's ball of knitting yarn (Song 2); the buzz of menacing beetles (Song 3); an innocent lullaby to a doll (Song 4); the obligatory list of blessings at bedtime (Song 5); a wild rocking ride on the hobby horse (Song 6); and the stealthy cat stalking a caged bird (Song 7).

Musorgsky captures the inflections of the child's voice with amazing realism as he wheedles and cajoles his Nurse; occasionally (Songs 2 and 3) the voice of the Nurse is heard—deeper, more mature, and full of unquestioned authority. *The Nursery* is a group of vignettes that is highly entertaining as well as uniquely realistic.

Extended Study List

Bez solntsa (*Sunless*) • Pesnya Mefistofelya o blokhe (Mephistopheles' Song of the Flea) • Gopak (Hopak) • Klassik (The Classicist) • Gornimi tikho letela dusha nebesami (Softly the Spirit Flew Up to Heaven) • Spes' (Pride) • Strekotun' ya beloboka (Chattering Magpie) • Sirotka (The Orphan) • Gde ty, zvyozdochka? (Where Art Thou, Little Star?) • Po griby (Gathering Mushrooms) • Chto vam slova lyubvi? (What are Love's Words to You?) • Noch' (Night) • Kozyol: svetskaya skazochka (The he-goat: a worldly story) • Po nad Donom sad tsvetyot (The Garden by the Don)

Selected Reading

James Bakst, *A History of Russian-Soviet Music* (Westport, CT: Greenwood Press, 1977).

M. D. Calvocoressi, *Mussorgsky*. Completed and revised by Gerald Abraham (London: J. M. Dent & Sons, 1974).

Jay Leyda and Sergei Bertensson, ed. and trans. *The Mussorgsky Reader* (New York: W. W. Norton & Co., 1947).

Bennie Middaugh, "Modest Mussorgsky's *Songs and Dances of Death*," *The NATS Bulletin*, 26:2 (1969), 2-10.

Alexandra Orlova, ed., *Mussorgsky Remembered* (Bloomington: Indiana University Press, 1991). Accounts of Mussorgsky's life and personality as seen in a collection of material by his contemporaries.

Oskar von Riesemann, *Mussorgsky*. trans. from the German by Paul England (Westport, CN: Greenwood Press, 1970). Chapter 5 deals with Mussorgsky's songs.

Laurence R. Richter, *Mussorgsky's Complete Song Texts* (Geneseo, NY: Leyerle, 2002).

Notes

1. In a letter to Ilya Repin, Russian artist. Quoted in Richard Anthony Leonard, *A History of Russian Music* (London: Jarrolds, 1956), 92.
2. Ibid., 96.
3. Bennie Middaugh, "Modest Mussorgsky's *Songs and Dances of Death*," *The NATS Bulletin*, 26:2, 6.
4. Quoted in Leonard, 95.

PYOTR IL'ICH TCHAIKOVSKY (1840-1893)

His talent does not possess the flexibility required for real vocal music... He did not acknowledge the equal rights of poetry and music... He regarded the text with despotic presumption...

—César Cui[1]

In contrast to Musorgsky's distinctly Russian style, Tchaikovsky's compositions are cosmopolitan. He was the first conservatory trained Russian composer, and a member of the first graduating class of the newly opened St. Petersburg Conservatory (presently known as the Rimsky-Korsakov Conservatory).

His musical style shares characteristics with the Europeans—Brahms, for instance. He did not consider the elements of Russian culture and folk music to be of great importance, though he used folk materials in some of his songs. For his 100-odd songs, he chose texts by Russian poets that display the Russian fondness for melancholy, unrequited passion, and plaintive sentiment, but Tchaikovsky treated the majority of these texts with an overwhelming and spacious lyricism, which is often at odds with Russian declamation. Rather than fusing words and music into a single entity, he subjugated the text to sweeping melodies. This put him at odds with César Cui and the other members of the "Mighty Handful."

Tchaikovsky wrote piano accompaniments that are overtly romantic and often have a contrasting countermelody or share melodic motives with the voice. He also used piano preludes, interludes, and postludes in his songs. Taken as a whole, his songs are striking in contrast—by turn dramatic, intensely emotional, solemn, sumptuously lyric, or reminiscent of folk songs.

Net, tol'ka tot, kto znal, Op. 6, No. 6   **No, only one who knows.* 1869**
(Johann Wolfgang von Goethe,   **(Song of Mignon)**
"Nur wer die Sehnsucht kennt", trans. L. Mey)

This is one of Tchaikovsky's most familiar songs, and probably the best known of all Russian art songs. He was twenty-nine when he composed it, and its romantic melancholy is typical of his music.

A syncopated chordal accompaniment throbs throughout the piece, paired with melodic figures above or below. A poignant opening theme is introduced in the piano, then taken up by the voice; melodic materials are shared by voice and piano at various points in the song. After a typical romantic climax, a moment of silence precedes the restatement of the opening motive in the piano, accompanied by a new melody in the voice. The emotional mood is one of intense loneliness and longing for understanding of grief. It is full of restrained and elegant melancholy, often too exaggerated and sentimental in performance. In the hands of a sensitive interpreter, this *romance* is poignant and touching.

*In the 1930s and 40s, this song was popularly known as "None but the lonely heart."

Sred' shumnogo bala, Op. 38, No. 3   **At the ball. 1878**
(Alexey Tolstoy)

A Tchaikovsky waltz tune of lyric beauty sweeps through this *romance*. Both the musical setting and the text call to mind the ballroom scenes in Tchaikovsky's opera *Evgeny Onegin*. The melodic phrases are intensely lyric, but interspersed with repeated falling intervals—the musings of the poet, remembering the grandeur of the ballroom where he saw a strange and beautiful woman whom he cannot forget. The piano introduction is used again to close the song.

Serenada Don-Zhuana, Op. 38, No. 1   **Don Juan's Serenade. 1878**
(Alexey Tolstoy)

Tchaikovsky set this poem at the suggestion of his patroness Mme. Von Meck, who marked several of Tolstoy's poems for Tchaikovsky's consideration. This waltz has a quite different character than that of "At the ball." Beneath a lady's balcony, Don Juan sings a brilliant bravura song. It is operatic in style and unrelenting in its tempo, capturing the impatience of the Don in his romantic pursuits. Tchaikovsky's piano introduction presents a quick, almost frenzied theme tinged with a bit of violence. There is even a short melodic fragment reminiscent of material from "At the ball" near the end of the piece.

Zakatilas' solntse, Op. 73, No. 4   **The sun has set. 1893**
(D.M. Rathaus)

This song belongs to a set of six (Op. 73) composed in the last year of Tchaikovsky's life. Outstanding in quality, each song is a highly lyrical work that evokes a particular mood. This set displays Tchaikovsky's interest in impressionism.

The themes expressed in this song are passionate romance and nostalgia for past youth. Vocal phrases are short variations of the opening piano line. The piano expresses great passion, driven by wide textures and syncopated chords in the treble. The nightingale, symbol of lovers' despair, is present in the last lines of the poem.

Ya li v pole da ne travushka byla,   **Was I not a tiny blade of grass.**
Op. 47, No. 7   **1880**
(Ivan Surikov)

Most of Ivan Surikov's poetry treats the hard lot of the Russian peasant, of Russian nature, and of Russian children. The *romance* is often called "The Bride's Lament,"—its text, the poignant words of a young girl forced to marry against her wishes. It is one of Tchaikovsky's few *romances* in the Russian folk style, and reveals his less-familiar nationalist side. Tchaikovsky discarded the poem's original title "Little-Russian Melody" (Ukrainian Melody), and left one stanza unset.

A young girl's parents have married her to a much older man whom she does not love; the text is her bitter, despairing soliloquy. The first two stanzas of the text use metaphor—the grass cut down for straw, the bush cut down for thatch—but the third, concluding section is the most dramatic in the song. It speaks directly to what has been done to her life by this marriage.

Tchaikovsky employs mixed meters—$\frac{3}{2}$ and $\frac{4}{4}$—in the song. There are three poetic stanzas, interleaved with a three-line refrain "Okh, ty, gore mayo goryushko!" (O woe, you heavy woe of mine!). This is sung twice, followed by "Znat', znat' takaya moya dolyushka!" (So that is what fate had in store for me!). Melodic material in this section is melismatic, and was inspired by a folk lament.

Tchaikovsky later transcribed the song for voice and orchestra.

459

Rastvoril ya okno, Op. 63, No. 2   **I opened the window wide. 1887**
(K. Romanov)

The *romances* of Op. 63 are noteworthy for Tchaikovsky's attention to text. In these songs, he achieved a closer coordination of music and poetry. Cui wrote that Tchaikovsky often treated his texts "unceremoniously,"[2] often rearranging, eliminating, or repeating words. He sometimes repeated verses or parts of verses, at times adding his own words. In the songs of Op. 63, Tchaikovsky also makes less use of extended piano postludes.

Romanov's text has a theme commonly found in Russian songs—the longing for home. A traveler opens the window for a breath of air, and falls to his knees as he smells the scent of lilacs. A nightingale begins to sing. The combination of birdsong and the fragrance of the flowers overwhelm him with a great longing for his homeland.

The song is in $\frac{9}{8}$ meter and consists of two stanzas, set strophically. The vocal lines are warmly lyrical and intensely felt, but remain graceful and controlled.

To bylo ranneyu vesnoy, Op. 38, No. 2   **It was in early spring. 1878**
(Aleksey Tolstoy)

Tchaikovsky was inspired by compose this song by Beethoven's setting of Goethe's text "Mailied." Tolstoy's poem is a recollection of young love, recounted with intense emotion. The lovers sit under the shade of a birch tree, with all the sights and sounds of nature around them. She accepts his declaration of love, and he weeps for happiness.

Tchaikovsky's setting is buoyant and full of energy. The first rapturous vocal phrase launches the song forward in one long arc that finally comes full circle, as the opening piano introduction is repeated in the final measures for closure. Piano figures echo material from the vocal line, and a strong bass line maintains the vibrant, dramatic mood.

Extended Study List

Blagoslovlyayu vas, lesa (I bless you, forests) • Pogodi (Wait) • Legenda (A Legend) • Ya tebe nichego neskazhu (I'll tell you nothing) • Otchego? (Why?) • Ne dolgo nam gulyat' (We have not far to walk) • Korol'ki (The Corals) • Serenada (Serenade) • Gornimi tikho letala dusha nebesami (Softly the spirit flew up to heaven) • Snova, kak prezhde, odin (Again, as before, alone) • Solovey (The nightingale)

Selected Reading

Alshvang, "The Songs," in *The Music of Tchaikovsky,* ed. Gerald Abraham (New York: W. W. Norton & Co., 1946).

Laurence R. Richter, *Tchaikovsky's Complete Song Texts* (Geneseo, NY: Leyerle Publications, 2001).

Richard D. Sylvester, *Tchaikovsky's Complete Songs: a companion with texts and translations* (Bloomington: Indiana University Press, 2002).

Notes

1. Cui's book *The Russian Song* (1896) vilified Tchaikovsky's free treatment of the texts of his songs, criticizing in particular the repetition of separate words and often, whole sentences in musical context. Quoted in *The Music of Tchaikovsky,* ed. Gerald Abraham (New York: W. W. Norton & Co., 1946), 197.

2. César Cui, *The Russian Romance: An Outline of Its Development,* published in St. Petersburg, 1896. Trans. James Walker, 63. The author is indebted to Michael Cochran for sharing this material from his personal library.

NIKOLAY ANDREYEVICH RIMSKY-KORSAKOV (1844-1908)

> I consider that the singers and the large audiences are justified in demanding harmonic melodiousness, sweetness and richness...
> —Nikolay Rimsky-Korsakov[1]

Nikolay Andreyevich Rimsky-Korsakov was one the "Mighty Handful." He was born in Tikhvin, near Novgorod, into an artistocratic family. From 1856 to 1862, he attended the naval academy in St. Petersburg, training as a naval officer. In 1861, he met the composer Mily Balakirev and joined the group that became known as the "Mighty Handful." As a musician, he was large self-taught. He later became professor of composition at the St. Petersburg Conservatory. Among his students were Sergey Prokofiev and Igor Stravinsky.

Rimsky-Korsakov was a brilliant orchestrator; he became famous for his imaginative and colorful blend of orchestral sounds. His orchestral works have achieved international fame, among them, *Sheherazade, Sadko, Easter Festival Overture,* and *Capriccio Espagnol*; but his operas far outweigh the importance of his compositions in other fields. Rimsky-Korsakov composed fifteen operas, many of them based on Russian history and folklore. Gerald Abraham observes that Rimsky-Korsakov's finest vocal writing is found in his operas.[2]

Rimsky-Korsakov composed over seventy *romances*, which may be divided into two periods: the twenty-two *romances* written from 1866-1870, and the fifty-two *romances* written from 1897-1898. The last group of songs contains multiple settings of Tolstoy and Pushkin. His last group of *romances* also displays a much more careful integration of music with texts.

His songs are notable for their wealth of color and programmatic settings, using classical musical form. In his songs, he was able to distill his skill at orchestration into a much smaller musical form. He was drawn to texts representing various aspects of nature. Oriental rhythms and melodies are often found in his *romances*. His songs are not overtly passionate, but lyrically expressive.

Plenivshis' rozoy, solovey,　　　　　　**The Nightingale and the Rose. 1866**
Op. 2, No. 2
(A. Kol'tsov)

A number of Rimsky-Korsakov's early *romances* that contain Oriental themes. In this lovely example, a nightingale sings day and night to a rose, and somewhere, a youth sings to his lovely maiden. A languorous, swaying introduction of twelve measures sets the scene. The first vocal phrase is unaccompanied. Melodic material from the opening piano introduction closes the first section. As the text describes the lover's serenade, chords in the accompaniment illustrate his lyre. The seductive introduction is heard for the last time at the end of the *romance*.

Redeyet oblakov letuchaya gryada,   **The Clouds Begin to Scatter.** 1897
Op. 42, No. 3
(Aleksandr Pushkin)

This beautiful *romance* is another of Rimsky-Korsakov's nature pictures, a miniature tone poem compressed into song form. The unhurried movement of floating clouds is heard in the arpeggiated piano figures. As the clouds continue their calm journey, the piano figures change slightly, gathering more texture, but maintaining the ongoing arpeggiated shape. Vocal phrases are equally broad-lined—beautiful melodic lines that create a peaceful mood. Rimsky-Korsakov has created a shimmering musical texture that vividly illustrates the text.

Noch', Op. 8, No. 2   **Night.** 1868
(A. Pleshcheev)

"Night was flying through the world, sending dreams to people...."

This *romance* is another of Rimsky-Korsakov's tonal landscapes that depicts not one, but a series of scenes. Each one flashes by with its own color, scents, and sounds. These nature pictures are depicted programmatically in the piano figures: the peaceful night as it descends on earth, the noble forest trees with their heady scent, the flowing water of the forest stream, the smell of meadow grass, the song of the nightingale borne on the breeze, the starry night. The musical texture is fresh and beautiful; the listener feels submerged in the musical landscape.

A beautiful motive, reminiscent of Borodin's *In the Steppes of Central Asia,* introduces the song and is used throughout as a linking motive. It appears at the end of the song, creating a balanced and circular form. "Noch'" is an excellent example of Rimsky-Korsakov's skill at creating a complete microcosm of sound and color.

Extended Study List

Iz slyoz moikh • Nochevala tuchka zolotaya • Na kholmakh Gruzii • V tyomnoy roshche zamolk solovey • Pesnya Zyuleyki • Dlya beregov otchizny dalney • Pridi, kak dalnaya zvezda • Yel i pal'ma • Ti i vy

Suggested Reading

Gerald Abraham, *Rimsky-Korsakov: A Short Biography.*
Gerald R. Seaman, *Nikolai Andreevich Rimsky-Korsakov: A Guide to Research* (New York: Garland Publishing Co., 1989).
V.V. Yastrebtsev, *Reminiscences of Rimsky-Korsakov,* ed. and trans. Florence Jonas (New York: Columbia University Press, 1985).

Notes

1. Rimsky-Korsakov, Foreword to *The Complete Works of Nicolai Rimsky-Korsakov: Songs with piano accompaniment,* vol. 4, trans. Dr. Olga Browning (Melville, NY: Belwin Mills Publishing Co., 1981).
2. Gerald Abraham, "Nikolay Andreyevich Rimsky-Korsakov," *The New Grove Dictionary of Music and Musicians,* ed. Stanley Sadie, vol. 16, 33.

SERGEY VASIL'EVICH RAKHMANINOV (1873-1943)

> Composing is as essential a part of my being as breathing or eating; it is one of the necessary functions of living.
>
> —Sergey Rakhmaninov[1]

As a pianist, Rakhmaninov was one of the most celebrated artists of his time. As a composer, his works for the keyboard are the most characteristic of his compositions, but his seven sets of songs, published between 1890 and 1916, contain the same spacious lyric approach as his piano works. As expected, the songs are filled with beautiful melodies and expressive piano accompaniments. Extensive use of introductions, interludes and postludes may be found throughout the songs. Rakhmaninov was drawn to poetic subjects having to do with nature; the majority of his texts are by Russian romantic poets.

Unlike his Russian contemporaries, Rakhmaninov's compositions do not reflect the same nationalistic characteristics; he is closer to Tchaikovsky than any other Russian composer. His approach to song is also analogous to Robert Schumann; both were pianists and the treatment of the accompaniment in their songs is collaborative with the voice in stating musical material. Rakhmaninov's accompaniments are often brilliant and rich in harmonic color and texture. Taken as a whole, his compositional output changes little from beginning to end in musical approach, style, or content. His songs continue to delight for their skillful blend of melodic writing, colorful pianism, and ability to generate immediate emotional excitement.

Ne poy, krasavitsa, pri mne, Op. 4, No. 4   **O never sing to me. 1893**
(Aleksandr Pushkin)

Op. 4 contains six love songs of intense passion, expressed in varying moods. This song is one of Rakhmaninov's masterpieces. The poet begs a young girl not to sing songs from Grusia (Georgia); they hold unhappy memories of a life and love gone forever. Emotionally, the poem expresses tormented hope as well as longing for lost beauty. The piano melody and vocal imitation "ya pominayat mne, o ne…" is an old Georgian melody.

A beautiful sinuous melody of descending phrases is stated by the piano — an exotic blend of melancholy Russian folk style and oriental color, reminiscent of Borodin *(In the Steppes of Central Asia)*. The vocal lines blend declamation and a restatement of the piano's theme to create one of those haunting melodies that remains with the listener long after the song ends.

After leaving Russia in 1917, Rakhmaninov stopped composing songs, declaring exile from his beloved homeland left him bereft of the desire to write: "Having lost my native land, I lost myself. An exile, who is deprived of his musical roots, traditions and native soil, has no other consolation but an inviolable silence of undisturbed reminiscences."[2] This deeply felt bond with Russia is at the heart of his musical setting of Pushkin's powerful poem.

Pushkin's text was also set to music by more than twenty composers, among them Balakirev, Glinka, Rimsky-Korsakov, and Lyadov.[3] Rakhmaninov dedicated this song to his cousin and future wife, Natalya Satina.

Uzh ty, niva moya, Op. 4, No. 5   **The Harvest of Sorrow. 1893**
(Aleksey Tolstoy)

A field of ruined corn becomes, for the poet, a metaphor for his lost love. Like the field that cannot be harvested, his love will never be realized. Of all the songs in Op, 4, this one is the most patently "Russian"—suffused with melancholy and filled with Russian folk music idioms.

Rakhmaninov uses folk song figures in the vocal phrases, above an arpeggiated piano texture that suggests the wind blowing through the field of grain. Emotionally, the song might be termed one long crescendo of sorrow. The ultimate expression of grief is given to the voice in a wordless cadenza on "Ah!"

Vesenniya vody, Op. 14, No. 11   **Spring Waters. 1896**
(Fyodor Tyutchev)

This dramatic, florid song quickly became famous throughout Russia and remains one of Rakhmaninov's most recognized vocal pieces. The poet, Fyodor Tyutchev, is critically acclaimed as the greatest nature poet that Russia has produced.

Scenes of thawing ice and rushing streams herald spring's approach. These appear in a thickly textured, turbulent piano accompaniment and an equally passionate, impetuous vocal line. This joyful momentum is maintained from start to finish. Rakhmaninov dedicated the song to his first piano teacher, Anna Ornatskaya.

Siren', Op. 21, No. 5   **Lilacs. 1902**
(Ekaterina Beketova)

Images of nature always attracted Rakhmaninov. This song blends successfully blends Russian folk material with European idioms. The melodic line expands from the singer's opening phrase through variation and rising sequences. A typical Rakhmaninov high-note climax creates a beautiful, effective moment.

K detyam, Op. 26, No. 7   **To the Children. 1906**
(Aleksey Khomyakov)

A parent recalls happy memories of when the children were at home, and also reflects the sense of loss at their leaving. Rakhmaninov sets a very simple vocal line (almost prayer-like) over an equally calm chordal accompaniment. Only at the climax "O 'deti!" (Oh! children) does the accompaniment become arpeggiated and the vocal line leap upward as the passage of time overwhelms the poet.

This song is often performed and much loved; Rakhmaninov composed it when his daughter Irina was three years old and Tatyana not yet born.

Vokaliz, Op. 34, No. 14   Vocalise. 1915

"Vocalise" is probably the most familiar wordless song in the repertoire. It has been transcribed for violin, viola, and cello and appropriated for other instrumental arrangements as well. Its opulent lyricism may seem overly romantic but in the hands of a sensitive singer, it retains a lyric elegance that has made it a staple in the repertory. Vocal phrases are broad and long-lined. The piano accompaniment is primarily chordal, but Rakhmaninov gives it small countermelodies derived from the opening vocal phrase which intertwine with the voice, maintaining a sense of forward motion and variety.

The song is dedicated to coloratura Antonina Nezhdanova. When she expressed regret that there was no text, Rakhmaninov replied flatteringly, "What need is there of words, when you will be able to convey everything better and more expressively than anyone could by your voice and interpretation?"[4]

Son, Op. 38, No. 5   A Dream. 1916
(F. Sologub)

The six songs of Op. 38 reveal the influence that impressionism had made upon Rakhmaninov's musical style. Concern for tonal color becomes the dominant factor in all the songs. A bolder harmonic palette appears in his writing for both voice and piano; fluctuating rhythms and ambiguous tonalities permeate the songs.

Rakhmaninov chose texts by Symbolist poets, whose style had become an important force in Russian literature. The vague imagery and musical word sounds of these poems melded beautifully with Rakhmaninov's harmonic approach.

"Son" is not a long song. The vocal phrases are intensely expressive, but almost meditative in character. Melodic interest is carefully balanced between voice and piano lines, giving the musical texture a translucent, otherworldly quality. The song concludes with a substantive postlude that extends the atmospheric mood of the last lines of poetry.

The songs of Op. 38 were the last Rakhmaninov wrote. Soon after they were completed, he and his family left Russia for the last time.

Zdes' khorosho, Op. 21, No. 7   It is beautiful here. 1902
(Glafira Galina)

In this exquisite song, Rakhmaninov skillfully balances melodic materials in voice and piano to create a microcosm of ethereal calm. Melodic phrases are built gradually, similar to the slowly sung Russian folk song form called *protyazbnye*, in which images of nature portray the spiritual and emotional state of the singer.[5]

The mood is one of tranquility and wonder. The vocal phrases slowly gather momentum, building in emotional intensity to the last line of text, "and you, my dream!," which features an ethereal high note that seems suspended in space. This phrase does not cadence conclusively; instead, a piano postlude provides tonal closure, ending the song with its own moving meditation.

Rakhmaninov completed this song on his honeymoon with Natalya Satina.

Extended Study List

V mal'chanyi nochi taynoy (In the Silence of the Night, Op. 4, No. 3) • O, ne grusti (O Do Not Grieve, Op. 14, No. 8) • Ya zhdu tebya (I Wait for Thee, Op. 14, No. 1) • Ditya kak tsvetok ty prekrasna (Child, Thou Art Fair as a Flower, Op. 8, No. 2) • Khristos voskres (Christ is Risen, Op. 26, No. 6) • U mayego okna (At My Window, Op. 26, No. 10) • Burya (The Storm, Op. 34, No. 3) • Arion (Arion, Op. 34, No. 5) • Veter perelyotny oblaskal menya (A Passing Breeze, Op. 34, No. 4) • Sey den' ya pomnyu (The Morn of Life, Op. 34, No. 10)

Selected Reading

Natalia Challis, ed., *The Singer's Rachmaninoff* (New York: Pelion Press, 1989).

Barrie Martyn, *Rachmaninoff: Composer, Pianist, Conductor* (Brookfield, VT: Scolar Press, 1990).

Geoffrey Norris, *Rachmaninoff* (New York: Schirmer Books, 1994). Chapter 11-The Songs.

Laurence R. Richter, *Rachmaninov's Complete Song Texts* (Geneseo, NY: Leyerle, 2000).

Notes

1. Quoted in Barrie Martyn, *Rachmaninoff: Composer, Pianist, Conductor* (Brookfield, VT: Scolar Press, 1990), 32.
2. Quoted in *The Singer's Rachmaninoff*, Natalia Challis, ed., 45.
3. Ibid., 48.
4. Martyn, 240.
5. Challis, 102.

SERGEY SERGEYEVICH PROKOFIEV (1891-1953)

> A sort of naive simplicity was always a feature of his musical idiom, and this tempered even his most iconoclastic works.
>
> —Rita McAllister[1]

In addition to eight operas, several cantatas and choral works, Sergey Prokofiev composed several sets of songs and romances as well as some folk song arrangements. For his early songs, he turned to texts of Konstantin Balmont and Anna Akhmatova; his later vocal works use poetry by Soviet poets or popular texts glorifying controversial sentiments.

Early studies with Reinhold Glière prepared him for entry to the St. Petersburg Conservatory where his list of teachers reads like a "who's who" of Russian music: among them, Liadov, Rimsky-Korsakov, and Tcherepin. Prokofiev's outspoken personality and aggressive leftist views won him more enemies than friends. His earliest musical works exhibit unique energy, and an exciting dramatic approach that borders on being mechanical. In his autobiography he outlined five principal elements that dominated his style: classical forms, search for innovation (an individual harmonic language and the means of expressing strong emotions), the "toccata, or motor element," lyricism, and the element of the joke (scherzo) or the grotesque.[2]

In 1932, Prokofiev returned to Russia after an extended trip to the United States and Europe and reexamined his artistic principles, outlining a new direction for his music, one that included "greater simplicity and more melody."[3]

Tonality was always central to his work; his harmonic language is varied but expressive, with atonal passages used primarily for contrast. In his early works, Prokofiev's approach to melody was generally angular, but extremely lyric in later pieces; he often flavored his melodies with pentatonic materials.

Given his prolific compositional output, it is small wonder that song did not occupy a consistent part of his musical *oeuvre*. Nonetheless, the songs have a sense of the dramatic springing from Prokofiev's artistic style.

Gadky utyonok, Op. 18   **The Ugly Duckling. 1914**
(Sergey Prokofiev, adapted from Hans Christian Andersen)

Prokofiev's musical creations for children include the wildly popular *Peter and the Wolf* and twelve piano pieces *Music for Children*, Op. 65, both written to commissions from the State. "The Ugly Duckling" is an extended song adapted from Andersen's familiar fairy tale of the ugly grey duck that was really a swan. Prokofiev's humorous setting of the story is really a miniature operatic drama. The vocal writing is freely declamatory rather than lyrical—in this sense, it is like Musorgsky. This natural approach to setting speech allows the animal characters in the story to assume realistic natural qualities.

The piano is assigned the larger task in telling the story; Prokofiev invests the accompaniment with vividly descriptive moments. At twelve minutes, the narrative is lengthy for song, but the pace of musical writing keeps the sections tightly joined, and the scenes seem to change quickly from situation to situation, with the piano accompaniment in charge of setting the emotional or atmospheric mood. The song is charming and fresh and has a lightness about it characteristic of the composer's early works.

Tri romansa na slova A. Pushkina, **Op. 73**   **Three Romances. 1936**
(Aleksandr Pushkin)

Sosny (Pine trees) • Rumyanoy zaryoyu pokrylsya vostok
(The East was Covered with a Rosy Dawn) • V tvoyu svetlitsu
(In your brightness)

These three songs on texts by Pushkin (Prokofiev's favorite poet) are the only songs Prokofiev composed after his return to Russia in 1932 that did not deal with partisans and Soviet heroes. They were composed for Russia's commemoration of the centenary of Pushkin's death in 1937; Prokofiev also created music for theatrical events linked to that celebration, and music for films about Pushkin.

Each song is of a different mood: hymn-like, intimate and pastoral, and intensely romantic. Lyricism stands out as the central element in the set, which is sprinkled throughout with altered chords, and expressive rhythms.

Extended Study List
Five Poems of Anna Akhmatova, Op. 27 • *Five Poems*, Op. 23 • *Three Children's Songs*, Op. 68 • *Twelve Russian Folk Songs*, Op. 104 • *Three Songs from Alexander Nevsky*, Op. 75bis • *Two Songs from Lieutenant Kijé*, Op.60bis • *Seven Songs*, Op. 79

Selected Reading
James Bakst, *A History of Russian-Soviet Music* (Westport, CT: Greenwood Press, 1977).
Richard Anthony Leonard, *A History of Russian Music* (London: Jarrolds, 1956).

Notes

1. Rita McAllister. Liner notes for *Elisabeth Söderström: Mussorgsky, Prokofiev, Grechaninov.* London Records. LP recording OS 26579.
2. Richard Anthony Leonard, *A History of Russian Music* (London: Jarrolds, 1956), 311.
3. Ibid.

IGOR FYODOROVICH STRAVINSKY (1882-1971)

> Music is given to us to establish an order in things; to order the chaotic and the personal into something perfectly controlled, conscious and capable of lasting vitality.
>
> —Igor Stravinsky[1]

Igor Stravinsky's music is somewhat analogous to his cosmopolitan lifestyle—one of constant exploration, assimilation, and new venues. During his lifetime he composed in numerous forms and styles, and in every case created significant and lasting works in each. For years Stravinsky was one of several composers who dominated the international music scene, and his music has influenced countless composers.

Stravinsky was a master craftsman; his music has been characterized as "intellectual"—not necessarily detached, but striving for classic order in opposition to overt emotional concerns. Most of Stravinsky's songs fall into the early period of his musical composition, and are strongly Russian in flavor. Later vocal works, such as *In Memoriam Dylan Thomas* and *Three Songs from Shakespeare* date a few years after his opera, *The Rake's Progress,* and exhibit his interest in serial techniques. His songs cannot be considered as indicative of his musical style. He devoted little attention to them, and in his long catalog of works, their number is quite small.

Pastorale   1907

This is the second entry in Stravinsky's vocal catalog, a brief song in the style of a vocalise. It is dedicated to Nadezhda Rimsky-Korsakov. A serene vocal line is set above an accompaniment that features a drone-like figure in the bass and a light countermelody in the treble.

In 1923 Stravinsky scored "Pastorale" for soprano, oboe, English horn, clarinet and bassoon. Ten years later, two instrumental transcriptions were composed: one for violin and piano; and one for violin, oboe, English horn, clarinet and bassoon. "Pastorale" is significant for its neoclassical style, which Stravinsky employed in his compositions of the 1920s.[2]

Berceuses du chat   **Cat's Cradle Songs. 1915-16**

Sur le poêle (On the Stove) • Intérieur (At Home) • Dodo (Dodo) •
Ce qu'il a le chat (The Cat Has...)

Stravinsky originally created these tiny songs (duration: 5 minutes) for contralto voice and three clarinets, and also made a reduction for voice and piano. In his early works Stravinsky tended to treat texts as part of the entire musical fabric, as conveyors of rhythmic accents rather than units of emotional-dramatic meaning. Stravinsky created this miniature work in France, based on Russian popular texts in the *pribaoutki* style. According to Stravinsky, *pribaoutki* "denotes a form of popular Russian verse to which the nearest English parallel is the limerick...according to popular tradition, they derive from a type of game in which someone says a word, which someone else then adds to, and which third and fourth persons develop, and so on, with utmost speed."[3]

Stravinsky blends folk-like declamation in the voice with flexible melodic materials for the clarinets these songs. The group resembles a set of little jingles, terse and fleeting. Song 2 is particularly striking for the use of melismas that recall a cat's lazy movements; Song 3 is a lullaby; Song 4 uses a single vocal phrase of dance-like rhythm repeated over and over.

Two Poems of Konstantin Balmont   **1911**
(Konstantin Balmont)

Nezabudochka—tsvetochek' (The Little Forget-Me-Not) • Golub' (The Dove)

Stravinsky composed these lyrical settings in Russia shortly after the success of *Petrushka*. Both songs lack a key signature and are contrasted in tempo. "The Flower" features an angular but lyric vocal line set over an intricate harmonic texture in a fairly slow tempo; "The Dove" is quicker, its vocal lines explore different combinations of two intervals (E-natural/F-sharp, and D-sharp/F-natural). These brief songs (2:30 minutes) are complemented by Stravinsky's manipulation of melodic fragments and bitonal processes. Stravinsky transcribed the two songs for high voice and chamber orchestra in 1954.

Three Songs from William Shakespeare   **1953**
(mezzo-soprano, flute, viola, clarinet)

Musick to Heare (*Sonnet VIII*) • Full Fadom five (Ariel's song from *The Tempest*)
• When Dasies pied (*Love's Labour's Lost*)

This chamber work belongs to Stravinsky's period of experimentation with twelve-tone works. He had composed no vocal music since the *Four Russian Songs* of 1919. Three rows are used for the piece: four notes, seven notes, and ten notes, respectively. These are freely presented in all three songs, with repetition of pitches before the entire series is stated.[4] The work exhibits one of Stravinsky's favorite devices, that of layered relationships. There is a piano reduction by the composer, although the interplay of instrumental colors with the voice makes the chamber version more effective in performance.

Song 1 is contrapuntal in style and almost pointillistic in its phrase shapes. The vocal part is peppered with rests, a characteristic of Stravinsky, who used tiny pauses to sharpen attention. Stravinsky treats the voice like one of the instruments; its rhythmic interplay, pitted against an angular accompaniment, maintains interest and forward motion. Song 2 features a tolling bell in the piano's first measure, complemented by a highly rhythmic vocal treatment in free canonic style. Bell-like figures are found hidden throughout the brief song and in the syncopated vocal line. Song 3 is dance-like in mood, highly rhythmic throughout and features short little thirty-second note figures depicting the cheery mocking song of the cuckoo. The song is strophic in structure, a surprising contrast to the two preceding pieces. A short postlude presents more birdcall motives in a humorous postscript.

In setting these texts, Stravinsky often disregarded the natural accents of the English words; this poses a problem for performers in keeping the indicated rhythmic pulsations while expressing the dramatic-emotional nuances of the text.

Extended Study List

Tri pesenki iz vospominanie yunosheskikh godov (Three songs from Childhood Recollections) • *Pribaoutki* (medium voice and eight instruments) • *Favn' i patushka (Faune et bergère) (Faun and Shepherdess)* • *Two Songs*, Op. 6 • *Two Poems by Verlaine* • *Tri stikhotvoreniya iz yaponskoy liriki (Three Japanese Lyrics)* • *In Memoriam Dylan Thomas* (tenor, string quartet, four trombones) • *Four Russian Songs*. 1918 • *Four Russian Songs*. 1954 • *Elegy for J.F.K.* (baritone, three clarinets)

Selected Reading

Ruth C. Friedberg, "The Solo Vocal Works of Igor Stravinsky: A Review," *The NATS Bulletin,* 23:1 (1966), 6-13.

Sharon Schafer, "Igor Stravinsky: Composer of Songs," *The NATS Bulletin* 39:1 (1982), 11-13.

Igor Stravinsky and Robert Craft, *Conversations with Igor Stravinsky* (New York: Doubleday and Co., Inc., 1959).

Roman Vlad, *Stravinsky* (London: Oxford University Press, 1960).

E. W. White, *Stravinsky: A Critical Survey* (New York: Philosophical Library, 1948).

Notes

1. Quoted in Vlad, *Stravinsky*, 113.
2. Sharon Schafer, "Igor Stravinsky: Composer of Songs," 11.
3. Quoted by Robert Craft. Liner notes to *Stravinsky Songs Conducted by the Composer.* Columbia Masterworks LP recording MS 7439.
4. Schafer, 11.

DMITRY DMITRIYEVICH SHOSTAKOVICH (1906-1975)

Music was what motivated him. This alone remained constant throughout a turbulent, often tortured life.

—Laurel E. Fay [1]

Dmitry Dmitriyevich Shostakovich was a musical icon of contemporary Russian music. His music has been characterized as eclectic, rooted in traditional tonal style, yet using dissonance and occasional atonality for expressive means.[2]

Shostakovich left a vast legacy of music that is diverse in style, inventive and inspired, often anguished, but always arresting. His formidable catalog of works contains 147 opus numbers, among them: fifteen symphonies, fifteen string quartets, two operas, an operetta, six concertos for various instruments, solo piano music, chamber music for piano and strings, three ballets, thirty-six film scores, incidental music for eleven plays, and numerous vocal works.

Shostakovich lived his adult life in the USSR and his music was greatly affected by political events there, especially under Stalin. Working as an artist during the cold war and post-cold war years was a daunting experience. Shostakovich had a troubled relationship with the government, which denounced him and his music twice—in 1936 and 1948. In public, he remained loyal, joining the party in 1960 and serving in the Supreme Soviet. Amazingly, he managed to survive the Stalinist cultural purges to rise to international fame.

Since his death in 1975, his life and career have been the subject of political and musical debate over the extent to which he may have been a secret dissident. His music remains his monument, and recent careful scholarship, coupled with numerous recordings in his centenary year, 2006, have attracted new legions of listeners to his music.

Spanish Songs, **Op. 100**   **1956**
(Trans. Sergey Bolotin-Nos. 1, 3
and Tatyana Sikorskaya-Nos. 2,4,5
and jointly-No. 6)

Adios, Granada (Farewell, Granada!) *Largo* • Mozuca (Little Stars)
Allegro • El samir (The First Meeting) *Largo* • Ronda
(Round Dance [A Birth]) *Allegro* • Morena salada (Black Eyes)
Allegretto • [No Spanish title] (The Dream [Barcarole]) *Allegretto*

Spanish music has had special attraction for Russian composers, among them, Glinka, Dargomyzhsky, Rubinstein and Minkov. Spanish subjects were popular in Russia from the mid-1930s on, when volunteers went to Spain to help the Spanish Communists in their fight against Franco's regime. Poems and songs with Spanish themes were created and Spanish names appeared with some regularity in various places.

This is a cycle of traditional folk songs for mezzo-soprano and piano, with the anonymous Spanish lyrics translated into Russian by Sergei Bolotin and Tatyana Sikorskaya. Shostavkovich adapted these charming melodies with their texts of love, separation, and longing for soprano Zara Dolukhanova,[*] who had given him the melodies and texts, asking him to harmonize them. The Russian translations did not fit easily with the Spanish melodies, and went through a series of revisions.

Spanish Songs is one of the most popular vocal works of Shostakovich. The faster tempo songs sparkle; the songs in slower tempos evoke the moods of the texts expressively. Shostakovich has adapted the folk melodies in a variety of settings that capture the color and passion of the words. After listening to one or two of the songs, one forgets that the texts are in Russian, since the musical texture is idiomatically Spanish.

*Dolukhanova gave the first performance of Shostakovich's vocal cycle *From Traditional Jewish Poetry.*

***Satires*, Op. 109**   **1960**
(Sasha Chorny)*

Kritiku (To a Critic) • Probuzhdenie vesny (The Awakening of Spring) •
Potomki (Descendants) • Nedorazumenie (Confusion) •
Kreytserova sonata (Kreutzer-Sonata)

Shostakovich wrote *Satires,* five romances for soprano and piano, for soprano
Galina Vishnevskaya. Vishnevskaya is the wife of Russian cellist Mstislav
Rostropovich; the couple was close friends with the composer.

The poems are quite brief. On the surface, the verses seem humorous, but
beneath the droll surface is sarcasm and anger. Werner Pfister observes, "Although
these texts date from the pre-Revolutionary period, Shostakovich and his contemporaries had no difficulty in hearing in them a malicious and critical allusion to
run-down Soviet reality."[3]

The controversial words to the third song, "Descendants," kept the Soviet
authorities from giving permission for the cycle's premiere performance. The
words were a metaphor indicting the Soviet regime and its political ideology.
Vishnevskaya suggested that subtitling the cycle "Pictures of the Past" might
diminish the problem. Only at the last minute was permission for the premiere of
the cycle to take place. Vishnevskaya reported that at the conclusion of the cycle,
the audience shouted to hear it again, and the performers repeated the work two
more times.**

Shostakovich clothes these texts in brilliant musical textures that sparkle and
bite. Under it all lies a darker mood and a melancholy chill. Musically, the little
cycle is full of musical quotations and witty touches. The vocal writing might have
come from the music hall. It embraces a number of styles: musical theater, narrative declamation, quick patter diction, abrupt interval leaps and one scream. Not
to be left out, the piano accompaniment reveals its share of colorful touches, prosaic waltz rhythms, gallops, and fragmentary "asides" in response to the texts. The
songs are joined by a repeated note motive that opens each song.

In the last satire, Shostakovich embeds quotations from Rakhmaninov's
"Spring Waters," Beethoven's "Kreutzer" Sonata and Tchaikovsky's *Evgeny Onegin.*

*Chorny, an early twentieth century writer, was known for his ironic and caustic poetry, but he also wrote
charming books for children.

**Vishnevskaya's account of the historic evening is detailed in the liner notes to the historic recording of
Satires, which also includes the premiere other the two other works Shostakovich wrote for her: *Seven
Romances on Poems by Aleksandr Blok*, (soprano, violin, cello, and piano) and his orchestration of
Musorgsky's *Songs and Dances of Death*. On BMG Music, Melodiya. Vishnevskaya, Rostropovich, violin-
ist David Oistrakh, and the Gorki State Philharmonic Orchestra. CD 74321 53237-2. Released 1998.

Suite on Verses of Michelangelo Buonarroti, Op. 145   **1974**
(Trans. into Russian by A. Efros)

Istina (Truth)	Sonnet 3 to Pope Julius II
Utro (Morning)	Sonnet 20
Lyubov' (Love)	Sonnet 25
Razluka (Separation)	Madrigal-Com' arò dunque ardire
Gnev (Anger)	Sonnet 4 on Rome in the Pontificate of Julius II
Dante (Dante)	Sonnet 1 on Dante Alighieri
Izganniku (To the Exile)	Sonnet 2 on Dante Alighieri
Tvorchestvo (Creativity)	Sonnet 61 on the death of Vittoria Colonna
Noch' (Night)	A Dialogue (Dialogue between Giovanni Strozzi and the Sculptor)
Smert' (Death)	Sonnet 69
Bessmertiye (Immortality)	Epitaph for Cecchino Bracci Fiorentio—Epigrams 14 and 12

This extended work—forty-odd minutes—was originally composed for bass and piano, and later orchestrated by Shostakovich as Op. 145a. Both the voice/piano and the orchestral versions should be listened to and contrasted.

Shostakovich composed the work to mark the 500th anniversary of Michelangelo's birth. He chose thirteen poems from Michelangelo's *Sonnets* and set them in eleven songs, titling the songs himself.

Shostakovich chose poems dealing with the theme of separation: the separation of lovers by impending death; exile, and the alienation of man and artist in a corrupt society; and death itself as a refuge from the corrupt world.[4] Shostakovich's musical settings reflect his feelings about life, love, art, and mortality.

Stark in its linear simplicity, the vocal writing is largely a combination of declamatory and arioso lines. The accompaniment is equally sparse, but Shostakovich creates a wide variety of melodic effects and changes of tempo and range. It is a work of unsettling power, and one of Shostakovich's masterpieces for the voice.

Michelangelo wrote the sonnets near the end of his life. Shostakovich was diagnosed with lung cancer in 1973. In reading Michelangelo's words, one cannot help but be struck by the symbolic parallels to Shostakovich's own artistic and personal struggles during his life. Perhaps the last lines of the last song, "Immortality," provide a personal benediction, asserting that the only immortality for man will lie in the hearts of those who loved him.

Extended Study List
Chetyre stikhotvoreniya Kapitana Lebyadkina (Four Verses of Captain Lebyadkin) • *Song-cycle: From Jewish Folk Poetry,* Op. 79 • *Four romances to words by Pushkin,* Op. 46 • *Five romances on texts from the periodical "Krokodil"* Op. 121 • *Four monologues to words by Pushkin,* Op. 91 • *Six romances to verses by English poets,* Op. 62 • *Two romances to lyrics by M. Lermontov,* Op. 84 • *Four songs to lyrics by E. Dolmatovsky,* Op. 86

Selected Reading
Laurel E. Fay, *Shostakovich: A Life* (New York: Oxford University Press, 2000).

Derek. C. Hulme, *Dmitri Shostakovich: A Catalogue, Bibliography, and Discography* (New York: Oxford University Press, 1991).

Richard Taruskin, *Defining Russia Musically* (Princeton: Princeton University Press, 1997).

Solomon Volkov, ed. *Testimony: The Memoirs of Dmitri Shostakovich.* trans. Antonina W. Bouis (New York: Limelight Editions, 1995). This book is falsely purported to be Shostakovich's transcribed memoirs.

Elizabeth Wilson, *Shostakovich, A Life Remembered* (Princeton: Princeton University Press, 1994).

Notes

1. Laurel E. Fay, Shostakovich: A Life, 5.

2. Boris Schwartz, "Shostakovich," *The New Grove Russian Masters Series* (London: Macmillan, 1986), 202.

3. Werner Pfister, liner notes to *Magdalena Kozená: Songs,* trans. Stewart Spencer. Magdalena Kozená, mezzo-soprano; Malcolm Martineau, piano, Henschel Quartett, Paul Edmund-Davies, flute. Deutsche-Grammophon B00021224-02, 2004.

4. Richard Longman, liner notes to *Shostakovich: The Orchestral Songs,* Vol. 2. Elena Zaremba, Ilya Levinsky, Sergei Leiferkus; Gothenburg Symphony Orchestra, Neeme Järvi, conductor. Deutsche-Grammophon, 447 085-2, 1995.

Scandinavian Song

Scandinavian music is based on the various folk traditions of the countries that make up its geographical area: Norway, Finland, Sweden, and Denmark. German *Lieder* and French *mélodie* were important in shaping song style in Scandinavia and throughout Europe; however, Scandinavian composers also drew upon their musical heritage and folk traditions, blending them into their songs.

Scandinavian composers have remained true to their cultural heritage, setting many songs with texts by famous Scandinavian poets—among them, Hans Christian Andersen, Henrik Ibsen, Vilhelm Krag, Aasmund O. Vinje, Holger Drachmann, and Andreas Munch. Scandinavia's lyric song form is known as the *romanse*. Its strophic form and simple melody and accompaniment make it somewhat similar to the nineteenth-century English ballad.

NORWAY

Norwegian art song tradition is very strong. Buoyed by its rich folk song literature, the quantity and quality of its songs developed more rapidly than in the other Scandinavian countries.

Norway gained political independence in the nineteenth century, and nationalism in the arts became a predominant part of the "new" Norway. Art song composition was a part of this movement. Halfdan Kjerulf was the first important song composer in Norway, but it was Edvard Grieg (1843-1907) who achieved international fame and brought Norwegian music to the attention of the world. His music and his songs have an innate lyricism and a simplicity that springs from Norway's natural beauty. For years Grieg's songs were the only Scandinavian art songs known outside the region.

Among Grieg's contemporaries, Johan Svendsen and Christian Sinding were notable song composers; in the late part of the century composers Agathe Backer-Gröndahl and Johan Backer-Lunde added more works to Norwegian song literature.

FINLAND

Finland has a long history of religious songs, which were a familiar form of vocal music for centuries. Song composition was sporadic during the nineteenth and twentieth centuries. Jean Sibelius (1865-1957) is credited with establishing a national musical style for his native Finland. He set many songs to Swedish texts (Swedish was the literary language of Finland for most of the nineteenth century). Although Sibelius wrote nearly 100 songs, he was not comfortable working in miniature forms.

Conversely, Yrjö Kilpinen (1892-1959) concentrated more on composing songs than any other form of music, and he is known primarily for his large body of songs. His songs have been compared to Hugo Wolf's in their close fusion of music and poetry, and he is known in his own country as "the Finnish Schubert."[1]

SWEDEN

Swedes have always loved to sing, and the country has produced a number of prominent singers. Jenny Lind, the "Swedish Nightingale," and Christine Nilsson concertized widely in Europe and the United States during the nineteenth century. More recently, these Swedish singers have continued the tradition of great singing: Jussi Björling, Set Svanholm, Nicolai Gedda, Birgit Nilsson, Elisabeth Söderström, Anne Sofie von Otter, and Håkan Hagegård.

Helmich Roman, a contemporary of Handel, was the first Swedish composer to gain a reputation outside Swedish borders. Eighteenth-century vocal music in Sweden was largely operatic, fueled by the presence of German opera composers and conductors living in Sweden, and supported by King Gustavus III. Gustavus III gave his patronage to Carl Mikael Bellman, a well-known poet, performer, and composer. Bellman set his own poems to music and performed them widely. Sweden honors Bellman every July with a celebration.

Inspired by Swedish lyric poetry, late nineteenth-century composers began to write a substantial body of songs. Song composition peaked during this period, and continued into the first decades of the twentieth century. Style varies widely in these works, shaped by individual approaches to a national sound, with elements of romanticism and impressionism added into the mix. Ture Rangström, Wilhelm Peterson-Berger, Sigurd von Koch, Emil Sjögren, Hugo Alfvén, and Wilhelm Stenhammar are Swedish composers whose songs deserve to be better known.[2]

DENMARK

Denmark's early history of solo song is not well known. Lutenist-composer John Dowland was employed in the Danish royal court in the sixteenth century; we can imagine that he brought Britain's musical style with him to the court. Musical activities during the seventeenth and eighteenth centuries were dominated by European musicians from Italy, Germany, and France, but one of the most famous musicians of the time was Danish—organist-composer Dietrich Buxtehude.

German *singspiel* was influential in the development of Danish song in the late eighteenth and early nineteenth centuries. But song composition did not tempt composers, and song developed in an unconnected manner.

The songs of Danish composer Carl Nielsen (1865-1931) are greatly admired in Denmark but little known outside the country. Nielsen's pupil, Knud Jeppesen, wrote some songs, but is better known for editing *La flora*, the classic collection of early Italian arias. Other Danish composers of songs are Peter Lange-Müller and Hakon Børresen.

***

Despite their quality and number, Scandinavian art songs have remained largely unknown. Happily, in recent years, excellent recordings and DVDs have helped make this repertory more accessible. Books and articles have been published that serve as references to this literature and its sung diction. This beautiful body of art song is being programmed more and more frequently, sung in the original languages.

Notes

1. Noni Espina, *Repertoire for the Solo Voice*, 791.
2. An excellent introduction to Swedish song literature is the compact disc *Wings in the Night: Swedish Songs*, Anne Sofie von Otter, mezzo-soprano; Bengt Forsberg, piano, Deutsche Grammophon 449-189-2, 1996.

NORWAY

EDVARD GRIEG (1843-1907)

> I loved a young woman with a marvelous voice and an equally marvelous gift as an interpreter. This woman became my wife and has remained my life's companion to this day. She has been, I daresay, the only true interpreter of my songs...My songs came to life naturally and through a necessity like that of a natural law, and all of them were written for her.
>
> —Edvard Grieg[1]

Edvard Grieg's songs number over 140 and fall into four main groups, divided by his settings in German, Danish, and Norwegian (Riksmål and Landsmål) poetry.[2] Grieg lived in the golden age of Norwegian lyric poetry, and was extremely sensitive to poetry and correct musical setting of words. Grieg's publishers were German and, during his lifetime, his songs were able to have wider dissemination in German translations. Grieg was never happy with this situation and worried about compromising the prosody. In a letter to Finck he lamented: "If a Scandinavian poet, whose language the foreigner neither sings nor understands, is garbled in translations, not only he but also the composer suffers. Unfortunately I have often had bad luck in my attempts to get good translations...the result, even in favorable circumstances, is usually that the translations are made to fit the music and seem unnatural."[3]

Many of Grieg's songs were published in translations and although he tried to supervise this process, he was not always happy with the results. Until quite recently, most performances of Grieg songs were sung in German translations; fortunately, new recordings are available of Grieg songs in their original languages, and singers are performing these beautiful works in the original versions.

Grieg used strophic form and its variants frequently in his songs, which gives them a folk-like quality. Schumann was a major influence for Grieg, whose songs exhibit some similar stylistic characteristics, especially in his writing for piano. Often, however, his unique and fresh ideas proved incompatible with the structured song forms he used.

Med en vandlilje, Op. 25, No. 4   **With a Water Lily. 1876**
(Henrik Ibsen)

A rustling piano accompaniment complements the ardent text. It doubles the voice throughout in both hands and echoes every vocal phrase an octave higher. Only with the third stanza does the major tonality shift gradually into minor, as the water sprite makes an appearance in the text, symbolizing the perils of love hidden beneath the surface. The original key returns for the fifth and last stanza, reached through a series of sequences and chromatic modulations in the melody. Grieg precisely indicates all instances of *crescendo-diminuendo* and *poco tenuto* throughout the song.

Jeg elsker dig, Op. 5, No. 3 (Ich liebe dich)   I love you. 1865
(Hans Christian Andersen)
Original text in Danish

"Jeg elsker dig" (I love you) is probably Grieg's best-known melody. It is an early work, one of four songs published as Op. 5. Grieg composed it during his courtship of Nina Hagerup and the set may be thought of as an engagement present to her. Grieg chose the four poems from a collection titled *Hjertets Melodier* (Melodies of the Heart) written in 1830 by the famous storyteller Hans Christian Andersen. The original version contained only one verse, but was changed later in the French and German versions of the song.

Musically, the fresh, tender sentiments are captured completely in one verse as Grieg originally composed it. The vocal line is beautifully lyric; chromaticism is present in the accompaniment but does not detract from the lyricism of the voice. The bass line doubles the voice, and sequentially rising phrases underscore the youthful ardent quality of the text. Beryl Foster observes that the chromatic style Grieg used in this song seems to foreshadow Roger Quilter's use of harmony, especially in such songs as "Now sleeps the crimson petal."[4]

To brune øjne (Zwei blanke braune Augen),   Two Brown Eyes. 1864-65
Op. 5, No. 1
(Hans Christian Andersen)

This tiny song is the first of the set that Grieg presented to Nina Hagerup as an engagement present. The Op. 5 songs were his first attempts at setting Danish poetry.

A gently dotted dance rhythm accompanies the charming folk-like vocal line, each independent of one another. Absent is the chromaticism usually found in Grieg's vocal compositions; instead, the melody shifts between major and minor.

En svane, Op. 25, No. 2   A Swan. 1876
(Henrik Ibsen)

Norway's great lyric poet Henrik Ibsen provided the text for this song —one of Grieg's greatest efforts in the genre. The brief poem is filled with symbolism. In Norse mythology and literature, the swan is a familiar image that symbolizes the soul. Foster points out that swans also appear in Celtic mythology, linked by a silver chain as divine beings in metamorphosis, and cites the fifth song text in Samuel Barber's *Hermit Songs* which refers to Christ as "O Swan."[5] Grieg uses a simple chordal accompaniment that contains some chromatic alterations to evoke the gliding movement of the swan and echoes the vocal line. The emotional mood is one of quiet intensity.

Våren   Spring. 1880
(Aasmund Olavsson Vinje)

"Våren" is one of Grieg's most beautiful melodies. Within its strophic form is a special portrait of Norway's short period of springtime when winter's snows are transformed to mountain green. This song is a striking example of Grieg's skill in text setting; though the rhythms of the lines are almost identical, there is no sense of monotony. Instead, the music gradually unfolds toward a climatic high point on F-sharp. Grieg's characteristic echoing of the ends of vocal phrases is found here, as well as an intensely emotional text setting that underlines his love for Norwegian nature.[6] A simple accompaniment underpins the exquisite melodic line. Grieg's manuscript copy shows he originally set four verses, but only two are found in all the printed versions.

Haugtussa, Op. 67   The Mountain Maid. 1895
(Arne Garborg)

Det syng • Veslemøy • Blåbaer-li • Møte • Elsk • Killingdans • Vond Dag • Ved Gjaetle-Bekken

Haugtussa contains the last of Grieg's Norwegian songs and the cycle is among his finest achievements. He described them as "the best songs I have written."[7] Garborg's original collection of poems numbered seventy lyric poems in Landsmål poetic style. Grieg was enthusiastic about the collection. He originally set twelve poems and added two to those; the published version in 1898 only contains eight songs. The remaining six are still in sketches and were printed for the first time in *Edvard Grieg Complete Works Vol. 15* (1991).

Haugtussa bears more than a passing resemblance in mood and story to Schubert's *Die schöne Müllerin*. Garborg's heroine is Veslemøy, a young herd girl with clairvoyant powers who has earned the nickname "Troll-maiden" because of her ability to see the troll and fairy-folk. Discarded by her lover, she tries to escape the harsh realities of life and the indifference of those around her, who shun her as strange and perhaps bewitched. Her visions put her in contact with nature itself and the powers of the underworld. Grieg chose to juxtapose these two forces as themes for his *Haugtussa*, alternating songs about love and nature in the song cycle. In the initial song Veslemøy is lured into the high mountains by the sounds of nature; in the final song, like Schubert's miller, she seeks comfort by the banks of the brook.

Like the songs in *Die schöne Müllerin*, the songs of *Haugtussa* are strophic in form, with the exception of Nos. 5 and 8. Strophic structure seems characteristically appropriate for the texts—which are modeled on Norwegian folk poetry—and for the style of the cycle as a whole.

DET SYNG (THE SINGING). Veslemøy attracts the advances of a troll who tries to lure her to his home in the mountain. His tactics alternate between rough threats and a seductive, alluring vocal line.

VESLESMØY (VESLESMØY). This song is a portrait of the heroine, a description of her features. Grieg varies the vocal and piano parts to portray different aspects of her character and personality.

BLÅBAER-LI (BLUEBERRY SLOPES). Vesleymøy, in high spirits, takes her sheep and goats out to graze on the hillsides covered with blueberries. Dance rhythms are used to portray her happy mood; a playful introduction is used as a postlude and its figures are found throughout the accompaniment. This song provides a fine contrast to the pensive character of the preceding song.

MØTE (MEETING). She meets her lover. The young couple awkwardly makes each other's acquaintance; they share a lunch and spend the afternoon together. As the cool evening descends they draw together longingly and pass the night in each other's arms.

ELSK (LOVE). This is a through-composed song. Veslemøy sings she is captured like a bird in the cage of love. The opening vocal phrase is reminiscent of the previous song, but is in the minor key, as if she knows this relationship will not end happily.

KILLINGDANS (KIDS' DANCE). Baby goats frolic on the hillside in this song , which provides a cheery moment in the cycle. The text is full of alliterations and rhyming words. The clumsy happy movements of the kids are found in the piano part; triplets and eighth-note figures alternate.

VON DAG (EVIL DAY). Even though he promised he would come to her through the bad weather, her lover does not appear. Chromatic movement in the inner parts of the accompaniment underscores Veslemøy's sorrow as she learns her lover is to marry a rich woman.

VED GJAETLE-BEKKEN (BY THE GJAETLE BROOK). This is another through-composed song, filled with descriptive nature sounds in piano—pedals, melodic sequences, tempo changes, water figures, 7th, 9th, 11th, and 13th chords, modulations. Vesleymøy brings her broken heart to the brook and seeks escape in its swirling waters.

Extended Study List

Mens jeg venter • Med en primula veris • Solveig's Sang • Forårsregn • Lok • Fra Monte Pincio • Gruss* • Ein Traum* • Zur Rosenzeit* • Die verschwiegene Nachtigall*

*Original poem in German

Selected Reading

Finn Benestad, "Edvard Grieg: Songs." Liner notes for recital of *Grieg Songs.* Anne Sofie von Otter/Bengt Forsberg. Deutsche-Grammophon 437 521-2, 1993.

Astra Desmond, "The Songs," in *Grieg: A Symposium,* ed. Gerald Abraham (Norman, OK: University of Oklahoma Press, 1950). Chapter 6, 71-92.

Bradley Ellingboe, "The Role of Language in the Songs of Edvard Grieg," *The NATS Journal* 43:3 (Jan/Feb 1987), 5-8+.

Beryl Foster, *The Songs of Edvard Grieg* (Brookfield, Vermont: Scolar Press, 1990). Excellent source which discusses all Grieg's songs in biographical context. Discography and chronological list of songs.

John Horton, *Grieg* (London: J. M. Dent & Sons, 1974).

Edvard Grieg, *Grieg and Delius: A chronicle of their friendship in letters.* Compiled and trans. by Lionel Carley (New York: Marion Boyers Publishers, 1993).

Sandra Jarrett, *Edvard Grieg and His Songs* (Burlington, VT: Ashgate, 2003).

Notes

1. In a letter to Henry Finck, Grieg's American biographer. Quoted in Benestad, liner notes to *Grieg Songs*, Deutsche-Grammophon 437 521-2, 1993.
2. After declaring independence, Norwegians began to purge their language of Danish words. Riksmål, literally meaning "language of the realm," was later renamed Bokmål, "language of the books." In 1853, Landsmål, "language of the land," joined Riksmål as the other official Norwegian language. Composed of many old Norwegian dialects, it was felt by many to be the "truer" of the two tongues, the one most directly descended from the Vikings. In Ellingboe, "The Role of Language in the Songs of Edvard Grieg," *The NATS Journal* 43:3, 5-6.
3. John Horton, *Grieg*, 194.
4. Foster, *The Songs of Edvard Grieg*, 47.
5. Ibid., 111.
6. Ibid., 141.
7. Ibid., 245.

FINLAND

JEAN SIBELIUS (1865-1957)

> ...the handful of songs that are Sibelius's most popular and most easily approachable may have created an image that does not do justice to his scope as a composer of songs.
>
> —Kimmo Korhonen[1]

Jean Sibelius was Finland's leading nationalist composer, and the first composer to bring the voice of the North to the rest of the world, fully articulated.[2] Throughout his lifetime, he came to symbolize, through his music and personality, not only Finland but all of the Scandinavian culture. His tone poem *Finlandia* (1899) is often thought of as the Finnish national anthem.

Jean Sibelius was a composer who drew inspiration from two crucial sources: nature and mythology. His music captured an emotional response to landscape, weather, and the natural rhythms of the world. He was deeply involved with Finnish myth as chronicled in the national epic poem, the *Kalevala*. Honored as a distinguished symphonist, he also composed nearly 100 songs, melodic in style, and—like his instrumental music—highly intense in mood. He continued to compose songs throughout his career.

Most of the poets whose texts he set were Swedish, which was the literary language of Finland for most of the nineteenth century, but he also set German and Finnish texts. Most of his songs are published in collections; he did not compose song cycles. He drew inspiration from "nature" poets writing in Swedish: Runeberg, Wecksell, Tavaststjerna (all Finnish), and Karlfeldt, Rydberg, Fröding (Swedish). The earliest songs date from the 1890s, and the last, the *Six Runeberg Settings*, Op. 90 were composed in 1917. Sibelius's songs are somewhat uneven and cannot be cited as his most characteristic musical works. Working on a small scale obviously did not come as easily to him as composing in a larger framework. His songs are often austere and have a brooding simplicity reminiscent of his symphonic works.

He wrote vocal parts that are technically demanding, frequently broad in phrase, but with articulation that is often like recitative. His piano accompaniments can be sparse in texture, or often too heavy, as if distilled from an orchestration. Although the songs do not have the wide range of expression found in Sibelius's orchestral works, there are works among them that may be considered masterpieces.

Song titles are listed in Finnish; since Sibelius's songs are often published and sung in German, German titles are listed also. Opus numbers are supplied to aid in locating songs. The name of the Finnish poet is given, but not the German translator.

Svarta rosor, Op. 36, No. 1   **Black Roses. 1899-1900**
(Schwarze Rosen)
(E. Josephson)

All the song texts in Op. 36 are tinged with the presence of Death. This early song is rich in romantic style with a strong undercurrent of melancholy. Glistening arpeggios in the piano underscore a declamatory, almost folk-like melody. Interleaved between the quick-moving sections are two identical vocal phrases—pauses for thought—"sorrow has black-petal'd roses." This phrase is repeated at the end of the song, this time more intense, *fortissimo* and an octave higher. This song and the two that follow are a handful of Sibelius's most popular songs; however, the poem is not a particularly strong one and translation from the original language dilutes the impact of this piece.

Säv, säv, susa, Op. 36, No. 4   **Sigh, Sedges, Sigh. 1899-1900**
(Schilfrohr, säus'le)
(G. Fröding)

This is a beautiful example of one of Sibelius's best songs. It is quasi-recitative in style, accompanied by harp-like arpeggios. Sibelius begins the song lyrically—a sighing section is heard as the text recounts a young girl's suicide. This section builds to a powerful climax, which is accompanied by a tremolo in the high register of the piano. Sibelius reprises the opening section to close the romantic story.

Flickan kom ifrån sin älsklings möte,* Op. 37, No. 5   **The Tryst. 1901**
(Mädchen kam von Stelldichein)
(J.L. Runeberg)

The text of this song has a folk-like quality: a girl returns from a meeting with her lover with reddened fingers and lips and, to her mother's questioning, makes excuses that she has eaten raspberries and scratched her hands with rose thorns. The next time she returns her cheeks are blanched; she tells her mother to make her grave and write on it how her lover betrayed her.

Despite its ballad-like story, Sibelius sets it in a sweeping, grandiose style, using a syncopated chordal accompaniment in the piano to highlight the girl's passion, followed by an intense melodic phrase in octaves. This phrase underscores the vocal line as the girl makes excuses to her mother, and appears at the end of the song as the girl tells of her lover's betrayal. Tension is maintained as the conversation unfolds through overlapping materials in the voice and piano and in the dramatic accompaniment figures used throughout. Like many folk ballad texts, this one has a tragic ending.

*See also Wilhelm Stenhammar's setting of this poem.

Marssnön, Op. 36, No. 5
(Märzschnee)
(J.J. Wecksell)

March Snow. 1899

This song in $\frac{5}{4}$ time gives the illusion of having no bar lines but drifting gently along like the white powdered snow it describes. The mood of the song takes on a new tone of urgency as spring is invoked: "Sleep so that your blossoming may be glorious, and your death, more rich." At the mention of death, the rhythm switches to $\frac{6}{4}$. This is a beautiful and evocative song. It has a companion piece in the same opus—"Demanten på marssnön" (The Diamond on March snow), No. 6— both songs are great favorites in Scandinavia and Finland.

Illalle, Op. 17, No. 6
(A.V. Foresman-Koskimies)

To Evening. 1898

This song is one of Sibelius's rare settings in the Finnish language. It is sometimes sung in Swedish as "Om kvällen." It features a beautifully simple, declamatory line that remains almost motionless for the entire song. Phrases are built on one repeated note, and move only slightly at the end of each poetic line. The piano accompaniment of alternating chord figures creates a beautiful shimmering texture.

Finnish is a highly inflected language, rich in vowel sounds. Sibelius's approach to vocal writing in this song highlights the resonance of the words and their unique verbal music.

The title of this song is a pun, as "Illalle" can mean either "to the evening," or "to Ilta." Ilta was the name of the poet's future wife.[3]

Var det en dröm? Op. 37, No. 4
(Josef Julius Wecksell)

Was it a Dream? 1902

Wecksell's poem is filled with emotion: "Was it a dream that I once was your heart's true love?" The words go on to recall the passion and sweetness of a love that is now over. But at night, through bitter tears, the poet hears a voice that says "hide this memory in your heart. It was your best dream!"

Sibelius translates the text musically into a rich-textured, dramatic setting, writing sustained vocal phrases of considerable breadth and intensity. Piano figures create a complicated, rippling rhythmic texture that seems to clash against the rhythms in the vocal line, producing a highly emotional mood. The middle section of the song is quieter; material in piano and voice changes as the sweetness of the lovers' relationship is recalled. The first turbulent musical section returns, driving to a dramatic ending.

Extended Study List

Demanten på marssnön , Op. 36, No. 6 • Höstkväll • Vilse, Op. 17, No. 4 • Den första kyssen, Op. 37, No. 1 • Spånet på vattnet, Op. 17, No. 7 • Till kvällen, Op. 17, No. 6 • Se'n har jag ej frågat mera, Op. 17, No. 1 • Jägargossen, Op. 13, No. 7 • Drömmen , Op. 13, No. 5 • Våren flyktar hastigt, Op. 13, No. 4 • Kyssens hopp, Op. 13, No. 2 • Hållilå, uti storm och i regn, Op. 60, No. 2 • Kom nu hit, död!, Op. 60, No. 1

Selected Reading

Gerald Abraham, ed., *The Music of Sibelius* (New York: Da Capo Press, 1975). Chapter 6: "The Songs."

Glenda Dawn Goss, *The Sibelius Companion* (Westport, CT: Greenwood Press, 1996).

Daniel M. Grimley, *The Cambridge Companion to Sibelius* (New York: Cambridge University Press, 2004).

Robert John Keane, *The Complete Solo-Songs of Jean Sibelius.* Ph.D. diss., University of London, 1993.

Robert Layton, *Sibelius* (New York: Schirmer, 1993). Chapter 13-The Songs.

Notes

1. Kimmo Korhonen, "Jean Sibelius: Solo Songs" trans. Jaakko Mäntyjärvi. Liner notes for *Jean Sibelius: Songs.* Tom Krause, baritone; Gustav Djupsjöbacka, pianist. Finlandia Records compact disc 4509-96871-2.
2. James Burnett, *The Music of Jean Sibelius* (East Brunswick, NJ: Associated University Presses, 1983), 17.
3. Liner notes Kari Kilpeläinen, liner notes to *Sibelius Songs.* Karita Mattila, soprano; Ilmo Ranta, piano. Ondine, ODE 856-2, 1995.

YRJÖ KILPINEN (1892-1959)

> Yrjö Kilpinen was one of those great figures...whose life work is tuned faithfully and consistently to the laws laid down by their own individuality, heedless of the changing fashions and labels of the world around them.
>
> —E. Marvia[1]

Yrjö Kilpinen is considered one of Finland's greatest composers, known above all as a composer of songs. He was born in Helsinki during a period of rising nationalism; studies in Berlin and Vienna grounded him in the German *Lieder* tradition, and he was content to compose in terms of a generally accepted idiom, choosing not to break new ground. Hallmarks of his songs are lyricism and a spontaneous response to the poetry of his native Finland.

With the exception of a few chamber works and compositions for chorus, Kilpinen's entire compositional output consists of his songs. There are 381 published songs; Kilpinen composed well over 700. Many were damaged in a bank vault flood; some were lost during the war with Russia in 1939 as Kilpinen hurriedly packed to escape the Russian advance. Perhaps the greatest disappointment is the loss of his personal catalog of compositions, presumed lost after his death.

Kilpinen considered his songs to be chamber music, that is, an inseparable fusion of music-making between singer and pianist. His songs are highly individual within an essentially traditional frame. In Europe, Kilpinen is often compared to Hugo Wolf, who also devoted himself almost entirely to composing songs; scholars place him in the great tradition of Schubert, Schumann, Brahms, and Wolf.[2] Like Wolf, he absorbed the works of one poet and then worked with those texts exclusively, composing with great speed.

Kilpinen's songs are simple but direct in dramatic impact, covering a wide range of styles and moods. He was a master of the vignette; his songs show his ability to distill intense atmosphere and emotion and present these with great economy of means. Most of the songs are published in short groups, organized by subject or mood, and these he preferred to be sung together.[3] He did not object to transpositions of his songs as long as the character of the music was not affected, and supervised all translations of his songs. He marked his scores carefully but in some cases allowed deviations from the printed page to suit the individual artist.

Like his contemporary, Jean Sibelius, he received a state pension from the Finnish government in recognition of his art and its significance for Finnish culture. Kilpinen's songs are uniquely individual and distinctive and deserve wider dissemination.

Kilpinen comosed four sets of songs to poetry by Christian Morgenstern (*Sechs Lieder,* Op. 59, *Lieder der Liebe I* and *II*, Op. 60 and 61, and *Lieder um den Tod,* Op. 62). These are German texts, as are the songs to poems by Albert Sergel, Hermann Hesse, Berta Huber, and Hans Fritz von Zwehl. Kilpinen composed numerous songs to Finnish and Swedish texts as well.[4]

Kirkkorannassa, Op. 54, No. 2   **Come, oh wave. 1926**
(V.E. Törmänen)

The text of this song exhorts a wave to abandon the wide spaces of the sea and come to the shore—to leave an imprint on the shore and join the singing of summer songs. Vocal phrases are constructed beginning on upbeats on the second step of the scale, maintaining a steady feeling of forward movement like that of lapping waves on the shoreline. Piano figures also maintain movement throughout, but do not overwhelm the voice.

Deine Rosen an der Brust   **Roses on your bosom. 1928**
(Christian Morgenstern)
(*Lieder der Liebe II*, Op. 61, No. 3)

This delicate, animated song is only one of many settings by Kilpinen of the German poetry of Christian Morgenstern. Op.60 and 61 (*Lieder der Liebe I* and *II*) use poetry on the theme of personal, intimate love. The sets are marked by different moods; Op. 60 is darker and melancholy, while the songs in Op. 61 have a folk-like quality. Here the piano accompaniment begins with a rhythmic pattern from which the song unfolds.

Tunturille, Op. 52, No. 4   **Away to the mountains. 1926**
(V.E. Törmänen)

This is a song of longing for the mountains of the poet's childhood—there to look down like an eagle on the earth below. The vocal line is sweeping and triumphant in emotion; the piano texture is heavy throughout, using rapid figures and chords that emphatically punctuate the singer's line. These syncopated chords fall in uneven patterns, and maintain a feeling of elation throughout the song.

Extended Study List

Ihr ewigen Sterne *(Spielmannslieder)* • Im Walde liegt ein stiller See (Op. 75, *Sommersegen)* • Kesäyö, Op. 23, No. 3 • Laululle, Op. 52, No. 3 • Vanha kirkko, Op. 54, No. 1 • Suvilaulu, Op. 54, No. 3 • Jänkä, Op. 54, No. 1 • Rannalta I, Op. 23, No. 1 • Unsere Liebe, Op. 60, No. 3

Selected Reading

Robert H. Cowden, "Yrjö Kilpinen: Neglected Master of the Lied," *The NATS Bulletin* 24:4 (May/1968), 2-6, 34. Excellent source on Kilpinen, includes information gathered from interviews with Mme. Kilpinen.

E. Marvia, "Kilpinen—Master of the Lied," *Yrjö Kilpinen Printed Works* (Helsinki, 1960).

Bennie Middaugh, "The Lieder of Yrjö Kilpinen," *The NATS Bulletin* 27:2 (December 1970). Good source for overview of Kilpinen's song style.

Frank Pullano, "The German Song Groups of Yrjö Kilpinen," *The NATS Bulletin* 21:5 (May/June 1971). All the German groups are listed at the end of the article, with range of individual songs, overall range, tessitura and duration of each opus.

Notes

1. E. Marvia, "Kilpinen—Master of the Lied," *Kilpinen Printed Works*, 16.
2. Robert H. Cowden, "Yrjö Kilpinen: Neglected Master of the Lied," *NATS Bulletin* 24:4, 4.
3. Ibid.
4. Kilpinen was trilingual; he spoke Finnish with his father, Swedish with his mother, and learned German as a student.

SWEDEN

WILHELM STENHAMMAR (1871-1927)

The melody must be everything in a song. The rest shall be unessential, only supporting, explaining, the means but not the end, or more correctly, both melody and harmony must jointly develop from the poem, come into existence through the poem and for the poem.

—Wilhelm Stenhammar[1]

Wilhelm Stenhammar is perhaps Sweden's most significant composer. His music is widely recognized in his native country, but has only recently begun to attract wide international interest as well. As Scandinavian song literature becomes better known and more frequently programmed, Stenhammar's songs appear with regularity on recital and concert programs.

Stenhammar studied in his native Stockholm, and then in Berlin, where he also established himself as a virtuoso pianist, appearing in recitals and orchestral concerts. He performed his own first *Piano Concerto* with the Berlin Philharmonic, conducted by Richard Strauss. In later years, he turned to conducting, first at the Royal Swedish Opera, and then with the Gothenburg Symphony Orchestra.

He composed cantatas, operas, chamber music, two symphonies and other orchestral works, six string quartets, and a piano concerto. His choral song *Sverige* (Sweden) is considered an unofficial national anthem.

Stenhammar composed approximately 110 songs; sixty-five are published. They represent Scandinavian song at the height of the Romantic period. For his texts, Stenhammar often chose poetry that dealt with nature themes. His songs are notable for their expressive melodic lines and for their rich, complex accompaniments. Stenhammar's music offers singers a wealth of beautiful lyric repertoire.

Flickan kom ifrån sin älsklings möte, Op. 4b, No. 1
(J.L. Runeberg)

The girl came home from meeting her lover. 1896

Stenhammar set this text seven years before Sibelius.* The two songs offer interesting comparisons; both settings are beautiful, and represent the styles of both composers.

The text is a conversation between a mother and daughter, revealing the young girl's secret meetings with her lover, her passion for him, and ultimately, the pain she suffers because of his unfaithfulness.

In contrast to Sibelius's heavier musical textures, Stenhammar approaches the poem from a more conservative and lyric perspective. Compare especially the piano writing in the two songs. Stenhammar's accompaniment is more intimate and linear, growing from a melancholy melody; Sibelius's is more dramatic and thicker-textured. It is interesting to note that both composers make use of syncopation in the opening piano figures of the songs.

Each question the mother asks is in the major; a minor triad precedes the girl's first answers. When the final stanza is reached, Stenhammar creates a powerful emotional moment through an unexpected tonality shift that mirrors the young girl's anguish. The accompaniment figures become repeated chords that hammer the girl's painful remembrances to her last despairing phrase. The piano repeats the opening melody to finish the poignant story.

*See Sibelius section for an annotation of this song.

I skogen
(Albert Thedor Gellerstedt)

In the Forest. 1887

Sweden has a great tradition of singing and a great love of nature. This song typifies the Swedish spirit in a simple setting of extraordinary impact.

"I skogen" is the earliest of Stenhammar's songs, written when he was sixteen years old. There are two stanzas; the form is ABA'. Moving eighth-note figures in broken chords and arpeggios gently push the song forward. The singer's line is beautifully lyric, stunning in its simplicity, and difficult to forget.

Speaking of this song, soprano Barbara Bonney observes: "Many Swedes say this is this is, without a doubt, *the* most perfect song from Scandinavia that was ever written—and it really is."[2]

Fylgia, Op. 16, No. 4
(Gustav Fröding)

Guiding Spirit. 1897

"Fylgia" is a passionate, ecstatic song. The text, by Gustav Fröding, one of Sweden's greatest lyric poets, is a breathless plea to the *fylgia*, the guiding spirit, to remain with him and comfort him. His beautiful "guardian angel" fulfills his longing for beauty and inspires his actions. In her commentary on Stenhammar's songs, Annette Johansson writes: "In early Scandinavian mythology, the term 'fylgia' (follower) referred to a supernatural being, the human soul, thought to be separate from the body."[3]

Fast-moving sixteenth-note patterns in the right hand of the piano accompaniment act as a rhythmic ostinato for most of the song. This figure and the very fast tempo (*Allegro agitato*) thrust the song forward and create a shimmering texture for the voice. Vocal phrases are lyrically shaped within the fast tempo. There are some phrases of uneven length, which also perpetuate the ardent, effusive tone of the piece. The piano closes the song with a postlude of eight measures that flies, like the *fylgia*, into the night.

Till en ros, Op. 8, No. 4   **To a Rose. 1895**
(J.L. Runeberg)*

The poet asks a beautiful red rose: "To whom shall I give you? Perhaps my mother? She is gone. Perhaps my sister? She is far away with her husband. Perhaps my brother? He is off at war. Then perhaps, my sweetheart? Oh! He is far from me, three forests and three rivers away…"

This haunting song is set in the minor key. Its form is extremely simple. The piano introduction is a melancholy, lonely little tune, folk-like in quality. The song text is set in three-part form: ABA. Vocal phrases are built of two rhythmic patterns: one used for the A section, one for the B section. Piano figures are extremely simple, and the overall texture is sparse.

Its very simplicity gives this song its elegance.

*Runeberg, a national poet of Finland, was from a Swedish speaking-family. "Flickan kom ifrån sin älsklings möte" is another Runeberg poem set to music by Stenhammar.

Vandraren, Op. 26, No. 1   **The Wanderer. 1908**
(Vilhelm Ekelund)

"Vandraren" is a most singable and delightful melody inspired by a poem describing a Scandinavian landscape. Amid the sounds and sights of a Scandinavian spring landscape, the poet exults in his surroundings.

The song's form is ABA'. Stenhammar marks the tempo "Lightly rippling along" (quarter note=144). Lyrical vocal phrases of uneven length combined with constant eighth-note motion in the piano, create a softly flowing texture that illustrates all the images in the text.

Extended Study List

Det far ett skepp • Melodi • Månsken • Flickan knyster i Johannenatten • Dottern sade till sin gamla moder • Prins Aladin av Lampan • Stjärnoga • Adagio • Irmelin Rose • Holder du af mig • Jungfru Blond och jungfru Brunett • I lönnens skymning • Ingalill

Selected Reading

Annette Johansson, trans. and commentary, *Thirty Songs of Wilhelm Stenhammar* (Geneseo, NY: Leyele Publications, 1999). See especially pp. 107-169.

Notes

1. Quoted in Annette Johansson, "Wilhelm Stenhammar and His Romanser." In *Thirty Songs of Wilhelm Stenhammar,* 159.
2. Barbara Bonney, in an interview segment, *Voices of Our Time: Barbara Bonney*, with Malcom Martineau, piano. Théâtre Musical de Paris-Chatelet. DVD Video. RM Associates, 2001.
3. Ibid., 122.

HUGO ALFVÉN (1872-1960)

My best ideas have come during my sea voyages a night, and, in particular, the wild autumns have been my most wonderful times for composition.
—Hugo Alfvén[1]

Hugo Alfvén's songs have been described as having a "popular" feeling about them. This is perhaps due to his strong gift for melody and his ability to create a programmatic atmosphere. Overall, his music shows an affinity with the late romantic style.

He attended the Stockholm Conservatory where he studied composition with Lindegren and violin with Zetterquist. He also studied painting.

For most of his career, Alfvén was a choral conductor. He conducted the Siljan Choir, a group of five church and regional choirs. He was also the director of choral studies at the University of Uppsala, and the director of the celebrated men's choir, Orphei Dränger (Sons of Orpheus). He made twenty-two tours throughout Europe with this group.

His interest in Swedish folk music and Swedish folk songs greatly influenced his own compositions, and, in turn, his works perpetuated an international interest in Swedish folk music. *Sveriges flagge* (Swedish Flag) has become an unofficial national anthem of Sweden. His musical compositions include five symphonies, ballets, songs, many chamber music pieces, and rhapsodies. His *Swedish Rhapsody*, Op. 19, became internationally popular and is his best-known work. It is frequently performed and recorded, and has been widely transcribed.

The great Swedish tenor, Jussi Björling, regularly performed Alfvén's songs on his recitals, and helped to popularize them. Alfvén's piano writing in his songs is very colorful, and almost orchestrally conceived. His gift for writing beautiful melodies produced songs that have great appeal for singers and for audiences.

Skogen sover, Op. 28, No. 6
(Ernest Thiel)

The Forest Sleeps. 1908

"Skogen sover" is a text that celebrates nature, and Alfvén creates an atmospheric musical setting for it. The first vocal pitch emerges from a silky piano figure ("Skogen sover" – the forest is asleep). The merry sounds of the forest are stilled as day stands guard over her treasure through the June night.

The form is through-composed. Elegantly shaped vocal phrases float over a simple accompaniment, whose patterns change with each musical section. Alfvén's setting resembles a chamber music texture, with touches of text painting (example: the forest's laughter) and interesting chord progressions in the piano that create the magical atmosphere of nature asleep.

This is a strikingly beautiful song.

Så tag mit hjerte
(Tove Ditlevsen)

So Take My Heart. 1946

Then take my heart in your hands / But take it carefully, take it gently / The red heart, now it is yours. It has loved and suffered / Now it is still / Now is it yours. It can also be broken, but only by you.

This charming love song is simple and understated, and has an innate warmth that communicates directly to the listener. The form is AABA. In the first two A sections, piano and voice end on the dominant, suspended. When the A section returns for the last time, a conclusive cadence is finally reached.

This lovely song is a good example of the "popular" feeling found in Alfvén's musical style. It might have come from one of the lavish movie musicals of the 1940s. In the hands of an excellent interpreter, it is quite effective.

Extended Study List

Vandrarens julsång • I bruset • Det unga hemmet • Julsång • Minnesskrift • Marias sånger • Vaggvisa • 10 Sånger, Op. 4 • Jag kysser din vita hand • Pioner

Selected Reading

Rolf Haglund, "Hugo Alfvén," in *The New Grove Dictionary of Music and Musicians,* ed. Stanley Sadie (New York: Macmillan, 1980), v.1, 253.

Notes

1. Rolf Haglund, "Ture Rangström," The New Groves Dicdtionary of Music and Musicians, ed. Stanley Sadie vol. 1 (New York: Macmillan, 1980), 253.

TURE RANGSTRÖM (1884-1947)

However influenced these composers were by what they learned abroad, you sense that Swedish nature, the seasons, the light, stayed with them, influencing them just as much as it did painters and writers.

—Anne Sofie von Otter[1]

Ture (Anders Johan) Rangström was one of the last composers in the Swedish romantic style. His music also contains influences from baroque music as well as neoclassicism. Ture Rangström belongs to the generation after Carl Nielsen and Wilhelm Stenhammar. He studied composition with Lindgren and with Pfitzner in Berlin. He also studied voice in Berlin, and later in Munich.

For many years, Rangström was a music critic in Stockholm, working for three Swedish news publications. In 1921, he succeeded Stenhammar as conductor of the Gothenburg Symphony Orchestra, and was later press advisor for the Swedish Royal Opera. He founded the Society of Swedish Composers in 1918.

He composed four symphonies and a variety of other musical works, but Rangström is best remembered for his songs. Although he was a trained singer, Rangström chose not to pursue a performing career, but he was active as a voice teacher in the decade after 1910. His thorough knowledge of the voice is readily apparent in the expressive vocal writing in his songs.

Rangström composed over 250 songs, and is considered one of Sweden's major song composers. Stylistically, his songs have an almost improvisatory quality, a feeling of unstructured harmonic scheme, and always, an expressive melodic line that is integrated with the poem. He wrote many of his songs in simple strophic structure.

He was absorbed by poetry and word sounds, and his song settings were influenced by a theory he called "speech melody"—a technique of developing vocal phrases from the inflection and intonation of an expressive reading. Many of his musical works are typically driven by programmatic ideas.

Rangström was especially inspired by the poetry of Bo Bergman. Four of his Bergman settings are annotated here. Bergman (1869-1967) wrote highly sophisticated lyric poetry—verses that often dealt with nature and with love, always mixed with a sense of melancholy or nostalgia.

Vingar I natten   Wings in the Night. 1917
(Bo Bergman)

Bergman's poem describes the flight of a silent black bird, flying in the world's wide spaces with the wind of anxiety in its wings. It has no home, nor rest. It is like the poet's longing; like the bird, he is driven by unrest. Both have whispering wings in the night.

A strong, declamatory vocal line and a restless, driving accompaniment combine to produce a dramatic, thick-textured song. Its astonishing energy is maintained continuously throughout the piece. The style of this song shares kinship with some Sibelius's dramatic settings.

Melodi*   Melody. 1917
(Bo Bergman)

You have only to walk over the fields and ever spring comes to life, clouds shine, parks whisper, and all nature resonates to your charm. Who gives you the power to become melody?

This song and "Afskedet" are excellent examples of Rangström's "speech melody" technique. Word inflection and rhythm are primary guidelines for shaping vocal lines.

Vocal phrases are sustained and lyric, over an arpeggiated accompaniment that slips easily through many colorful harmonies before finally reaching the ending cadence.

Rangstöm's ability to extract the essence of the poem and translate it into musical sound is readily apparent here.

*Wilhelm Stenhammar also set this text.

Serenad   Serenade. 1924
(Bo Bergman)

Arpeggiated piano figures create a serene backdrop for a tranquil vocal line in this quiet serenade. The musical texture has an unhurried character. This is not a serenade of a lover under his sweetheart's window; it is a nostalgic remembrance of someone grown old, recalling youth in a lovely evening where the moonlight made everything shine. It is a serenade given as a gift to someone younger.

Both piano and vocal lines seem to shift slightly through the song—the harmonies are often subtly altered, and the vocal line wanders just enough to create a feeling of weightlessness. It is an atmospheric texture full of wonder and yearning.

Afskedet   **The Farewell. 1924**

(Bo Bergman)

Piano figures are constantly in motion throughout this song, creating a rippling, shimmering texture. Sinuously shaped vocal phrases describe the parting of lovers—he to serve as a seaman, she to wait until the next homecoming, and then, the next parting. The text is set syllabically (see "Melodi"). The poem is suffused with the melancholy that is so often found in Bergman's verses.

Extended Study List
Dan enda stunden • Bön till natten • Villemo • Pan • Somm arnatten • Vinden och trädet • Gammalsvenskt • En gammal dansrym • Flickan under nymånen • Sköldmön

Notes
1. Anne Sofie von Otter, quoted in Nick Kimberley, "A Singing Country," liner notes to *Watercolors: Swedish Songs*. Anne Sofie von Otter and Bengt Forsberg, piano. Deutsche-Grammophon B000 1857-02, 2003.

DENMARK

CARL NIELSEN (1865-1931)

His importance lies in the very fact that he was not typical. He took comfortable old Danish music by the scruff of its neck and shook hard; his was a big fist breaking windows to let in fresh air.

—John H. Yoell[1]

Carl Nielsen stood at the forefront of Danish music during the opening years of the twentieth century. His style was rooted in diatonic harmony, but his use of materials was bold and individual; interval and rhythm were the bedrock of his compositions, which have an amazing sense of force and energy. He composed six symphonies and numerous other instrumental works; he also had an abiding interest in solo song. Despite this rugged, almost raw quality that pervades his works, Nielsen's music also contains a serene strength derived from the countryside where he was raised.

Nielsen's songs are greatly admired in his native Denmark but have yet to achieve the popularity or recognition of the two Scandinavian composers from Finland: Sibelius and Kilpinen. Nielsen's style is charming and contains naive, lovely melodies with simple accompaniments—an attempt on his part to create songs that Danish schoolchildren would be able to sing.

Nielsen's interest in solo song continued throughout his life; in his efforts to channel the solo song from classic romanticism back into popular areas, he contributed many songs to official school songbooks, creating a new, populist type of song. For this reason, only a few really deserve to be labeled "art" songs. Two early collections on the poems of Jens Peter Jacobsen are excellent examples of Nielsen's songs; also notable are the Op. 10 Holstein songs and selected miscellaneous songs. By age forty, he had produced two operas, one serious (*Saul and David*), one comic (*Maskarade*). The latter is highly popular with Danish audiences, and is considered Denmark's national opera.

Irmelin Rose* 1891
(Jens Peter Jacobsen)

This song is considered a Nielsen "classic." It belongs to the set of *Jacobsen Songs* of 1891. It retains links with the *romanse* tradition, and bears some relation to the songs of Edvard Grieg. Its mood and style recall the chivalric past.

*Also set by Frederic Delius and Wilhelm Stenhammar.

Aebleblomst Apple Blossoms. 1894
(Ludvig Holstein)

One of Nielsen's loveliest songs, this piece belongs to the Holstein songs, a set of six songs designated as Op. 10. In style and mood, it falls within the area of the Nordic *romanse*. Not until later did Nielsen create his own popular style, breaking with musical character of the earlier, more sentimental type song.

Extended Study List
Erindringens sø • Vi sletternes sønner • Jaegersang • Sommersang • I Aften • Sang bag ploven • Du Danske Mand • Genrebillede • Hilsen

Some examples of Nielsen's Folk High School gebrauchsmusik: Jeg baerer med smil min byrde (I Carry My Burden With Joy) • Saenk kun dit hoved, du blomst (Lower Your head, Pretty Flower) • Grøn er vårens haek (Green Hedges in Spring)

Selected Reading
Mina F. Miller. *Carl Nielsen: A Guide to Research* (New York: Garland Publishing, 1987).
Anne-Marie Reynolds, *The Songs of Carl Nielsen.* Ph.D. diss., University of Rochester, 1998.
John Y. Yoell, *The Nordic Sound: explorations into the Music of Denmark, Norway, Sweden* (Boston: Crescendo Publishing Co., 1974).

Notes
1. John Y. Yoell, *The Nordic Sound: Explorations into the Music of Denmark, Norway, Sweden*, 150.

Spanish Song

Spanish art song has ancient roots. Today's Spanish art song is preceded by a long tradition of vocal music dating from the sixteenth century. Spain's "Golden Age" of music refers to music of the Renaissance; during this era, part songs, solo songs, and choral works were composed in great numbers.

Sixteenth-century solo song was usually accompanied by the *vihuela*, a plucked viol whose timbre made it well suited for accompanying the voice. *Villancicos* and *romances* were popular solo song forms of this era; both were sung in Castilian. *Villancicos* ("rustic songs") flourished at the courts of Charles V and Philip II. Piano-accompanied Spanish song, as we know and perform it, belongs to the nineteenth and twentieth centuries, and is largely composed of songs written by the composers annotated in this section.

In the seventeenth and eighteenth centuries, theater music dominated vocal music in Spain. Literally thousands of works were written and performed yearly. The two main forms of music theater were the *zarzuela* and the *tonadilla*. *Zarzuelas* were a Spanish operatic form geared toward the aristocracy; *tonadillas* began life as an entr'acte with song, a light-natured Spanish "opera buffa." *Tonadillas* disappeared in the early decades of the nineteenth century, but their style greatly influenced Spanish vocal music. Probably the most famous examples are Enrique Granados's *Colección de tonadillas*, songs that pay homage to the Spanish artist Francisco Goya, and the *majos* and *majas* who appear so frequently in his paintings.

Zarzuelas, which had been eclipsed by the popularity of the *tonadilla*, made a strong comeback in the nineteenth century. Some composers wrote many successful works that filled the concert halls, but rather than becoming a serious "operatic" form, the *zarzuela* remained a popular type of theatrical entertainment.

Solo song was not really important again as a vocal form until the twentieth century. Falla, Nin, Turina, Guridi, Obradors, and Mompou (all born in the last years of the nineteenth century), and Rodrigo and Montsalvatge (born in the early years of this century), are the composers whose names come to mind when Spanish art song is mentioned.

Apart from composing his own vocal works, Joaquín Nin restored interest in Spain's earlier song heritage. In the 1920s, he collected and published important collections of folk songs and songs from seventeenth-century *tonadillas*, which he harmonized with appealing representative accompaniments. Among these were *Veinte cantos populares españoles* and *Quatorze airs anciens*.

Within its rich palette of sound, Spanish music is full of complexities and different styles; each separate province has a special musical flavor unique to its geography. Pianist Graham Johnson learned that regional differences matter enormously in Spanish music.[1] Articulation of Granados's rhythms in his *Tonadillas*, evocations of eighteenth-century Madrid, need to be much more elegant and crisp than the rhythms of Andalusian music, which is freer and more uninhibited in its Moorish style. Each of Spain's geographical regions has its own musical flavor and roots.

Despite its diversity, Spanish song maintains a seamless and enduring character. Johnson observes that very early Spanish song sounds as though it might have been composed in modern times, and that much of twentieth-century Spanish song can sound quite old.[2]

Piano figures in Spanish song accompaniments usually contain patterns reminiscent of the Spanish guitar and heel-clicking Spanish dances. These colorful and vibrant rhythms are unmistakably Spanish in flavor, and help give Spanish song its unique and distinctive style. Unfortunately, these same features also "stereotype" Spanish song for many people. Not all Spanish song is fast and colorful; apart from the usual musical clichés, there are many beautiful examples of quiet and expressive songs as well.

Apart from Falla's *Siete canciones populares españolas* and Montsalvatge's *Cinco canciones negras,* which are performed with regularity, some of the real treasures of Spanish song are still largely unknown and unperformed. In recent years, publications of Spanish song and publications about Spanish vocal music have proliferated. Spanish song literature is as highly individual as its various composers, and a wealth of beautiful, appealing literature is waiting to be discovered.

Notes

1. Johnson, who was accompanying Victoria de los Angeles, was gently upbraided by the soprano for playing an accompaniment from Castile as "if it were from the South." In Jacqueline Cockburn and Richard Stokes *The Spanish Song Companion*, with an introduction and notes on the composers by Graham Johnson, 14.
2. Ibid., 20.

ARNE DØRUMSGAARD (1921-2006)

Arne Dørumsgaard was a Norwegian composer, whose arrangements of early songs and arias, titled *Canzone scordate,* have provided beautiful recital fare for distinguished singers for the past fifty years. Dørumsgaard's excellent realizations for voice and piano include twenty-two volumes of folk songs and early song literature from Italy, Spain, France, Germany, England, and Scandinavia. Once available only in libraries, they are now published by Recital Publications.

Distinguished pianist Dalton Baldwin terms Dørumsgaard's arrangements "unique in their imagination and inspired realizations for the piano." Frederica von Stade describes the early French aria realizations as having "a transparency and a simplicity and sensitivity that are unique and special and infinitely valuable to the world of song literature."[1] Selections from Book I (*Ten Early Spanish Songs*) are annotated here as examples of early Spanish song literature.

From *Ten Early Spanish Songs* (1450-1550)

Juan de Anchieta (1462-1523)   **Composer**
(arr. Arne Dørumsgaard)

CON AMORES, LA MI MADRE (WITH LOVE IN MY HEART, MOTHER). "With love in my heart, mother, I fell asleep. As I slept, I dreamed what my heart secretly hid. While love consoled me more than I deserved."

Anchieta was one of the outstanding Basque musicians of his time. He was related to San Ignacio de Loyola, and was a composer and singer at the court of

Queen Isabella. He traveled constantly, for the queen moved her court frequently. He subsequently was appointed *maestro de capilla* to her son, Prince Juan. After the queen's death he was transferred to the service of her daughter Joanna and her consort Philip the Fair; with their court he visited Flanders and the south of England. A characteristic example of Anchieta's music is the celebrated *Cancionero de palacio,* a collection of 550 songs, probably composed for use in the Duke of Alba's household.

This song has an simple, serene melody which is decorated with some delicate vocal *fioritura*. In his arrangement, Dørumsgaard tastefully embroiders the introductory measures also. The introductory material, abbreviated by four measures, closes the song.

Francisco de la Torre (fl. 1483-1504)   **Composer**
(arr. Arne Dørumsgaard)

PÁMPANO VERDE (GREEN VINE). "Green pampano trees cluster white. Whoever saw duennas out at this hour? In their midst the young girls are seen."

Francisco de la Torre was a fifteenth-century Sevillian composer, singer at the court of Ferdinand V of Aragon, and choirmaster at the Cathedral. To him we owe an enormous number of dances as well as secular and religious compositions.

This song has a tender lyrical melody with an accompaniment of pizzicato figures that evoke the *vihuela.*[*] It concludes with the voice humming the first two vocal phrases. The delicacy of this setting and the beauty of the vocal melody perfectly captures the atmosphere of fifteenth-century Spain.

Cristóbal de Morales (1500-1553)   **Composer**
(arr. Arne Dørumsgaard)

DE ANTEQUERA SALE EL MORO (THE MOOR SET OUT FROM ANTEQUERA). "From Antequera came the Moor. In his hands were letters of sorrow/Written in blood and not for lack of ink/With the blood of a hundred twenty years of suffering."

One of his contemporaries considered Morales to be "the light of Spain in music."[2] Almost all of his music is liturgical (eight volumes of his *Monumentos de la música española),* but he composed a few secular pieces as well. Morales's style was influenced by Josquin, and his own music influenced Palestrina. He had a thorough command of the musical techniques practiced on the Continent during the first half of the sixteenth century.

Morales received his initial musical training in Seville, and spent time in Rome as a member of the papal choir. In addition to music, his lengthy Latin dedications show him to be a scholar as well. He was later employed in the cathedrals of Toledo and Málaga.

Morales was deeply concerned with expressing the meaning of the text as well as with the musical structure of his compositions. "De Antequera sale el Moro" is a mysterious, dramatic narrative: a Moor leaves his home, Antequera, carrying letters of sorrow, written with his own blood—the blood of 120 years of suffering. Its meter fluctuates with the text: $\frac{2}{2}$, $\frac{3}{2}$, $\frac{4}{2}$. Morales's setting is abundant proof of his mastery of the polyphonic style.

Alonso Mudarra (c. 1510-1580)   Composer
(arr. Arne Dørumsgaard)

TRISTE ESTABA EL REY DAVID (KING DAVID WAS SORROWFUL). "King David was sorrowful and full of grief/At the news of Absalom's death."

Mudarra was a Spanish vihuelist and composer, brought up in Guadalajara in the households of the third and fourth dukes of Infantado, Diego Hurtado de Mendoza (1461-1531) and Iñigo López de Mendoza (1493-1566).[3] He was trained in Seville, and spent the better part of his life in the service of that cathedral, as canon. In 1546 he published a tablature book of vihuela and guitar music (*Tres libros de musica en cifras para vihuela*) that included a number of songs with *vihuela* accompaniment. These included settings on texts by Horace, Ovid, and Virgil as well as the Italians Petrarch and Sannazaro.

This song captures the intense sorrow of King David at the news of the death of his son, Absalom. "Absalón" is repeated four times, each time with different rhythmic stresses and increasing emotional impact.

Gabriel Mena (fl. 1511-1516)   Composer
(arr. Arne Dørumsgaard)

A LA CAZA, SUS, A CAZA (TO THE CHASE, EVERYONE). "To the chase, everyone! Young lovers, go in search of love! With wings of sweetness you will soar and fly/You will hunt for love with sadness and joy."

Gabriel Mena was a Spanish poet and composer who served as a singer in the court chapel of Ferdinand V, then entered the service of the Admiral of Castile. Nineteen of his *villancicos*** are found in the *Cancionero de palacio*. Their style is marked by freshness and charm. At least two quote folk tunes.

"A la caza, sus, a caza" is a charming evocation of the hunt for love, in which everyone who joins finds sweetness as well as sadness. Mena's melodic setting of the words is highly rhythmic and energetic.

*Vihuela: a plucked instrument of the viol family and the Spanish equivalent of the Elizabethan lute.

**Villancicos: songs of folk origin (often on a Nativity theme) with a refrain. The mood and rhythms of these rustic carols were usually vibrant and energetic. This form emerged and flourished in Spain at the court of Charles V and his son Philip II.

Extended Study List
Canzone Scordate. 22 volumes

Selected Reading
Jacqueline Cockburn and Richard Stokes, *The Spanish Song Companion*. Introduction and notes by Graham Johnson (London: Victor Gollancz, 1992). Information on early Spanish song and its composers may be found here.

Notes
1. Quoted in flyer/brochure announcing the publication of *Canzone Scordate*. Recital Publications, Huntsville, TX.
2. Graham Johnson, "Cristóbal Morales," in *The Spanish Song Companion*, 36.
3. Robert Stevenson, "Alonso Mudarra," *The New Grove Dictionary of Music and Musicians*, 757.

ENRIQUE GRANADOS (1867-1916)

> The songs of Granados are the first in Spanish music where the piano... is
> permitted to enter into an important role in its own right.
>
> —Graham Johnson[1]

Enrique Granados is so identified with the Madrid of Goya, it is easy to forget
that he was born a Catalán. Recent discovery of the scores of his Catalán stage
works, which enjoyed widespread local success but never became known outside
Barcelona, has added a new dimension to Granados's musical history. His reputation has, until recently, rested almost solely on his numerous compositions for the
piano. Granados was essentially a miniaturist; his music is full of finely crafted
details, and his mature stage works seem to be a series of cameos. His songs share
an abundance of delicate musical touches.

Granados studied composition with Felipe Pedrell[2] in 1881, and after two
years study at the Paris Conservatoire, began a career as a pianist in Barcelona.
He established a fine reputation as a fine performer; many of his compositions
were written for his use on the concert platform. Also, a magnificent teacher, he
eventually founded his own teaching institution, the Academia Granados, in 1901.

Granados's fame as a composer rests squarely on his masterpiece, *Goyescas*
(1911), a suite of six imaginative, colorful piano pieces inspired by the paintings
and sketches of Spanish painter Francisco Goya, for whom Granados had an abiding fascination. He later composed an opera of the same title on a libretto by
Fernando Periquet, drawn from scenes in Goya's paintings and used the piano
suite as the basis for the vocal parts. The opera *Goyescas* (1916) was premiered to
great acclaim at the Metropolitan Opera in New York with the composer present.
Returning home after the triumphant debut, Granados and his wife tragically
drowned at sea after the HMS Sussex was torpedoed in the English Channel.

Granados was an remarkable pianist; his song accompaniments are exceptional in their partnering of the voice, using figures derived from the national accompanying instrument of Spain, the guitar. The spontaneity and brilliance of these
accompaniments combine fine piano technique and style with a melodic line rooted firmly in Spanish vocal idioms. Eighteenth-century Madrid as immortalized by
Goya in his paintings became both the setting and the theme for Granados's
compositions for voice and piano. His most popular vocal work is the *Coleccíon
de tonadillas* (Collection of Character Songs). In these songs, Granados tried to
reproduce the musical style found in the theater of Goya's day.

Granados's song style and treatment of the piano influenced the vocal music
of his younger contemporary Falla, and of Turina; all used piano figures that
imitate techniques of guitar performance: arpeggiated chords, fast repeated chords
(*rasgueados*), and repeated notes (*punteado*).

Selections from *Tonadillas*
(Fernando Periquet)

La maja dolorosa No. 1 • La maja dolorosa No. 2 • La maja dolorosa
No. 3 • El tra la la y el punteado • Amor y odio • El majo discreto •
El mirar de la maja

Granados's admiration for the paintings of Francisco Goya (1746-1828) inspired this set of songs. The texts—like Goya's paintings—illustrate the "majas" and "majos" (women and men) of eighteenth-century Madrid.[3] *Tonadilla* is a term derived from *tonada*, a song of theatrical character. In the eighteenth century, *tonadillas* were often performed by a costumed singer between the acts of plays as a sort of vocal *intermezzo*. From this, the *tonadilla* gradually developed into a miniature opera, in dramatic content and cast not unlike the Italian *intermezzi*.[4] In his *Tonadillas*, Granados—himself an excellent painter—attempted to musically recreate the picturesque era of Goya. Vocal phrases are firmly rooted in Spanish vocal traditions and the guitar is graphically illustrated in the piano. Fernando Periquet, the librettist for Granados's opera *Goyescas*, provided the texts for these songs.

Granados composed his *Colección de tonadillas escritas en estilo antiguo* (Collection of little songs in the antique style) between 1896 and 1900. The twelve songs (only one in the bass clef, suitable for a male singer) were premiered in Paris in 1916. The work is a brilliant set of songs that captures the mood and color of Spain and of Goya's paintings as well.

LA MAJA DOLOROSA NOS. 1, 2, 3 (THE GRIEVING MAJA NOS. 1, 2, 3). These three songs form a triptych—a heartrending lament of a woman mourning the death of her lover. With each song, her emotions change: the first is full of intense anger and despair; the second, a remembrance of shared romantic passion; and the third, a recollection of all the couple's joyful past together.

In Song 1, as the maja dramatically bemoans her loss, disjunct intervals characterize the vocal phrases and the range encompasses more than two octaves (A-flat above the staff to G-natural below). In Song 2, the maja remembers the deep passion of their love in a lyrical lament. The two stanzas are separated by a lovely piano interlude, which also returns as a postlude. In Song 3, a gentle staccato melody in the piano ushers in the first vocal phrases. The text refers to specific locations in Madrid where the couple shared joyful moments.[5]

The three songs are related thematically. The final portrait, "La Maja de Goya" (the last song in the *Tonadillas* set) reprises material from the first song; in the original version the singer recites an extended poem about Goya's amorous liaison with the Duchess of Alba over a long guitar-like piano background accompaniment before the song proper begins. It is an exceptional piece of spoken-sung theater.

EL TRA LA LA Y EL PUNTEADO (TRA LA LA AND THE PLUCKED GUITAR). An unmistakable Spanish flavor is found in this charming, light song based on graceful dance rhythms. The piano accompaniment is composed of guitar figures; a brilliant flourish by the guitar (piano) echoes each "tra-la-la" section.

AMOR Y ODIO (LOVE AND HATE). This gentle folk-like melody bemoans the sorrow which love has caused and the majo who inspired the love but does nothing to encourage it. The comparison between love and hate is heightened musically by a major-minor alteration. (The first section of the song is in minor, the second in major.) The easy rhythmic flow is interrupted by an exclamation in the vocal line—an ascending scale that climbs emotionally through the phrase "por quien me olvida sin que una luz alentadora" to a high note, then descends to the cadence. A discreet piano accompaniment is made up of delicate guitar figures.

EL MAJO DISCRETO (THE DISCREET MAJO). The maja describes her majo, who is said to be ugly, but—she says slyly—he is more than adequate in other ways, one of which is keeping secrets! A piano introduction of octaves underlines the maja's certainty, then dissolves into a lilting waltz as she relates the attributes of her majo. A final vocal flourish leaves no doubt as to her mindset.

EL MIRAR DE LA MAJA (THE MAJA'S GAZE). A single accompaniment line holds forth throughout the entire song, built on a rhythmic ostinato in triple meter. Vocal phrases contain sensual descending *portamenti* that express the restrained anger of the maja, as she turns a sultry gaze full of smoldering anger on her lover. The combination of lovely melodic vocal lines with the unrelenting staccato accompaniment is both musically engaging and unsettling. Only for the concluding measures does the accompaniment take leave of the staccato articulation and pedal is used for a tiny postscript ending.

Extended Study List

El majo olvidado • Las currutacas modestas • *Canciones amatorias* • La maja y el ruiseñor

Selected Reaading

Jacqueline Cockburn and Richard Stokes, *The Spanish Song Companion*. Introduction and notes by Graham Johnson (London: Victor Gollancz, 1992). Chapter 5.

Carol A. Hess, *Enrique Granados: A Bio-Bibliography* (New York: Greenwood Press, 1991).

Mark Larrad, "Enrique Granados," *The New Grove Dictionary of Opera,* edited by Stanley Sadie (New York: Grove's Dictionaries of Music, 1992), v. 2, 508.

Notes

1. Graham Johnson, "Enrique Granados," in *The Spanish Song Companion* by Jacqueline Cockburn and Richard Stokes (London: Victor Gollancz, 1992), 80.
2. Felipe Pedrell (1841-1922), Catalonian composer, is considered the father of Spanish nationalism. He unearthed early Spanish music and researched its living folklore, publishing vocal music of past centuries in four volumes titled *Cancionero musical popular español* (1918-19). He greatly influenced Granados and Falla to compose contemporary music using elements of Spanish folk music.
3. In his liner notes to *A Spanish Songbook* (Jill Gomez, soprano; John Constable, pianist. Conifer Classics compact disc 75605-51243-2), Patrick Carnegy identifies the majas and majos as "street-wise boys and girls" as contrasted with the more aristocratic señors and señoritas.
4. For a succinct and informative discussion of the *tonadilla* and *zarzuela*, see Graham Johnson, "Song in the Theatre," in *The Spanish Song Companion,* 56.
5. Carnegy (see Note 3) identifies the locations as follows: Mentidero (a small eighteenth-century square in Madrid, now the entrance to the Calle de León) and Florida (the district around the church of San Antonio de la Florida, where Goya painted his frescos of the Miracle of St. Anthony).

MANUEL DE FALLA (1876-1946)

It was Falla who brought Spanish music into the twentieth century—his knowledge and use of folk song, and his fidelity to the Spanish spirit make him the Bartók or Kodály of Spain.

—Graham Johnson[1]

Manuel de Falla received his early musical education in Cadiz and Madrid. In Madrid he dutifully composed *zarzuelas*, and studied for a short time with Spain's eminent composer and greatest folklorist, Felipe Pedrell.[2] Pedrell was a decisive influence on Falla's musical development.

In 1904, Falla won two competitions, one for piano, one for composition. His opera *La vida breve* became his ticket to Paris. Instead of a short stay, he lived there from 1907 to 1914. He was befriended by Dukas, Debussy, Fauré, Ravel, and the Spaniards Albéniz, Turina, and pianist Ricardo Viñes (who was to be Poulenc's teacher). In Albéniz's work, Falla found a model for his own national musical style.

Falla's travel to Paris couldn't have been at a more opportune time. Albéniz was composing his fourth book of *Iberia* for the piano; Debussy was completing his *Ibéria* (a section of his *Images* for orchestra), and Ravel was writing *L'Heure espagnole* and the *Rapsodie espagnole.* When Dukas saw the score of *La vida breve,* he suggested the opera be presented at the Paris Opéra Comique. It received a first performance in Nice in 1913, then a production at the Opéra Comique in the same year.

When Falla returned to Madrid, he brought with him the revised version of *La vida breve,* the yet unperformed *Siete canciones populares españolas* and sketches for *Noches en los jardines de España. La vida breve* was produced in Madrid to great success, and Falla's reputation was assured. He became the leading figure of the modern Spanish school.

Falla's music combines the sensuous charm of Spanish music with an intellectual approach; the finished product is an appealing mixture of authentic Spanish flavor and classical style. His career was not one of sustained creativity; his reputation was made on half a dozen works, most composed in his forties or earlier: *La vida breve* (1913); *El amor brujo* (1915); *Noches en los jardines de España* (1911-1915); *Concerto for Harpsichord* (1926); and *The Three-Cornered Hat* (1919). His most important contribution to song literature was the set titled *Siete canciones populares españolas* (Seven Spanish Popular Songs).

Falla's music has been compared in style and atmosphere to the haunting poetry of Federico García Lorca, whom Falla mentored musically.[3] A decisive influence on all of Falla's work was the *cante jondo*, the deep song of Andalusia, the most primitive source of Spanish music and the purest form of flamenco. Falla called it "the backbone of popular Andalusian song." Both Lorca and Falla believed that *cante jondo* was the "thread that joins us to the impenetrable Orient" and that it origins sprang from Byzantine chant and Moorish music.[4]

Falla received France's Cross of the Legion of Honor and succeeded Edward Elgar in the Academie des Beaux Arts of France. In later life Falla produced relatively few compositions. In 1939 he moved to Argentina to escape the stifling artistic aftermath of the Spanish Civil War, and died there in 1946, leaving a large-scale opera *Atlántida*, unfinished.

Siete canciones populares españolas   **Seven Spanish Popular Songs. 1914**

El paño moruno • Séguidilla murciana • Asturiana •
Jota • Nana • Canción • Polo

Siete canciones populares españolas consists of folk melodies from various regions of Spain—Murcia, Asturias, Aragon, and Andalucia—arranged by Falla with beautifully crafted accompaniments that preserve the spirit of folk music, but are brilliantly pianistic.

Falla differed from Pedrell in his use of folk song materials. While Pedrell used them in their original form, including quoting sections of old music, Falla set them in harmonies which evoked the guitar and in themes and figures derived from the songs themselves. The words and tunes of the seven songs are traditional, though Falla developed and extended all the melodies except in the first and third songs. He wrote:

> In all honesty, I think that in popular song, the *spirit* is more important than the letter. The essential features of these songs are rhythm, tonality, and melodic intervals. The people themselves prove this by their infinite variations on the purely melodic lines of the songs...[5]

Using an abundance of motives and techniques from Spanish folk music, Falla blended dance rhythms, folk rhythms, and virtuoso piano accompaniments into a song collection of unique quality and imagination. Falla's treatment of rhythm and harmony in the piano accompaniments creates a series of vibrant textures in which the folk melodies are set like jewels.

Seven Spanish Popular Songs occupies a secure place in the repertory as probably the most performed work in Spanish vocal literature. The seven songs make the strongest effect when performed as a group; their order, balance, and contrast in mood and tonality is meticulously planned. The songs were published in Paris by Max Eschig, with a French version by Paul Milliet, translator of *La vida breve*. The work is dedicated to Ida Godebski.

EL PAÑO MORUNO (THE MOORISH CLOTH). This song is based on a celebrated ancient folk song of Murcia. Exotic Moorish rhythm is heard in the accompaniment. A lively rustic melody in the bass line is featured in the extended piano introduction to this song.[*] In both piano and vocal line, the second beat is accentuated. Two brief vocal sections are ushered in with a typical *accacciatura*.[**] The poem archly compares the lover to a stained cloth on the counter which will now sell for less, for it has lost its value. ¡Ay!

*Falla later borrowed the first four bars of the bass line to illustrate the miller (from Murcia) in *The Three-Cornered Hat*.

**A discordant note sounded with a principal note or chord and immediately released.

SEGUIDILLA MURCIANA (SEGUIDILLA FROM MURCIA). The *seguidilla* is the popular dance form in quick triple time from the south of Spain.[*] The vocal line is a series of repeated notes with melismatic phrase endings; the accompaniment (as in the preceding song) suggests the Spanish guitar in fast running triplets, *allo spiritoso*, in the *punteado* or contrapuntal style, with *pianissimo* passages. The tempo is breathless, racing without pause to the final measures where the voice and piano end together with a brilliant flourish.

*Murcia is a maritime province in southeast Spain. The *seguidilla* was an ancient Castilian dance and folk poem.

ASTURIANA (ASTURIAN SONG). This is a plaintive melody from Asturias in northern Spain.* The accompaniment is centered on the dominant of F minor in alternating octaves throughout the song, creating a "weeping" pattern and sustaining a mood of unvarying melancholy. In spite of the mood, the song is beautifully lyrical. The green pine tree in the text is said to be an ancient Spanish symbol of sexual desire.[6]

*Asturias is a province of highlands. Its indigenous instruments is the *gaita* or bagpipe.

JOTA (JOTA). A *jota* is one of the most widely known Spanish dance-song forms, mainly associated with Aragon.* It is usually accompanied by the guitar, castanets, or other instruments. Figures illustrative of these folk instruments are found in the colorful piano accompaniment. Instrument and voice alternate sections; the piano is in a strongly marked, vigorous $\frac{3}{8}$; the voice enters in $\frac{3}{4}$ in a more declamatory, slower tempo.

*The jota is popular throughout Spain, but especially in Aragon and Navarre where it is part of a ritual, sung in honor of Our Lady of Pilar in Saragossa. It has been said that in the *jota* we hear the sound of helmets, the roaring of cannon, the neighing of horses and a clang of swords. The present *jota* is more characteristic of Mediterranean Spain.

NANA (LULLABY). This tender lullaby is an Andalusian cradle song, oriental in quality.[7] The key is E major/minor; there is a tonic pedal sounded on the off-beats. Descending stepwise figures in the piano, alternating in right and left hands, create a hypnotic lullaby mood. The vocal line is sensuous, with melismatic turns at the ends of phrases. The simple, clear texture and rhythmic interest created by the juxtaposition of voice and piano is striking.

CANCÍON (SONG). A flirtatious love song in G major creates a welcome change of mood between the preceding song and the one that follows. A rhythmic ostinato figure in the bass line of the piano holds forth throughout, a double pedal point (V-I) punctuated by syncopated chords in the right hand. The vocal line has tiny uneven stresses that appear at various points within the four-bar phrases. The overall atmosphere is graceful and charming.

POLO (POLO). This vibrant song belongs to the Gypsy world of the flamenco and the *cante jondo*.* Both love and sadness are united in a high-spirited, passionate setting. Falla's rapid repeated-note piano accompaniment evokes heel-clicking flamenco dance steps (*zapateado*). It begins with a brilliant *punteado* with accents that evoke the *palmadas* (hand-clapping) of the spectators. The voice enters, singing "¡Ay!" the plaintive cry of Andalusian singers, and the vocal line features held notes and vivid melismas that depict the passionate despair of the text.

Cante jondo (deep song) was an Andalusian flamenco song—a highly emotional, tragic song originated by prisoners In the late nineteenth century it was adopted by Gypsies, who made it even more
expressive and florid. The *siguiriya gitana* or Gypsy *seguidilla* and its derivative forms evolved from
the *cante jondo*. Characteristics of the *cante jondo* include: limited melodic range, conjunct intervallic movement, repetition of tones within the melody, use of micro tones, and shouts of "ay" and "olé."
The ritualistic cry of "¡Ay!" usually precedes improvisation.

Trois mélodies   **1910**
(Théophile Gautier)

Les colombes • Chinoiserie • Séguidille

Falla composed this group of songs during his sojourn in Paris (1907-1914).
Each song is characterized by a colorful, brilliant piano accompaniment and a vocal
line of considerable flexibility. The third song features its own very "Spanish"
sounding tune—not a folk melody but Falla's own creation. The poems by
Théophile Gautier, one of the forerunners of symbolism, are full of evocative visual images. Falla's skill with French prosody is meticulous; great care is taken with
accents, long and short syllables, and silent letters.

These songs are unjustly neglected works, perhaps because they exude more
French elements than Spanish. Certainly the texts are French, but so is much of
the musical language, a tribute to the styles of the composers whom Falla knew
and worked with in France. Falla's friendship with Debussy was important in the
birth of these songs, which look ahead to his chamber piece *Psyché*. The songs also
display his understanding of French style, which he admired greatly, a style that
was to infiltrate not only his songs, but his orchestral works as well, without
destroying the innate Spanish character of his music.

The first performance of *Trois mélodies* was given at the Salle Gaveau in
November, 1910 by Mme. Ada Adiny-Millet, with Falla accompanying. The concert
was part of the Société Musicale Indépendante (S.M.I.) of Paris, a newly formed
society of which Falla was one of the founders. Composer Paul Dukas had the songs
published by Rouart-Lerolle in Paris in 1910.

LES COLOMBES (THE DOVES). Tints of color from Debussy and Ravel
permeate this subdued setting. Vague and impressionistic patterns figure
prominently in the accompaniment texture. Modulations take place subtly; a
melodic line in sextuplets is reminiscent of a Debussian recitative. The text
contains the quintessential French dove, found throughout French poetry,
used here as a symbol for the poet's inner dreams and fantasies. This song is
dedicated to Mme. Adiny-Milliet, the wife of the translator of *La vida breve*,
and the singer who gave the first performance of these songs.

CHINOISERIE[*] **(CHINOISERIE).** This song owes much to the oriental settings of
Debussy and Ravel and also calls to mind the *Poèmes chinois* of Roussel, composed several years earlier. Debussy thought the original opening of Falla's
song was too heavy and advised him to try and find something else for the initial phrases. Falla pruned the accompaniment except for the opening chord and
one that later punctuates the recitative of the voice at the word "*Chine* (China)."

Like Debussy, Falla was fascinated by the Orient and was fond of visiting the Musée Guimet, a museum of Oriental art near his lodging.[8]

Chinoiserie: A Chinese curio.

SÉGUIDILLE (SEGUIDILLA). "Alza! Ola!" This is a picture of a cigarette-smoking, dancing Spanish beauty, "la véritable Manola," complete with tight ruffled skirt, hair comb, and fiery temperament. Falla invokes the rhythm of the *seguidilla*; with the final triplet stress we can see Manola's swirling skirt.

The tonality is C major, with colorful modulations, vibrant accompaniment and a vocal line that retains its elegance in spite of the exuberant musical setting. Triplets and marked rhythms in the vocal phrases recall a "typical" Spanish melody. The descriptive text is punctuated by shouts of "Alza! Ola!" as Manola captivates her admirers. Falla dedicated this song to Mme. Claude Debussy.

Extended Study List

Soneto à Cordoba (voice and harp) • *Psyché* (voice and chamber ensemble) • Tus ojillos negros • Olas gigantes

Selected Reading

James Burnett, *Manuel de Falla and the Spanish Musical Renaissance* (London: Victor Gollancz, 1979).

Gilbert Chase and Andrew Budwig, *Manuel de Falla: A Bibliography and Research Guide* (New York: Garland Publishing Inc., 1986).

Jacqueline Cockburn and Richard Stokes, *The Spanish Song Companion*. Introduction and notes by Graham Johnson (London: Victor Gollancz, 1992). Chapter 7.

Ronald Crichton, *Falla* (London: British Broadcasting Corporation, 1982). BBC Music Guides series.

Suzanne Demarquez, *Manuel de Falla*. Translated from the French by Salvator Attanasio (Philadelphia: Chilton Book Company, 1968).

Jaime Pahissa, *Manuel de Falla: His Life and Works* (London: Museum Press, Ltd., 1954). Trans. from the Spanish by Jean Wagstaff.

Notes

1. Graham Johnson, "Manuel de Falla," in *The Spanish Song Companion,* 105.
2. Walter Starkie. Liner notes to *Spanish Songs*. Shirley Verrett, mezzo-soprano, Charles Wadsworth, piano. RCA Victor. LP recording LM/LSC 2776, 1964.
3. Graham Johnson, 198.
4. Quoted in Ronald Crichton, *Falla* (BBC Music Guides), 96.
5. Joseph Miquel Sobrer and Edmon Colomer, *The Singer's Anthology of 20th Century Spanish Songs* (New York: Pelion Press, 1987), 97.
6. Walter Starkie. Liner notes to *Spanish Songs*.
7. According to the composer, the sources of the Andalusian lullaby appear to be India (as is true of Andalusian vocal music in general), whereas instrumental musical forms derive more from music of Persian or Moorish origins.
8. Suzanne Demarquez, *Manuel de Falla*, 51.

JOAQUÍN NIN (1879-1949)

> Nin...did even more valuable work than Falla in editing and publishing Spanish folk songs.
>
> —Charles Osborne[1]

Joaquín Nin was a composer, piano virtuoso, and musicologist. He was Cuban by birth, but was taken to Spain as a child. Piano studies in Barcelona were followed by six years in Paris, where he studied with Moszkowski. He studied counterpoint and composition at the Schola Cantorum. In 1905, he was appointed to teach piano at that institution, and was named honorary professor in 1908. He also taught in Berlin. In 1910, he returned to Havana where he founded a concert society and a music magazine.

Nin concertized throughout the world as a pianist, specializing in performing the works of Bach and early Spanish composers. It was Nin who brought the sonatas of Padre Soler* to the world's attention.

His devotion to the music of the Spanish Baroque can be seen in his compositions, whose style is marked by clarity and delicate modulation as well as by influences of French impressionism. In this regard, his style resembles that of Mompou. Nin classified his songs in extended series and wrote copious notes for his editions. He took existing melodies—folk songs or popular tunes from the *tonadilla* age—and set them in elaborate and often demanding piano accompaniments.

In 1923, Nin published two volumes of popular songs, *Veinte cantos populares españolas*, as well as two sets of *Airs anciens,* both published by his principal publisher, Eschig.** There are two sets of *villancicos* (Christmas songs) published in 1932, and two works for low voice and piano, one with violin.

Nin's family was also interesting; he was the brother of Anaïs Nin, famed for her chronicles of sensual Parisian adventures and her letters to Henry Miller; and he was the father of the composer Joaquín Nin-Culmell (b. 1908). Nin-Culmell made his home in the United States, teaching at Williams College and the University of California at Berkeley where he chaired the music department for a number of years and conducted the university orchestra. His music, like his father's, is influenced by neoclassic principles and by Spanish melody and rhythm. Nin-Culmell created a large number of folk song arrangements from Catalonia, Andalusia and Salamanca.

---

*Soler was the most gifted of the eighteenth-century Spanish composers for the harpsichord.

**Twenty Popular Spanish Songs* is published by Eschig with a French title, *Vingt chants populaires espagñols.*

Minué cantado	Minuet in Song.

José Bassa (from *Four Ancient Spanish Songs*)

"If Amaryllis's eyes hurl their arrows cruelly, sweetly wounding the heart/ What is Cupid's naughty quiver to him, and why should Love need a dart?"

The musical setting is intimate and like a serenade. A simple accompaniment, reminiscent of the *vihuela*, creates graceful counterpoint with the vocal line throughout this charming minuet.

Paño murciano   **The Murcian Cloth.**
(from *Twenty Popular Spanish Songs*)

"Tell me, Señor Silversmith, how much silver do I need for you to set in silver
the kiss my lover gave me? I've heard you are a master of your art. Here is a job
worthy of your craftsmanship. How much silver do I need?"

This vibrant setting is introduced by a guitar-like cadenza that settles into
even rhythmic patterns that propel the song forward. Its rhythm is that of a
characteristic Spanish dance, the *guajira*, alternating $\frac{6}{8}$ and $\frac{3}{4}$ meter. The "guitar"
cadenza, capped with a brilliant flourish, finishes the song.

Montañesa   **Mountaineer.**
(from *Twenty Popular Spanish Songs*)

"That afternoon I was reaping and she was gathering hay, and she was ruddy
and dark like cherries in the spring. Four pine trees are in your woodland glade.
I tend them for you. Four majos wish to cut them but none has dared."

A reflective mood is created by open fifths in the piano introduction. Languid
melismas embellish the vocal phrases throughout and are repeated at various
points in the accompaniment. The meter is $\frac{3}{4}$; the tempo is marked *Lento,* quarter
note=88. Melodic material is the dominant element here, underscored with a
chordal accompaniment of wide range and open texture—an elegant *sarabande*.[2]

Extended Study List
Cantos populares españoles • *Diez villancicos españoles*. Two sets of ten Christmas songs each •
Le chant du veilleur (mezzo, violin, piano) • Canto andaluz • Polo

Selected Reading
A. Menéndez Aleyxandre, "Joaquín Nin (y Castellanos)," *The New Grove Dictionary of Music and
Musicians,* edited by Stanley Sadie (New York: Grove's Dictionaries of Music, 1980), Vol. 13, 250.
Jacqueline Cockburn and Richard Stokes, *The Spanish Song Companion*. Introduction and notes by
Graham Johnson (London: Victor Gollancz, 1992). Chapter 8.

Notes
1. Charles Osborne, *The Concert Song Companion* (New York: Da Capo Press, 1974), 216.
2. The saraband was a seventeenth- and eighteenth-century dance in slow triple meter and
   dignified style, with an accent or prolonged tone on the second beat. It appeared in Spain in the
   early sixteenth century. (*Harvard Dictionary of Music*, 2nd edition, 1972).

JOAQUÍN TURINA (1882-1949)

Turina was a master at sensitive text settings.
—Suzanne R. Collier Draayer[1]

Joaquín Turina was a native of Seville and, like Manuel de Falla, was drawn
to Paris, where he was influenced by French musical style. He studied at the Schola
Cantorum with d'Indy, although his music never lost "sevillanismo," the
flavor of Seville. In Paris, Turina met and was befriended by Falla and mentored
by Albéniz. Although Turina was strongly influenced by French music, especially

that of Debussy, Albéniz urged him to seek inspiration in the folk music of his native Spain. As a result, Turina's music is a colorful and diverse mixture of styles.

Turina loved simplicity and beauty and often responded in music to literary or visual ideas.[2] His songs always illustrate the text, and his guitar music explores the full range of the instrument's capabilities. His music blends both his Sevillian character with Andalusian elements. His orchestral works are linked musically with European models, but contain Sevillian grace and style.

Turina's song style is extremely colorful for its distinctive use of Spanish elements. His songs are highly emotional and intensely rhythmic, with lyrical melodies and sensitive text settings. Often cast in Spanish dance rhythms, they make considerable use of Spanish folk materials and Andalusian melodic effects, such as blending major and minor modes. Like Falla and Granados, Turina was fond of using guitar figurations in the piano—arpeggiated chords, repeated notes, and quick repeated chords. Turina was an outstanding pianist, which is reflected in his song accompaniments.

In addition to his music, Turina wrote a book on music history *Enciclopedia musical abreviada* (1917) and one on composition, *Tratado de composicion* (1946). Both are considered important contributions to Spanish music.

Poema en forma de canciones, **Op. 19**   **Poem in the Form of Songs. 1918**
(Ramon de Campoamor)

Dedicatoria (piano solo) • Nunca olvida... • Cantares •
Los dos miedos • Las locas por amor

The texture and harmony of these songs are more complex than Granados's *Tonadillas*, though they are immediately appealing for their romantic lyricism, color, and dramatic interpretation of the text.

DEDICATORIA (DEDICATION). With this dramatic introductory piano solo, Turina introduces and sets the tone for the song cycle—its mood a contrast of lyricism and intensity. Turina was fond of combining vocal and instrumental movements in his works.[*] In Andalusian folk music, it is standard practice for the guitarist to preface his song with an instrumental piece that sets the mood and sometimes develops the rhythm of the song to come. The piano prelude serves that function here. An guitar-like figure of alternating notes from this piece is used in Songs 2, 3, and 4, and the contrasting moods introduced here are also found in Songs 3 and 4.

---

[*]Turina used this same structure in *Canto a Sevilla* (1927), which begins with a "Preludio" for solo piano and features another piano solo piece midway through the cycle.

NUNCA OLVIDA... (DO NOT FORGET). The first twelve bars of the piano introduction are filled with gliding thirds and descending chordal figures, which are all lyrical in mood. Four of these twelve bars are repeated between the two stanzas, and a motive fragment (three descending chords) appears under the last held note in the voice. Melodic material for the voice is simple. The text contrasts the generosity of love that is willing to forgive with the hurt of love that cannot.

Cantares (Songs). "Cantares" is cast in the *cante jondo* mold. It is a popular song, often excerpted from the cycle for performance. The piano introduction is constructed from a flowing figure of two alternating notes (derived from the introductory material of the "Dedicatoria") that are punctuated by emphatic chords. After opening with a brilliant unaccompanied melisma ("¡Ay!"), the voice soon retreats to an expressive dance-like melody, supported by a gently moving accompaniment in triple meter. The singer's opening cry of despair ends the song with a vibrant flourish.

Los dos miedos (The Two Fears). This text juxtaposes yearning and fear with striking effect. The two emotions are divided by a piano interlude that repeats the passionate central section of the opening "Dedicatoria."

The piano introduction is comprised of lyrical singing figures in the right hand over arpeggios in the bass. The vocal line has a narrow range and is underscored with the same figure that appeared in the piano prelude and in Song 3—a figure of alternating notes, an interval of a second apart. After the emotional piano interlude, the voice enters again, building to its own climax, full of intense lyricism. Figures from the piano introduction are heard again before the voice sings the last two words, "sin tì" (without you).

Las locas por amor (Frantic for Love). This song is gay, rapidly moving, and seems more French than Spanish. The goddess Venus says that, like all women, she prefers to be loved passionately for a brief time, rather than forever with restraint! Turina combines a delightful dance tune with a wildly intense vocal line, which pauses only near the end to allow the Goddess to confide her secret preferences, and before reiterating the initial vocal lines in a forceful, exciting finish.

Tu pupila es azul *(Tres Poemas)*   **Your Eyes Are Blue. 1933**
(Gustavo Adolfo Bécquer)

"Tu pupila es azul" is the second song in a group of three poems by Gustavo Adolfo Bécquer; the text is one of Bécquer's best. Vocal phrases are romantic and lyrical. After the opening phrase ("Tu pupila es azul") each stanza is given a different melodic treatment. Accompaniment figures are varied, ranging from a small staccato motive based on chords (they answer the opening statement) to romantic arpeggiated figures and guitar-like gestures at the end of the piece. Turina unifies the three stanzas by using the same melodic fragment for "Tu pupila es azul." A colorful vocal cadenza ends the song with an idiomatic Spanish flourish.

Extended Study List

Triptico • Rima • *Canto a Sevilla* (1927) (soprano and orchestra or piano) • Olas gigantes • Saeta, en forma de Salve • Vocalizaciones • Corazon de mujer • Cantares (high voice, guitar) • Homenaje a Lope de Vega • *Tres Arias* • *Tres Sonetos* • *Tres Poemas*

Selected Reading

Jacqueline Cockburn and Richard Stokes, *The Spanish Song Companion*. Introduction and notes by Graham Johnson (London: Victor Gollancz, 1992). Chapter 9.
Suzanne R. Draayer, "Joaquín Turina: *Tres Arias, Tres Poemas* and *Tres Sonetos*," *The NATS Journal*, 50:1 (Sept/Oct 1993).

____, "Contemporary Spanish song: Cycles for soprano by Turina and Rodrigo." D.M.A. diss., University of Maryland, College Park, 1987.

Notes

1. Suzanne R. Draayer, "Joaquín Turina: *Tres Arias, Tres Poemas* and *Tres Sonetos*," *The NATS Journal*, 50:1, 15.
2. Carlos Gomez Amat, "Joaquín Turina," in *The New Grove Dictionary of Music and Musicians,* 1980, 265.

JESÚS GURIDI (1886-1961)

From the beginning Guridi put his cards on the table as a composer willing to write in his own language.

—Graham Johnson[1]

Jesús Guridi was born in Vitoria in the Alava province of northeastern Spain. His musical aptitude and early studies attracted enough attention and support so that, in 1904, he was sent to Paris to study at the Schola Cantorum with Grovlez (piano), d'Indy (counterpoint and fugue), Decaux (organ), and Sérieyx (composition). He went on to study organ and composition with Joseph Jongen in Brussels and instrumentation with Neitzel in Cologne.

Returning to Bilbao, he distinguished himself as an organist at the Basilica of Señor Santiago in Bilbao and as conductor of the Bilbao Choral Society, posts he held for many years. In Bilbao, he composed almost all of his polyphonic choral works, which he based on popular song. Guridi became one of the relatively few successful Basque composers. He was especially acclaimed as a composer of operas and orchestral music.

Guridi's musical works were always a tribute to his Basque heritage; he published an album of twenty-two Basque songs and his *zarzuelas* make frequent use of Basque folk music. Although he wrote three sets of songs in his native Basque language, Jesús Guridi is known principally for one work: *Seis canciones castellanas*. Unfortunately, the Franco regime suppressed works related to the Basque culture, so Guridi's two successful Basque operas *Mirentxu* (1910) and *Amaya* (1920), a popular *zarzuela (El caserio)*, and his three Basque song cycles are hardly known outside Spain. The one vocal work published by Union Musical Española, the state publishing company, is this set of Castilian songs.

Seis canciones castellanas	**Six Castilian Songs.**

Allá arriba, en aquella montaña • ¡Sereno! • Llámale con el pañuelo • Non quiero tus avellanas • ¡Como quieres que adivine! • Mañanita de San Juan

These six songs are popular Castilian melodies, harmonized in highly original settings, blending vocal lines of folk song melodies with colorful, modern harmonies. Great variety in dramatic mood is found in the set.

ALLÁ ARRIBA, EN AQUELLA MONTAÑA (HIGH UP ON THAT MOUNTAIN). A beautiful folk-like melody with varied repetitions is sung by a young girl comparing imagined lovers—a ploughman ("labrador") with a miller ("molinero"). She prefers a ploughman who takes his mules to plough—here a piano interlude interrupts her thoughts, using the opening material reiterated in an unsettled tonality—and at midnight, comes to serenade her. She imagines his serenade, accompanied by light, glistening arpeggios. In the last lines of the poem, the girl gives careful directions to her house.

¡SERENO! (WATCHMAN!). This song germinates from a motive of four sixteenth notes descending chromatically, coupled with a second pattern of chromatic thirds. Alternation from bass to treble clef creates a feeling of mystery and agitation.

In the first vocal phrase, the singer calls to the watchman using a melodic pattern reminiscent of the call of the watchman himself. With each repetition of "Sereno!" the initial pitch rises. The form is a modified ABA, punctuated by passionate and intense connecting material. The piano introduction is used for the last four measures.

LLÁMALE CON EL PAÑUELO (BECKON TO HIM WITH YOUR KERCHIEF). This is a bullfighter's song, full of grace and charm, with colorful meslismas in the voice derived from the *cante jondo* tradition. Three quick chords in the piano introduce a Spanish rhythmic figure that descends sequentially into the bass register; the voice enters unaccompanied, answered by a rhythmic figure in the piano. Accompaniment figures are chordal in one section, rhythmically punctuating the vocal line, then change to a driving ostinato rhythm that punctuates the graceful twisting vocal line.

NON QUIERO TUS AVELLANAS (I DO NOT WANT YOUR HAZELNUTS). "I do not want your hazelnuts, nor your gillyflowers. The promises you made turned out to be empty. As I drew water from the fountain, the water bore the words of love away." This song is a sweet, deeply felt lament in which the lover's empty promises are caught in the reiteration of a simple melodic fragment. The meter is $\frac{7}{8}$; the accompaniment is, for the most part, simple chords interspersed with melodic fragments drawn from the introductory measures, evocative of softly moving water.

¡COMO QUIERES QUE ADIVINE! (HOW DO YOU EXPECT ME TO GUESS?). A lilting rhythmic pattern in $\frac{3}{8}$ time alternates open fifths and sixths with chords. Chordal accents shift from beat 2 to beats 1 and 3; this two-bar rhythmic ostinato continues almost without interruption throughout this love song.

Vocal phrases are also rhythmic and declamatory, becoming more lyrical and embellished in the second section ("Cuando voy por leña al monte, ole ya, mi niña"). Despite the infectious rhythmic treatment, the poetic mood remains calm and elegant. The first vocal phrase is repeated unaccompanied at the end of song as a little suspended coda.

MAÑANITA DE SAN JUAN (EARLY ON ST. JOHN'S DAY).[*] Of all the songs in the set, this is the most unabashedly lyric. It is a love song, with a playful and symbolic text; the Spanish dove is the messenger of love. The form is ABA; the meter is $\frac{6}{4}$. Both A and B sections have measures of $\frac{9}{4}$ for rhythmic interest and lyric extension. Chordal figures and a higher register characterize the B section, as the dove and its mission are described, followed by a brief transition leading back to the repeat of A.

*St. John's day is Midsummer day, June 24th.

Selected Reading
Jacqueline Cockburn and Richard Stokes, *The Spanish Song Companion*. Introduction and notes by Graham Johnson (London: Victor Gollancz, 1992). Chapter 10.

Notes
1. Graham Johnson, "Jesús Guridi," in *The Spanish Song Companion* (London: Victor Gollancz, 1992), 139.

FEDERICO MOMPOU (Catalán, 1893-1987)

If you were to pinpoint what it is that makes Mompou inimitable...it is this: a love and sensitivity for the subtleties of sound quality.
—Pierre Huybregts[1]

I composed only for myself. I hate bravura music, the big things. I am a simple person...I compose on the moment, when I feel the inspiration. I don't think of being listened to by thousands of people or just one person. I just compose because I have the inspiration and the need to compose.
—Federico Mompou[2]

Federico Mompou has been referred to as the personification of Catalán song. Half French and half Catalán by birth, Mompou mastered the art of the miniature—Graham Johnson labels him "an unashamed petit maître"[3]— composing a body of song and piano pieces that successfully blend the flavor of his Catalán roots with French stylistic influences from his studies.

Mompou was among many Spanish and Catalán composers who sought out Paris in the closing years of the nineteenth century as a place to study and to work. After early studies at Barcelona's Conservatorio del Liceo, Mompou went to Paris, living there from 1911 to 1914 and again from 1921 to 1941. Many of his songs were published in Paris by Editions Salabert.

Critics affirm his most creative writing is found in his songs. Mompou composed thirty-seven songs for voice and piano, written at various times between 1915 and 1971. They reflect the elegant understatement of Fauré, the miniaturism of Satie, and the skillful technique of Poulenc. His search for "pure poetry" and a lean, understated quality for his music is reflected in these small forms—detailed without mannerism. His musical style is not complex, but retains a musical sophistication nonetheless.

Mompou's melodies are immediately appealing. Folk-like melodies form the basis for many songs—short phrases in the style of the Catalán folk tune. Harmonically, his songs reflect influences from Debussy and a harmonic sense that is discreet but provocative. He was drawn to poetry of a melancholy, pensive nature. His songs are a rich addition to the literature, and are appearing on recitals with increasing regularity. They are accessible to audiences and are still musically sophisticated and gratifying for performers.

Combat del somni	**Dream Combat. 1942-48**
(Josep Janés)	

Damunt de tu només les flors (1942) • Aquesta nit un mateix vent (1946) •
Jo et pressentia com la mar (1948)

Combat del somni is perhaps closest to the characteristic style of Mompou's music, elegant and streamlined settings of atmospheric poetry. Texts for the three songs come from a book of sonnets by Catalán poet and publisher Josep Janés (1913-1959) who wrote the poems after the death of his beloved, a woman named Maria Victòria. The texts for all three songs are melancholy, dreamlike and abstract. In its original form, the cycle contained four songs; the fourth, "Fes-me la vida transparent," is now frequently performed on its own, apart from the set.

For melodic appeal and richness of piano writing, Mellars compares this set to the later songs of Poulenc.[4] Songs 1 and 3 have flowing melodies that are simple and folk-like, but with accompaniments that are quite French in style. Song 1 has an extended piano interlude that divides the two verses; in the repeated section, themes from the piano and the vocal line are heard, intertwined. Song 2 has a vocal line that grows out of the rhythm of the introduction. In all three songs , vocal phrases are repeated rather than developed.

Extended Study List

Trois comptines • Olas gigantes • Cantar del alma • Llueve sobre el río • Rosa del cami • Cortina de fullatge • Incertitud • Neu • Le Nuage • Primeros pasos • Fes-me la vida transparent • Pastoral • *Charmes*

Selected Reading

Jacqueline Cockburn and Richard Stokes, *The Spanish Song Companion.* Introduction and notes by Graham Johnson (London: Victor Gollancz, 1992). Chapter 12.

Frieda Elaine Holland, "Federico Mompou: A Performer's Guide to the Songs for Voice and Piano." D.M.A. diss., The University of Texas at Austin, 1987.

Wilfred Mellers, "Mompou's Elegy." *Chesterian,* 26:169, 1952, 46-54.

Joseph T. Rawlins, "The Songs of Federico Mompou," *The NATS Journal, 41:5,* 1985, 11-15.

Notes

1. Joseph T. Rawlins, "The Songs of Federico Mompou," *The NATS Journal,* 41:5, 15.
2. Ibid.
3. Graham Johnson, "Frederic Mompou" in *The Spanish Song Companion*, 145.
4. Quoted in Rawlins, 12.

FERNANDO OBRADORS (1897-1945)

> Obradors is the Spanish song writer par excellence for our times, which is to say his music unfailingly provides what many of today's English-speaking singers demand...when they want to close their recitals with a "bang."...
> —Graham Johnson[1]

Fernando Obradors was born in Barcelona and studied the piano with his mother. He was largely self-taught in harmony, counterpoint and composition. He conducted the Liceo and Radio Barcelona Orchestras, and composed a number of symphonic works and *zarzuelas*. He is known principally for his *Canciones clásicas españolas* (Classical Spanish Songs), published in four volumes. The Spanish publisher is Unión Musical Española; International Music Company publishes the first volume in the United States under the title *Obradors: Classical Spanish Songs*.

Most of Obradors's songs are arrangements of light weight and texture, but they epitomize the popular conception of Spanish song. They fall into a generic neoclassic style acquired from folk song and *tonadilla*, using texts that range from charming verses of the fifteenth century to popular poetry of the eighteenth and nineteenth centuries. The settings generally contain dance rhythms, lyricism, and colorful vocal display. They are performed often.

Del cabello más sutil   From the Finest Hair.

This is Obradors at his most romantic—a beautiful long-lined melody over a piano accompaniment of arpeggios. Despite its passionate avowal of love, Obradors's musical treatment remains delicate. With two quatrains, set in varied strophic form, and a brief twenty-two measures, this exquisite song is over far too soon.

El Vito   El Vito.

"An old woman is worth a *real*, and a young two *cuartos*. I'm so poor, I'll choose the cheapest."[*] This is a transcription from a popular song that was all the rage in Madrid around 1800. The dance of this name (*vito*) is typically Spanish, designed to be danced atop a tavern table for an audience of bullfighters. Obradors captures its vibrancy and fire in his highly rhythmic setting. Variations in rhythmic stresses in voice and piano (reminiscent of castanets) help build excitement. Each stanza ends with three decisive, stamping chords.

*A *real* is a silver coin; a *cuarto* is copper.

Extended Study List

¿Corazon, porqué pasáis... • Al amor • La mi sola, Laureola • Chiquitita la novia • El majo celoso • Con amores, la mi madre • Consejo • El Tumba y lé • Tres morillas • Confiado jilguerillo • Aquel sombrero del monte

Selected Reading

Jacqueline Cockburn and Richard Stokes, *The Spanish Song Companion*. Introduction and notes by Graham Johnson (London: Victor Gollancz, 1992). Chapter 16.

Notes

1. Graham Johnson, "Fernando Obradors," in *The Spanish Song Companion* (London: Victor Gollancz, 1992), 188.

JOAQUÍN RODRIGO (1901-1999)

Song is the microcosm for Rodrigo.

—Antonio Machado[1]

Joaquín Rodrigo was born in Sagunto, near Valencia. He was blinded at the age of three as a result of a diphtheria epidemic. In 1927, Rodrigo traveled to Paris to begin a five-year period of study with composer Paul Dukas at the Schola Cantorum; a subsequent grant enabled further studies with André Pirro at the Sorbonne and with Maurice Emmanuel at the Paris Conservatoire. During his stay in Paris, Rodrigo became active in the group of Spanish composers living there—Falla, Turina, Albéniz, and Granados.

Falla in particular urged Rodrigo to incorporate Spanish nationalistic elements into his music: Moorish and Gypsy melodies, Spanish dance rhythms and accompaniments that evoke the guitar. Rodrigo returned to Madrid after the Spanish Civil War where the Manuel de Falla chair was created for him at the University in 1947.

Rodrigo composed around 100 songs, many of which have not been heard outside his native Spain. Like Turina, Rodrigo's vocal music has distinctive nationalistic characteristics: dance rhythms, folk materials, and lyric plaintive melodies. His musical style shows little deviation or development, remaining squarely in a colorful, but fairly conservative Spanish idiom, highly reminiscent of the Golden Age of Spanish poetry and song. This style served him well; for many, his *Concierto de Aranjuez* for guitar embodies the Spanish spirit and is certainly one of the most popular pieces of Spanish music ever written.

Rodrigo was fond of using ostinati as unifying devices in his piano accompaniments. His approach to melody is extremely lyrical. Draayer observes that both Turina and Rodrigo's melodies have "what the Spaniards call *evocacíon*, that is, a sense of the poetry—something felt rather than something explainable."[2]

Cuatro madrigales amatorios   1947
(Inspirados en música española del siglo XVI)

¿Con qué la lavaré? • Vos me matásteis • ¿De dónde venís, amore? •
De los alamos vengo, madre

Four amatory* madrigals provide the texts and melodies for this cycle, probably the best-known of Rodrigo's vocal works. The songs are skillful and attractive arrangements of well-known Spanish songs of the sixteenth century. There is also an arrangement for voice and orchestra.

*Expressions of love

¿CON QUÉ LA LAVARÉ? (WITH WHAT SHALL I WASH?). The tonality alternates between D minor and D major in this mournful lament, set in a beautifully clear, sparse texture. The vocal line is set syllabically in graceful lyric lines that rise in pitch with the singer's emotion. The manipulation of the motives is tightly structured with canonic imitation between voice and piano that continues throughout and sustains the melancholy mood.

VOS ME MATÁSTEIS (YOU KILLED ME). Though in a slightly faster tempo than the previous song, this is a reflective, lyric setting—"You have killed me—girl with the flowing tresses." As in the first song, short motives interact frequently between the voice and piano. The vocal phrase "Vos me matásteis" is transposed at several pitch levels; the first incidence is repeated five times during the song. The phrase "Riberas de un río" is also repeated. By repeating these small phrases, Rodrigo creates a feeling of length and perpetuates a mood of loneliness and reflection.

¿DE DÓNDE VENÍS, AMORE? (WHERE HAVE YOU BEEN, MY LOVE?). This is a spirited, flirtatious text: "Where have you been, my love? Ah…I know very well…" The tempo is marked *Allegro grazioso*. The setting is a highly rhythmic treatment in which the voice borrows a phrase from the piano ("Bien sé yo de dónde") and repeats it twice at the ends of verses. In the piano, this phrase is divided between upper and lower registers, the final fragment punctuated emphatically in octaves—a sly commentary on the text. Rodrigo has the voice join in as well in a four-bar staccato coloratura passage of laughing disbelief. Alternating the motives in different registers in the accompaniment also serves to express the lover's flighty behavior.

This song is a famous *villancico* by Enriquez de Valderrábano (fl. 1550), who published a seven-volume book of *vihuela* music.[3]

DE LOS ALAMOS VENGO, MADRE (I COME FROM THE POPLARS, MOTHER). A lover returns from a tryst with his beloved; the mood of the song is an excited remembrance of their meeting. Repetitive rhythmic figures evoke the strumming of guitars—or perhaps the pounding of a horse's hooves—is he riding back?

Vocal phrases are graceful and melodious, with a tiny syncopation on the word "madre." Word-painting at the word "aire" (breeze) initiates coloratura passages and melismatic word settings, which appear with increasing frequency to the end of the song. The ostinato in the accompaniment combined with the flexible vocal line is elegant as well as exciting.

The original *villancico* from which Rodrigo made his arrangement was by Miguel de Fuenllana (fl. 1550), a blind *vihuela* virtuoso who dedicated the set of songs (from which this one is taken) to Philip II. He prefaced the set with an "avisos y documentos" or "guide to the performing practice of the time."[4]

Extended Study List

Tres villancicos • *Dos poemas* (voice w/flute or piano) • *Dos canciones para cantar a los niños* • *Cantos de amor y de guerra* • Romance de la infantina de Francia • Serranilla • Soneto • Cantiaga • *Doce canciones españolas*

Selected Reading

Jacqueline Cockburn and Richard Stokes. *The Spanish Song Companion*. Introduction and notes by Graham Johnson (London: Victor Gollancz, Ltd., 1992). Chapter 18.

Suzanne R. Draayer, "Joaquín Rodrigo and his *Doce Canciones Españolas* and *Cantos de amor y de guerra*." *The NATS Journal* 51:4 (March/April 1995).

_____, "Contemporary Spanish song: Cycles for soprano by Turina and Rodrigo." D.M.A. diss., University of Maryland, College Park, 1987.

_____, Joaquín Rodrigo, 1901-1999. *The Journal of Singing* 56:2 (November/December 1999).

_____, *A Singer's Guide to the Songs of Joaquín Rodrigo* (Lanham, MD: Scarcrow Press, 1999).

Notes

1. Antonio Machado, "The Vocal Microcosm of Joaquín Rodrigo." Liner notes to *Joaquín Rodrigo Intégrale des mélodies*, vol. 1 Margarita Castro-Alberty, soprano; Carlos Cebro, pianist. Lys Records. Lys D-025, 1995.
2. Suzanne R. Draayer, "Joaquín Rodrigo and his *Doce Canciones Españolas* and *Cantos de amor y de guerra*," 5.
3. Patrick Carnegy. Liner notes to *A Spanish Songbook*. Jill Gomez/John Constable. Conifer Classics. Compact Disc 75605 51243 2, 1994.
4. Ibid.

XAVIER MONTSALVATGE (Catalán, 1912-2002)

Montsalvatge represents a new direction in Spanish music...
—Graham Johnson[1]

Xavier Montsalvatge, composer and critic, was born in Gerona and studied at the Barcelona Conservatory. His early works won the prestigious Pedrell Prize. He soon gained recognition as a composer of ballets, acknowledging Stravinsky and the French composers of *Les Six* as inspirations for his musical approach. He lived in Barcelona most of his life, writing as a critic for several publications and teaching on the faculties of the San Jorge Academy, the Destino Seminary, and the Barcelona Conservatory.

Montsalvatge's musical style is not avant-garde, but his deft use of twentieth-century idioms mixed with a strong exotic flair imported from the West Indies, gives his works great individuality. West Indian musical style was strongly Spanish; in importing this music back to Spain and reuniting it with its original roots, Montsalvatge produced works infused with "a new, vague, and evocative manifestation of musical lyricism."[2] His music is an elegant mixture of color, rhythm and theatrical flair. He had an abiding interest in children's music and poetry as well.

Montsalvatge is best-known in Spain for his opera *El gato con botas* (Puss-in-Boots), several ballets, film music, and other symphonic music. His song cycle *Cinco canciones negras* is an excellent example of Montsalvatge's distinctive musical style. It has attained enormous popularity and is a favorite of singers worldwide.

Cinco canciones negras   **Five Negro songs. 1945**

Cuba dentro de un piano (Rafael Alberti) • Punto de Habanera (Néstor Luján) •
Chèvere (Nicolás Guillén) • Canción de cuna para dormir a un negrito
(Ildefonso Pereda Valdés) • Canto negro (Nicolás Guillén)

This is a cycle full of contrasts. Montsalvatge deftly integrates lush harmonic textures, sensual melodies, and a diverse array of moods. West Indies rhythms and musical style permeate the music, set to a seemingly eclectic set of poems by modern poets Rafael Alberti, Néstor Luján, Nicolás Guillén, and Ildefonso Pereda Valdés. But the five texts are all bound by underlying themes: the disintegration of a native culture, colonialism, and racism. Poetic order is subtly and carefully ordered.

The work was composed for the Catalán singer Mercedes Plantada. There is an orchestral version of the songs, and, as might be imagined, Montsalvatge's lush harmonic textures translate beautifully into instrumental colors.

CUBA DENTRO DE UN PIANO (CUBA IN A PIANO). Rafael Alberti's poetry is full of vivid images—a bittersweet reminiscence of Havana at the turn of the century, redolent with languid lifestyle, colorful *fandangos* and *habaneras*. With the loss of Cuba in the Spanish-American war, Spanish influence gave way to that of the United States, and (in the angry words of the poet) that is when the Spanish "Sí" became the Yankee "YES!"

Montsalvatge's musical approach features a highly chromatic piano accompaniment, held together by a swaying *habanera* rhythm. The song begins with a recitative-like narrative that dissolves into more rhythmic vocal phrases as the story unfolds. Rhythms and vocal declamation change with the poet's thoughts as other pictures come to mind. Chromatic harmonies and dissonances between voice and piano create an atmosphere of sensual calm that is violently interrupted by the last phrase. A piano postlude restores the relaxed feeling of the opening, and strains of the *habanera* fade into nothingness through the last measures.

PUNTO DE HABANERA (SIGLO XVIII) (HABANERA RHYTHM). In this vignette of old Havana, a lovely young Creole girl passes down the street to admiring glances from a group of watching sailors. The tempo and rhythm is that of the Cuban *guajiras* (folk song and dance in alternating $\frac{6}{8}$ and $\frac{3}{4}$ time). The song is subtitled "A Humorous Flirtation—18th century." Staccato articulation and dance rhythms mirror the light step of the young "criolla." Only in the last sixteen bars of the song (marked "Coda") do we catch a glimpse of something darker in the poem.

CHÉVERE (THE DANDY). Cuban poet Guillén belongs to the Afro-Cuban school of poetry. His poems are often use the language of Cuba's poor blacks and mirror images from his mulatto heritage. "Chévere" is a dramatic picture of a young black, trapped in his social and cultural status. He vents his anger by wielding a knife, which becomes a metaphor for his own twisting and turning. Vocal phrases contain melismas that are echoed in the piano. Another piano figure consists of a set of violent chords—a picture of a slashing knife.

CANCIÓN DE CUNA PARA DORMIR A UN NEGRITO (LULLABY FOR A LITTLE BLACK BOY). Montsalvatge's tender lullaby is intimately drawn. Over a rocking *habanera* bass line, vocal phrases of supple lyricism float freely. Soft syncopations in the voice play against rhythmic figures in the piano; there is a small amount of shared material that also links the two together. This is a beautifully effective song, hypnotic in its blend of musical materials.

CANTO NEGRO (NEGRO SONG). Montsalvatge's exciting setting incorporates Afro-Cuban themes into a colorful rhythmic texture. Guillén's poem is full of African rhythms and Yoruba words, employed for their sound value, especially in refrains. Their rhythmic repetition resembles a tongue-twisting incantation. A colorful piano accompaniment of highly syncopated dance rhythms is pitted against the rhythmic vocal line, producing a vivid and brilliant song to end the set.

Extended Study List
Cinco invocationes al crucificado • *Canço amorosa* • *Oraçao* • *Habaneras de la Costa Brava* • Soneta à Manuel de Falla • *Canciones para niños*

Selected Reading
Jacqueline Cockburn and Richard Stokes, *The Spanish Song Companion*. Introduction and notes by Graham Johnson (London: Victor Gollancz, 1992). Chapter 19.

E. Franco: *Xavier Montsalvatge* (Madrid, 1975).

Nke Aka Nori, "The Songs for Solo Voice and Piano by Xavier Montsalvatge, with emphasis on the *Cinco Canciones Negras*." D.M.A. diss., Boston University, 1994.

M. Valls: *Xavier Montsalvatge* (Barcelona, 1969).

Notes
1. Graham Johnson, "Xavier Montsalvatge," in *The Spanish Song Companion*, 223.
2. Quoted in Enrique Franco, "Xavier Montsalvatge," *The New Grove Dictionary of Music and Musicians*, Vol. 12, 543.

South American Song

South America's music is a kaleidoscope of influences reflected from its colonial history and shaped by the musical traditions of its immigrants, notably those from Portugal and Spain. In Brazil, European musical sounds and traditions held sway. In the last part of the nineteenth century Brazilian musical life was dominated by the afternoon salon concert, which featured works by Schumann, Liszt, and Chopin on the programs. Italian opera was heard in the opera houses. Spanish *boleros*, *habaneras*, and *seguidillas* were an influential part of Brazil's musical heritage, and in the twentieth century, American jazz added yet another ingredient into the mix.

But other music is also found in Brazil—ethnic musical treasures from slaves brought over in trade traffic that lasted over 150 years (until 1850), and from Brazil's own Indian natives. Not until the early years of the twentieth century did South American music begin to find a voice of its own. Brazilian composer Heitor Villa-Lobos spent time traveling through Brazil absorbing its various folk styles and influences. Stimulated by his findings, he began to blend native elements into his music, re-created and combined with his own unique and eclectic style. Villa-Lobos was a prolific composer, writing in many musical forms. He composed over 100 songs—uneven in quality, but the best of them are exciting and expressive, and had a decided influence in shaping and developing the art song in Brazil. His harmonizations of familiar folk melodies, *Brazilian Typical Songs* (1919), are excellent examples of some indigenous sounds of Brazilian music.

Brazil's most prolific composer of songs was Camargo Guarnieri, who wrote over 200 songs. Another Brazilian composer of note is Francisco Braga, who studied with Massenet in Paris. Like his pupil, Villa-Lobos, he integrated Afro-Brazilian rhythms into his songs, but significant traces of his European training appear in them.

In Argentina, composer Alberto Ginastera helped shape a national musical style by integrating native and folk elements into his musical works. Carlos Guastavino, another Argentinean, has composed over 200 songs, adding a substantial body of vocal music to South American literature. His songs combine Argentina's folk idioms and dance rhythms with beautiful fluid melodies.

Twentieth-century composers in Uruguay, Ecuador, Peru, Chile, Colombia, and Venezuela have produced numerous songs, but they are largely unknown outside their own countries.

Songs of South America and Central America are largely unexplored. It is still difficult to obtain published music for voice and piano, but well worth the effort. Fortunately, there are some recordings of South American song literature available by artists such as Bidú Sayão, Teresa Berganza, Alicia Nafé, Carmen Balthrop, and Margot Pares-Reyna, José Cura, and Bernarda Fink.

ALBERTO GINASTERA (Argentina, 1916-1983)

His works reflect a unique heritage of Argentine folkloric elements combined with the best of the classical tradition...He is a cultural representative of his country par excellence.

Raúl A. Quijano[1]
Permanent Representative of Argentina
to the Organization of American States

Alberto Evaristo Ginastera was born in Buenos Aires and studied composition at the National Conservatory there. He later held a teaching position on its faculty from 1941 to 1945. After World War II he traveled to the United States to study and founded the League of Argentinean Composers. He founded a conservatory in La Plata, Argentina and was its director from 1948 to 1958. His later years were spent in residence in Switzerland.

Ginastera is recognized and honored as a pioneer in developing contemporary Latin American music. His music incorporates the rich heritage of Argentina's folklore and musical idioms and spans many forms: ballets, operas, cantatas, orchestral works, and chamber music. A large percentage of his compositions were commissioned and premiered in the United States, where his work has received critical acclaim since 1946, when he received a Guggenheim Fellowship.

Ginastera's music integrates the folk music tradition of his native Argentina with twentieth-century techniques and his own changing creative needs. His songs strongly reflect the nationalistic color and flavor of his native Argentina, stamped with his individual personal style.

He composed three successful operas: *Don Rodrigo* (1964), *Bomarzo* (1967), and *Beatrix Cenci* (1971). The last two works were composed for United States premieres; *Beatrix Cenci* was commissioned by the Opera Society of Washington for the opening of the John F. Kennedy Center for the Performing Arts.

Cinco canciones populares argentinas   **Five Popular Argentine Songs.**
(Traditional)

Chacarera • Triste • Zamba • Arrorró • Gato

Ginastera's *Five Argentine Popular Songs* correspond to Falla's *Seven Popular Spanish Songs* in that they are stylized settings of folk songs. Using anonymous traditional texts, Ginastera set five types of Argentine folk song/dance forms: *chacarera*, *triste*, *zamba*, *arrorró*, and *gato*, whose melodies are closely patterned on the traditional models. Piano accompaniments retain the characteristic rhythms and harmonies of the folk material, but also display Ginastera's personal musical touch.

Argentine dances and songs are full of complicated rhythmic patterns which the performers take pride and enjoyment in performing. Popular music in Buenos Aires is a blend of European elements: Spanish, French, and Italian. Music of the Argentinean countryside displays strong Spanish traditions, although it has taken on the unique flavor of idiomatic Argentinean culture.

CHACERERA. The group opens with a spirited driving song with displaced rhythmic stresses. The dance is performed by four dancers and involves vigorous and spirited footwork. Its style and form is closely related to the *gato*.

TRISTE (SADNESS). The *triste* is a melancholy love song, generally thought to have originated in Peru and then spread to northern Argentina. Its melody has both Indian and European characteristics. It is closely related to the *vidala* or *vidalita* which developed among the gauchos. Two verses feature a repeated motive of four notes in the piano over a chordal accompaniment.

ZAMBA. This song/dance has its roots in the *tango*, a familiar form in Argentina, Brazil, and Uruguay. As it traveled into other areas, the *zamba* (also spelled *samba* in some locations) acquired characteristics of African folk elements. The accompaniment somewhat resembles the *habanera*; the song is a lilting dance-like melody.

ARRORRÓ. The rolled consonants of this tender lullaby produce a soothing sound. Set in ABA' form, the first stanza begins with an unvarying piano figure that approximates rocking. A tiny piano interlude of expanded range and varied accompaniment introduces the second short stanza. The last measures of the song are a return of the musical material of the first stanza. This time the voice hums the initial phrases and finishes the lullaby quietly, as it began.

GATO. This energetic dance of the Argentina gaucho is marked by driving rhythms. It is the most important dance of the Argentine countryside, and many dances are derived from it. It is danced by two couples.

A definite formal structure is assigned and followed precisely. Introduction, vocal part, and guitar interludes are all a prescribed number of measures. The dancer improvises the dance with rapid movements consisting largely of stamping steps, but always based firmly on a pattern established at the outset of the dance.

Canción al árbol del olvido
(Fernán Silva Valdés)

Song to the Tree of Oblivion. 1938

This is one of Ginastera's earliest songs, a haunting melody in a *tango* rhythm. The poem consists of three stanzas; the first two are accompanied by a single line in the piano, reminiscent of a guitar. The second stanza migrates to the major key. Two short piano interludes, varied slightly in harmonic materials, separate the stanzas. Each is a miniature commentary on the previous poetic content—intimate, intense in mood and softly syncopated. The final verse is accompanied by a two-hand piano accompaniment, fuller and varied slightly to complement the alterations in the vocal line. Ginastera maintains unity throughout the song with the hypnotic ostinato rhythm that underpins both accompaniment and vocal line throughout.

Valdés's poem refers to the tree of oblivion where souls near death go to find relief. A lovesick lover lies down under the tree and sleeps, in hopes of forgetting his sweetheart. Upon waking, he realizes he forgot to blot her from his mind beforehand.

Characteristics of the *vidalita* are found in the song. The *vidala* and *vidalita* (little vidala) are songs and dances that have their roots in the life of the Pampas. The word itself means "life." Each *vidala* has many verses, with a repetition of the word "vidalita" after the third line of each stanza. This song/dance belongs to the season of the year when the fruit of the algarrobo tree is ripening and the people of the ranches celebrate with music and merrymaking.

Extended Study List

Canción a la luna lunanca • Milena (cantata for soprano and orchestra) • String Quartet No. 3 (with soprano) • Serenata (male voice, cello and chamber ensemble) • Las horas de una estancia

Notes

1. Slipcase notes to *Homage to Alberto Ginastera.* Inter-American Musical Editions, Organization of American States. Recording available in the University of California, San Diego Music Library.

CARLOS GUASTAVINO (Argentina, 1912-2000)

The music comes by itself. I am not responsible; one part of my brain has music.

—Carlos Guastavino[1]

Carlos Guastavino composed 200 solo songs, choral and chamber works, and compositions for piano and guitar. His songs were inspired by the dance rhythms and folklore of his native Argentina. Nature, flowers, murmuring water, the vast pampas, and birds (especially the dove) are frequent images found in his songs. Guastavino's amiable personality and enthusiasm for living are mirrored in his music.

Guastavino was an excellent pianist with a profound love for and knowledge of the human voice, nurtured by many years of accompanying in studios of voice teachers. His prolific compositions for the voice earned him the nickname of the "Argentine Schubert," although he modestly protested the title. His passion for his country was intense. He set only Spanish texts and his reaction to poetry was spontaneous:

When I read poetry that touches me, I become very agitated, my whole body contorts, I vibrate totally, and tears appear in my eyes. It's very strong! I then take the manuscript paper and write the notes. The melody comes easily; everything is very quick; I cannot stop...it's as if I were possessed; suddenly, when I become aware that I have found what I wanted, I stand, make gestures, walk, go in circles, laugh or cry, and give thanks to God.[2]

Guastavino's integration of popular elements into his songs gives them an almost improvisatory style. Indeed, there is little formal complexity; the songs are eminently singable, the melodies are fluid and immediately engaging. Their chief element is a natural lyricism rooted in the folk traditions of his native country that are integrated into his songs with sophistication. With his songs, Guastavino developed a bona fide Latin American style that synthesizes the musical and cultural idioms of Argentina with the classical art song form.

In the past few years, compact disc recordings have made Guastavino's songs better-known in this country. He did not object to their transposition. The songs discussed here are well-known in Argentina and are available from the Lagos Publishing Co. in Buenos Aires.

La rosa y el sauce   **The Rose and the Willow. 1940**
(Francesco Silva)

"The rose was starting to open, embracing the willow. The passionate tree loved her so much. A frivolous girl robbed her [of the rose] and the desolate willow is crying."*

Guastavino's penchant for lyricism is given full rein in this lovely song. A spacious melody in the piano introduces an equally opulent vocal line, laced with graceful melismas. A dramatic, almost operatic climax occurs at the word "apassionado," followed by a change of mood as the girl plucks the rose. The piano's opening melody is given to the voice in the closing measures; it is sung with a humming sound that emulates the weeping willow.

Hermano   **Brother.**
(Hamlet Lima Quintana)

"Notice my brother, how you are singing. All the earth listens with me. From the time to the tenderness of true life it is precious to have a bleeding heart. From the scream to the prayer the man living in pain sings blood from his history. Notice, my brother."*

This song has no metronomic marking, and is often performed in too rapid a tempo and with a rough, "earthy" delivery. This is contrary to the composer's concept.[3] The quarter note should equal 44 or the eighth note should equal 88. A too-fast tempo dilutes the song's basic rhythmic thrust. The vocal writing is a lyric recitative. The text is a narrative of the gauchos and the Argentine pampas; it reflects the solitary peacefulness of the pampas, their life and livelihood.

Pampamapa   **Song of the Pampas.**
(Hamlet Lima Quintana)

"I'm not from this neighborhood but it's all the same. I have stolen the magic of the roads. If my name hurts you, throw it in the water. I don't want your mouth to become bitter. As an old bird I know when the wheat is green and when we have to love. I'm leaving—crying. I will give you my dreams. Give me your peace."*

The song is part of a set titled *Popular Songs*. Like many of Guastavino's songs, this one is based on a dance rhythm—the *huella*. This strongly accented, rhythmic dance is heard in the piano in the form of a prelude that returns to alternate with intensely lyric vocal sections, underpinned by a simpler chordal accompaniment pattern. Guastavino cautioned against using too much *portamenti* in performing this song.[4]

Bonita rama de sauce   **The Pretty Willow Branch.**
(Arturo Vazquez)

"The pretty branch of the willow never bloomed. It always remains saying good-bye to the river, which passes and combs her hair. The river swears that he loves her, but the river lies. Under the tree a poet is seated, singing and dreaming."*

This is a lilting melodic setting that employs syncopation and some alternation of major-minor materials.

Milonga de dos hermanos   **Milonga of Two Brothers.**
(Jorge Luis Borges)

> *"When the fire was blazing the guitar told stories of stories of the Iberra brothers, the best of the ones who work with the knife and now are covered with dirt. Pride and greed cause a man to get lost. Juan Iberra shot his brother. It is the story of Cain who keeps killing Abel."**

The *milonga* is a popular dance song with *habanera* rhythm, which originated as a song of the lower social strata of Argentina. The Argentine tango, so typical of the country, evolved from a hybrid mixture of the Argentine *milonga*, the Andalusian *tango*, and the Cuban *habanera*.

Se equivocó la paloma   **The Confused Dove. 1941**
(Rafael Alberti)

> *"The confused dove made so many mistakes...In order to go to the north, she went south. She believed the sea was sky, the stars dew. She was mistaken. She fell asleep on the shore, on top of a branch."**

Quiet intensity colors the beginning of this song. Guastavino uses a five-note melodic cell "se equivocaba" to link dramatic content and maintain musical unity. Using the pitches of the cell (D, F, A, G) he creates an ostinato figure for the piano. By juxtaposing both vocal and piano figures, the flustered dove is vividly drawn in musical terms.

Viniendo de Chilecito   **Coming from Chile. 1949**
(Francisco Silva)

> *"On my way from Chile I met a pretty girl from La Rioja. No matter where I go, I remember her."**

This is an effervescent song with alternating rhythmic patterns; the first comprises two melodic fragments that form the first vocal phrase, the second heavily underscores the syllabic stresses of "Chilecito," and the last is a lilting declamatory melody of three notes. The melodic materials are integrated into an animated dance-like setting with the flavor of a popular folk song.

*Translations and paraphrases courtesy of Mary MacKenzie.

Extended Study List

Desde que te conocí • Mi viña de Chapanay • El Sampedrino • Nana • Pueblito, mi pueblo • Mi garganta • Pampa sola • Romance de José Cubas • La palominta • Ya me voy a retirar • Abismo de sed • Encantamiento • *Cuatro canciones coloniales*

Selected Reading

Carlos Vilo, Editorial Lagos, "Carlos Guastavino," liner notes to *Las Puertas de la Mañana: Canciónes Argentinas de Carlos Guastavino* (New Albion Records NA 058CD). Trans. by Ulises Espaillat.

Notes

1. Quoted in Vilo liner notes.
2. Ibid.
3. Mary MacKenzie. Lecture recital. National Association of Teachers of Singing winter workshop. Pasadena, California, January 1990.
4. Interview with Mary MacKenzie. December, 1993.

FRANCISCO ERNANI BRAGA
(Brazil, 1868-1945)

Braga wrote numerous songs; unfortunately, most of them are known only in South America. The great Brazilian soprano Bidú Sayão and Spanish mezzo-soprano Teresa Berganza brought his songs to the attention of the world through recital performances. Recordings by Teresa Berganza and Carmen Balthrop have made these lovely works available for larger audiences.

In 1890 Braga traveled to Paris on a fellowship where he studied for a time with Massenet; he later lived in Germany where he was strongly influenced by Wagner. While in Europe he composed symphonic poems and during a stay in Italy, an opera. He returned to Brazil in 1900 and was influential in the musical life of Rio de Janeiro and São Paulo, as composer, conductor, and professor of composition at the National Institute of Music in Rio de Janeiro.

Like his pupil, Villa-Lobos, Braga's musical style integrates influences from Europe with the culture of Brazil; in particular, he takes the speech rhythms of the Afro-Brazilian dialect and blends them into his songs. In many songs, specific word sound imitations or repetitions of sounds are used to colorful effect, producing an onomatopoeia that is almost hypnotic, and does not depend on literal meanings. Braga's skill in combining these speech rhythms into his essentially lyric style makes his songs fascinating and appealing.

Capim di pranta   **The Persistent Weed.**

(Canción Jongo)

This is a Jongo song from Alagôas with Afro-Brazilian rhythm. In the colonial age, singing farmworkers are fighting against the capim, a stubborn weed that grows again as soon as it is pulled out. The queen's order makes them stop the thankless task. Braga has fashioned an infectious rhythmic setting calling for rapid diction from the singer. A rhythmic ostinato in the piano propels the song along; each section is delineated by *ritardandi* as the workers pause in their efforts, then the determined rhythmic pattern commences as the unyielding weed has to be attacked again.

Sâo Joâo-dâ-ra-râo   **Saint John's Day.**
(Canción de ronda infantil, Piani)

This is a children's song from Piani, a region in Brazil. The children sing on
the day of Sâo Joâo (St. John's Day, June 27th) in a manner typical of this region—
repeating the last syllable of the words. It is literally "playing with the words" for
no other reason than to hear the repetition. This theme alternates in rondo form
with two contrasting sections, both slower and extremely lyric in quality. The first
section returns for a final time, sung on the syllable "la."

Nigue-nigue-ninhas   **Lullaby.**
(Canción de cuna afro-brasileña, Pariba do Norte)

This is an Afro-Brazilian lullaby from Paraibo do Norte. The words are a blend
of Portuguese and African dialect and do not have a clear sense, but seem to be of
deep lovingness. Simple rocking figures accompany a beautiful lyric line, intimate
in mood. "Nigue" is a lullaby sound and may be compared with "Ninghe" in
Montsalvatge's "Lullaby" (*Cinco canciones negras*).

Extended Study List
Engenho Novo! • A casinha pequenina • O'Kinimbá

HEITOR VILLA-LOBOS (Brazil, 1887-1959)

I compose in the folk-style. I utilize thematic idioms in my own way and
subject them to my own development. An artist must select and transmit
the material given him by his people.

—Heitor Villa-Lobos[1]

Brazil's nationalistic musical movement found its leader in Heitor Villa-Lobos,
a largely self-taught composer with an intuitive approach to composition. He
resisted imitating the style of other musicians, choosing instead to create his own
musical language by blending Brazil's native music with European influences and
his own intense imagination. After a short period of formal training at the National
Institute of Music in Rio de Janeiro, he journeyed throughout Brazil ingesting its
folklore and indigenous music.

In the 1920s Villa-Lobos visited Paris where he absorbed the music of Debussy
and d'Indy. French and other European musical traditions are found in his music,
combined with elements of Brazilian folk music. Brazilian popular music and the
use of nontraditional folk instruments are also integrated freely and spontaneous-
ly into his music.

Villa-Lobos composed close to 2,000 works (some sources say 3,000), so vast a
body of music that cataloguers have had problems with an authentic listing.
His music shows marked unevenness in quality within a diversity of styles—
not unlike his own eccentric nature. He composed with great speed and in an
almost automatic way.

His strong interest in improvisational popular music of his country is evident in the character of his songs. He approached life with the same nonconformist attitude, traveling widely throughout Brazil, taking as his lifestyle the bohemian existence of the *choreo.** Villa-Lobos mastered both the guitar and the cello; both instruments are central to many of his works.

One of his most familiar and beautiful vocal compositions is the *Bachianas brasileiras* No. 5 for soprano and eight cellos, which features exquisite lyric vocal phrases. Composed between 1930 and 1945, *Bachianas* comprises nine suites dedicated to the genius of Johann Sebastian Bach whom Villa-Lobos believed to be "a universal and rich folkloristic source deeply rooted in the folk music of every country in the world."[2] Each movement of the *Bachianas* has two titles; one traditionally European, the other Brazilian.

Villa-Lobos's music is characterized by vitality and color, integrating the diverse variety of Brazil's geographical areas and cultures into a distinct musical idiom that captures the essence of the country. He stated: "It is only nature and humanity that can lead an artist to the truth...I study the history, the country, the speech, the customs, the background of the people. I have always done this, and it is from these sources, spiritual as well as practical, that I have drawn my art."[3]

He was the first composer of Latin America to achieve universal fame as a modernist. During the latter part of his life, Villa-Lobos became an important force in the field of musical education in Brazil. He spent the 1930s and early 1940s attempting to reorganize musical instruction in the public schools of São Paulo. In 1932, he was appointed director of the Superintendencia de Educação Musical e Artistica (S.E.M.A.) in Rio de Janeiro. During his tenure in the post he presented gigantic mass choral concerts aimed at establishing patriotism in Brazil's youth through music education.

*A *choro* was one of the many groups of serenading instrumentalists who roamed the streets of Rio de Janeiro. These musicians (*choreos*) played improvisatory popular style music, usually both amorous and melancholy in mood (the term *choro* is related to the verb "chorer"—to weep). The word refers to both the music and the instrumental groups.

Canção do poeta do século XVIII   Song of an Eighteenth-Century Poet.
(Alfredo Ferreira)

When Villa-Lobos sets South American poets, the songs always have a close proximity to popular music. Although the texture and form of this song has an archaic quality, the harmonic materials are distinctly contemporary. Dreamy, reflective and free-flowing speech rhythms dominate the vocal line, which is doubled by the piano with an occasional altered chord.

The poet is dreaming of a walk in the moonlight with his sweetheart. Ferreira is a Portuguese poet.

Viola quebrada *(Canções tipicas brasileiras)*
Modinha de M de A

Folk music set by Villa-Lobos often takes on the character of art music. This song is found in a collection of Brazilian folk songs; Villa-Lobos's musical setting invests it with features of an art song. "Viola quebrada" is a *modinha*, a Brazilian musical form brought from Portugal. Its meaning—*Moda* (style or mood) and *inha* (the diminutive)—implies a fragment in a certain mood or a little song in a given mood.

The song is cast in three alternating sections, contrasting quick dotted rhythms with broader, more lyric passages accompanied by simple chords. The text describes a *Fado*-player* who takes on a heavy work schedule because of his lady love.

*A performer of Portuguese folk songs.

Xangô
(Canto fetiche de Makumba do Brasil)

Rhythmic energy and color dominate this song; musical materials incorporate Brazil's native Indian elements. Xangô, a god of the Macumba,* is master over fire and lightning. He loves war and women, but he also helps people to withstand the storms of life and protects them from sorcery.

Heavy, dramatic textures predominate throughout the song; the vocal line is like a repeated incantation, underpinned by colorful writing for the piano, including *glissandi*. The piece is highly emotional from beginning to end.

*A religious ritual originating from Africa.

Extended Study List
Bachianas Brasileiras No. 5 (Cantilena) • *Suite for Voice and Violin* • *Serestas* • Canção des aguas claras • Canção de crystal • Adeus êma • Estrélla é lua nova • *Modinhas y cançãoes* • *Tres poemas indigenas* • *Duas Paisagens* • Pai-do-mato • Samba classico • Desejo

Selected Reading
David Appleby, *The Music of Brazil* (Austin: University of Texas Press, 1983).
_____, *Heitor Villa-Lobos: A Bio-Bibliography* (New York: Greenwood Press, 1988).
Vasco Mariz, *Heitor Villa-Lobos: Brazilian Composer* (Gainesville: University of Florida Press, 1963).
Simon Wright, *Villa-Lobos* (New York: Oxford University Press, 1992). Oxford Studies of Composers.

Notes
1. Quoted in liner notes, *Villa-Lobos: Bachianas Brasileiras,* Nos. 2, 5, 6, 9 (Angel S-36979 LP recording, 1973).
2. Ibid.
3. Ibid.

Eastern European Song

In the eastern European countries, there is not a body of song literature comparable to that of Germany, France, Great Britain, or America. Although eastern Europe produced its share of distinguished musicians and composers, only a small number were interested in song composition. Eastern European musical styles were forged in the late nineteenth century as each country tried to assert a national identity through music, especially by using folk elements in art music.

CZECHOSLOVAKIA

The Czechoslovak peoples have a great love of singing and a strong heritage of folk music. Despite this, there is not a strong tradition of solo song in the country. Instead, many amateur musical organizations cultivated choral music. Composers wrote symphonies, choral and chamber works, and operas, but little solo song.

For many years, Czechoslovakia was bilingual; both German and Czech were spoken, so it is not surprising that the German *Lied* strongly influenced the development of Czech solo song. Bedřich Smetana (1825-1884) and Antonín Dvořák (1841-1904) stand out as composers of vocal music. Smetana wrote only a few songs and is known primary for his operas. Dvořák wrote around seventy songs, influenced by German *Lied* style, but suffused with Bohemian melodies and rhythms. Dvořák's style influenced the early work of Leoš Janáček (1854-1928), the most important twentieth-century Czech composer. His operas have gained international recognition; his songs are few in number but highly individual and expressive.

HUNGARY

In Hungary, Béla Bartók (1881-1945) and his colleague Zoltán Kodály (1882-1967) were deeply involved in researching, gathering, and codifying the folk music of their country. In addition to their arrangements of folk music, these composers also composed classical song. Kodály's pupil Mátyás Seiber (1905-1960) wrote a number of songs to Hungarian, German, French, and English texts.

POLAND

Polish songs developed from Polish theatrical music and late-eighteenth-century French song; their popular style was modified and influenced by the German *Lied*. Famous pianist-composer Frédéric Chopin (1810-1849) composed nineteen songs. They are early works and not indicative of his musical style, although some of them are delightful. In the twentieth century, composer Karol Szymanowski (1882-1937) expressed his nationalism in a number of songs. The earliest were influenced by Chopin, but his later songs are highly individual, blending elements from Scriabin, Schoenberg, and Stravinsky's music into his own personal style.

ROMANIA

Romanian composer George Enescu (1881-1955) received his musical training in Vienna and Paris. He was considered the guiding spirit of Romanian music. His song cycle *Sept chansons de Clément Marot* is an example of his expressive musical style and his opera *Oedipe* still awaits the recognition it deserves.

Each of the countries of eastern Europe has a colorful and rich heritage of folk traditions and music, which has been assimilated into the solo song literature of these countries. With the exception of the songs of Dvořák , this literature is largely unknown. The various original languages involved and the difficulties encountered in obtaining music scores have contributed to this neglect.

CZECHOSLOVAKIA

ANTONÍN DVOŘÁK (1841-1904)

It is...unselfish nationalism—broadly melodic, original, exotic, full of unexpected twists, enchanting in its harmony—that gives Dvořák's music its great charm and beauty.

—Harold C. Schonberg[1]

The music of the people is like a rare and lovely flower growing amidst encroaching weeds. Thousands pass it, while others trample it under foot, and thus the chances are that it will perish before it is seen by one discriminating spirit who will prize it above all else.

—Antonín Dvořák [2]

Antonín Dvořák composed approximately seventy songs; most are stylistically related to the German *Lied*. They are often compared with those of his friend and mentor, Johannes Brahms. Among his songs are three sets of Moravian duets, Op. 20, 32, and 38, after Moravian folk songs, as well as several other single duets.

Melody is the overriding element in the songs, although Dvořák's piano accompaniments are full of interest and harmonic color. His approach to text setting is often uneven, although his songs manage to assimilate the atmosphere and essence of the poetry. His early songs are experimental in style, and it was not until middle age that he began to produce his best work in the genre. If his songs break no new ground, they nonetheless have variety and immediate emotional appeal. Great dramatic strength is found in his *Zigeunermelodien* (*Cigánské melodie*).

Although we think of Dvořák primarily as a composer of symphonies and chamber music, he thought of himself as a composer of operas. Dvořák's eleven operas offer further insights into his dramatic, expressive, and structural approach to vocal writing. His best songs deserve to be heard more frequently, and, if possible, in their original language.

Cigánské melodie (Zigeunermelodien), Op. 55 (Adolph Heyduk)		Gypsy Songs. 1880
Czech	**German**	**English***
Má píseň zas	Mein Lied ertönt	My Song of Love
Kterak trojhranec můj	Ei, wie mein Triangel	Ei! Ring Out My Triangle
A les je tichý kolem kol	Rings ist der Wald	Here in the Wood
Když mne stará matka	Als die alte Mutter	Songs My Mother Taught Me
Struna naladěna	Reingestimmt die Saiten!	Set the Fiddles Scraping
Široké rukávy a široké gatě	In dem weiten, breiten, luft'gen	Flowing Sleeve and Trouser
Dejte klec jestřábu	Darf des Falken Schwinge	Cloudy Heights of Tatra

*Titles are given in Czech, German, and English. Dvořák originally composed the cycle in German for the premiere in Vienna, using translations from the Czech by the poet. The songs are often performed and recorded in the German translation.

The *Zigeunermelodien (Cigánské melodie)* represent Dvořák's finest achievement in song. The work celebrates the music and culture of the nomadic Gypsies (now known as Sinti and Roma) of eastern Europe. Their free life style and unrestrained passion for life perpetuated romantic images in nineteenth-century music and literature. Hungarian music is rich in influences from these peoples.

Dvořák set the songs to texts of Czech poet Adolf Heyduk, who drew on folk sources for his verses. Since the premiere of these songs was to take place in Vienna, Dvořák was under considerable pressure to produce songs with German texts and wrote the music to German versions prepared by Heyduk.

The *Zigeunermelodien* have one overriding theme: the joyous freedom of Gypsy life and the passionate emotional makeup of the Gypsy personality. The first and last songs are majestic and bardic in quality, underlining the theme of the unfettered freedom of the Gypsy life. Songs 2, 5, and 6 are spirited, joyous dances that draw heavily on Czech and Hungarian dance rhythms. Song 2 is an animated dance with accelerated tempo and dramatic rhythmic treatment. Song 3, "Rings ist der Wald" (Here in the Wood) is reminiscent of Brahms in its long-lined melodies and hushed atmosphere. Song 4 is the familiar "Als die alte Mutter" (Songs My Mother Taught Me)—in a sense, the center of the cycle. Dvořák maintains a nostalgic atmosphere—almost suspended in time—by using two simple meters simultaneously. The vocal line is written in $\frac{2}{4}$, the piano in $\frac{6}{8}$; the resultant texture is rich in color. Piano figures reminiscent of the Gypsy *cimbalom*[*] appear in Song 5.

Dvořák's *Zigeuenermelodien* should be contrasted with Johannes Brahms's *Zigeuenerlieder*. Each composer captures the flavor of the free-spirited Gypsy life, although Dvořák's treatment provides a wider and richer variety of musical textures.

*Hungarian hammered dulcimer

Biblícké písně, **Op. 99**   **Biblical Songs. 1894**

Oblak a mrákota jest vůkol Něho	Clouds and Darkness are round about Him (Psalm 97, vs. 2-6)
Skrýše má a pavéza má Ty jsi	Thou Art My Refuge and Shield (Psalm 119, vs. 114, 115, 117, 120)
Slyš, ó Bože! slyš modlitbu mou	Give Ear, O God, Unto My Prayer (Psalm 55, vs. 2-9)
Hospodin jest můj pastýř	The Lord Is My Shepherd (Psalm 23, vs. 1-4)
Bože! Bože! Píseň novou	God! God! I Will Sing A New Song (Psalm 144, vs. 9; Psalm 145, vs. 2, 3, 5, 6)
Slyš, ó Bože, volání mé	Hear My Prayer, O Lord (Psalm 61, vs. 2, 4, 5; Psalm 63, vs. 1, 4, 5)
Při řekách babylonských	By the Waters of Babylon (Psalm 137, vs. 1-5)
Popatřiž na mne a smiluj se nade mnou	Look Unto Me and Have Mercy (Psalm 25, vs. 16-18, 20)
Pozdvihuji očí svých k horám	I Lift My Eyes to the Mountains (Psalm 121, vs. 1-4)
Zpívejte Hospodinu píseň novou	Sing to the Lord a New Song (Psalm 96, vs. 1, 4, 7, 8; Psalm 96 vs. 12, 11)

Dvořák composed the *Biblical Songs* in New York in 1894. They represent his last set of songs. Unfortunately, most of them are uneven and disappointing in quality. They tend to be sentimental rather than devout. Among the best are the poignantly simple "The Lord Is My Shepherd" and "By the Waters of Babylon." The texts are excerpts from the Psalms. Dvořák originally set them from a seventeenth-century Czech Protestant Bible, but realizing that a German translation would have to be made, he rewrote the voiceparts and, in changing them, drastically altered their rhythmic vitality. In 1894, Dvořák orchestrated Nos. 1-4. The songs are published in Czech, German, French, and English.

Extended Study List

Vier Lieder, Op. 82 • Kralové Dvur • *Three Modern Greek Songs*, Op. 50 (baritone) • *Moravian Duets*, Op. 32 (soprano, contralto) • Operas: *Rusalka, The Devil and Kate*

Selected Reading

Gerald Abraham, *Essays on Russian and East European Music* (Oxford: Clarendon Press, 1985). Chapter 12: Czechoslovakian Song.

Michael Beckerman, ed., *Dvořák and His World* (Princeton: Princeton University Press,1993).

Timothy Cheek, *Singing in Czech: A Guide to Czech Lyric Diction and Vocal Repertoire* (Lanham, MD: Scarecrow Press, 2001). Part 2 contains sections on Smetana, Dvořák, Janáček, Martinů, and Haas.

Astra Desmond, "The Songs," in *Antonín Dvořák: His Achievement,* ed. Viktor Fischl (Westport, CT: Greenwood Press, 1970).

Alec Robertson, *Dvořák* (London: J. M. Dent and Sons, 1964). Chapter 12: The Songs.

Notes

1. Harold C. Schonberg, *The Lives of the Great Composers* (New York: W.W. Norton and Company, 1970), 368.
2. Antonín Dvořák, "Music in America," *Harper's New Monthly Magazine*, 1895. Although this statement was made in reference to the American "Negro songs," it offers a general, but presumably accurate, interpretation of his feeling towards folk music in general.

LEOŠ JANÁČEK (1854-1928)

The proof that folk songs originated from words lies in the special character of their rhythm.

—Leoš Janáček[1]

Leoš Janáček's compositions may be divided into three style periods: 1854-1903; 1903-1918; and 1918-1928.* The first period contains a slender list of songs; most are folk songs and include the Moravian *Folk Songs*. The second period contains *Twenty-six Popular Ballads* and *Songs of Silesia;* the third and most mature period includes *Folk Songs of Moravia, Love Songs of Moravia* and *The Diary of One Who Vanished.***

Janáček's use of folk materials in his music was influenced by Dvořák. Janáček was obsessed with speech patterns, and his vocal works are bound up with the Czech language whose patterns and stresses became an integral part of his melodic approach. He believed that speech motives were of utmost importance in defining and shaping melodic elements. In the late 1800s, he began to take down examples of everyday speech in musical notation for study, seeking to discern moods and emotions within them as well as inherent factors of rhythm and pitch.

He called these rhythmic units *sčasovka*.[2] The "melodic curve of speech" was a theory of Janáček's, and his musical style is heavily influenced by this view.

Janáček's approach to melody is folk-like, using short phrases—usually disjunct—that emphasize one interval and often resemble recitative. Since Janáček's melodic writing springs from the irregular patterns of everyday speech, it is not surprising that his "speech melodies" became the basis of his vocal writing and indeed, his entire musical style. Many times the piano accompaniment is derived from the vocal line, using vocal material in variation or as an echo. Much of Janáček's music is dramatic and full of sudden contrasts.

Folk elements permeate the form of his works; short phrases and asymmetrical rhythmic groupings are found in abundance. Each piece's form is unique. Janáček's vocal music is generally considered superior to his instrumental works. His operas have a personal, natural style: *Jenůfa, Kát'a Kabanová, The Cunning Little Vixen (Příhody líšky Bystroušky), The Makropoulos Affair (Věc Makropulos),* and *From the House of the Dead (Z mrtvé domu),* his final and most pessimistic score. In the last decade, Janáček's operas have become part of the repertoire.

*Approximate dates
**It is difficult to obtain Janáček's songs in English translation.

Zápisník zmizelého **The Diary of One Who Vanished. 1917-19**

This work is a large cycle for tenor, alto, three female voices, and piano. Most of the songs are short. The tenor sings eighteen of the twenty-two songs and there is one piano solo in the group. Texts are a sequence of short poems found by the police in an exercise-book belonging to a young Moravian peasant of good character whose mysterious disappearance they were investigating.[3] Clearly autobiographical, the poems outline the story of his seduction by a Gypsy woman, his resultant shame, and his resolve to leave home and run away with her. The poems were published in a Brno newspaper and attracted Janáček's attention.

The cycle is a semi-dramatic setting on a half-darkened stage; the tenor is the hero Janik, the alto is the Gypsy, Zefka. A trio of female voices acts as a Greek chorus, commenting (offstage) on the action. Janáček's sensitivity to verbal intonation is reflected throughout the work; the words are set with impeccable prosody and motives inspired from verbal articulation often generate instrumental texture as well. Timothy Cheek observes: "The song cycle demonstrates Janáček's operatic inclinations, with lighting and staging directions written into the score, and is based on speech melody."[4]

The Diary of One Who Vanished belongs to Janáček's third style period, extending roughly from 1918 to 1928, which includes his operas *Kát'a Kabanová, Příhody líšky Bystroušky (The Cunning Little Vixen), Věc Makropulos (The Makropulos Affair),* and *From the House of the Dead.*

Extended Study List

Morvaská lidová poesie v písních (Moravian folk poetry in songs. Fifty-three songs for medium voice and piano) • *Slezské písně* (Silesian Songs. Ten songs for medium voice and piano)

Selected Reading

Timothy Cheek, *Singing in Czech: a guide to Czech lyric diction and vocal repertoire* (Lanham, MD: Scarecrow Press, 2001). Part 2 contains sections on Smetana, Dvořák, Janáček, Martinů, and Haas.
Hans Hollander, *Leoš Janáček: His Life and Work.* trans. Paul Hamburger (London: John Calder, 1963).
Ian Horsbrugh, *Leoš Janáček* (New York: Charles Scribner's Sons, 1982).
Jaroslav Vogel, *Leoš Janáček: A Biography.* Rev.and ed. Karel Janovicky (New York: W.W. Norton, 1981).

Notes

1. Harlow Robinson, "The Folk Connection," *Opera News* 50 (January 4, 1986), 20.
2. Timothy Cheek, *Singing in Czech*, 217.
3. Gerald Abraham, "Czechoslovakian Song," *Essays on Russian and East European Music*, 182.
4. Cheek, 227.

HUNGARY

BÉLA BARTÓK (1881-1945)

> To handle folk tunes is one of the most difficult tasks; equally difficult
> if not more so than to write a major original composition...We must
> penetrate into it, feel it, and bring it out in sharp contours by the
> appropriate setting...It must be a work of inspiration just as much as any
> other composition.

—Béla Bartók[1]

Béla Bartók wrote two types of vocal works for voice and piano: art songs and settings of Hungarian and Slovak folk texts and melodies. During his maturity, two sets of five songs were composed: *Five Songs*, Op. 15, to texts that Bartók never identified; and *Five Songs,* Op. 16, to symbolist texts of Endre Ady. Both works belong in his first style period, characterized by strong folk music associations.

In 1907, Bartók became professor of piano at the Royal Academy of Music. During his lifetime, he and his friend Zoltán Kodály traveled through Hungary, collecting folk songs.

The ten-year period of 1920-1930 delineates Bartók's rhythmic-polyphonic period, characterized by a thorough assimilation of folk idioms into the overall texture of his music. Denser rhythms and textures are found in these works, which are less defined tonally. *Five Village Scenes* (1924) and *Eight Hungarian Folk Songs* (1907-1917) are characteristic of the numerous vocal compositions based on folk tunes. Blending his vast knowledge of Hungarian (Magyar) folk music idioms into his personal style, Bartók created a uniquely Hungarian body of art music, culminating in his opera, *Bluebeard's Castle,* whose roots can be traced to the modes and rhythms of Hungarian folk song.

Extended Study List
Five Songs, Op. 15 • *Five Songs*, Op. 16 • *Five Village Scenes* • *Eight Hungarian Folksongs*

Selected Reading
Malcom Gillies, *Bartók Remembered* (New York: W. W. Norton Co., 1990).
Paul Griffiths, *Bartók* (London: J. M. Dent, 1984). Master Musicians series.
Vera Lampert, "Works for Solo Voice with Piano," in *The Bartók Companion,* ed. Malcom Gillies (Portland: Amadeus Press, 1994). Chapter 24.

Notes
1. Quoted in liner notes to *Béla Bartók: Songs, Op. 15, Op. 16; Hungarian Folksongs, Village Scenes.* Turnabout Records. LP recording TV-S 34592. 1973.
2. Vera Lampert, in *The Bartók Companion*, 388.

ZOLTÁN KODÁLY (1882-1967)

> Kodály's compositions are characterized in the main by rich melodic invention, a perfect sense of form, [and] a certain predilection for melancholy and uncertainty.
>
> —Béla Bartók[1]

Zoltán Kodály was primarily a composer of vocal music. His songs are well-written for the voice and are not musically complex, although they are rich in melodic elements. In them may be found the basis of Hungarian musical declamation, using traditional folk song structures.

Kodály's parents were amateur musicians; he earned a Ph.D. in philology and, in addition to his career as a composer, was also a music critic and essayist. In Paris, Kodály met Debussy, whose musical style figures prominently in Kodály's work, coupled with the influences of Hungarian (Magyar) folk music.

Kodály's earliest works are late romantic in sound quality, reminiscent of Brahms. Melody is the most conspicuous element in Kodály's style; many melodies are characterized by the interval of a fourth (a trait of Magyar music). With his friend Béla Bartók, Kodály began collecting and studying the folk songs of Hungary in 1905. Kodály's arrangements of folk songs and ballads were published in a ten-volume series titled *Hungarian Folk Music*.

The following characteristics may be found in Kodály's music: melodic shapes that contain many repeated notes; harmonies derived from melodic shapes; use of pentatonic scales; simple, balanced forms, generative in style; rhythms based on Magyar folk elements (example—a short unaccented note followed by long accented note); and a free rhapsodic but basically conservative style.

Lyricism is the outstanding quality in Kodály's songs; melodies are generally nostalgic and introspective. Melodic materials are given prominence; accompaniments provide a harmonic background of broken chords, sophisticated pedal points and inventive figures. Song forms are often strophic, interspersed with descriptive interludes. Word stresses and inflections of the Magyar language dominate the structure of his vocal phrases. Vocal accents in the poetry always determine the contour of his melodic lines.

From 1908 to 1942, Kodály taught composition at the Budapest Academy of Music. From the 1920s on, he was extremely active in the field of Hungarian music education. In the late 1920s, he was appointed head of music education for the country; the 1930s saw the establishment of a "Singing Youth Movement." Kodály's prolific writings on music and the teaching of music not only guided music education in his own country, but permeated systems of music teaching in other countries as well.

Kodály believed singing to be the foundation of all music since the "mother tongue" is itself a vocal idiom and the act of singing produces immediate musical experience. In teaching and developing musicianship, he stressed the use of solmization, using song material drawn from the folk songs and folk music of Hungary. Kodály's writing and activity in the field of music education were revolutionary and resulted in a "democratization" of music education. Through his work, the Hungarian people developed a musical consciousness based on their own country's musical materials.

He remained in Budapest during both world wars. After the end of World War II, Kodály was the most highly respected figure in Hungarian cultural life: he was president of the Budapest Academy of Music, the Hungarian Council of Arts, and the Hungarian Academy of Sciences.

Extended Study List
Sixteen Songs, Op. 1 (1907-09) • *Twenty Hungarian Folksongs* (1906)

Notes
1. Max Wegner, "Zoltan Kodály," *The New Grove Dictionary of Music and* Musicians, Vol. 10, 39.

POLAND

FRÉDÉRIC CHOPIN (1810-1849)

> Nothing is more hateful than music without hidden meaning.
>
> —Frédéric Chopin[1]

Frédéric Chopin composed nineteen songs, all set to Polish texts. They are early works and many show the influence of his teacher, Joseph Elsner. The earliest Chopin songs preserved were those he copied into Elsner's daughter's album some time before he left Poland.

Seventeen songs were published posthumously, as Op. 74; the last two were discovered and published in 1910. As might be expected, the songs feature lyrical melodic lines. Surprisingly, Chopin's accompaniments are fairly simple and unpretentious. Song forms are similarly modest. Chopin uses mazurka rhythms in a number of the songs; texts range from dramatic narrative to folk tales, many suffused with melancholy emotion or patriotic fervor. Stylistically, they are close to the Polish song of that day and show little of his personal style that was to develop and flower in his piano compositions.

Songs (Op. 74)
Zyczenie (The Maiden's Wish) • Wiosna (Spring) • Smutna rzeka (The Troubled Stream) • Dumka (Reverie) • Hulanka (A Drinking Song) • Czary (Witchcraft) • Gdzie lubi (There where she loves) • Precz z moich oczu (Out of my sight) • Posel (The Messenger) • Sliczny Chlopiec (Handsome boy) • Melodya (Elegy) • Wojak (The Warrior) • Dwojaki koniec (The Two Corpses) • Moja Pieszczotka (My Darling) • Nie ma czego trzeba (I want what I do not have) • Pierscien (The Ring) • Narzeczony (The Bridegroom) • Piomska Litweska (Lithuanian Song) • Spiew z mogily (Hymn from the tomb)

Selected Reading
Gerald Abraham, *Essays on Russian and East European Music* (Oxford: Clarendon Press, 1985). Chapter 10: "Polish Song."
Beverly True, "Frédéric Chopin as a Song Writer," *The NATS Journal,* 43:5 (May/June 1987).

Notes
1. Quoted in Arbie Orenstein, *A Ravel Reader,* 335.

KAROL SZYMANOWSKI (1882-1937)

> The Polish collections, intersected by settings in German, French and English—to the late embrace of a specifically Polish song of the earth renders his trove of song one of the richest, most varied, and piquantly, teasingly fantastic of all excursions through the soundscape of twentieth-century music.
>
> —Adrian Corleonis[1]

Karol (Maciej) Szymanowski was the central figure in Polish music in the first half of the twentieth century. His works are highly varied in form; he composed works for the stage (including opera, ballet and operetta); orchestral music; chamber music; songs and choral works; and piano music.* His song output was substantial, influenced musically by Wolf, Ravel, and Stravinsky, but assimilated into his own unique and expressive style.

He was born in the Ukraine, then part of the former kingdom of Poland. His well-to-do parents encouraged their children to pursue artistic endeavors. Szymanowski began to compose and play the piano at an early age. In 1901, he went to Warsaw and studied harmony, counterpoint, and composition. In 1904, he traveled to Berlin, where he and a few colleagues founded the "Young Composers' Publishing Co.," which promoted concerts and publication of new Polish music. One of Szymanowski's compositions from this period was his first opera, *Hagith* (1913). With the advent of World War I in 1914, he returned to Poland and remained there through the war, writing music and reading. At the end of the war, Poland became an independent nation again, and Szymanowski became deeply interested in the Polish folk idiom, attempting to create a national Polish style in his compositions.

Szymanowski was a voracious reader and a highly educated individual. His cultural background is reflected in his music, particularly in his choice of texts. Two-thirds of his output consists of settings of, or reactions to literary texts.[2] A number of his works for orchestra include the voice: *Love Songs of Hafiz (Third Symphony)*; *Songs of a Fairy Princess*; *Songs of the Infatuated Muezzin*; *Stabat Mater*; and *Veni Creator*, among others.

Szymanowski's music is extremely colorful harmonically, but also delicate and detailed. His early music shows marked influences of Reger, Richard Strauss, and Wagner. French impressionism, and the works of Scriabin, Schoenberg, and Stravinsky were to inform his later musical style. Some of the songs in Op. 17 and Op. 20 teeter on the brink of atonality.

Szymanowski was also deeply attracted to and moved by the Arabic-Persian culture; a number of his musical compositions sprang from this attraction.

Symanowski's music is not part of the mainstream repertoire, and much of his work is not known outside of Poland. In recent years, however, there has been a resurgence of interest in his music.

*Szymanowski's music is published by Eschig, Polskie Wydawnictwo Muzyczne, and Universal Edition.

Extended Study List

Three Fragments from Poems by Jan Kasprowicz, Op. 5 • The Swan, Op. 7 • *Four Songs*, Op. 11 • Vocalise-étude (1928) • *Three Lullabies*, Op. 48 • *Bünte Lieder*, Op. 22 • *Des Hafis Liebeslieder*, Op. 24 • *Songs of the Fairy Princess*, Op. 31 • Lonely Moon, Op. 32/1 • *Songs of the Infatuated Muezzin*, Op. 42 • *Seven Songs to Poems by James Joyce*, Op. 54 • *Soldiers' Songs* (1920) • *Kurpian Songs*, Op. 58

Selected Reading

Teresa Chylinska, "Karol Szymanowski," *The New Grove Dictionary of Music and Musicians,* ed. Stanley Sadie, (London: Macmillan Publishers Ltd., 1980), Vol. 18, 499-504.

_____, *Szymanowski,* Polish Music History Series, 1993. (Friends of Polish Music, University of Southern California, School of Music, Los Angeles, CA 90089). This volume available in the Emory Library, USC.

Stephen C. Downes, *Szymanowski as Post-Wagnerian: The Love Songs of Hafiz, Op. 24* (New York: Garland Publishers, 1994).

Christopher Palmer, *Szymanowski* (London: BBC, 1983).

Notes

1. Adrian Corleonis, review of "Szymanowski: Complete Songs" in *Fanfare,* 29:1 (Sept/Oct 2005), 299.
2. Teresa Chylinska, "Karol Szymanowski," *New Grove Dictionary of Music and Musicians,* 502.

ROMANIA

GEORGE ENESCU (1881-1955)

> Enescu was, with Bartók, the greatest musician I have ever known; whatever he did in music—composing, playing the violin, viola or piano, conducting—he was deeply inspiring. He is still to be discovered.
>
> —Yehudi Menuhin[1]

George Enescu was born in Romania in 1881. His studies at the Vienna Conservatory (1888-1894) and at the Paris Conservatoire (1895-1899) resulted in a brilliant multifaceted career as a virtuoso violinist, composer, conductor, and teacher. In France, he studied with Jules Massenet, Gabriel Fauré, and André Gédalge at the Paris Conservatory; these teacher-mentors had considerable influence on his compositional style.

In 1913, his *Second Romanian Rhapsody* was performed by the Chicago Symphony. Subsequently, his music entered the repertoire of the New York Symphony, Cincinnati Symphony, Minneapolis Symphony, and Boston Symphony orchestras. He toured the United States and Canada numerous times as a performer; in 1923 he conducted the Philadelphia Orchestra and in 1938, the New York Philharmonic. As a teacher, Enescu was a member of the faculty at the Ecole Normale de Musique in Paris; one of his pupils there was Yehudi Menuhin.

Enescu composed a small handful of songs[*]; most are settings of French texts.[2] His most significant vocal work is the cycle of seven poems by sixteenth-century poet Clément Marot, a work that ranks among the masterpieces of early twentieth-century song. Enescu seemed drawn to texts of a sad, meditative nature.

Enescu's catalog of compositions included concerti, chamber music, orchestral works, and one opera, *Oedipe,* which consumed him for twenty-five years. Although it is still largely unknown, it is one of the outstanding operas of the twentieth century. *Oedipe's* first draft was completed two years after he composed the Marot song cycle.

Enescu's compositional style reflects wide-ranging European influences. Enescu understood that his far-flung talents as a performer, composer, conductor, and teacher made it difficult to "categorize" his career and his music: "People have been puzzled because they have been unable to catalogue and classify me in the usual way; they could not decide exactly what type of music mine was. It was not French, after the manner of Debussy; it was not exactly German, they declared...

I naturally absorbed French influences to a certain extent, which combined with the German, gave a further character to my writings."[3]

During his lifetime, Enescu worked to encourage a new national school of composition, and was considered the guiding force in Romanian music. His vocal music deserves wider recognition and performance.

Cintece is the Romanian word for song.

Sept chansons de Clément Marot, Op. 15   1908

Estrene à Anne • Languir me fais… • Aux damoyselles paresseuses d'escrire à leurs amys • Estrene de la rose • Présent de couleur blanche • Changeons propos, c'est trop chanté d'amours… • Du confict en douleure

Enescu's seven settings early sixteenth-century French poetry are beautifully crafted and musically appealing. Elegant lyric vocal lines, combined with harmonies tinged with modality evoke the world of Clément Marot (c. 1495-1544), court poet to François I. Marot continued to use medieval forms (*chansons, ballades)* in his poetry, while experimenting with developing poetic forms (*rondeaux, epîtres*, and *estrenes)*. Marot's work is a blend of the old and the new, and Enescu captures this quality in his musical setting. Although the poetry of Marot is old French, the cycle should be sung using the contemporary pronunciation of the French language (*maulvaise=mauvaise*; *estioient=etaient*, etc.).[4]

Enescu's musical style in these songs has a distinctly French flavor, although it does not directly resemble his French contemporaries (Duparc, Debussy, Roussel, Fauré). The settings capture the ambience of Marot's time, portraying the poet as a troubadour. Accompaniments are full of figures that suggest the lute or a small harp.

ESTRENE À ANNE (GIFT TO ANNE). "For this New Year, take my heart as a gift; a painful heart scarred by a new and deep wound…"

The troubadour offers his heart to his beloved—a heart rich in love, but also pained and wounded by the experience. The vocal phrases are deceivingly simple, but never lose their elegance and fluid melodic character. Enescu's marking for the vocal line is *bien declamé*. A lute is suggested by the piano accompaniment, structured primarily of arpeggiated chords. An archaic flavor is imparted by the use of modal harmonic materials.

LANGUIR ME FAIS…(YOU MAKE ME LANGUISH…). "I languish, though I meant not to offend you. You write no more, nor inquire after me; but nonetheless I desire no other lady. Better to die than change my thoughts. But I complain of the grief I suffer and far from you, humbly implore that you will not be angry with me."

This song is often excerpted from the set for single performance. It is fashioned of a delicate vocal line above a highly ornamented piano accompaniment that brings to mind an archaic, improvisatory serenade. Enescu's tempo indication is *Assez lent, tristement*; the piano introduction is marked *Avec gracilité et abandon*, while the vocal line is *Très doux*. Vocal phrases are intensely lyric, though simple; a final melisma on the word "faschée" implores the beloved not to be angry and points up the nostalgic longing of the poet.

Aux damoyselles paresseuses d'escrire à leurs amys (To the young ladies too lazy to write to their friends). "Hello, what is the good news? You neither write nor answer me. If in brief you give me none, I'll make up my own. Since you're so stubborn...good eventide, good night, good evening, good day. But if you pick currants, send me some. You know I sigh for them, but am more eager to see you, my dears...some time. Good day."

The song is subtitled "Rondeaux." Its fragmented vocal lines portray the breathless, agitated state of the poet, eager to hear from his long overdue correspondents. The piano figures are equally brief and are used to both punctuate and underline the vocal phrases.

Estrene de la rose (Gift of the Rose). "A suitor relates the fable of the red rose to his lady love: One day Venus was pursuing her lover Adonis through gardens full of thorns and branches. Her feet and arms were bare and a rose-tree scratched her with its thorns. From her blood some of the white roses were made red. I present this rose to you; your sweet soft face is like the fresh, crimson rose."

This song is the center of the set and is one of the loveliest of the group. Harmonically, Enescu evokes Venus and Adonis's chase by small detours away from the tonal center, D. Figures in the accompaniment imitate a delicate lute accompaniment, embroidered with turns; as the story of the chase is related, the turns stretch out into chord outlines of running sixteenth notes. Enescu also employs a mixture of meters; the vocal line is notated in $\frac{2}{8}$, $\frac{3}{8}$, $\frac{4}{8}$, $\frac{5}{8}$ and $\frac{8}{8}$, the piano accompaniment in $\frac{6}{16}$, $\frac{9}{16}$, $\frac{12}{16}$, $\frac{15}{16}$, and $\frac{24}{16}$.

*The rose was the flower of the Goddess Venus, and in the beginning all roses were white in color.

Présent de couleur blanche (Gift of white color). "My gift to you is white like a dove, flying to you to tell you of my love...to fall at your feet and softly tell you without hesitation that I am longing for you. I will say more, since I abandon you to him—the lord to whom you are given will never love you like I do."

Alternating meters—$\frac{3}{8}$, $\frac{4}{8}$, $\frac{2}{8}$—give this song a unique narrative quality. Enescu highlights the plaintive mood with a simple and affecting setting, quite lyrical but nostalgic. The song is dedicated to Maggie Teyte.*

*Teyte created the role of Mélisande in Debussy's opera *Pelléas et Mélisande*. When in Paris for her first season at the Opéra-Comique in 1906-7, she had an affair with Enescu. She knew nothing of the dedication of this song until sixty years later, when she confessed to the liaison.[5]

Changeons propos, c'est trop chanté d'amours... (Let's change the subject, we've sung enough of love). "Let's change the subject, we've sung enough of love. Let's sing of the pruning knife, all wine-growers use it. O little pruning knife, by you the little vines are cut down from which the good wines come. The god Vulcan forged the knife in heaven with fine steel tempered with good old wine. Bacchus boasts about it; in those days he came to bless the vineyards in his hat of vine-leaves. Silenus followed behind him, carrying flagons. He could drink as straight as a line and then would dance. His nose was red as a cherry; many people come from his race."

The last two songs present highly divergent emotional moods. With this song, Enescu travels far afield with a rollicking drinking song. Its heavy texture complements its robust mood, which humorously races to the end of the text, becoming more animated and less controlled, as though the narrator is drinking his way to the end of the tale. As the final measures approach, the vocal phrases become less controlled (Enesco marks: *Fort, d'une voix trainard d'ivrogne, Presque parlé, En trainant*) and increasingly tipsy before finally collapsing in a drunken stupor. The piano punctuates the singer's last phrase with a final humorous flourish.

DU CONFICT EN DOULEURE (IF I SUFFER). "If I suffer in spite of myself I bear it...if someone wants to comfort me, he cannot appease my pain. Thus I languish, with no hope of greater joy."

Marot's text is a blend of pain and resignation, in which the poet discovers that the inevitability of his suffering will also allow him to enjoy it at the same time. His pain underlies all his existence, and its persistent ache strengthens his character. This is underlined by the phrase, "Si j'ay du mal," which is repeated three times. The song is subtitled "Rondeaux." As the poet's passion increases, the accompaniment texture thickens and widens in range. A last persistent repetition of "Si j'ay du mal" appears in the voice and the piano finishes the piece with a brief but expressive postlude.

Selected Reading

B. Gavoty, *Les Souvenirs de Georges Enesco* (Paris, 1955).
Noel Malcolm, *George Enescu: His Life and Music* (Exeter: Toccata Press, 1990).
Yolanda Marcoulescou, "Georges Enesco: Sept Chansons sur vers de Clément Marot," *The NATS Bulletin*, 33:2 (December 1976).

Notes

1. Yehudi Menuhin, "*Oedipe* and Enesco." Prefatory notes to recording of Enesco's opera *Oedipe* (EMI. Two digital compact discs CDS 7 54011-2, 1990).
2. Cultural and social ties with France led Romanian poets to write in the French language, which remained the language of choice for many Romanian poets and composers until around 1935. Today, French remains the second language for many well-educated people.
3. Georges Enescu. Program notes in the Chicago Symphony program (1931-32 season). Quoted in Marcoulescou, "Georges Enesco," *The NATS Bulletin*, 32.
4. Ibid., 34. Mme. Marcoulescou's voice teacher gave the first performance of this cycle, accompanied by the composer. Marcoulescou's article is one of the only authoritative sources dealing with this beautiful cycle. Marcoulescou recorded the work (*Yolanda Marcoulescou Sings Enesco and Roussel*. Orion Recordings, LP ORS 75184. Another recording by mezzo-soprano Sarah Walker and Roger Vignoles piano was released in 1984. *French Songs: Enesco, Roussel, Debussy*. Unicorn/Kachana. LP recording DKP 9035).
5. Noel Malcolm, *Enescu*, 100.

OTHER REPRESENTATIVE EAST EUROPEAN COMPOSERS

Joseph Elsner (1769-1854)	Poland
Józef Nowakowski (1800-1865)	Poland
Stanislaw Moniuszko (1819-1872)	Poland
Bedřich Smetana (1825-1884)	Czechoslovakia
Bohuslav Martinů (1890-1959)	Czechoslovakia
Mátyás Seiber (1905-1960)	Hungary
Felicia Donceanu (b. 1931)	Romania
Mihail Jora (1891-1971)	Romania

Index of Songs and Cycles

Each annotated song or cycle is listed with its composer and the national section in which it may be found.

Song Composers by Nationality

Each composer annotated in the text is indicated by an asterisk.*

AMERICAN

Albert, Stephen (1941-1992)
Argento, Dominick* (b. 1927)
Babbitt, Milton (b. 1916)
Bacon, Ernst* (1898-1990)
Baley, Virko (b. 1938)
Barber, Samuel* (1910-1981)
Beach, Amy Marcy Cheney* (1867-1944)
Beeson, Jack (b. 1921)
Berger, Jean (1909-2002)
Bernstein, Leonard* (1918-1990)
Blitzstein, Marc (1905-1964)
Bolcom, William* (b. 1938)
Bowles, Paul* (1910-1999)
Burleigh, H.T.* (1866-1949)
Cadman, Charles Wakefield (1881-1946)
Cage, John (1912-1992)
Carpenter, John Alden (1876-1951)
Carter, Elliott (b. 1908)
Chanler, Theodore* (1902-1961)
Charles, Ernest (1894-1984)
Citkowitz, Israel (1909-1974)
Cloud, Judith (b. 1954)
Copland, Aaron* (1900-1990)
Corigliano, John (b. 1938)
Crumb, George (b. 1929)
Dello Joio, Norman (b. 1913)
Del Tredici, David (b. 1937)
Diamond, David (1915-2005)
Dougherty, Celius (1902-1986)
Duke, John* (1899-1984)
Edwards, Clara (1887-1974)
Faith, Richard* (b. 1926)
Farwell, Arthur* (1872-1952)
Fennimore, Joseph (b. 1940)
Fine, Irving (1914-1962)
Finney, Ross Lee (1906-1997)
Floyd, Carlisle (b. 1926)
Foss, Lukas (b. 1922)
Foster, Stephen* (1826-1864)
Gordon, Ricky Ian (b. 1956)
Griffes, Charles* (1884-1920)
Hageman, Richard (1882-1966)
Hagen, Daron Aric* (b. 1961)
Harris, Roy (1898-1979)
Heggie, Jake (b. 1961)
Hindemith, Paul (1895-1963) (German,
    American citizenship 1945)
Hoiby, Lee* (b. 1926)
Hopkinson, Francis (1737-1791)
Howe, Mary (1882-1964)

Hundley, Richard* (b. 1931)
Ives, Charles* (1874-1954)
Kilpatrick, Jack (John) Frederick (1915-1967)
    (Native American Indian-Cherokee)
Laitman, Lori* (b. 1955)
Larsen, Libby* (b. 1950)
Lekberg, Sven (1900-1984)
Loeffler, Charles Martin (1861-1935)
MacDowell, Edward (1861-1908)
Moore, Ben (b. 1960)
Moore, Douglas (1893-1969)
Musto, John* (b. 1954)
Naginski, Charles (1909-1940)
Niles, John Jacob (1892-1980)
Nordoff, Paul (1909-1977)
Pasatieri, Thomas* (b. 1945)
Paulus, Stephen* (b. 1949)
Persichetti, Vincent* (1915-1987)
Pinkham, Daniel (b. 1923)
Powell, Mel (1923-1998)
Previn, André (b. 1929)
Rochberg, George, (1918-2005)
Rorem, Ned* (b. 1923)
Siegmeister, Elie (1909-1991)
Still, William Grant (1895-1978)
Thompson, Randall (1899-1984)
Thomson, Virgil* (1896-1989)
Zaimont, Judith Lang* (b. 1945)
Zwilich, Ellen Taafe (b. 1939)

BRITISH

Alwyn, William (1905-1985)
Arne, Dr. Thomas Augustine (1710-1778)
Bax, Arnold (1883-1953)
Benjamin, Arthur (1893-1960)
Bishop, Sir Henry R. (1786-1855)
Bliss, Arthur (1891-1975)
Boyce, Dr. William (1711-1779)
Bridge, Frank (1879-1941)
Britten, Benjamin* (1913-1976)
Bush, Geoffrey* (1920-1998)
Butterworth, George* (1885-1916)
Byrd, William (1543-1623)
Campion, Thomas* (1567-1620)
Carey, Henry (1690-1743)
Clarke, Rebecca* (1886-1979)
Corkine, William (early 17th century)
Delius, Frederick* (1862-1934)
Dickinson, Peter* (b. 1934)
Dowland, John* (1563-1626)
Dring, Madeleine* (1923-1977)

Elgar, Sir Edward (1857-1934)
Finzi, Gerald* (1901-1956)
Gardiner, H. Balfour (1877-1950)
Gibbs, C. Armstrong (1889-1960)
Glanville-Hicks, Peggy (1912-1990) (Australia)
Grainger, Percy (1882-1961)
Gurney, Ivor* (1890-1937)
Head, Michael* (1900-1976)
Heseltine, Philip (see Warlock, Peter*)
　　(1894-1930)
Holloway, Robin (b. 1943)
Holst, Gustav (1874-1934)
Horder, Mervyn* (1910-1997)
Howells, Herbert (1892-1983)
Hume, Tobias (d. 1648)
Ireland, John* (1879-1962)
Jones, Robert (d. 1617)
Lawes, Henry (1595-1662)
Lehmann, Liza (1862-1918)
Linley, William (1771-1835)
Maconchy, Elizabeth (1907-1994)
Maxwell Davies, Peter (b. 1934)
Moeran, E.J. (1894-1950)
Morley, Thomas (1557-1603)
Musgrave, Thea (b. 1928) (Scotland)
Orr, Charles* (1893-1976)
Parry, Sir Hubert (1848-1918)
Pilkington, Francis (1582-1638)
Purcell, Henry* (1659-1695)
Quilter, Roger* (1877-1953)
Rands, Bernard (b. 1934) (American citizenship
　　1983)
Rosseter, Philip (1575-1623)
Rowley, Alec (1892-1958)
Rubbra, Edmund (1901-1986)
Scott, Cyril (1879-1970)
Smith, John Christopher (1712-1795)
Stanford, Charles Villiers (1852-1924)
Thiman, Eric H. (1900-1975)
Tippett, Michael (1905- 1998)
Vaughan Williams, Ralph* (1872-1958)
Walton, William (1902-1983)
Warlock, Peter (Philip Heseltine)* (1894-1930)
Weir, Judith (b. 1954)

CANADIAN

Archer, Violet (1913-2000)
Bissell, Keith (1912-1992)
Coulthard, Jean (1908-2000)
Fleming, Robert (1921-1976)
Morawetz, Oskar (b. 1917)
Schafer, R. Murray (b. 1933)
Willan, Healey (1880-1968)

CENTRAL AMERICAN/CARIBBEAN

Campos-Parsi, Héctor (1925-1998) (Puerto Rico)
Chávez, Carlos (1899-1978) (Mexico)
Orbón, Julián (1925-1991) (Cuba)
Ponce, Manuel (1882-1948) (Mexico)
Revueltas, Silvestre (1899-1940) (Mexico)
Sandoval, Miguel (1903-1953) (Guatemala)
Vega, Aurelio de la (b. 1925) (Cuba; American
　　citizenship 1966)

EASTERN EUROPEAN

Bartók. Béla* (1881-1945) (Hungary)
Chopin, Frédéric* (1810-1849) (Poland)
Donceanu, Felicia (b. 1931) (Romania)
Dvořák, Antonín* (1841-1904) (Czechoslovakia)
Elsner, Joseph (1769-1854) (Poland)
Enescu, George* (1881-1955) (Romania)
Janáček, Leoš* (1854-1928) (Czechoslovakia)
Jora, Mihail (1891-1971) (Romania)
Kodály, Zoltán* (1882-1967) (Hungary)
Martinu, Bohuslav (1890-1959) (Czechoslovakia)
Moniuszko, Stanislaw (1819-1872) (Poland)
Nowakowski, Józef (1800-1865) (Poland)
Poldowski (Lady Dean Paul) (1880-1932) (Poland)
Seiber, Mátyás (1905-1960) (Hungary)
Smetana, Bedřich (1825-1884) (Czechoslovakia)
Syzmanowski, Karol* (1892-1937) (Poland)

FRENCH

Auric, Georges (1899-1983)
Bachelet, Alfred (1864-1944)
Berlioz, Hector* (1803-1869)
Bizet, Georges* (1838-1875)
Boulanger, Lili* (1893-1918)
Boulanger, Nadia (1887-1979)
Canteloube, Joseph (1879-1962)
Caplet, André (1879-1925)
Chabrier, Emmanuel* (1841-1894)
Chaminade Cécile* (1857-1944)
Chausson, Ernest* (1855-1899)
d'Indy, Vincent (1851-1931)
Debussy, Claude* (1862-1918)
Delage, Maurice (1879-1961)
Delibes, Léo (1836-1891)
Duparc, Henri* (1848-1933)
Dupont, Gabriel (1878-1914)
Durey, Louis (1888-1979)
Dutilleux, Henri (b. 1916)
Fauré, Gabriel* (1845-1924)
Françaix, Jean (1912-1997)
Franck, César* (1822-1890)
Gounod, Charles* (1818-1893)
Hahn, Reynaldo* (1874-1947)
Holmès, Augusta (1847-1903)
Honegger, Arthur (1892-1955)
Ibert, Jacques* (1890-1962)
Jolivet, André (1905-1974)
Koechlin, Charles (1867-1951)
Lalo, Edouard (1823-1892)
Leguerney, Jacques* (1906-1997)
Martin, Frank (1890-1974) (Switzerland)
Massenet, Jules (1842-1912)
Messiaen, Olivier (1908-1992)
Migot, Georges (1891-1976)
Milhaud, Darius* (1892-1974)
Pierné, Gabriel (1863-1937)
Poulenc, Francis* (1899-1963)
Ravel, Maurice* (1875-1937)
Rivier, Jean (1896-1987)
Rosenthal, Manuel (1904-2003)
Roussel, Albert* (1869-1937)
Saint-Saëns, Camille (1835-1921)
Satie, Erik* (1866-1925)

Sauguet, Henri (1901-1989)
Séverac, Déodat de (1842-1912)
Tailleferre, Germaine (1892-1983)
Viardot, Pauline* (1821-1910)
Vieu, Jane (1871-1955)

GERMAN

Arnim, Bettine von (1785-1859)
Bach, Johann Sebastian (1685-1750)
Beethoven, Ludwig van* (1770-1827)
Berg, Alban* (1885-1935) (Austria)
Brahms, Johannes* (1833-1897)
Cornelius, Peter (1824-1874)
Eisler, Hanns (1898-1962)
Franz, Robert* (1815-1892)
Haydn, Franz Joseph* (1732-1809) (Austria)
Hensel, Fanny Mendelssohn* (1805-1847)
Korngold, Erich* (1897-1957) (Austria; American
    citizenship 1943)
Lang, Josephine (1815-1880)
Liszt, Franz* (1811-1886) (Hungary)
Loewe, Johann Carl Gottfried* (1796-1869)
Mahler, Alma Schindler (1879-1964) (Austria)
Mahler, Gustav* (1860-1911) (Austria)
Marx, Joseph* (1882-1964) (Austria)
Mendelssohn, Felix* (1809-1847)
Mozart, Wolfgang Amadeus* (1756-1791) (Austria)
Pfitzner, Hans* (1869-1949)
Reger, Max (1873-1916)
Reichardt, Johann Friedrich (1752-1814)
Reichardt, Louise (1779-1825)
Schoeck, Othmar (1886-1957) (Switzerland)
Schoenberg, Arnold* (1874-1951) (Austria;
    American citizenship 1941)
Schröter, Corona (1751-1802)
Schubert, Franz* (1797-1828) (Austria)
Schumann, Clara* (1819-1896)
Schumann, Robert* (1810-1856)
Spohr, Louis (1784-1859)
Strauss, Richard* (1864-1949) (Austrian
    citizenship 1947)
Wagner, Richard* (1813-1883)
Webern, Anton (1883-1945) (Austria)
Weill, Kurt* (1900-1950) (American citizenship
    1943)
Wolf, Hugo* (1860-1903) (Austria)
Zelter, Carl (1758-1832)
Zemlinsky, Alexander von (1871-1942)
Zumsteeg, Johann (1760-1802)

ITALIAN

Alfano, Franco (1876-1954)
Arditi, Luigi (1822-1903)
Bellini, Vincenzo* (1801-1835)
Berio, Luciano* (1925-2003)
Bononcini, Giovanni (1672-1748)
Buzzi-Peccia, Arturo (1856-1943)
Caccini, Francesca (1587-1640?)
Caccini, Giulio* (c. 1546-1618)
Caldara, Antonio (1670-1736)
Carissimi, Giacomo (1605-1674)
Casella, Alfredo (1883-1947)

Castelnuovo-Tedesco, Mario* (1895-1968)
Cavalli, Francesco (1602-1676)
Cesti, Marc'Antonio (1623-1669)
Colbran, Isabella (1785-1845)
Cimara, Pietro* (1887-1967)
Dallapiccola, Luigi (1904-1975)
Davico, Vincenzo (1889-1969)
Donaudy, Stefano* (1879-1925)
Donizetti, Gaetano* (1797-1848)
Durante, Francesco* (1684-1755)
Falconieri, Andrea (1586-1656)
Ghedini, Giorgio Federico (1892-1965)
Giordani, Giuseppe (1744-1798)
Gluck, Christoph Willibald* (1714-1787)
    (German: listed under Italian for his
    contributions to Italian opera and vocal music)
Handel, George Frideric* (1685-1759)
    (German: listed under Italian for his
    contributions to Italian opera and vocal music)
Legrenzi, Giovanni (1626-1690)
Leoncavallo, Ruggiero (1858-1919)
Lotti, Antonio (1667-1740)
Malipiero, Gian Francesco (1882-1973)
Menotti, Gian Carlo (1911-2007)
Monteverdi, Claudio* (1567-1643)
Paisiello, Giovanni (1741-1816)
Pasquini, Bernardo (1637-1710)
Pergolesi, Giovanni Battista* (1710-1736)
Pizzetti, Ildebrando* (1880-1968)
Puccini, Giacomo (1858-1924)
Respighi, Ottorino* (1879-1936)
Righini, Vincenzo* (1756-1812)
Rosa, Salvator (1615-1673)
Rossini, Gioachino* (1792-1868)
Santoliquido, Francesco* (1883-1971)
Scarlatti, Alessandro* (1660-1725)
Stradella, Antonio (1645-1681)
Strozzi, Barbara* (c. 1619-1664)
Tosti, Francesco Paolo* (1846-1916)
Verdi, Giuseppe* (1813-1901)
Vivaldi, Antonio* (c. 1680-1741)
Wolf-Ferrari, Ermanno* (1876 -1948)

RUSSIAN

Arensky, Anton (1861-1906)
Balakirev, Mily (1837-1910)
Borodin, Aleksandr* (1833-1887)
Cui, César* (1835-1918)
Dargomyzhsky, Aleksandr (1813-1869)
Glazunov, Aleksandr (1865-1936)
Glière, Reinhold (1875-1956)
Glinka, Mikhail* (1804-1857)
Gretchaninov, Aleksandr (1864-1956)
Medtner, Nicholas (1880-1951)
Musorgsky, Modest* (1839-1881)
Prokofiev, Sergey* (1891-1953)
Rakhmaninov, Sergey* (1873-1943)
Rimsky-Korsakov, Nicolay* (1844-1908)
Rubinstein, Anton (1830-1894)
Shostakovich, Dmitry* (1906-1975)
Stravinsky, Igor* (1882-1971) (French citizenship
    1934; American citizenship 1945)
Sviridov, Georgii (1915-1998)
Tchaikovsky, Pyotr Il'ich* (1840-1893)

SCANDINAVIAN

Ahlström, Olof (1756-1838) (Sweden)
Alfvén, Hugo* (1872-1960) (Sweden)
Aulin, Tor (1866-1914) (Sweden)
De Frumerie, Gunnar (1908-1987) (Sweden)
Gade, Niels (1817-1890) (Denmark)
Grieg, Edvard* (1843-1907) (Norway)
Kilpinen, Yrjö* (1892-1959) (Finland)
Kjerulf, Halfdan (1815-1868) (Norway)
Lange-Müller, Peter (1850-1926) (Denmark)
Larsson, Lars-Erik (1908-1986) (Sweden)
Linde, Bo (1933-1970) (Sweden)
Lindblad, Adolf (1801-1878) (Sweden)
Nielsen, Carl* (1865-1931) (Denmark)
Nordqvist, Gustav (1886-1949) (Sweden)
Nystroem, Gösta (1890-1966) (Sweden)
Peterson-Berger, Wilhelm (1867-1942) (Sweden)
Rangström, Ture* (1884-1947) (Sweden)
Sibelius, Jean* (1865-1957) (Finland)
Sinding, Christian (1856-1941) (Norway)
Sjöberg, Carl (1861-1900) (Sweden)
Sjögren, Emil (1853-1918) (Sweden)
Söderman, August (1832-1876) (Sweden)
Stenhammar, Wilhelm* (1871-1927) (Sweden)
Voch Koch, Sigurd (1879-1910) (Sweden)

SOUTH AMERICAN

Braga, Francisco Ernani* (1868-1945) (Brazil)
Caamaño, Roberto (1923-1993) (Argentina)
Camps, Pompeyo (b. 1924) (Argentina)
Ginastera, Alberto* (1916-1983) (Argentina)
Guarnieri, Camargo (1907-1993) (Brazil)
Guastavino, Carlos* (1912-2000) (Argentina)
Orrego-Salas, Juan (b. 1919) (Chile)
Ovalle, Jaime (1894-1955) (Brazil)
Pedrell, Carlos (1878-1941) (Uruguay)
Plaza, Juan Bautista (1898-1964) (Venezuela)
Santa Cruz, Domingo (1899-1987) (Chile)
Sas, Andrés (1900-1967) (Peru)
Uribe-Holguín, Guillermo (1880-1971) (Colombia)
Villa-Lobos, Heitor* (1887-1959) (Brazil)

SPANISH

Albéniz, Isaac (1860-1909)
Dørumsgaard, Arne* (arr.) (1921-2006)
(Norwegian arranger, early Spanish songs)
Esplá, Oscar (1886-1976)
Esteve, Pablo (d. 1794)
Falla, Manuel de* (1876-1946)
García Lorca, Federico (1898-1936)
Gerhard, Roberto (1896-1970) (Catalán)
Granados, Enrique* (1867-1916)
Guridi, Jesús* (1886-1961)
Laserna, Blas de (1751-1816)
Malibran, Maria Felicitá (1808-1836)
Mompou, Frederic* (1893-1987)
Montsalvatge, Xavier* (1912-2002)
Nin, Joaquín* (1879-1949) (b. Cuba)
Nin-Culmell, Joaquín (1908-2004)
Obradors, Fernando* (1897-1945)
Plá, Manuel (d. 1766)
Rodrigo, Joaquín* (1901-1999)
Sor, Fernando (1778-1839)
Toldrá, Eduardo (1895-1962) (Catalán)
Turina, Joaquín* (1882-1949)
Valverde, Joaquín (1846-1910)
Vives, Amadeo (1871-1932) (Catalán)

Composers and Selected Works

Each annotated composer, song, or cycle is indicated by an asterisk.*

Albéniz, Isaac (1860-1909), Spanish
    Rimas de Bécquer
    Seis baládas italianas

Albert, Stephen (1941-1992), American
    Flower of the Mountain
    Into Eclipse
    To Wake the Dead
    Treestone

Alfano, Franco (1876-1954), Italian
    Tre poemi di Rabindranath Tagore

Alfvén, Hugo* (1872-1960), Swedish   *489*
    Jag kysser din vita hand
    Så tag mit hjerte*
    Skogen sover*

Alwyn, William (1905-1985), British
    Invocations
    Leavetaking, A
    Mirages

Anchieta, Juan de* (1462-1523), Spanish   *496*
    Con amores, la mi madre*

Archer, Violet (1913-2000), Canadian
    Moon Songs (V. Lindsay)
    Under the Sun

Arditi, Luigi (1822-1903), Italian
    Il bacio

Argento, Dominick* (b. 1927), American   *311*
    Andrée Expedition, The
    Casa Guidi
    *From the Diary of Virginia Woolf**
    Letters from Composers (high voice, guitar)
    Miss Manners on Music
    *Six Elizabethan Songs**
    songs about spring
    To Be Sung Upon the Water
    (high voice, clarinet, piano)

Arne, Dr. Thomas Augustine (1710-1778),
  British
    Lass With the Delicate Air, The
    On a day, alack the day
    Soldier Tir'd of War's Alarms

Auric, Georges (1899-1983), French
    Huit poèmes de Jean Cocteau
    Trois poèmes de Léon-Paul Fargue
    Trois poèmes de Louise de Vilmorin
    Trois poèmes de Max Jacob

Babbitt, Milton (b. 1916), American
    Head of the Bed, The
    Philomel
    Three Theatrical Songs
    Two Sonnets
    Virginal Book, The
    Vision and Prayer

Bach, Johann Sebastian (1685-1750), German
    Bist du bei mir
    Komm, süsser Tod
    Meine Seele, lass es geben

Bachelet, Alfred (1864-1944), French
    Chére nuit

Bacon, Ernst* (1898-1990), American   *269*
    Five Poems of Emily Dickinson
    Fond Affection*
    It's All I Have to Bring*
    Lingering Last Drops
    Omaha*
    One Thought Ever at the Fore*
    Quiet Airs
    To Make a Prairie*

Baley, Virko (b. 1938), American
    Journey After Loves
    Klytemnestra
    Poems of Emily Dickinson, Books I, II, III
    Two Poems in the Olden Style

Barber, Samuel* (1910-1981), American   *283*
    Bessie Bobtail
    Daisies, The
    Despite and Still, Op. 41
    Dover Beach, Op. 31
    Green Lowland of Pianos, A*
    *Hermit Songs**
    I Hear An Army*
    Knoxville: Summer of 1915
    Mélodies passagères
    Monks and Raisins
    Nocturne
    Nun takes the veil, A
    O boundless, boundless evening*
    Queen's face on the summery coin, The
    Rain has fallen*
    Secrets of the Old, The*
    Sleep now
    Sure on this Shining Night*
    With rue my heart is laden

Ginastera, Alberto* (1916-1983)   *522*
South American (Argentina)
Canción a la luna lunanca
Cancíon al árbol del olvido*
Cinco canciones populares argentinas*
Las horas de una estancia
Milena
Serenata

Giordani, Giuseppe (1744-1798), Italian
Caro mio ben

Glinka, Mikhail* (1804-1857), Russian   *448*
Somnenie*
V krovi gorit ogon' zhelan'ya*
Ya pomnyu chudnoye mgnoven'ye*

Gluck, Christoph Willibald* (1714-1787),   *422*
in Italian section
Die frühen Gräber
Der Jüngling
Die Neigung
O del mio dolce ardor*
Ode an den Tod
Die Sommernacht
Spiagge amate

Gordon, Ricky Ian (b. 1956), American
Afternoon on a Hill
Air
Coyotes
My Sister's New Red Hat
Once I Was
Will There Really Be A Morning

Gounod, Charles* (1818-1893), French   *162*
L'Absent*
Au rossignol
Biondina
Chanson de printemps
Chant d'automne
Envoi de fleurs
Fountain mingles with the river, The
If thou art sleeping, maiden
Mignon
My true love hath my heart
O ma belle rebelle*
Où voulez-vouz aller?
Rêverie
Sérénade*
Le Temps des roses
Le Vallon
Venise*
Viens, les gazons sont verts*

Grainger, Percy (1882-1961), British
Folk Song Arrangements

Granados, Enrique* (1867-1916), Spanish   *499*
Amor y odio*
Canciones amatorias
Las Currutacas modestas
La maja dolorosa (Nos. 1, 2, and 3)*
La Maja y el ruiseñor
El majo discreto*
El majo olvidado
El mirar de la maja*
El tra la la y el punteado*

Grieg, Edvard* (1843-1907), Norwegian   *477*
Forårsregn (Frühlingsregen)
Fra Monte Pincio
Gruss
Haugtussa*
Jeg elsker dig*
Med en primula veris
Med en vandlilje*
Mens jeg venter (Derweil ich warte)
Solveig's Sang
En svane*
To brune øjne*
Ein Traum
Våren*
Die verschwiegene Nachtigall
Zur Rosenzeit

Griffes, Charles* (1884-1920), American   *263*
Auf geheimem Waldespfade*
Auf ihrem Grab
Fountain of the Acqua Paola, The
Half-ring Moon, The
Lament of Ian the Proud*
Meeres Stille
Mein Herz ist wie die dunkle Nacht
Phantoms
Pierrot
Rose of the Night, The
Song of the Dagger
Symphony in Yellow*
Tears
Thy Dark Eyes to Mine
Two Birds Flew into the Sunset Glow
Vale of Dreams, The
We'll to the Woods, and Gather May

Guarnieri, Camargo (1907-1993),
South American (Brazil)
Canções de Amor

Guastavino, Carlos* (1912-2000),   *524*
South American (Argentina)
Abismo de Sed
Bonita rama de Sauce*
Cuatro Canciones Coloniales
Desde que te conocí
El Sampedrino
Encantamiento
Hermano*
Mi garganta
Mi viña de Chapanay
Milonga de dos hermanos*
Nana
La Palominta
Pampa sola
Pampamapa*
Pueblito, mi pueblo
Romance de José Cubas
La rosa y el sauce*
Se equivocó la paloma*
Viniendo de Chilecito*

Guridi, Jesús* (1886-1961), Spanish   *511*
Seis canciones castellanas*

Epipalinodie*
Invocation
Je me lamente
Je vous envoie
Ma douce jouvence est passée*
La Nuit
Le Paresseux
*Le Paysage ou La Description de Port-Royal
des Champs*
Le Présent
Sept poèmes de François Maynard
Sérénade d'un Barbon
La Solitude
Sonnet pour Hélène
Le Vallon

Lekberg, Sven (1900-1984), Swedish
Four Poems of Edna St. Vincent Millay

Leoncavallo, Ruggiero (1858-1919), Italian
Mattinata

Linde, Bo (1933-1970), Swedish
Den ängen där du kysste mig
Äppelträd och päronträd
Är jag intill döden trött
Tag mig

Linley, William (1771-1835), British
Lawn, as white as driven snow
No flower that blows
O, bid your faithful Ariel fly

Liszt, Franz* (1811-1886), in German section   *94*
Comment, disaient-ils
Die drei Zigeuner*
Du bist wie eine Blume
Es muss ein Wunderbares sein*
Freudvoll und leidvoll*
Ihr Glocken von Marling*
Kennst du das Land
Der König von Thule
Oh! quand je dors*
S'il est un charmant gazon
Tre Sonetti di Petrarca
Das Veilchen
Vergiftet sind meine Lieder
Wanderers Nachtlied

Loeffler, Charles Martin (1861-1935), American
Dream within a Dream, A
To Helen

Loewe, Johann Carl Gottfried* (1796-1869),   *49*
German
Archibald Douglas
Edward*
Elvershöh
Erlkönig*
Frauenliebe
Herr Oluf*
Hinkende Jamben
Der Mohrenfürst auf der Messe
Der Mummelsee
Der Nöck
Odins Meeresritt
Tom der Reimer
Der wandelnde Glocke
Wanderers Nachtlied

Lotti, Antonio (1667-1740), Italian
Pur dicesti, o bocca bella

MacDowell, Edward (1861-1908), American
Sea, The
Thy Beaming Eyes
To a Wild Rose

Maconchy, Elizabeth (1907-1994), British
Shakespeare Songs
Three Donne Songs

Mahler, Alma Schindler (1879-1964), German
(Austria)
Bei ihr ist es Traut
Ich wandle unter Blumen
Laue Sommernacht
Die stille Stadt
Waldseligkeit

Mahler, Gustav* (1860-1911),   *127*
German (Austria)
Ablösung im Sommer
Erinnerung
Hans und Grete
Ich atmet' einen linden Duft'*
Ich bin der Welt abhanden gekommen*
Das irdische Leben*
Kindertotenlieder
Liebst du um Schönheit*
Das Lied von der Erde
Lieder aus 'Des Knaben Wunderhorn'
Lieder eines fahrenden gesellen
Scheiden und Meiden
Selbstgefühl
Wer hat dies Liedlein erdacht?*

Malipiero, Gian Franco (1882-1973), Italian
Ballata
I sonetti delle fate
Quattro Sonetti del Burchiello

Martin, Frank (1890-1974), Swiss
Quatre Sonnets à Cassandre

Marx, Joseph* (1882-1964),   *142*
German (Austria)
Am Fenster*
Die Begegnung
Bitte
Die Elfe
Hat dich die Liebe berührt
Jugend und Altger
Maienblüten
Marienlied
Nocturne*
Pierrot Dandy
Regen*
Schliesse mir die Augen beide
Selige Nacht
Ständchen
Valse de Chopin*
Die Verslassene
Waldseligkeit
Wanderers Nachtlied

Massenet, Jules (1842-1912), French
Elégie
Nuit d'espagne
Ouvre tes yeux bleus
Que l'heure est donc brève

*Le Travail du peintre**
Trois poèmes de Louise de Vilmorin
Tu vois le feu du soir

Powell, Mel (1923-1998), American
Little Companion Pieces
Settings
Strand Settings
Two Prayer Settings
Die Violine

Previn, André (b. 1929), American
Friday Night in the Royal Station Hotel
Morning Has Spread Again
Sallie Chisum Remembers Billy the Kid
Vocalise

Prokofiev, Sergey* (1891-1953), Russian   466
Five Mélodies
Five Poems
Gadky utyonok, Op. 18*
Poems by Anna Akhmatova
Russian Songs, Op. 104
Three Children's Songs
Three Romances, Op. 73*

Puccini, Giacomo (1858-1924), Italian
A te
Canto d'anime
E l'uccellino
Sole e amore
Terra e mare

Purcell, Henry* (1659-1695), British   357
Ah, how sweet it is to love
Bess of Bedlam
Evening Hymn, An
Fairest Isle
Fatal hour comes on apace, The
Hark! Hark! the Echoing Air*
I Attempt from Love's Sickness to Fly
If music be the food of love*
I'll Sail Upon the Dog Star*
Knotting Song, The
Let the dreadful engines
Music for a while*
Oh! Lead Me to Some Peaceful Gloom
One charming night
Since from my dear Astrea's sight
Sweeter than Roses*
There's not a swain on the plain
We sing to Him
What can we poor females do?

Quilter, Roger* (1877-1953), British   367
Arnold Book of Old Songs, The
Blow, blow, thou winter wind
Bracelet, The
Brown is my love
By a fountainside
Cherry ripe
Come away, death
Constant lover, The
Damask roses
Daybreak
Dream Valley
Fair House of Joy*
Faithless shepherdess, The
Fear no more the heat of the sun
Fuschia tree, The

Go, Lovely Rose*
Hey, ho, the wind and the rain
I arise from dreams of thee
It was a lover and his lass
Julia's hair
Love's Philosophy*
Maiden blush, The
My life's delight
Night piece, The
Now Sleeps the Crimson Petal*
O Mistress Mine*
Orpheus with his lute
Take, O take those lips away
To daisies
Under the greenwood tree
Weep you no more, sad fountains
When icicles hang by the wall
Wild flower's song, The

Rakhmaninov, Sergey* (1873-1943),   463
Russian
K detyan*
Ne poy, krasavitsa pri mne*
Siren'*
Son*
Uzh ty, niva moya*
Vesenniya vody*
Vocaliz*
Zdes' khorosho*

Rands, Bernard (b. 1934), British
(American citizenship 1983)
Ballad 1
Ballad 2
Ballad 3
Canti del sole
Canti lunatici
Déjà
Der Nachsommer
Serena
Walcott Songs

Rangström, Ture* (1884-1947), Swedish   490
Afskedet*
Bön till natten
Den enda stunden
Flickan under nymånen
Gammalsvenskt
Melodi*
Pan
Serenad*
Villemo
Vingar I natten*

Ravel, Maurice* (1875-1937), French   212
Chansons madécasses
*Cinq mélodies populaires grecques**
Deux mélodies hébraïques
*Don Quichotte à Dulcinée**
*Histoires naturelles**
Sainte*
Shéhérazade
Sur l'herbe*
Trois poèmes de Stéphane Mallarmé
Vocalise en forme de habanera

Reger, Max (1873-1916), German
Maria's Wiegenlied

Heimkehr
Ich trage meine Minne
Ich wollt ein Sträusslein binden
Kling!
Meinem Kinde
Morgen!*
Die Nacht*
Ophelien Lieder
Ruhe, meine Seele
Säusle, liebe Myrte!
Schlagende Herzen
Schlechtes Wetter*
Ständchen*
Traum durch die Dämmerung
Vier letzte Lieder
Wie sollten wir geheim sie halten
Die Zeitlose
Zueignung*

Stravinsky, Igor* (1882-1971), Russian   *468*
(French citizenship 1934;
American citizenship 1945)
Berceuses du chat*
Elegy for J.F.K.
Le faune et la bergère
Four Russian Songs. 1918
Four Russian Songs. 1954
In Memoriam Dylan Thomas
Pastorale*
Pribaoutki
Three Japanese Lyrics
Three Songs from William Shakespeare*
Two Poems by Verlaine
Two Poems of Konstantin Balmont*

Strozzi, Barbara* (1619-1664), Italian   *412*
Amor, non dormir pìu*
Amore è bandito
Che si può fare?
Gite, o giorni dolenti
Lagrime mie
Non pavento io non di te*
Rissolvetevi pensieri
Soccorrete, luci avare
Spesso per entro al petto*
Tradimento!*
Voglio morire

Sviridov, Georgi (1915-1998), Russian
Blown by the Wind from Afar
Moscow Morning
Silvery Road, Where are You Leading Me
Spring

Szymanowski, Karol* (1882-1937), Polish   *539*
Bünte Lieder
Des Hafis Liebeslieder
Four Songs
Kurpian Songs
Lonely Moon
Seven Songs to Poems by James Joyce
Soldiers' Songs
Songs of the Fairy Princess
Songs of the Infatuated Muezzin
Swan, The
Three Fragments from Poems by Jan Kasprowicz
Three Lullabies
Vocalise-étude

Tailleferre, Germaine (1892-1983), French
Six chansons françaises

Tchaikovsky, Piotr Il'ich* (1840-1893),   *457*
Russian
Net, tol'ka tot, kto znal*
Rastvoril ya okno*
Serenada Don-Zhuana*
Sred' shumnogo bala*
To bylo ranneyu vesnoy*
Ya li v pole da ne travushka byla*
Zakatilas' solntse*

Thiman, Eric (1900-1975), British
I Love All Graceful Things

Thompson, Randall (1899-1984), American
Velvet Shoes

Thomson, Virgil* (1896-1989), American   *266*
At the Spring
La Belle en dormant
Berceau de Gertrude Stein
English Usage
Five Songs from William Blake
Four Songs of Thomas Campion
If Thou a Reason Dost Desire to Know*
My Crow Pluto
Old English Songs
Praises and Prayers
Prayer to St. Catherine, A*
Preciosilla
Sigh no more, ladies*
Take, o take those lips away*
Tiger, The

Tippett, Michael (1905-1998), British
Songs for Ariel

Toldrá, Eduardo (1895-1962), Spanish (Catalán)
A l'ombra del lledoner
Anacreòntica
As froliñas dos toxos
Cançó de passar cantant
Canticel
Festeig
Seis canciones

Torre, Francisco de la* (fl. 1485-1504),   *497*
Spanish
Pámpano verde*

Tosti, Francesco* (1846-1916), Italian   *434*
A Vucella
Addio! (Goodbye)
L'alba sepaera dalla luce l'ombra
Aprile
Ave Maria
E Morto Pulcinella
Ideale*
Lamento d'Amore
Luna d'estate
Malìa*
Non mi guardere
Non t'amo più
Quel di!
La serenata*
Serenata d'un angelo
L'Ultima canzone

Walton, William (1902-1983), British
 Daphne
 Old Sir Faulk
 Through gilded trellises

Warlock, Peter (Heseltine)* (1894-1930), *382*
British
 As ever I saw
 Balulalow
 Bayly Berith the Bell Away, The
 Bethlehem Down
 Captain Stratton's Fancy
 Contented lover, The
 Curlew, The
 Fox, The
 Good ale
 Ha'nacker mill
 Jillian of Berry*
 Lilligay
 Love for Love
 Lover's maze, The
 Mourn no Moe
 My Own Country*
 Piggésnie
 Pretty Ring Time*
 Rest sweet nymphs*
 Robin Goodfellow
 Roister Doister
 Sigh no more, ladies
 Sleep*
 Spring
 Sweet and twenty
 Take, o take those lips away
 The First Mercy
 Twelve Oxen
 Wind from the West, The
 Yarmouth Fair

Webern, Anton (1883-1945), German (Austria)
 Eight Early Songs
 Five Songs, Op. 3
 Four Songs, Op. 4
 Four Songs, Op. 12

Weill, Kurt* (1900-1950), German *150*
(American citizenship 1943)
 Ballad of Sexual Dependency
  (*Threepenny Opera*)
 Berlin im Licht-Song*
 Complainte de la Seine
 Les Filles de Bordeaux
 Frauentanz
 J'attends un navire
 Je ne t'aime pas
 Lonely House* (*Street Scene*)
 Lost in the Stars
 Die Muschel von Margate
 My Ship* (*Lady in the Dark*)
 Nanna's Lied*
 Ofrah's Lieder
 Pirate Jenny
 Le Roi d'Acquitaine
 September Song
 Sing Me Not a Ballad
 Somehow I Never Could Believe
  (*Street Scene*)
 Speak Low (*One Touch of Venus*)*
 Stay Well

 Surabaya Johnny (*Happy End)*
 The Saga of Jenny
 Three Walt Whitman Songs
 Und was bekam des Soldaten Weib?
 What Good Would the Moon Be? (*Street Scene*)
 Youkali: Tango Habanera*

Weir, Judith (b. 1954), British
 King Harald's Saga

Willan, Healey (1880-1968), Canadian
 Chansons Canadiennes (2 vols.)
 Drake's Drum
 Music, when soft voices die
 O Mistress Mine
 Oh Death! Thou Art the Colling Night

Wolf, Hugo* (1860-1903), German (Austria) *111*
 Ach, des Knaben Augen...(*Spanisches*
  Liederbuch)
 Agnes (*Möricke Lieder*)
 An eine Aolsharfe (*Möricke Lieder*)
 Anakreons Grab* (*Goethe Lieder*)
 Auch kleine Dinge...* (*Italienisches*
  Liederbuch)
 Auf eine Christblume I and II (*Möricke Lieder*)
 Auf ein altes Bild* (*Möricke Lieder*)
 Bedeckt mich mit Blumen* (*Spanisches*
  Liederbuch)
 Begegnung* (*Möricke Lieder*)
 Cophtisches Lied I and I (*Goethe Lieder*)
 Du sagst mir... (*Italienisches Liederbuch*)
 Ein Stündlein wohl vor Tag (*Möricke Lieder*)
 Elfenlied* (*Möricke Lieder*)
 Er ist's* (*Möricke Lieder*)
 Erwartung (*Eichendorff Lieder*)
 Der Feuerreiter (*Möricke Lieder*)
 Fussreise (*Möricke Lieder*)
 Ganymed (*Goethe Lieder*)
 Der Gärtner* (*Möricke Lieder*)
 Geh, Geliebter, geh jetzt* (*Spanisches*
  Liederbuch)
 Gesang Weylas (*Möricke Lieder*)
 Gleich und Gleich (*Goethe Lieder*)
 Harfenspieler I* (*Goethe Lieder*)
 Harfenspieler I, II, III (*Goethe Lieder*)
 Heb' auf dein blondes Haupt... (*Italienisches*
  Liederbuch)
 Heimweh (*Eichendorff Lieder*)
 Herr, was trägt der Boden hier* (*Spanisches*
  Liederbuch)
 Heut nacht erhob ich mich...* (*Italienisches*
  Liederbuch)
 Ich esse nun mein Brot... (*Italienisches*
  Liederbuch)
 Ich hab in Penna...* (*Italienisches*
  Liederbuch)
 Ihr jungen Leute (*Italienisches Liederbuch*)
 In dem Schatten meiner Locken*
  (*Spanisches Liederbuch*)
 In der Frühe (*Möricke Lieder*)
 Kennst du das Land* (*Goethe Lieder*)
 Kling klinge, mein Pandero (*Spanisches*
  Liederbuch)
 Der Knabe und das Immlein (*Möricke Lieder*)
 Mausfallen-Sprüchlein
 Mein Liebster hat zu Tische... (*Italienisches*
  Liederbuch)

Mein Liebster ist so klein... (*Italienisches Liederbuch*)
Mein Liebster singt...* (*Italienisches Liederbuch*)
Mögen alle bösen Zungen... (*Spanisches Liederbuch*)
Morgentau
Mühvoll komm ich und beladen... (*Spanisches Liederbuch*)
Der Musikant* (*Eichendorff Lieder*)
Nachtzauber* (*Eichendorff Lieder*)
Nein, junger Herr... (*Italienisches Liederbuch*)
Nimmersatte Liebe* (*Möricke Lieder*)
Nixe Binsefuss (*Möricke Lieder*)
Nun lass uns Frieden schliessen...* (*Italienisches Liederbuch*)
Nun wandre, Maria* (*Spanisches Liederbuch*)
Prometheus (*Goethe Lieder*)
Der Rattenfänger* (*Goethe Lieder*)
Sagt, seid ihr es, feiner Herr... (*Spanisches Liederbuch)*
Schweig einmal still... (*Italienisches Liederbuch)*
Sie blasen zum Abmarsch (*Spanisches Liederbuch*)
Die Spröde* (*Goethe Lieder*)
Das Ständchen (*Eichendorff Lieder*)
Sterb' ich, so hüllt in Blumen... (*Italienisches Liederbuch*)
Storchenbotschaft (*Möricke Lieder*)
Der Tambour (*Möricke Lieder*)
Trau nicht der Liebe... (*Spanisches Liederbuch*)
Um Mitternacht (*Möricke Lieder*)
Verborgenheit* (*Möricke Lieder*)
Das verlassene Mägdlein* (*Möricke Lieder*)
Verschwiegene Liebe* (*Eichendorff Lieder*)
Wenn du mich mit den Augen streifst... (*Italienisches Liederbuch*)

Wenn du zu den Blumen gehst (*Spanisches Liederbuch*)
Wer rief dich denn... (*Italienisches Liederbuch*)
Wie glänzt der helle Mond (*Keller Songs*)
Wie lange schon...* (*Italienisches Liederbuch*)
Wiegenlied im Sommer
Die Zigeunerin* (*Eichendorff Lieder*)
Zitronenfalter im April (*Möricke Lieder*)

Wolf-Ferrari, Ermanno* (1876-1948),   *435*
Italian
Quattro Rispetti, Op. 11*

Zaimont, Judith Lang* (b. 1945),   *325*
American
Ages of Love, The
Chansons Nobles et Sentimentales
Chant
Coronach
Four Songs
From the Great Land: Women's Songs
Greyed Sonnets*
In the Theatre of Night: Dream Songs on Poems by Karl Shapiro
Magic World, The
New-fashioned Songs*
Solemn music, A
Two Songs for Soprano and Harp
Vessels—Rhapsody for Mezzo and Piano
Will's Words
Woman of Valor, A

Zemlinsky, Alexander von (1871-1942), German
Das bucklichte Männlein
Elend
Harlem Tänzerin

Zwilich, Ellen Taafe (b. 1939), American
Einsame Nacht

Selected Bibliography

This bibliography is by no means exhaustive. General references are provided by national area; books that contain informative material on interpretation are also included. Selected diction books treating specific areas of song literature also appear. Books treating the work of more than one composer are listed by national area. Books, journal articles, and dissertations dealing specifically with a single composer's songs may be found listed in the "Selected Reading" at the end of that composer's section. Readers are also directed to explore general search engines and composers' websites on the Internet.

Since new vocal literature is being added to the repertoire yearly, readers should note that surveys of literature are only as current as their publication date.

GENERAL REFERENCES

Kurt Adler. *The Art of Accompanying and Coaching.* (University of Minnesota, 1965). Thorough discussion of style, diction, interpretation from the coach/pianist's point of view.

Alan Blyth, ed., *Song on Record* (New York: Cambridge University Press, 1986-1988). Two volume set of essays reviewing recordings of song. Volume 1 deals with German *Lieder,* Volume 2 contains French *mélodie,* Spanish, Scandinavian, British, and American song.

Berton Coffin, ed., *Singer's Repertoire.* Second edition (New York: The Scarecrow Press, 1960-62). In five volumes. Volume 1: Coloratura Soprano, Lyric Soprano and Dramatic Soprano; Volume 2: Mezzo Soprano and Contralto; Volume 3: Lyric Tenor and Dramatic Tenor; Volume 4: Baritone and Bass. Song lists suited for each listed voice, categorized by arbitrary categories.

____, and Werner Singer, eds., *Singer's Repertoire.* Second edition (New York: Scarecrow Press, 1962). Volume 5 in the series: Program Notes for the Singer's Repertoire. Sketchy paraphrases of selected song literature for use in programs.

Shirlee Emmons and Stanley Sonntag, *The Art of the Song Recital* (New York: Schirmer Books, 1979). Excellent reference covering all facets of the song recital including program building, musical resources and research. Extensive appendix of repertoire lists.

____, and Wilbur Watkin Lewis, *Researching the Song: A Lexicon* (New York: Oxford University Press, 2006). More than 2,000 entries supply information on most of the mythological, historical, geographical, and literary references contained in western art song. Brief biographies of poets, composers who set their poems, synopses of major works from which song texts were taken.

Noni Espina, *Repertoire for the Solo Voice* (Metuchen, NJ.: Scarecrow Press, 1977). Extensive, two-volume reference of works for solo voice with annotations, covering material from the thirteenth century to the present.

H. Plunket Greene, *Interpretation in Song* (New York: Da Capo Press, 1979).

James H. Hall, *The Art Song* (Norman, Oklahoma: University of Oklahoma Press, 1953). General survey of French, German, English song. Selected songs discussed.

Donald Ivey, *Song: Anatomy, Imagery, and Styles* (New York: Free Press, 1970). A study of the component elements of song. Also covers principal style elements of representative composers in a compact but informative history of song.

Diane Peacock Jezic, *Women Composers: The Lost Tradition Found* (New York: The Feminist Press, 1988).

Sergius Kagen, *Music for the Voice* (Bloomington, Indiana: University of Indiana Press, 1968, rev.). Provides an annotated listing of available songs, airs, operatic excerpts and folk songs from the seventeenth century to 1968. Entries are arranged by composer and list song titles, general style and form of each song, tessitura and compass, problems of execution for singer and accompanist, available editions and recommended translations and transpositions.

Lotte Lehmann, *More Than Singing: The Interpretation of Songs* (Westport: Greenwood Press, 1975).

____, *Eighteen Song Cycles: Studies and Their Interpretation* (New York: Praeger, 1972). Lehmann's highly personalized comments on interpretation of eighteen selected French and German song cycles.

Carol McClintock, ed., *The Solo Song: 1580-1730* (New York: W.W. Norton, 1973). Selected English, French, German, Italian songs of the Renaissance-Baroque periods. Contains important introductory chapter on performance practices.

Barbara Meister, *An Introduction to the Art Song* (New York: Taplinger Publishing Co., 1980). A general overview of the genre.

____, *Art Song: The Marriage of Music and Poetry* (Wakefield, NH: Hollowbrook Publishing, 1992). Selected song literature is examined as to the fusion of poetic and musical elements.

Philip Miller, ed., *The Ring of Words: An Anthology of Song Texts* (New York: Doubleday & Company, Inc., 1962). An anthology of selected poetry set by major composers of song, arranged by poet.

Gerald Moore, *Singer and Accompanist: The Performance of Fifty Songs* (Westport, CT: Greenwood Press, 1975). The noted accompanist-coach provides performance notes for fifty selected songs. Written from a pianist's viewpoint.

Charles Osborne, *The Concert Song Companion* (New York: Da Capo Press, 1974). The art song 1650-1950, according to language and country.

Julie Anne Sadie and Rhian Samuel, eds. *Norton / Grove Dictionary of Women Composers* (New York: W.W. Norton, 1994).

Douglass Seaton, *The Art Song: A Research and Information Guide* (New York: Garland Publishing Co., 1987).

Denis Stevens, *A History of Song* (London: Hutchinson Company, 1960). [Also published in paperback by W.W. Norton.] Comprehensive narrative of the history of the genre from the *troubadours* to the twentieth century.

Miriam Stewart-Green, *Women Composers: A Checklist of Works for Solo Voice* (Boston: G.K. Hall, 1980). Listing of 3,746 composers. Song titles, sources for obtaining performance materials. Separate listings for operas, oratorios, cycles, vocal works with instruments, and dramatic scenes.

James Winn, *Unsuspected Eloquence: A History of the Relations between Poetry and Music* (New Haven: Yale University Press, 1981).

GERMAN LIEDER

Elaine Brody and Robert Fowkes, *The German Lied and Its Poetry* (New York: New York University Press, 1971). A study of selected nineteenth-century *Lieder* from Mozart through Berg, from the standpoint of poetry and text setting.

Dietrich Fischer-Dieskau, *The Fischer-Dieskau Book of Lieder* (New York: Limelight Editions, 1984). English trans. by George Bird and Richard Stokes. Texts and translations for over 750 songs by every major composer of *Lieder*.

Lorraine Gorrell, *The Nineteenth-Century German Lied* (Portland, Oregon: Amadeus Press, 1993). In-depth discussion of the *Lieder* of Schubert, Schumann, Brahms, Wolf as well as lesser-known composers of the period. Examines social and literary factors that impacted the development of the *Lied* as a genre.

Rufus E. Hallmark, ed., *Nineteenth-Century German Lieder* (New York: Schirmer Books, 1995). Collection of essays by prominent scholars on representative works by major composers, discussing styles, forms, and poetry that characterize their *Lieder*.

Anneliese Landau, *The Lied: The Unfolding of Its Style* (Washington, DC: University Press of America, Inc., 1980). General introduction to the genre.

Marie-Thérèse Paquin, *Ten Cycles of Lieder* (Montreal: University of Montreal Press, 1977). Translations (poetic and word-for-word) of ten selected cycles by Beethoven, Brahms, Mahler, Schubert, and Schumann.

Lois Phillips, *Lieder Line by Line* (New York: Charles Scribner's Sons, 1980). Word-for-word and poetic translations of selected *Lieder* of Beethoven, Schubert, Schumann, Wagner, Brahms, Wolf, Mahler, and Strauss.

S.S. Prawer, ed., *The Penguin Book of Lieder* (Baltimore: Penguin Books, 1964). Contains selected texts and translations of important *Lieder* composers with brief biographical notes.

Charles Rosen, *The Romantic Generation* (Cambridge: Harvard University Press, 1995). A thorough exploration of the musical language, styles, and spirit of the Romantic period. See especially Chapter 3: "Mountains and Song Cycles."

Aksel Schiøtz, *The Singer and His Art* (New York: Harper & Row, 1970). Last section of the book is a discussion of *Winterreise* and *Die schöne Müllerin* with Schiøtz's suggestions for interpretation.

Elisabeth Schumann, *German Song* (New York: Chanticleer Press, 1948).

J.W. Smeed, *German Song and Its Poetry* 1740-1900 (London: Croon Helm, 1987).

Lawrence D. Snyder, *German Poetry in Song* (Berkeley, CA: Fallen Leaf Press, 1995). Indexes 9,800 *Lieder* composed after 1770, and the poetry from which composers drew their inspiration.

Jack M. Stein, *Poem and Music in the German Lied from Gluck to Hugo Wolf* (Cambridge: Harvard University Press, 1971). A study of the fusion of poetry and music in the songs of Schubert, Schumann, Brahms, and Wolf and the evolution of the German *Lied* between 1750-1900.

Kenneth S. Whitton, *Lieder: An Introduction to German Song* (New York: Franklin Watts, 1984).

FRENCH MÉLODIE

Betty Bannerman, ed. and trans., *The Singer as Interpreter: Claire Croiza's Master Classes* (London: Victor Gollancz, Ltd., 1989). Notes from the master classes of Claire Croiza, concerning the art of singing and interpretation, with particular reference to the composers for whom she had been a chosen interpreter.

Pierre Bernac, *The Interpretation of French Song* (New York: W.W. Norton, 1978). Classic acclaimed reference to French song study. Texts of 200 selected songs, with translations, indicated liaisons and elisions, and suggestions for performance.

Elaine Brody, *Paris: The Musical Kaleidoscope,* 1870-1925 (New York: George Braziller, 1987). A fascinating panorama of the movements, people and works that flourished in the cultural ferment of Paris during the decades of the Great Expositions.

Laurence Davies, *The Gallic Muse* (New York: A.S. Barnes, 1967). Biographical sketches and discussion of the songs of Fauré, Duparc, Debussy, Satie, Ravel, and Poulenc.

Thomas Grubb, *Singing in French.* Second edition (New York: Schirmer Books, 1990). A definitive guide to French diction for singers, accompanists, and coaches. Contains an excellent repertoire list of *mélodies* and arias.

David Hunter, *Understanding French Verse: A Guide for Singers* (New York: Oxford University Press, 2005). Covers the basics of French versification, using examples drawn from a wide range of well-known song settings.

Timothy LeVan, *Masters of the French Art Song* (Metuchen, NJ: Scarecrow Press, 1991). Texts and translations of the complete songs of Chausson, Debussy, Duparc, Fauré and Ravel.

Barbara Meister, *Nineteenth-Century French Song* (Bloomington: Indiana University Press, 1980). Discussion of every published song by Fauré, Chausson, Debussy, and Duparc from the standpoint of text setting and noteworthy musical elements. All texts and translations.

Frits Noske, *French Song from Berlioz to Duparc* (New York: Dover, 1970). A study of nineteenth-century French song. Analysis of the *mélodies* of Berlioz, Liszt, Gounod, Bizet, Delibes, Massenet, Saint-Saëns, Lalo, Franck, Fauré, Duparc, and others.

Charles Panzéra, *Fifty Mélodies Françaises* (Brussels: Schott Frères, 1964). Brief lessons in style and interpretation from one of France's major singers.

Nancy Perloff, *Art and the Everyday: The Impact of Parisian Popular Entertainment on Satie, Milhaud, Poulenc, and Auric* (New York: Oxford University Press, 1991).

Roger Shattuck, *The Banquet Years: the origin of the avant-garde in France 1885 to World War I* (New York: Vintage Books, 1968). Excellent discussion of the arts in France during this period. Chapters on Rousseau, Satie, Jarry, and Apollinaire.

ENGLISH SONG

Stephen Banfield, *Sensibility and English Song: Critical Studies of the Early 20th Century* (New York: Cambridge University Press, 1985). Two volumes examining British song and its composers. Volume 2 contains extensive song lists by composer.

Edward Doughtie, *English Renaissance Song* (Boston: Twayne Publishers, 1986).

Philip Heseltine (Peter Warlock), *The English Ayre* (Westport: Greenwood Press, 1926).

Trevor Hold, *Parry to Finzi: Twenty English Song-Composers* (Woodbridge: The Boydell Press, 2002).

Elise B. Jorgens, *The Well-tun'd Word: Musical Interpretations of English Poetry 1597-1651* (Minneapolis: University of Minnesota Press, 1982). The relation of text to music in songs by England's lutenists.

Sydney Northcote, *Byrd to Britten: A Survey of English Song* (New York: Roy Publishers, Inc., 1966).

Michael Pilkington, *Gurney, Ireland, Quilter, and Warlock* (Bloomington: Indiana University Press, 1989). Covers all songs (in print or not) of these four composers, giving ranges, voice types, comments, specific technical problems, publishers.

____, *Campion, Dowland, and the Lutenist Songwriters* (Bloomington: Indiana University Press, 1989).

Stephen Ratcliffe, *Campion: On Song* (Boston: Routledge and Kegan Paul, 1981). An investigation of Campion's songs with style and poetic analysis.

Louise Schleiner, *The Living Lyre in English Verse from Elizabeth through the Restoration* (Columbia: University of Missouri Press, 1984).

Ian Spink, English Song: *Dowland to Purcell* (New York: Charles Scribner's Sons, 1974).

AMERICAN SONG

Christine Ammer, *Unsung: A History of Women in American Music* (Westport: Greenwood Press, 1980).

Judith E. Carman, William K. Gaeddert, Rita M. Resch, Gordon Myers. *Art Song in the United States, 1759-1999: An Annotated Bibliography* (Lanham, MD: Scarecrow Press, 2001).

Ruth C. Friedberg, *American Art Song and American Poetry* (Metuchen: Scarecrow Press, 1981-1987). Three volumes, focusing on "the interrelationships between the composer and the poet and the ways in which these have influenced the completed songs." Selected examples of important contributions to the performing literature by the selected composers. Volume 1: America Comes of Age: Edward MacDowell, Charles Loeffler, Charles Griffes, Charles Ives, Roy Harris, Aaron Copland, Douglas Moore, Ernst Bacon, William Grant Still; Volume 2: Voices of Maturity: Virgil Thomson, John Duke, Ross Lee Finney, Paul Nordoff, Sergius Kagen, Mary Howe, Charles Naginski; Volume 3: The Century Advances: Samuel Barber, Norman Dello Joio, Paul Bowles, Hugo Weisgall, David Diamond, Jack Beeson, Richard Owen, Jean Eichelberger Ivey, William Flanagan, Ruth Schonthal, Richard Cumming, Vincent Persichetti, Ned Rorem, Richard Hundley, John Corigliano, and Robert Baksa.

Harold Gleason and Warren Becker, *20th Century American Composers* (Bloomington: Frangipani Press, 1980). Outline form with brief biography, list of compositions, and discussion of style. Composers include Barber, Carpenter, Carter, Copland, Cowell, Hanson, Harris, Ives, Moore, Piston, Riegger, Rogers, Ruggles, Schuman, Sessions, Thompson, and Thomson.

Jane Manning, *New Vocal Repertory: An Introduction* (New York: Taplinger, 1987). Suggestions for extending the English-language repertory with specific pieces grouped according to technical difficulty. Composers include Babbitt, Musgrave, Carter, Bernstein, Sessions, Rands.

Sharon Mabry, *Exploring Twentieth-Century Vocal Music: A Practical Guide to Innovations in Performance and Repertoire* (New York: Oxford University Press, 2002).

Victoria Etnier Villamil, *A Singer's Guide to the American Art Song 1870-1980* (Metuchen, NJ: The Scarecrow Press., 1993). Arranged alphabetically by composer, this valuable reference gives brief biographies and selected song listings for American composers.

Helen Walker-Hill, *From Spirituals to Symphonies: African-American Women Composers and Their Music* (Westport: Greenwood Press, 2002).

ITALIAN SONG

Ruth C. Lakeway and Robert C. White, Jr., *Italian Art Song* (Bloomington: Indiana University Press, 1989). Brief history of solo Italian song. Deals specifically with representative songs of composers Alfano, Respighi, Pizzetti, Malipiero, Casella, Davico, Wolf-Ferrari, Cimara, Santoliquido, and Castelnuovo-Tedesco, among others.

Timothy LeVan, *Masters of the Italian Art Song* (Metuchen, NJ: Scarecrow Press 1990). Word-by-word and poetic translations of the complete songs for voice and piano of Bellini, Donaudy, Donizetti, Puccini, Rossini, Tosti, and Verdi.

RUSSIAN SONG

Gerald Abraham, *Essays on Russian and Eastern European Music* (Oxford: Clarendon Press, 1985). Chapter 1-Russian Song; Chapter 10-Polish Song; Chapter 12-Czechoslovakian Song.

James Bakst, *A History of Russian-Soviet Music* (Westport: Greenwood Press, 1977).

M.D. Calvocoressi and Gerald Abraham, *Masters of Russian Music: Biographical Studies of the Great Russian Composers* (New York: Tudor Publishing Co., 1944).

Stuart Campbell, ed. and trans., *Russians on Russian Music 1830-1880* (Cambridge: Cambridge University Press, 1994).

Richard Anthony Leonard, *A History of Russian Music* (London: Jerrolds, Ltd., 1956).

Jean Piatek and Regina Arashov, *Russian Songs and Arias* (Dallas: Pst...Inc., 1991). Phonetic readings, word-by-word translations for 150 songs and arias, with a concise guide to Russian diction.

SCANDINAVIAN SONG

See listings in specific composer sections.

SPANISH/SOUTH AMERICAN SONG

Stela Maria Santos Brandao, *The Brazilian Art Song: a performance guide utilizing selected works by Heitor Villa-Lobos.* Ed.D. dissertation, Columbia University Teachers College, 1999.

Jacqueline Cockburn and Richard Stokes,*The Spanish Song Companion,* with an introduction and notes by Graham Johnson (London: Gollancz, 1992). Texts, translations, and introductory notes on early Spanish song, *tonadillas, zarzuelas*, and representative literature by major Spanish song composers. An excellent source in this area.

Josep M. Sobrer and Edmon Colomer, *The Singer's Anthology of 20th Century Spanish Songs* (New York: Pelion Press, 1987). Concert songs of Enrique Granados, Manuel de Falla, and Frederic Mompou. Some discussion of composers and poets. Word-by-word and poetic translations, IPA transcriptions.

Kathleen L. Wilson, *The Art Song in Latin America* (Stuyvesant, N.Y.: Pendragon Press, 1998).

ABOUT THE AUTHOR

CAROL KIMBALL is Professor of Voice and Vocal Literature and a Barrick Distinguished Scholar at the University of Nevada, Las Vegas. A member of UNLV's music faculty since 1972, Dr. Kimball founded the UNLV Opera Theatre, directing its productions from 1972 until 1981. She holds degrees from New York University, Arizona State University, and the University of Arizona.

In addition to *Song*, her publications include *Interpreting the Songs of Jacques Leguerney: A Guide for Study and Performance* (with Mary Dibbern and Patrick Choukroun), and the *Singer's Edition* opera anthology series. For Hal Leonard, she has edited *The French Song Anthology, Women Composers: A Heritage of Song*, and *Art Song in English: 50 Songs by British and American Composers*. Her articles and reviews on opera and song literature have appeared in many professional journals, including *The Opera Quarterly, The Journal of Singing,* and *The Opera Journal*. She has served as the editor of *The Opera Journal* for the National Opera Association, and editor pro-tem of *The Journal of Singing* for the National Association of Teachers of Singing.

A specialist in French vocal repertoire, Carol Kimball has studied and coached with Pierre Bernac, Gérard Souzay, Martial Singher and Thomas Grubb. Her recital of French *mélodies* for Orion Records with pianist Thomas Grubb remains a staple recording in many college and university libraries. She is recognized for her work in promoting the songs of French composer Jacques Leguerney in the United States.

For her accomplishments in and for the Arts, Dr. Kimball was honored with the 1992 Nevada Governor's Arts Award for Excellence in the Arts. She was awarded the Regents' Creative Activities Award in 1997, the Outstanding Faculty Award given by the UNLV Alumni Association, a Nevada State Council for the Arts Artist Fellowship, the Morris Teaching Award for the College of Arts & Letters, and awards for research in French song from the National Endowment for the Humanities and the UNLV Research Council. Carol Kimball is listed in *Distinguished Women in Southern Nevada*. She remains active as a clinician and adjudicator.